FOUNDATIONS OF AI...

*To my wife Behnoosh, to my mother Maliheh, to my son Majid,*
*and my sisters, Gitty, Jaleh and Shahin with love and gratitude*
Bijan Vasigh

*This book is dedicated to the new arrivals, Madison and Hanorah;*
*hopefully, they will be able to read it sooner rather than later*
Ken Fleming

*To all those that have helped me along the way and for all those that*
*share a passion for aviation...*
Liam Mackay

# Foundations of Airline Finance
## Methodology and Practice

BIJAN VASIGH
*Embry-Riddle Aeronautical University, USA*

KEN FLEMING
*Aviation Consulting Group, USA*

*&*

LIAM MACKAY
*Continental Airlines, USA*

ASHGATE

Published by
Ashgate Publishing Limited
Wey Court East
Union Road
Farnham
Surrey, GU9 7PT
England

Ashgate Publishing Company
Suite 420
101 Cherry Street
Burlington
VT 05401-4405
USA

www.ashgate.com

**British Library Cataloguing in Publication Data**
Vasigh, Bijan.
  Foundations of airline finance : methodology and practice.
  1. Airlines--Finance. 2. Airlines--Accounting.
  3. Airlines--Cost of operation.
  I. Title II. Fleming, Ken. III. Mackay, Liam.
  387.7'1-dc22

  ISBN: 978-0-7546-7769-7 (hbk)
       978-0-7546-7770-3 (pbk)

**Library of Congress Cataloging-in-Publication Data**
Foundations of airline finance : methodology and practice / edited by Bijan Vasigh, Ken Fleming, and Liam Mackay.
     p. cm.
  Includes bibliographical references and index.
  ISBN 978-0-7546-7769-7 (hc) -- ISBN 978-0-7546-7770-3 (pbk.)  1. Aeronautics, Commercial--Finance. 2. Airlines--Cost of operation.  I. Vasigh, Bijan. II. Fleming, Ken. III. Mackay, Liam.
  HE9782.F56 2010
  387.7068'1--dc22
                                                                                                    2009045929

Printed and bound in Great Britain by the
MPG Books Group, UK

# Contents

# List of Figures

# List of Tables

# Glossary of Terms

**A**

**Accounts Payable (AP)**: Money the company owes to another party.

**Accounts Receivables (AR)**: Accounts receivable consists of monies due from customers as a result of a credit sale. On a balance sheet, accounts receivable is often recorded as an asset because this represents a legal obligation for the customer to pay cash for its short-term debts.

**Aircraft Utilization**: Aircraft utilization is calculated by dividing aircraft block hours by the number of aircraft days assigned to service on air carrier routes and presented in block hours per day.

**Air Carrier**: Any airline that undertakes directly, by lease, or other arrangement to engage in air transportation.

**Aircraft Crews Maintenance Insurance (ACMI)**: A lease between two parties where the first party is a lessor with an AOC responsible for the aircraft crews, maintenance, and insurance and the second party is the lessee, usually with an AOC, who is responsible for schedules, flight charges, cargo handling, crew support, flight operations, ramp handling, and aircraft servicing and fueling.

**Airport and Airway Trust Fund**: Fund established by Congress to pay for improvements to the nation's airports and air traffic control system. Money in the fund comes solely from users of the system, principally via taxation of domestic airline tickets.

**Airport Improvement Program (AIP)**: Provides grants for public-use airports that are included in the National Plan of Integrated Airport Systems (NPIAS). These grants are given to public agencies, private owners and entities for planning and development.

**Annuity**: A series of consecutives payments of equal amounts.

**Available Seat Kilometer (ASK)**: A measure of a passenger airline's carrying capacity that is calculated as follows:

$$ASK = \text{Number of seats} \times \text{number of kilometers flown}$$

**Available Seat Mile (ASM)**: A measure of a passenger airline's carrying capacity that is calculated as follows:

$$ASM = \text{Number of seats} \times \text{number of miles flown}$$

**Available Ton Mile (ATM)**: A measure of a cargo airline's carrying capacity that is calculated as follows:

$$ATM = \text{weight in non-metric tons} \times \text{number of miles flown}$$

**Average Stage Length (ASL)**: The ASL is the average distance flown per aircraft departure.

$$ASL = \frac{Plane\ Miles}{Departures}$$

**Average Collection Period**: The average time accounts receivable have been on the book.

$$ACP = \frac{ACR \times 365\ days}{Credit\ Sales}$$

**B**

**Balance Sheet**: A financial statement that summarizes a company's assets, liabilities and shareholders' equity at a specific point in time.

**Bankruptcy**: The inability of an airline to meet its financial obligations is called bankruptcy.

There are two basic types of Bankruptcy proceedings. A filing under Chapter 7 is called liquidation. Chapter 11 bankruptcy allows an airline to reorganize and refinance to be able to prevent final insolvency.

**Block Hour**: Block hour is the time from the minute the aircraft door closes at departure of a revenue flight until the moment the aircraft door opens at the arrival gate.

**Book Value**: The book value of an asset is its original cost minus accumulated depreciation.

**Break-Even Load Factor**: The load factor that covers the necessary operating costs for scheduled traffic revenue.

$$\text{Break-Even}_{LF} = \frac{CASM}{R/RPM} = \frac{CASM}{Yield}$$

**C**

**Cabotage Law**: The term cabotage, which has a Spanish origin, denotes the transport of passengers and cargo within the same country.

**Call Option**: A contract that gives the option holder the right, but not the obligation, to buy an agreed quantity of a particular financial asset from the seller at a particular time (the expiration date) for a predetermined price (the strike price).

**Capital Lease**: A lease structure whereby the lessee essentially assumes full ownership of the asset, including all associated risks.

**Carrying Costs**: Carrying costs, or holding costs, is the cost associated with carrying inventories. For most inventories carrying costs include the warehouses charges, damage, obsolescence, shrinkage and relocation costs.

**Certificated Air Carrier**: An air carrier that is certified by the DOT to conduct scheduled or non-scheduled services interstate. The certificate issued to the air carrier by the DOT is the Certificate of Public Convenience and Necessity.

**Code-sharing**: An arrangement where an airline may place its own code on to another carrier's flight. The airline that is actually operating the flight is called the operating carrier, and the airline that is marketing the flight is called the marketing carrier. Both carriers may sell tickets for the flight.

**Collar**: A collar is a hedging strategy of limiting both upside and downside protection of a commodity by simultaneously buying a put option and selling (writing) a call option on the same asset.

**Commercial Service Airport**: Airport receiving scheduled passenger service and having 2,500 or more enplaned passengers per year.

**Commuter Air Carrier**: A passenger air carrier operating aircraft with 30 seats or fewer and performing at least 5 scheduled roundtrips per week. It operates for hire or compensation under FAR Part 135.

**Computer Reservation System (CRS)**: CRS systems provide travel agencies with airline schedules, fares and seat availability. They also enable travel agents to book seats and issue tickets.

**Cost per available seat mile (CASM)**: It is represented in cents and is calculated as follows:

$$\text{CASM} = \frac{Operating\ Costs}{ASM}$$

**Current Assets**: Assets that can be converted into cash without significant loss of value in a very short period of time.

**D**

**Degree of Financial Leverage (DFL)**: Financial leverage involves using debt to finance the company, and results in having greater interest expense. DFL is defined as the percentage change in EPS for a given percentage change in EBIT.

$$DFL = \frac{Q(P-V)}{Q(P-V)-FC-I}$$

**Degree of Operating Leverage (DOL)**: Operating leverage involves using a large proportion of fixed costs in the operations of the firm. DOL measures the degree to which a project incurs a combination of fixed and variable costs.

$$DOL = \frac{Q(P-V)}{Q(P-V)-FC}$$

**Depreciation**: Reduction in the price of an asset during its estimated useful life owing to wear and tear, age, deterioration and obsolescence.

**Deregulation**: The term refers to the Airline Deregulation Act of 1978, which ended U.S. government regulation of airline routes and charges. Under deregulation, airlines are free to choose where to fly and set appropriate fares.

**Discount**: For a debt security, discount is the difference between the promised future payment and the present value.

**Dry-Lease**: A leasing arrangement between two airlines where the first airline leases an aircraft from the second airline (lessor) to operate. Under dry-lease, the lessee pays for the crew, fuel, and maintenance.

**E**

**Enplanement**: The boarding of a revenue passenger, including an in-transit passenger, on a scheduled/non-scheduled flight, both domestically and internationally.

**Essential Air Service (EAS)**: The program intended to guarantee small communities a minimal level of scheduled air service. The EAS program subsidizes commuter airlines to serve the rural communities across the country that otherwise would not receive any scheduled air service.

**F**

**Federal Aviation Administration (FAA)**: A United States government agency responsible for regulating air safety and the operation of the air-traffic control system.

**Federal Air Regulation (FAR)**: Title 14 of the U.S. government's Code of Federal Regulations. The FAR covers all the rules regarding aviation in the U.S.

**Finance Lease**: A long-term lease, generally lasting the life of the asset, where the lessee essentially assumes ownership of the asset and the associated risk.

**Financial Leverage**: A measure of the amount of debt used in the capital structure of the airlines.

An airline with high leverage is more vulnerable to downturns in the business cycle because the airline must continue to service its debt regardless of how bad business is.

**Financial Risk**: The risk that an airline may not have sufficient cash to meet current financial obligations.

**First Freedom**: The privilege to fly across another state (country) without landing.

**Fifth Freedom**: The privilege for an airline that is en route to or from the state it is registered in to take on revenue passengers, mail and freight in a second state and to transport it to a third state.

**Fixed Cost**: Costs are identified as fixed if they do not change as volume changes. Fixed costs cannot be eliminated in the short run.

**Form 41 Data**: Information derived from airline filings with the Bureau of Transportation Statistics. Airline financial data is filed with the BTS quarterly; traffic and employment numbers are filed monthly.

**Fourth Freedom**: The privilege for an airline to transport revenue passengers, mail and freight from one state to the state where it is registered.

**Freight**: Any commodity other than mail and passenger baggage transported by air.

**Freight-Ton Mile**: A ton-mile is defined as one ton of freight shipped one mile.

**Frequent Flyer Programs**: A service in which airline customers accrue points corresponding to the distance flown on an airline. These points can be used for free air travel, increased benefits such as airport lounge access, or priority bookings, and other products or services.

**Future Value**: The value that a current investment grows to at a given interest rate over a specified period of time.

**Future Value of an Annuity**: The value that a series of consecutive equal payments grows to at a given interest rate.

**G**

**Goodwill**: Goodwill is a business advantage of customer loyalty and patronage and developed with continuous business under the same name over a period of time.

**Gross Domestic Product (GDP)**: The total output of goods and services produced by all the different productive resources within a given country, valued at market prices.

**H**

**Hedging**: Hedging is similar to buying insurance policies intended to minimize and transfer risk.

**Hub and Spoke**: Many airlines designate an airport as a hub through which they transit passengers from spoke (origin) to spoke (destination).

**I**

**Income Statement**: A financial statement that summarizes the various transactions of an airline during a specified period, showing the net profit or loss. Income statement is based on the fundamental accounting equation:

$$\text{Income} = \text{Revenue} - \text{Expenses}$$

**Internal Rate of Return (IRR)**: The IRR is the discount rate that makes the net present value of all cash flows from a project equal to zero.

**In-transit Passengers**: Revenue passengers at an airport that are transferring from an international flight to a domestic flight, and vice versa.

**J**

**Just In Time (JIT)**: JIT (also known as lean production or stockless production) is an inventory strategy that stresses taking possession of inventory just before the time it is needed in production.

**L**

**Lease**: A lease is a contract granting use or occupation of property during a specified period in exchange for specified lease payments.

**Lessee**: A person who leases a property from its owner (lessor).

**Lessor**: The owner of an asset who grants another party to lease the asset.

**Leverage**: The use of debt to supplement investment.

**Liquidity**: The ability of an asset to be converted into cash quickly and without any loss of value.

**Load Factor**: Load factor is the ratio of revenue passenger miles over available seat-miles, representing the proportion of aircraft seating capacity that is actually sold and utilized.

**M**

**Major Airlines**: Airlines earning revenues of $1 billion or more annually in scheduled service.

**Modified Accelerated Cost Recovery System (MACRS)**: MACRS allows for more depreciation towards the beginning of the life of the capital asset and allowing the tax-deductible depreciation expense to be taken sooner.

## N

**National Plan of Integrated Airport Systems (NPIAS)**: A program that identifies more than 3,300 airports that are eligible to receive Federal grants under the Airport Improvement Program (AIP) based on their significance to national air transportation.

**Net Present Value (NPV)**: The net present value (NPV) equals the total present value of all cash inflows and outflows.

**Net Profit Margin**: Net profit (or loss) after interest and taxes as a percent of operating revenues.

**Nonscheduled Service**: Revenue flights not operated as regular scheduled service, such as charter flights.

## O

**Operating Expenses**: Expenses directly incurred to conduct a flight.

**Operating Lease**: Typically a shorter term lease whereby the lessor retains ownership.

**Operating Leverage**: A measure of the extent to which fixed assets are utilized in the business firm.

**Operating Profit Margin**: Operating profit (operating revenues minus operating expenses) as a percent of operating revenues.

**Operating Revenues**: Revenues from air transportation and related incidental services.

**Options**: An option is a contract that gives the holder the right, but not the obligation, to buy or sell a security at a predestined price for a given period of time.

## P

**Par Value**: Par value is the same as the face value, the principal value or maturity value of the bond. The par value is the amount of money the investor will receive once the bond matures.

**Passenger Load Factor**: Load factor is the ratio of revenue passenger miles over available seat-miles, representing the proportion of aircraft seating capacity that is actually sold and utilized.

$$LF = \frac{RPM}{ASM} \times 100$$

**Passenger Revenue per Available Seat Mile (PRASM)**: The average passenger revenue received per unit of output. PRASM is calculated by taking total passenger revenue divided by total ASMs.

**Payback**: The payback period represents the time required to recover the initial investment.

**Perpetuity**: A constant stream of cash flows without a definite end (assumed to be forever).

**Preferred Stocks**: A hybrid security combing some of the characteristics of bonds and common stocks but usually carrying no voting rights.

**Primary Market**: The market for raising new capital for the first time.

**Prime Rate**: The rate that a commercial bank charges its most creditworthy customers.

**Profitability Ratios**: A group of ratios that are used to assess the return on assets, sales, and invested capital.

**Put Option**: A put option is a contract that gives the holder the right, but not the obligation, to sell a security at a predetermined price for a given period of time.

**R**

**Return on Investment (ROI)**: The percentage amount that is earned on a company's total capital, calculated by dividing the total capital into earnings before interest, taxes, or dividends.

**Revenue Management**: A management approach to optimizing revenue that is based on managing revenues for different market segments or from different sources of funding around capacity and timing (yield management).

**Revenue Passenger Enplanement**: The total number of revenue passengers boarding aircraft including origination, stopover or connecting passengers.

**Revenue Passenger Load Factor**: (See *Passenger Load Factor*)
   Revenue passenger load factor is the ratio of revenue passenger miles over available seat-miles, representing the proportion of aircraft-seating capacity that is actually sold and utilized

**Revenue Passenger Mile (RPM)**: RPM is the principal measure of an airline's revenue generating ability. An RPM is one revenue passenger transported for one mile.

**Revenue per available seat mile (RASM)**: The average total revenue received per unit of output. RASM is calculated by taking total revenue divided by total ASMs.

**Revenue Ton Mile (RTM)**: One non-metric ton of revenue traffic transported one mile.

**Risk Aversion**: The propensity of investors or individuals to avoid risk unless it is properly compensated.

**Risk free assets**: Assets free of risk of default.

**Risk Premium**: The minimum difference an investor requires investing on a risky investment.

S

**Safety Stocks**: The inventory that is held in excess to regular demand to protect against being out of stock.

**Seat Pitch**: A measure of seat legroom. It is the distance from one seat in an aircraft to the next seat.

**Second Freedom**: The privilege to land in another state for non-traffic purposes such as refueling or mechanical issues.

**Secondary Market**: The markets for securities that have already been issued and traded among investors with no proceeds go to the company.

**SEC**: U.S. Securities and Exchange Committee.

**Seventh Freedom**: The privilege for an airline to pick up revenue passengers and freight from one state to another without originating, stopping or terminating in the state of registration.

**Sixth Freedom**: The privilege for an airline to transport revenue passengers, mail and freight from one state to another, while passing through its state of registry.

**Small Certificated Air Carrier**: An air carrier holding a certificate issued under section 401 of the Federal Aviation Act of 1958, as amended, that operates aircraft designed to have a maximum seating capacity of 60 seats or fewer or a maximum payload of 18,000 pounds or less.

**Stage 2**: Term used to describe jets meeting certain noise parameters on takeoff and landing.

**Stage 3**: Term used to describe the quietest jets in service today.

**Straight-line Depreciation**: A method of depreciation that is calculated by taking the purchase price of an asset subtracted by the salvage value divided by the total productive years the asset can be reasonably expected to benefit the company.

**Supplemental Air Carrier**: An air-carrier authorized to perform passenger and cargo charter services.

**Swap**: Transactions involving an exchange of cash flows between two parties, such as interest rate swap (fixed rate and floating rate).

**T**

**Third Freedom**: The privilege to put down revenue passengers, mail and freight taken from the state where the airline is registered to another state.

**Treasury Bills (or T-bill)**: Treasury bills are short obligations of the federal government. They mature in one year or less, and like zero-coupon bonds, they do not pay interest prior to the maturity.

**Treasury Notes (T-notes)**: Treasury notes are short obligations of the federal government and they mature in two to ten years.

**U**

**U.S. Flag Carrier**: One of a class of air carriers holding a Certificate of Public Convenience and Necessity issued by the U.S. Department of Transportation (DOT) and approved by the President, authorizing scheduled operations over specified routes between the United States and one or more foreign countries.

**V**

**Variable Costs**: A variable cost is a cost that changes in proportion to a change in a company's activity or business.

**W**

**Walk Away Lease**: A lease that allows the airline to return the aircraft at specified times without penalty.

**Warrant**: A security issued by a corporation along with a bond or preferred stock, giving the holder right to buy a specific amount of securities at a specific price.

**Weighted Average Cost of Capital (WACC)**: The average cost of capital for an airline is found by multiplying the cost of each capital item (i.e. debt, equity) by its weight in the capital structure.

**Wet-Lease**: A leasing arrangement between lessor and lessee to lease aircraft and crew from the second party which operates services on behalf of the first party.

**Y**

**Yield**: The average amount of revenue received for every paid seat mile flown.

**Z**

**Zero Coupon Bonds**: Zero coupon bonds are sold at discount and don't make regular interest payments as other bonds do. The bond holder receives all the interest in one lump sum when the bond matures.

# List of Abbreviations

| | |
|---|---|
| ACI | Airports Council International |
| ACMI | Aircraft, Crew, Maintenance and Insurance |
| AFC | Average Fixed Cost |
| AMEX | American Stock Exchange |
| AOC | Air Operator's Certificate |
| AOPA | Aircraft Owners and Pilots Association |
| ASL | Average Stage Length |
| ASM | Available Seat Miles |
| ATA | Air Transport Association |
| ATC | Air Traffic Control |
| ATI | Air Transport Intelligence |
| BAA | British Airport Authority |
| BTS | Bureau of Transportation Statistics |
| CAPM | Capital Asset Pricing Model |
| CASM | Cost Per Available Seat Mile |
| CCC | Cash Conversion Cycle |
| CD | Certificate of Deposit |
| CEO | Chief Executive Officer |
| CFO | Chief Financial Officer |
| CPA | Certified Public Accountant |
| CRS | Computer Reservation Systems |

| | |
|---|---|
| DCF | Discounted Cash Flow |
| DFL | Degree of Financial Leverage |
| DOC | Direct Operating Cost |
| DOL | Degree of Operating Leverage |
| DOT | Department of Transportation |
| EAC | Equivalent Annual Cost |
| EBIT | Earnings Before Interest and Taxes |
| EOQ | Economic Order Quantity |
| EPS | Earnings per share |
| EU | European Union |
| FAA | Federal Aviation Administration |
| FASB | Financial Accounting Standards Board |
| FC | Fixed Cost |
| FFP | Frequent Flyer Programs |
| FIFO | First In, First Out |
| FTSE | London Stock Exchange |
| FV | Future Value |
| GAAP | Generally Accepted Accounting Principles |
| GDP | Gross Domestic Product |
| GECAS | GE Commercial Aviation Services |
| IATA | International Air Transport Association |
| ICAO | International Civil Aviation Organization |
| IFRS | International Financial Reporting Standards |
| ILFC | International Lease Finance Corporation |

| | |
|---|---|
| IOC | Indirect Operating Cost |
| IPO | Initial Public Stock Offering |
| IRR | Internal rate of return |
| IRS | Internal Revenue Services |
| JAA | Joint Aviation Authorities |
| JIT | Just-in-time inventory strategy |
| LCC | Low-Cost Carrier |
| LIBOR | London Interbank Offered Rate |
| MACRS | Modified Accelerated Cost Recovery System |
| MC | Marginal Cost |
| MIRR | Modified Internal Rate of Return |
| NASDAQ | National Association of Securities Dealers Automated Quotations |
| NOC | Non Operating Cost |
| NPIAS | National Plan of Integrated Airport Systems |
| NPV | Net Present Value |
| NWC | Net Working Capital |
| NYMEX | New York Mercantile Exchange |
| NYSE | New York Stock Exchange |
| O&D | Origin and Destination |
| OAG | Official Airline Guide |
| P/E | Price-to-Earnings ratio |
| PI | Profitability Index |
| PV | Present Value |
| RASM | Revenue per Available Seat Mile |

| ROA | Return on Assets |
| ROE | Return on Equity |
| ROI | Return on Investment |
| RPM | Revenue Passenger Mile |
| RRPM | Revenue per Revenue passenger Miles |
| RRTM | Revenue per Revenue Ton Miles |
| RTM | Revenue Ton Miles |
| SEC | Security Exchange Commission |
| SML | Security Market Line |
| TC | Total Cost |
| TFC | Total Fixed Cost |
| TOC | Total Operating Cost |
| VC | Variable Cost |
| WACC | Weighted Average Cost of Capital |

# Acknowledgements

The writing and development of any text book is always a long and difficult task. We have received a great deal of assistance and encouragement from a number of individuals whose efforts we would like to acknowledge.

Many ERAU graduate students helped in the preparation for this manuscript. We owe a special debt to the graduate assistants, Matthew Dixon, Duane Miner, Halnettige Perera, Joost Vlek, Clara Hudson, Omar Haddadeen, and William R. Harris.

The professionals at Ashgate Publishing have done an admirable job in being patient with the text and turning the raw manuscript into an actual book. Especially, we are grateful to Guy Loft, Gillian Steadman, Luigi Fort and Peter Stafford.

We also wish to thank the following individuals who helped in various stages of editing and/or commenting on the final draft. Among these are Fariba Alamdari, Boeing; Brian Pearce, the International Air Transport Association; David Gillen, The University of British Columbia; Zane Row, Continental Airlines; Brent Bowen, Purdue University; Alessandro Oliveira, Aeronautics Institute of Technology, Brazil. Our academic colleagues and reviewers Bert Zarb, James Baldwin, Christina Frederick, Dan Petree, Reza Taleghani, Darryl Jenkins, Vitaly Guzhva, Chris Tarry, Alfred Lupi, Joubine Motaharian, Javad Gorjidooz, Vedapuri Raghavan, Richard Tame, and Christian Vogel, all provided comments and suggestions that were thoughtful and valuable.

Any mistakes that may still be in the text are, of course, the sole responsibility of the authors.

# *Reviews of* Foundations of Airline Finance

'Vasigh has created a highly readable and accessible text which provides an understanding of the complexities of airline financial management. He covers not only the essential techniques in financial analysis but also provides key material on aviation industry valuation, capital budgeting and importantly risk management. This excellent book should be essential reading for students of aviation as well as air transport industry professionals.'

David Gillen, University of British Columbia, Canada

'Dr Vasigh has produced that rare thing – a book on applied finance that is readable and illuminating. Since the industry routinely destroys shareholder value, despite creating tremendous consumer value, this expertly guided tour behind airline financial statements should be required reading for analysts, policy-makers and newcomers to airline management.'

Brian Pearce, Chief Economist, IATA

'Dr Vasigh's book is a valuable source of information for those who have a keen interest in understanding airline industry finance and accounting. The systematic approach adopted in writing it successfully navigates the readers through the complexities of airline financial statements, airline capital structure, cost classifications, and more.'

Fariba Alamdari, Boeing Commercial Airplanes, USA

'Bijan Vasigh's book offers the reader a good overview of the considerations and analyses that are important in evaluating the financial performance of the airline industry. It offers many real-life examples and insights into the challenges facing today's airlines. Vasigh links traditional financial concepts with airline examples, giving the reader a better avenue for understanding the metrics and methods that are particular to the industry. Foundations of Airline Finance offers good insight into how the airlines stay aloft financially despite consistently strong economic headwinds.'

Zane Rowe, Continental Airlines, USA

'As we have come to expect, this book represents the continuing high standard of scholarship that Dr Vasigh is known to contribute. His latest work is absolutely necessary for students and practicing professionals alike. I commend Dr Vasigh for the rigor of this text and its contribution to our academic discipline. We are fortunate to have this work added to the body of literature in our field. The area of airline finance needs this methodological approach to solve the decades-old problems the industry has not resolved. I am confident that airline managers of the future will be better prepared as a result of Dr Vasigh's text.'

Brent Bowen, Purdue University, USA

'This book is a fantastic introduction to the complexities of airline finance. It would be an invaluable guide for anyone just entering the management side of an airline, whether they be students or ex-line employees, allowing them to confidently discuss and understand the basics of airline finance.'

Richard Tame, Airline Consultant

'In order to survive in an ever-increasing competitive market, airlines must manage their finances properly. This book is a comprehensive guide for the finance-related issues that emerge in the airline industry. In a time of global crisis, the concepts thoroughly addressed by Dr Vasigh are critical. It is of inestimable value for airline executives, managers, researchers and students.'

Alessandro Oliveira, Aeronautics Institute of Technology, Brazil

# Preface

From a financial management perspective, it is undoubtedly true that probably the most challenging industry in the world today is the airline industry. The industry is faced with significant internal competition, while from the outside it is subject to sometimes capricious government controls in the form of security requirements that are levied on no other industry of comparable size. Low-cost airlines have intensified fierce domestic competition, while legacy airlines have been burdened with holdover labor contracts (that date from the inefficient period of regulation) and severe merger problems that have arisen owing to different cultures between merged airlines. In addition, heightened security concerns have disrupted schedules, forced flight cancellations, and severely inconvenienced the traveling public. Since almost all decisions in this (and any other industry) depend on an appropriate financial management background, the authors of this text, with many years of teaching aviation finance in an academic setting, active consulting in the industry, and actual industry decision-making with individual airlines, feel that there is a need to prepare prospective participants in airline management (as thoroughly as possible) in the intricacies of managerial finance as it applies to the industry. Therefore, for all of the reasons mentioned above and more, it seems to us that this is an appropriate time to publish a basic financial textbook that covers the fundamentals of financial management in the airline industry. The textbook covers the fundamentals of financial management that are appropriate to any firm or industry and, more importantly, the differences that characterize managerial finance in the modern airline industry. To that end, we have developed a step-by-step approach that addresses financial decision-making from both a theoretical and a practical point of view. And, while the text can certainly be used as a basic introduction to finance, it is mainly aimed at aviation professionals and students who have a desire to enter the aviation industry in a management capacity.

The text is divided into four more or less self-contained sections that progress from the theoretical foundations of financial management to more sophisticated practical applications of the theoretical concepts. The first section lays the necessary theoretical foundation for the critical concepts that are needed to understand financial management in the airline industry. Chapter 1 gives an overview of the importance of finance in the industry. The chapter describes the truly global nature of the industry and introduces the reader to important concepts that are covered in more detail later in the text. This chapter is followed by a chapter that gives a detailed discussion of the true nature of costs within the industry. The misconception surrounding the nature of fixed costs and their application to financial decision-making is one issue (among many others) that receives much needed coverage. Following this chapter the critically important topic of the time value of money is explained in clear and straightforward terms. Informative and simple numerical examples are used to illustrate this important concept, thought by some to be the most important theoretical idea in the field of financial management. Finally, the last chapter discusses the important roles of risk and return in financial management. Various methods that are used to evaluate these concepts are discussed and illustrated in the context of the aviation industry.

The second section of the text introduces the reader to the use of financial statements to evaluate the actual position of the firm in the industry. And, some significant differences between airline accounting and more traditional accounting are highlighted and explained; for example, the treatment of frequent flyer miles in the accounting statement. The first chapter of this section covers the accounting statement and how to read and understand it. This is followed by the role of financial statements in understanding the position and prospects of the individual firm. Finally, the actual techniques for analyzing all of this information are explained and illustrated with concrete examples.

The third section of the text provides a clear exposition of capital budgeting within the industry. This topic is yet another critically important financial concept that differentiates the airline industry from other large capital intensive industries. The reason for this is the fact that the fungible nature of the capital assets (that is, aircraft) makes the situation unique for the airline industry. Among other important topics, capital budgeting in the context of the Capital Asset Pricing Model (CAPM), the Weighted Average Cost of Capital (WACC) and various stock valuation models are covered in the opening chapter of this section. This chapter is followed by a chapter that discusses the overall airline capital structure and the important methods (equity, debt, retained earnings, etc.) associated with acquiring that capital. The final chapter of this section discusses the ideas of working capital and current asset management.

The last section of the text is quite probably the part that will be of greatest interest to airline professionals, since it explains and gives examples of some important practical applications of financial management. The section is introduced with the important practical concept of hedging. Hedging protects an industry or airline from the fluctuations of price in the marketplace and, in particular, the volatility of fuel prices, which is generally the single highest expense for any airline. However, hedging is not without its own risks, and these are discussed at length in the chapter. The next chapter in the applications section concerns the all-important buy versus lease decision for any airline within the industry. This topic, although covered at some length in various articles on aviation finance, has not received (in our opinion) sufficient in-depth coverage in basic aviation finance texts. The underlying ideas and quantitative assumptions and rationale for either decision are discussed and evaluated in the chapter. Finally, the issue of valuation is covered in the last chapter of this section. The critical question of what an aviation asset (generally an aircraft but sometimes an airport in the era of privatization) is worth is addressed and, more importantly, a method for actually calculating this value is presented in some detail.

In summation, it is our hope that the text will find an interested audience in both academia and the aviation industry.

# PART I

# Theoretical Aspects of Airline Finance

# 1

# The Role of Finance in the Airline Industry

"With the pressure on in our cost structure due to energy prices, the importance of the work for which these groups are responsible has soared. Southwest must develop a new long-term financial plan as we reengineer our company to combat higher fuel prices."

Laura Wright, Chief Financial Officer, Southwest Airlines

This text aims to provide students who plan to enter the aviation industry, operational aviation professionals, and aviation finance managers, with many of the fundamental tools required to successfully analyze an airline's business and help shape the organization for financial prosperity. It has been said that finance is the life blood of business, and that is why some U.S. carriers appoint their former Chief Financial Officers (CFOs) as their new CEOs.

While the tools of finance are universal, in attempting to analyze the airline industry, the goal of this text is to present finance in a real and practical sense. However, prior to a detailed understanding of various financial tools, this chapter will provide an overview of the role of finance in industry, and in particular, for the airline industry. The globalization of the airline industry, and the financial consequences of these developments, will be discussed. The chapter will also introduce the reader to the important concepts of accounting and economic profits. It will provide an overview of the various forms of business organizations that a firm might choose and how they may affect finances (particularly in the aviation industry) and the complications that may arise (agency problems) from the organization selected. The following topics will be covered in this introductory chapter:

- Introduction and Historical Background
- The International Nature of the Aviation Industry
- Objectives of Airlines
- Accounting Profit
- Economic Profit
- Business Organizational Structures
- Sole Proprietorships
- Partnership

## INTRODUCTION AND HISTORICAL BACKGROUND

Finance is a diverse and wide-encompassing field that deals with ensuring that a company has the financial resources (i.e. cash) to not only operate successfully in the short-term, but also to help position the company for long-term prosperity. While long-term prosperity may not aptly describe the airline industry, financial management, together with accounting, play a critical role in maintaining a sound and efficient airline operation. Finance is diverse because it touches every facet of an airline, affecting not only short-term decision making, but also long-term strategic planning.

Historically, airlines have operated in two very distinct environments. Prior to 1978 in the United States and 1999 in the European Union, airlines operated in a regulated environment where governments had full control over where airlines could fly and what rates they could charge. Even today this is still common in international aviation; however, like domestic airline deregulation, the trend is towards less regulation. Additionally, while the practice did not occur in the United States, globally many airlines were owned and controlled by the government, creating further regulation in the airline industry. During the regulated era in the United States, airlines received protection from competition, with government limiting the number of airlines serving a particular route. Pricing was largely based on a cost-plus formula, where airlines told the government what it cost to fly a route, and the government merely tacked on a profit margin. Because of regulation, carriers earned relatively stable and healthy profits. As a result, financial analysis was not of the utmost importance to the airlines, as most of the financial issues dealt with stating the financial performance of the company (much in the realm of accounting) and securing the necessary funds for capital investment.

The post airline-deregulation era has brought a much more high-stakes environment, where airlines are afforded the opportunity to earn greater profits than under regulation, but are also subject to increased competition, placing downward pressure on air fares. As a result, the post-deregulation airline industry has become much more risky, with many airlines, such as Eastern and Pan American, finding it difficult to compete, resulting in their liquidation.[1]

Eastern fell victim to the takeovers and labor conflict that characterized the industry and subsequently Eastern began losing money as it faced competition from low-cost airlines, such as People Express, which offered low airfares. Recently, major United States carriers such as United, Delta, and Northwest Airlines have all entered

---

1    Eastern Airlines commenced its service as Pitcairn Airways in Pennsylvania in 1929 and ceased operations on January 1991.

bankruptcy protection, succumbing to the stark realties of the post-deregulation world, where operating profit margins are narrowly thin. Increased competition, declining unit revenue, and highly volatile fuel-prices have caused the worldwide airline industry to be in a financial crisis for the past several years. To quote British Airways chief executive Willie Walsh, "We are in the worst trading environment the industry has ever faced" (Wardell, 2008).

Deregulation and financial distress have placed greater importance on finance, since strategic financial planning and implementation are at the root of determining whether an airline will succeed or cease to operate. Figure 1.1 shows the cyclical nature of profits in the airline industry during the past decade, with airlines posting profits for a few years, followed by losses for the next few years. After six straight years of losses, it appeared the industry was on its way to starting the cycle of profitability again in 2007; however, skyrocketing fuel costs and the financial crisis in the U.S. during 2008 have led analysts to predict that the airline industry will once again return to an extended period of operating losses (IATA, 2008).

One of the greatest trends in the post-deregulation airline industry is the proliferation of low-cost carriers (LCCs), or airlines with significantly lower cost structures than their original, so-called, legacy carrier counterparts (when we refer to legacy carriers in the United States, we typically refer to the big six U.S. Airlines: American, Continental, Delta, Northwest, United, U.S. Airways; however, more generally legacy carrier can describe any traditional, full-service, major hub-and-spoke airline). Table 1.1 provides a comparison of U.S. legacy and low-cost carriers through a common-size income statement between 2005 and 2008. As Table 1.1 displays, low-cost carriers have outperformed legacy carriers in terms of operating and profit margins, partly a result of lower overhead costs. This, combined with lower operating costs as a result of operating a much simpler operation, have resulted in low-cost carriers placing tremendous pressure on the legacy carriers,

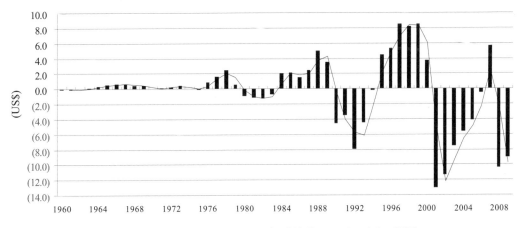

*Source*: International Civil Aviation Organization (ICAO), International Air Transport Association (IATA).

**Figure 1.1     Global airline industry profits**

**Table 1.1    Common-size income statement, comparison between low-cost and legacy carriers**

|  | 2004 | | 2005 | | 2006 | | 2007 | |
|---|---|---|---|---|---|---|---|---|
|  | LCC | Legacy | LCC | Legacy | LCC | Legacy | LCC | Legacy |
| **Revenues** | | | | | | | | |
| Passenger Revenues | 91.0% | 76.9% | 87.6% | 75.2% | 83.7% | 70.8% | 83.1% | 71.7% |
| Other Revenues | 9.0% | 23.1% | 12.4% | 24.8% | 16.3% | 29.2% | 16.9% | 28.3% |
| Total Revenues | 100.0% | 100.0% | 100.0% | 100.0% | 100.0% | 100.0% | 100.0% | 100.0% |
| **Expenses** | | | | | | | | |
| Flying Operations (Labor, Fuel, Other Direct Expenses) | 41.1% | 32.2% | 42.6% | 35.2% | 52.0% | 34.7% | 52.4% | 34.8% |
| Maintenance | 11.0% | 9.5% | 9.6% | 8.9% | 8.8% | 8.4% | 8.6% | 8.7% |
| Depreciation and Amortization | 4.9% | 5.4% | 4.4% | 4.7% | 3.2% | 4.2% | 3.4% | 4.0% |
| Total Aircraft Operating Expenses | 57.1% | 47.0% | 56.7% | 48.8% | 64.1% | 47.3% | 64.5% | 47.5% |
| Servicing and Administration Expenses | 41.2% | 38.3% | 38.4% | 34.9% | 32.5% | 33.1% | 31.9% | 33.4% |
| Transport-related Expenses | 1.7% | 14.8% | 4.9% | 16.3% | 3.4% | 19.6% | 3.6% | 19.1% |
| Total Expenses | 100.0% | 100.0% | 100.0% | 100.0% | 100.0% | 100.0% | 100.0% | 100.0% |
| Operation Margin | 10.2% | 5.0% | 0.2% | -2.8% | -0.1% | 3.8% | 0.7% | 5.4% |
| Profit Margin | 5.6% | 1.8% | -5.9% | -30.3% | -1.4% | -9.6% | -1.0% | 6.4% |

*Source*: Complied by Authors using Back Form 41.

whose cost structures are still heavily weighted with the inflated costs from the regulated era. This cost advantage has enabled LCCs to expand aggressively, whittling away market share from legacy carriers. This theme has played out in both North America and Europe in the past ten years and is also slowly beginning to be played out in Asia. The result of increased low-cost competition has been a reduction in passenger yields (revenues) in domestic markets, and a reduction in service standards for legacy carriers. Particularly in the United States, domestic air travel has been turned into a commodity where airlines compete almost exclusively on cost. When competition is based on cost, low-cost carriers have an advantage over legacy carriers owing to their comparative cost structures. Cost competition has created a situation where U.S. airlines find it difficult to make a profit domestically and European carriers struggle in intra-European air travel. These forces, combined with other factors, have placed significant financial pressure on legacy carriers, creating financial distress in many situations.

Table 1.2 shows the top ten global low-cost carriers ranked by the passengers carried in 2009. Low-cost carriers have experienced a steady growth throughout the airline industry with average traffic growth of around 9%, and with some European carriers such as Ryanair and easyjet obtaining double digit growth rates. Southwest Airlines really invented the low-cost carrier model when it began flying within Texas in 1971. Today it is the largest LCC by a fairly considerable amount with the airline carrying 88.5 million passengers in 2008. In Europe, Ryanair and easyJet have posted double-digit passenger growth with 13.2% and 16.6% respectively, while carrying over 100 million passengers combined. In Asia, the LCC business model is not as developed; however, AirAsia of Malaysia, Adam Air of Indonesia, and Cebu Pacific Air of Philippines are just a few Asian LCCs that have experienced considerable growth. Deregulation has been a little slower in development in Asia; however, if the trend continues, as the airline industry experiences more deregulation, LCCs in Asia should experience dramatic growth.[2]

**Table 1.2      Top 10 low-cost carriers in the world by passenger volume**

| Rank | Carrier | Passengers (millions) |
|:---:|---|:---:|
| 1 | Southwest Airlines | 88.5 |
| 2 | Ryanair | 57.6 |
| 3 | easyjet | 44.6 |
| 4 | Air Berlin | 28.6 |
| 5 | GOL Transportes Aeros | 25.7 |
| 6 | AirTran Airways | 24.6 |
| 7 | JetBlue Airways | 21.9 |
| 8 | Virgin Blue Airlines | 16.7 |
| 9 | WestJet Airlines | 14.3 |
| 10 | Thomsonfly | 12.2 |

*Source*: Airline Business—May 2009, p. 74.

Simply owing to their size and international presence, legacy carriers generate more revenue than low-cost carriers. The largest airlines, in terms of revenue, in the U.S. and Europe are shown in Tables 1.3 and 1.4, respectively. While legacy carriers earn more revenue than low-cost carriers, in terms of what is most important, low-cost carriers have been more profitable than legacy carriers. The exception to this trend, in the United States, was in 2007 where in terms of margins, legacy carriers outperformed low-cost carriers (see Table 1.1). The low-cost carriers' performance was mired by the poor financial performance of ATA (American Trans Air) and Frontier Airlines, who filed for Chapter 11 bankruptcy protection. This was largely the result of poor performance by ATA (American

---

2      Other low-cost airlines in Asia include: Jazeera Airways from Kuwait, Air Blue and Shaheen Air from Pakistan, Eastar Jet and Jeju Air from South Korea and finally Nok Air and One-Two-GO from Thailand.

**Table 1.3     Top 10 largest airline groups: Europe**

| Rank | Airline Group | Revenue ($ millions) |
|------|---------------|----------------------|
| 1 | Lufthansa Group | 36,533 |
| 2 | Air France-KLM Group | 33,739 |
| 3 | British Airways | 15,013 |
| 4 | Iberia | 8,101 |
| 5 | SAS Group | 8,056 |
| 6 | Air Berlin | 4,995 |
| 7 | THY Turkish Airlines | 4,684 |
| 8 | easyJet | 4,649 |
| 9 | Virgin Group | 4,488 |
| 10 | Ryanair | 4,141 |

*Source*: Airline Business—August 2009, p. 67.

**Table 1.4     Top 15 largest airline groups: North America**

| Rank | Airline Group | Revenue ($ millions) |
|------|---------------|----------------------|
| 1 | AMR Corporation | 23,766 |
| 2 | Delta Air Lines | 22,697 |
| 3 | Fedex | 22,364 |
| 4 | United Airlines | 20,194 |
| 5 | Continental Airlines | 15,241 |
| 6 | U.S. Airways Group | 12,118 |
| 7 | Southwest Airlines | 11,023 |
| 8 | ACE Aviation Holdings | 10,381 |
| 9 | United Parcel Service | 5,800 |
| 10 | Alaska Air Group | 3,663 |
| 11 | SkyWest Airlines | 3,496 |
| 12 | JetBlue Airways | 3,388 |
| 13 | AirTran Airways | 2,552 |
| 14 | WestJet Airlines | 2,389 |
| 15 | Atlas Air | 1,607 |

*Source*: Airline Business—August 2009, p. 66.

Trans Air) and Frontier who filed for Chapter 11 bankruptcy on April 10, 2008, indicating that LCCs are not immune from financial distress. On June 22, 2009, Frontier announced that, pending court approval, the airline would be a wholly owned subsidiary of Republic Airways, once Frontier emerged from Chapter 11 bankruptcy.

Table 1.5 shows the top 15 international airlines, in terms of operating profit margin, for 2007 and 2008. While the list contains a multitude of low-cost and regional carriers, no legacy airlines from North America or Europe are in the top 15. This depicts the maturation of the legacy carrier model in North America and Europe. Additionally, Table 1.5 depicts how airlines in developing economies are reporting solid financial results. In essence, the profitability of an airline is partly the byproduct of the region's economy, for increased business activity helps spur increased revenue.

**Table 1.5      Top 15 airline groups by operating margin**

|  |  | Operating Margin | |
| --- | --- | --- | --- |
| Rank | Airline Group | 2008 | 2007 |
| 1 | AirAsia | 26.80% | 34.70% |
| 2 | Middle East Airlines (MEA) | 21.00% | 15.10% |
| 3 | Kuwait Airways | 19.10% | -12.20% |
| 4 | Copa Airlines | 17.40% | 18.40% |
| 5 | Republic Airways Holdings | 17.20% | 17.80% |
| 6 | Air Arabia | 14.00% | 19.20% |
| 7 | LAN Airlines | 11.80% | 11.70% |
| 8 | WestJet Airlines | 11.50% | 14.10% |
| 9 | Allegiant Air | 11.10% | 12.20% |
| 10 | Air Wisconsin | 10.30% | 9.80% |
| 11 | Avianca | 9.90% | 0.00% |
| 12 | THY Turkish Airlines | 9.60% | 14.90% |
| 13 | Air Canada Jazz | 9.10% | 10.20% |
| 14 | Omini Air International | 8.80% | 5.80% |
| 15 | Cebu Pacific | 8.80% | 17.00% |

*Source*: Airline Business—August, 2009.

To help offset the airlines' troubles in domestic markets, airlines have placed greater focus on international travel.[3] Since regulation still exists in international travel, competition is severely limited, so greater profits can be made in this sector. Additionally, international markets have not yet seen significant competition from low-cost carriers

---

3    Airline Industry Outlook, Henry Joyner, Senior Vice President of Planning, American Airlines, March 15, 2007.

and may not for the foreseeable future since the success of the low-cost model in international markets is unknown. These factors have encouraged legacy carriers to shift capacity out of domestic markets and onto international flights. For example, Delta Airlines embarked on a massive international expansion in 2006, transitioning numerous 767 aircraft from domestic flights to Europe and Africa. Additionally, Continental has configured their 757–200s, an aircraft used predominantly for domestic flying in the United States, for international flying. Table 1.6 displays the trend of US legacy carriers shifting more capacity to international flying by detailing the proportion of international ASMs from 2004 to 2008.

**Table 1.6     International available seat miles (millions)**

| Carriers | 2004 | 2005 | 2006 | 2007 | 2008 |
|----------|------|------|------|------|------|
| Continental | 39% | 42% | 44% | 45% | 48% |
| Northwest | 38% | 39% | 40% | 42% | 46% |
| United | 35% | 40% | 39% | 41% | 44% |
| Delta | 24% | 26% | 34% | 39% | 44% |
| American | 34% | 36% | 38% | 38% | 39% |
| U.S. Airways | 25% | 25% | 28% | 27% | 23% |

*Source*: Compiled by Authors using Back Aviation Form 41.

From 2004 to 2008, the majority of U.S. network carriers increased their proportion of international flying, with Delta increasing international capacity the most. This increase on the network carriers' reliance on international flying is the result of adding new flights to new international markets and by cutting domestic capacity. This shifting of capacity has enabled legacy carriers to reap short-term profits; however, it does not address the problems legacy carriers are facing in domestic markets. Legacy carriers still operate extensive domestic networks to feed their international flights, but they sometimes do so at a loss. This strategy may not prove to be effective in the long-term unless legacy carriers are able to improve their performance in domestic markets by largely reducing unit costs.

It should be noted that trends in the aviation industry are generally regional rather than global. For instance, the African aviation industry differs significantly from the Asian aviation industry. However, similarities do exist between regions and these are usually based on the level of maturity of the industry. Mature aviation industries in Europe and North America have a high degree of similarity, as do the aviation sectors in India and China. It should come as no surprise that the aviation industry exhibits similar trends with respect to the macro economies of the regions, since the industry is strongly tied to the general economy. When the economy is doing well, business is thriving, thus increasing business trips. Additionally, consumers have increased disposable income, which they are more willing to spend on vacations. This creates a high degree of correlation between the economy and the aviation industry. Generally speaking, the aviation industry lags behind the economy by approximately 6–12 months. Therefore, the high growth economies of China and India are attracting suppliers and investors in the industry. Table 1.7 displays the forecast annual growth rate of passenger traffic in and between regions based on Boeing's market outlook.[4] As would be expected, for inter-region growth, Asia Pacific is forecast to outperform all the other regions, with North America and Europe displaying modest growth rates. The inter-region passenger growth forecast is likely to coincide with long-term economic forecasts, whereby Europe and North America are mature markets.

**Table 1.7　Airline passenger growth rates (RPMs): 2008 to 2028**

|  | Africa | Latin America | Middle East | Europe | North America | Asia Pacific |
|---|---|---|---|---|---|---|
| Asia Pacific | 9.2% | 9.1% | 6.3% | 5.5% | 4.9% | **6.9%** |
| North America | 7.4% | 4.7% | 6.9% | 4.6% | **2.5%** | |
| Europe | 5.4% | 4.3% | 5.5% | **3.4%** | | |
| Middle East | 6.1% | - | **6.2%** | | | |
| Latin America | 5.5% | **6.4%** | | | | |
| Africa | **6.4%** | | | | | |

*Source*: Boeing Current Market Outlook 2009.

One major concern to the aviation industry is the price of oil. The airline industry is one of the largest users of oil in the economy, requiring huge amounts of jet fuel to operate every day. Because of this, the impact of a change in the price of oil has a substantial impact on the airlines, and it may ultimately be the difference between profitability and loss. Several years ago wages and salaries were the largest cost item to the airlines; however, with the recent upward trend in the price of oil, fuel has surpassed salaries as the largest cost (Figure 2.6). Based on cash-flow structure, significant price elasticity, and increased competition, airlines have struggled to pass on the increased price of fuel to the customers. Therefore, the airlines have had to bear the majority of the additional cost of fuel, resulting in poor financial performance. To combat this, airlines have invested in fuel-efficient aircraft, new technologies (such as blended winglets), aircraft weight saving programs, and increased ancillary revenues. In all of these reactions, financial managers have played a critical role in helping combat the rising cost of fuel.

To some, the price of jet fuel appears out of the control of airlines; however, airlines such as Southwest have been successful through fuel hedging strategies. Since airlines consume such large amounts of fuel, their risk exposure is substantial; therefore, strategies to minimize the risk in the price of oil are prudent. Fuel hedging strategies and the financial tools used to implement them are discussed in detail in the chapter on minimizing risks.

---

4　Both Boeing and Airbus produce frequent worldwide market forecasts.

## THE INTERNATIONAL NATURE OF THE AVIATION INDUSTRY

One of the unique aspects of airline transportation is the international nature of the business. The principal reason for this is, of course, the fact that no other mode of transportation can compete with the obvious speed advantage that the aircraft possess over longer distances. Airlines shuttle passengers and freight of different nationalities all over the globe, from destinations such as New Delhi, India to exotic places and cities like Rio de Janeiro and Bangkok. To be successful, globalization requires intimate knowledge of the local market and this in turn presents unique challenges to finance. However, international business in the aviation industry is not just limited to airlines, but also includes many suppliers to the airline industry, such as aircraft and engine manufacturers. Table 1.8 provides an overview of the major corporations (and their nationality) competing in the various aviation industries.

**Table 1.8     Major companies in the aviation industry**

|                                      | Company Name        | Nationality          |
| ------------------------------------ | ------------------- | -------------------- |
| **Commercial Aircraft Manufacturing** | Boeing              | United States        |
|                                      | Airbus              | France               |
|                                      | Bombardier          | Canada               |
|                                      | Embraer             | Brazil               |
| **General Aircraft Manufacturing**   | Cessna              | United States        |
|                                      | Cirrus              | United States        |
|                                      | Dassault            | France               |
| **Commercial Airlines**              | American Airlines   | United States        |
|                                      | United Airlines     | United States        |
|                                      | Air France          | France               |
|                                      | Lufthansa           | Germany              |
|                                      | British Airways     | United Kingdom       |
|                                      | Emirates            | United Arab Emirates |
|                                      | Cathay Pacific      | Hong Kong            |
|                                      | Qantas              | Australia            |
| **Aircraft Engine Manufacturing**    | General Electric    | United States        |
|                                      | Pratt & Whitney     | United States        |
|                                      | Rolls Royce         | United Kingdom       |
|                                      | Snecma              | France               |
|                                      | MTU Aero Engines    | Germany              |

*Source*: Compiled by Authors using manufacturers' information, 2008.

Commercial aircraft manufacturing is an industry dominated by just a few companies. This fits the economic definition of an oligopoly market—a market in which only a few companies compete. Although these companies reside in just a few countries, the scope of their products requires that their supply chain be spread across the globe. For instance, Boeing's new 787 Dreamliner has a supply chain stretching from Japan to Italy. By having such a widely spread supply chain, Boeing can draw upon technological knowledge from across the globe. However, with such a diverse and global supply chain, problems can easily arise. Supplies from half way around the world may not arrive at the necessary time, causing delays in production. Also, for aircraft manufacturers to be successful, they need to sell aircraft not only to airlines located in their home country, but also to airlines located around the globe. This is because the enormous capital requirements of a new aircraft program cannot be recouped by sales from only one country, not even the United States. The reason for this is the fact that the United States has a declining proportion of world air-traffic—largely the result of economic growth in other regions of the globe. Table 1.9 shows that, while North America still accounts for the largest number of passengers per year among the world's top 200 airlines, the Asia-Pacific region and European regions could potentially equal North America in the future.

**Table 1.9    Passenger airline traffic by region (2008)**

| Region | Passenger Numbers (billions) | Change |
|---|---|---|
| Africa | 92 | 5.30% |
| Asia-Pacific | 1208 | 2.00% |
| Europe | 1282 | 5.60% |
| Middle East | 262 | 9.30% |
| North America | 1495 | -0.40% |
| Latin America | 180 | 8.10% |

*Source*: Airline Business—August 2009.

Globalization in any industry, including the commercial aircraft manufacturing industry, is a double-edged sword. For airlines, globalization enables them to purchase aircraft manufactured across the globe. This increased competition lowers costs and provides the airlines with more products that suit their particular needs, thereby increasing economic efficiency. However, this is not the case universally. Airlines in some countries, such as Iran and Cuba, have political sanctions imposed on them that prohibit the airlines from purchasing aircraft manufactured in specific countries. This creates economic inefficiency that ultimately increases the costs of the airlines in those countries. The other side of globalization is that local companies must now compete against companies across the globe. This puts increased pressure on the local companies to provide better products and become more efficient. This pressure will cause some companies to transform themselves and become better, while others will suffer and fail. In this scenario, companies may go bankrupt and jobs will be lost. Therefore, to some, globalization will not appear to be a win-win scenario. In the aircraft manufacturing industry, the demise of Russian companies such as Ilyushin, Sukhoi, Tupolev, Antonov, and Yakolev can be attributed to globalization. Prior to the collapse of the Soviet Union, the Russian manufacturers were protected by the state. However, afterwards the companies were competing against products from Boeing, Airbus, and McDonnell Douglas, which were superior to their own. As a result, orders dwindled and the manufacturers struggled to sell existing models and design new products. Globalization essentially caused the Russian commercial aircraft manufacturing industry to no longer exist. The major problem with Russian commercial aircraft in the past has been the poor after-sales support compared with Western manufacturers such as Boeing and Airbus.

In the new globalized environment, airlines must also embrace globalization to be successful. In the United States, domestic competition has increased and passenger yields have decreased, so airlines have placed more focus on international flying. In fact, the current U.S. domestic environment is so difficult that some airlines will post corporate profits by making money on international flying while recording losses on domestic flights. The reason for continuing to operate domestically is that the U.S. legacy carriers still require the domestic flights to feed their international flights through hubs. Without such traffic feed, the carriers' international flights alone would not be profitable. In fact, the lack of domestic feed for international flights is one reason for the collapse of the original Pan American World Airways.[5]

Operating in multiple countries provides unique issues to airlines, including financial issues. By operating internationally, airlines collect and spend money in multiple currencies. With currency exchange rates fluctuating, airlines bear the risk that the money they collect today may be substantially less in value than the expenses they pay in the future. Additionally, some currencies may not be freely traded, making it difficult to convert revenue earned in a foreign country into domestic currency. Because of currency fluctuations, airlines must hedge to help minimize the risk in dealing in multiple currencies.

## OBJECTIVES OF AIRLINES

> "Safety is the very foundation of the aviation industry, and it must be Southwest's priority to ensure the personal safety of each Southwest Airlines customer and employee."
>
> Gary Kelly and Colleen Barrett, Southwest Airlines

While airline executives' mandate includes a variety of objectives, their primary objective should be to increase shareholder wealth through maximizing revenue and minimizing costs. Other objectives for airlines include:

- Shareholder wealth maximization
- Customer satisfaction
- Employee satisfaction
- Positive image with stakeholders, employees, passengers, and the community
- Safety.

---

5    Pan American World Airways began life in 1927 and in 1991 after 64 years of service, finally submitted to years of financial pressures.

In an ideal world, every business decision undertaken should consider all factors in determining if shareholder value is increased or decreased. Unfortunately, not all business decisions are made with maximizing the shareholder wealth in mind. These "incorrect" decisions may be made due to a variety of issues, such as personal egos/agendas, politics, or ethics. Such issues can lead to destructive behavior that may ultimately lead to the failure of the business. A common issue involves disagreements between the head of a company (chief executive officer) and the shareholders. A CEO may push for a certain business direction (e.g. merger) where he personally stands to gain, while shareholders may oppose such a deal believing that the merger is a bad idea for the company and ultimately their invested wealth. In this example, both sides differ based on their objectives, presenting a difficult situation that may ultimately lead to an "incorrect" decision.

Maximizing shareholder value can be accomplished in either of two ways: an increase in the stock price of the company, allowing investors to achieve greater capital gains; or the redistribution of profits to shareholders in the form of dividends. In order to accomplish either of these two outcomes, a company must be able to achieve a long-term profit. Therefore, the objective of an airline manager is to maximize profits, influenced by the rules established and enforced by government. Passengers seek to buy transportation at the lowest possible price with the best possible service and the most convenient schedules. For customers to be satisfied and the airline to receive enough business to make a profit, airlines must offer customers the best value proposition based on those three elements: price, service and convenience (weighted to varying degrees depending on the passenger). Profit can be defined and calculated as either an accounting profit or economic profit.

## ACCOUNTING PROFIT

Accounting profit can be defined as total revenue minus total explicit costs. Total revenue is the sum of cash received from the operation of the business, while costs, or expenses, are the outflows of assets used to provide the good or service. Explicit costs are those costs directly linked to the operation of the business, and they may either be cash outlays or non-cash items, such as depreciation. Therefore, it is important to remember that accounting profit is not simply the difference between cash inflows and cash outflows, but the difference between assets generated from the operation of the business and the assets lost as a result of performing the business function. To many, accounting profit is the "normal" profit, as it is stated on the income statement which must be prepared according to strict accounting rules and regulations.[6]

Accounting Profit = Total Revenue-Total Expenses (explicit costs)

## ECONOMIC PROFIT

From an economic standpoint, profit must also take into consideration opportunity costs. Opportunity costs are defined as the cost of choosing one option over the next best alternative. As an example, consider an airline that has only one aircraft and has a choice

---

6      Prior to the deregulation act of 1978, ticket prices, as well as the routes an airline could fly, were set by the Civil Aeronautical Board as a part of the regulation of air travel.

of three routes. Assume that the cost of operating on all three routes is the same and that the revenue from the three routes is as listed in Table 1.10.

**Table 1.10    Airline's choices**

|          | Annual Revenue |
|----------|----------------|
| City A   | $450,000       |
| City B   | $275,000       |
| City C   | $150,000       |

Since the goal of the airline is to maximize shareholder wealth, the airline decides to fly to city A. Based on the airline's decision to fly to city A, the airline's next best alternative would be to fly to city B. This means that the airline's opportunity cost would be $275,000. The principle behind opportunity costs is helping to ensure that the best option is chosen. For example, if a company was losing money year after year and eroding shareholder value, then the next best option may be to close the company and earn zero profit. This option would stop the company from losing money, preventing further decreases in shareholder value. Another example, the interest that could be earned from the proceeds of the sale of an aircraft, is an opportunity cost for the use of that aircraft. Many airlines have frequent flyer programs that promise passengers free flights. The opportunity costs that airlines incur because the seats are given to non-revenue passengers, is the lost revenue from paying passengers.

Economic profit is defined as total revenue minus total explicit costs and opportunity costs. Therefore, for a business to be profitable from an economic standpoint, the business must have positive revenue over both explicit and opportunity costs. As a result of the inclusion of opportunity costs, the barrier to achieve a profit from an economic standpoint is significantly greater than earning an accounting profit. Economic profit is rarely explicitly calculated since determining opportunity costs can be difficult, since all the alternative business opportunities may not be known. Because of these issues, economic profit is usually the result of an individual's judgment, and is used implicitly in business decision-making and strategy crafting.

Economic Profit = Total Revenue - Total Expenses (explicit costs + opportunity costs)

The major categories of explicit costs are listed below:

* Selling and general administrative expenses
* Fuel costs
* Flight and cabin crew expenses
* Direct maintenance expenditures
* Landing fees and capital equipment charges
* Distribution cost (sales and promotion)
* Station cost
* Ground expenses

- Passenger services
- Interest expenses
- Taxes.

## BUSINESS ORGANIZATIONAL STRUCTURES

Around the globe, organizations differ based on their ownership and management structure. Ownership structure varies depending on a host of factors, such as the number of employees, overall size of the business, extent of liability, and the number of owners. When starting a business, one of the most critical early decisions is selecting the appropriate ownership structure, since that decision can have a lasting impact on the success of the business. While ownership structures vary from country to country, in the United States there are four common organizational structures: sole proprietorships, partnerships, corporations, and non-business entities.

### Sole Proprietorships

By definition, a sole proprietorship is "a simple, informal structure that is inexpensive to form; it is usually owned by a single person or a family" (SBA, 2008). In essence, it is the most basic form of business since a single person owns the business. Because of this, sole proprietorships are usually small in size, providing the owner with full control over the organization. The proprietor personally owns all of the assets of the company and personally receives all of the profits generated by the company. In fact, there is no legal difference between the proprietor and the company; they are viewed as being the same business entity. Income of sole proprietorship is considered to be the personal income of the individual owner and taxation is based upon the income of the owner (Chambers and Lacey, 2007). Depending on the specific taxation laws, this may either be beneficial or detrimental.

One major downside to sole proprietorships is that the owner assumes full liability for the company's actions. In the United States this represents a significant risk to the owner, since in the event of a liability lawsuit, the litigation can go after not only the assets of the company but also the owner's personal assets. Therefore, for businesses operating where liability risks are high, a sole proprietorship is usually not the best organizational structure.

An example of a sole proprietorship would be an individual who wants to start his or her own lawn care service. In most cases, all this individual needs to do is to file for an occupational license from the governing body in his or her area (i.e. county government) and maintain proper records for tax purposes. In this case, a sole proprietorship is likely a good choice since the liability risk of lawn care is minimal and the business is likely to be initially small. This in turn provides the owner with full control over all business activities. From a taxation standpoint, the individual is taxed on all income generated from the lawn care service, less operational expenses, at his or her personal taxation rate.

### Partnerships

As defined by the Internal Revenue Service (IRS) a partnership is, "an unincorporated organization with two or more members is generally classified as a partnership for federal tax purposes if its members carry on a trade, business, financial operation, or venture and divide its profits" (Internal Revenue Service, 2008). A general partnership has properties similar to a sole proprietorship, but is controlled by two entities instead of one. Because of this, each partner maintains full liability and the partnership is not a legal entity, so that each partner is taxed individually. Partnerships are easy to create and in the United States require no written agreement between partners, although most partnerships do have some form of written terms (SBA, 2008). By legal definition, a partner does not have to be an individual, but may also be a corporation. Therefore, partnerships may be formed between two individuals, two corporations, or an individual and a corporation. As a result, multiple forms of partnerships exist, such as general partnerships, limited partnerships, and joint ventures. While partnerships exist in all forms of business, they are particularly common in professional service areas, such as accounting and legal services. By forming a partnership, accountants and lawyers can split their overhead costs—overhead costs that would have to be borne individually if in a sole proprietorship. Therefore, the creation of a partnership has some very practical value.

As an example, suppose two lawyers want to combine their practices. To do so, all they would need to do is enter into some form of partnership agreement and ensure that both parties have all the necessary requirements to practice law in their area. As is the case with sole proprietorships, from an accounting standpoint, the partners' personal expenses and business expenses must be tracked separately; however, their total income will be taxed on a personal tax level. Business expenses incurred from the partnership can be used as deductions; therefore, it is critical to keep documentation differentiating business expenses among partners.

## Corporations

A corporation can be defined as "an organization recognized by the law as an entity with rights, privileges, assets, and liabilities distinct from those of its owners" (Lewellen, Halloran, and Lanser, 2000). Therefore, a corporation is a separate legal entity with the unique feature of limited liability, which means that the liability of the company ends with the company and that investors are not fully liable for the actions of the corporation. Therefore, the worst-case scenario for investors in corporations is that they just lose just their original investment and not their personal assets. Limited liability is the greatest advantage of a corporation over other forms of organizations and it is the recommended organizational form for businesses with any liability exposure.

Another advantage of a corporation is the greater ease by which capital can be raised. While all three forms of business can receive debt financing, corporations also have the ability to raise funds through the issuance of equity, or stock. Equity provides investors with a proportional share of ownership of the company. For example, Southwest Airline has 611,137,000 shares of common stock outstanding with 536 institutional investors and 1,007 mutual fund companies as share holders. The shareholders' interests are managed and protected by the corporation's board of directors. While the issuance of stock reduces the founder's share of ownership, it is an effective way to raise funds for expansion. When the stock of a corporation is publicly traded, the corporation is referred to as a public corporation, and it must provide financial reports to the general public. Private corporations also exist, where ownership of the company is composed of one or a few entities.

While corporations have many advantages, the greatest disadvantage of a corporation is double-taxation. Since a corporation is a separate legal entity, corporations are taxed on their profitability. After the corporation is taxed, the company may wish to distribute dividends, or cash payments, to their investors based on the profitability of the company. When the investor receives the dividend income, the investor will be taxed on the income in their personal tax bracket. Therefore, as the profits of the corporation are transferred from the company to the individual, the income has been taxed twice, hence double-taxation. This is in contrast to sole proprietorships and partnerships which only have single tax, at the individual's personal tax bracket. Since the tax brackets for corporations and individuals vary significantly, the total dollar impact of double-taxation depends on a host of factors and can vary widely.

## Not for Profit Organizations (NPO)

Another form of organization worth mentioning is not for profit entities. This is a wide range of organizations formed for purposes other than to make a profit. In America, the non-profit sector has more than $2 trillion in assets.[7] These organizations typically fulfill social roles, such as education and medical care. Non-business entities lack identifiable ownership and have goals that vary considerably from organization to organization. These issues create substantial challenges to accounting policies and procedures, usually requiring specialized knowledge.

While many assume non-profit organizations do not earn a profit, in fact profitability is necessary for the organization to achieve its goals. All profits generated from the organization are generally re-invested in the organization, to further its goal of providing better education or health care. However, since the profit motive is not central to these organizations, they are usually less efficient than for profit entities. This organizational inefficiency is particularly damaging in industries where the non-business entity has substantial market power. For example, many government organizations have monopoly power and, since their goals are not profit-based, they are plagued with inefficiency.

Non-business entities are particularly important in the aviation industry, with several major entities falling under the classification of non-business entities. For example, most airports in the United States, and for that matter the globe, are non-business entities with vaguely defined goals such as *"providing the best passenger experience"*. It is sometimes argued that airports are not created to generate a profit, but to serve the population. However, airports routinely generate a profit in order to fund future projects.

Since most airports are essentially monopolies, there is little competition to limit the profitability of an airport. This creates agency issues between passengers, airlines, and the airport since all their goals differ. Therefore, understanding the organizational structure of entities in the aviation industry can substantially increase one's knowledge of the industry.

## COMPARISON BETWEEN BUSINESS STRUCTURES

As mentioned above, the key aspects that help differentiate organizational structures are: amount of liability, amount of control, taxation, and the ability to raise capital. Table 1.11

---

7     Nonprofit GPS, 2009.

**Table 1.11    Advantages and disadvantages of business structures**

| Business Type | Advantages | Disadvantages |
|---|---|---|
| **Sole Proprietorships** | • Simple to start<br>• Owner has full control<br>• Easily can be resolved<br>• Taxation limitations<br>• Secrecy. | • Unlimited liability<br>• Harder to raise capital<br>• Lack of continuity<br>• Limited sources of funds. |
| **Partnerships** | • Simple to start<br>• Partners still have a relative large amount of control when compared with that of corporations<br>• Decision making. | • Unlimited liability<br>• Each individual has less control when compared with that of a sole proprietorship<br>• Life of partnership<br>• Limited sources of capital. |
| **Corporations** | • Limited liability (LLC) (Shareholders are only liable for their investment)<br>• Easier to raise capital<br>• Ease of transfer of ownership<br>• Potential for expansion. | • Double-Taxation<br>• Loss of control<br>• Expensive to form<br>• Information disclosure requirement. |

*Source*: Small Business Administration.

summarizes the key advantages and disadvantages for the major organizational structures. To summarize, sole proprietorships are simple to start, with the owner maintaining full control; however, the owner assumes unlimited liability and, while the capital required to start may be minimal, it is usually more difficult to raise in the future. Partnerships provide the owner with less control as it is divided between the partners; however, each partner still retains unlimited liability. Finally, corporations provide the least amount of control as multiple shareholders may own the company, and this provides limited liability because the shareholders merely helped the corporation raise capital. Additionally, corporations experience double-taxation when dividends are distributed to their shareholders or when shareholders exercise capital gains.

Since there is no one universally suitable organizational structure, the decision as to which structure to use will depend on the industry and the goals/objectives of the business. In the United States, where the threat of liability lawsuits is greater than most countries, corporations, while more complex, provide the safety of limited liability. In the aviation industry, an industry with a high exposure to liability, organizations involved in the industry are almost always corporations. The risk of unlimited liability in the United States is greater than the disadvantages of double-taxation. The loss of control issue for corporations can be alleviated if the corporation decides to remain private; however, by remaining private, the corporation could have greater difficulty in raising capital.

Table 1.12 provides a comparison of organizational structures, in terms of the number of registered organizations in the United States, and their corresponding total annual income, less any losses. From the data, a clear paradox exists between sole proprietorships and corporations. In terms of the total number of registered organizations in the United

**Table 1.12    Comparison of types of business structure and annual incomes**

| Organization Type | Number of Organizations | Percentage | Total Annual Income (thousands) | Percentage |
|---|---|---|---|---|
| Sole Proprietorships (non-farm) | 19,710,079 | 72% | $230,308,100 | 20% |
| Partnerships | 2,375,375 | 8.50% | $154,485,912 | 13% |
| Corporations | 5,401,237 | 19.50% | $779,988,635 | 67% |
| **Total** | **27,486,691** | | **$1,164,782,647** | |

*Source*: Internal Revenue Service website accessed on 1/11/2008.

States, sole proprietorships, excluding farms, are the vast majority of organizations operating in the business environment. However, in terms of total annual income, sole proprietorships represent only 20% of the total annual income reported to the IRS. In contrast, corporations only represent roughly 20% of the total number of organizations, yet generate approximately 67% of the total income. This disparity clearly shows that the majority of sole proprietorships are small, while corporations are relatively large.

As mentioned, the reason for this is the fact that corporations have limited liability and a much greater ability to raise capital. Intuitively this makes sense, as family-run grocery stores (sole proprietorships) are small, while Fortune 500 corporations, such as Boeing and American Airlines, are extremely large, even by corporate America's standards. While sole proprietorships outweigh corporations in sheer quantity, the state of the nation's economy depends more on corporations. This is the reason why most political decision-making and media attention is directed towards corporations. Also, this focus on corporations is one of the reasons why small business organizations and better business bureaus have been established to help promote small business.

## AGENCY ISSUES

"I left a legacy of shame. It is something I will live with for the rest of my life."

Bernard Madoff [8]

Agency issues are concerns between members of organizations which have different objectives. A principal-agent problem occurs[9] when an agent pursues personal objectives that conflict with the principal's (shareholders) contractual rights. The recent Enron and Tyco scandals are examples of the principal-agent problem. Another example, WorldCom did not report in its filed compensation tables any implicit income to CEO from the over $400 million of loans he received from the company at a low interest rate (2.15%).[10] Agency

---

8    Bernard Madoff, a former financier and convicted felon, apologizing at U.S. court hearing where he was sentenced to 150 years in prison for fraud.
9    It occurs when the owner of a company and the manager are different individuals and have different preferences.
10    Bebchuk and Fried, *Executive Compensation as an Agency Problem*, John M. Olin Center for Law, and Economics, Harvard, 2003.

issues are particularly prevalent in corporations where control of the company, especially publicly-traded corporations, is extremely decentralized. For example, the manager with stock-option contracts can gain immensely through such manipulations by driving up the price of a stock, exercising a call option, and then selling the stock. In public corporations, the Board of Directors (BOD) is the representation for shareholders since its members have been elected by the shareholders. However, how accurately does the board of directors represent the interest of all the shareholders? Board members typically receive extensive perks from the corporation. As a result, boards of directors are often criticized for rubber-stamping the desires of management. In that case, an agency issue exists between the representatives of the stockholders and the stockholders themselves.

The other major agency issue, and the more common one, is the difference in objectives between management and shareholders. The major objective for shareholders is to increase their wealth, which is the result of the corporation maximizing its profit. However, executive management may have other objectives, which can result in catastrophic corporate damage. Recent scandals with companies like Enron, Tyco, and WorldCom have raised the awareness of principal-agent issues and corporate ethics. Table 1.13 below highlights a few of the more highly publicized principal-agent problems.

**Table 1.13     Recent examples: Principal–agent problems**

| Company | Alleged Problems | Results | Loss to Shareholder |
|---|---|---|---|
| Adelphia | Management looted assets | Filed for bankruptcy, stock was delisted, fines and criminal charges | Over $3.5 billion loss in value |
| Arthur Andersen | Destroyed audit documents for Enron | Liquidated | |
| Madoff Investment Securities LLC | Securities fraud | 150 years imprisonment and forfeiture of $170,179 billion | $18 billion in losses to investors |
| Enron | Fraudulent Accounting | Filed for bankruptcy and stock delisted | $64.2 billion loss in value |
| Imcolone | Insider trading | Prison Term for CEO | Significant price drop |
| Merrill Lynch | Inflated Internet Stocks | Fines | Significant price drop |
| Tyco | Management looted assets | Fines and criminal charges | $6.3 billion loss in value |
| WorldCom | Fraudulent accounting | Filed for bankruptcy, fines and criminal charges | $2.6 billion loss in value |

*Source*: Compiled by the Authors.

A prime example of the destruction that agency issues can cause was Tyco. Executives spent excessively on non-business related activities, using corporate money to fund all their leisure activities. As a result of this looting of assets, Tyco shareholders lost a combined $6.3 billion in value. When a company loses value owing to management goals that are different from shareholder goals, the lost value is referred to as agency costs (Ross, Westerfield and Jordan, 2008). As a result of these fraudulent activities, investors lost billions of dollars when the stock plunged in value the day Tyco's activities came to light.

Since principal-agent problems between shareholders and management can be catastrophic, how can they be avoided? The simplest answer is to align the objectives of management and shareholders by issuing management stock or stock options, so that management personnel are also stockholders. This creates the incentive for management to increase shareholder value, since they are now shareholders themselves. Other methods used for aligning objectives are providing top management seats on the board of directors, profit sharing, and having other incentive based pay schemes. The value of incentive pay has proven particularly successful when offered to front-line employees and middle management. All these methods help solidify a strong corporate culture and reduce agency issues. The principal-agent problem has become so high-profile in recent years that the U.S. Congress decided that it needed legislation to control corruption at the corporate level, and President George Bush signed the Sarbanes-Oxley Act into law on July 30, 2002 (Edison, 2006).

## FINANCIAL MARKETS

If Delta Air Lines wants to borrow $500 million to finance new aircraft, or London Heathrow needs more money to finance the construction of new runway, they need to access capital markets. Capital markets are the markets for long term securities with a security representing an interest in a corporation (Brigham and Houston, 2000). In general, capital market brings together suppliers and demanders of capital.[11] We have pointed out that one of the goals of airline finance is to maximize shareholder wealth, but how do airlines, or any other businesses, get shareholders in the first place? Shares of stock in a company are sold through financial markets. There are two major types of financial markets: primary markets and secondary markets (Ross, Westerfield and Jordan, 2008). Table 1.14 shows the differences in attributes between primary markets and secondary markets. The money market is where short-term securities with maturities of one year or less are traded. Money market instruments include Treasury bills (T-Bills), negotiable CD's, money market funds and Eurodollar deposits.

### Primary Markets

A *primary market* involves a corporation which raises capital by issuing new stock. Assume EZjET wanted to raise capital by offering a share of ownership; they would invite the public to purchase shares of stock in the form of an initial public offering (IPO) or privately sell shares to a bank, brokerage firm or other financial institution. The initial offering of a class of stock is done so in the primary markets. An IPO is the financial mechanism by which an airline offers stock to the general public for the first time and becomes a publicly traded company. IPOs are essentially very risky investment. As a result, there is potential for huge financial gains and losses. On June 8, 1971, Southwest Airlines through an IPO issued 650,000 shares at approximately $11.[12] JetBlue Airways raised $158.4 million from its $27 per share stock National Association of Securities Dealers Automated Quotations (NASDAQ) initial public offering.[13] In 1999, WestJet Airlines announced the airlines raised

---

11    Baumol, W. 1990. "Entrepreneurship: Productive, Unproductive and Destructive." *Journal of Political Economy*. 98, 893–921.
12    Southwest Airlines, 2009.
13    The Business Journal, Friday, April 19 2002.

**Table 1.14    Financial markets: Primary vs. Secondary**

| Primary Markets | Secondary Markets |
|---|---|
| Initiated by corporation | Does not directly involve corporation |
| Direct sale | Sale between two independent parties; investors and/or financial institutions |
| May be offered publicly or privately | Sold through Dealer and/or Auction Markets |

*Source*: Ross, Westerfield and Jordan, 2008.

$25 million from the sale of 2,500,000 common shares of the company.[14] Brazilian low-cost airline GOL successfully priced its IPO at $9 per share and raised $281 million in June, 2004.[15] On December 19, 2006, Genesis Lease Limited, a global commercial aircraft leasing company, raised more than $640 million by issuing 27,860,000 shares at a public offering price of $23.00 per share.

## Secondary Markets

*Secondary markets*, on the other hand, involve two parties totally outside the corporation; that is, one investor or institution selling to another investor or institution. Secondary markets can consist of dealer markets or auction markets. Dealer markets involve dealers of stock and other financial securities who actually buy and sell the securities to/from investors. Auction markets involve actual locations and make use of brokers who match buyers and sellers (Ross, Westerfield and Jordan, 2008).

One example of an auction market is the New York Stock Exchange (NYSE). Other secondary markets in the United States included the American Stock Exchange (AMEX) and NASDAQ. Other major world exchanges include the NYSE Euronext, FTSE International in London (London Stock Exchange), the Tokyo Stock Exchange (TSE)[16] and the Shanghai Exchange. Table 1.15 provides a listing of the major global stock exchanges, as well as the combined market capitalization of the companies listed on the exchange.

The NYSE is the largest and oldest of the U.S.stock exchanges, dating back to 1792 (Investopedia, 2009a). The NYSE had been a privately held company until its acquisition of electronic exchange Archipelago in 2005. Trading on the NYSE used to all be done on the floor of the exchange; however, the NYSE now has more electronic trading, yet the NYSE still makes use of trading specialists who are assigned a certain number of stocks and are responsible for maintaining as close to continuous trading as possible (Investopedia, 2009a). The NASDAQ is a computerized system of trading that was invented in 1971 (Investopedia, 2009b). Today the NASDAQ has become the second largest exchange in the U.S., providing quotes on over 5,000 stocks which are traded actively, including companies like Dell and Microsoft (Investopedia, 2009b). The AMEX is the third largest

---

14    Calgary, Alberta, Business Wire, July 13, 1999.
15    Bloomberg, December 30, 2004.
16    The Tokyo Stock Exchange was created under the direction of the Finance Ministry and began trading on June 1, 1878.

Table 1.15     Major world stock exchanges

| Exchange Company | Listings | Market Capitalization |
| --- | --- | --- |
| NYSE/NYSE Euronext | Over 8,500 | $16.7 Trillion |
| Nasdaq | About 3,100 | $4.0 Trillion |
| London Exchange | About 3,300 | $3.9 Trillion |
| Tokyo Exchange | About 2,200 | $4.3 Trillion |
| Shanghai Exchange | About 800 | $3.7 Trillion |

Source: NYSE Euronext and World Federation of Exchanges.

of the U.S.stock exchanges; however, the exchange has taken on a much smaller role and has since been merged with the parent company of the NYSE (NYSE Euronext, 2009). The AMEX lists about 10% of securities traded within the U.S. (Investopedia, 2009c). NYSE Euronext (NYSE's parent company) announced that the AMEX will no longer be an active exchange effective March 1, 2009 (NYSE Euronext, 2009).

Two independent Federal agencies, the U.S. Securities and Exchange Commission (SEC) and the Commodity Futures Trading Commission (CFTC) are the industry watch dogs and oversee the financial markets.

## SUMMARY

This chapter was an introduction to the basics of business in general, and the airline industry specifically. Finance plays a critical role in business, and it is used in all levels of decision-making, from top-level structural decisions down to simple operational choices. As a result, an effective financial manager needs to not only understand finance, but also the industry in which his or her company operates. To that end, this chapter discussed the international aspects of aviation and the concepts of accounting and economic profits. This chapter also recognizes the emergence of the low-cost carriers as the powerhouses of the future airline industry, estimated to grow up to 50% of the market share. Finally, the chapter covered the organizational forms that businesses might adopt and the problems that may arise from those forms. The overall goals of the remainder of the text are to provide students and professionals with an understanding of finance in the industry and the ability to use this knowledge more effectively.

## DISCUSSION QUESTIONS

1. Discuss the impact that low-cost carriers have had on the airline industry and the reasons for their success. Include a brief description of the history of the industry that has facilitated this success.
2. Differentiate between accounting income and economic income. Why might these two numbers differ?
3. What strategy have legacy carriers adopted to counter the competition from low-cost carriers and why have they adopted this particular strategy.

4.  Discuss the pros and cons of globalization, from a financial perspective, as far as the airline industry is concerned.
5.  Describe the difference between primary and secondary markets.
6.  If an airline has a single owner, what is the major objective of a financial manager?
7.  Describe some current examples of agency issues in today's business environment and cite their impact on shareholder wealth.
8.  Analyze the basic forms of business organization and their respective strengths and weaknesses from a financial point of view.
9.  Name the three major types of organizational structures and list their advantages and disadvantages.
10. What are the advantages and disadvantages of strategic alliances?
11. Explain the difference between accounting costs and economic costs.

## REFERENCES

CBS Market Watch Scandal Sheet. Retrieved February 13, 2008, from Market Watch Web site: http://www.marketwatch.com/news/features/scandal_sheet.asp

Chambers, D., and N. Lacey (2008). *Modern Corporate Finance* (5th ed.). Hayden-McNeil.

Ezard, K.and A. Panariello (2008, August). "Sunny intervals". *Airline Business*, 42–43.

*Internal Revenue Service* (n.d.). Retrieved January 11, 2008, from http://www.irs.gov

International Air Transport Association (2008, September). *Financial forecast: Significant losses continue into 2009*. www.iata.org/economics

International Civil Aviation Organization (n.d.) Retrieved January 14, 2008, from http://www.icaodata.com/default.aspx

Investopedia (2009a). New York Stock Exchange. Retrieved February 27, 2009 from http://www.investopedia.com/terms/n/nyse.asp

Investopedia (*2009b). Nasdaq. Retrieved February* 27, 2009 from http://www.investopedia.com/terms/n/nasdaq.asp

Investopedia (*2009c). American Stock Exchange-AMEX*. Retrieved February 27, 2009 from http://www.investopedia.com/terms/a/amex.asp

Lewellen, W., J. Halloran, and H. Lanser (2000). *Financial Management: An introduction to principles and practice*. Cincinnati, Ohio: South-Western College Publishing.

NYSE Euronext (2009). Amex.com website integration. Retrieved February 27, 2009 from http://www.nyse.com/attachment/amex_landing.htm

Small Business Administration (n.d.). Retrieved January 21, 2008, from http://www.sba.gov

Ross, A., R. Westerfield, and D. Jordan (2008). *Fundamentals of Corporate Finance (8)*. New York: McGraw-Hill/Irwin.

Wardell, J., (August 1, 2008). "Oil price rise hits British Airways Q1 profits," *USA Today*. Retrieved July 12, 2009 from http://www.usatoday.com/travel/flights/2008 –08–01-ba-earn_N.htm?csp=34

# 2

# Airline Cost Classifications

"Today, the situation is exacerbated with costs exceeding revenues at four times the pre-September 11 rate. Today, we are literally hemorrhaging money. Clearly this bleeding has to be stopped—and soon—or United will perish sometime next year."

James Goodwin, chairman and CEO of United's parent company UAL, October, 2001

Costs are an important part of any business. Without a fundamental understanding of controlling costs, companies will struggle to earn a profit. To increase profitability, either revenue should go up or costs must come down. One of the reasons that low-cost carriers (LCC) are outperforming legacy carriers is their lower cost structure. Airlines with higher productivity in terms of employees per ASM, high aircraft utilization, faster aircraft-turnaround time, and higher load factors have inherent cost advantages. Cost control is important in any business, but especially important in the airline industry since the airline industry has been in a financial crisis for much of this new century, a crisis exacerbated by the current global financial trouble. Declining revenue and high costs have resulted in many airlines entering bankruptcy during the 2000s.[1] To further compound the problem, with airlines competing in an extremely competitive marketplace, increasing fares is often difficult, leaving cost control as the only real solution to profitability. Many airlines throughout the globe have managed to make progress in lowering non-fuel unit costs since 2001. Airlines can control many of the costs related to the level of service they provide; however, airlines cannot always directly control many other types of costs, such as the price of fuel, labor costs, aircraft prices, landing fees, and air navigation charges. This chapter analyzes the different types of costs that airlines incur and analyzes techniques by which the airline industry has tried to reduce costs. The understanding of cost principles is applicable to any business since without the knowledge of where the cost of a product originates, the business may not be able to make a profit selling that product. The chapter starts with a discussion of accounting costs in general and then moves to the specifics of the airline industry. The following topics are covered in the chapter.

- Startup Costs
- Production Costs
- Fixed Costs
- Variable Costs
- Marginal Costs
- The Use of Costs for Managerial Decision-Making

---

1    Examples are United, U.S. Airways, Delta and Northwest in the United States.

## STARTUP COSTS

A cost is generally defined as the sacrifice made, usually in terms of resources, to perform a task. From an accounting perspective, costs are generally defined as expenses for goods received or services performed. From an economics standpoint, businesses can also incur opportunity costs, as these are the costs of giving up the next best alternative. This chapter primarily focuses on explicit, quantifiable costs, yet opportunity costs should still be considered from a decision-making standpoint.

To start a business there are certain start-up costs that are necessary to begin operation. Start-up costs are the expenses investors incur from inception until the business becomes functional. All businesses must procure licenses and any other type of permits necessary to legally operate a business in the country/state/county/city where they operate. In addition, specific types of businesses have other set-up costs which must be taken into account when starting the business. Manufacturing companies must have a physical facility, the necessary machinery, and inventory. In highly regulated industries, such as the airline industry, the necessary permits, such as an air operators certificate (AOC), can take considerable time and money. Additionally, airlines must procure aircraft, secure landing rights and gates at airports, find office space, create a robust information technology infrastructure, and most importantly, hire and train employees. This entire process is extremely lengthy with the airline incurring sizeable costs as time goes by. By first flight, an airline will have spent multi-millions of dollars to commence business. As such, significant start-up capital must be secured to finance an airline's start-up costs. These capital requirements represent a barrier to entry in the airline industry.

Once these initial starting costs have been incurred, they should not be taken into consideration for future decisions since once the costs have been incurred they cannot generally be recuperated.[2] By definition, sunk costs are any expenses that have already been incurred and therefore cannot be recuperated. As mentioned, sunk costs should not be used in making any future operating decisions as they have no bearing on any future outcome; however, managers often let sunk costs factor into their decision making, especially when deciding whether to continue to stay in business. Managers may think that they should remain in business, even when there is no hope of making a profit, because the company has already "spent all the money". Often called the sunk cost fallacy, managers believe that they must get use out of their start-up equipment even when it is not profitable.

---

2    For purposes of the following discussion, salvage value for the costs already incurred is assumed to be zero. Salvage (or resale) value can be incorporated for real-world decisions, but the basic conclusions of the following discussion are not altered by the inclusion of salvage costs. In general, salvage value merely reduces the sunk costs that have already been incurred.

Airline managers may also potentially fall into the sunk cost fallacy with regard to aircraft purchases. For example, an airline may have bought a new Boeing 757 eight years ago; however, at today's current fuel prices, the plane is not profitable flying the routes it is operating on. The airline could replace the 757 with a new Boeing 737–900ER, an airplane with similar capacity, but with better fuel economy. However, the manager may think that the 757 is "still pretty new" and decides to keep it in order to get as much use out of it as possible. This would be an example of the sunk cost fallacy at work since the airline has already paid for the 757 and the cost of that airplane should not have anything to do with the business decision of whether or not to buy the 737–900ER. This is not to say that the manager should definitely buy the 737, but rather should look at all the factors surrounding buying the 737, such as whether the airline can raise the capital to purchase the airplane and whether buying the airplane will increase profitability.

Another example could be an airline that pays to secure access to a slot-restricted airport. For instance, with the commencement of the Open Skies agreement between the United States and the European Union, all U.S. carriers were granted access to slot-congested London Heathrow Airport. However, in order to fly there, airlines had to pay to secure access rights. Such investments in slots would be considered a sunk cost when evaluating route performance in the future. Based on the sunk cost fallacy, if several years later the airline deems Heathrow Airport to be unprofitable owing to increased trans-Atlantic competition, the airline should not continue operation if profits are not foreseeable. The fact that the airline incurred considerable costs to enter the market should not be considered.

## PRODUCTION COSTS

"They must be very cautious that they don't get to the point where a customer will say it's just not cost-effective to fly."

David Castelveter, Air Transport Association

In accounting, any asset incurs a depreciation expense which helps assign the cost of the asset over its useful life. This is the result of the asset being worth less after several years instead of being new. Depreciation is just one of the many costs associated with a product over its useful life. As an example, a brand new commercial aircraft will incur maintenance costs, routine service costs, and regulatory costs over its lifetime just to remain operational. Additionally, over time the asset will depreciate in value as a result of technical innovation, advanced aircraft that come on the market, and depreciation of the asset. All of these costs will exist over the life of an aircraft. When determining what type of aircraft to order, managers must not only look at the purchase price of the airplane, but also the maintenance and operating costs of the aircraft over its useful life. For this reason, many low-cost carriers use only one type of aircraft to save on maintenance parts and training costs, even if the original purchase price is higher.[3]

---

3    Usually the reverse is true, since low-cost carriers have a penchant for placing sizeable aircraft orders, receiving volume discounts from manufacturers.

There are also opportunity costs associated with using an asset. If an asset is out of service, revenue cannot be generated from that asset, representing an opportunity cost to the company. Aircraft are routinely out of service for either scheduled or unscheduled maintenance, resulting in opportunity costs to the airline. In addition to opportunity costs associated with time, there are also opportunity costs associated with other uses of a product. For example, a piece of machinery that is used to join together body components on a car assembly line could be used to mold bumpers. Along with other uses for the product, the product could be sold to another party. In the airline business, an airline operating an aircraft has the opportunity cost of selling that airplane to another airline or to an aircraft leasing company. The airline may be able to record a onetime gain if they sell the aircraft at a price greater than the book value. Also, according to Air Transport Association, the booking of Federal Air Marshals into first-class seats particularly at a time when every additional revenue dollar is so important to the industry is producing opportunity costs in excess of $100 million annually.[4] If an airline is operating efficiently with its fleet deployed throughout the market, then a decision to redeploy equipment to another market to compete with other airlines will certainly incur opportunity costs.[5]

## FIXED COSTS (FC)

One of the fundamental characteristics of the airline industry is the presence of large fixed costs. Fixed costs are defined as costs of production which do not change with the rate of output. For an airline, fixed costs are those costs which do not directly relate to flying an additional seat or passenger. Examples of fixed costs in the airline industry include rental expenses and aircraft ownership costs. Fixed costs are unavoidable in the course of the short-term and are the same dollar amount no matter how efficient or inefficient the airline is. Figure 2.1 shows a fixed-cost curve, where total fixed costs (TFC) are represented as a horizontal line, since the cost is the same for all levels of production.

**Figure 2.1      Fixed cost curve**

4      ATA, 2009.
5      Gerald Smith Boston College, 2009.

A derivation of fixed costs is semi-fixed costs, which are costs that do not vary for a broad range of production outcomes. For example, gate rental expenses at an airport may be deemed a semi-fixed cost as renting one gate may be sufficient to handle up to ten daily flights; however, if the airline wants to introduce an eleventh flight, an additional gate would need to be leased. With two gates, the airline would be able to handle up to 20 flights a day at the airport. Under this scenario, the cost of one gate lease would be fixed for one to ten daily flights, while gate rental expenses would also be fixed for 11 to 20 daily flights, but at a higher step rate. This ladder effect creates fixed costs for portions of production.

The airline industry is one in which fixed costs encompass a large part of the total cost of operation. Aircraft ownership expenses, terminal/gate leases, liability insurance and even wages (to a certain extent with the presence of labor agreements) could be deemed fixed or semi-fixed costs.[6] Since fixed costs do not vary in relation to the amount of production, businesses should try to get as much production as they can out of assets that have a fixed cost associated with them. By increasing production, a company can reduce its average fixed cost. Therefore, the airlines with the lowest cost structures utilize their assets the most efficiently. For example, Southwest Airlines has achieved its cost leadership strategy by having high aircraft utilization rates, using terminal gates to operate at least ten daily flights, and by achieving high employee productivity.

*Average fixed costs* (AFC) are simply the total fixed cost divided by the level of production.

Table 2.1 shows the comparison of fixed cost and average fixed cost for an aircraft maintenance facility with $10,000 in fixed costs. As production increases, average fixed cost decreases. By servicing more aircraft with an asset that has a fixed cost, the maintenance facility is able to spread the fixed cost over a greater number of units, reducing the unit cost. Similarly, airlines are able to decrease cost per aircraft by increasing aircraft utilization (the number of hours per day that an aircraft is in the air). Although total fixed costs remain the same no matter how many passengers or cargo are carried, the average fixed cost will decrease as the number of operations increases.

## VARIABLE COSTS (VC)

While costs vary significantly among airlines, there are some common cost characteristics. Fuel is typically the largest component of operating costs and generally amounts to about 30% of operating costs. Labor is the next largest component of the costs. Costs that directly vary with changes in production are deemed variable costs. There are many costs that an airline incurs that are based on the number of passengers, the number of departures, or the volume of cargo carried. Some of these are aircraft fuel, some labor costs, supplies, and replacement parts. Whereas total variable costs (TVC) change based on the level of output, average variable cost (AVC) may not change for varying levels of production. However, as a result of scale efficiencies and semi-variable costs, average variable costs do not always remain constant for all levels of production. Just as with fixed costs, the average variable cost can be calculated by dividing the total variable cost (TVC) by the total production.

---

6    Airlines generally carry sizeable liability insurance.

**Table 2.1       Fixed cost (FC) and average fixed cost (AFC)**

| Total Fixed Costs | Production (in units) | Average fixed cost |
|---|---|---|
| $10000.00 | 10 | $1000 |
| $10000.00 | 20 | $500 |
| $10000.00 | 30 | $333 |
| $10000.00 | 40 | $250 |
| $10000.00 | 50 | $200 |
| $10000.00 | 60 | $167 |
| $10000.00 | 70 | $143 |
| $10000.00 | 80 | $125 |
| $10000.00 | 90 | $111 |
| $10000.00 | 100 | $100 |
| $10000.00 | 110 | $91 |
| $10000.00 | 120 | $83 |
| $10000.00 | 130 | $77 |
| $10000.00 | 140 | $71 |
| $10000.00 | 150 | $67 |
| $10000.00 | 160 | $63 |
| $10000.00 | 170 | $59 |
| $10000.00 | 180 | $56 |
| $10000.00 | 190 | $53 |
| $10000.00 | 200 | $50 |

While some costs may be classified as mixed, displaying tendencies of both variable and fixed costs, and when these are not present, then variable and fixed costs are added together, the total cost function is known. This represents the total, fully burdened cost of production.

$$Total\ Cost\ (TC) = TFC + TVC$$

$$Average\ Total\ Cost\ (ATC) = AFC + AVC$$

The average total cost for an airline, on a per unit basis, is measured by total cost per available seat mile (CASM), which takes into consideration both fixed and variable costs.

$$CASM = \frac{Total\ Cost}{ASM}$$

$$CASM_{Operating} = \frac{Operating\ Cost}{ASM}$$

Figure 2.2 displays the CASM for the major U.S. carriers, with Southwest Airlines (WN) having the lowest unit costs as a result of high fixed cost utilization.

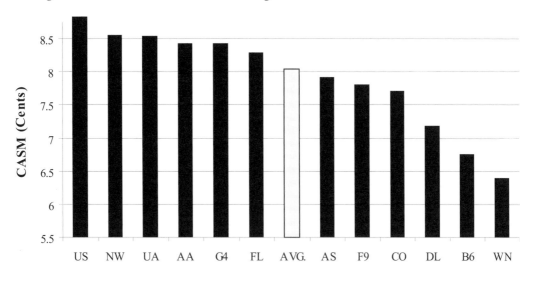

*Source*: Back Aviation Form41 Data 2008.

**Figure 2.2      Total cost per available seat mileage (CASM)**

## MARGINAL COSTS (MC)

The cost to produce one additional unit is called the marginal cost (MC). In an airline, the incremental cost per passenger on any given day on any given flight with low load factor is very small. This is a result of economies of scale. That is, a business may be able to increase production without a significant increase in costs because it is able to use unused capacity of fixed assets. An example of this would be an airline increasing flights from an airport it already serves. There may be very little additional cost to operating one additional flight out of a city where ground staff, equipment, and gate space are already in place. Another reason that marginal costs (MC) may vary is due to mixed costs, such as labor. Flight crews may be paid a fixed salary; however, additional flight crew may be needed if the airline increases the number of flights or the capacity of its planes. The formula for marginal cost is as follows:

$$MC = \frac{\Delta TC}{\Delta Q} = \frac{\partial TC}{\partial Q}$$

where the change in output ($\Delta Q$) is usually assumed to be 1 unit and ($\Delta TC$) is the change in total cost.

As a result of the large fixed costs in the airline industry, airlines tend to have very low marginal costs. In essence, the cost to an airline of carrying one additional passenger is minimal since the only significant marginal cost is incremental fuel burn and catering costs.

As a result, airlines are able to offer deeply discounted fares that can cover their marginal costs. For any pricing strategy, the minimum price should always be the marginal cost, with any incremental revenue providing a contribution to covering the fixed costs.

To understand the differences between total costs, variable costs, marginal costs, and fixed cost, refer to Table 2.2 displaying the cost structure of U.S.A. Aircraft Catering service. U.S.A. Aircraft Catering is a catering service that sells meals to airlines. U.S.A. Aircraft Catering has fixed costs of $200,000 per year for catering truck and building leases. The variable costs of preparing the meals are equal to $100,000 for every one thousand airplanes. Using information from Table 2.2, cost curves can be graphed to show the behavior of each cost category. Graphs of the cost curves for U.S.A. Aircraft Catering are shown in Figures 2.3 and 2.4.

**Table 2.2      U.S.A. aircraft catering cost**

| Airplanes catered (thousands) | TC | FC | VC | AFC | AVC | ATC | MC |
|---|---|---|---|---|---|---|---|
| 0 | $200,000 | $200,000 | $0 | $0 | $0 | $0 | $0 |
| 1 | $300,000 | $200,000 | $100,000 | $200,000 | $100,000 | $300,000 | $100,000 |
| 2 | $400,000 | $200,000 | $200,000 | $100,000 | $100,000 | $200,000 | $100,000 |
| 3 | $500,000 | $200,000 | $300,000 | $66,667 | $100,000 | $166,667 | $100,000 |
| 4 | $600,000 | $200,000 | $400,000 | $50,000 | $100,000 | $150,000 | $100,000 |
| 5 | $700,000 | $200,000 | $500,000 | $40,000 | $100,000 | $140,000 | $100,000 |
| 6 | $800,000 | $200,000 | $600,000 | $33,333 | $100,000 | $133,333 | $100,000 |
| 7 | $900,000 | $200,000 | $700,000 | $28,571 | $100,000 | $128,571 | $100,000 |
| 8 | $1,000,000 | $200,000 | $800,000 | $25,000 | $100,000 | $125,000 | $100,000 |
| 9 | $1,100,000 | $200,000 | $900,000 | $22,222 | $100,000 | $122,222 | $100,000 |
| 10 | $1,200,000 | $200,000 | $1,000,000 | $20,000 | $100,000 | $120,000 | $100,000 |
| 11 | $1,300,000 | $200,000 | $1,100,000 | $18,182 | $100,000 | $118,182 | $100,000 |
| 12 | $1,400,000 | $200,000 | $1,200,000 | $16,667 | $100,000 | $116,667 | $100,000 |

The cost curves show that the total fixed cost and the average variable cost are both constant. Average variable cost is constant because for every additional 1,000 aircraft that U.S.A. caters, variable cost increases by $100,000.

A constant variable cost means that the company is achieving constant returns to scale. For every additional input ($100,000) it is receiving one level of output (1,000 aircraft catered). Some companies do not receive constant returns to scale, meaning that they have either increasing returns or decreasing returns to scale. When a company operates with increasing returns to scale, the average cost is decreasing and the company is receiving the benefits of economies of scale. Decreasing returns to scale exhibit the opposite characteristics; that is, marginal cost is increasing and diseconomies of scale

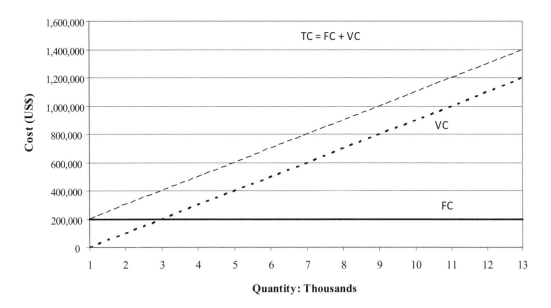

**Figure 2.3      Total cost curves for U.S.A. aircraft catering**

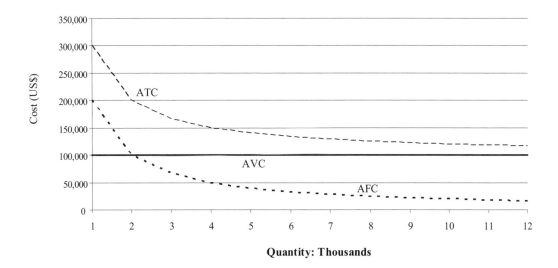

**Figure 2.4      Average cost curves for U.S.A. aircraft catering**

occur. Increasing and decreasing returns are depicted in Figure 2.5 through a non-linear total cost curve.

Figure 2.5 provides an example of an airline hub to show a variable cost function that exhibits increasing returns to scale for up to 120 flights per day and then decreasing returns to scale. As the number of flights per day at the hub begins to increase from 20, the variable cost is rising at a slower rate (average variable cost is decreasing). The airline is achieving economies of scale by using the same gates and ground personnel for multiple flights per day. At some point, however, variable costs begin to rise at an increasing rate. This is the

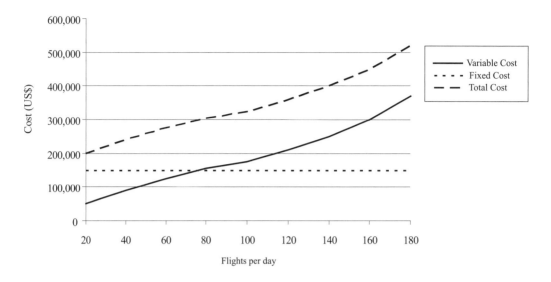

**Figure 2.5    Returns to scale: Airline hub**

inflection point, which in Figure 2.5 is at approximately 120 flights per day. After this point the airline is incurring diseconomies of scale. As the number of flights increase from 120 per day, more ground staff, ground equipment and gates have to be hired and/or leased. Furthermore, airspace at the airport becomes congested causing aircraft to circle in the air burning more jet fuel. As flights continue to increase, the marginal cost of adding another flight at the hub grows higher and higher. Airlines must be aware of diseconomies of scale as they grow larger, either through mergers or increased frequency of flights, as it represents inefficiency.

## USING COST FUNCTIONS FOR MANAGERIAL DECISIONS

While it is instructive to review the cost categories, it is even more important to understand how they affect managerial decision making. In this regard the cost curves provide the following rules for managerial decision-making:

- Marginal cost tells us where (how much) to produce
- Average total cost tells us whether we should produce
- Average variable cost tells us when we should cease production.

The intuitive explanation for this is the following: Since marginal cost is incurred for producing one additional unit of output, then it is obvious that as long as the revenue from the extra unit exceeds its cost, then we will want to produce that unit since it is adding to profit. Conversely, if the cost for that unit exceeds the revenue, then we will not want to produce that unit. Hence, we will continue production up to the point where marginal cost and marginal revenue are equal but not beyond.

Average total cost can be multiplied by total output to back solve for total cost. As long as total revenue exceeds total cost we will, of course, continue production. In the event that total cost falls below total revenue, but is still above variable costs, then we would still continue production (in the short run) since we are still making a contribution to fixed costs. This is an acceptable solution in the short-term; however, eventually fixed costs need to be paid and, if the cost curves remain the same, the company will be unable to generate sufficient revenue to pay for fixed costs and therefore such a scenario is not practical in the long run.

$$ATC = \frac{TFC + TVC}{Q} = \frac{TC}{Q}$$

$$TC = ATC \times Q$$

Finally, average variable costs can be translated into total variable costs by multiplying by the level of output. In this case, if total revenues do not cover our total variable costs, then production should cease since money is being lost on every unit being produced. That is, since revenue does not cover average variable costs, then the airline must consider either bankruptcy or ceasing operations (a complex and difficult decision).

## STRUCTURE OF AIRLINE COSTS

"Certainly, airlines like JetBlue, airlines like Southwest, they've got a different cost structure, they've got a different rationale, they've got a different model."

David Field, *Airline Business* Magazine

This section provides more detail on the cost structure found in the airline industry. Managing costs not only improves the profitability of a company and can provide better service levels to customers, but is the primary point of differentiation found in an oligopolistic airline industry. Table 2.3 lists some of the more common fixed and variable costs that airlines may incur. The airline industry in United States is an oligopoly market dominated by a few major airlines, so that industry dynamics, or cost factors impact the profit structure of airlines. Examples of cost factors include the size and type of aircraft, fuel efficiency and distance traveled. Furthermore, the costs of airline resources can be divided into operating costs and non-operating costs. Non-operating costs are costs not directly linked to the airline's operation, but are required to conduct business. The major non-operating cost to airlines is interest expense.

### Operating Costs (OCs)

Airline operating costs are those costs that are incurred in the process of providing air transport services to passengers which include aircraft expenses, fuel, maintenance, employee expenses, landing fees and other operating expenses. Operating costs are both fixed and variable, yet all relate to the core operation of the business. The sharp rise in jet fuel prices since 2008, the largest direct operating cost to airlines, has increased the pressure for airlines to improve their overall cost efficiency and productivity levels.[7] Through the use of fuel hedging programs many airlines have been able to reduce their operating expenses with a predetermined and acceptable fuel cost. However, hedges placed at oil's peak may also represent realized hedging losses for the carriers.[8]

---

7    Given the significance of fuel costs to the industry's economic viability and the volatility of fuel prices, airlines typically engage in hedging programs to eliminate price variation.
8    See Chapter 11 for a more in-depth discussion of fuel hedging.

**Table 2.3      Airline fixed and variable costs**

FIXED COSTS

Fixed salaries, benefits and training costs for flight crews, which do not vary according to aircraft usage

Maintenance costs

• Maintenance labor for maintenance scheduled on an annual basis
• Maintenance contracts for maintenance scheduled on an annual basis

Lease costs based on a length of time

Depreciation

Operations overhead

Administrative overhead

Self-insurance costs

VARIABLE COSTS

Crew costs (travel expenses, overtime charges, wages of crew hired on an hourly or part-time basis)

Maintenance costs scheduled on the basis of flying time or flight cycles

• Maintenance labor (includes all labor salaries, wages, benefits, travel, training)
• Maintenance parts (cost of materials and parts consumed in aircraft maintenance and inspections)
• Maintenance contracts (all contracted costs for unscheduled maintenance, maintenance scheduled on flight-hour basis, on flight-cycle basis or on condition)
• Engine overhaul, aircraft refurbishment, major component repairs

Modifications

Fuel and other fluids

Lease costs (leasing costs based on flight hours)

Landing fees, airport and en-route charges

Operating costs can be further broken down into direct and indirect operating costs. In the airline industry, direct operating costs comprise the greatest portion of operating costs, with labor wages and aircraft fuel comprising the bulk of airline operating costs. To examine the specific operating costs that airlines incur, Table 2.5 shows the operating expenses section of the income statement for Southwest Airlines.

The expenses shown in Table 2.5 can also be expressed as percentages of the overlying cost structure of Southwest Airlines. This is commonly called a common-size income statement and it expresses the dollar amounts as percentages.

The common-size income statement is particularly useful to compare changes in a cost structure over time. Table 2.6 provides a common-size income statement for Southwest Airlines which displays the increasing proportion of jet fuel in Southwest's cost structure. Other than this significant change, most other airline operating cost categories did not exhibit a significant shift in the airline's operating cost structure. Depending on the level of output for the periods, such costs could potentially be deemed fixed or semi-fixed costs.

*Direct Operating Costs (DOC)*[9]      Direct operating costs are those costs which can be directly traced to a specific level of production, which for the airline industry is generally classified as a block hour, aircraft mile, or available seat mile.[10] Labor and fuel are the two largest direct operating costs for an airline, as evidenced by the operating expense section for Southwest Airlines. As mentioned previously, labor exhibits tendencies of a mixed cost, with some

9      Direct operating costs are generally calculated as a cost per aircraft mile or aircraft block hour.
10     An available seat mile (ASM) represents one seat flown for one mile.

## Table 2.4    Airline operating and non-operating costs

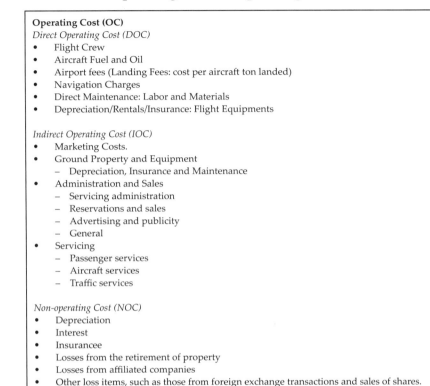

**Operating Cost (OC)**
*Direct Operating Cost (DOC)*
- Flight Crew
- Aircraft Fuel and Oil
- Airport fees (Landing Fees: cost per aircraft ton landed)
- Navigation Charges
- Direct Maintenance: Labor and Materials
- Depreciation/Rentals/Insurance: Flight Equipments

*Indirect Operating Cost (IOC)*
- Marketing Costs.
- Ground Property and Equipment
  - Depreciation, Insurance and Maintenance
- Administration and Sales
  - Servicing administration
  - Reservations and sales
  - Advertising and publicity
  - General
- Servicing
  - Passenger services
  - Aircraft services
  - Traffic services

*Non-operating Cost (NOC)*
- Depreciation
- Interest
- Insurancee
- Losses from the retirement of property
- Losses from affiliated companies
- Other loss items, such as those from foreign exchange transactions and sales of shares.

## Table 2.5    Operating expenses for Southwest Airlines ($ millions)

|                                   | 2006  | 2007  | 2008   |
| --------------------------------- | ----- | ----- | ------ |
| Salaries, wages, and benefits     | 3,052 | 3,213 | 3,340  |
| Fuel and oil                      | 2,138 | 2,536 | 3,713  |
| Maintenance materials and repairs | 468   | 616   | 721    |
| Aircraft rentals                  | 158   | 156   | 154    |
| Landing fees and other rentals    | 495   | 560   | 662    |
| Depreciation and amortization     | 515   | 555   | 599    |
| Other operating expenses          | 1,326 | 1,434 | 1,385  |
| **Total operating expenses**      | 8,152 | 9,070 | 10,574 |

*Source*: Southwest Airlines-Investor Relations (2009).

wages, salaries, and benefits (WSB) components largely fixed, while other components, such as overtime and profit sharing, act more like variable costs.[11] As Table 2.6 displayed,

---

11    Labor costs include total salaries, and all benefits and other costs that are paid out to employees either directly or indirectly.

**Table 2.6      Common-size operating expenses for Southwest Airlines**

|                                        | 2006 | 2007 | 2008 |
|----------------------------------------|------|------|------|
| *Operating Expenses*                   |      |      |      |
| Salaries, wages, and benefits          | 37%  | 35%  | 32%  |
| Fuel and oil                           | 26%  | 28%  | 35%  |
| Maintenance materials and repairs      | 6%   | 7%   | 7%   |
| Aircraft rentals                       | 2%   | 2%   | 1%   |
| Landing fees and other rentals         | 6%   | 6%   | 6%   |
| Depreciation and amortization          | 6%   | 6%   | 6%   |
| Other operating expenses               | 16%  | 16%  | 13%  |
|                                        | 100% | 100% | 100% |
| **Total operating expenses ($ millions)** | **8,152** | **9,070** | **10,574** |

the composition of Southwest Airlines operating expenses are changing. Increases in the price of fuel have meant that fuel has become the largest operating expense. For Southwest Airlines, fuel has increased from 26% of operating costs in 2006 to 35% of operating costs in 2008. On the other hand, salaries have decreased from 37% of operating costs to 32% of operating costs, even though salaries have increased in real terms.

Together labor costs and fuel make up two-thirds of the operating expenses for Southwest Airlines in 2008. Other operating costs include aircraft rentals, landing fees, maintenance, depreciation and other operating expenses, and these comprise the remaining 33% of operating expenses for Southwest in 2008. While understanding direct-operating costs is important from an external standpoint, internal analysis requires detailed understanding of the differentiation between variable direct operating costs and fixed direct operating costs. Such differentiation is required to understand not only methods to reduce an airline's cost structure, but to also to shape business strategy.

As mentioned earlier, an airline's fixed operating costs are those costs of operation that occur whether or not specific flights are operated. These costs include aircraft leases, terminal leases, and crew salaries. Variable direct operating costs are those costs that are incurred based on the level of activity (number of flights) an airline operates. Fuel, landing fees, passenger services, and maintenance are all considered variable operating costs since they vary depending on the number of flights taken over the course of a year. Some flight crew costs, such as overnight accommodations, could also be deemed variable operating costs.

In determining a particular flight's profitability, an airline should examine variable direct operating costs, since fixed costs are going to be incurred regardless of whether the flight operates or not. Table 2.7 provides detailed financial information concerning a DirectJet Airways flight between Tampa Bay (TPA) and Pittsburgh (PIT).

Based solely on the bottom line it appears that the flight is losing money, yet based on contribution analysis the flights should still be operated as all the variable costs are being covered. The revenues from the flights are covering the direct variable operating costs and therefore are contributing to the fixed costs of the airline. The fixed operating and indirect costs are being allocated to the flights based on the percentage of operations that these

**Table 2.7        Income statement for DirectJet Airways Flights 100 and 101**

| DirectJet Airways | | | | | |
|---|---|---|---|---|---|
| Partial Income Statement (in thousands) | | | | | |
| For the Quarter Ending December 31, 2008 | | | | | |
| **Flight #100 (TPA-PIT)** | | | **Flight #101 (PIT-TPA)** | | |
| **Revenues** | | | | | |
| Ticket revenue | $ | 900.00 | Ticket revenue | $ | 851.18 |
| In-flight sales revenue | | 4.00 | In-flight sales revenue | | 3.80 |
| Cargo and other revenue | | 86.00 | Cargo and other revenue | | 67.00 |
| Total Revenue | $ | 90.00 | Total Revenue | $ | 921.98 |
| **Operating Costs** | | | | | |
| *Direct Costs* | | | *Direct Costs* | | |
| *Variable* | | | *Variable* | | |
| Fuel | $ | 503.00 | Fuel | $ | 505.25 |
| Cabin Crew Expenses | | 45.00 | Cabin Crew Expenses | | - |
| Passenger service | | 36.00 | Passenger service | | 37.10 |
| Maintenance | | 67.50 | Maintenance | | 67.50 |
| Landing fees | | 90.00 | Landing fees | | 94.50 |
| Passenger facility fees | | 40.50 | Passenger service fees | | 39.28 |
| Government segment tax | | 31.50 | Government segment tax | | 30.56 |
| Security fees | | 22.50 | Security fees | | 21.82 |
| Total Variable costs | $ | 836.00 | Total Variable costs | $ | 796.02 |
| *Fixed* | | | *Fixed* | | |
| Aircraft lease | $ | 66.67 | Aircraft lease | $ | 66.67 |
| Cabin Crew Salaries | | 0.74 | Cabin Crew Salaries | | 0.74 |
| Insurance | | 45.00 | Insurance | | 45.00 |
| Total Fixed costs | $ | 12.41 | Total Fixed costs | $ | 112.41 |
| *Indirect Costs* | | | *Indirect Costs* | | |
| Gate and Terminal fees | $ | 0.00 | Gate and Terminal fees | $ | 12.50 |
| Ground staff | | 5.00 | Ground staff | | 5.00 |
| Selling and Admin. Expenses | | 52.00 | Selling and Admin. Expenses | | 52.00 |
| Advertising | | 9.00 | Advertising | | 9.00 |
| Total Indirect costs | $ | 76.00 | Total Indirect costs | $ | 78.50 |
| Net Operating Profit (Loss) | $ | (34.41) | Net Operating Profit (Loss) | $ | 64.95) |

*Note*: Cabin crew expenses are hotel/meal costs for crew overnighting between flights.

two flights make up. The fixed direct costs and the indirect costs would still be incurred even if the flights were dropped.

At times, an airline may still decide to operate a flight even if the direct variable operating costs exceed revenue. One reason for this is that the flight may be providing a passenger feed to a connecting flight that is profitable but without the connecting passengers would turn unprofitable. Additionally, there could potentially be direct costs associated with not operating the flight and having the aircraft sit around, such as routine maintenance and parking fees.

If these costs exceed the negative contribution, then the flight should also be permitted to fly. Finally, analyzing only historical information is insufficient as it ignores future forecasts. If the TPA-PIT flight was to have significant growth prospects, then the airline should continue operating with a negative contribution margin in the hope of achieving profitability in the long-run.

*Indirect Operating Costs*   Indirect operating costs are those costs not directly related to the core function of the airline, such as some labor training costs, selling expenses, and administration costs. These costs are necessary for an airline to operate; however, indirect costs cannot be directly linked to a specific flight since the expenses provide support to all operations. Since they do not directly impact an airline's operation, indirect costs represent the first area of concentration a manager might focus on to reduce total operating costs.

## Non-Operating Costs

Airlines also incur costs that are not related to airline operations. Non-operating costs are expenses arising from activities not associated with the rendering of air transport services. Typically non-operating costs are related to the financial structuring of the company and are the result of the financial strategy of the airline. Interest expense is the most common non-operating cost in the airline industry and this is a result of the sizeable debt loads airlines carry. While the debt is necessary to fund the operations, interest expense is considered a non-operating cost because the cost is not directly related to an airline's operations. Other non-operating costs for an airline include any loss on the sale of aircraft and other assets and expenses in non-aviation activities. Airlines may receive income from investments or from non-core activities, such as hotel management.

Since airlines are in business to maximize shareholder wealth, understanding the composition of costs, regardless of if they are fixed or variable, is the starting point to understanding the airline industry. Figure 2.6 provides a breakdown of various cost categories on a unit basis. As has been the theme throughout this chapter, fuel and labor comprise the majority of an airline's cost structure, and some part of these costs are out of an airline's control. Fuel is based on the market bearing rate, while labor is highly unionized and fixed for periods of time. As a result, while other categories may not comprise a significant portion of an airline's cost structure, they should be the initial focus points for financial managers since they may provide the greatest opportunity for cost reduction.

One particular area where cost reduction can be achieved is maintenance costs. Just like an automobile, as an aircraft ages, maintenance becomes more prevalent and expensive. As a result, airlines desire not only the lower operating costs of new aircraft, but also the lower maintenance costs. However, fleet managers must be able to balance these benefits against higher ownership costs of new aircraft.

Figure 2.7 displays the composition of aircraft maintenance as a percentage of total operating costs for major U.S. carriers. As shown, low-cost carriers tend to have maintenance

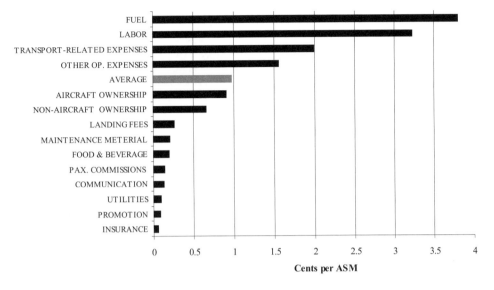

*Source*: ATA, 2009.

**Figure 2.6     U.S passenger airlines: Cost per available seat mile, 2008**

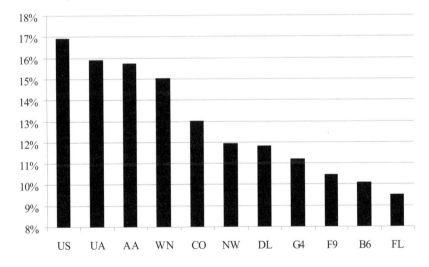

*Source*: Compiled by the Authors from Back Aviation Form41 Data.

**Figure 2.7     Maintenance cost as a percentage of CASM**

costs that make up a smaller percentage of their total operating costs. This is largely the result of carriers like Frontier (F9), AirTran (FL), and JetBlue (B6) having newer airplanes, which result in lower maintenance costs than their legacy carrier counterparts.

As their fleets age, maintenance costs will become a greater percentage of their total operating costs. However, some airlines such as Singapore Airlines and Ryanair have policies where aircraft are removed from the fleet fairly quickly to avoid more costly maintenance costs down the road.

## AIRLINE COST REBALANCING/RESTRUCTURING

While airlines have continually focused on reducing costs, the rise in the price of fuel has forced airlines to take many steps to try and reduce costs for company survival. As part of their cost rebalancing efforts, several network carriers reduced their costs by adopting uniform aircraft types, flexible work rules and operating at lower-cost and less congested airports. These traditional methods of cost-cutting have been the staple of low-cost carriers such as Southwest Airlines and Ryanair since their inception. As an example, Southwest operates a fleet of only Boeing 737s, flight attendants pick up trash in between flights (saving expenses on ground cleaning staff), and Southwest flies to alternate airports in some large cities such as Chicago-Midway, Ft. Lauderdale, Dallas Love Field and Houston-Hobby (Southwest Airlines, 2009).

Legacy carriers have historically been reluctant to adopt these practices, largely as a result of operating considerably different networks, although some are trending towards fleet commonality. For example, Continental Airlines has an all-Boeing fleet, with the bulk of the domestic fleet comprising 737s (Continental Airlines, 2009). In addition to fleet commonality, many airlines are cutting costs by retiring older aircraft that are less fuel efficient than newer aircraft. In 2008 Continental announced plans to retire forty-eight older 737s, over a two-year period, replacing them with newer 737NGs (Continental Airlines, 2009). American Airlines also announced plans to retire older aircraft in 2008, retiring about 40–45 MD-80s and A300s (Kirby, 2008 May 21).

Newer aircraft and flying into less-crowded airports are cost-cutting measures that generally received high approval from passengers; however, airlines have also been forced to resort to other cost-cutting measures which reduce the level of service. Airlines have cut cabin amenities and reduced other services such as onboard food service. On June 1 2008, U.S. Airways stopped providing pretzels and other complementary snacks in coach for domestic flights (Kirby, 2008 May 23). However, U.S. Airways was not the first airline to do so, as American Airlines eliminated free food in domestic coach in 2004 (Ezard, 2005). Moreover, U.S. Airways went one step further by experimenting with charges for non-alcoholic drinks, including water. Free food and beverages have been replaced with Buy on Board (BOB) food options, representing incremental revenue for the airlines. The BOB food offerings are of higher quality than the previous free airline meals and have received a positive response from passengers since they were first introduced by America West Airlines in 2003 (Field, 2004). On the other hand, such service cuts were only possible in an oligopoly market if the majority of the airlines followed with the same service cuts. While most initiatives have proved successful, no other airline followed U.S. Airways in charging for beverages, including water. Because of negative publicity, U.S. Airways reversed their decision. Much like pricing, changes in service level need to be accepted by the industry in order to be successful.

In addition to charging for food, airlines have begun charging for other services that were previously free, such as pet transportation, telephone reservations, seat selection and checked baggage. All major U.S. carriers (except for Southwest and JetBlue as of this writing) have started charging to check one or more bags domestically, a service that was previously free. American Airlines (and some other carriers) have gone a step further, increasing other fees for services such as pet transportation (American Airlines, 2009). The aim of these fees is not only to increase revenue, but also to reduce costs by having fewer people use these services. By charging for checked luggage, passengers are likely to check in fewer bags, reducing the need for luggage handlers. Charging for phone reservations pushes customers to automation (the internet), reducing the need for reservations staff. However, airlines must be wary about adding all of these new fees and reducing service since it makes airline travel less attractive (in comparison to substitutes such as driving or taking a train). Also, by reducing service, legacy carriers no longer have product differentiation over their low-cost counterparts. Without product differentiation, airlines cannot charge a higher price than their competitors since consumers will simply buy the lowest-price ticket. Therefore, cost-cutting by reducing service may actually make an airline less profitable if fares have to be reduced to attract passengers.

In addition to reduced service, many airlines have reduced capacity to cope with high costs and depressed demand in the face of a global recession. In Europe, Austrian Airlines dropped service to Mumbai and two other cities as part of an overall reduction in capacity of 10% in 2009 (Yahoo Finance, 2009, January 30). Austrian Airlines expects the capacity reductions to save about 115 million Euros. In the United States, airlines have been at the forefront of capacity reductions since the end of 2008, cutting capacity in the fourth quarter and in 2009. Delta Air Lines announced even further capacity cuts since it plans to cut 10% of international capacity beginning in September 2009 (Weber, 2009, March 10). However, simply reducing capacity only eliminates variable operating costs in the short term. Since airlines have significant fixed costs, cost savings experience a lag effect as it takes time to return aircraft to lessors and to furlough employees. Such lag effects have caused some airlines to operate less efficiently during the downturn in hopes of being able to ramp up capacity quicker than their competitors when the economy improves.

There are additional cost-cutting measures that can be implemented by airlines that do not necessarily affect the level of service. Productivity enhancement is an excellent way for airlines to reduce cost. Oum and Yu (1998) published a study of productivity and cost competitiveness of world airlines, including the consideration of numerous financial indicators.[12]

$$\text{Productivity} = \frac{\text{Outputs}}{\text{Inputs}}$$

As mentioned in the section on fixed costs, as output increases for the same number of fixed inputs, the average fixed cost decreases. Thus, the concept of productivity implies that each input is able to produce more output and therefore average costs decrease. There are many ways by which airlines can increase productivity. One obvious way to become more productive is to increase the daily utilization rate of the aircraft. The aircraft utilization rates for 2008 for eleven major U.S. carriers are shown in Figure 2.8. JetBlue (B6) and Frontier (F9) have the highest utilization rate of major U.S. airlines shown in Figure 2.8, allowing them to spread the fixed costs of the aircraft over a greater amount of production.

A high utilization rate allows airlines to lower their average fixed cost per block hour. High utilization rates can be achieved by minimizing aircraft ground time, operating flights with longer stage lengths, and by operating aircraft during off-peak time periods (i.e. redeye flights). Since JetBlue has one of the longest average stage lengths in the industry, it results in a high aircraft utilization rate (Vasigh et al, 2008). One notable exception is Allegiant Airlines (G4) that has a very low aircraft utilization rates. However, as a result of operating older aircraft with low ownership costs and a cost structure that is highly variable, Allegiant believes high aircraft-utilization is not of the utmost importance, nor is it more efficient. In fact, high utilization rates would only accelerate costly maintenance checks for its aging fleet.

Another measure of productivity that can be analyzed is the relationship between cost per available seat mile and the average stage length of an airline's flights. Average

---

12    Productivity is defined as the ratio of outputs to inputs.

stage length is the average length of a flight in miles. Based on economies of scale, as the average stage length increases, CASM should decrease as a result of spreading the fixed costs over a greater number of available seat miles. Figure 2.9 plots CASM and average stage length (ASL) for the airlines listed in Figure 2.8. General expectations suggest that increasing stage length lowers unit costs, with all else equal, as the increase in operating expenses attributed to longer stage length is less than proportional to the increase in ASMs.

The data in Figure 2.9 does not completely reflect the assumption that higher average stage length results in lower CASM for both LCC and Legacy airlines.[13] However, the assumption does hold fairly well within classes of carriers. For example, as stage length

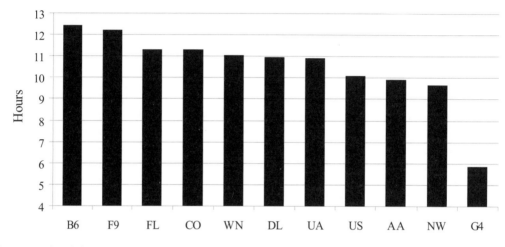

*Source:* Back Aviation Form41 Data.

**Figure 2.8     Aircraft utilization (block hrs. /day)**

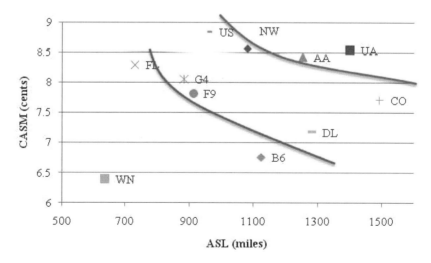

**Figure 2.9     CASM vs. Average stage length**
*Source:* Compiled by the Authors from Back Aviation Form41 Data.

---

13    Longer stage lengths allow the fixed costs of each flight to be spread over more ASMs.

increases within the legacy carriers (American, U.S. Airways, United, etc.), CASM tends to decrease. The same holds true for the low-cost carriers (AirTran, Allegiant, JetBlue, etc.); that is, as stage length increases within the low-cost carriers, CASM decreases. The outlier of the group is Southwest Airlines (WN) which has a lower average stage length and lower CASM than any of the other carriers. Southwest has been able to counter this trend through exceptional airport operations that include the ability to turnaround aircraft very quickly and the overall efficiency in its operations structure.

Airlines can increase productivity through many other methods as well. The use of automation to reduce the number of employees needed in certain areas is another way to enhance productivity. A good example of this is the use of self-service kiosks at check-in counters or the expansion of online check-in. Instead of needing one agent for each passenger, the check in procedure needs only one employee for approximately four kiosks to tag bags and check identification. In fact, Ryanair has gone one step further by eliminating airport check-in and providing online check-in as a passenger's sole option (BBC News, 2009). Airlines can also increase productivity by increasing their use of assets, more specifically, by increasing aircraft and gate utilization. As one of the leaders in cost reduction, U.S. Airways reduced costs by an estimated $1.1 billion in 2005, including $285 million in savings achieved through increased productivity (Lowry, 2005). In Asia, Cathay Pacific Airways implemented a series of measures aimed at cutting costs, including the deferral of aircraft deliveries and offering unpaid leave to employees, as the airline faced a significant drop in both cargo and passenger revenue . Airlines the world over reduced employment with Japan Airlines planning on reducing its workforce by 13% to 14,100, by the end of March 2011 (The Economic Times, 2009, January 8).

Another method used to reduce costs has been salary reduction. This difficult action has been a necessary step in the tough economic times that airlines face. Legacy carriers have been able to work with labor unions to come up with wage concessions to keep the struggling airlines afloat and to prevent further job losses in the industry. In fact, $480 million of U.S. Airways $1.1 billion in cost savings came from a new labor contracts (Lowry, 2005).

## Cost Restructuring

The airline industry seems to continually experience tough economic and financial conditions. To understand actions airlines must take for survival, consider the only U.S. legacy carrier that has not been in recent bankruptcy protection: American Airlines.

In 1982 jet fuel increased to $1.10 per gallon, which at that time was higher than it had ever been before (Horn, 1990). Faced with high oil prices and competition from deregulation, legacy airlines like American Airlines were confronted with the reality of record losses. Despite being the leading domestic airline, American needed to restructure costs quickly owing to a fuel-inefficient fleet, a large ratio of debt, and costly labor and other operating costs (Horn, 1990). In order to combat high costs, American Airlines drastically changed employee-compensation rates by developing a "two-tier" system. Created in 1983, the two-tier system allowed American to pay new hires at rates that were less than the wages currently being paid to its existing ground workers, pilots, and flight attendants (Loveman, 1990). The new employees were still union members but were paid on a lower scale than the current employees. Unions agreed to go along with this idea since it increased union membership and protected current union members from pay cuts or job losses.

The two-tier pay scale allowed American to hire new employees who were necessary for the expansion strategy that American was to undertake in the 1980s. For American, expansion occurred both domestically and internationally. The airline went from two U.S. hubs to seven and expanded service to Europe and the Far East (Loveman, 1990). American's growth strategy was also predicated on providing excellent customer service. According to American CEO Robert Crandall, the important elements of customer service were on-time arrivals, good baggage-handling, and friendly employees (Horn, 1990). American largely achieved their customer service objectives when it was named Air Transport World's airline of the year in 1988 (Horn, 1990).

However, by 1990 fuel prices had begun to increase again. The Iraq invasion of Kuwait, coupled with declining revenues owing to a U.S. recession, made the prospect of profits for American look slim (Loveman, 1990). Another round of cost reductions was in order to keep American profitable; however, this time American was not as successful in negotiations with its unions as it was in 1983. The pilots were demanding higher wages in return for the success the company had achieved during the 1980s.

In 1991 the pilots' union negotiated a new contract with American that increased wages and profit sharing compensation. This contract increased costs for American (Loveman, 1990). The contract negotiation with the ramp and maintenance workers union, the TWU, was a little more successful in keeping costs down. The union agreed to reduce demands for higher wages in exchange for an incentive and profit-sharing based compensation structure (Loveman, 1990). The goals of the union and management were more aligned since workers received incentives based on on-time flight performance and the reduction of mishandled baggage rates at the airports where they worked.

The history of American Airlines through the 1980s and early 1990s shows that airlines can get through hard economic times; however, airlines must change their fundamental cost structure to deal with economic realities. Restructuring is important to the survival of today's airlines. In order for the legacy carriers of today to restructure, labor costs must be lowered. The prevailing sentiment with workers in 1990 at American Airlines was that job security was more important than wages. Said a former American agent, "I want a career with AA, so though I would like more money, I am most concerned about keeping my job'" (Loveman, 1990). In a climate where airlines such as Aloha, American Trans Air (ATA), and Skybus have gone out of business, many airline employees probably feel the same sentiments as the former agent today. Even with reductions in labor costs, layoffs are still likely as part of any restructuring; Continental Airlines announced 3,000 layoffs in June 2008 to take effect by the end of the year (New Mexico Business Weekly, 2008). In this uncertain business climate, employees may have to accept wage concessions to prevent more job losses or going out of business.

Restructuring involves more than just lowering labor costs; it also involves optimizing an airline's route network and strategy. Airlines may shift to more profitable routes, such as trans-Pacific and trans-Atlantic flights. Using wide-bodied aircraft on domestic flights may be an inefficient use of the aircraft when they could be making more money on international routes. Domestic routes need to be structured to feed profitable international routes. An example of this is Delta Airlines' hub at New York's Kennedy Airport (JFK) where domestic flights are structured to feed the over 30 trans-Atlantic destinations that Delta flies to from JFK (Delta Airlines, 2008). Structuring domestic routes to feed international routes means that legacy carriers will probably need to eliminate low-yield point-to-point routes. For example, Delta announced it will cut all flights out of Orlando International Airport (MCO) that are not flights to hubs (Adams, Lollis and Hansen, 2008).

One of American Airlines' problems when fuel prices began to rise in the early 1980s was a fuel-inefficient fleet (Horn, 1990). Today many airlines are facing the same problem with older fuel-inefficient fleets. To reduce costs, airlines may have to restructure their fleets to newer, more fuel-efficient aircraft. For example, Alaska Airlines finished a fleet transition by the end of 2008 that included retiring MD-80s and 737–200s (Fiorino, 2006). These planes are being replaced by new 737–800s. A table showing Alaska's fleet transition is shown in Table 2.8.

An overview of different cost-cutting measures employed by major U.S. airlines is shown in Table 2.9 overleaf.

**Table 2.8    Alaska Airlines fleet plan and transition 2005–2008**

| Alaska Airlines Fleet Plan | | | | |
|---|---|---|---|---|
| Aircraft Type | 2005 | 2006 | 2007 | 2008 |
| MD-80 | 26 | 21 | 15 | 0 |
| Boeing 737-200 | 7 | 3 | 0 | 0 |
| 737-400 | 40 | 40 | 40 | 40 |
| 737-700 | 22 | 22 | 20 | 20 |
| 737-800 | 3 | 15 | 28 | 42 |
| 737-900 | 12 | 12 | 12 | 12 |
| Total Fleet Count: | 110 | 113 | 115 | 114 |

*Source*: Aviation Week and Space Technology.

While restructuring costs are important, airlines must not lose sight of the customer. As Robert Crandall mentioned with American in the 1980s, good customer service is what separates airlines from one another (Horn, 1990). It is no secret that the most profitable U.S. airline in recent years, Southwest, is known for its friendly customer service. If customers will not fly on an airline, then no amount of cost-cutting will keep an airline in business. Additionally, customers require airlines to operate a sound operation, with on-time departures and arrivals. Flight punctuality provides multiple benefits since it not only helps increase customer service, but it also reduces costs as a result of delays and cancellations.

## SUMMARY

In this chapter we have looked at the structure of airline costs. Airlines are highly capital-intensive, and as such, have a very high level of fixed costs. Because of these high fixed costs airline efficiencies are generated when a high level of output is achieved since doing so spreads the fixed costs over a broader range, reducing the average fixed cost. Airline costs are generally categorized as operating costs or non-operating costs. Operating costs are those costs incurred in the operation of providing air transport services. When deciding on whether to operate a particular route or service, airlines should look at the marginal cost. The marginal cost is the incremental cost to provide an additional good or

**Table 2.9      U.S. airlines' recent cost cutting measures**

| Airline | Area | Amount (million) |
|---------|------|------------------|
| Continental | Labor cost reductions | $169 |
| Northwest | Labor cost reductions | $667 |
| | Fleet costs | $400 |
| | Routes, debt, other | $700 |
| United | Aircraft leases | $850 |
| | Flight attendant labor | $125 |
| | Changes in pension plan | $645 |
| | Productivity gains | $7,000 |
| | | by 2010 |
| Delta | Pilot labor | $145-$300 |
| | Other labor | $605 |
| | Leases, pensions, debt relief, fleet modifications | $970 |
| Southwest | Slower cruising speeds | $42 |
| U.S. Airways | New labor contracts | $480 |
| | Non-labor productivity improvements | $285 |
| | Pension plan terminations | $250 |
| | Aircraft leasing/ maintenance costs | $80 |

*Sources*: Air Transport World online (September, 23 2005), Aviation Week & Space Technology (January 24, 2005; October 24, 2005; January 9, 2006; March 6, 2006; March 27, 2006), Associated Press (May 2, 2008).

service (in the case of airlines, an additional flight or additional capacity). With the rising costs of fuel, labor and other expenses, airlines must look to restructure (reduce) their costs. This chapter has looked at many of the ways that airlines have reduced costs from the increase of automation to reductions in capacity and staffing levels.

## DISCUSSION QUESTIONS

1.  Explain why fixed or semi-fixed costs are irrelevant for financial decision-making.
2.  Discuss the concept of opportunity cost.
3.  What is the nature of operating costs in the airline industry?
4.  Explain the concept of marginal cost.
5.  How are marginal cost, average total cost, and average variable cost related to managerial financial decision-making?
6.  How may airlines reduce their operating costs?
7.  List and explain the types of accounting costs that are covered in the chapter.

8. What has been the single most effective method for cost reduction in the airline industry?
9. Describe some of the largest start-up costs for an airline. Additionally, what are some of the largest cost items that airlines routinely incur?
10. Why is the airline industry commonly referred to as a high fixed cost industry and what is the impact of this on the industry's operating environment?
11. Does the airline industry have low marginal costs? What impact does an airline's marginal cost having on pricing?
12. How are low-cost carriers able to maintain their cost leadership advantage?
13. What are the benefits of an airline entering bankruptcy protection? How does an airline entering bankruptcy shape the industry's competitive dynamics?
14. Explain the relationship between CASM and ASL.
15. Explain how maintenance costs affect airlines' profit and why maintenance costs change over the course of time. Why do airlines typically avoid trimming maintenance costs during periods of cost reductions?
16. You are given the following cost functions:
    $TC = 2500 + 2000Q$
    $TC = 2500 + 200Q + 2Q^2$
    a.  Compute the average variable cost, average cost, and marginal cost for each function.
    b.  For each function, discuss the relationship between MC and AVC.

## REFERENCES

Adams, M., B. Lollis, and B. Hansen (2008). "Fliers in for pain as airlines pack it in". *USA Today*, June 3, 2008. Retrieved June 5, 2008 from http://usatoday.com/travel/flights/2008-06-03-airlines-cuts-flights-fares_N.htm?imw=Y

American Airlines (2008). AMR Corporation announces significant capacity reductions, aircraft retirements and additional revenue growth efforts. Retrieved June 2, 2008 from http://www.aa.com/content/amrcorp/pressReleases/2008_05/21_capacity.jhtml

BBC News (2009). Ryanair to abolish check-in desks. Retrieved on March 30, 2009 from http://news.bbc.co.uk/1/hi/business/7903656.stm?lss

Continental Airlines (2008). Continental's fleet plan. Retrieved on June 2, 2008 from http://www.continental.com/web/en-UScontent/travel/inflight/aircraft/default.aspx

Delta Airlines (2008). Delta's interactive route map. Retrieved on June 5, 2008 from http://delta.innosked.com/

Ezard, K. (2005). "American stresses need to further reduce costs in 2005". *Air Transport Intelligence News*, January 19, 2005.

Field, D. (2004). "No more free lunches". *Airline Business*, Jan. 2004.

Fiorino, F. (2006, March). A Single Approach: Exit MD-80s, enter new 737s as Alaska simplifies operations. Aviation Week and Space Technology, 164(12), 63. Retrieved June 5, 2008, from ABI/INFORM Global database. (Document ID: 1008499671).

Horn, J. (1990). *American Airlines: Strategy in the 1990s*. Harvard Business School Publishing, Case # 94–910–44, Boston.

Kirby, M. (2008, May 21). "Fleet slashed as American unveils new capacity plan". *Air Transport Intelligence News*.

Kirby, M. (2008, May 23). "Snacks out in domestic coach as U.S. Airways seeks to cut costs". *Air Transport Intelligence News*.

Loveman, G. (1990). *American Airlines: Compensation and cost reduction*. Harvard Business School Publishing, Case # 9–491–060, Boston.

Lowry, M. (2005). "AirWatch report". *Aviation Week and Space Technology*.

New Mexico Business Weekly (2008, June 5). Continental will cut 3,000 jobs, reduce flights. Retrieved June 6, 2008 from http://www.bizjournals.com/sanantonio/othercities/albuquerque/stories/2008/06/02/daily26.html

Oum, T. and Yu, C. (1998) Winning Airlines: Productivity and Cost Competitiveness of the World's Major Airlines, Kluwer Academic Publishers, Transportation Research, Economics and Policy.

Southwest Airlines (2008). *Southwest Airlines cities. Retrieved* on June 2, 2008 from http://www.southwest.com/travel_center/routemap.html

The Economic Times (2009, January 8). Japan Airlines to cut 1,640 jobs by 2011: Spokesman. Retrieved March 10, 2009 from http://economictimes.indiatimes.com/News/International_Business/Japan_Airlines_to_cut_1640_jobs_by_2011_spokesman/articleshow/3952409.cms

Vasigh, B., Fleming, K. and Tacker, T. (2008). *Introduction to Air Transport Economics: Theory to Applications*. Ashgate Publishing Co., Burlington, Vermont.

Weber, R. (2009, March 10). Delta Air Lines to cut intl flights in Sept. Associated Press. Retrieved March 10, 2009 from http://www.google.com/hostednews/ap/article/ALeqM5glGh0iEU-Dw035o7AhmcFw1MqdXAD96R8MN83

Yahoo Finance (2009, January 30). Austrian Airlines in emergency cost-cutting program. Retrieved March 10, 2009 from http://uk.biz.yahoo.com/30012009/323/austrian-airlines-emergency-cost-cutting-programme.html

# 3

# Time Value of Money

"People who invest in aviation are the biggest suckers in the world."

David G. Neeleman[1]

The purpose of this chapter is to introduce the reader to the concept of the time value of money and how its applicability can affect decision-making in the airline industry. The basic idea of the time value of money is that a dollar in hand today is worth more than a dollar in the future .The time value of money has many useful applications. One of the most important is that it helps you measure the trade-off in spending and saving. Consequently, individuals or airlines must be compensated if they invest present dollars for a future return. This compensation is commonly called the interest rate. Conversely, the present value of future dollars is not worth as much as it is today and this difference is commonly called the discount rate. Along with present value and future value, the concept of an annuity, or the actual value (present or future) of a stream of income, is critical to any student of finance, since it is the basis for most of the topics in finance. This chapter has the following outline:

- Future Value
- Present Value
- Compounding Interest
- Annuities
- Perpetuities
- Amortization Schedule
- Summary
- Discussion Questions
- Appendix 1: Time Value of Money Calculations in Excel
- Appendix 2:
    - Present Value of an Annual Ordinary Annuity
    - Future Value of an Annual Ordinary Annuity
    - Present Value of $1
    - Future Value of $1.

## FUTURE VALUE

The future value of an investment is the amount in which a cash flow or series of cash flows will grow over a given period of time when compounded at a given interest rate (IATA, 2007). This

---

1    After raising a record $128 million to start JetBlue Airways, May 1999.

is very useful when performing investment valuations analysis, especially for investments like certificates of deposits (CDs) and bonds. Suppose that the rate of return of return on investments is 10%. Assuming DirectJet invests in a bond worth $100 today, the bond will be worth $110 in a year. Working backwards, DirectJet is willing to pay up to $100 for a payment of $110 a year from now. Simple mathematical computations can be performed to determine the future value of an investment; this concept can also be referred to as compounding, since its objective is to determine a future value based upon a set of parameters that include its present value and a given rate of interest. We calculate the present value of a future payment as follows. The present value is compounded until the value for the desired year is achieved. Therefore, the future value (FV) is equal to the present value plus the interest earned.

$$FV = PV + I$$
$$FV = PV + i \times PV$$

Symbolically, the equation is represented as:

$$FV = (1+i) \times PV$$

where:
$PV$ = the initial investment at the time 0
$i$ = the interest rate associated with the investment[2]
$I$ = the amount of interest

According, to this formula, if you invested $100 at an interest rate of 10%, the future value at the end of one period would equal $110 (as pointed out above).

$$FV = PV \times (1+i)$$
$$FV = 100 \times (1+.10)$$
$$FV = 110$$

This formula can be expanded to include situations where a sum of money is invested for multiple periods of time at stated interest rates. For example, assume that one has $1,000 that he or she wishes to invest and the interest rate is 10% (that is calculated annually) with a three-year term. After the first year, the investment would return the original $1,000 plus 10% interest for a total of $1,100. Notice that the second year present value is the future value of the cash flow after year 1.

$$FV = PV (1+i)^n$$
$$PV = 1000$$
$$i = 10\%$$
$$n = 3$$

$$FV_1 = 1000 \times (1+.10) = 1100$$
$$FV_2 = 1000 \times (1.10)^2 = 1210$$
$$FV_3 = 1000 \times (1.10)^3 = 1331$$

2    Because of interest, the value of an investment will increase over time.

where:

n    = the length of time of the investment

After calculations, it is determined that the future value of the investment of $1,000 will reach $1,331 at the end of year three (assuming that the interest rate remains constant). After the three years, the investment would return the original $1,000 plus $331 of interest for a total of $1,331.

To illustrate the use of the equation above, consider Table 3.1. The table displays the growth of $1,500 over a period of twenty years at an interest rate of 10%. In the example provided below, interest is calculated on an annual basis.

This function can also be calculated in Microsoft Excel under the financial formula function. The methodologies of how to use financial functions is presented in the appendix to this chapter. The following graph displays the exponential growth of the investment calculated in Table 3.1 over time.

In addition to the time period of an investment, the interest rate (also known as the rate of return or discount rate) of an investment is also critical in determining the future value. To illustrate the effect of interest rates on future values, the following example

**Table 3.1    Future value table of $1500 at 10%**

| Year | Beginning Amount | Interest | Ending Amount |
|------|------------------|----------|---------------|
| 1 | $1,500.00 | $150.00 | $1,650.00 |
| 2 | $1,650.00 | $165.00 | $1,815.00 |
| 3 | $1,815.00 | $181.50 | $1,996.50 |
| 4 | $1,996.50 | $199.65 | $2,196.15 |
| 5 | $2,196.15 | $219.62 | $2,415.77 |
| 6 | $2,415.77 | $241.58 | $2,657.34 |
| 7 | $2,657.34 | $265.73 | $2,923.08 |
| 8 | $2,923.08 | $292.31 | $3,215.38 |
| 9 | $3,215.38 | $321.54 | $3,536.92 |
| 10 | $3,536.92 | $353.69 | $3,890.61 |
| 11 | $3,890.61 | $389.06 | $4,279.68 |
| 12 | $4,279.68 | $427.97 | $4,707.64 |
| 13 | $4,707.64 | $470.76 | $5,178.41 |
| 14 | $5,178.41 | $517.84 | $5,696.25 |
| 15 | $5,696.25 | $569.62 | $6,265.87 |
| 16 | $6,265.87 | $626.59 | $6,892.46 |
| 17 | $6,892.46 | $689.25 | $7,581.71 |
| 18 | $7,581.71 | $758.17 | $8,339.88 |
| 19 | $8,339.88 | $833.99 | $9,173.86 |
| 20 | $9,173.86 | $917.39 | $10,091.25 |

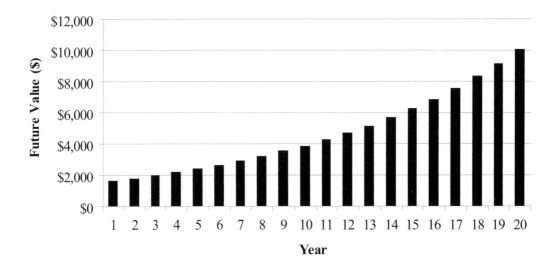

**Figure 3.1     Future value of $1500 at 10% interest**

compares an initial investment of $100 over ten years over interest rates of zero, 10, 20, 30, and 40%.

Table 3.2 illustrates the effect that the interest rate has on the future values. The difference between the initial investment earning 10 and 40% interest is $2,633.17 after ten years.[3] This is considerable given the fact that both investments had the same starting (present)

**Table 3.2     Future values of various interest rates over time**

| Period | FV at 0% | 10% | 20% | 30% | 40% |
|--------|----------|-----|-----|-----|-----|
| 0 | $100.00 | $100.00 | $100.00 | $100.00 | $100.00 |
| 1 | $100.00 | $110.00 | $120.00 | $130.00 | $140.00 |
| 2 | $100.00 | $121.00 | $144.00 | $169.00 | $196.00 |
| 3 | $100.00 | $133.10 | $172.80 | $219.70 | $274.40 |
| 4 | $100.00 | $146.41 | $207.36 | $285.61 | $384.16 |
| 5 | $100.00 | $161.05 | $248.83 | $371.29 | $537.82 |
| 6 | $100.00 | $177.16 | $298.60 | $482.68 | $752.95 |
| 7 | $100.00 | $194.87 | $358.32 | $627.49 | $1,054.14 |
| 8 | $100.00 | $214.36 | $429.98 | $815.73 | $1,475.79 |
| 9 | $100.00 | $235.79 | $515.98 | $1,060.45 | $2,066.10 |
| 10 | $100.00 | $259.37 | $619.17 | $1,378.58 | $2,892.55 |

---

3      $2633.17 = $2892.55 - $259.37

value and the time period of the investment was the same. This is a concrete example of the power of compound interest.[4]

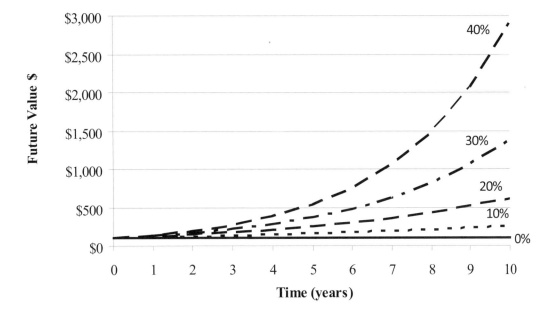

**Figure 3.2    Future value of $100 at various interest rates**

## PRESENT VALUE

Present value is also important as it puts future cash flows in present dollar terms. Ross defines the concept as the price or value put on time, so that the time value of money reflects the opportunity cost of investing at a risk-free rate (Ross, Westerfield and Jordan, 2008). It is at the base of almost all theories that deal with the valuation of money. Most commonly, the concept is used to determine whether an investment is feasible or not. Since the time value of money states that a dollar today is worth more than a dollar in the future, dollars over different time periods cannot be simply added together. Instead, these dollars must be compared using some common denominator, either as a present or as a future value. There are several methods that have been developed to accurately compare the values of these "different dollars" and these include the present value, future value, compounding, and discounting.

As an example of the types of issues the time value of money helps solve, assume that the government loans a local airport 5 million dollars to repair damages caused by a natural disaster, with the promise that the airport will repay the 5 million in one year. Because of the discussion above, when the airport repays the 5 million at the end of the year, it is worth less than the original 5 million. Thus, the government is giving the airport an interest free loan which is ordinarily not a good investment idea, but it may be a good public policy idea to get the airport up and running again.

---

4    As a simple rule of thumb, if one divides the given rate of interest into 72 the answer gives the approximate time for the investment to double. So, for example, $100 invested at 9% would double in 8 years.

The present value concept can be used to determine the present value of expected future cash flows by including the discount rate that is associated with the situation. Basically, this means that present value is used to determine how much a future dollar is worth today in relationship to the discount (interest) rate associated with the situation. Using the future value of a cash flow, the present value can be determined by discounting the future values with the interest rate. Hence, this function is known as discounting, since the objective is to discount a future value to determine its present value.

$$PV = \frac{FV}{(1+i)^n}$$

where:
$FV$ = the future (terminal) value of the initial investment
$i$ = the discount (interest) rate per period
$n$ = the time in years

To determine the present value of $110 to be received in one year at a discount rate of 10%, we use the formula above and divide $110 by one plus the discount rate:

$$PV = \frac{FV}{(1+i)^n}$$

$$PV = \frac{110}{(1+.10)^1} = \$100$$

Calculating the present value of multiple periods is similar to calculating the future value of multiple periods. The present value of $1 to be received in n periods in the future at a discount rate of $i$ is:

$$PV = \frac{FV}{(1+i)^n}$$

As an example, assume you receive a savings bond as a birthday gift. This bond has a stated interest rate of 10% and will pay you $121 in two years time. Based on this information, the present value of the bond is found to be $100.

$$PV = \frac{\$120}{(1+0.10)^2} = \$100$$

As found by the original equation, at the start of the first year (t = 0), the value of the bond is $100 and at the start of second year, the bond is worth $110, and at the end of the second year, the bond is worth $121. Microsoft Excel is also able to compute complex present value calculations using the present value (PV) function.

Table 3.3 and Figure 3.4 illustrate the present value of $1,500 at 10% over the period of twenty years. For this example interest is calculated on an annual basis. In the latter part of the chapter interest calculations based on different frequency of calculations is explained. An investment, such as a savings bond, worth $1,500 in five years has a present value of $931.38 today. This information is important when buying/selling bonds to determine if the acquisition price is a fair price.

$$PV = 110/1.1 = 100 \quad PV = 121/1.1 = 110$$

**Figure 3.3     Present value**

**Table 3.3     Present value table of $1,500 at 10% over 20 years**

| Years to Maturity | Beginning of Year | Ending of Year |
|:---:|:---:|:---:|
| 1 | $1,363.64 | $1,500.00 |
| 2 | $1,239.67 | $1,363.64 |
| 3 | $1,126.97 | $1,239.67 |
| 4 | $1,024.52 | $1,126.97 |
| 5 | $931.38 | $1,024.52 |
| 6 | $846.71 | $931.38 |
| 7 | $769.74 | $846.71 |
| 8 | $699.76 | $769.74 |
| 9 | $636.15 | $699.76 |
| 10 | $578.31 | $636.15 |
| 11 | $525.74 | $578.31 |
| 12 | $477.95 | $525.74 |
| 13 | $434.50 | $477.95 |
| 14 | $395.00 | $434.50 |
| 15 | $359.09 | $395.00 |
| 16 | $326.44 | $359.09 |
| 17 | $296.77 | $326.44 |
| 18 | $269.79 | $296.77 |
| 19 | $245.26 | $269.79 |
| 20 | $222.97 | $245.26 |

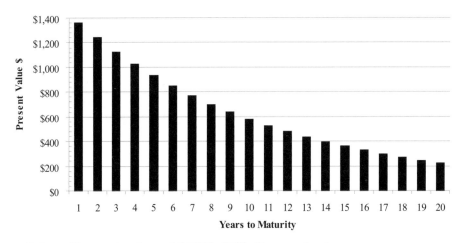

**Figure 3.4    Present value of $1500: 10% discount rate**

An investment, such as a savings bond, worth $1,500 in five years has a present value of $931.38 today.

To further illustrate the time value of money over the life of an investment, Table 3.4 compares the effect of the interest rate on the present value of an investment over different time periods. As an example, assume that you wish to purchase a $500 savings bond, but you have the option of choosing different maturity dates for the bonds. With these different maturity dates, the purchase price of the bond is adjusted for the present value, as shown in Table 3.4.

**Table 3.4    Present values of various interest rates over time**

| Period | PV at 0% | 10% | 20% | 30% |
|--------|----------|-----|-----|-----|
| 0 | 500 | 500.00 | 500.00 | 500.00 |
| 1 | $500.00 | $454.55 | $416.67 | $384.62 |
| 2 | $500.00 | $413.22 | $347.22 | $295.86 |
| 3 | $500.00 | $375.66 | $289.35 | $227.58 |
| 4 | $500.00 | $341.51 | $241.13 | $175.06 |
| 5 | $500.00 | $310.46 | $200.94 | $134.66 |
| 6 | $500.00 | $282.24 | $167.45 | $103.59 |
| 7 | $500.00 | $256.58 | $139.54 | $79.68 |
| 8 | $500.00 | $233.25 | $116.28 | $61.29 |
| 9 | $500.00 | $212.05 | $96.90 | $47.15 |
| 10 | $500.00 | $192.77 | $80.75 | $36.27 |
| 11 | $500.00 | $175.25 | $67.29 | $27.90 |
| 12 | $500.00 | $159.32 | $56.08 | $21.46 |
| 13 | $500.00 | $144.83 | $46.73 | $16.51 |
| 14 | $500.00 | $131.67 | $38.94 | $12.70 |
| 15 | $500.00 | $119.70 | $32.45 | $9.77 |

To understand Table 3.4, the present value of a $500 bond with a 10% rate that matures in one year is $454.55 and the same bond purchased with a maturity in 5 years is $310.46. The same $500 savings bond with an interest rate of 30% at year 5 has a present value of $134.66. Figure 3.5 displays the decreasing present value associated with the different interest rates and time periods.

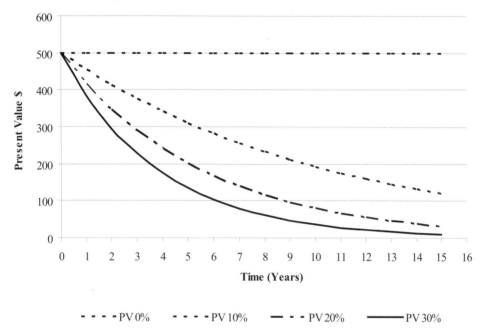

**Figure 3.5      Present value of $500 with different interest rates**

## COMPOUNDING INTEREST

Up to this point, all the examples in this chapter have had their interest rates calculated on an annual basis. Although this makes it extremely easy to calculate, in the real world interest is normally calculated in other frequencies, such as quarterly, monthly, daily, and even continuously.

To illustrate how to calculate interest that is accrued on a basis other than annually, assume that the future value of a bond is $100 in ten years, the interest rate is 5%, and is compounded quarterly (m=4).

$$PV = \frac{FV}{(1+\dfrac{i}{m})^{n \times m}}$$

where:
m    − number of compounding periods
FV  = 100
i      = 5%
m    = 4
n     = 10

$$PV = \frac{\$100}{1+(\frac{0.05}{4})^{10\times4}}$$

$$PV = \frac{100}{1.6436}$$

$$PV = \$60.84$$

The present value of the 10-year bond is $60.84 which is a different value than what would have been calculated using annual compounding; therefore, when the value is calculated using a rate that is compounded on a more frequent basis then annually, it yields a lower present value. This means that more interest is applied to this bond over its life than for an investment that is compounded on an annual basis. To illustrate this point, consider the same examples except with a different compounding rate. Using the same parameters as the above example, except with monthly compounding instead of quarterly compounding, the present value of the bond is found to be $60.72 which is slightly less than the example above, as a result of the more frequent compounding.

$$FV = 100$$

$$i = 15\%$$

$$n = 3$$

$$m = 12$$

$$PV = \frac{FV}{(1+\frac{i}{m})^{n\times m}}$$

$$PV = \frac{100}{(1+\frac{0.05}{12})^{3\times12}}$$

$$PV = \frac{100}{1.5639}$$

$$PV = 63.94$$

Table 3.5 displays the effect of different periodic compounding periods on present value. In this example, assume a future value of 2 million dollars for an aircraft lease with an interest rate of 8%. The table below displays the present value of this aircraft lease at different time points. Interest is compounded on a yearly, quarterly, weekly, and daily basis in the example. As stated before, as the number of periods in which interest is compounded increases, the present value of the investment decreases. (This should make intuitive sense since interest is being added to the initial amount of the investment on a more frequent basis.)

**Table 3.5**      **Present value of $2 million at 8% using different years to maturity and compounding methods**

| Years to Maturity | Yearly | Quarterly | Monthly | Daily |
|---|---|---|---|---|
| 1 | $1,851,851.85 | $1,847,690.85 | $1,846,722.91 | $1,846,249.10 |
| 2 | $1,714,677.64 | $1,706,980.74 | $1,705,192.75 | $1,704,317.87 |
| 3 | $1,587,664.48 | $1,576,986.35 | $1,574,509.26 | $1,573,297.67 |
| 4 | $1,470,059.71 | $1,456,891.63 | $1,453,841.16 | $1,452,349.70 |
| 5 | $1,361,166.39 | $1,345,942.67 | $1,342,420.89 | $1,340,699.67 |
| 6 | $1,260,339.25 | $1,243,442.98 | $1,239,539.70 | $1,237,632.78 |
| 7 | $1,166,980.79 | $1,148,749.11 | $1,144,543.18 | $1,142,489.20 |
| 8 | $1,080,537.77 | $1,061,266.61 | $1,056,827.06 | $1,054,659.83 |
| 9 | $1,000,497.93 | $980,446.30 | $975,833.37 | $973,582.38 |
| 10 | $926,386.98 | $905,780.83 | $901,046.92 | $898,737.80 |

Future value of an investment is also impacted by the rate of compounding with the future value formula modified in a similar manner. As an example, assume we have $1,500 to invest at a discount rate of 7% for ten years and interest is calculated on a quarterly basis.

$$PV = 1500$$

$$m = 4$$

$$i = 7\%$$

$$n = 10$$

$$FV = PV(1 + \frac{i}{m})^{n \times m}$$

$$FV = 1500(1 + \frac{.07}{4})^{10 \times 4}$$

$$FV = 1500(2.00157)$$

$$FV = 3002.40$$

To illustrate the difference in future value that interest rate compounding has, reconsider the above example; however, instead of quarterly compounding, interest is compounded monthly. With monthly compounding, the $1,500 investment has a future value of $3,014, which is an increase over the $3,002 future value of quarterly compounding. Therefore, as the number of periods in which interest is compounded increases, the future value of an investment also increases.

$$PV = \$1,895$$

$$m = 12$$

$$i = 8.9\%$$

$$n = 15$$

$$FV = PV(1 + \frac{i}{m})^{n \times m}$$

$$FV = 1700 \times (1 + \frac{0.07}{12})^{10 \times 12}$$

$$FV = 1500 \times (2.0097)$$

$$FV = \$3,014$$

## ANNUITIES

An annuity is defined as an equally distributed set of payments that occur over a predetermined amount of time. IATA defines an annuity as a series of payments of an equal amount at fixed intervals for a specified number of periods. The most common payment intervals are yearly, semi-annually, quarterly, and monthly. With this definition in mind, several examples of annuities are readily available, such as aircraft leases, mortgages, car payments, rent, pension fund payments, and insurance premiums.

Based on when payments are made, there are two types of annuities: ordinary annuity and an annuity due. An ordinary annuity is when payment is made at the end of the interval, while an annuity due has payment made at the beginning of the interval.

As with the previous examples, present and future value can be calculated for annuities. The present value of an annuity can be calculated by the following equation:

$$PV_{Annuity} = \frac{PMT}{(1+i)} + \frac{PMT}{(1+i)^2} + ... + \frac{PMT}{(1+i)^n}$$

$$PV_{Annuity} = PMT \times [\frac{1}{i} - \frac{1}{i(1 + \frac{i}{m})^{n \times m}}]$$

where:
$PMT$ = the amount of the payment or cash flow
$i$ = the discount rate associated with the payment
$n$ = time in years
$m$ = number of compounding periods per year

$$PV_{Annuity} = PMT \times [\frac{1}{\frac{i}{m}} - \frac{1}{\frac{i}{m} \times (1 + \frac{i}{m})^{n \times m}}]$$

$$PV_{Annuity} = \$10,000,000 \times [\frac{1}{.05} - \frac{1}{0.05 \times (1 + .05)^4}]$$

$$PV_{Annuity} = \$35,459,505.04$$

For an example of the present value of an annuity (PVA), assume that DirectJet Airlines decides to invest in an annuity fund that will pay \$10,000,000 at the end of each of the next four years. The annuity fund has an interest rate of 5% compounded annually. In order to receive the annuity, DirectJet Airlines would need to pay \$35,459,505 today.

One type of annuity mentioned earlier is a car loan, which most are probably familiar with. Aviation-related companies usually take out loans for vehicles that operate on the ramp, shuttle crews, and so on. In the following example, assume a local Fixed Base Operator (FBO) has taken out a note on a new ramp vehicle and the terms of the note are as follows: the monthly payments are \$337 for a period of five years, or sixty months, with an interest rate of 6%.

$$PMT = 337$$

$$i = 6\% \div 12$$

$$n = 5 \times 12$$

$$PVA = PMT \times [\frac{1}{i} - \frac{1}{i(1 + \frac{i}{m})^{n \times m}}]$$

$$PVA = 337 \times [\frac{1}{(\frac{0.06}{12})} - \frac{1}{(\frac{0.06}{12}) \times (1 + \frac{.06}{12})^{5 \times 12}}]$$

$$PVA = 337 \times [\frac{1}{0.005} - \frac{1}{(0.005) \times (1.005)^{60}}]$$

$$PVA = 337 \times [51.7255]$$

$$PVA = \$17,431.51$$

The present value of the annuity is \$17,431.51. The present value represents the fair value of the loan and if the vehicle is worth this much or more, the FBO is receiving a good deal on the financing of the vehicle. If the vehicle is not worth this much, then the FBO is not getting a good deal from the financing company.

Another example of an annuity in the aviation industry is aircraft leasing. For example, assume that an airline is in need of an Airbus A320 aircraft and wishes to lease the aircraft.

The airline would approach one of the many leasing companies like General Electric's GECAS[5] or the International Lease Finance Corporation (ILFC)[6] and negotiate terms of the lease. They might for instance agree on a twenty year lease with annual payments of two million dollars. The interest rate associated with these payments may be 10%. Table 3.6 and Figures 3.6 and 3.7 illustrate the present value of these payments.

As with the previous examples, the same basic principle applies if payments are made on a basis that occurs more frequently than on an annual basis.

**Table 3.6    Present value of an annuity**

| Period | PMT | Rate | Present Value |
|--------|-----|------|---------------|
| 0 | $2,000,000.00 | 10% | $0.00 |
| 1 | $2,000,000.00 | 10% | $1,818,181.82 |
| 2 | $2,000,000.00 | 10% | $3,471,074.38 |
| 3 | $2,000,000.00 | 10% | $4,973,703.98 |
| 4 | $2,000,000.00 | 10% | $6,339,730.89 |
| 5 | $2,000,000.00 | 10% | $7,581,573.54 |
| 6 | $2,000,000.00 | 10% | $8,710,521.40 |
| 7 | $2,000,000.00 | 10% | $9,736,837.64 |
| 8 | $2,000,000.00 | 10% | $10,669,852.40 |
| 9 | $2,000,000.00 | 10% | $11,518,047.63 |
| 10 | $2,000,000.00 | 10% | $12,289,134.21 |
| 11 | $2,000,000.00 | 10% | $12,990,122.01 |
| 12 | $2,000,000.00 | 10% | $13,627,383.65 |
| 13 | $2,000,000.00 | 10% | $14,206,712.41 |
| 14 | $2,000,000.00 | 10% | $14,733,374.91 |
| 15 | $2,000,000.00 | 10% | $15,212,159.01 |
| 16 | $2,000,000.00 | 10% | $15,647,417.28 |
| 17 | $2,000,000.00 | 10% | $16,043,106.62 |
| 18 | $2,000,000.00 | 10% | $16,402,824.20 |
| 19 | $2,000,000.00 | 10% | $16,729,840.18 |
| 20 | $2,000,000.00 | 10% | $17,027,127.44 |
| | | Total Payments | $40,000,000.00 |
| | | NPV | $17,027,127.44 |

---

5    GECAS is a leading global commercial aircraft leasing and financing company, with over 1,800 owned and managed aircraft.
6    ILFC is the world's largest aircraft lessor by value.

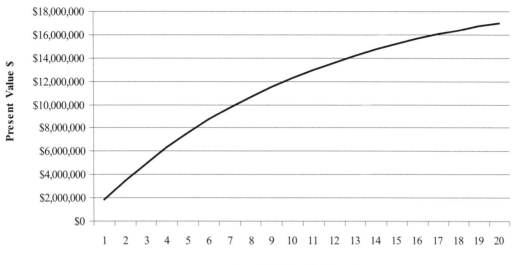

**Figure 3.6    Present value of an annuity with $2,000,000 payments compounded yearly**

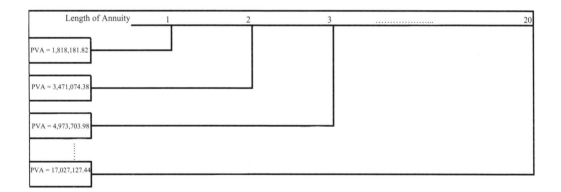

**Figure 3.7    Present value of an annuity**

Another important issue of annuity valuation is that of net present value or NPV. The net present value is the difference between the cost of the annuity and its present value at any given time. The formula for NPV is:

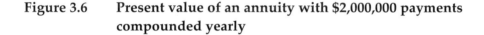

$$NPV_{Annuit} = \sum_{n=0}^{n}\left(\frac{PMT}{(1+i)^n}\right) \quad PMT \times [\frac{1}{i} - \frac{1}{i(1+i)^n}] = PMT \times PVIVA_{i,n}$$

The first term in square brackets is called the present value interest factor for the annuity and it shows the present value of $1 paid in each of n periods discounted at 1%. For the aircraft leasing company in the previous example, the NPV is calculated by taking the sum of the present value for each year's lease payment. Therefore, for the lease the NPVA is $17,027,127.44 even though the total payments equal $40 million. Discounting the future payments shows a large difference between the amount paid out over time and its present value. Once again, this result reinforces the concept of the time value of money. The NPV function is available in Microsoft Excel and is listed under the financial formulas. To do the calculation, simply enter the discount or interest rate and then the amount for each payment. Excel will then display the value of the NPV.

As a further practical example, assume an employee has $368,000 in his retirement account when he approaches retirement and he wants to know how long the funds will last if he withdraws $50,000 a year. The account pays 6% interest compounded yearly. In this case, the present value of the annuity and the annual interest rate and payments are known, but the period is unknown. We can solve this problem by using a special version of the present value of an annuity equation and an annuity table. In annuities with annual compounding the $m$ term can be eliminated to develop a term called the Present Value Interest Factor of an Annuity (PVIFA). This modified equation is shown below:

$$PV_{Annuity} = PMT \times [\frac{1}{i} - \frac{1}{i(1+i)^n}]$$

$$PVIFA_{i,n} = [\frac{1}{i} - \frac{1}{i(1+i)^n}]$$

$$PV_{Annuity} = PMT \times PVIFA_{i,n}$$

In the above equation there are four factors that are used in solving for an annual annuity. These are present value, payment, interest rate and the number of years the annuity lasts. (Moyer, McGuigan and Kretlow, 2006). If three of the terms are known, the fourth can be solved for using an annuity table. An annuity table is included as an appendix to this chapter. In the example of the employee with the retirement account, we have three of the variables (interest rate, present value of the annuity, and the payment). With these three factors we can solve for PVIFA and determine $n$ through the annuity table.

$$PV_{Annuity} = PMT \times PVIFA_{i,n}$$

$$368,000 = 50,000 \times PVIFA_{i,n}$$

$$PVIFA_{i,n} = 7.36$$

In the annuity table we find 7.360 under the column for annuities with an interest rate of 6%. We see that the number of periods this corresponds with is 10; therefore, the retirement will last for 10 years with the current present value and payments of $50,000 per year.

As with everything dealing with the time value of money, the future value of an annuity can also be calculated. Suppose one invested $1,000 at the end of one year in an account paying 10%. Each year one will deposit another $1,000. How much will the account have at the end of the third year? To determine the future value of an annuity, a formula similar to the present value formula is used:

$$FV_{Annuity} = PMT \times \left[ \frac{(1+\frac{i}{m})^{n \times m} - 1}{\frac{i}{m}} \right]$$

where:
$PMT$ = the amount of the payment
$i$     = the discount rate
$m$    = the number of compounding periods per year
$n$     = time in years

First Year: $FV_{Annuity} = 1000 \left[ \frac{(1+.10)^1 - 1}{.10} \right] = 1000$

Second Year: $FV_{Annuity} = 1000 \left[ \frac{(1+.10)^2 - 1}{.10} \right] = 2100$

Third Year: $FV_{Annuity} = 1000 \left[ \frac{(1+.10)^3 - 1}{.10} \right] = 3310$

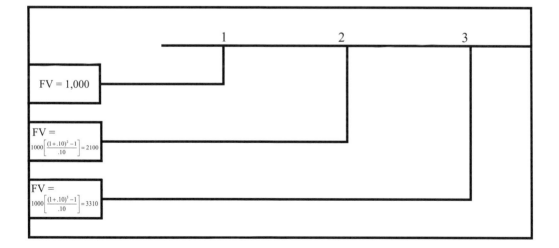

**Figure 3.8      Future value of an annuity**

To further illustrate the concept, refer back to the ramp vehicle example previously mentioned and determine the future value. As a reminder, the ramp vehicle's lease was $337 per month for five years with an annual interest rate of 6%. The future value of this annuity is expected to be $23,512.50 at the end of the sixty months. The difference between the present value and the future value of the loan can be viewed as the difference between the price of the vehicle and the interest associated with the note.

$$PMT = 337$$
$$m = 12$$
$$i = 6\%$$
$$n = 5$$

$$FVA = 337\left[\frac{(1+\frac{0.06}{12})^{5\times12} - 1}{\frac{.06}{12}}\right]$$

$$FVA = 337[69.77]$$

$$FVA = 23,512.50$$

Just as with the present value of an annuity, we can use a special form of the annuity formula for annuities with annual compounding. The future value of an annual annuity formula uses elements similar to the present value function and these are the interest rate, payment, number of time periods and a future value investment factor.

$$FV_{Annuity} = PMT \times \left[\frac{(1+i)^n - 1}{i}\right]$$

$$FVIFA_{i,n} = \left[\frac{(1+i)^n - 1}{i}\right]$$

$$FV_{Annuity} = PMT \times FVIFA_{i,n}$$

As an example to illustrate the use of the future value investment factor, suppose that an employee wants to put $10,000 into his retirement account at the end of every year until the employee retires. The employee wants to know how many years of savings will be needed until the account reaches $470,000. Assume the retirement account pays 6% interest.

$$FV_{Annuity} = PMT \times FVIFA_{i,n}$$
$$470,000 = 10,000 \times FVIFA_{i,n}$$
$$FVIFA_{i,n} = 47.00$$

By finding the value that we calculated for FVIFA in the future value annuity table in the appendix, we see that the corresponding value is 23; the retirement account will take 23 years to reach $470,000.

## PERPETUITIES[7]

A perpetuity is a stream of cash flows that lasts forever. A perpetuity follows the same principle as an annuity, except for the fact that it is a set of never-ending cash flows. An example of a perpetuity is preferred stock that yields a constant dollar dividend indefinitely. The calculation of a perpetuity follows the same basic principle as that of an annuity. The present value of a perpetuity is calculated by determining the cash flow for a given period and its rate.

Calculate the present value of a perpetuity (PVP) paying PMT dollars at the end of every year

$$PVP = \frac{PMT}{(1+i)} + \frac{PMT}{(1+i)^2} + \frac{PMT}{(1+i)^3} + \frac{PMT}{(1+i)^4} + \frac{PMT}{(1+i)^5} + \quad + \frac{PMT}{(1+i)^n}$$

Factor $\dfrac{PMT}{(1+i)}$ out from right hand side of above equation:

$$PVP = \frac{PMT}{(1+i)} \times \left[ 1 + \frac{1}{(1+i)^1} + \frac{1}{(1+i)^2} + \frac{1}{(1+i)^3} + \frac{1}{(1+i)^4} + \quad + \frac{1}{(1+i)^n} \right]$$

$n \to \infty$

*Then*

$$PVP = PMT \times \left( \frac{1}{i} \right)$$

$$PVP = \frac{PMT}{i}$$

where:
PMT  = the cash flow or payments, and
i      = the interest rate associated with the payment.

As a specific example of a perpetuity, assume that you are interested in investing in perpetual bonds.[8] After careful research you have determined that this investment will yield an annual cash flow of $1,500 with a required return rate of 6.5%. Using the equation from above, the present value of this perpetuity is found to be $23,076.92:

$$PVP = \frac{1500}{0.065}$$

$$PVP = \$23,076.92$$

The value of a perpetuity changes drastically when interest rates change. In the above example, the value of the perpetuity drops to $15,000 when the interest rate increases to 10% or increases to $30,000 when the interest rate drops to 5%.

---

7    Perpetuity is a stream of cash flows that lasts forever.
8    These bonds are called consols.

## AMORTIZATION SCHEDULE

Amortization is the payment of a loan where the payments contribute toward both interest and principal over the life of the loan. An amortization schedule is a tool that can help an airline manager to know just how much he is paying for the aircraft purchased or leased. This information is provided to the manager when signing the contract or purchasing an aircraft or other equipment. We can also look at amortization as the schedule of payments for the loan. When signing a mortgage for a house, the amortization schedule is usually also broken out. Technically speaking, amortization is the distribution of a single cash flow into smaller cash flows. The process is accomplished with the aid of an amortization schedule that displays the number of payments, the beginning balance at each period, the total payments, how much paid to interest and principal and finally, the ending balance. An example of an amortization schedule is found in Table 3.7 for a loan of $150,000 to build an aircraft hangar at a general aviation airport. The rate of interest is 5.50% for a period of ten years and the payments are made on an annual basis.

**Table 3.7     Amortization schedule**

| Payment No. | Payment Date | Beginning Balance | Scheduled Payment | Total Payment | Principal | Interest | Ending Balance |
|---|---|---|---|---|---|---|---|
| 1 | 31/01/2009 | $150,000.00 | $19,900.17 | $19,900.17 | $11,650.17 | $8,250.00 | $138,349.83 |
| 2 | 31/01/2010 | $138,349.83 | $19,900.17 | $19,900.17 | $12,290.92 | $7,609.24 | $126,058.91 |
| 3 | 31/01/2011 | $126,058.91 | $19,900.17 | $19,900.17 | $12,966.93 | $6,933.24 | $113,091.99 |
| 4 | 31/01/2012 | $113,091.99 | $19,900.17 | $19,900.17 | $13,680.11 | $6,220.06 | $99,411.88 |
| 5 | 31/01/2013 | $99,411.88 | $19,900.17 | $19,900.17 | $14,432.51 | $5,467.65 | $84,979.37 |
| 6 | 31/01/2014 | $84,979.37 | $19,900.17 | $19,900.17 | $15,226.30 | $4,673.87 | $69,753.07 |
| 7 | 31/01/2015 | $69,753.07 | $19,900.17 | $19,900.17 | $16,063.75 | $3,836.42 | $53,689.32 |
| 8 | 31/01/2016 | $53,689.32 | $19,900.17 | $19,900.17 | $16,947.25 | $2,952.91 | $36,742.07 |
| 9 | 31/01/2017 | $36,742.07 | $19,900.17 | $19,900.17 | $17,879.35 | $2,020.81 | $18,862.72 |
| 10 | 31/01/2018 | $18,862.72 | $19,900.17 | $18,862.72 | $17,825.27 | $1,037.45 | $- |
| | | | | | Total: | $49,001.65 | |

From the Table 3.7 the total interest paid over the life of the loan can be calculated by adding the separate interest payments to reach a figure of $49,001.65. The table also displays how the payments are broken into interest and principal and how the payments reduce their respective balances. In this type of loan format both parties know the exact amount of interest that will be charged and it is easy to determine the amount of principal and interest that will be repaid over the life of the loan. This loan has the interest rate fixed. The interest payment is largest in the first year, and it declines as the outstanding balance of the loan declines. However other types of loans may have variable interest rates.

## SUMMARY

This chapter introduces the crucial concept of the time value of money. This is probably one of the most significant concepts in the finance literature. The basic idea can be expressed in the notion that a dollar today is worth more than a dollar tomorrow. The difference between the two values is always expressed in terms of the interest or discount rate. That is, the interest rate is the amount that an individual would be willing to pay in the future in order to borrow money in the present. The chapter shows how the interest rate can be used to calculate the present value of future streams of income or the future value of a present stream of income. The chapter also discusses more complicated variations of these ideas such as annuities, perpetuities, and amortization schedules. The appendices to the chapter contain instructions as to how to use these financial functions in Excel.

## DISCUSSION QUESTIONS

1. Explain why, using the formulas from the chapter, that compound interest and discounted present value are essentially two ways of looking at the same thing.
2. Using the same formula show why as the interest rate goes up the present value goes down.
3. Assume that EZjET airlines have a financial decision to make between purchasing an aircraft for $20 million right now or leasing the aircraft at a cost of $2 million per annum for the next 20 years. Further assume that the going rate of interest in the economy is 6%. Using the tables in the appendix to the chapter, discuss what financial decision EZjET should make and why.
4. Now assume that the interest rate has gone up to 10%. Answer the same question as that in question number three and explain in economic terms what the difference between the two situations is.
5. Give the definition of an annuity.
6. What is the relationship between discounting and compounding?
7. Provide an example of a perpetuity. How does an annuity differ from a perpetuity?
8. Construct a loan amortization schedule for a 10 year, 10% loan of $45,000,000. The loan requires 10 equal payments.
9. You deposit $20,000 at the end of each year of the next five years into an account that pays 8% per year, compounding monthly, how much would be in the account at the maturity?
10. What is the future value of a $1,500 investment in five years that earns 4.5%
    a. Compounded annually?
    b. Compounded quarterly?
    c. Compounded monthly?
11. How much is $7,000 in three years worth today assuming one can earn a nominal interest rate of 1.25%
    a. Compounded annually?
    b. Compounded quarterly?
    c. Compounded monthly?
12. What is the present value of an annuity that generates a $2,000 income for the next ten years, given an interest rate of 3%, compounded annually?

13. If one were to place $6,000 in a bank account earning 2.25% annually, every year, for the next five years, how much would be in the account at the end of five years?

14. What is the present value of perpetuity of $5,000 annually at a 5% annual interest rate?

15. How long would it take for you to quadruple your money if you invest your money and it is expected to give you 6% interest compounded monthly?

16. What is the relationship among an annuity, a perpetuity, and a growing cash stream?

## APPENDIX 1: TIME VALUE OF MONEY CALCULATIONS IN EXCEL

### Time Value of Money Calculations in Excel

This section shows the reader how to run the financial functions referenced in the chapter using Microsoft Excel. Note that this chapter references use of Microsoft Excel 2004; however, a similar format is also used in Excel 2007. The formula functions are available by clicking the formula function button, or $F_x$, in Excel. Simply follow the format that Excel provides and Excel will solve for the desired variables.

### Future Value in Excel

The future value function is easily calculated in Excel. For example, if you want to determine the future value of $1,500 at the end of five years with an interest rate of 10%, open the future value function in Excel. This formula is listed under the financial formulas option or by entering = FV in the formula bar. Once this step is accomplished, the user can simply answer the formula questions and then Excel will solve this function. In the example given (see Figure 3.9) enter in 10% or 0.10 in the rate line. The number of periods will be 5 on the Nper line and the present value is entered as -1500 so that Excel can return a positive value for the future value. In this particular example the future value is $2,415.76.

Using this same example, suppose that interest in this case was compounded over the five years on a monthly basis. In this case the inputs into Excel would vary slightly.

The example in Figure 3.10 displays how the user would input the new variables.

In this example $^{10}/_{12}$ or .008333 would be entered for the interest rate since the annual rate is 10% and it is calculated on a monthly basis. The number of periods entered would be 5×12 or 60 since this is the number of times that interest will be calculated. The present value remains the same as in the previous example. This will yield a future value of $2467.96. The only difference between these two examples is merely the way in which interest is compounded over the life of the example.

### Present Value in Excel

Figure 3.11 shows how to enter a present value calculation in Excel. This function is listed under the financial formulas option or you can also type =PV in the formula bar. As before,

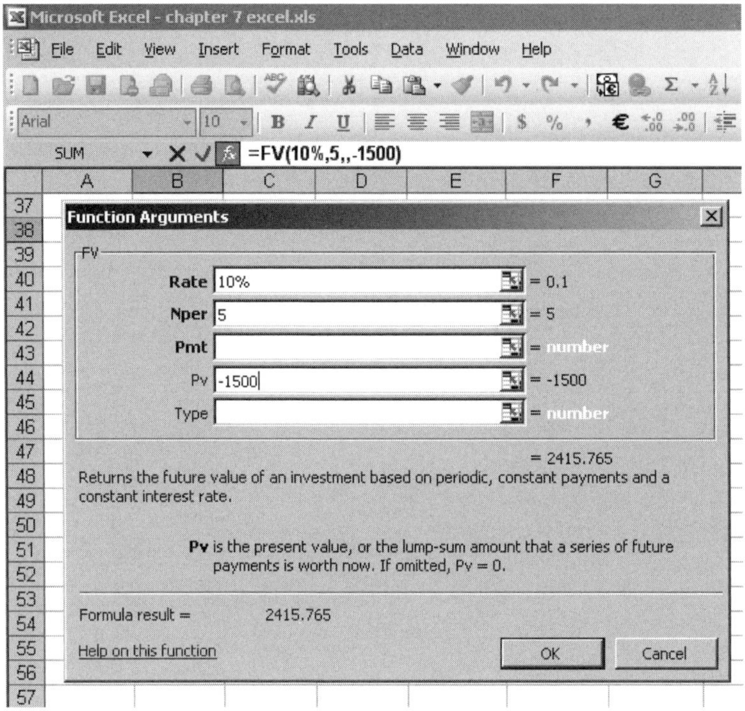

**Figure 3.9     Future value in Excel**

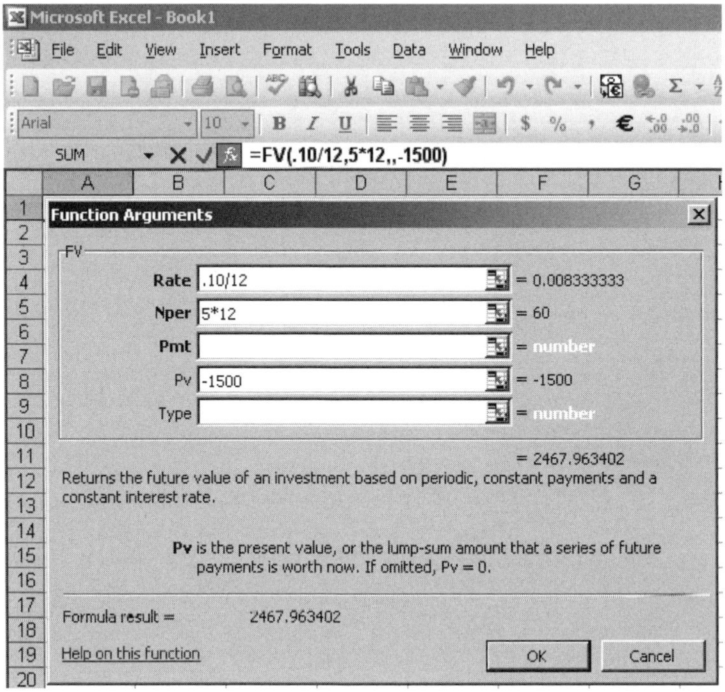

**Figure 3.10     Future value in Excel-monthly compounding**

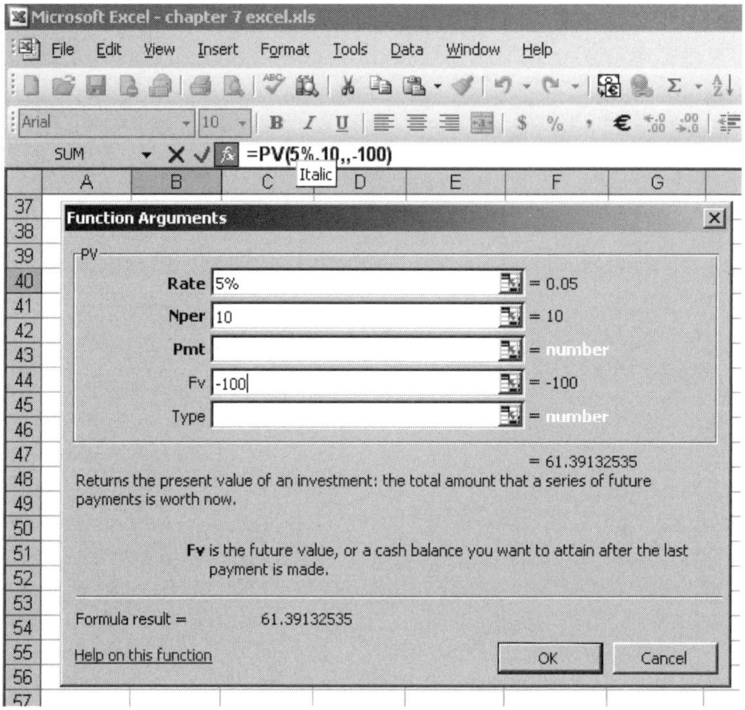

Figure 3.11     Present value in Excel

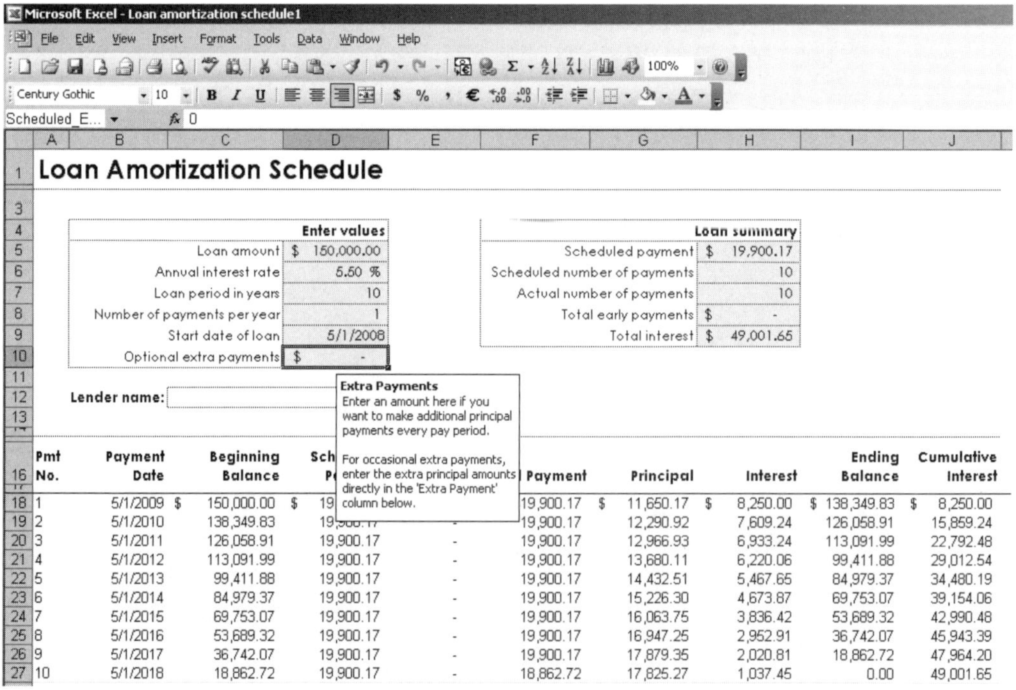

Figure 3.12     Amortization schedule in Excel

follow the formula outline to achieve the results. For this example, the interest rate is assumed to be 5%, the time period 10 years and the future value 100. On the rate line insert 5% or .05. On the Nper line enter 10 and on *Fv* line enter -100. In this case insert a negative value for the future value amount so that excel can return a positive value for the present value.

## Amortization Tables

Under the template options in Excel, there is an amortization schedule option. For this choice the user simply enters the required information and the table will auto populate. Figure 3.12 opposite shows the output for the example of $150,000 at a discount rate 5.50% for a period of ten years.

## APPENDIX 2

Table 3.8 is for an ordinary annuity where payments occur at the end of the year. For annuity dues, where payments occur at the beginning of the year, a different table must be used.

**Table 3.8　　　Present value of an annuity of $1**

$$PVIFA_{i,n} = \frac{1}{i} - \frac{1}{i(1+i)^n}$$

| Periods | 1% | 2% | 3% | 4% | 5% | 6% | 7% | 8% | 9% | 10% |
|---|---|---|---|---|---|---|---|---|---|---|
| 1 | $0.99 | $0.98 | $0.97 | $0.96 | $0.95 | $0.94 | $0.93 | $0.93 | $0.92 | $0.91 |
| 2 | $1.97 | $1.94 | $1.91 | $1.89 | $1.86 | $1.83 | $1.81 | $1.78 | $1.76 | $1.74 |
| 3 | $2.94 | $2.88 | $2.83 | $2.78 | $2.72 | $2.67 | $2.62 | $2.58 | $2.53 | $2.49 |
| 4 | $3.90 | $3.81 | $3.72 | $3.63 | $3.55 | $3.47 | $3.39 | $3.31 | $3.24 | $3.17 |
| 5 | $4.85 | $4.71 | $4.58 | $4.45 | $4.33 | $4.21 | $4.10 | $3.99 | $3.89 | $3.79 |
| 6 | $5.80 | $5.60 | $5.42 | $5.24 | $5.08 | $4.92 | $4.77 | $4.62 | $4.49 | $4.36 |
| 7 | $6.73 | $6.47 | $6.23 | $6.00 | $5.79 | $5.58 | $5.39 | $5.21 | $5.03 | $4.87 |
| 8 | $7.65 | $7.33 | $7.02 | $6.73 | $6.46 | $6.21 | $5.97 | $5.75 | $5.53 | $5.33 |
| 9 | $8.57 | $8.16 | $7.79 | $7.44 | $7.11 | $6.80 | $6.52 | $6.25 | $6.00 | $5.76 |
| 10 | $9.47 | $8.98 | $8.53 | $8.11 | $7.72 | $7.36 | $7.02 | $6.71 | $6.42 | $6.14 |
| 11 | $10.37 | $9.79 | $9.25 | $8.76 | $8.31 | $7.89 | $7.50 | $7.14 | $6.81 | $6.50 |
| 12 | $11.26 | $10.58 | $9.95 | $9.39 | $8.86 | $8.38 | $7.94 | $7.54 | $7.16 | $6.81 |
| 13 | $12.13 | $11.35 | $10.63 | $9.99 | $9.39 | $8.85 | $8.36 | $7.90 | $7.49 | $7.10 |
| 14 | $13.00 | $12.11 | $11.30 | $10.56 | $9.90 | $9.29 | $8.75 | $8.24 | $7.79 | $7.37 |
| 15 | $13.87 | $12.85 | $11.94 | $11.12 | $10.38 | $9.71 | $9.11 | $8.56 | $8.06 | $7.61 |
| 16 | $14.72 | $13.58 | $12.56 | $11.65 | $10.84 | $10.11 | $9.45 | $8.85 | $8.31 | $7.82 |
| 17 | $15.56 | $14.29 | $13.17 | $12.17 | $11.27 | $10.48 | $9.76 | $9.12 | $8.54 | $8.02 |
| 18 | $16.40 | $14.99 | $13.75 | $12.66 | $11.69 | $10.83 | $10.06 | $9.37 | $8.76 | $8.20 |
| 19 | $17.23 | $15.68 | $14.32 | $13.13 | $12.09 | $11.16 | $10.34 | $9.60 | $8.95 | $8.36 |
| 20 | $18.05 | $16.35 | $14.88 | $13.59 | $12.46 | $11.47 | $10.59 | $9.82 | $9.13 | $8.51 |
| 21 | $18.86 | $17.01 | $15.42 | $14.03 | $12.82 | $11.76 | $10.84 | $10.02 | $9.29 | $8.65 |
| 22 | $19.66 | $17.66 | $15.94 | $14.45 | $13.16 | $12.04 | $11.06 | $10.20 | $9.44 | $8.77 |
| 23 | $20.46 | $18.29 | $16.44 | $14.86 | $13.49 | $12.30 | $11.27 | $10.37 | $9.58 | $8.88 |
| 24 | $21.24 | $18.91 | $16.94 | $15.25 | $13.80 | $12.55 | $11.47 | $10.53 | $9.71 | $8.98 |
| 25 | $22.02 | $19.52 | $17.41 | $15.62 | $14.09 | $12.78 | $11.65 | $10.67 | $9.82 | $9.08 |
| 26 | $22.80 | $20.12 | $17.88 | $15.98 | $14.38 | $13.00 | $11.83 | $10.81 | $9.93 | $9.16 |

**Table 3.8** *Concluded*

| Periods | 1% | 2% | 3% | 4% | 5% | 6% | 7% | 8% | 9% | 10% |
|---------|------|------|------|------|------|------|------|------|------|------|
| 27 | $23.56 | $20.71 | $18.33 | $16.33 | $14.64 | $13.21 | $11.99 | $10.94 | $10.03 | $9.24 |
| 28 | $24.32 | $21.28 | $18.76 | $16.66 | $14.90 | $13.41 | $12.14 | $11.05 | $10.12 | $9.31 |
| 29 | $25.07 | $21.84 | $19.19 | $16.98 | $15.14 | $13.59 | $12.28 | $11.16 | $10.20 | $9.37 |
| 30 | $25.81 | $22.40 | $19.60 | $17.29 | $15.37 | $13.76 | $12.41 | $11.26 | $10.27 | $9.43 |

**Table 3.9** **Future value of an annuity of $1**

$$FVIFA_{i,n} = \frac{(1+i)^n - 1}{i}$$

| Periods | 1% | 2% | 3% | 4% | 5% | 6% | 7% | 8% | 9% | 10% |
|---------|--------|--------|--------|--------|--------|--------|--------|--------|--------|--------|
| 1 | $1.00 | $1.00 | $1.00 | $1.00 | $1.00 | $1.00 | $1.00 | $1.00 | $1.00 | $1.00 |
| 2 | $2.01 | $2.02 | $2.03 | $2.04 | $2.05 | $2.06 | $2.07 | $2.08 | $2.09 | $2.10 |
| 3 | $3.03 | $3.06 | $3.09 | $3.12 | $3.15 | $3.18 | $3.21 | $3.25 | $3.28 | $3.31 |
| 4 | $4.06 | $4.12 | $4.18 | $4.25 | $4.31 | $4.37 | $4.44 | $4.51 | $4.57 | $4.64 |
| 5 | $5.10 | $5.20 | $5.31 | $5.42 | $5.53 | $5.64 | $5.75 | $5.87 | $5.98 | $6.11 |
| 6 | $6.15 | $6.31 | $6.47 | $6.63 | $6.80 | $6.98 | $7.15 | $7.34 | $7.52 | $7.72 |
| 7 | $7.21 | $7.43 | $7.66 | $7.90 | $8.14 | $8.39 | $8.65 | $8.92 | $9.20 | $9.49 |
| 8 | $8.29 | $8.58 | $8.89 | $9.21 | $9.55 | $9.90 | $10.26 | $10.64 | $11.03 | $11.44 |
| 9 | $9.37 | $9.75 | $10.16 | $10.58 | $11.03 | $11.49 | $11.98 | $12.49 | $13.02 | $13.58 |
| 10 | $10.46 | $10.95 | $11.46 | $12.01 | $12.58 | $13.18 | $13.82 | $14.49 | $15.19 | $15.94 |
| 11 | $11.57 | $12.17 | $12.81 | $13.49 | $14.21 | $14.97 | $15.78 | $16.65 | $17.56 | $18.53 |
| 12 | $12.68 | $13.41 | $14.19 | $15.03 | $15.92 | $16.87 | $17.89 | $18.98 | $20.14 | $21.38 |
| 13 | $13.81 | $14.68 | $15.62 | $16.63 | $17.71 | $18.88 | $20.14 | $21.50 | $22.95 | $24.52 |
| 14 | $14.95 | $15.97 | $17.09 | $18.29 | $19.60 | $21.02 | $22.55 | $24.21 | $26.02 | $27.97 |
| 15 | $16.10 | $17.29 | $18.60 | $20.02 | $21.58 | $23.28 | $25.13 | $27.15 | $29.36 | $31.77 |
| 16 | $17.26 | $18.64 | $20.16 | $21.82 | $23.66 | $25.67 | $27.89 | $30.32 | $33.00 | $35.95 |
| 17 | $18.43 | $20.01 | $21.76 | $23.70 | $25.84 | $28.21 | $30.84 | $33.75 | $36.97 | $40.54 |
| 18 | $19.61 | $21.41 | $23.41 | $25.65 | $28.13 | $30.91 | $34.00 | $37.45 | $41.30 | $45.60 |
| 19 | $20.81 | $22.84 | $25.12 | $27.67 | $30.54 | $33.76 | $37.38 | $41.45 | $46.02 | $51.16 |
| 20 | $22.02 | $24.30 | $26.87 | $29.78 | $33.07 | $36.79 | $41.00 | $45.76 | $51.16 | $57.27 |
| 21 | $23.24 | $25.78 | $28.68 | $31.97 | $35.72 | $39.99 | $44.87 | $50.42 | $56.76 | $64.00 |
| 22 | $24.47 | $27.30 | $30.54 | $34.25 | $38.51 | $43.39 | $49.01 | $55.46 | $62.87 | $71.40 |

**Table 3.9** *Concluded*

| Periods | 1% | 2% | 3% | 4% | 5% | 6% | 7% | 8% | 9% | 10% |
|---|---|---|---|---|---|---|---|---|---|---|
| 23 | $25.72 | $28.84 | $32.45 | $36.62 | $41.43 | $47.00 | $53.44 | $60.89 | $69.53 | $79.54 |
| 24 | $26.97 | $30.42 | $34.43 | $39.08 | $44.50 | $50.82 | $58.18 | $66.76 | $76.79 | $88.50 |
| 25 | $28.24 | $32.03 | $36.46 | $41.65 | $47.73 | $54.86 | $63.25 | $73.11 | $84.70 | $98.35 |
| 26 | $29.53 | $33.67 | $38.55 | $44.31 | $51.11 | $59.16 | $68.68 | $79.95 | $93.32 | $109.18 |
| 27 | $30.82 | $35.34 | $40.71 | $47.08 | $54.67 | $63.71 | $74.48 | $87.35 | $102.72 | $121.10 |
| 28 | $32.13 | $37.05 | $42.93 | $49.97 | $58.40 | $68.53 | $80.70 | $95.34 | $112.97 | $134.21 |
| 29 | $33.45 | $38.79 | $45.22 | $52.97 | $62.32 | $73.64 | $87.35 | $103.97 | $124.14 | $148.63 |
| 30 | $34.78 | $40.57 | $47.58 | $56.08 | $66.44 | $79.06 | $94.46 | $113.28 | $136.31 | $164.49 |

**Table 3.10**    **Present value of $1 due at the end of n periods**

$$PVIF_{i,n} = \frac{1}{(1+i)^n}$$

| Periods | 1% | 2% | 3% | 4% | 5% | 6% | 7% | 8% | 9% | 10% |
|---|---|---|---|---|---|---|---|---|---|---|
| 1 | $0.99 | $0.98 | $0.97 | $0.96 | $0.95 | $0.94 | $0.93 | $0.93 | $0.92 | $0.91 |
| 2 | $0.98 | $0.96 | $0.94 | $0.92 | $0.91 | $0.89 | $0.87 | $0.86 | $0.84 | $0.83 |
| 3 | $0.97 | $0.94 | $0.92 | $0.89 | $0.86 | $0.84 | $0.82 | $0.79 | $0.77 | $0.75 |
| 4 | $0.96 | $0.92 | $0.89 | $0.85 | $0.82 | $0.79 | $0.76 | $0.74 | $0.71 | $0.68 |
| 5 | $0.95 | $0.91 | $0.86 | $0.82 | $0.78 | $0.75 | $0.71 | $0.68 | $0.65 | $0.62 |
| 6 | $0.94 | $0.89 | $0.84 | $0.79 | $0.75 | $0.70 | $0.67 | $0.63 | $0.60 | $0.56 |
| 7 | $0.93 | $0.87 | $0.81 | $0.76 | $0.71 | $0.67 | $0.62 | $0.58 | $0.55 | $0.51 |
| 8 | $0.92 | $0.85 | $0.79 | $0.73 | $0.68 | $0.63 | $0.58 | $0.54 | $0.50 | $0.47 |
| 9 | $0.91 | $0.84 | $0.77 | $0.70 | $0.64 | $0.59 | $0.54 | $0.50 | $0.46 | $0.42 |
| 10 | $0.91 | $0.82 | $0.74 | $0.68 | $0.61 | $0.56 | $0.51 | $0.46 | $0.42 | $0.39 |
| 11 | $0.90 | $0.80 | $0.72 | $0.65 | $0.58 | $0.53 | $0.48 | $0.43 | $0.39 | $0.35 |
| 12 | $0.89 | $0.79 | $0.70 | $0.62 | $0.56 | $0.50 | $0.44 | $0.40 | $0.36 | $0.32 |
| 13 | $0.88 | $0.77 | $0.68 | $0.60 | $0.53 | $0.47 | $0.41 | $0.37 | $0.33 | $0.29 |
| 14 | $0.87 | $0.76 | $0.66 | $0.58 | $0.51 | $0.44 | $0.39 | $0.34 | $0.30 | $0.26 |
| 15 | $0.86 | $0.74 | $0.64 | $0.56 | $0.48 | $0.42 | $0.36 | $0.32 | $0.27 | $0.24 |
| 16 | $0.85 | $0.73 | $0.62 | $0.53 | $0.46 | $0.39 | $0.34 | $0.29 | $0.25 | $0.22 |
| 17 | $0.84 | $0.71 | $0.61 | $0.51 | $0.44 | $0.37 | $0.32 | $0.27 | $0.23 | $0.20 |
| 18 | $0.84 | $0.70 | $0.59 | $0.49 | $0.42 | $0.35 | $0.30 | $0.25 | $0.21 | $0.18 |

**Table 3.10** *Concluded*

| Periods | 1% | 2% | 3% | 4% | 5% | 6% | 7% | 8% | 9% | 10% |
|---------|------|------|------|------|------|------|------|------|------|------|
| 19 | $0.83 | $0.69 | $0.57 | $0.47 | $0.40 | $0.33 | $0.28 | $0.23 | $0.19 | $0.16 |
| 20 | $0.82 | $0.67 | $0.55 | $0.46 | $0.38 | $0.31 | $0.26 | $0.21 | $0.18 | $0.15 |
| 21 | $0.81 | $0.66 | $0.54 | $0.44 | $0.36 | $0.29 | $0.24 | $0.20 | $0.16 | $0.14 |
| 22 | $0.80 | $0.65 | $0.52 | $0.42 | $0.34 | $0.28 | $0.23 | $0.18 | $0.15 | $0.12 |
| 23 | $0.80 | $0.63 | $0.51 | $0.41 | $0.33 | $0.26 | $0.21 | $0.17 | $0.14 | $0.11 |
| 24 | $0.79 | $0.62 | $0.49 | $0.39 | $0.31 | $0.25 | $0.20 | $0.16 | $0.13 | $0.10 |
| 25 | $0.78 | $0.61 | $0.48 | $0.38 | $0.30 | $0.23 | $0.18 | $0.15 | $0.12 | $0.09 |
| 26 | $0.77 | $0.60 | $0.46 | $0.36 | $0.28 | $0.22 | $0.17 | $0.14 | $0.11 | $0.08 |
| 27 | $0.76 | $0.59 | $0.45 | $0.35 | $0.27 | $0.21 | $0.16 | $0.13 | $0.10 | $0.08 |
| 28 | $0.76 | $0.57 | $0.44 | $0.33 | $0.26 | $0.20 | $0.15 | $0.12 | $0.09 | $0.07 |
| 29 | $0.75 | $0.56 | $0.42 | $0.32 | $0.24 | $0.18 | $0.14 | $0.11 | $0.08 | $0.06 |
| 30 | $0.74 | $0.55 | $0.41 | $0.31 | $0.23 | $0.17 | $0.13 | $0.10 | $0.08 | $0.06 |

**Table 3.11** **Future value of $1 due at the end of n periods**

$$FVIF_{i,n} = (1+i)^n$$

| Periods | 1% | 2% | 3% | 4% | 5% | 6% | 7% | 8% | 9% | 10% |
|---------|------|------|------|------|------|------|------|------|------|------|
| 1 | $1.01 | $1.02 | $1.03 | $1.04 | $1.05 | $1.06 | $1.07 | $1.08 | $1.09 | $1.10 |
| 2 | $1.02 | $1.04 | $1.06 | $1.08 | $1.10 | $1.12 | $1.14 | $1.17 | $1.19 | $1.21 |
| 3 | $1.03 | $1.06 | $1.09 | $1.12 | $1.16 | $1.19 | $1.23 | $1.26 | $1.30 | $1.33 |
| 4 | $1.04 | $1.08 | $1.13 | $1.17 | $1.22 | $1.26 | $1.31 | $1.36 | $1.41 | $1.46 |
| 5 | $1.05 | $1.10 | $1.16 | $1.22 | $1.28 | $1.34 | $1.40 | $1.47 | $1.54 | $1.61 |
| 6 | $1.06 | $1.13 | $1.19 | $1.27 | $1.34 | $1.42 | $1.50 | $1.59 | $1.68 | $1.77 |
| 7 | $1.07 | $1.15 | $1.23 | $1.32 | $1.41 | $1.50 | $1.61 | $1.71 | $1.83 | $1.95 |
| 8 | $1.08 | $1.17 | $1.27 | $1.37 | $1.48 | $1.59 | $1.72 | $1.85 | $1.99 | $2.14 |
| 9 | $1.09 | $1.20 | $1.30 | $1.42 | $1.55 | $1.69 | $1.84 | $2.00 | $2.17 | $2.36 |
| 10 | $1.10 | $1.22 | $1.34 | $1.48 | $1.63 | $1.79 | $1.97 | $2.16 | $2.37 | $2.59 |
| 11 | $1.12 | $1.24 | $1.38 | $1.54 | $1.71 | $1.90 | $2.10 | $2.33 | $2.58 | $2.85 |
| 12 | $1.13 | $1.27 | $1.43 | $1.60 | $1.80 | $2.01 | $2.25 | $2.52 | $2.81 | $3.14 |
| 13 | $1.14 | $1.29 | $1.47 | $1.67 | $1.89 | $2.13 | $2.41 | $2.72 | $3.07 | $3.45 |
| 14 | $1.15 | $1.32 | $1.51 | $1.73 | $1.98 | $2.26 | $2.58 | $2.94 | $3.34 | $3.80 |

**Table 3.11**    *Concluded*

| Periods | 1% | 2% | 3% | 4% | 5% | 6% | 7% | 8% | 9% | 10% |
|---|---|---|---|---|---|---|---|---|---|---|
| 15 | $1.16 | $1.35 | $1.56 | $1.80 | $2.08 | $2.40 | $2.76 | $3.17 | $3.64 | $4.18 |
| 16 | $1.17 | $1.37 | $1.60 | $1.87 | $2.18 | $2.54 | $2.95 | $3.43 | $3.97 | $4.59 |
| 17 | $1.18 | $1.40 | $1.65 | $1.95 | $2.29 | $2.69 | $3.16 | $3.70 | $4.33 | $5.05 |
| 18 | $1.20 | $1.43 | $1.70 | $2.03 | $2.41 | $2.85 | $3.38 | $4.00 | $4.72 | $5.56 |
| 19 | $1.21 | $1.46 | $1.75 | $2.11 | $2.53 | $3.03 | $3.62 | $4.32 | $5.14 | $6.12 |
| 20 | $1.22 | $1.49 | $1.81 | $2.19 | $2.65 | $3.21 | $3.87 | $4.66 | $5.60 | $6.73 |
| 21 | $1.23 | $1.52 | $1.86 | $2.28 | $2.79 | $3.40 | $4.14 | $5.03 | $6.11 | $7.40 |
| 22 | $1.24 | $1.55 | $1.92 | $2.37 | $2.93 | $3.60 | $4.43 | $5.44 | $6.66 | $8.14 |
| 23 | $1.26 | $1.58 | $1.97 | $2.46 | $3.07 | $3.82 | $4.74 | $5.87 | $7.26 | $8.95 |
| 24 | $1.27 | $1.61 | $2.03 | $2.56 | $3.23 | $4.05 | $5.07 | $6.34 | $7.91 | $9.85 |
| 25 | $1.28 | $1.64 | $2.09 | $2.67 | $3.39 | $4.29 | $5.43 | $6.85 | $8.62 | $10.83 |
| 26 | $1.30 | $1.67 | $2.16 | $2.77 | $3.56 | $4.55 | $5.81 | $7.40 | $9.40 | $11.92 |
| 27 | $1.31 | $1.71 | $2.22 | $2.88 | $3.73 | $4.82 | $6.21 | $7.99 | $10.25 | $13.11 |
| 28 | $1.32 | $1.74 | $2.29 | $3.00 | $3.92 | $5.11 | $6.65 | $8.63 | $11.17 | $14.42 |
| 29 | $1.33 | $1.78 | $2.36 | $3.12 | $4.12 | $5.42 | $7.11 | $9.32 | $12.17 | $15.86 |
| 30 | $1.35 | $1.81 | $2.43 | $3.24 | $4.32 | $5.74 | $7.61 | $10.06 | $13.27 | $17.45 |

# REFERENCES

Chambers, D., and N. Lacey (1999). *Modern Corporate Finance* (2). Reading, MA: Addison-Wesley.

IATA (2007). *Airline Finance and Accounting Management* (2). International Air Transport Association, Montreal.

Moyer, C., J. McGuigan, and J. Kretlow (2006). *Contemporary Financial Management* (4). St. Paul, MN.

Palmiter, R. (2003). Law and Valuation: Financial valuation in legal contexts. Wake Forest University School of Law. Retrieved November 13, 2008 from http://www.wfu.edu/%7Epalmitar/LawandValuation/Index.htm

Ross, S., R. Westerfield, and J. Jaffe (2008). *Corporate Finance* (8). McGraw-Hill Irwin.

Ross, S., R. Westerfield, and B. Jordan (2008). *Fundamentals of Corporate Finance* (8). McGraw-Hill Irwin.

# 4

# Risk and Return

"He gave me a lot of very useful advice when I set up Virgin Atlantic 21 years ago. Perhaps his best advice was to make sure that I took BA to court before they bankrupted us—not after, as he did."[1]

Sir Richard Branson, Virgin Atlantic

Every decision in life contains some degree of risk, no matter how trivial the risk factor. When an airline makes a decision to buy an aircraft, its decision is influenced by what it expects the return on that aircraft to be and the associated risk. For example, there is a risk that a recently purchased car will incur mechanical defects that are not covered by warranty. However, the degree of risk that the car will incur a defect and that the defect is not covered by warranty can depend on a host of factors, such as the car's reliability, the manufacturer's reputation, and how the car is driven. Ultimately in finance, analyzing the risk of a company undergoes a similar process such as determining the company's market position, analyzing financial statements and identifying the company's long-term threats and opportunities. However, in finance, determining the benefit received from a decision, called a return, can be calculated since it is usually stated in currency terms. For instance, while an airline may be facing bankruptcy, an investor may be willing to provide equity. For this investor, the risk factor would be the airline going bankrupt and losing the investment, while the return factor would be the perceived gain of investing in the airline. Hence, airlines might display considerable variation in risk and returns. This chapter will help the reader understand the concept of risk and return by understanding the different risk preferences and how risk applies to the airline industry. The capital asset pricing model (CAPM) is explained and, to more fully understand the concept of risk and return, the question as to whether the airline industry is a risky investment is discussed. Therefore, this chapter highlights the dichotomy between risk and return and how it impacts the financial environment. The following topics are covered in the chapter:

- Expected Rate of Return
  - Portfolio Risks and Returns
- Risk Analysis
- Financial Risk Preferences
  - Risk-Averse Investors
  - Risk-Neutral Investors

---

1    Referring to the late Sir Freddie Laker who was the pioneer of the low-cost concept and started Laker Airways in the mid 1960s.

## EXPECTED RATE OF RETURN

While the term "return" in finance may appear to be a rather elementary term, in fact it contains many subtle connotations that need to be explained. Simply put, return is the profit received on capital investments or securities. For example, suppose a company invested in a new piece of machinery which resulted in a $5,000 annual increase in profits. In dollar terms, the return would simply be $5,000 since that was the profit received attributed to the incremental increase in investment. Returns can also be stated in percentage terms, with such metrics as return of investment, return on assets, and return on equity. Assuming the piece of machinery cost $40,000, the return on investment would have been 12.5% per year.

$$\text{Return on Investment} = k_i = \frac{Net\,income}{Investment} = \frac{Net\,income}{Average\,total\,asets}$$

$$k_i = \frac{\$5,000}{\$40,000} = 12.5\%$$

The above example concerning additions to property, plant, and equipment is a classic example of a company's returns. The return can be stated in dollar terms as the cash received from the investment or expressed in percentage terms. However, the return on a financial investment is a little less definitive, as the total dollar return is comprised of two components: dividend income and capital gains.

$$\text{Total Dollar Return} = \text{Dividend Income} + \text{Capital Gain (or loss)}$$

Dividend income is commonly received from purchases in stock as profitable companies typically re-direct a portion of their earnings back to their shareholders. Dividends are usually paid by corporations with stable historical profits and a sound financial outlook. Dividends can be distributed annually, bi-annually, or quarterly and are up to the sole discretion of the company's management. Companies are free to increase or slash dividend payments; however, such changes will trigger a shift in the company's stock price, as the dividend amount is ultimately imbedded within the price of the stock.

Capital gains represent the change in the stock price ($P_{s,t}$) from one period to the next ($P_{s,t+1}$). For instance, assume the share price for Continental Airlines increased from $10 to $15 during a month. For one share of stock, the capital gain recorded would be merely $5, the difference in share price between the two periods.

$$\text{Capital Gain (Loss) } P_{s,t+1} - P_{s,t} = \$15 - \$10 = \$5$$

However, one important distinction needs to be made with respect to capital gains, in that the profit is never actually received until the equity investment has been sold. Therefore, any increase in stock price is merely an unrealized gain, or loss, and it becomes realized upon the sale of the stock. In the Continental Airlines example above, if the shareholder retained the stock at the end of the month, the $5 gain would have been unrealized. However, if the stock was sold at the end of the month, the $5 gain would have been realized. This distinction becomes particularly important when evaluating financial statements and determining the financial impact of valuation in investment and derivative instruments.

Gain on stock can also be stated as a percentage return by calculating both the dividend yield and capital gain percentage of the stock. Consider a stock that issued a $3 annual dividend per share and increased in value from $15 per share to $30 per share during the year. By using the formula shown below, the total return on an investment in the stock would yield the shareholder a 120% annual return, a great return on investment by anyone's standards.

$$\text{Total Return} = k_i = \text{Dividend Yield} + \text{Capital Gain } \%$$

$$k_i = \left(\frac{\text{Dividend}_{t+1}}{\text{Share Price}_t}\right) + \left[\frac{(\text{Share Price}_{t+1} - \text{Share Price}_t)}{\text{Share Price}_t}\right]$$

$$k_i = \frac{\$3}{\$15} + [\frac{\$30 - \$15}{\$15}] = 0.20 + 1.0 = 1.20 \, or \, 120\%$$

Another key when measuring the return on investment is the holding period, or the length of time in which the security is held. In other words, the holding period is the time in which any gains or losses are unrealized. Since smart investing usually requires holding onto an investment for extended periods of time, the holding return on a stock is merely the return on investment for the extended period of time. For instance, consider a stock that provides zero dividends and which experiences a –8% return in the first year, +6% in the second year, and +14% in the third year. While the annual return varies considerably by year, the three-year holding return is merely the sum of the annual returns:

$$K_t = \sum_{i=1}^{3} k_i = (-8\% + 6\% + 14\%) = 12\%$$

Therefore, the holding period return is fundamentally different than average return which merely states the holding period return on an annualized basis. For example, the average annual return for the stock above would be 4%.

$$\hat{k} = \frac{\sum_{i=1}^{3} k_i}{N} = \frac{12\%}{3} = 4\%$$

*Portfolio Risks and Returns*

The expected return on a portfolio is the weighted average of the expected return on the securities included in that portfolio, with the weight of a security in a portfolio simply being the percentage of assets invested in that security. A key investment strategy used to reduce risk is to hold a portfolio of stocks, as it reduces the investor risk that one stock performs badly. While this risk minimization technique reduces the potential gain, it also greatly diminishes downside losses. Portfolio theory is a key reason why mutual funds have grown to be a very popular and effective investment tool. The expected return on a portfolio ($K_p$) is the weighted average of the expected returns on the securities included in the portfolio, weighted by the percentage of the portfolio invested in that security.

$$\hat{k}_p = \text{Expected Return on Portfolio}$$

$$\hat{k}_p = \sum_{i=1}^{n} w_i \times \hat{k}_i$$

where :

$$w_i = \frac{\text{value of investment i}}{\text{value of portfolio}}$$

$$\hat{k}_i = \text{expected return of investment i}$$

In order to calculate the return on an investment portfolio, the weighted average annual return needs to be calculated. Consider the following portfolio highlighted in Table 4.1, which contains three stocks with varying annual returns.

**Table 4.1        Sample portfolio**

|           | Shares Held | Closing Price | Stock Value | Annual Return |
|-----------|-------------|---------------|-------------|---------------|
| Stock A   | 100         | $60           | $6,000      | 8%            |
| Stock B   | 20          | $120          | $2,400      | -12%          |
| Stock C   | 40          | $40           | $1,600      | 15%           |
|           | 160         |               | $10,000     |               |

Portfolio return is calculated by weighting the annual return of an individual security based on the security's dollar value of the portfolio. For the portfolio contained in Table 4.1, stock A represents 60% of the portfolio based upon its stock value compared with the total portfolio value, while stock B and stock C represent 24% and 16% of the portfolio respectively. From the portfolio values of the individual securities, the portfolio return is found to be 4.3%.

$$k_p = \sum_{i=1}^{n} w_i \times k_i$$

$$k_i = (8\% \times .60) + (-12\% \times .24) + (15\% \times .16)$$

$$k_i = 4.8\% - 2.9\% + 2.4\% = \mathbf{4.3\%}$$

As another example, consider the portfolio contained in Table 4.2. Assume the portfolio consists of seven stocks with a total value of $1,000,000. The value of each stock ranges from $100,000 to $300,000 or 10% to 30% of the portfolio; returns on each of the stocks range from –9% to 10%. By multiplying each of the returns by the stocks weight, the individual weighted return for each stock is found ($W_i \times K_i$); all weighted returns added together provide the portfolio return, which equals 4.1% for the portfolio contained in Table 4.2.

**Table 4.2     Portfolio return**

| Stock | Ki | Value | Wi | Wi*Ki |
|-------|------|-----------|-----|--------|
| A | 6% | $200,000 | 0.2 | 1.20% |
| B | 2% | $100,000 | 0.1 | 0.20% |
| C | 10% | $300,000 | 0.3 | 3.00% |
| D | -3% | $100,000 | 0.1 | -0.30% |
| E | -9% | $100,000 | 0.1 | -0.90% |
| F | 4% | $100,000 | 0.1 | 0.40% |
| G | 5% | $100,000 | 0.1 | 0.50% |
| | | $1,000,000 | | |
| Kp | | | | 4.10% |

A similar methodology can be used to determine the expected return of an individual stock or portfolio. Expected return is the return that an individual expects in a future period. Since expected return is a projection of the future, the actual return of a stock can vary considerably. Additionally, the expected return of the same security can vary based upon one's beliefs, projections, knowledge, and skill. One methodology for calculating expected return is to assign varying probabilities of an expected annual return. For instance, consider a stock (Table 4.3) with different expected returns based upon the state of the economy. Additionally, one has varying probabilities of the state of the economy. Based on these factors, the expected return of the stock can be calculated.

Expected Return on Investment = $\hat{k}_i$

$$\hat{k}_i = p_{depression} \times k_{depression} + p_{recession} \times k_{recession} + p_{normal} \times k_{normal} + p_{boom} \times k_{boom}$$

$$\hat{k}_i = \sum_{i}^{n} p_i \times k_i$$

$$\hat{k}_i = (5\% \times -.20) + (10\% \times -5\%) + (65\% \times .10) + (20\% \times .35)$$

$$\hat{k}_i = -1\% - 0.5\% + 6.5\% + 7.0\% = 12\%$$

Based upon one's assumptions of the economy and the associated return, the expected return of the stock is 12%. For this stock, there was a 55% range (–20% to 35%) in which

**Table 4.3      Expected annual return of an individual security**

|  | Probability | Expected Annual Return | Weighted Return |
|---|---|---|---|
| Depression | 5% | -20% | -1.00% |
| Recession | 10% | -5% | -0.50% |
| Normal | 65% | 10% | 6.50% |
| Boom | 20% | 35% | 7.00% |
| $\hat{k_i}$ |  |  | 12.00% |

the stock's expected return could vary. Other stocks could potentially have smaller ranges in which the return might vary. This variance of expected returns is sometimes thought to represent risk.

## RISK ANALYSIS

"Every time I fly and am forced to remove my shoes, I'm grateful Richard Reid[2] is not known as the Underwear Bomber."

Douglas Manuel, aerospace executive regards airport security

While there is no universal financial definition of risk, the variance of return is usually the most agreed upon definition. A stock or portfolio whose returns are fairly stable over time would be considered less risky than a stock whose returns swing wildly from one period to the next. Ultimately, the expected return of investment is based upon this risk. The expected return of an investment can be constructed from two categories: risk-free return and risk premium.

Expected return = Risk-free return + Risk premium

Risk-free return is a security with zero to little risk as the return is guaranteed. As a result of the return being guaranteed, risk-free securities are usually debt instruments. However, all financial institutions have some probability of bankruptcy where the return would not be received; therefore, there is no corporate financial instrument that has absolutely zero risk. The only true risk-free securities available are instruments that are backed by the government, since from a finance perspective it is assumed that the government will never default. Therefore, U.S. treasury bills are considered a risk-free investment as their return is guaranteed, with the risk-free return being the return on a standard U.S. treasury bill.

---

2      Richard Reid is known for attempting to destroy a commercial aircraft in-flight by *detonating* explosives hidden in his shoes. On December 25, 2009, Umar Abdulmutallab attempted to detonate plastic explosives hidden in his underwear while on board Northwest Airlines Flight 253.

The risk premium represents the excess return over the risk-free rate, since the underlying principle of the risk and return dichotomy is that the more risk an individual bears, the greater the return that is expected. Thus, the risk premium is the difference between the expected return and the risk-free return. When the risk-free return and the risk premium are combined together, the total risk is the result.

The basic definition of risk is the variance of expected return. Using the same stock contained in Table 4.3 and the expected return of 12%, the variance and standard deviation of the stocks' return can be calculated using the following formula:

$$Variance = \sigma^2 = \sum_{i=1}^{n} P_i \times (\hat{k}_i - k_i)^2$$

$$Standard\ Deviation = \sigma = \sqrt{\sum_{i=1}^{n} P_i \times (\hat{k}_i - k_i)^2}$$

If we return to the example in Table 4.4 of a stock with various returns that depend on the state of the economy, we can calculate the standard deviation:

$$\sigma = \sqrt{0.01885} = 0.1373\ or\ 13.73\%$$

**Table 4.4      Standard deviation of a weighted individual security**

| | Probability | Expected Annual Return | Weighted Return | $P_i \times (\hat{k}_i - k_i)^2$ |
|---|---|---|---|---|
| Depression | 5% | -20% | -1.00% | 0.005 |
| Recession | 10% | -5% | -0.50% | 0.003 |
| Normal | 65% | 10% | 6.50% | 0.000 |
| Boom | 20% | 35% | 7.00% | 0.011 |
| | | | 12.00% | 1.89% |
| $\hat{k}_i$ | | | $\sigma$ | 13.73% |

The standard deviation of the security is 13.73%, which means that on average the expected return can vary by a degree of 13.73%. In terms of judging if this stock is risky, the stock needs to be compared to another stock or portfolio. On a standalone basis, it is difficult to determine risk, as risk needs to be compared with the next best alternative. Additionally, the riskiness of this stock relates to one's viewpoint of risk and how much risk one is willing to bear.

Standard deviation is an important measure when determining the risk of a security or portfolio. Standard deviation is often associated with the normal distribution curve; that is, in a normal distribution, 68% of all measurements will fall within one standard deviation of the mean, 95% within two standard deviations, and 99% within three standard deviations (Brase, 2008). Figure 4.1 shows a normal distribution curve with a mean of 50. Figure 4.1 shows that as the standard deviation (risk) increases for a normal distribution with the same mean, the shape of the standard normal curve becomes more flat.

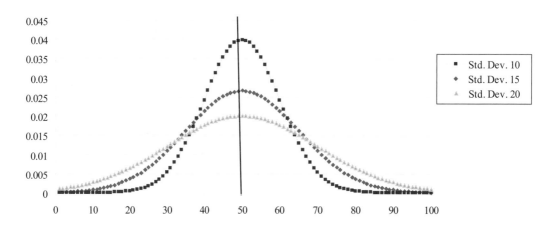

**Figure 4.1     Normal distribution curve: Mean = 50**

Risk can be classified into two separate categories, systematic and unsystematic, based upon the driver of the risk.

*Systematic risk* is risk that is inherent to the entire market or industry, usually affecting all industries and companies across the board.[3] Also commonly called market risk, systematic risk contains factors such as recessions and wars. For instance, during a recession/depression period, economic factors impact the entire market, providing negative returns for the majority of the companies in the market. While systematic risk can impact some companies/industries more than others, it is really difficult to avoid; therefore, it is rather out of an investor's control and goes with the territory of investments.

*Unsystematic risk* is of far greater concern to an investor as it represents risk inherent to a specific industry or company. As a result, unsystematic risk is avoidable and therefore represents the risk of choosing one investment strategy over another. The airline industry is filled with unsystematic risk, with the largest risk factor being the price of oil. With jet fuel being the greatest cost to the airline industry, soaring fuel prices will have an adverse effect on the profitability of the airline industry. As a result, the price of oil represents a major unsystematic risk factor in the aviation industry. Other industry-specific unsystematic risk factors include the threat of labor action that could potentially halt an airline's operations and aviation safety that could potentially cause people to choose other airlines or modes of transport in response to an accident. The degree to which these unsystematic factors exist ultimately helps decide how much risk an investor is willing to bear. Unsystematic risk can be reduced or eliminated through diversification (Ross, Westerfield and Jordan, 2008). Investing in a portfolio with stocks from many different industries spreads out unsystematic risk among many different investments with the intent that the unsystematic risk throughout the different industries will balance each other out.

---

3     Changes in the gross domestic product (GDP), unemployment, interest rates, and inflation are examples of systematic risk. Strikes, terrorism, accidents, and takeovers are examples of unsystematic risk.

# FINANCIAL RISK PREFERENCES

"Why would Northwest let PNCL (Regional carrier, Pinnacle Airlines) profit during their demise? If PNCL was reaping profits from the avoidance of fuel price risk and customer risk, why couldn't Northwest change the agreement in a way that would be detrimental to Pinnacle and beneficial to Northwest?"

Jeff Annello Author, Seekingalpha.com

An important understanding of risk is the fact that all investors are not alike. Different investors will assume varying degrees of perceived risk, and as a consequence, will have varying degrees of optimal return. Risk tolerance is the degree of risk or uncertainty that an investor is willing to absorb. An investor's level of risk tolerance is based on a host of factors, both economic and social. For instance, retirees on fixed income generally desire a low level of risk as a result of their desire not to lose their life savings. There are generally three primary categories of risk tolerance based upon one's level of assumed risk and expected return: risk adverse, risk neutral, and risk seeking.

## Risk-averse Investors

Risk-averse investors are the typical investors who stay away from adding high-risk assets to their portfolio. While risk-averse investors will take on some level of risk, the declining returns of risk will typically stop risk averse investors from absorbing high levels of risk unless adequately compensated for it. The prime example of a risk adverse investor is one whom when faced with two investment options with similar expected return, will choose the option with the lowest amount of risk. While this investment strategy may appear to be the only correct strategy, in actuality, risk-averse investors will stick to safe investments, such as government bonds and mutual funds. As a result of their lower levels of risk tolerance, risk-averse investors typically obtain lower yield returns; however, during recessionary periods, risk-averse investors will also not lose as much, relative to other investors. As a result, risk-averse investors usually have fairly stable returns over time, which is good for investors looking to retain their money. As mentioned, retirees are a good example of risk adverse investors as they do not want their retirement income to swing violently at the whim of the economy.

## Risk-neutral Investors

Risk-neutral investor is an investor who does not consider the underlying risk when making an investment decision. To a risk-neutral investor, risk is implicit in every investment and therefore should not be the discerning factor when making a decision. Risk-neutral investors will typically focus much of their attention on expected returns as opposed to analyzing potential factors that could result in losses. Many individuals likely fall into the category of risk neutral, believing that the underlying factors of a company stock will spur positive gains, as opposed to the issues that could cripple the company.

## Risk-seeking Investor

Risk-seeking investor is an investor who will take on additional risk without the necessary increase in return. While a risk lover may be expecting high levels of returns, by definition the increased amount of risk is not justified by the higher returns. Risk lovers are investors who diverge from conventional investing wisdom, as they seek increased amounts of risk for the allure of higher returns. While very few investors are pure risk lovers, hedge firms routinely absorb a significant amount of risk in an effort to obtain higher returns on their investments.

## RISK DIVERSIFICATION

To reduce risk, the most common and successful investment strategy applied is diversification. *Diversification* is the technique of mixing a wide variety of investments in a single portfolio in order to reduce risk (Marshall, 1989). The goal of diversification is to minimize risk by smoothing out unsystematic risk while helping to maximize investment return (Ross, Westerfield and Jordan, 2008). A truly diversified portfolio is one that crosses multiple industries covering a variety of unsystematic risk factors while ensuring that no one risk factor is heavily weighted in the investment portfolio. By trying to minimize the importance of any single risk factor, investors help eliminate most unsystematic risk, providing themselves with a portfolio where systematic risk is prevalent. In essence, a fully diversified portfolio acts like the market, where any one individual investment will not significantly help or harm the investment portfolio. Mutual funds are a prime example of a diversified investment, with the strategy proving largely successful.

As was mentioned, constructing a diversified investment portfolio involves taking a host of individual investments with differing properties in order to help cancel out unsystematic risk. The key in creating a fully diversified portfolio is having individual investments that are extremely poorly correlated or highly negatively correlated. In order to highlight the process of determining a diversified portfolio, consider an investor who holds only an interest in American Airlines (AMR) common stock, but wishes to diversify his or her portfolio to minimize the risk and swings in price volatility. As an example, the investor is looking at four other sectors in which to diversify: gold with Barrick Gold Corporation (ABX),[4] oil with Exxon Mobil (XOM), technology with Google (GOOG), and aerospace/defense with Boeing (BA). Table 4.5 provides historical monthly closing prices for all five investment options as well as the monthly return, on an annualized basis.

From the historical monthly closing stock price data, a simple correlation matrix can be constructed to compare the relationships between the five stock prices. Table 4.6 displays the correlation matrix of the five stocks.

From Table 4.6, three of the stocks have a negative correlation with American Airlines stock (ABX, XOM, GOOG). A negative correlation means that when AMR's stock price increases, the other stocks will decrease in price, and vice versa. Such negative correlation may help guard against significant losses; however, the three stocks are not strongly negatively correlated to AMR. In fact Google, with a correlation coefficient of

---

4      Barrick Gold Corporation (ABX) is the largest gold exploration and development company, in terms of market capitalization and traded on the New York Stock Exchange (NYSE).

**Table 4.5**    **Monthly closing prices and returns for AMR, ABX, XOM, GOOG, and BA**

|       | AMR | ABX | XOM | GOOG | BA | AMR Return | ABX Return | XOM Return | GOOG Return | BA Return |
|-------|-----|-----|-----|------|----|-----------|-----------|-----------|------------|-----------|
| 8-Nov | $7.05 | $20.81 | $68.93 | $291.00 | $42.52 | -30.95% | -8.49% | -6.47% | -19.02% | -18.28% |
| 8-Oct | $10.21 | $22.74 | $73.70 | $359.36 | $52.03 | 3.97% | -38.11% | -4.56% | -10.28% | -8.59% |
| 8-Sep | $9.82 | $36.74 | $77.22 | $400.52 | $56.92 | -4.94% | 5.79% | -2.93% | -13.55% | -12.52% |
| 8-Aug | $10.33 | $34.73 | $79.55 | $463.29 | $65.07 | 14.40% | -17.99% | -0.01% | -2.21% | 7.95% |
| 8-Jul | $9.03 | $42.35 | $79.56 | $473.75 | $60.28 | 76.37% | -6.92% | -8.74% | -10.01% | -7.02% |
| 8-Jun | $5.12 | $45.50 | $87.18 | $526.42 | $64.83 | -28.79% | 12.93% | -0.71% | -10.14% | -20.60% |
| 8-May | $7.19 | $40.29 | $87.80 | $585.80 | $81.65 | -18.02% | 4.84% | -4.21% | 2.00% | -2.00% |
| 8-Apr | $8.77 | $38.43 | $91.66 | $574.29 | $83.32 | -2.77% | -11.12% | 10.04% | 30.38% | 14.11% |
| 8-Mar | $9.02 | $43.24 | $83.30 | $440.47 | $73.02 | -29.59% | -16.36% | -2.79% | -6.52% | -10.17% |
| 8-Feb | $12.81 | $51.70 | $85.69 | $471.18 | $81.29 | -8.11% | 1.00% | 1.96% | -16.50% | 0.02% |
| 8-Jan | $13.94 | $51.19 | $84.04 | $564.30 | $81.27 | -0.64% | 22.35% | -8.52% | -18.39% | -4.89% |
| 7-Dec | $14.03 | $41.84 | $91.87 | $691.48 | $85.45 | -33.76% | 3.80% | 5.08% | -0.22% | -5.50% |
| 7-Nov | $21.18 | $40.31 | $87.43 | $693.00 | $90.42 | -11.75% | -7.86% | -2.70% | -1.98% | -5.79% |
| 7-Oct | $24.00 | $43.75 | $89.86 | $707.00 | $95.98 | 7.67% | 9.54% | -0.61% | 24.63% | -6.10% |
| 7-Sep | $22.29 | $39.94 | $90.41 | $567.27 | $102.21 | -9.06% | 23.88% | 7.97% | 10.10% | 8.57% |
| 7-Aug | $24.51 | $32.24 | $83.74 | $515.25 | $94.14 | -0.69% | -1.16% | 1.11% | 1.03% | -6.19% |
| 7-Jul | $24.68 | $32.62 | $82.82 | $510.00 | $100.35 | -6.34% | 13.19% | 1.48% | -2.43% | 7.56% |
| 7-Jun | $26.35 | $28.82 | $81.61 | $522.70 | $93.30 | -7.05% | -0.21% | 0.85% | 4.98% | -4.41% |
| 7-May | $28.35 | $28.88 | $80.92 | $497.91 | $97.60 | 8.66% | 4.15% | 5.23% | 5.63% | 8.57% |
| 7-Apr | $26.09 | $27.73 | $76.90 | $471.38 | $89.90 | -14.32% | -1.53% | 5.21% | 2.89% | 4.60% |
| 7-Mar | $30.45 | $28.16 | $73.09 | $458.16 | $85.95 | -10.65% | -4.41% | 5.26% | 1.94% | 1.90% |
| 7-Feb | $34.08 | $29.46 | $69.44 | $449.45 | $84.35 | -8.02% | 0.82% | -2.85% | -10.38% | -2.19% |
| 7-Jan | $37.05 | $29.22 | $71.48 | $501.50 | $86.24 | 22.56% | -3.50% | -3.30% | 8.91% | 0.81% |
| 6-Dec | $30.23 | $30.28 | $73.92 | $460.48 | $85.55 | -5.41% | -2.35% | -0.23% | -5.02% | 0.35% |
| 6-Nov | $31.96 | $31.01 | $74.09 | $484.81 | $85.25 | 12.77% | 1.81% | 8.00% | 1.77% | 11.25% |
| 6-Oct | $28.34 | $30.46 | $68.60 | $476.39 | $76.63 | 22.47% | 0.89% | 6.44% | 18.53% | 1.28% |
| 6-Sep | $23.14 | $30.19 | $64.45 | $401.90 | $75.66 | 12.06% | -8.24% | -0.83% | 6.17% | 5.27% |
| 6-Aug | $20.65 | $32.90 | $64.99 | $378.53 | $71.87 | -6.14% | 8.69% | 0.36% | -2.09% | -2.88% |
| 6-Jul | $22.00 | $30.27 | $64.76 | $386.60 | $74.00 | -13.45% | 4.06% | 10.42% | -7.81% | -5.48% |
| 6-Jun | $25.42 | $29.09 | $58.65 | $419.33 | $78.29 | 3.08% | -3.29% | 0.72% | 12.78% | -1.61% |
| 6-May | $24.66 | $30.08 | $58.23 | $371.82 | $79.57 | 0.08% | 0.77% | -2.95% | -11.04% | 0.10% |
| 6-Apr | $24.64 | $29.85 | $60.00 | $417.94 | $79.49 | -8.91% | 11.92% | 3.64% | 7.16% | 7.07% |

**Table 4.5**    *Concluded*

|  | AMR | ABX | XOM | GOOG | BA | AMR Return | ABX Return | XOM Return | GOOG Return | BA Return |
|---|---|---|---|---|---|---|---|---|---|---|
| 6-Mar | $27.05 | $26.67 | $57.89 | $390.00 | $74.24 | 7.77% | -0.49% | 2.51% | 7.55% | 7.22% |
| 6-Feb | $25.10 | $26.80 | $56.47 | $362.62 | $69.24 | 10.57% | -13.02% | -4.88% | -16.19% | 6.85% |
| 6-Jan | $22.70 | $30.81 | $59.37 | $432.66 | $64.80 | 2.11% | 12.90% | 11.70% | 4.29% | -2.75% |
| 5-Dec | $22.23 | $27.29 | $53.15 | $414.86 | $66.63 |  |  |  |  |  |

**Table 4.6**    **Correlation matrix of the stock prices of AMR, ABX, XOM, GOOG, and BA**

|  | AMR | ABX | XOM | GOOG | BA |
|---|---|---|---|---|---|
| AMR | 1 |  |  |  |  |
| ABX | -0.484 | 1 |  |  |  |
| XOM | -0.410 | 0.680 | 1 |  |  |
| GOOG | -0.041 | 0.625 | 0.768 | 1 |  |
| BA | 0.551 | 0.203 | 0.405 | 0.630 | 1 |

–0.0408, has practically no relationship with AMR; this indicates that these companies probably have different unsystematic risk factors. This makes practical sense since Google operates in a completely different environment from American Airlines. Both commodity companies (ABX and XOM) are marginally negatively correlated and this also makes implicit sense. The reason for this is that as commodity prices rise (especially oil), the input costs to the airline also increase. This hurts the airline's profitability and ultimately the company's long-term earnings potential. Therefore, Exxon Mobil would be a good stock to add to an AMR investment portfolio as it tends to move in the opposite direction from the airline stock, thereby helping to minimize any potential losses. On the other hand, Boeing would not be a good choice to diversify one's portfolio as it is marginally correlated to American Airlines, indicating that both companies have similar unsystematic risk factors. This is straight forward since Boeing's success ultimately depends on the success of the airline industry; therefore, when an airline's financial performance falls and the stock price goes down, so too does Boeing's. Based on the correlation coefficients alone, a portfolio of solely American Airlines stock could be better diversified with the addition of Barrick Gold Corporation (ABX) stock (the stock with the greatest negative correlation to AMR) and Google (GOOG). Based on correlation alone, such a portfolio might help to smooth out the unsystematic risk, while also increasing expected returns.

As was mentioned previously, the degree of risk can also be measured through the standard deviation of the portfolio. Using the annualized return data contained in Table 4.5, the average monthly return of American Airlines (AMR) stock for the three year period was –1.57%. The average annual return of American Airlines (AMR) stock for the three year period was –17.30%. Using the assumption that the historical three year average

**Table 4.7       Standard deviation of AMR returns**

| AMR Return | Variance |
|:---:|:---:|
| -30.95% | 0.0863 |
| 3.97% | 0.0031 |
| -4.94% | 0.0011 |
| 14.40% | 0.0255 |
| 76.37% | 0.6074 |
| -28.79% | 0.0741 |
| -18.02% | 0.0271 |
| -2.77% | 0.0001 |
| -29.59% | 0.0785 |
| -8.11% | 0.0043 |
| -0.64% | 0.0001 |
| -33.76% | 0.1036 |
| -11.75% | 0.0104 |
| 7.67% | 0.0085 |
| -9.06% | 0.0056 |
| -0.69% | 0.0001 |
| -6.34% | 0.0023 |
| -7.05% | 0.0030 |
| 8.66% | 0.0105 |
| -14.32% | 0.0163 |
| -10.65% | 0.0083 |
| -8.02% | 0.0042 |
| 22.56% | 0.0582 |
| -5.41% | 0.0015 |
| 12.77% | 0.0206 |
| 22.47% | 0.0578 |
| 12.06% | 0.0186 |
| -6.14% | 0.0021 |
| -13.45% | 0.0141 |
| 3.08% | 0.0022 |

**Table 4.7**     *Concluded*

|  | AMR Return | Variance |
|---|---|---|
|  | 0.08% | 0.0003 |
|  | -8.91% | 0.0054 |
|  | 7.77% | 0.0087 |
|  | 10.57% | 0.0147 |
|  | 2.11% | 0.0014 |
| Avg. Return | -1.57% |  |
| Variance |  | 1.2857 |
| Std. Dev. |  | 1.1339 |

return can be used as a proxy for the future expected return of an investment in AMR, the standard deviation of the return is 113.39%.[5]

$$\sigma^2{}_{AMR} = 0.00892$$

$$\sigma_{AMR} = 0.0944501 = 9.45\%$$

While the standard deviation of American Airlines equity return may appear minimal, diversifying the portfolio can further reduce risk. Based on the correlation coefficients contained in Table 4.6, an investor wishes to diversify his or her portfolio by adding an equal share of Exxon Mobil (XOM) to the portfolio. From the data in Table 4.5, the average annualized return of an XOM investment yielded a 0.07% return. With an equal 50/50 share of the investor's portfolio, the expected return on the portfolio is

$$\hat{k}_p = \sum_{i=1}^{n} w_i \times \hat{k}_i$$

$$\hat{k}_p = w_{AMR} \times \hat{k}_{AMR} + w_{XOM} \times \hat{k}_{XOM}$$

$$\hat{k}_p = 0.50 \times (-0.13) + 0.50 \times (0.07) = -0.03\%$$

where:
$w_{AMR}$  = the percentage of the portfolio held in AMR
$k_{AMR}$  = the expected return on AMR
$w_{XOM}$  = the percentage held in XOM
$k_{XOM}$  = the expected return on XOM

---

5      Note that both variance and standard deviation of a dataset can be calculated in Microsoft Excel using the Variance and standard Deviation functions.

In this example, diversifying one's portfolio to include Exxon Mobil (XOM), increased (lower negative return) the expected return of the portfolio over a portfolio of only AMR. The reason for this is the obvious fact that the expected return on XOM was greater than AMR. However, if the expected return on XOM was worse than AMR, then the portfolio would have experienced a decline in expected return. In general, however, and over the longer term, diversification will yield a higher return than concentration in one or a small number of stocks. Additionally, it is important to note that adjustments in the percentage held of each stock in the portfolio can also result in significant changes to the expected return.

In order to illustrate the risk minimization properties of diversification, both the variance and standard deviation of the new portfolio can be calculated using the following formula.

$$\sigma_p^2 = W_{AMR} \times \sigma_{AMR}^2 + 2 \times W_{AMR} \times W_{XOM} \times COV_{AMR,XOM} + W_{XOM} \times \sigma_{XOM}^2$$

where:
$\sigma_{AMR}^2$ = the variance of AMR's return
$COV_{AMR,XOM}$ = the covariance between AMR's and XOM's annualized returns
$\sigma_{XOM}^2$ = the variance of XOM's return

Using the covariance function in Microsoft Excel and the data contained in Table 4.5, the covariance of the annualized returns between AMR and XOM was found to be –0.000012.[6] Additionally, the variance and standard deviation of XOM's annualized returns were found to be 0.00065 and 2.55%, respectively. Based on this information, the variance and standard deviation of the newly constructed portfolio is:

Variance of Portfolio = $0.5(0.00892)^2 + 2(0.5) \times (0.5)(-0.000012) + 0.5(0.00065)^2$

**Table 4.8      Standard deviation of AMR/XOM portfolio**

| | |
|---|---|
| Variance | 1.000034 |
| Standard Deviation | 1.000017% |

Based on the standard deviation of the portfolio, the inclusion of XOM into the portfolio helped reduce the amount of risk from 9.45% to 0.58%. This indicates that the actual return for a portfolio holding equal proportions of AMR and XOM will not vary greatly from the expected return. However, adjustments to the composition of the portfolio can dramatically affect both the risk and the expected return on the portfolio. Furthermore, the inclusion of additional securities to the portfolio will help mitigate risk, as the portfolio variance of the unsystematic risk will be further minimized. Figure 4.2 provides a visualization of the diminishing risk as greater numbers of securities are added to the portfolio. It is important to note that unsystematic risk will never equal zero, since the portfolio variance becomes asymptotic to the covariance of the portfolio (all pairs of covariances held within

---

6      Note that the covariance of the annualized returns between AMR and XOM is different than the correlation coefficient of the stock prices between AMR and XOM.

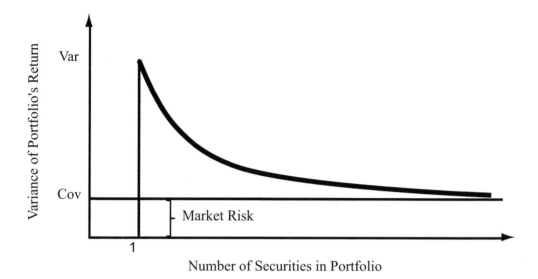

**Figure 4.2    Relationship between the variance of a portfolio and the number of securities in the portfolio**

the portfolio). Additionally, there will always be some component of systematic or market risk in the portfolio, as with any individual security.

## BETA

Another measure of risk is beta, which describes the relationship between the individual security's expected return to that of the market's return. Beta is also referred to as financial elasticity, and it helps measure a security's sensitivity to that of the market, thereby implicitly comparing the degree of risk in the security, compared with the market. Beta is calculated by measuring the correlation between the historical returns of the company's stock versus the historical return of the market. By mathematical definition, the beta value of a company's stock is calculated by:

$$\beta_i = \frac{Cov(K_i, K_M)}{\sigma^2(K_M)}$$

where:
$Cov(K_i, K_M)$ = the covariance of return on the asset and the return on the market
$\sigma^2(K_M)$    = the variance of the market's return.

Covariance can also be calculated between two securities as we did in the example with AMR and XOM. The covariance between AMR and XOM is displayed in Table 4.9.

Exxon and American Airlines display an extremely low covariance, which makes sense intuitively, since both are in industries which have an inverse relationship. That is, as oil companies do well, airlines typically do poorly. The covariance being near zero tells us

**Table 4.9    Covariance between AMR and XOM returns**

| AMR Return | Variance | XOM Return | Variance |
|---|---|---|---|
| -0.310 | 0.086 | -0.065 | 0.005 |
| 0.040 | 0.003 | -0.046 | 0.003 |
| -0.049 | 0.001 | -0.029 | 0.001 |
| 0.144 | 0.025 | -0.000 | 0.000 |
| 0.764 | 0.607 | -0.087 | 0.009 |
| -0.288 | 0.074 | -0.007 | 0.000 |
| -0.180 | 0.027 | -0.042 | 0.003 |
| -0.028 | 0.000 | 0.100 | 0.008 |
| -0.296 | 0.079 | -0.028 | 0.001 |
| -0.081 | 0.004 | 0.020 | 0.000 |
| -0.006 | 0.000 | -0.085 | 0.009 |
| -0.338 | 0.104 | 0.051 | 0.002 |
| -0.118 | 0.010 | -0.027 | 0.001 |
| 0.077 | 0.009 | -0.006 | 0.000 |
| -0.091 | 0.006 | 0.080 | 0.005 |
| -0.007 | 0.000 | 0.011 | 0.000 |
| -0.063 | 0.002 | 0.015 | 0.000 |
| -0.071 | 0.003 | 0.009 | 0.000 |
| 0.087 | 0.010 | 0.052 | 0.002 |
| -0.143 | 0.016 | 0.052 | 0.002 |
| -0.107 | 0.008 | 0.053 | 0.002 |
| -0.080 | 0.004 | -0.029 | 0.001 |
| 0.226 | 0.058 | -0.033 | 0.002 |
| -0.054 | 0.001 | -0.002 | 0.000 |
| 0.128 | 0.021 | 0.080 | 0.005 |
| 0.225 | 0.058 | 0.064 | 0.003 |
| 0.121 | 0.019 | -0.008 | 0.000 |
| -0.061 | 0.002 | 0.004 | 0.000 |
| -0.135 | 0.014 | 0.104 | 0.009 |
| 0.031 | 0.002 | 0.007 | 0.000 |

**Table 4.9**    *Concluded*

|              |          |          |          |          |
|--------------|----------|----------|----------|----------|
|              | 0.001    | 0.000    | -0.030   | 0.001    |
|              | -0.089   | 0.005    | 0.036    | 0.001    |
|              | 0.078    | 0.009    | 0.025    | 0.000    |
|              | 0.106    | 0.015    | -0.049   | 0.003    |
|              | 0.021    | 0.001    | 0.117    | 0.012    |
| Avg. Return  | -0.016   |          | 0.009    |          |
| Variance     |          | 1.286    |          | 0.093    |
| Std. Dev.    |          | 1.134    |          | 0.305    |
|              |          |          | Covariance | -0.002 |

that the return on each stock does not typically move in the same direction and they are not highly correlated.

The beta calculation is essentially a regression of the historical returns of the company versus the total market, which is a fairly complex undertaking. Thankfully most financial sources, such as Yahoo! Finance, provide a computed beta value for all publicly listed companies. While methodologies may vary slightly from source to source, the majority compute the covariance against the S&P 500. For instance, Yahoo! Finance computes the beta value of a company against the monthly price changes of the S&P 500 over a 36-month period (Yahoo! Finance, 2008). Other suitable barometers of the markets can be used so it is important to note that not all beta values are calculated from the same market.

For most companies, beta values typically range from zero to two; however, there is no absolute range of values for beta so other values are possible. A beta value of one indicates that there is a perfect correlation between the market and the individual security. This means that the historical returns of the company match perfectly with those of the market. It is sometimes assumed that the market has a beta value of one, and that any deviation on either side of this value shows the amount of risk that the security has. Typical companies with beta values close to the market are conglomerates such as Siemens (SI) and General Electric (GE) whose diversified business ventures enable their returns to approximate the market.

A security with a beta value greater than one indicates a security that varies greater than the market, and this can be interpreted as a greater amount of risk. As an example, and by definition, a company with a beta value of 1.5 will see a 1.5% movement in its stock price for every 1% movement in the market. This means that the company's returns vary 50% more than the market. In terms of elasticity, a beta value greater than one is more elastic, since the stock's returns will fluctuate more significantly than the market. A good example of high beta-value stocks are technology companies, whose earnings and returns tend to fluctuate over product life cycles and the macro-economic environment.

A beta coefficient less than one indicates that the firm's returns vary less than the market. This can be interpreted as a situation where these firms are thought to be more stable and hence less risky. For example, if historical data holds true, a company with a beta value of 0.50 will only provide a 0.50% return when the market achieves a 1% return; however, when the market loses 1%, the company will only lose 0.50%. Thus, the returns of low beta stocks are thought to be much more stable. Low beta stocks are typically utility companies where revenue and costs are relatively fixed and stable over time.

Negative beta values are also possible, representing companies that are negatively correlated to the market. Companies with negative beta coefficients provide negative returns when the market is experiencing positive gains, and vice versa. An investor might view negative beta stocks as a hedge or insurance policy providing a good addition to a well diversified portfolio. However, while negative beta coefficients are sometimes achieved in the short-term, long-run empirical evidence seems to indicate that virtually no stocks have negative beta values (Ross, Westerfield, and Jaffe, 2008).

## CAPITAL ASSET PRICING MODEL (CAPM)

Using the determinants of risk, beta, and various market forecasts, the expected rate of return of an individual security can be calculated by using the capital asset pricing model (CAPM). The basic underlying assumption of CAPM is that the expected return of a security is linearly related to its beta. Since beta values are readily calculated and supplied, the capital asset pricing model is obviously a valuable tool for investors. The reason for this is the fact that the CAPM provides investors with a baseline valuation tool to project expected returns for individual firms. Quantitatively, the capital asset pricing model is as follows:

$$k_i = k_{RF} + \beta_i \times (k_M - k_{RF})$$

where:
$k_{RF}$ = the risk-free rate of return
$\beta$ = the beta of the security
$k_M$ = the expected return on the market.

Interestingly, $(k_M - k_F)$ is also called the market risk premium, since it is the difference between the expected return on the market and the risk-free rate.

Since the risk-free rate of return is usually a known value, because it is commonly calculated based upon short-term U.S. treasury bills, the expected market return is largely based on the investor's projection of the future. In order to understand the capital asset pricing model, and the impact of beta, consider a market with an expected return of 10% and a risk-free rate of return of 2%. As pointed out above, for a company A with a beta equal to 1, the expected return to the company will equal the market return.

$$k_A = 2\% + 1.0(10\% - 2\%) = 2\% + 1.0(8\%) = 10\%$$

However, consider company B that has a beta value of 0.50. In this case the expected return on the security will fall to 6%. This is the result of the return on the risk premium being cut in half by the beta value of 0.5.

$$k_B = 2\% + 0.5(10\% - 2\%) = 2\% + 0.5(8\%) = 6\%$$

Conversely, if a company has a beta value of 1.5, then the expected return on the security will exceed the market with an expected return of 14%. This situation is favorable to individual investors, so that in a bull market investors might do well to focus their attention on stocks with high beta values.

$$k_C = 2\% + 1.5(10\% - 2\%) = 2\% + 1.5(8\%) = 14\%$$

However, as was mentioned, high beta stocks also contain greater risk. For example, consider the same scenario except that the market is projected to decrease by 6%. A company with a beta value of 0.50 will have an expected return of –2%, which outperforms the industry.

$$k_B = 2\% + 0.5(-6\% - 2\%) = 2\% + 0.5(-8\%) = -2\%$$

Under the same scenario, a company with a beta of 1.5 would have an expected return far worse than the industry at –10%.

$$k_C = 2\% + 1.5(-6\% - 2\%) = 2\% + 1.5(-8\%) = -10\%$$

Therefore, and as pointed out earlier, individual investment decisions will ultimately depend on an individual's outlook on the market and tolerance of risk.

To further understand the impact of beta using the capital asset pricing model, consider company D whose beta value is –1.25. A negative beta value indicates the company's return moves in the opposite direction of the market; therefore, using the expected market return of –6%, company D's expected return will actually be positive at 12%. While such companies are rare, they could represent good investment options during bear markets.

$$k_D = 2\% - 1.25(-6\% - 2\%) = 2\% - 1.25(-8\%) = 12\%$$

The relationship between the expected return of a security and the beta value of the security can be depicted graphically through the security market line (SML). The security market line, shown in Figure 4.3 shows the linear relationship between expected return and beta. The intercept of the line is the risk-free rate and the slope of the line is the risk premium, or the difference between expected market return and the risk-free rate. Based on long-term empirical evidence, the security market line generally has upward-slope. This is the result of the expected return in the market being greater than the risk-free rate of return (Ross, Westerfield, and Jaffe, 2008). However, during recessionary periods, the security market line could be downward-sloping. In this case the risk-free rate exceeds the market return. Based on the long-term SML shown in Figure 4.3, when the beta value of the security is equal to zero, the expected return on the security is the risk-free rate of return. As mentioned before, when the beta value is exactly one, the expected return of the security is equal to the expected return of the market.

## RISK IN THE AVIATION INDUSTRY

While it is important to understand the fundamentals of the risk/return dichotomy, it is particularly important for students of the aviation industry to understand how the

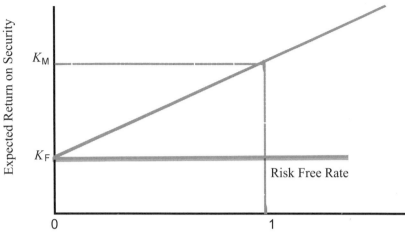

**Figure 4.3 General long-term security market line (SML)**

industry is viewed externally. In capital markets the amount of risk that a company has plays a big role in the company's ability to obtain capital at a reasonable cost.

Based on information contained in Figure 4.4, U.S. airlines have risk characteristics that span the spectrum. The majority of carriers have beta values between zero and one, while a few carriers have beta values greater than one, signaling an investment riskier than the market. Finally, both Republic Airways (RW) and Alaska Airlines (AS) actually have a negative beta coefficient indicating that the company acts opposite to the market.[7]

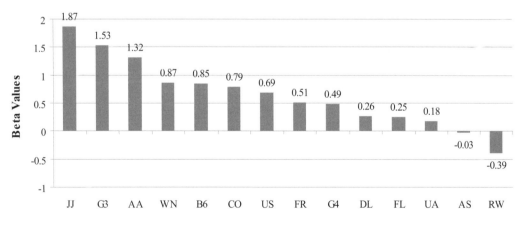

*Note:* Northwest and Delta have combined since Sept. 2008.

*Source:* Data compiled by Authors using publicly available financial data.

**Figure 4.4 Beta coefficients for U.S. airlines**

---

7    It should also be noted that Delta beta values reflects Northwest and Delta combined.

Furthermore, no generalization about airline industry risk can be stated as individual carriers exhibit varying levels of beta values. However, the two carriers with the highest beta values, TAM (JJ) and GOL (G3), are both from Brazil. Clearly, during this time period, some carriers in Brazil exhibited greater risk tendencies than the market and the industry. However, by and large, most of the carriers had variation in earnings that were on average less than the industry, indicating stability during this time period. Ultimately, the beta value of a company is at a point in time that looks historically on trading levels. During the time frame in question from Figure 4.4, airlines probably outperformed the market as the recession caused significant downwards pressure on equities. It would be interesting to take a similar snapshot of the industry beta values at a different point in time, as the story could be different. Timing, particularly with respect to mergers, could be one of the potential reasons for Republic Airways' negative beta value.

The fluctuation in the earnings of the airlines is another indication of the risk in the industry. Airlines have historically displayed significant variation in earnings not only over the long term, but also in the short term. The airline industry exhibits extreme cyclicality, much in the way the market does; however, this problem has been exaggerated as a result of airlines' significant fixed costs and the long development time in strategic planning (due mainly to aircraft construction). After deregulation in the United States in 1972, the airline industry experienced significant losses during the first half of every decade, closely followed by significant profitability in the latter half of every decade (Vasigh, Fleming, and Tacker, 2009). This volatile earnings cycle creates heightened risk since earnings might fluctuate severely in a downward direction and this may cause many bankruptcies.[8]

In the short term, the airline industry also exhibits seasonality where earnings vary from quarter to quarter. Historically, the third quarter (northern hemisphere summer) has proved to be the most profitable quarter while the first quarter (northern hemisphere winter) typically provides the year's worst earnings. Such seasonality is a result of air travel demand; however, the market as a whole does not exhibit the same degree of seasonality, causing a greater variance in earnings, and thus increased risk. With fuel hedging representing an increasing activity by all airlines, earnings have become even more volatile as airlines report realized/unrealized gains and losses. For airlines not practicing fuel hedge accounting, any fluctuation in the price of commodities will cause a significant change in the mark-to-market account, which ultimately needs to be recorded in the company's consolidated income statement.[9] To summarize, fuel hedging has created further variances in airline earnings, thus causing greater distortions in investor returns, while providing increased risk to investors. An example of the volatility between quarters for airline earnings in shown in Table 4.10.

As can be seen from the table, Southwest Airlines and Continental Airlines quarterly earnings followed the normal pattern in 2007 with higher earnings in Q2/Q3 than in Q1/Q4. However, the highest earning quarter varied between the two carriers. For Southwest Airlines in 2007 Q2 was the best quarter, while for Continental Airlines Q3 was the best. This difference is the result of travel demand and an airline's route network. For airlines with an expansive international network, such as Continental Airlines, Q3 typically outperforms Q2 as a result of greater international travel demand during the summer. For domestic U.S. carriers, such as Southwest, the reverse is usually the case with Q2 outperforming Q3.

---

8    See Table 4.11.
9    For further information on hedge accounting and mark-to-market changes, please refer to Chapter 11.

**Table 4.10      Earnings for selected airlines by quarter ($ millions)**

| Southwest Airlines | | | | |
|---|---|---|---|---|
| Year | Q1 | Q2 | Q3 | Q4 |
| 2007 | 93 | 278 | 162 | 111 |
| 2008 | 34 | 321 | -120 | -56 |
| 2009 | -91 | | | |
| **Continental Airlines** | | | | |
| Year | Q1 | Q2 | Q3 | Q4 |
| 2007 | 22 | 228 | 241 | 71 |
| 2008 | -80 | -3 | -236 | -266 |
| 2009 | -136 | | | |

*Sources*: Southwest and Continental Airlines Annual Filings 2007–2009.

The typical earnings trend did not hold true in 2008 as a result of rising fuel prices; that is, those airlines which hedged fuel when prices began to rise experienced losses on those hedges in the third and fourth quarter of 2008 when oil prices retreated back down. We can see the impact of fuel prices and fuel hedges with the quarterly earnings of Southwest and Continental; that is, earnings in the third and fourth quarter of 2008 were worse for both airlines than in the first and second quarters of that year. Therefore, while the common earnings trend may exist, certain management actions or external macro-economic events may ultimately cause the earnings trend to be distorted. Investors need to interpret such information when evaluating the quarterly performance of an individual carrier.

Finally, another barometer of industry risk is the number of firms that enter bankruptcy protection. The airline industry has a long history of airlines either going bankrupt or ceasing operations. Delta, Northwest, United, U.S. Airways, and Frontier have all entered bankruptcy protection in the last several years. Table 4.11 shows airline bankruptcies in the U.S since the terrorist attacks of September 11, 2001.

Bankruptcy ultimately causes shareholder wealth to be lost, representing a significant risk to investors; however, it is important to note that a majority of these aforementioned carriers have re-emerged. While airlines are deemed risky to equity investors, airlines do not appear to be as risky to debt holders, due to the significant fixed assets (i.e. aircraft, engines, slots, spare parts) that can be collateralized. However, in a twist of irony, the significant fixed assets of airlines ultimately cause them to experience significant swings in profitability, and this can  represent increased risk to equity investors. Therefore, depending on one's viewpoint, the aviation industry can be viewed as either a risky investment or a more stable investment; however, as this chapter has shown, an investor's rate of return in the airline industry will also vary significantly.

- Northwest Merged with Delta in September of 2008.
- Era Aviation, founded 1948 and in 2009 the company was acquired by rival Frontier Alaska Group. It forms the largest carrier in Alaska, serving more cities and carrying more passengers inter-state than any other Alaskan airline.

**Table 4.11     Recent airline bankruptcies in the U.S.**

| Date | Airline | Bankruptcy Chapter | Date | Airline | Bankruptcy Chapter |
|------|---------|--------------------|------|---------|--------------------|
| 02/01/2002 | Sun Country Airlines | 7 | 28/12/2005 | Era Aviation | 11 |
| 30/07/2002 | Vanguard Airlines | 11 | 01-1/6/06 | Independence Air | 7 |
| 11/08/2002 | U.S. Airways | 11 | 21/02/2006 | Florida Coastal Airlines | 11 |
| 09/12/2002 | United Airlines | 11 | 15/10/2007 | Kitty Hawk Aircargo | 11 |
| 21/03/2003 | Hawaiian Airlines | 11 | 24/12/2007 | MAXjet Airways | 11 |
| 30/10/2003 | Midway Airlines | 7 | 07/01/2008 | Big Sky | 7 |
| 23/01/2004 | Great Plains Airlines | 11 | 31/03/2008 | Champion Air | 11 |
| 30/01/2004 | Atlas Air/Polar Air Cargo | 11 | 31/03/2008 | Aloha Airlines | 7 |
| 12/09/2004 | U.S. Airways | 11 | 02/04/2008 | ATA Airlines | 11 |
| 26/10/2004 | ATA Airlines | 11 | 07/04/2008 | Skybus Airlines | 11 |
| 01/12/2004 | Southeast Airlines | 7 | 11/04/2008 | Frontier Airlines | 11 |
| 30/12/2004 | Aloha Airlines | 11 | 26/04/2008 | Eos Airlines | 11 |
| 14/09/2005 | Delta Air Lines | 11 | 14/05/2008 | Air Midwest | 7 |
| 14/09/2005 | Comair | 11 | 18/06/2008 | Gemini Air Cargo | 11 |
| 14/09/2005 | Northwest Airlines | 11 | 18/07/2008 | Vintage Props | 11 |
| 29/09/2005 | TransMeridian Airlines | 7 | 12/08/2008 | Gemini Air Cargo | 7 |
| 13/10/2005 | Mesaba Airlines | 11 | 06/10/2008 | Sun Country | 11 |
| 07/11/2005 | Independence Air | 11 | 15/10/2008 | Primaris Airlines | 11 |

*Source*: Air Transport Association

- MAXjet was all business-class and operated services to London Stansted Airport, from Las Vegas, Los Angeles, and New York. On 24 December 2007, the airline ceased operations.
- Originally MGM Grand Air; started in 1987and ceased all operations on May 31, 2008.
- ATA Airlines started operations on July 24, 1946 and ceased on March 31, 2008.
- As of 2009, Southwest Airlines has purchased the operating certificate and all assets held by ATA Airlines while the airline was in bankruptcy protection.
- In July 2009, acquisition procedure for Frontier Airlines underway by Republic Airways Holding Inc., together with Midwest Airlines. However, on July 30, 2009, Southwest Airlines announced that it would be making a bid for Frontier during a bankruptcy auction. The bid by SWA was not accepted.
- Vintage Props; started 1991; operations ceased July 2008.

## SUMMARY

Investors weigh both the riskiness of an investment and its expected return when deciding which securities to invest in. Assuming all other items (including expected return) are equal, the rational investor will choose an investment with less risk over one with more risk. There are two types of risk involved in investments: systematic risk and unsystematic risk. Unsystematic risk is the risk involved in investing in a particular industry and company, and this can be reduced through a well-diversified portfolio. Systematic risk refers to the general risk of financial markets and cannot be removed through diversification. The beta of a company's stock refers to how the stock moves in comparison to the overall stock market. Stocks which have a positive beta move up and down as the market does. On the other hand, stocks with a negative beta move opposite the market. If the absolute value of the beta is less than 1, the stock is not as volatile as the market; an absolute value greater than 1 indicates the stock is more volatile than the market. A company's beta can then be used to determine the expected or required rate of return from an investment in that company by using the capital asset pricing model (CAPM).

The airline industry is perhaps one of the more risky industries to invest in owing to the cyclicality and volatility of airline profits. Fluctuating fuel prices and demand often lead to losses in the airline industry and even bankruptcy. Owing to the riskiness of the industry, it is often difficult for airlines to raise capital. That is, the riskiness of the industry generally means that potential investors will require a greater rate of return on their investment.

## DISCUSSION QUESTIONS

1.  Suppose an investor purchased 150 shares of EZjET for $6.00 per share and then one year later sold all the stock at a price of $8.50 per share. During the year the airline declared an annual dividend of $0.10 per share. What was the total dollar return and the rate of return on investment?

2.  Consider the following small portfolio of an investor specializing in airline equities:

| Ticker symbol | Number of shares | Stock price | Expected return |
|---------------|------------------|-------------|-----------------|
| CAL           | 8,000            | $13.00      | (3%)            |
| LUV           | 13,000           | $8.60       | 5%              |
| GOL           | 7,000            | $9.50       | 2%              |
| CEA           | 2,000            | $30.00      | 9%              |

    a.   What is the expected return on the portfolio?
    b.   What is the variance of the portfolio?
    c.   What is the standard deviation of the portfolio?

3.  What is the difference between systematic risk and unsystematic risk? A global economic recession would be classified as what risk factor?

4.  Describe the three types of financial risk preferences.

5.  What is risk diversification? Using mathematical proof, propose one or more stocks that would diversify a portfolio of solely LCC stock. What is the standard deviation of the individual equities? What is the standard deviation of the portfolio assuming equal ownership levels?

6.  By using Yahoo! Finance, Google Finance or the company website obtain the historical quarterly returns for Southwest Airlines (LUV) and Continental Airlines (CAL) for the last three years and calculate the covariance of the stock equities. What is the most recent beta value for LUV and CAL? Based on its beta value, how do these stocks perform with regard to the market?

7.  Using online financial tools, find the latest rate for a 6-month U.S. treasury bill.
    a.   Assuming the 6-month U.S. Treasury bill is the risk free rate, what is the expected market return of UAUA assuming the market is expected to increase 12%?
    b.   What is the expected market return of UAUA assuming the market is expected to decrease 5%?

8.  Discuss some of the reasons for the airline industry's high volatility in earnings and its prevalence of bankruptcies.

9.  Explain the difference between dividend returns and capital gain returns. Which type of investor will be more likely to pick stocks that had one or the other as its prominent return and why?

10. What would be the expected return on a portfolio that contained three airline stocks that had expected returns up 8% with a 30% probability, 6% with a 45% probability and 9% with a 25% probability?

11. Explain why the variance of the return on a stock is sometimes equated with risk.

12. List some of the quantitative ways that diversification can be achieved.

13. Define what a Beta is either in words or by a formula. What does it mean if Beta is greater than one, or less than one?

14. What is the basic underlying assumption of the Capital Asset Pricing Model?
15. Assess the amount of risk in the aircraft industry. In your answer discuss the difference between fixed assets and stock prices of airline companies.
16. Go to Yahoo! Finance at finance.yahoo.com, and click on "Stock Research" then "historical quotes." Get daily prices, LAN Chile, for July 31, 2009 through July 31, 2010. At the bottom of the page you will have an option to save that data in a spreadsheet file.
    a.  Collect returns data over the past 1 year for the LAN Chile. Also collect data about the return on the stock index on the airline industry.
    b.  Find the LAN's beta from any published sources. Is your computed beta the same? If not, why do you think it's different?

## REFERENCES

Brase, C. (2008). *Understandable Statistics* (9th ed). Cengage Learning.

Burton, J. (1998, May/June). Revisiting the capital asset pricing model. Dow Jones Asset Manager, 20–28. Retrieved March 24, 2009 from http://www.stanford.edu/~wfsharpe/art/djam/djam.htm

Marshall, J. (1989). *Futures and Option Contracting: Theory and Practice*. South-Western Publishing Company.

Michaels, J. (2008, June 12). More capacity cuts at U.S. Airways. Retrieved April 8, 2009 from http://www.aviationweek.com/aw/generic/story_channel.jsp?channel=commandid=news/USCUT06128.xmlandheadline=More%20Capacity%20Cuts%20At%20US%20Airways

Ross, S., R. Westerfield, and J. Jaffe (2008). *Corporate Finance* (8th ed.). McGraw-Hill.

Ross, A., R. Westerfield, and B. Jordan, (2008). *Fundaments of Corporate Finance* (8). McGraw-Hill Irwin, New York.

Vasigh, B., Fleming and Tacker (2008). *Introduction to Air Transport Economics: Theory to Applications*. Ashgate Publishing Co., Burlington, Vermont.

# PART II

# Airline Accounting and Finance

# 5

# The Role of Accounting in Airlines

"Sarbanes-Oxley in particular has imposed a tremendous burden on corporate America and certainly on Southwest Airlines."

Gary Kelly, CEO Southwest Airlines

While similar to finance, the role of accounting is somewhat different in the airline industry. This role will be explained by examining the impact that accounting has not only in the airline internally, but also on the external industry environment. The American Accounting Association defines accounting as "the process of identifying, measuring and communicating economic information to permit informed judgments and decisions by users of information".

With this in mind, the chapter will cover those accounting principles that permit aircraft manufacturers, airports, and creditors to know whether the airline to which they grant credit is having trouble paying its bills or even at risk of bankruptcy.

The chapter will also discuss the role of accounting in international airlines and not only the financial risks that international airlines are exposed to, but also the different techniques to lower these risks. The outline for this chapter is as follows:

- Role of Accounting in Business
- Financial Accounting
- Managerial Accounting
- Differences in Airline Accounting
- International Trade and IATA Clearing House
- Issues Pertaining to the Airline Industry
  - Frequent-flyer Programs
- Accounting treatment of frequent-flyer miles
- Incremental cost method
- Deferred revenue method
- Frequent-flyer miles sold to third parties
- Interline Frequent-flyer miles
- Accounting changes related to frequent-flyer programs
- Disclosures
- Revenue Recognition
- U.S. Airlines vs. European Airlines

- International Operations
  - Currency Risk
- Airline Consolidation
- Summary
- Discussion Questions.

## ROLE OF ACCOUNTING IN AIRLINES

As with all industries, accounting plays a critical role in the airline industry. Accounting permits both managers and non-managers to make informed decisions that not only affect individual investors, but entire companies and industries. Some of the roles of accounting are:

- giving managers a snap shot of the financial position of the airline at a certain point in time;
- evaluating the performance of an airline over similar time periods;
- allowing managers to evaluate important strategic decisions, such as whether to cut a product from the company's offerings or make lease vs. buy decisions;
- allowing investors to compare accurately two different companies and determine which one will "best fit" his or her investment strategy.

Accounting provides the quantitative data that allows one to accomplish all of these goals. In accounting, there are two major fields that will be outlined: financial accounting and managerial accounting. Accounting for airlines has the same basic principles as accounting for other industries; however, airlines tend to require more information both for internal and external users. Moreover, the airline industry in the United States is required by law to disclose a considerable amount of extra information, especially when compared with other industries. Therefore, it makes good business sense for airlines to use this information, thereby adding value to these data. This collection of publicly available information also has significant value to both investors and managers alike. For example, using these data, airlines can determine the cost of one seat on a particular aircraft, during any particular flight. This allows an airline to accurately measure how changes to the cost structure affect their product (seats in this case). Additionally, airlines can easily benchmark themselves against their competitors owing to the full dissemination of information. Most of the data that airlines disclose are available on various government websites, including www.bts.gov. However, in its raw form these data do not have too much value, as the data can be difficult to utilize and require extensive data scrubbing. Several companies have realized the need for up-to-date accurate data that have more value and they have processed the data so that managers and investors are able to use it more easily.

There are usually two different heads of accounting within a company: the controller and the treasurer. The controller is responsible for instituting control mechanisms over a company's finances, as well as financial reporting and audits of the company's accounting systems and any internal audits of a company's books (Siegel and Shim, 2005). The treasurer, on the other hand, is responsible for the receipt and disbursement of a company's funds (Downes and Goodman, 2006). The treasurer has control over payments which the company makes and is responsible in some companies for the actual custody of cash or other financial instruments (such as a checkbook). In addition, the treasurer is also responsible for maintaining a market for the company's securities, including common stock and bonds (Downes and Goodman, 2006).

**Table 5.1    Responsibilities of controller and treasurer**

| Controller | Treasurer |
|---|---|
| Chief accounting executive | Financial planning |
| Planning and control | Management of working capital |
| Financial reporting | Assigning credit policy |
| Taxes | Managing investements |
| Development/audit of accounting systems | Receipt, custody and disbursement of funds |
| Internal audits | Developing market for company's securities |

*Source*: Siegel and Shim, 2005 & Downes and Goodman, 2006.

## FINANCIAL ACCOUNTING

Generally there are also two different branches of accounting: financial accounting and managerial accounting. Financial accounting "is the subdivision of accounting concerned with the preparation of financial statements for outsider use" (Porter and Sawyer, 2006). According to this definition, financial accounting is concerned with preparing financial statements for individuals who are not involved with the day-to-day operations of the company. Since these statements are for, in effect, non-managers, they must be prepared and presented in a format that can be easily understood by individuals with a basic understanding of the accounting system. In the United States, the financial statements of companies must adhere to the United States Generally Accepted Accounting Principles (U.S. GAAP).[1] These standards allow those with a basic knowledge of the accounting system to accurately compare the financial standings of various companies across various industries. These standards ensure that the items being recorded and stated are comparable. This means that companies are required to report items according to certain criteria, so that current assets in one company can be compared to current assets in a different company. The subheadings of these reports, such as the balance sheet, income statement, and cash flow statements are discussed in further detail in the following chapters.

Financial accounting also involves auditing a company's books to ensure their accuracy. An audit is an unbiased look at the statements and numbers in a company's financial statements to ensure that they are truthful and accurate (Libby, Phillips, Whitecotton, 2009). Audits may be performed internally by employees of the company or externally by an independent party, such as an accounting firm. An internal audit is usually led by the controller of the organization (Siegel and Shim, 2005). As a result of the Sarbanes-Oxley Act, internal audits have become a more important part of the accounting process tying

---

1    Generally Accepted Accounting Principles is determined by the Governmental Accounting Standards Board, which operates under a series of principles and restrictions.

up valuable time and effort on the part of the controller and those employees who report to the controller. An external audit is performed by an outside independent auditor. The external auditor is a CPA (Certified Public Accountant) who is qualified to form an auditor's report (Libby, Phillips, Whitecotton, 2009). The independent auditor renders his opinion on the validity of the financial statements; however, the independent auditor report is not a certification of the financial statements or the accounting records of the company (Credit Research Foundation, 1999). Audits of financial statements, whether internal or external, are extremely important to a company. Investors such as banks and private equity companies must be able to trust what is reported in the financial statements of a company so that they can make decisions on whether or not to provide capital. Without accurate financial statements, investors will not have the information necessary to make an informed financial decision about the company.

## MANAGERIAL ACCOUNTING

Porter (2006) defines managerial accounting as "the branch of accounting concerned with providing management with information to facilitate planning and control." Managerial accounting is concerned with preparing statements for use by the "insiders" of a company, which basically means the preparation of statements for the use of managers. Therefore, these statements can be tailor-made for the individual needs of managers to reflect any benchmarks that the company chooses to measure and track. As can be imagined from the above definition, there is a considerable amount of freedom in the design and layout of these statements, since different company's management will track and chart different objectives. There are no pre-set GAAP standards for managerial accounting statements with certain metrics and statements considered non-GAAP financial measures. Table 5.2 further compares and contrasts the similarities between managerial accounting and financial accounting.

**Table 5.2    Comparison between financial accounting and management accounting**

| Differences | Financial Accounting | Managerial Accounting |
|---|---|---|
| Intended audience | External users<br><br>• Shareholders<br>• Creditors<br>• Banks<br>• Financial institutions<br>• Potential investors | Internal Users<br><br>• Executives<br>• Managers |
| Guidelines followed | Adheres to GAAP | Based upon the individual needs of the managers |
| Purpose | Allows shareholders to accurately compare the performance of a company | Allows managers to view certain areas of interest and compare in such a manner that the manager dictates |
| Source data | Based strictly on historical data | Can use projected rates and not solely based on historical performance |

## DIFFERENCES IN AIRLINE ACCOUNTING

Owing to the unique industry that airlines operate and compete in, airline accounting differs somewhat from that of traditional industries. Not only is the industry unique, but the services offered by each airline tend to differ by numerous factors including, but not limited to, target market segment, region or regions served, desired level of prestige, and so on. Additionally, the historically high level of government involvement in the airline industry still has a lasting effect on airlines, including accounting. To determine a very specific definition of airline accounting we turn to the International Air Transport Association (IATA). According to IATA (2009), the purpose of airline revenue accounting systems are "to manage the control, reporting, use and accounting of tickets, excess baggage tickets and other 'accountable' documents. In doing so it should be accurate and flexible, and provide maximum efficiency in processing ticket data, and posting and billing accurate values. It should validate all transaction, and initiate recoveries where under-collections or errors have occurred."

This may appear to be a massive, over-defined definition, but the basic purpose of an airline's accounting system is to accurately and efficiently account and track all performance and financial transactions of the airline. This in turn provides both shareholders and managers detailed information that is both relevant and accurate. Some of the ways in which airline accounting can be complicated are the international trade and currency issues, liabilities through unearned revenue, loyalty programs, and exposure to risk. We deal with each of these airline accounting issues in the remainder of this chapter.

## INTERNATIONAL TRADE AND IATA CLEARING HOUSE

IATA Clearing Services, or ICS, is the area within IATA that deals with airline-to-airline financial transactions. IATA's Clearing House, or ICH, falls under this area. According to IATA, the purpose of the ICH is to "provide the means to settle all the billed items sent to and from airlines around the world" (IATA Clearing House). IATA claims that this service clears more than 40 billion U.S.D. each year for the participating members. The service is used by more than 450 companies worldwide and on average, more than 350 airlines monthly (IATA Clearing House). The ICH therefore provides a "common ground" in which airlines can conduct business with each other. The IATA Clearing House provides an environment which is relatively safe and secure, while reducing costs and providing minimal risk to the individual airline. The following examples will further explain and clarify the IATA Clearing House.

Assume that British Airways and Emirates Airlines are purchasing seats on each other's flights through a code-share agreement. The financial transactions would go through the IATA Clearing House and then would be sent to the respective airline. This reduces the overall cost associated with the transaction and lowers the risk exposure for each airline. Figure 5.1 further depicts this situation. The solid lines depict a transaction where British Airways is sending currency to Emirates, while the dotted line depicts the opposite situation.

This setup allows the airlines to take a situation in which a large amount of financial risk can exist and lessen that amount of risk. With the utilization of this service, airlines have lowered the amount of risk they are exposed to and have also increased their efficiency. The reason for this is that, with the IATA Clearing House handling the transaction, there is an assurance that it will be completed. All parties benefit from the IATA Clearing House

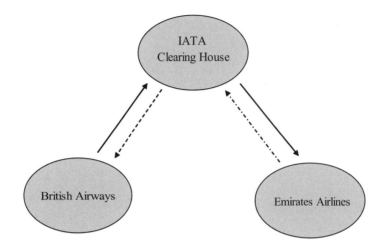

**Figure 5.1     IATA clearing house**

by eliminating the costs associated with having one or more of the airline's own employees working on processing accounting transactions between airlines.

## ISSUES PERTAINING TO THE AIRLINE INDUSTRY

This section primarily focuses upon issues that affect accounting in the airline industry. These issues tend to be specific in nature, and pertain primarily to the airline and aviation industries. Specifically, airline loyalty programs are discussed with a focus primarily on frequent flyer programs and their effect on customer loyalty in the industry. Later we will discuss the specifics of revenue recognition and how airlines record transactions in their accounting equation, as well as how these transactions affect the industry. Finally this section closes with a closer look at issues affecting international airlines, especially that of currency risk and how airlines have taken steps to lessen the effect of this risk.

### *Frequent-flyer Programs*[2]

One interesting program developed by many airlines to ensure customer loyalty is the frequent flyer program. These programs vary from airline to airline, but most include some form of perks or incentives for a passenger who continues to choose the airline. Most often this is in the form of frequent-flyer miles. One popular example of this program is the Delta SkyMiles frequent-flyer program. Delta's SkyMiles program, like many other frequent-flyer programs, has several different levels of membership based on certain criteria and accumulated points. Each level has its own unique benefits which may include free upgrades to business or first class on certain flights. These programs cost the airlines large sums of money to administer, yet they provide the airlines with loyal customers who could potentially choose one of their rivals. As will be shown in the revenue recognition section of this chapter, frequent-flyer miles represent a liability on the airline's accounting

---

2     This section was mainly authored by Bert J. Zarb Ph.D, CPA. He is a professor of accounting at Embry-Riddle Aeronautical University, Daytona Beach, Florida.

**Table 5.3      Airline frequent-flyer miles liabilities ($ millions) as of December 31, 2008**

| Airline | Program | Liability | |
|---------|---------|-----------|---|
| United Airlines | Mileage Plus | Current Liability | 1,414 |
| | | Long-term Liability | 2,768 |
| Delta Air Lines | SkyMiles | Current Liability | 1,624 |
| | | Long-term Liability | 3,489 |
| Continental Airlines | OnePass | Current Liability (combined with other air travel liability) | 1,881 |

*Source*: Airline 2008 SEC 10K Filings.

books, as they can be redeemed in the future for travel. Table 5.3 above contains some liability balances for frequent-flyer programs of different airlines. For instance, at the end of December 31, 2008, Delta's total liability associated with their frequent-flyer program was $5,113MM.

In an industry where price competition by low-cost airlines has caused legacy airlines to cut back on service, frequent-flyer programs remain intact. However, airlines are starting to make cuts to their frequent-flyer programs, with airlines like United and U.S. Airways eliminating minimum mileage earnings on flights. With the cost that they represent, frequent-flyer programs must be accounted for and they must also produce some measurable financial results.

One benefit of these programs is that they allow the airline to easily track the trends of their different frequent-flyer groups. These can be tracked using several factors, but also can be as simple as what groups are taking what flights. Frequent-flyer programs provide airlines with data on how customers are earning their points as well as how they are redeeming them. Another way in which airlines can make money from frequent-flyer programs is to sell their miles to other companies who then try to persuade consumers to purchase their product or service by offering them airline miles for doing so. Credit card companies have entered into these types of agreements with airlines to buy credit card miles. The credit card companies offer reward incentives in which consumers are given rewards on certain airlines based upon their credit card purchasing habits. Increasingly, credit card companies are being used as a short-term source of financing for airlines through the pre-sale of miles. In essence, the credit card company will purchase a lump sum of miles upfront, providing the airlines with a one-time cash impact, in return for free miles in the future. Many credit card companies like Chase and American Express offer co-branded credit cards, as listed in Table 5.4.

Frequent-flyer programs were introduced in 1981 by American Airlines with a program called AAdvantage. Soon other airlines followed creating their own reward programs (Zarb, 2009). The basic concept of a frequent-flyer program is to encourage passenger loyalty and induce higher levels of repeat business from premium-fare passengers by providing those passengers awards according to their frequency of travel on the sponsoring airline. These rewards are typically in the form of frequent-flyer miles, points, or points that can be accumulated and converted into free or discounted travel.

**Table 5.4　　　Frequent-flyer miles credit cards**

| American Express | Visa |
|---|---|
| Virgin Atlantic | Air Tran |
| Delta Skymiles Credit Card | United Chase Plus Visa Card |
| JetBlue Card from American Express | United Mileage Plus Visa Signature Card |
| Virgin America | Southwest Rapid Rewards Visa Card |
| | Continental Airlines World Mastercard |
| | British Airways Visa Signature Card |

With arrangements such as code-sharing and alliances, some airlines not only allow members of their frequent-flyer programs (FFP) to use their mileage credits to obtain awards on another participating airline, but also earn mileage credits for flights taken on another participating airline, or both. In the mid 1990s, many airlines established marketing partnerships with hotels, restaurants, car rental companies and credit card issuers, which enabling their members to earn additional credit by patronizing these firms. In 2007, banks spent an estimated $4 billion on airline miles for credit-card rewards.[3]

Mileage credits do not only offer free travel awards, but also the ability to buy tickets at discount prices, free companion tickets, first class upgrades, and other non-travel awards. However, in order not to displace fare-paying passengers, airlines have imposed restrictions on redemption rates of frequent flyer miles. Such restrictions include the limitation of capacity that is available for frequent-flyer passengers on some flights during peak travel periods.

Unused awards must be accounted for on carriers' books. There are two methods of accounting for free or discounted travel earned through FFPs: the incremental cost method and the deferred revenue method. However, there is no specific authoritative guidance on the accounting for FFPs as the FASB has not yet reached a consensus on the accounting for FFPs.

*Incremental cost method*　The incremental cost method is based on the concept that passengers redeeming their FFP awards are simply filling what would have otherwise been an empty seat. Therefore, the cost for an airline to fly a FFP member is the cost the airline will incur to provide travel to one additional passenger or an airline's marginal cost. Under the incremental cost method, a liability is recorded for the cost associated with rewarding the FFP members expected to redeem mileage credits. These incremental costs typically include the cost of fuel, food and drinks, ticketing, and so on. When awards are expected to be redeemed for free travel on other airlines or for non-travel awards, the incremental cost is the amount the sponsoring airline will be obligated to pay the other airline or other third-party providing the award.

In order to estimate the FFP obligation using the incremental cost method, airlines must estimate the number of mileage credits that are expected to be used by FFP members. Several factors influence this estimation:

- the minimum amount of mileage credits required before a FFP member can claim an award

---

3　　*Chicago Tribune*, September 23, 2008.

- the expiration period established for the program
- historical data: frequency of redemptions, overall number of mileage credits redeemed, proportion of air/non-air travel awards.

Some airlines have been able to build up experienced-based statistical models for estimating the likelihood and type of redemptions. However, if FFP awards are without limitations or if special promotional programs are used, the value of the award could be more significant compared to the value of the purchases earning the award. Thus, the use of incremental cost method may be not appropriate.

*Deferred revenue method*   Under the deferred revenue method, the fair value of all mileage credits is deferred until the mileage credits are used. The use of the deferred revenue method has been limited, even though some airlines have used the method in their business combinations and when emerging from bankruptcy. The deferred revenue method is required under International Financial Reporting Standards (IFRS). Reference may be made to International Financial Reporting Interpretations Committee (IFRIC) interpretation No. 13 Customer Loyalty Programs.

In evaluating the fair value of mileage credits, airlines usually derive the value from purchased tickets with the same or similar restrictions as frequent-flyer awards, or even from the transportation element of transactions of sales of mileage credits. Consequently, the fair value of mileage credits is determined upon issue of the credits with the resulting liability not marked-to-market.

As the fair value of mileage credits issued changes over time, it becomes necessary to change the deferral rate resulting in a pool of mileage credits that are valued at different rates. Since these mileage credits are easily exchangeable, it is difficult for airlines to track individual mileage credits from issuance to usage. In order to mitigate this difficulty, airlines determine the value of mileage credits used for awards by using a weighted average, or a first-in first-out method (FIFO) to determine which miles have been redeemed and which ones remain outstanding.

Under the deferred revenue method, airlines have to estimate and account for mileage credits which are not likely to be redeemed or will expire. This is known as "breakage", and should be recognized using either the Expiration Recognition Method, or the Redemption Recognition Method.

- Expiration Recognition Method: Under this method, "breakage" is recognized at the expiration of the mileage credits or when the probability of those mileage credits to be redeemed is remote.
- Redemption Recognition Method: Under this method, "breakage" is estimated as well as recognized in proportion to actual mileage redeemed.

Figure 5.2 overleaf shows the economic model of the Qantas Frequent-flyer program. As can be seen in the figure, Qantas Airways is using the deferred revenue method for its accounting of mileage credits. Frequent-flyer points are recorded as a liability on the balance sheet until they are either used or expire, at which point the profit/loss is recorded on the income statement. Therefore, the main principle of the deferred revenue method is that frequent-flyer miles and any associated revenue stays on the balance sheet until the miles are either used or expired. At such point in time, the miles are removed from the balance sheet with any revenues and/or expenses transferred to the income statement.

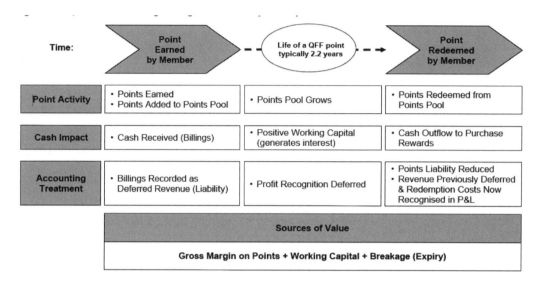

**Figure 5.2    Qantas accounting recognition of frequent flyer points**

*Source:* Quantas Group 2007/08 Half Year Results Investor Briefing, p. 46.

*Frequent-flyer miles sold to third parties*    With the rise in the popularity of frequent-flyer programs, other industries have entered into partnerships with airlines. The hotel, car rental, and banking industries were among the first external participants in airline frequent-flyer programs. However, upon analyzing the cost as an airline partner, some companies decided to withdraw from the FFP relationship. This was the decision made by Hertz, the first car rental company to establish a FFP partnership, even though the company later rejoined the partnership. Today, non-travel award-earning activities include credit-card purchases, long-distance telephone services, and even mortgages and stock trades.

Frequent flyer third party relationships involve the buying and selling of miles between parties. To provide an example of potential transactions, consider Delta's frequent flyer program, SkyMiles. As part of the SkyMiles program, members can earn and redeem miles from loyalty to other companies, such as rental car company Avis. Under most FFP agreements, when a SkyMiles member earns points from Avis, Avis purchases the miles from Delta as a result of obtaining the loyalty of the Delta customer. However, when a SkyMiles member redeems a free car rental from Avis, Delta will pay Avis for the privilege of being able to redeem miles on non-airline travel activity. The individual agreement with the third party then stipulates the payments.

Most airline loyalty programs feature mileage credits issued under co-branded credit card programs. These co-branded credit card programs have been seen by airlines as an additional source of financing. To protect the credit card issuers in the event the airline goes into bankruptcy, the financing arrangement can be structured as a pre-purchase of mileage credits by the credit card issuer to be used for fulfillment of awards offered to cardholders. Pre-purchased mileage credits are recorded as deferred revenue or debt by the airline based on the terms of the arrangement. When the credit card issuer grants mileage credits to its customers, deferred revenue or debt is reduced and the credit is broken up into its travel and marketing components respectively.

*Interline frequent-flyer miles* Over the years, airlines have created alliances that include their airline partners' FFPs with a view to extending their programs not only in order to attract and retain premium passengers, but also to offer their FFP members extended options for the use of their accumulated mileage credits. Under the terms of such alliances, FFPs are administered on a reciprocal basis between airlines. In most cases, the airlines establish a settlement contract of net activity between their partners. This settlement of net activity is usually done once a year at a rate per mileage credit that is usually higher than the carriers' own incremental cost necessary to provide a FFP seat. Most of the time, these rates are frequently up to ten times higher than the incremental cost as they tend to represent the equivalent of the fair value of a ticket. If an airline accounts for FFPs under the deferred revenue method, this is not an issue as their deferral rates approximate or exceed the settlement rates.

The following example, taken from the AICPA Frequent-flyer Program Guide, illustrates the accounting for FFP activity between one airline and its partner using the incremental cost method. Four activities can affect the settlement between Home Airline (HA) and Partner Airline (PA).

1. Home Airline FFP members earn mileage credits in the Home Airline FFP for travel that occurred on Partner Airline. Partner Airline is obligated to pay Home Airline for the mileage credits earned.
2. Home Airline FFP members use mileage credits to fly on Partner Airline. Home Airline is obligated to pay Partner Airline for the seats provided to Home Airline FFP members.
3. Partner Airline members earn mileage credits in the Partner Airline FFP for flights on Home Airline. Home Airline is obligated to pay Partner Airline for the mileage credits earned.
4. Partner Airline FFP members use their mileage credits to fly on Home Airline. Partner Airline is obligated to pay Home Airline for the seats provided to the Partner Airline FFP members.

In Table 5.5 the payment received for activity 1 is treated as deferred revenue and is recognized as travel occurs, following the same method used for mileage credits sold to third parties. The payment to Partner Airline for activity 2 is recognized as a liability. It has no effect on Home Airline revenue or expense. The payment in activity 3 is recorded by Home Airline as an operating expense to reflect the cost of purchasing the mileage credits back from Partner Airline. Activity 4 is recognized as passenger revenue for Home Airline as it would normally be when FFP members use their mileage credits to fly with Home Airline.

Airlines evaluate the effect of the anticipated settlement of their FFP liability on other airline partners in different ways. The most used approach is to use the airline's recent history to estimate a trend for the FFP awards that will be settled with travel on partner airlines based on the settlement rates contracted with its airline partners. When an airline enters into an agreement with a new airline partner, it should accrue an additional liability based on the best estimate of the portion of its mileage credits that will be settled on the new partner airline. The airline has to consider several factors while making its estimate: these include the contractual terms of agreement with the new airline and the number of FFP members who can reasonably redeem mileage credits on the new airline.

**Table 5.5      Mileage accrual on FFP partner airlines**

| Activity Number | Activity | Effect on settlement | Miles | Settlement rate per mile | Net receipt by home airline | Accounting treatment by home airline |
|---|---|---|---|---|---|---|
| 1 | HA earn on PA | PA pay HA | 240,000,000 | 0.01 | $2,400,000 | Deferred revenue |
| 2 | HA burn on PA | HA pay PA | 440,000,000 | 0.01 | -4,400,000 | Frequent flyer liability |
| 3 | PA earn on HA | HA pay PA | 172,000,000 | 0.01 | -1,720,000 | Operating expense |
| 4 | PA burn on HA | PA pay HA | 772,000,000 | 0.01 | 7,720,000 | Current revenue |
| | Amount due from PA | | | | $4,000,000 | |

*Source*: AICPA Frequent Flyer Program Guide, p. 11.

*Accounting changes related to frequent-flyer programs*    As can be seen, the accounting of an airline's FFP is complicated and involves many estimates and assumptions. Some of the more important assumptions include the type and value of incremental costs, estimates of how FFP obligations will be settled, the fair value of elements in the sale of mileage credits, and the period over which mileage credits will be used by members when not tracked on a specific identification basis. Clearly, it is imperative for an airline to document the rationale in using its estimates and assumptions in accounting for its FFP.

Thus, because of the inherent nature of these assumptions and estimates, it is common for airlines to change their estimates, and this in turn affects the amount of their obligations and deferred revenues. As with all changes in estimates, reference should be made to FASB No. 154 *Accounting Changes and Error Corrections*, which specifies:

> A change in accounting estimate shall be accounted for in (a) the period of change if the change affects that period only or (b) the period of change and future periods if the change affects both. A change in accounting estimate shall not be accounted for by restating or retrospectively adjusting amounts reported in financial statements for prior periods or by reporting pro forma amounts for prior periods.

Table 5.6 provides some examples of common changes in estimates in frequent-flyer accounting and how each would be evaluated under FASB guidance.

*Disclosures*    Historically, the disclosure of frequent-flyer rules and restrictions has been part of each airline's operating policy. In 2006, the Department of Transportation issued a report entitled "Follow-up Review: Performance of U.S. Airlines in Implementing Selected Provisions of the Airline Customer Service Commitment". This report found that airlines had failed to deliver on their own promises in a number of key areas. These included their commitment to provide consumers with frequent-flyer program performance data that could be used to make meaningful comparisons between competing programs.

Airline companies belonging to The Air Transport Association (ATA) committed to disclose an annual report on frequent-flyer redemptions, but the Commitment provision

**Table 5.6      Accounting changes associated with FFPs**

| FFP common changes in estimate | Period of accounting recognition |
|---|---|
| • Changes to estimates of incremental cost | • Current period charge or credit to operations to reflect the updated estimate of the obligation or liability |
| • Changes to the settlement rate or portion of mileage credits to be used on airline partners | • Current period charge or credit to operations to reflect the updated estimate of the obligation |
| • Changes in the fair value of the deferred component of the sale of mileage credits | • Applied prospectively to future sales of mileage credits with respect to the initial recognition |
| • Changes in the period over mileage credits sold are expected to be used by program members to claim travel. | • Applied prospectively to future sales of mileage credits and any unamortized deferred revenue balances. |

*Source*: FASB Statement No. 54.

was not specific about where the information should be published.[4] Since no clear method was provided as to where the redemption information should be disclosed, such information could not be easily located and furthermore, airlines do not always tell customers where they can find the information. The report reviewed all 15 member airlines of Air Transport Association and found the following:

- Two ATA airlines and two non-ATA airlines do not report redemption information to the public. Of these, two ATA airlines report this information on Internet sites only available to members of their frequent-flyer programs.
- The remaining 11 ATA airlines report redemption information to the public, but it is not readily available.
- Three airlines report redemption information in both their annual submissions to the Securities and Exchange Commission (10K report) and on their Internet sites.
    - Seven airlines only report redemption information in their 10K reports.
    - One airline reports redemption information only on its Internet site.

Another study published in the International Journal of Accounting in 2002 found that only about 40% of the airlines were disclosing information about their frequent-flyer accounting policy.

## REVENUE RECOGNITION

Airlines in the United States operate under the accrual basis of accounting, since this is the standard for most U.S. corporations. In preparing financial statements, airlines should adhere to a uniform set of rules called generally accepted accounting principles (GAAP). The standard is set by U.S. GAAP, and is primarily concerned with the manner in which companies recognize income and expenses and note them on their respective

---

4      The ATA is the trade group of the principal U.S. airlines and their members transport more than 90% of U.S. airline passenger and cargo traffic.

financial statements. According to Briner (2001), and based on Financial Accounting Standards Board (FASB) principal No.5 "revenue is recognized when a transaction occurs and 1) the revenue is realized or realizable and 2) the revenue is earned". Practically speaking, this means that revenue is realized when monetary units exchange hands and earned when the actual exchange of goods or services takes place. A comparison of the recognition of revenues and expenses under the accrual and cash basis of accounting is shown in Table 5.7.

**Table 5.7     Recognition of revenues and expenses under accrual and cash accounting**

| | Recognition Criteria | |
|---|---|---|
| | **Accural** | **Cash** |
| Revenue | When realized and earned | When $ received |
| Expenses | When incurred | When $ paid |

Under the cash basis of accounting a transaction is recorded only when money changes hands. This may be practical for a very small company or in personal finance; however, for large companies, revenues and expenses must be tracked if the companies are going to be able to effectively manage their finances. In addition, accounting principles tell businesses that they must match revenues and expenses to the period in which they occur and not later when the actual cash is paid. In the airline industry this is important because the reverse actually occurs; that is, cash is collected before revenue is earned and expenses are incurred. Revenue is collected or realized when a consumer purchases and therefore pays for a ticket. This revenue is then earned and expenses are incurred for that customer when the customer utilizes the ticket and the exchange of the product is recognized.[5]

Assume a passenger buys a plane ticket on U.S. Airways at the cost of $300.00 on February 1st for a flight on February 25th. According to accounting standards, this transaction cannot be counted as revenue on February 1st since it has not yet been "earned". The $300.00 would be recognized as revenue on February 25th when the revenue is earned by the actual flight and the use of the sold ticket.

Table 5.8 depicts how transactions are reflected on the accounting equation for an airline. The equation is divided into two main parts which are: items that affect the balance sheet (assets, liabilities and owners equity) and items which are reflected on the income statement (revenue and expenses). As seen in the table, a pre-sold ticket represents a liability to the airline since it is responsible for providing the service that the customer has already paid for. As previously mentioned, frequent-flyer miles also represent a liability to the airline. The miles earned entitle the passengers to free round-trip tickets or other perks such as first-class upgrades. Therefore the frequent-flyer miles earned carry a dollar value that shows up as a liability on the airline balance sheet. The reason for this is the obvious fact that the airline must provide a future benefit to the customer. The earning and redemption of frequent-flyer miles and its effect on the accounting equation is shown in Table 5.9.

---

5     The U.S. Securities and Exchange Commission (SEC) has issued a Staff Accounting Bulletin (SAB No. 104) that gives additional guidance on revenue recognition. It can be accessed from the SEC website http://www.sec.gov

**Table 5.8      Revenue recognition**

|  | Balance sheet | | | Income statement |
|---|---|---|---|---|
|  | Assets = Liabilities + Owners Equity + | | | Revenue - Expenses |
| Feb. 1 |  |  |  |  |
| Cash | $300 |  |  |  |
| Presold tickets |  | $300 |  |  |
|  |  |  |  |  |
| Feb. 25 |  |  |  |  |
| Presold ticket liability |  | ($300) |  |  |
| Revenue from ticket sales |  |  |  | $300 |

**Table 5.9      Frequent-flyer miles**

|  | Balance sheet | | | Income statement |
|---|---|---|---|---|
|  | Assets = Liabilities + Owners Equity + | | | Revenue - Expenses |
| Feb. 1 |  |  |  |  |
| Miles awarded to customer x |  |  |  |  |
| (25000 @.01/mile) |  | $250 |  |  |
| Customer loyalty | $250 |  |  |  |
|  |  |  |  |  |
| Feb. 25 |  |  |  |  |
| Frequent-flyer miles liability |  | ($250) |  |  |
| Frequent-flyer award expense |  |  |  | $250 |

The accounting equation contained in Table 5.9 shows an example where a customer earns 25,000 frequent-flyer miles on February 1 and redeems them for a ticket on February 25. When these miles are awarded on February 1, it not only creates a liability for the airline that will be on the books until the customer redeems, it also creates the expense of the free travel that the airline provides on February 25. In return, the airline hopes to garner goodwill and customer loyalty from the ability of customers to earn and redeem frequent-flyer miles. In order to reduce the liability and expense of frequent-flyer miles, many airlines have recently changed the quantity of miles awarded or have given other options for customers to redeem frequent-flyer miles, such as car rentals, hotel stays or magazine subscriptions. Airlines hope that alternative options for redeeming miles will allow the airline to get rid of the liability of frequent-flyer miles more quickly.

## U.S. AIRLINES VS. EUROPEAN AIRLINES

U.S. airlines operate in an environment that is different from other airlines across the world. This section compares and contrasts the differences that occur between these two groups. In the United States, carriers compete both in domestic and international markets, just as do many other air carriers across the globe. However, in the U.S., domestic flights play a huge and vital role for carriers so that American carriers have a higher percentage of domestic travel as compared with their European counterparts. Table 5.10 highlights the high percentage of domestic flights in the U.S.

**Table 5.10    Comparison of the top 8 U.S. Airlines and their percentage of international and domestic flights for April 2009**

| Airline | | Total [million] | Domestic | International |
|---|---|---|---|---|
| American | | | | |
| | ASM | 12644.1 | 61% | 39% |
| | RPM | 10283.7 | 63% | 37% |
| Alaska | | | | |
| | ASM | 1868 | 88% | 12% |
| | RPM | 1475 | 88% | 12% |
| Continental | | | | |
| | ASM | 7907.3 | 51% | 49% |
| | RPM | 6620.2 | 53% | 47% |
| Delta (including Northwest) | | | | |
| | ASM | 16190.7 | 55% | 45% |
| | RPM | 13327.7 | 57% | 43% |
| Southwest | | | | |
| | ASM | 8463.5 | 100% | 0% |
| | RPM | 6517.9 | 100% | 0% |
| United | | | | |
| | ASM | 10348.4 | 55% | 45% |
| | RPM | 8305.9 | 58% | 42% |
| U.S. Airways | | | | |
| | ASM | 5884.8 | 76% | 24% |
| | RPM | 4988.5 | 77% | 23% |
| Combined | | | | |
| | ASM | 63306.8 | 65% | 35% |
| | RPM | 51518.9 | 66% | 34% |

*Source*: Compiled by the Authors based upon data from The Airline Monitor.

Table 5.10 lists the domestic and international proportions for the top seven U.S. airlines for the period of April 2009. As shown, Continental and Delta have the highest percentage of international flights for this period based upon Available Seat Miles (ASM) flown. Southwest Airlines does not fly any international routes, which explains why 100% of ASMs are domestic for Southwest. The carrier with the second highest percentage of domestic ASMs to total ASMs is Alaska. It should also be noted that the figures for U.S. Airways includes those of America West, since the two airlines have merged. The route structure of an airline can be viewed as a form of diversification. In this regard, an airline can view its domestic and international services as two different product lines. However, by legacy carriers operating the hub and spoke model, the domestic network is needed to provide feed for the international network. Together, both networks must work closely together to be profitable. A lack of a domestic network was a primary reason for the demise of the original Pan Am.

Assume for example that Continental Airlines' routes are, for the most part, evenly distributed between its international and domestic markets. With this approach, Continental could hope that if one market segment is down, the other market will counterbalance the effect of the failing market. For example, if domestic leisure travel is down, Continental could hope that the international market for leisure travel has increased, thus balancing out the negative effect of the domestic market.

In Europe, on the other hand, carriers have traditionally been primarily focused on what would be considered international markets. This has been due to several circumstances, including geographic size and inter-modal competition. However, recent route expansion within Europe has been led by low-fare carriers which now have 76% of the intra-Europe market. As of 2007, European carriers are operating 2,655 more nonstop non-domestic routes within Europe than existed in 2003 (Beckerman, 2007). Table 5.11 shows the European carriers that have opened up the most new routes within Europe between 2003 and 2007, with all of these carriers being low-cost carriers.

**Table 5.11    Intra-Europe expansion 2003–2007**

| Rank | Carrier | New routes in operation as of 2007 |
| --- | --- | --- |
| 1 | Ryanair | 465 |
| 2 | easyJet Airline | 153 |
| 3 | Hapag-Lloyd Express | 130 |
| 4 | Jet2.com | 100 |
| 5 | Wizz Air | 99 |
| 6 | Norwegian Air Shuttle | 74 |
| 7 | SkyEurope | 70 |
| 8 | Flybe | 65 |
| 9 | Air Berlin | 58 |
| 10 | Centralwings | 52 |

*Source*: Association of European Airlines, Issue 4-2007 p. 7.

Geographic size plays a huge factor in Europe where countries tend to be considerably smaller than in the U.S. Belgium would be one example of a small country in Europe where there is little domestic airline travel. Inter-modal competition is another factor that affects European air carriers in their domestic markets. In highly developed areas such as Europe, a passenger usually has the option of choosing either rail or air service. For example, in France, domestic air carriers compete against passenger trains that travel at speeds that approach those of aircraft. Also, with the use of train service, passengers need not worry about long lines at security checkpoints, carryon baggage restrictions, or other travel concerns associated with air travel.

In the United States, domestic air travel has less competition from other modes of travel, owing to the vast size of the country and the lack of a highly developed passenger rail system in most areas. The travel history of the United States has made it a country that is highly dependent on personal passenger vehicles (i.e. cars) and air travel. After World War II, the U.S. focused its concerns on developing a vast interstate highway system and not on rail development.

## INTERNATIONAL OPERATIONS

Figure 5.3 shows the several major passenger airlines according to operating revenue, and all have significant international operations in addition to their domestic operations. However, with the increased revenues from international operations come increased risks. International airlines are exposed to more risk than typical non-international airlines or businesses. These risks exist in many different areas and some of these unique risks are listed in Table 5.12.

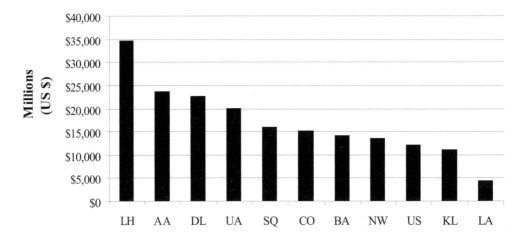

*Source*: Back Aviation Form 41.

**Figure 5.3      Major airlines by operating revenue (2008)**

**Table 5.12    Risks affecting airlines**

Currency risks

Fuel price risk

Aircraft costs and maintenance costs

Government regulations (taxes and sanctions)

International events (terrorism)

Threat of substitutions in some areas (high-speed rail)

Threat of new entrants

*Source*: U.S. DOT Form 41 via BTS, Schedule P12.

## Currency Risk

Currency risk is the risk a company is exposed to by operating within several different currency systems. An example is when, in the case of an airline, costs are incurred in one currency and income is received in the form of a different currency. For example, Delta Air Lines has its maintenance facilities in the United States and is currently operating an international route that flies from New York to France. Income in the form of ticket sales could potentially be received in euros, while the maintenance costs associated with this aircraft would be spent in U.S. dollars. Typically, the dollar and the euro have fluctuating exchange rates, meaning that one dollar is not always equal to one euro. Therefore, Delta Air Lines would have to exchange the euros received into dollars. Depending on the current market this could either put the airline at an advantage or a disadvantage. This can also distort earnings since currency exchange rates affect revenues. If the euro is relatively high compared to the dollar and income was received as euros, then Delta Air Lines would recognize a financial benefit when it converts euros to dollars. This is due to the fact that the euros Delta has will exchange for more dollars (i.e. one euro = $1.20 instead of $1). On the other hand, assume Air France is based in France and has its maintenance facilitates there. On its Boston to France route many of its customers are paying in U.S. dollars. Air France must now convert these dollars into euros. When converting from dollars to euros and the dollar is worth less than the euro, Air France receives fewer euros than they receive in dollars (i.e. $1= 0.80 euros instead of $1= 1 euro). Therefore, costs could be incurred in a monetary unit that currently has more or less value than the monetary unit a company's income is recognized in. Airlines must take into account currency risk and trends in exchange rates when setting prices in various currencies.

To reduce currency risk, airlines may engage in currency hedging (guarding against fluctuations in exchange rates) by locking in an exchange rate or a range of exchange rates. For example, Northwest Airlines engaged in currency hedging against the Japanese Yen and Canadian dollar at the end of 2007. Northwest estimated that 42.6% of anticipated sales in Yen and 66.4% of sales in Canadian dollars were hedged in 2008 (Northwest Airlines Corp., 2008, February 29). Currency hedging is discussed in more detail in the chapters on risk and fuel hedging. Similarly, many airlines such as Southwest have benefited from the rapidly growing fuel costs in the past few years, through fuel hedging strategy. Qantas increased its fuel hedging level to 90% of its needs during 2007.

## AIRLINE CONSOLIDATION

"Consolidation of the airline industry is inevitable."

W. Douglas Parker, CEO, U.S. Airways

## CONSOLIDATION IN THE U.S. AIRLINE INDUSTRY

In recent years, both in the U.S. and the EU, there has been an increased amount of airline consolidation. Airline mergers and acquisitions have been especially common place in the U.S. If one looks at the history for any major legacy carrier in the United States, it is apparent that its history is made up of mergers. Delta for example, in its long history as an air carrier, has merged with Southern, Northeast, and Western Airlines (Delta). In 2008 Delta was back in the spotlight by merging with fellow Skyteam alliance member Northwest Airlines. The merger was approved in October, 2008 by the United States Department of Justice (Associated Press, 2008, October 29). Recently, there has also been discussion of a possible merger between United Airlines and Continental.[6] U.S. Airways and America West merged in 2005; this merger uncovered many problems with the way mergers take place. According to the Wall Street Journal, U.S. Airways still has several issues concerning employee relations in the new combined carrier with different labor unions battling issues out in court (Trottman, Carey & Prada 2008, February 21). Other examples of recent mergers in the U.S. include American Airlines' acquisitions of Reno Air and TWA in 1998 and 2001 respectively. Figure 5.4 illustrates a framework of the major airline mergers that have happened in the United States since deregulation of 1978. Because of economic problems, labor disputes, and rising fuel costs many airlines such as Eastern Airlines, Pan American Airways, and ATA were forced into liquidations and Delta Airlines, Northwest Airlines and United Airlines filed for bankruptcy protection.

### Consolidation in the EU

In 2003, Air France and KLM merged with each other. This merger formed the largest air transport company in the EU.[7] In recent news, Air France-KLM is currently in negotiation to purchase Alitalia Airlines.[8] The Italian government has shown some signs of approval of this merger. Air France-KLM states that they will handle this merger in the same manner as the KLM merger that occurred just a few years earlier with the carrier operating as a separate brand and entity. Air France-KLM anticipates only 1,100 layoffs in the process

---

6      Source: *Wall Street Journal*.
7      Source: www.airfrance.com
8      Source: *Aviation Week*.

of the merger with Alitalia. Negotiations have recently been discontinued because of politics; that is, the unions of Alitalia would not back the deal and in the opinion of Prime Minister Berlusconi, Alitalia was to remain Italian (he even won the national elections in Italy in 2008 partly because of that statement). Elsewhere in Europe, British carrier EasyJet purchased GB Airways, a franchise operator for British Airways (Hanson, 2007, October 29). These examples prove that mergers and acquisitions in the airline industry are not just confined to the U.S., but occur constantly on a global scale. In 2006, Lufthansa acquired Swiss and made it a wholly-owned subsidiary. However, Lufthansa decided not to merge the two airline identities. Lufthansa then set its sites on merging with Austrian Airlines and investing in both British Midland Airlines and Brussels Airlines.

## Consolidation in Other Parts of the Aviation Industry

"Any combination among the top six carriers has anticompetitive tendencies, which will probably mean a net loss for consumers."

Samuel Buttrick, an analyst at UBS Warburg.

Mergers are not just confined to the airline industry since aircraft manufacturers have also been a source of mergers. Boeing acquired rival McDonnell Douglas in 1997 to move the market for large passenger jets from an oligopoly to a duopoly with Airbus (Boeing, 2008). As noted earlier, mergers and acquisitions of airlines are commonplace. These mergers can have both a positive and a damaging effect on the companies involved. The industry has come to understand that challenges are part of mergers and it has now become educated on issues affecting the overall health of the resulting organization (see Figure 5.4 overleaf). These issues include existing routes structures, hub issues, aircraft types, and employee seniority and relations.

## SUMMARY

This chapter discussed accounting in both general businesses and airlines in the U.S. and internationally. It covered how airlines diversify their business and gave examples of U.S. airlines and their respective route structures. Specific accounting issues that all airlines incur, including collection of revenue before it is earned, were discussed. The chapter also explained the accounting practices regarding the frequent-flyer programs .The chapter explained how international airlines reduce the amount of risk associated with doing business relating to issues of passenger transport, maintenance, and currency risks. The IATA Clearing House function was discussed as a way for airlines to reduce their risks.

## DISCUSSION QUESTIONS

1. What are the major differences between managerial accounting and financial accounting?
2. Discuss the role of the IATA Clearing House and how it provides benefit to the airline industry.

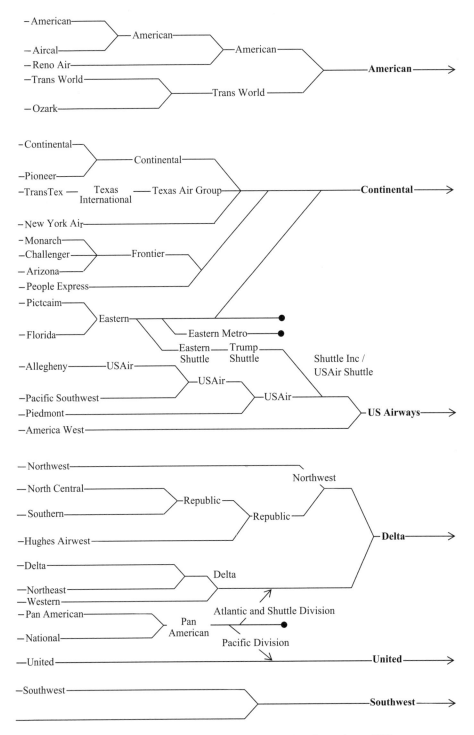

*Source*: Introduction to Air Transport Economics: Vasigh, Fleming and Tacker, Ashgate, 2008.

**Figure 5.4      Evolution of U.S. airline industry**

3. What are the major differences between the incremental cost method and the deferred revenue method of airline frequent-flyer mileage accounting treatment?
4. How do airlines benefit from frequent-flyer programs and cobranded credit card agreements?
5. What are the major differences between the accrual method of accounting and cash accounting?
6. Airline mergers have propagated in the industry because they generate profits by reducing costs and eliminating competition. What are the benefits from industry consolidation? Do the U.S. or European airline industries require further consolidation?
7. Discuss the principle of accrual accounting and why it is preferred to cash basis accounting.
8. Accounting is sometimes called the language of finance. Can you give some concrete reasons why this is so?
9. List at least three ways in which airline accounting is different from what might be called normal accounting.
10. What are some of the advantages and disadvantages of airlines conducting frequent-flyer programs?

## REFERENCES

AICPA, (2008). Airlines AICPA Audit and Accounting Guide.

Air France KLM, a Global Leader in Air Transport. Retrieved February 29, 2008, from Air France Web site: www.airfrance.com

Airline Monitor, The. "A Review of Trends in the Airline and Commercial Jet Aircraft Industries". Volume 20, No.7.

American Airlines. American Airlines History. Retrieved May 20, 2008, from http://www.aa.com/content/amrcorp/corporateInformation/facts/history.jhtml

Associated Press (2008, October 29). Justice Department OKs Delta-Northwest merger. Retrieved November 4, 2008 from http://www.foxnews.com/story/0,2933,444926,00.html

Beckerman, D. (2007). "New routes across Europe: Here to stay?" Association of European Airlines (4), 7.

Boeing (2008). Boeing: History-Higher, faster, farther- McDonnell Douglas Corp...Goshawks and MDs. Retrieved May 16, 2008, from the Boeing Company: http://www.boeing.com/history/narrative/n085mdc.html

Briner, R. (2001). Subtle Issues in Revenue Recognition. The CPA Journal.

Carey, S., D. Berman, and P. Prada (2008, February 7). Airline merger talks accelerate; Megadeals in works: Delta-Northwest, UAL-Continental. Wall Street Journal (Europe), p. UK.31. Retrieved February 29, 2008, from ProQuest Newsstand database.

Chambers, D., and N. Lacey (1999). Modern Corporate Finance (2nd ed.). Reading, MA: Addison-Wesley.

Choose a Card. Retrieved February 29, 2008, from Chase Credit Cards Web site: http://www.chase.com.

Credeur, Mary J. (Sep. 20, 2008). "Passengers burn up frequent-flyer miles". Calgary Herald, p. C8.

Delta Airlines. Retrieved January 28, 2008, from Delta Airlines Web site: http://www.delta.com

Hanson, L. (2007, October 29). EasyJet builds Gatwick base through GB Airways purchase. Retrieved November 4, 2008 from Aviation Week Intelligence Network Database.

Holloway, S. (2003). *Straight and Level: Practical Airline Economics*. Hampshire, England: Ashgate.

IATA. (2006). *Airline Finance and Accounting Management*

IATA Clearing House. From IATA Web site: http://www.iata.org/whatwedo/finance/clearing/index. htm

Northwest Airlines Corp. (2008, February 29). *Form 10-K (2007)*. Retrieved August 8, 2008 from www.nwa.com/corpinfo

Personal Cards. Retrieved February 29, 2008, from American Express Web site: http://www. americanexpress.com

Peterson, R. (1999), "Buy a home, fly to Rome", *American Bankers Association. ABA Banking Journal*, *91*(9), 62-63.

Porter, N., and R. Sawyers (2006). *Accounting for Decision Making*. Mason: Thomson South-Western.

QantasGroup, (2008), 2007/08 Half Year Results Investor Briefing. Retrieved from www.asx.com. au/asxpdf/20080221/pdf/317kqrh3frdhpf.pdf.

Tan, W., G. Tower, P. Hancock, and R. Taplin (2002) "Empires of the sky: determinants of global airlines' accounting-policy choices", *The International Journal of Accounting*, 37(3), 277-299.

Trottman, M., S. Carey, and P. Prada (2008, February 21) Labor Sees Opportunity in Airline Tie-Ups; Unions Weigh Support as a Way to Extract Better Contract Terms. Wall Street Journal (Eastern Edition), p. A.12. Retrieved February 29, 2008, from ABI/INFORM Global database.

U.S. Department of Transportation. (2006). Performance of U.S. Airlines in Implementing Selected Provisions of, the Airline Customer Service Commitment (AV-2007-012).

# 6

# Airline Financial Statements

"With the pressure on in our cost structure due to energy prices, the importance of the work for which these [financial] groups are responsible has soared, Southwest must develop a new long-term financial plan as we re-engineer our Company to combat higher fuel prices."

Laura Wright, CFO, Southwest Airlines

As a result of steady decline in traffic, the Airline industry may lose up to $US10 billion in 2009. The average ticket price is expected to drop as airlines are unable to cut capacity at the rate the demand is falling. Currently, there is an extreme pressure on the industry cash flow, revenue and balance sheet. In this chapter we introduce the reader to various financial statements (i.e. income statement, balance sheet, cash flow statement) by analyzing real-world airline financial statements. These statements are important sources of information about airlines for internal and external use. Financial statements are crucial because they can help to both reveal problems and identify counteractive measures. These statements are financial descriptions of economic activity and status required by law for all businesses. The steps used in the creation of financial statements are also presented to provide the reader with a greater understanding of the impact that managerial decisions and actions have on financial statements. The following topics are covered in the chapter:

- Balance Sheet
  - Current Assets
  - Fixed Assets
  - Depreciation
- Straight line
- Double declining balance methods
- Modified Accelerated Recovery System (MACRS)
- Sum-of-years digits
  - Current Liabilities
  - Long Term Debt
  - Stockholders' Equity
- Income Statement
- Common-Size Income Statement
- Statement of Retained Earnings
- Cash Flow Statement
  - Operating Activities
  - Investing Activities
  - Financing Activities

- Summary
- Discussion Questions.

*The analysis of financial* statements is the basic starting point for understanding the financial strength (or weakness) of any company. Financial statements help provide an overall perspective on a company, enabling both outsiders and insiders to understand the past fiscal health of a company, and provide information on the company's future prospects. Analysis of financial statements also enables companies to benchmark themselves with competitors in their industry—knowledge that aids overall corporate strategy. Since financial statements are the origin of most of the financial analysis used in finance and managerial accounting, it is critical to understand the buildup of financial statements. An entire field of study, financial accounting, deals with the preparation of financial statements; therefore, this chapter will merely provide an overview of the financial statements used in the airline industry in order to provide the foundation for further study.

In the airline industry (as well as many other industries), the preparation of financial statements is the domain of financial and corporate accounting. However, finance departments also provide input into the creation of financial statements, usually at a more operational level. In order to reduce confusion, financial statements are prepared according to generally accepted accounting principles (GAAP).[1] GAAP is a collection of policies and methods that show how financial statements are to be prepared. In the United States, the Financial Accounting Standards Board (FASB) is the current non-governmental body that helps set the accounting standards required by GAAP. Other countries have similar boards that administer GAAP, providing GAAP with a global presence. Based on GAAP, corporate accounting departments will produce the following financial statements that are legally mandated to be made available for public corporations:

- The balance sheet
- The income statement
- The statement of retained earnings
- The cash flow statement.

## BALANCE SHEET

"Well, of course all three financial statements should be studied in conjunction with one another, but if I had to choose just one, it would be the balance sheet because it represents the foundation upon which a business is built."

Matthew Richey[2]

The balance sheet provides an overall financial snapshot of a company, or an airline, at a given point in time. Unlike other financial statements that provide an overview of a company's finances for a period of time, the balance sheet only looks at the company on an individual day. When combined with past balance sheets, an overall financial time series of the company can

---

1       For more information on GAAP visit www.fasab.gov/accepted.html
2       Portfolio Manager, Centaur Capital.

be constructed (Brealey, Myers, and Marcus, 2009). The balance sheet basically tells someone what the company owns and how it is financed. In order to illustrate, Table 6.1 contains the balance sheet for Southwest Airlines on December 31, 2006 through 2008.

The balance sheet is divided into two halves: assets and liabilities plus stockholders' equity. Assets indicate what the firm owns; liabilities indicate what the firm has borrowed, while equity is the investment put into the business. Since corporations are owned by stockholders, stockholders' or shareholders' equity is commonly denoted on the balance sheet. In balance sheets, accounts are categorized according to common characteristics from those with the greatest liquidity (ability to be converted to cash quickly) to the least liquid (Gitman, 2006):

1.  Assets:
    Current assets
        Cash
        Marketable securities
        Accounts receivable
        Inventory
    Fixed (non-current) assets
        Property, plant and equipment
        Land
        Intangible assets
2.  Liabilities:
    Current liabilities
        Accounts payable
        Notes payable
        Current portion of long-term debt
        Unearned revenue
        Taxes payable
        Wages payable
    Long term (Non-current liabilities)
        Long-term debt
3.  Owners' Equity:
    Preferred Stock
    Common Stock
        Additional Paid-In Capital.

Typically from a theoretical standpoint, an airline lists its assets on the left side of the balance sheet and its debts and liabilities on the right. The accounting equation states that assets equal liabilities and shareholders' equity. The accounting equation holds true since the equation is simply stating that whatever the airline owns, it must have been financed either through borrowings (liabilities) or owner's investment equity. As Table 6.1 shows, Southwest Airlines balance sheet "balances" for years 2008, 2007 and 2006, indicating that total assets equals total liabilities and shareholders' equity, with values of $14,308 million $16,772 million and $13,460 million respectively.

Assets = Liabilities + Shareholders' Equity

Assets - Liabilities - Preferred stock = Common stockholders' equity

The left hand side of LAN Chile's years 2007 and 2008 balance sheet, which is given in Table 6.12, provides the airline's assets, while the right hand side gives the liabilities and equities, or it is safe to say the claims against LAN Chile's assets.

## Current Assets

Accounting standards are one in classifying assets into two major categories: current assets and fixed assets. Current assets are assets that are easily convertible into cash (usually within a year). The ease and quickness with which assets are convertible into cash is called liquidity. Therefore, by definition, current assets are highly liquid (Ross, Westerfield, and Jordan, 2008). For Southwest Airlines (and other companies), the major current assets are cash, short-term investments, accounts receivable, inventories, fuel-derivative contracts, and prepaid expenses.

While no definition of cash is needed, the cash balance of an airline is a fine balance between having too much or too little. Too much cash represents opportunities lost (i.e. expansion—new routes/aircraft) while too little cash can put an airline precariously close to not being able to finance daily operations. Therefore, the cash policy of an airline is critical to the strategic success in the industry. Short-term investments are securities that Southwest Airlines plans on holding for a short period of time. Short-term investments act like cash as they are highly liquid, yet enable the company to earn a nominal amount of interest. Typical short-term investments for airlines are auction rate securities. If Southwest decided to hold onto the investments for a period greater than a year, then they would be classified as long-term investments, which would then fall out of the current asset account and into a separate category under assets on the balance sheet. Accounts receivable are amounts not yet collected by the airline, but that are owed to it. However, since there is the possibility that not everyone will pay, there is an accounting adjustment that subtracts an allowance for doubtful accounts, providing a proxy for the amount of receivables that the company will not collect. While the size of the proxy amount is determined by the company, it is usually based on historical receivable trends. Inventories represent parts that are owned by the airline that can be easily sold. Inventories are valued at book value (the historical price paid less any accumulated depreciation). The reason for using book value, as opposed to market value, would be that the value of inventories would be at the discretion of the accountant,[3] which may not properly reflect the airlines real financial situation. In essence, market value may not only lead to greater swings in asset values over time, but could result in over-valuing a company's total tangible assets. Fuel derivative contracts are contained in Southwest's current assets when the contracts are expected to provide a gain in the future. If the contracts turn bad and are expected to provide a loss in the future, this account will shift to a current liability account.[4] Prepaid expenses are expenses for services that have been paid, but not yet rendered. The creation of this account is based on the accounting principle that expenses are recognized when they are incurred, and not when they are paid. They are recorded as a current asset, since they represent a value to the company that will be redeemed in the future. In total, Southwest Airlines held $2,893 million in current assets at December 31, 2008, which was a considerable decrease from the previous year. Therefore, Southwest had more highly

---

3    Discussion of the calculation of book value and accumulated depreciation follows later in this chapter.
4    Fuel hedging strategies are discussed in Chapter 11.

## Table 6.1    Southwest Airlines balance sheet December 31, 2008

Balance sheet

|  | 2008 | 2007 | 2006 |
|---|---|---|---|
| **ASSETS** | | | |
| Current assets: | | | |
| Cash and cash equivalents | 1368 | $2,213 | $1,390 |
| Short-term investments | 435 | 566 | 369 |
| Accounts and other receivables | 209 | 279 | 241 |
| Inventories of parts and supplies, at cost | 203 | 259 | 181 |
| Deferred income taxes | 365 | | |
| Fuel derivative contracts | | 1,069 | 369 |
| Prepaid expenses and other current assets | 313 | 57 | 51 |
| **Total current assets** | $ 2,893 | $ 4,443 | $ 2,601 |
| Property and equipment, at cost: | | | |
| Flight equipment | 13722 | 13,019 | 11,769 |
| Ground property and equipment | 1769 | 1,515 | 1,356 |
| Deposits on flight equipment purchase contracts | 380 | 626 | 734 |
| | 15871 | 15,160 | 13,859 |
| Less allowance for depreciation and amortization | 4831 | 4,286 | 3,765 |
| | $ 11,040 | $ 10,874 | $ 10,094 |
| Other assets | 375 | 1,455 | 765 |
| | $ 14,308 | $ 16,772 | $ 13,460 |
| **LIABILITIES AND STOCKHOLDERS EQUITY** | | | |
| Current liabilities: | | | |
| Accounts payable | 668 | $759 | $643 |
| Accrued liabilities | 1012 | 3,107 | 1,323 |
| Air traffic liability | 963 | 931 | 799 |
| Current maturities of long-term debt | 163 | 41 | 122 |
| **Total current liabilities** | $ 2,806 | $ 4,838 | $ 2,887 |
| Long-term debt less current maturities | 3498 | 2,050 | 1,567 |
| Deferred income taxes | 1904 | 2,535 | 2,104 |
| Deferred gains from sale and leaseback of aircraft | 105 | 106 | 120 |
| Other deferred liabilities | 1042 | 302 | 333 |
| Commitments and contingencies | | | |
| Stockholders equity: | | | |
| Common stock, $1.00 par value: 2,000,000,000 shares authorized; 807,611,634 shares issued in 2007 and 2006 | 808 | 808 | 808 |
| Capital in excess of par value | 1215 | 1207 | 1142 |
| Retained earnings | 4919 | 4788 | 4307 |
| Accumulated other comprehensive income | (984) | 1241 | 582 |
| Treasury stock, at cost: 72,814,104 and 24,302,215 shares in 2007 and 2006, respectively | (1005) | (1103) | (390) |
| **Total stockholders equity** | $ 4,953 | $ 6,941 | $ 6,449 |
| | $ 14,308 | $ 16,772 | $ 13,460 |

*Source*: Southwest Airlines.

liquid assets in 2007 than it did in 2008 however, to more fully understand the reasons behind the decrease in current assets, other parts of the balance sheet and other financial statements need to be analyzed. During the same period, LAN Chiles' current assets increased faster than current liabilities (see Table 6.12).

## Fixed Assets

The opposite of current assets are fixed assets, which are assets that are not highly liquid. Fixed assets also known as property, plant and equipment (PP&E), are usually large items that are difficult to convert into cash quickly and are held for a long time, such as terminal buildings and aircraft. As a consequence of rigidity of these fixed assets, airlines are not always able to fully adjust capacity to meet the falling demand.

The airline industry is highly capital intensive, requiring significant fixed assets to operate. These costs include items such as maintenance facilities and station costs. For airlines, the largest fixed assets are owned aircraft. In the case of Southwest Airlines in Table 6.1, it owns in excess of $13.72 billion of flight equipment. It is critical to note that fixed assets are only items that the company owns. For example, Southwest Airlines total aircraft fleet may be valued in excess of $13 billion; however, aircraft that are leased will not be shown as a fixed asset for the airline.[5] In addition to flight equipment, Southwest Airlines also has fixed assets from ground, property, and equipment, as well as aircraft purchase deposits. Note that fixed assets do not have to be tangible; that is, they may not have a physical existence, but can still be very valuable. In the airline industry, a prime example of intangible fixed assets is landing rights or airport slots. At some airports worldwide, airlines are required to purchase the right to be able to land or takeoff; therefore, the airline must purchase the intangible asset of a landing slot to be able to operate out of the airport. One such airport is London Heathrow; therefore, it is unsurprising that the airport's largest operator, British Airways, carries £205 million worth of landing rights on its balance sheet (British Airways, 2009). In February, 2008, Japan Airlines International (JAL) sold its Haneda Airport Maintenance Centers 1 and 2 (fixed Assets) to the Industrial and Infrastructure Fund Investment Corporation, to concentrate on its core air transport activities and making cost reductions to enhance profitability.

## DEPRECIATION

An important accounting concept to understand concerning fixed assets is depreciation. Depreciation is simply the allocation of the original cost of an asset over the period of its use.

Property, plant and equipment (PP&E) is a significant asset category for most airlines and often represents over half of the total assets of an airline. In income statements the depreciation of these assets is a substantial operating expense. In general, an airline's aircraft depreciation expense is influenced by estimating both the useful life and the perceived fair market value of the aircraft at the end of its estimated useful life. Depreciation is a non-cash accounting item used to show that an asset provides value to the company over an extended period of time (Brealey, Myers, and Allen, 2008). A major reason to purchase an aircraft is to take advantage of depreciation tax benefits from ownership. While a

---

5    The decision of buying or leasing an asset is discussed in Chapter 12.

depreciation expense appears on the income statement, the accumulated depreciation of the asset is deducted on the balance sheet to help provide an accurate representation of an asset's value. Before the Airline Deregulation Act of 1987, most major airlines depreciated the value of their aircraft around 20 years with an estimated residual value of 5% of the original cost of the aircraft.[6] Many Asian countries have adopted a more liberal depreciation policy. For example, Qantas CEO is using 10-year depreciation policy. To understand the principle of depreciation, consider a brand new automobile retailing for $40,000; however, two years later the same automobile re-sells for $30,000.[7] This difference in price can be thought of as the depreciation of the asset, reflecting the fact that a two-year old car is not worth the same as a brand new car. Since the true depreciation of an asset is not known until the asset is sold, accounting principles require most fixed assets to have an annual depreciation expense. The accumulated depreciation of the asset (the total depreciation of the asset from day one) minus the asset's original value is called book value, and the book value of the asset is what appears on the balance sheet. As the asset increases in age, the book value of the asset will decrease owing to an increase in accumulated depreciation.

$$\text{Book Value} = \text{Acquisition Cost} - \text{Accumulated Depreciation}$$

There are different methods for calculating depreciation expense. The depreciation methods and estimates used to determine the amount of this expense can vary widely from one airline to another airline. Once the useful life of the aircraft is determined, the annual depreciation can be calculated from one of the following methods:

- Straight-Line Depreciation
- Double-Declining-Balance Method
- Modified Accelerated Cost Recovery System (MACRS)
- Sum-of-Years Digits.

*Straight-line depreciation*   The simplest method for calculating depreciation is straight-line depreciation. The straight line method means that the annual depreciation expense will be the same for each full year of use. As mentioned above, before 2000, most major airlines' depreciable lives for a majority of their aircraft were around 20 years with an estimated residual value of generally around 5% of the cost of the asset.[8] The formula for straight-line depreciation is:

$$\text{Depreciation} = \frac{\text{Acquisition Cost - Residual Value}}{\text{Useful Life}}$$

where:
- the acquisition cost is the purchase price of the asset
- the useful life is the company's estimate on the expected life of the asset
- the residual (salvage) value is the estimated value of the asset at the end of its useful life.[9]

---

6    Overview of Airline Industry Depreciation Policies, the Center for Financial Research and Analysis, 1999.

7    Depreciation is a process of allocation not valuation of the asset.

8    The Center for Financial Research and Analysis, Inc. (CFRA), December 1999.

9    If the market for used aircraft at the time of sale is strong, one might assume that the residual value might be higher than expected.

Since airlines are highly capital intensive, depreciation can be a significant expense for an airline.[10] As an example, the 2009 list price for a brand new B787-8 is $167 million (Boeing, 2009). Assume that the useful life for the 787-8 is 20 years and that at the end of 20 years the aircraft can be sold for $5 million. From the following formula, the Boeing 787-8 will incur an annual depreciation expense of $8.1MM annually.

$$\text{Depreciation} = \frac{\text{Acquisition Cost - Residual Value}}{\text{Useful Life}}$$

$$\text{Depreciation} = \frac{\$167 - \$5}{20\,years} = \$8.1 \text{ million/year}$$

Based on the calculated depreciation expense of the 787-8, Table 6.2 calculates the accumulated depreciation and book value of the aircraft over time. At 2022, the balance will hold an asset value of $69.8 million for the 787-8. This will either be displayed on the balance sheet as a single line item as the book value of PP&E, or two separate line items: historical cost less accumulated depreciation.

**Table 6.2     Depreciation and book value of a Boeing 787-8 with a useful life of 20 years**

| Year | Depreciation expense | Accumulated depreciation | Book value |
|------|----------------------|--------------------------|------------|
| 2010 |                      |                          | $167,000,000 |
| 2011 | $8,100,000           | $8,100,000               | $158,900,000 |
| 2012 | $8,100,000           | $16,200,000              | $150,800,000 |
| 2013 | $8,100,000           | $24,300,000              | $142,700,000 |
| 2014 | $8,100,000           | $32,400,000              | $134,600,000 |
| 2015 | $8,100,000           | $40,500,000              | $126,500,000 |
| 2016 | $8,100,000           | $48,600,000              | $118,400,000 |
| 2017 | $8,100,000           | $56,700,000              | $110,300,000 |
| 2018 | $8,100,000           | $64,800,000              | $102,200,000 |
| 2019 | $8,100,000           | $72,900,000              | $94,100,000 |
| 2020 | $8,100,000           | $81,000,000              | $86,000,000 |
| 2021 | $8,100,000           | $89,100,000              | $77,900,000 |
| 2022 | $8,100,000           | $97,200,000              | $69,800,000 |
| 2023 | $8,100,000           | $105,300,000             | $61,700,000 |
| 2024 | $8,100,000           | $113,400,000             | $53,600,000 |
| 2025 | $8,100,000           | $121,500,000             | $45,500,000 |
| 2026 | $8,100,000           | $129,600,000             | $37,400,000 |

---

10    Depreciation expense is contained on the income statement.

**Table 6.2    Concluded**

| Year | Depreciation expense | Accumulated depreciation | Book value |
|------|---------------------|-------------------------|------------|
| 2027 | $8,100,000 | $137,700,000 | $29,300,000 |
| 2028 | $8,100,000 | $145,800,000 | $21,200,000 |
| 2029 | $8,100,000 | $153,900,000 | $13,100,000 |
| 2030 | $8,100,000 | $162,000,000 | $5,000,000 |

*Double-declining-balance method*    Another method for calculating depreciation is the double-declining-balance method. This method records depreciation at double the straight line depreciation rate (Keown, Martin, Petty, and Scott, 2005). The first step in calculating the double-declining-balance depreciation is to calculate the annual straight-line depreciation as a percentage. The simple formula is:

$$\text{Straight Line Depreciation Rate} = \frac{100\%}{\text{Useful Life}}$$

Based on the straight line depreciation rate, double-declining-balance depreciation is calculated as:

$$\text{Depreciation} = \text{Book Value} \times (\text{Straight Line Depreciation Rate} \times 2)$$

It is critical to note that the formula above is based on the asset's book value which changes each year when the double-declining method is used. For example, using the same 787-8 example from above, the depreciation in the first year will be:

$$\text{Straight Line Depreciation Rate} = \frac{100\%}{20} = 5\%$$

$$\text{Depreciation (Year 1)} = \$167 \text{ million} \times (5\% \times 2) = \$16.7 \text{ million}$$

Comparatively, the depreciation amount for the 787-8 in the first year is more than double the depreciation expense calculated using straight line depreciation, hence the method's title.[11] Using the double-declining-balance depreciation method for year two, the depreciation expense for the 787-8 would be $15.03 million.

$$\text{Depreciation (Year 2)} = (\$167 \text{ million} - \$16.7 \text{ million}) \times (5\% \times 2)$$

$$\text{Depreciation (Year 2)} = \$150.3 \text{ million} \times 10\% = \$15.03 \text{ million}$$

Unlike the straight-line depreciation method where the depreciation expense is uniform throughout the asset's useful life, the depreciation expense under the double-declining-balance method varies every year, with the depreciation expense declining every year

---

11    The double-declining-balance depreciation amount is more than double because the method ignores the residual value.

throughout the asset's useful life. This is why double-declining-balance depreciation is categorized as an accelerated depreciation method, since the company will incur greater depreciation at the start of the asset's useful life than at the end. The depreciation schedule using the double-declining-balance method for the 787 is shown in Table 6.3.

**Table 6.3    Double-declining balance method**

| Year | Depreciation expense | Accumulated depreciation | Book value |
|---|---|---|---|
| 2008 | | | $167,000,000 |
| 2009 | $16,700,000 | $16,700,000 | $150,300,000 |
| 2010 | $15,030,000 | $31,730,000 | $135,270,000 |
| 2011 | $13,527,000 | $45,257,000 | $121,743,000 |
| 2012 | $12,174,300 | $57,431,300 | $109,568,700 |
| 2013 | $10,956,870 | $68,388,170 | $98,611,830 |
| 2014 | $9,861,183 | $78,249,353 | $88,750,647 |
| 2015 | $8,875,065 | $87,124,418 | $79,875,582 |
| 2016 | $7,987,558 | $95,111,976 | $71,888,024 |
| 2017 | $7,188,802 | $102,300,778 | $64,699,222 |
| 2018 | $6,469,922 | $108,770,701 | $58,229,299 |
| 2019 | $5,822,930 | $114,593,630 | $52,406,370 |
| 2020 | $5,240,637 | $119,834,267 | $47,165,733 |
| 2021 | $4,716,573 | $124,550,841 | $42,449,159 |
| 2022 | $4,244,916 | $128,795,757 | $38,204,243 |
| 2023 | $3,820,424 | $132,616,181 | $34,383,819 |
| 2024 | $3,438,382 | $136,054,563 | $30,945,437 |
| 2025 | $3,094,544 | $139,149,107 | $27,850,893 |
| 2026 | $2,785,089 | $141,934,196 | $25,065,804 |
| 2027 | $2,506,580 | $144,440,776 | $22,559,224 |
| 2028 | $17,559,224 | $162,000,000 | $5,000,000 |

One problem with the double-declining balance method is that it can result in a large depreciation expense in the last year of the asset's estimated useful life. This expense occurs in order to reduce the book value of the asset to its residual value. In the example above, in order to align the book value of the 787 to its residual value the airline must record depreciation expense of over $17.5 million in year 20. To avoid such a large depreciation expense, the airline or company could estimate a higher residual value when it first acquires the asset.

Companies are free to choose any depreciation method for internal and external use, as long as they document their methodology and are consistent throughout. The disclosure of the depreciation methodology is usually contained in the notes accompanying the financial statements. Since companies are free to choose their depreciation methodology and useful life, the methods for depreciation calculation can vary considerably in the airline industry. For example, Southwest Airlines uses the straight-line method to calculate depreciation for all their assets, with aircraft having an estimated useful life ranging from 23 to 25 years and a residual value at the end of the useful life of 15% of the asset's original acquisition cost (Southwest Airlines, 2009, July 2009). As a comparison, Emirates Airlines also uses straight-line depreciation; however, passenger aircraft receive a useful life of only 15 years with a residual value of 10% of the asset's original acquisition cost (Emirates Group, 2008, March 31). This difference in depreciation methodology is largely a result of corporate strategy: that is, Emirates has a much more ambitious fleet plan where they will retire aircraft at a much younger age than Southwest Airlines. However, this will result in Emirates incurring greater annual depreciation expenses. In 1998, Continental Airlines extended the depreciable lives of certain type of aircraft from 25 to 30 years and increased the estimated residual values of those aircraft from 10% to 15%.[12] During same period America West increased the average depreciable life of its 737-200 aircraft by four years while keeping the residual value constant.

*Modified Accelerated Cost Recovery System (MACRS)*   Differences in the calculation of depreciation can lead to companies playing games in how they document depreciation. In the United States, the Internal Revenue Service (IRS) does not take kindly to such games, so for tax purposes all companies must adhere to a standardized depreciation scheme called the Modified Accelerated Cost Recovery System (MACRS). MACRS is an accelerated depreciation schedule based on various factors of the asset that are determined by the IRS. Because of MACRS, most companies prepare two sets of financial statements, one for internal/external use with the depreciation method of their choice, and another for tax purposes using MACRS. It is important to note that MACRS does not take into account the salvage value of the asset. In addition, the IRS classifies the depreciation period and depreciation rates for each asset. Based on the asset's classification, MACRs will establish a recovery period for the asset. From this recovery period, the MACRS table will assign the depreciation rate as a percentage of historical cost. Table 6.4 overleaf provides a sample MACRS table for assets with recovery periods ranging from three to ten years.

*Sum-of-years digits*   Many assets, such as automobiles and computers, lose a substantial portion of their value early in their lifetime. Assume an asset depreciates from price V to salvage value S in N years. Under this method depreciation is computed by multiplying book value (V) by the remaining periods of useful life at the start of the period divided by the sum of the digits in the original useful life. For an asset with a five-year useful life, N=5, depreciation in the first year would be:

$$\frac{5}{5+4+3+2+1} = \frac{5}{15} = 33.3\%$$

of depreciable value times (V-S).

---

12   The Center for Financial Research and Analysis, Inc. (CFRA), December 1999.

**Table 6.4    Depreciation rates under different recovery periods**

MACRS Recovery Table

| Year | 3 Year | 5 Year | 7 Year | 10 Year |
|------|--------|--------|--------|---------|
| 1 | 33.33% | 20.00% | 14.29% | 10.00% |
| 2 | 44.45% | 32.00% | 24.49% | 18.00% |
| 3 | 14.81% | 19.20% | 17.49% | 14.40% |
| 4 | 7.41% | 11.52% | 12.49% | 11.52% |
| 5 | | 11.52% | 8.93% | 9.22% |
| 6 | | 5.76% | 8.92% | 7.37% |
| 7 | | | 8.93% | 6.55% |
| 8 | | | 4.46% | 6.55% |
| 9 | | | | 6.56% |
| 10 | | | | 6.55% |
| 11 | | | | 3.28% |

*Source*: Compiled by the Authors using data provided by the Internal Revenue Service.

$$DEP = \text{Depreciation}$$

$$DEP\,\text{Year }1 = \frac{N}{\sum\limits_{i=1}^{N} Year_i}(V - S)$$

$$DEP\,\text{Year }2 = \frac{N-1}{\sum\limits_{i=1}^{N} Year_i}(V - S)$$

$$DEP\,\text{Year N-1} = \frac{(N-(N-2))}{\sum\limits_{i=1}^{N} Year_i}(V - S) = \frac{2}{\sum\limits_{i=1}^{N} Year_i}(V - S)$$

$$DEP\,\text{ Year N} = \frac{(N-(N-1))}{\sum\limits_{i=1}^{N} Year_i}(V - S) = \frac{1}{\sum\limits_{i=1}^{N} Year_i}(V - S)$$

where:
V       = Acquisition cost
S       = Salvage value
N       = Useful life of the asset

Total depreciation  $= \sum\limits_{i=1}^{N}(DEP_1 + DEP_2 + \cdots + DEP_n)$

## Comparison of Depreciation Methods

As depreciation is an expense item on the income statement, it can impact the stated profitability of a company. Since companies are free to choose their depreciation methodology, which impacts the depreciation expense, it is important to understand the differences in methodologies. To provide an accurate comparison of the different methods, we use the 787-8 example.

Assume that an airline purchases and receives a new 787-8 for $167 million at the beginning of a year and that the aircraft is expected to have a useful life of 10 years with a

**Table 6.5      Comparison of depreciation methods**

| Year | Straight-line | Double-declining balance | Sum-of-years digits | MACRS |
|------|--------------|-------------------------|---------------------|-------|
| 1 | $14,700,000 | $33,400,000 | $26,727,273 | $16,700,000 |
| 2 | $14,700,000 | $26,720,000 | $24,054,545 | $30,060,000 |
| 3 | $14,700,000 | $21,376,000 | $21,381,818 | $24,048,000 |
| 4 | $14,700,000 | $17,100,800 | $18,709,091 | $19,238,400 |
| 5 | $14,700,000 | $13,680,640 | $16,036,364 | $15,397,400 |
| 6 | $14,700,000 | $10,944,512 | $13,363,636 | $12,307,900 |
| 7 | $14,700,000 | $8,755,610 | $10,690,909 | $10,938,500 |
| 8 | $14,700,000 | $7,004,488 | $8,018,182 | $10,938,500 |
| 9 | $14,700,000 | $5,603,590 | $5,345,455 | $10,938,500 |
| 10 | $14,700,000 | $2,414,361 | $2,672,727 | $10,938,500 |
| 11 | | | | $5,494,300 |
| **Total** | **$147,000,000** | **$147,000,000** | **$147,000,000** | **$167,000,000** |

salvage value at that time of $20 million. Table 6.5 provides the depreciation expense over the useful life under the various depreciation methods.

From the data contained in Table 6.5, the double declining method produces the largest amount of depreciation within the first year. Note that the percentages listed for MACRS are the maximum allowed; however, owing to various tax regulations, an asset may be capped at a certain dollar amount, regardless of what the calculated amount from the percentage might be. Note also that using the MACRS method, depreciation is straight-line on the remaining value of the asset starting at year seven and continuing for four and a half years.

## Current Liabilities

As opposed to current assets, current liabilities are short-term financial obligations that will be satisfied within one year (Ogden, Jen, and O'Connor, 2003). Typical current liabilities include:

- Accounts payable
- Notes payable
- Accrued expenses or liabilities
- Unearned revenue
- Current maturities of long-term debt.

Accounts payable represents amounts owed for goods and services the company has bought. In essence, accounts payable are unpaid bills. They represent a complete representation of current obligations that arose from the purchase of goods and services that are due within a year. Accrued liabilities are amounts owed to parties who have provided services but have not yet been paid. Accrued liabilities are usually related to payroll and occur as a result of there being a cross-over between the date of the balance sheet and when employees are actually paid. Finally, current maturities of long-term debt represent the payments of long-term debt that fall due within one year of the date of the balance sheet. As seen in the balance sheet in Table 6.1, of Southwest Airlines with $3,661 million of long-term debt outstanding, only $163 million will be due within a year. For Southwest Airlines, its current liabilities totaled $2,806 million in 2008, accounting for nearly half of its total liabilities, up from approximately 45% of total liabilities in 2007. In 2010, Southwest Airlines enjoyed the highest capitalization rate among U.S. commercial airlines with $8.43 Billion assets.

## Long-term Debt

Long-term debt represents the total of the liabilities that are due after a one-year period (Emery et al 2007). Common to airlines, long-term debt are various financial instruments issued by the airlines (bonds/notes, debentures) that come due at some later point, less the maturities due within a year, which are current liabilities. While the total value of long-term debt can be useful, the notes to the financial statements usual provide a detailed breakdown of the long-term debt. To fully understand the company's debt structure, Table 6.6 displays the detailed breakdown of Southwest Airlines long-term debt as of December 31, 2008. As Table 6.6 shows, Southwest Airlines had a variety of financial instruments, mostly notes, which are due at various time periods. The value of the notes is the face value of the debt instrument, with the interest rate representing the amount of interest to be collected on the note. The interest rate represents the cost of the debt. Once the face value of the debt is due, it will be transferred to the current liability portion of the balance sheet.

**Table 6.6      Current liabilities and long term debts of selected airlines, 2008**

|                        | Fixed assets | Long-term debt | Current liabilities | Current assets |
|------------------------|--------------|----------------|---------------------|----------------|
| SouthWest Airlines     | 15,871       | 3,498          | 2,806               | 2,893          |
| American Airlines      | 19,240       | 9,001          | 9,374               | 5,935          |
| Delta Airlines         | 36,111       | 15,411         | 11,022              | 8,904          |
| United Airlines        | 14,600       | 8,286          | 7,281               | 4,861          |
| Continental Airlines   | 8,339        | 5,371          | 4,474               | 4,347          |
| U.S. Airways           | 4,796        | 3,634          | 3,044               | 2,418          |
| LAN Airlines           | 3,600        | 1,833          | 1,379               | 1,351          |
| Copa Airlines          | 1,432        | 800            | 502                 | 522            |
| TAM                    | 4,642        | 3,111          | 1,809               | 1,567          |
| GOL                    | 2,390        | 1,041          | 1,102               | 709            |

*Source*: Compiled by the authors.

## Stockholders' Equity

As mentioned previously, stockholders' equity represents the value invested by the owners in the company. Stockholders' equity is divided into two major components: contributed capital and retained earnings.

Total Stockholders' Equity = Contributed Capital + Retained Earnings

For Southwest Airlines, contributed capital is comprised of common stock and capital in excess of par value. Common stock is represented on the balance sheet at par value, an arbitrary value set by the company that is usually set at a very low value. For Southwest Airlines, par value is set at $1.00. Par value is multiplied by the total number of common stock shares issued by the company to determine the par value of the common stock. These shares can be outstanding through multiple means, including regularly traded shares that are held on the New York Stock Exchange (NYSE). The use of par value provides the legal basis for the value of common stock and is unrelated to the actual price of the stock listed on the stock market. Stock market value is not displayed on the balance sheet as it does not represent the money received by the airline for issuing the stock and because the value of the stock changes daily and it would therefore not provide an accurate measure of the value received for the issuance of equity. To account for the difference between par value and what the airline actually receives when they issue the stock, the balance sheet contains the capital in excess of par value account. For example, if Southwest Airlines issued 1,000 new shares of common stock and received $50 per share, the transaction would increase the common stock account by $1000 (1,000 new stock multiplied by par value ($1)) and increase the capital in excess of par value account by $49,000.[13]

The other major component contained under stockholders' equity is retained earnings. Retained earnings represent the net income generated by the company that is being re-invested into the company. The value of retained earnings is directly linked to the income statement, as it is essentially net income less any dividends paid out to stockholders (Ross et al 2008). Retained earnings are sometimes the best way to fund future activities; however, in the airline industry, the capital requirements are so immense that airlines must fund capital purchases with the help of other means (i.e. long-term debt).

## Income Statement

The second major financial statement, the income statement, provides a financial summary of a company's operating results during a specified time period (Keown et al 2005). The specified time period varies depending on the report, which is in contrast to the balance sheet, which merely looks at the company at a glimpse in time. The income statement is also commonly referred to as the profit and loss statement (P&L), statement of incomes and losses, or the report of earnings. Table 6.7 displays the income statement for Southwest Airlines on an annual basis for multiple time periods. Table 6.7 summarizes Southwest Airlines financial performance for the year 2008 (January 1 to December 31), as well as 2007 and 2006. Income statements may also be prepared that summarize the company's performance for a quarter or month. Income statements provide a record of revenue and

---

13    ($50 per share – $1 par value) * 1,000 shares = $49,000.

expenses and show the income an airline earns in a given accounting period, usually in one year.

The general purpose of the income statement is to determine the company's net income for the time period. Income is defined as:

$$Income = Revenue - Expenses$$

Based on the above formula, the income statement displays the company's revenue, subtracts the expenses, and finally accounts for interest and taxes. While every income statement will vary slightly, Southwest's income statement, shown in Table 6.7 opposite, is typical of many companies.

The first section in any income statement will detail the company's revenue generated during the operating period. Operating income is an airline's earnings from its core operations after it has deducted its cost of providing services and its general operating expenses. Operating income does not include interest expenses or income generated outside the normal activities of the airline, such as income on sales of aircraft or gains of fuel hedging contracts.[14]

Operating income is calculated as follows:

$$Operating\ Income = Gross\ revenue - Operating\ Expenses - Depreciation\ Expense$$

Southwest Airlines divides its operating revenue into three categories: passenger, freight, and other. Dividing operating revenue into categories is typical of companies operating in different sectors, but it is up to the discretion of the company. From Table 6.7, Southwest Airlines generated approximately $11 billion in revenue in 2008, which was a fairly substantial increase over the $9.9 billion generated in 2007.

Depending on the type of company, the income statement may contain the line item cost of goods sold directly after operating revenue. Cost of goods sold is the cost of the units of inventory sold during the period. For a retail company, cost of goods sold would be the cost of the product to the company. Gross profit is found by subtracting the cost of goods sold from the operating revenue during the period. However, in the airline industry, an aircraft seat is not inventoried and therefore cost of goods sold is not contained in the income statement. This is typical for most service-based companies.

Following operating revenues are operating expenses, which consist of the expenses to operate the company. In the airline industry the largest costs are fuel and WSB (wages, salaries, and benefits). The wages, salaries and benefits category contain the full cost for all the employees of the company, including pension expenses and bonuses. For Southwest Airlines, salaries and benefits represent approximately 32% of the company's total operating expenses. The second major category of operating expenses in the airline industry is fuel and oil. With the price of fuel increasing, this category is becoming a greater proportion of operating expenses for airlines. Other airline specific operating expenses are maintenance materials and repairs, which do not include maintenance salaries, but do include the materials used to maintain and repair the aircraft. Landing fees, the cost of flying into an airport, also receive their own line item on the Southwest Airlines income statement.

---

14    Typically most gains/losses on hedging contracts are stated outside operating income; however, depending on the accounting system being used, gain/losses could be found in the operating expense section. However, these are typically defined as special items and are excluded.

## Table 6.7     Southwest Airlines income statement at December 31, 2008

| | (U.S. $ Millions) | | | |
| | 2008 | 2007 | 2006 | 2005 |
|---|---|---|---|---|
| **OPERATING REVENUES:** | | | | |
| Passenger | 10549 | $9,457 | $8,750 | $7,279 |
| Freight | 145 | 130 | 134 | 133 |
| Other | 329 | 274 | 202 | 172 |
| **Total operating revenues** | **$11,023** | **$9,861** | **$9,086** | **$7,584** |
| **OPERATING EXPENSES:** | | | | |
| Salaries, wages, and benefits | 3340 | 3,213 | 3,052 | 2,782 |
| Fuel and oil | 3713 | 2,536 | 2,138 | 1,341 |
| Maintenance materials and repairs | 721 | 616 | 468 | 446 |
| Aircraft rentals | 154 | 156 | 158 | 163 |
| Landing fees and other rentals | 662 | 560 | 495 | 454 |
| Depreciation and amortization | 599 | 555 | 515 | 469 |
| Other operating expenses | 1385 | 1,434 | 1,326 | 1,204 |
| **Total operating expenses** | **$10,574** | **$9,070** | **$8,152** | **$6,859** |
| **OPERATING INCOME** | 449 | 791 | $934 | 725 |
| **OTHER EXPENSES (INCOME):** | | | | |
| Interest expense | 130 | 119 | 128 | 122 |
| Capitalized interest | -25 | -50 | -51 | -39 |
| Interest income | -26 | -44 | -84 | -47 |
| Other (gains) losses, net | 92 | -292 | 151 | -90 |
| **Total other expenses (income)** | **171** | **-267** | **144** | **-54** |
| **INCOME BEFORE INCOME TAXES** | 278 | 1,058 | 790 | 779 |
| **PROVISION FOR INCOME TAXES** | 100 | 413 | 291 | 295 |
| **NET INCOME** | **$178** | **$645** | **$499** | **$484** |
| **NET INCOME PER SHARE, BASIC** | 0.25 | $0.85 | $0.63 | $0.61 |
| **NET INCOME PER SHARE, DILUTED** | 0.24 | $0.84 | $0.61 | $0.60 |

*Source*: Southwest Airlines Annual Reports.

As discussed previously, depreciation is the allocation of the original cost of an asset over the period of its use. Using various depreciation methods (straight line, double-declining-balance, etc.), every owned asset has a depreciation expense which is summarized under the depreciation and amortization line item of the income statement. For Southwest Airlines, the bulk of depreciation is probably from owned aircraft. However, assets such as aircraft do not have to be owned, but may also be leased. Lease payments are also an expense and are contained under the aircraft rentals line item; however, the values of leased aircraft do not appear on the balance sheet unlike owned aircraft. The difference by which owned versus leased assets are represented on the financial statements is an important factor to consider in the decision-making process of whether to lease or buy, and an entire chapter is devoted to this issue later in the textbook.

After operating expenses have been subtracted, the operating income is determined. As the title implies, operating income is the profit generated solely from the operations of the company (Gitman, 2009). For Southwest Airlines in 2008, its operating income was $449 million U.S.D. The last remaining steps in calculating the net income for the company are to account for interest revenue and expenses and any taxes, if applicable.

One important line item to note contained under other expenses in Southwest Airlines annual income statement is the net other gains (losses). Referring back to depreciation and an asset's book value, an accounting adjustment may have to be made when a capital asset is sold. Assume an aircraft purchased 10 years ago has a current book of $40 million. If this aircraft is sold for $60 million, the airline has received an amount greater than the book value of the asset, and therefore needs to record a gain on their income statement. In this instance, the net other gains account would increase by $20 million. If the aircraft were sold for $20 million, a $20 million loss would have to be recorded. Finally, if the asset was sold for exactly book value, no accounting adjustment would be required. When selling an asset, an understanding of the asset's book value is critical as it can have an impact on the company's bottom line, net income. However, since such events are not considered routine, they are commonly denoted as special items.

Once all adjustments, interest revenue/expense, and taxes are taken into consideration, the net income of the company for the period can finally be computed. For Southwest Airlines in 2008, it recorded a net income, or profit, of $178 million. This is a decline from the previous year, mainly owing to the fuel costs and economic recession. Something that most income statements display, especially for publicly traded corporations, is the net income on a per share basis. Net income per share is calculated by dividing the total net income generated by the company for the period by the total number of shares outstanding at the statement date.

$$\text{Net Income per Share} = \frac{\text{Total Net Income}}{\text{Number of Shares Outstanding}}$$

Using information from the income statement (total net income) and the balance sheet (total number of shares outstanding), Southwest Airlines 2008 net income per share is calculated as follows:

$$\text{Net Income per Share} = \frac{\$178 \text{ million}}{808 \text{ million shares outstanding}}$$

EPS= $0.22

Net income per share represents the wealth generated for stockholders' and is the key measurement by which the financial community assesses the company. Net income per share helps provide a more even comparison between companies and better enables evaluation of the company to the industry. Therefore, arguably, net income per share has a greater impact on the company's stock price than the simple net income of the company.

To summarize this section, we provide another example. Table 6.8 provides the 2006, 2007, and 2008 income statement for LAN Chile. Passenger, cargo and other revenues are shown at the top of each statement, after which various operating expenses, including interest and taxes, are subtracted to obtain net income. The left hand side of LAN Chile's years 2007 and 2008 balance sheet, which is given in Table 6.9, provides the airlines' assets, while the right hand side gives the liabilities and equities, or it is safe to say, the claims against LAN Chile's assets. During the same period, LAN Chiles' current asset's increased faster than current liabilities (see Table 6.9).

**Table 6.8    LAN Airlines S.A. and subsidiaries, income statement December 31, 2008**

| | (US $ Millions) | | |
|---|---|---|---|
| | 2008 | 2007 | 2006 |
| **REVENUES:** | | | |
| Passenger | 2859 | $2,197 | $1,813 |
| Cargo | 1527 | 1,154 | 1,073 |
| Other | 148 | 173 | 147 |
| **Total operating revenues** | **$4,534** | **$3,524** | **$3,033** |
| **EXPENSES:** | | | |
| Salaries, wages, and benefits | 608 | 489 | 442 |
| Fuel and oil | 1424 | 930 | 763 |
| Commissions to Agents | 481 | 402 | 404 |
| Depreciation and amortization | 183 | 154 | 123 |
| Passenger Services | 85 | 72 | 56 |
| Aircraft Rentals | 151 | 159 | 158 |
| Aircraft Maintenance | 155 | 159 | 117 |
| Other Rentals and Landing Fees | 451 | 366 | 337 |
| Other Operating Expenses | 458 | 379 | 330 |
| **Total operating expenses** | **$3,996** | **$3,110** | **$2,730** |
| **OPERATING INCOME** | **$536** | **$413** | **$302** |
| **OTHER EXPENSES (INCOME):** | | | |
| Interest income | 16 | 18 | 7 |
| Interest Expense | -82 | -76 | -60 |
| Other (gains) losses, net | -68 | 12 | 37 |
| **Total other expenses (income)** | **-134** | **-46** | **-16** |
| **Income before minority Interest** | 401 | 367 | 286 |
| **Minority Interest** | -1.118 | 0.289 | 1 |
| Income Before Income Taxes | 400 | 368 | 288 |
| Income Taxes | -64 | 659 | 46 |
| **NET INCOME** | **$334** | **$308** | **$241** |

*Source*: Annual reports.

## Table 6.9      LAN Airlines S.A. Balance sheet December 31, 2008

|  | (US $ Millions) | |
|---|---|---|
|  | 2008 | 2007 |
| **ASSETS** | | |
| Current assets: | | |
| Cash and cash equivalents | 15 | $11 |
| Time Deposits | 256 | 308 |
| Marketable Securities | 138 | 148 |
| Trade accounts Receivable and Other | 438 | 468 |
| Notes and accounts receivable from related Companies | 1.117 | 0.226 |
| Inventories | 50 | 54 |
| Prepaid and recoverable taxes | 72 | 68 |
| Prepaid Expenses | 13 | 13 |
| Deferred income Tax Assets | 6545 | 4,624 |
| Other Current Assets | 358 | 13 |
| **Total current assets** | $    1,351 | $    1,089 |
| Property and equipment, at cost | 3093 | 2351 |
| Other assets | 460 | 460 |
|  | $    4,904 | $    3,901 |
| **LIABILITIES AND STOCKHOLDERS EQUITY** | | |
| Current liabilities: | | |
| Current Portion of Long term Loans | 151 | $102 |
| Current Portion of Long term Leasing Obligations | 63 | 62 |
| Securitization Obligations | 6.75 | 12.82 |
| Dividend Payable | 105 | 120 |
| Accounts Payable | 361 | 322 |
| Notes and accounts payable from related Companies | 303 | 357 |
| Air Traffic Liability and other unearned Income | 329 | 325 |
| Other Current Liabilities | 360 | 176 |
| **Total current liabilities** | $    1,379 | $    1,122 |
| **Long-Term Liabilities** | | |
| Loans from Financial Instituions | 1654 | 1,228 |
| Securitization Obligations | - | 6.75 |
| Other Creditors | 247 | 52 |
| Provisions | 92 | 94 |
| Obligations under Capital Lease | 179 | 233 |
| Deferred income Tax Liabilities | 228 | 170 |
| **Total Long Term Liabilities** | $    2,402 | $    1,785 |
| **Minority Interest** | 5721 | 5189 |
| **Share Holders Equity** | | |
| Common Stock (338,790,909 shares) | 453 | 453 |
| Reserves | 1.740 | -0.052 |
| Retained Earnings | 662 | 534 |
| **Total stockholders equity** | $    1,118 | $    988 |
| **Total Liabilities and stockholders equity** | $    4,904 | $    3,901 |

Source: LAN Airlines S.A

## COMMON-SIZE INCOME STATEMENT

A modified form of the income statement that is useful for analysis is the common-size income statement. This is a useful way of standardizing the income statement by expressing each item as a percentage of total sales. Hence, a common-size income statement shows every line item as a percentage of total revenue. By doing so, comparisons between various items can quickly be made to better understand the financial workings of the company. Table 6.10 provides a reconstructed common-size income statement for Southwest Airlines on December 31, 2008.

**Table 6.10      Common-size income statement. Southwest Airlines, December 31, 2008 (U.S.$ millions)**

| | | |
|---|---:|---:|
| **OPERATING REVENUES:** | | |
| Total operating revenues | $11,023 | 100.00% |
| Passenger | 10,549 | 95.70% |
| Freight | 145 | 1.32% |
| Other | 329 | 2.98% |
| **OPERATING EXPENSES:** | | |
| Salaries, wages, and benefits | 3,340 | 30.30% |
| Fuel and oil | 3,713 | 33.68% |
| Maintenance materials and repairs | 721 | 6.54% |
| Aircraft rentals | 154 | 1.40% |
| Landing fees and other rentals | 662 | 6.01% |
| Depreciation and amortization | 599 | 5.43% |
| Other operating expenses | 1,385 | 12.56% |
| Total operating expenses | 10,574 | 95.93% |
| | | |
| **OPERATING INCOME** | 449 | 4.07% |
| **OTHER EXPENSES (INCOME):** | | |
| Interest expense | 130 | 1.18% |
| Capitalized interest | (25) | -0.23% |
| Interest income | (26) | -0.24% |
| Other (gains) losses, net | 92 | 0.83% |
| | | |
| Total other expenses (income) | 171 | 1.55% |
| | | |
| **INCOME BEFORE INCOME TAXES** | 278 | 2.52% |
| **PROVISION FOR INCOME TAXES** | 100 | 0.91% |
| | | |
| **NET INCOME** | **$178** | **1.61%** |

*Source*: Southwest Airlines 10-k Filings, 2009.

The common-size income statement contained in Table 6.10 actually contains two percentage breakdowns: the second column is the percentage of the value to total operating revenue and the third column provides a percentage of sub-total for total operating revenue to total operating expenses, and total other expenses (income). The first area to look at when analyzing a common-size income statement is the bottom. From the common-size income statement, Southwest Airlines net income in 2008 represents 1.6% of total revenue. This ratio, also called the profit margin, is essential to look at when analyzing a company.[15] This implies that for every $100 of revenue generated, Southwest Airlines generates $1.60 in total profit. While the profit margin helps display an overall picture of the company, the operating profit margin is potentially more useful since it solely analyzes the company's operations and excludes the costs associated with financial structuring. The common-size income statement of Southwest Airlines shows an operating profit margin of 4.1% for 2008.

The common-size income statement also aids in comparing various revenues and costs of a company. For example, passenger revenue makes up 95.7% of Southwest Airlines total revenue,[16] which is unsurprising considering the airline's business model focuses on passenger travel; however, for conglomerate companies operating in multiple industries, a breakdown of revenue is extremely useful. The common-size income statement also quickly identifies that more than half of Southwest Airlines revenue is consumed by two cost categories: salaries, wages and benefits and fuel & oil. While a common-size financial statement does not provide any additional information, it enables analysis of the financial statement to be performed more quickly and easily.

## THE STATEMENT OF RETAINED EARNINGS

The third major financial statement presented by a company is the statement of stockholders' equity, which explains changes in stockholders' equity during the period. As mentioned previously, stockholders' equity is made up of contributed capital and retained earnings. While the statement of stockholders' equity displays all changes in stockholders' equity, a portion of that statement, the statement of retained earnings, deals with just one part of stockholders' equity. For our purposes, the statement of retained earnings provides the vital link between the income statement and the balance sheet. Table 6.11 provides a reconstructed statement of retained earnings for Southwest Airlines.

The statement of retained earnings starts off with the starting balance of the retained earnings account from the prior period. Referring back to Table 6.1 and Southwest Airlines balance sheet, notice that the retained earnings value of $4,788 million as of December 31, 2007 equal the starting point of the December 31, 2008 statement of retained earnings. The net income generated from the previous statement date to the date of the new statement (in this case one year) is added to the retained earnings. This represents new wealth that is generated by the company and it is available to fund future activities. In the case of Southwest Airlines, an issuance of common stock is deducted from retained earnings as it is a result of an employee stock purchase plan. Since the company provides a discounted

---

15    Further discussion of the profit margin ratio, and other financial indices, as well as airline industry benchmarking, is contained in Chapter 7.
16    American Airlines and Continental Airlines Passenger Revenues are 87.18% and 90.13% respectively for 2008.

**Table 6.11     Statement of retained earnings**

| | |
|---|---:|
| Balance at December 31, 2007 | $4,788 |
| Net income | 645 |
| Issuance of common and treasury stock | **(150)** |
| Cash dividends, $.018 per share | **(14)** |
| | |
| Balance at December 31, 2007 | $4,788 |

*Source*: Southwest Airlines, December 31, 2008.

stock price to its employees, they fund this program through their retained earnings account.

Finally, any dividends (cash payments by the company to stockholders) that are distributed throughout the period are also funded through retained earnings. For the year 2008, Southwest Airlines distributed dividends of $.018 per share. Therefore, if a stockholder held 1,000 shares of Southwest Airlines in 2008, they would receive a cash payment from the company for $18. The total amount of dividends distributed by Southwest Airlines in 2008 was $13 million.[17] While companies are not required to distribute dividends, they usually do so for a variety of reasons; these are discussed later on in the text.

Once all the adjustments are made to the retained earnings account, a December 31, 2008 retained earnings value of $4,919 million is calculated. This value, which is based on the prior period retained earnings account balance and net income, flows back through to the balance sheet. This is the critical link between the two financial statements and shows why the income statement is usually generated first. That is, the income statement creates the statement of retained earnings, and this in turn is used to balance the balance sheet. Figure 6.1 displays the accounting flow from the income statement to the balance sheet.

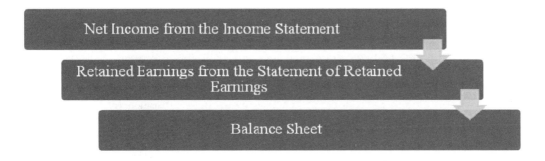

**Figure 6.1     Accounting flow from the income statement to the balance sheet**

---

17     Total Dividends Distributed = Dividends per Share × Number of Shares Outstanding
        Total Dividends Distributed = $.018 × 722,222,222 = $13 million.

## CASH FLOW STATEMENT

The final major financial statement used to analyze a company is the cash flow statement, which reports the company's cash inflows and outflows for a stated period. The cash flow statement represents a departure from typical accounting principles, as the flow of cash is the primary concern. No other financial statement provides a detailed understanding of a company's cash position, since a company may report an annual net income, yet its cash balance could increase or decrease during that period. Therefore, analysis of a company's cash flow is important in helping determine the company's immediate financial position, and if the company will be able to meet its short-term financial obligations (Ogden et al, 2003).

The cash flow statement is particularly important in the airline industry where cash inflows are generated in different periods than cash outflows. In order to understand the different cash inflows/outflows of an airline, consider one flight during the busy Christmas season. The cash inflow generated from the flight will vary depending on when passengers book the flight. This can occur anywhere from the time of departure up to a year prior to the flight. Cash outflows for the flight (expenses such as fuel and labor) will usually occur anywhere from 15-90 days after the flight has occurred, depending on the accounts payable policy of the airline. When this cycle is compounded over thousands of flights, airlines will have cycles where cash outflows may be greater than cash inflows and vice versa.

For any company, cash flows are divided into three categories:

1. Operating activities
2. Investing activities
3. Financing activities.

### Operating Activities

Operating activities represent the principal revenue-producing activities plus any cash flows that are not generated from investing or financing activities. In the example above, all of the cash flows described would fall under the category of operating activities. Investing activities are the acquisition and disposal of long-term assets and other investments. Financing activities are changes in the size and composition of the company's equity and borrowings (Lasher, 2008). As Table 6.12 displays, these three categories are separated on the cash flow statement.

The starting point in calculating the cash flows from operating activities is the net income of the period generated from the income statement. Net income is the logical starting point when calculating the operating cash flow since the income statement provides the financial summary of the company's operating activities. However, the income statement contains non-cash flow items that are included on the income statement but do not affect the cash balance of the company. The most glaring item that falls into this category is depreciation and amortization. Since no cash leaves the company as a result of depreciation or amortization, adjustments must be made on the cash flow statement to take into consideration but non-cash flow items contained on the income statement (Lasher, 2008).

From Southwest Airline's annual income statement generated on December 31, 2008, the airline generated $178 million in net income for the period. Included in the net income were debits for non-cash items such as depreciation and deferred income taxes. Therefore, the value of these items is credited back to the cash flow through the operating activities statement. For example, the $599 million depreciation expense recorded on the income statement is added back on the cash flow statement. Additionally, adjustments for changes on the balance sheet to current assets and current liabilities from one period to the next are made to display any movement in the company's cash from one period to the next. For example, Southwest Airlines air traffic liability account on December 31, 2007 was $931 million and $963 million on December 31, 2008. During the year, the air traffic liability account increased by $32 million, representing an increased liability, or positive cash flow, since more cash was collected to pay for air travel that had not yet occurred. Therefore, a $32 million positive adjustment is made on the cash flow statement to take into consideration the positive cash flow. Other adjustments are made for other current assets and current liabilities.[18] After these adjustments are made, the net cash provided from operating activities is calculated at $1,521 million for 2008, indicating that the company's operations had used a significant amount of cash, largely as a result of significant cash outflows related to accounts payable and accrued liabilities.

## Investing Activities

The second section of the cash flow statement details changes in cash flows resulting from investing activities. Any changes in fixed assets or investments are noted in this portion of the cash flow statement. For Southwest Airlines in 2008, the net purchase in property and equipment increased by $923 million, indicating that the company used cash to purchase additional fixed assets in the year, resulting in a sizeable cash outflow. Additionally during 2008, the airline sold short-term investments, providing a positive cash inflow to the tune of $5,831 million, and purchased new short-term investments worth $5,886 million.

As a result of various investing activities, a cash outflow of $978 million was recorded. A sizeable cash outflow for investing activities is perfectly acceptable, as one of the overall financial goals of a company is to use the cash generated from operations to invest in various projects in the hope of gaining net income in the future. The cash flows from investing activities help detail how a company attempts to position itself in the market for the future. Therefore, the cash flow from Southwest's investing activities is actually directly related to the cost structure of the airline's operations.

## Financing Activities

The third and final category contained on the cash flow statement details the cash flows from financing activities. During the year 2008, Southwest Airlines issued $1000 million of long-term debt, providing an immediate cash inflow to the company, while also receiving proceeds from employees purchasing stock in the company. Cash outflows relating to financing were also made as a result of long-term debt payments, payment of cash

---

18    Note that the adjustments to certain assets and liabilities in Southwest Airlines cash flow statement may not perfectly match the changes recorded on Southwest Airlines balance sheet since the details contained in the individual accounts are unknown.

dividends, and the repurchase of common stock. All activities that affect the equity of the company during the period are recorded under cash flows from financing activities, along with their corresponding impact on cash flow. As a result of all these activities, Southwest Airlines has a net cash flow of $1,654 million to finance its operations during the period. The issuance of long-term debt (1 billion) indicates the plans for asset acquisitions such as a fleet and equipment expansions. The line item of Proceeds from revolving credit of $400 million reflects the airline better positioning itself for the future shortfalls in net income. This is usually the case for companies that are stable financially, while companies that are seeking growth will usually have a positive cash flow from financing activities since they will use the cash to help fund future activities. Therefore, the cash flow from financing activities can aid in understanding a company's overall long-term goals.

As a result of cash inflows/outflows from operating, investing, and financing operations, Southwest Airlines cash and cash equivalents decreased during the period by $845 million. This decrease in cash is due to the large amount of cash generated in operations, some of which was used to invest and finance for the future. This decrease in cash is also depicted on the balance sheet from Table 6.1, where the current asset account, cash and cash equivalents, changed from $2,213 million in 2007 to $1,368 million, or a decrease of $845 million. Therefore, when constructing the statement of cash flows, an easy way in reconciling the statement and making sure it is correct, is to check the change in the cash account on the balance sheet. While the final result of the cash flow statement is easily determined from the balance sheet, the detail of the cash flow statement helps analyze the company and determines where the company has been financially. It may also be used to provide insight into where the company is heading financially.

Because of this detail, many investors believe the statement of cash flow is the most important financial statement that public companies are mandated to provide; however, all financial statements should be used when analyzing a company since they all provide different financial perspectives on the company (see Table 6.12 opposite).

## SUMMARY

In this chapter we have examined the four financial statements (balance sheet, income statement, statement of retained earnings, and the cash flow statement) and how they can be used to determine a company's financial position. Financial statements provide both internal and external users with information needed to make decisions about the company's performance and its future. The income statement details a company's operations for the quarter while the balance sheet provides a financial snapshot of the company's financial position. The income statement reports on financial operations of a company over a period of time, for example, during a calendar year of 2010, while the balance sheet can be thought of as a snapshot in time. With cash being so critically important in the airline industry, as in many other businesses, the cash flow statement provides important insight into how the company is positioning itself for the future and whether the company's operations are generating the cash necessary to run and finance the business. Moreover, the differences in size make it more difficult to compare financial statements of different airlines, so we presented a methodology to form common size financial statements. More in-depth analysis of all the financial statements is provided in the later chapters.

## Table 6.12     Annual cash flow statement: Southwest Airlines, December 31, 2008

| Cash Flows | 2008 | 2007 | 2006 | 2005 |
|---|---|---|---|---|
| **CASH FLOWS FROM OPERATING ACTIVITIES:** | | | | |
| Net income | 178 | 645 | 499 | 484 |
| Adjustments to reconcile net income to net cash provided by operating activities: | | | | |
| Depreciation and amortization | 599 | 555 | 515 | 469 |
| Deferred income taxes | 56 | 328 | 277 | 291 |
| Amortization of deferred gains on sale and leaseback of aircraft | -12 | -14 | -16 | -16 |
| Share-based compensation expense | 18 | 37 | 80 | 80 |
| Excess tax benefits from share-based compensation arrangements | | -28 | -60 | -47 |
| Changes in certain assets and liabilities: | | | | |
| Accounts and other receivables | 71 | -38 | -5 | -9 |
| Other current assets | -384 | -229 | 87 | -59 |
| Accounts payable and accrued liabilities | -1,853 | 1,609 | -223 | 855 |
| Air traffic liability | 32 | 131 | 150 | 120 |
| Other, net | -226 | -151 | 102 | -50 |
| Net cash provided by operating activities | -1,521 | 2,845 | 1,406 | 2,118 |
| **CASH FLOWS FROM INVESTING ACTIVITIES:** | | | | |
| Purchases of property and equipment, net | -923 | -1,331 | -1,399 | -1,146 |
| Purchases of short-term investments | -5,886 | -5,086 | -4,509 | -1,804 |
| Proceeds from sales of short-term investments | 5,831 | 4,888 | 4,392 | 1,810 |
| Payment for assets of ATA Airlines, Inc. | | | | -6 |
| Debtor in possession loan to ATA Airlines, Inc. | | | 20 | |
| Other, net | | | 1 | |
| Net cash used in investing activities | -978 | -1,529 | -1,495 | -1,146 |
| **CASH FLOWS FROM FINANCING ACTIVITIES:** | | | | |
| Issuance of long-term debt | 1,000 | 500 | 300 | 300 |
| Proceeds from Credit line Borrowing | 91 | | | |
| Proceeds from revolving credit agreement | 400 | | | |
| Proceeds from sale and leaseback transactions | 173 | | | |
| Proceeds from Employee stock plans | 117 | 139 | 260 | 132 |
| Payments of long-term debt and capital lease obligations | -55 | -122 | -607 | -149 |
| Payments of cash dividends | -13 | -14 | -14 | -14 |
| Repurchase of common stock | -54 | -1,001 | -800 | -55 |
| Excess tax benefits from share-based compensation arrangements | | 28 | 60 | 47 |
| Other, net | -5 | -23 | | -1 |
| Net cash provided by (used in) financing activities | 1,654 | -493 | -801 | 260 |
| | | | | |
| **NET INCREASE (DECREASE) IN CASH AND CASH EQUIVALENTS** | **-845** | **823** | **-890** | **1,232** |
| **CASH AND CASH EQUIVALENTS AT BEGINNING OF PERIOD** | **2,213** | **1,390** | **2,280** | **1,048** |
| **CASH AND CASH EQUIVALENTS AT END OF PERIOD** | **1,368** | **2,213** | **1,390** | **2,280** |

*Source*: www.southwest.com/investor_relations/fs_sec_filings

## DISCUSSION QUESTIONS:

1. What information is contained in the balance sheet, income statement, and statement of cash flows?
2. Go to finance.yahoo.com
   a. In the "Get Quotes" section, enter GOL for GOL Airlines.
   b. Along the left margin, click on "Balance Sheet."
   c. Compute the ratio of Total debt to Total assets for the past three years.
   d. Compute the ratio of Equity to Total assets for the same period.
   e. Find the same ratio for COPA (CPA) Airlines.
   f. Which airline is in better condition and why?
3. Why is depreciation defined as a noncash expense?
4. Why would an airline choose accelerated depreciation method over a straight line depreciation technique?
5. Provide a definition of cash flow. Give the reasons that accounting profit can differ from cash flow.
6. What are the advantages of debt financing?
7. DirectJet sold an aircraft with a book value of $10,000,000 and recorded a $2,000,000 gain. How should this transaction be recorded on the cash flow statement?
8. Distinguish between amortization and depreciation.
9. EZjET had purchased an aircraft push truck two years ago for $450,000. These types of tractors are the only All Wheel Drive (AWD) tugs in their weight class. The truck now can be sold for $350,000. The push truck has been depreciated using the MACRS 5 year recovery period, and the EZjET pays 35% taxes on both ordinary income and capital gain:
   a. Compute recaptured depreciation and capital gain (loss), if any.
   b. Find the airline's tax liability.
10. What is the accounting equation?
11. Consider DirectJet Airlines which recently purchased a new Boeing 737-700 for $42 million. At the end of ten years, the aircraft is expected to have a residual value of $10 million.
   a. What is the annual depreciation expense of the aircraft using straight line depreciation?
   b. What is the book value of the aircraft after five years using straight-line depreciation?
   c. What is the depreciation expense of the aircraft in the first year using double-declining balance depreciation?
   d. What is the depreciation expense of the aircraft in the third year using double-declining balance depreciation?
   e. Using the MACRS table in Table 6.4, what is the depreciation expense in year three for the aircraft?
   f. Using the MACRS table in Table 6.4, what is the depreciation expense in year seven for the aircraft?
   g. What is the depreciation expense of the aircraft in the first year using sum-of-years digits depreciation? What is the book value?
   h. What is the depreciation expense of the aircraft in the third year using sum-of-years digits depreciation? What is the book value?
12. State which accounting statement(s) the following line items would be found on:

a.   Accounts payable
b.   Depreciation expense
c.   Net income
d.   Issuance of common stock
e.   Fuel expense
f.   Accumulated other comprehensive income
g.   Proceeds from long-term debt
h.   Interest expense
i.   Long-term debt
j.   Air-traffic liability.

13. Assume DirectJet purchased a Boeing 737-900ER for $82 million dollars. The aircraft will be depreciated straight-line to a salvage value of $15 million dollars. Assume the relevant tax rate is 34 percent. Calculate:
    a.   The annual depreciation
    b.   Annual depreciation tax savings.

14. Refer to Table 6.11, LAN Chiles' income statement; complete the common-size statement by dividing each item on the income statement by net sales.

# REFERENCES

Brealey, R., S. Myers, and F. Allen (2008). *Principles of Corporate Finance*, (9th ed). McGraw-Hill.

Brealey, R., S. Myers, and A. Marcus (2009). *Fundamentals of Corporate Finance*, 6th edition. McGraw-Hill.

Brigham, E. and J. Houston (1998). *Fundamentals of Financial Management*, (8th ed). The Dryden Press.

British Airways (2008, March 31). *2007/08 Annual Report and Accounts*.

Emirates Group (2008, March 31). *Annual Report 2007-2008*.

Emery, D., J. Finnerty, and J. Stowe (2007). *Corporate Financial Management*, (3rd ed). Prentice Hall.

Gitman, L.. (2006). *Principles of Managerial Finance*, (11th ed). Addison Wesley Higher Education.

Gitman, L. (2009). *Principles of Managerial Finance*, (12th ed). Prentice Hall.

How to Depreciate Property. Retrieved February 20, 2008, from Internal Revenue Service web site: http://www.irs.gov/publications/p946/index.html

Keown, A., J. Martin, J. Petty, and D. Scott (2005). *Financial Management: Principles and Applications*, (10th ed). Prentice Hall.

Lasher, W. (2008). *Practical Financial Management*, (5th ed). South-Western.

Ogden, J., F. Jen, and P. O'Connor (2003). *Advanced Corporate Finance*. Prentice Hall.

Ross, S., R. Westerfield, and B. Jordan (2008). *Fundamentals of Corporate Finance Standard Edition*, (8th ed). McGraw-Hill.

Southwest Airlines (2008, April 17). *SWA Annual Report*.

Southwest Airlines (2008, September 10). *Southwest Airlines announces new finance leaders*.

# 7

# Financial Statement Analysis

"I think Southwest has a great model. They're used to efficiency. They bought new airplanes. They turned them (around) quickly on the ground. We loved the efficiency side of the business, but we thought they may be a little too much of a prisoner to their success."

David Neeleman[1]

While it is important to understand the composition and role of financial statements, to truly make the statements valuable, detailed analysis of the statements is required. One common methodology to analyze financial statements is ratio analysis, which utilizes a host of financial calculations to analyze different portions of a company. Such financial indices as return on investment (ROI), profit margin, debt-equity ratio, and price-earnings ratio are used not only internally by airlines, but also externally by the investment community. Airline industry-specific metrics, such as cost per available seat mile (CASM) and revenue per revenue passenger mile (R/RPM), are also introduced. Using ratios and other financial analysis techniques, airline benchmarking of U.S. carriers is performed to help recognize strong financial airlines and to understand how they are successful by dissecting their financial statements. This chapter covers the following topics:

- Financial ratio analysis
  - Profitability Ratios
  - Liquidity Ratios
  - Long-Term Risk Ratios
  - Stock Market Ratios
- Airline-Specific Financial Ratios
- Airline Industry Benchmarking
- Predicting Insolvency
  - Altman's Z-Score Model
  - Springate's Z-Score Model
  - Fulmers's H-Score Model
- Summary
- Discussion Questions
- Appendix 1 : Summary of Financial Ratios
- Appendix 2 : The DuPont Method.

---

1    The founder and former CEO of JetBlue Airway, and founder of Azul Linhas Aéreas Brasileiras.

Although financial statements are essential in helping to analyze a company, they are basically the starting point for successful financial management. Financial statements provide the raw figures on the company's financial position; however, these numbers are only meaningful when compared with other firms competing in the industry. The various quantitative methods that are used to compare financial statements to assess a firm's financial condition and performance are commonly referred to as ratio analysis. Ratio analysis encompasses a wide variety of calculations and metrics that enable a manager to quickly spot trends in the company's performance, highlighting historical performance and projections for the future.

## FINANCIAL RATIO ANALYSIS

There are two major comparisons that ratio analysis provides and these are comparisons of the firm across time and comparisons of the firm with the industry. Using ratio analysis, financial results can be standardized across time to help analyze a company's financial performance through various periods. This level of analysis helps understand a company's evolution over time in the industry; however, owing to potential macro-economic shocks on the environment it may not always be appropriate to compare a company's results from one year to the next. The more powerful ratio analysis comparison is with other firms competing in the same industry. With financial statements readily available for all publicly-traded companies, benchmarking of competing firms can easily be undertaken to help understand a company's financial position within the industry. This benchmarking effectively enables firms to recognize their strengths and weaknesses relative to the industry and since firms vary in size and composition is only possible through the standardization that ratio analysis provides.

The various metrics used in the ratio analysis can be classified into four broad categories based on what portion of the company that they are analyzing:

- Profitability ratios
- Liquidity ratios
- Long-term risk ratios
- Stock market ratios.

Profitability ratios help to describe the efficiency or success of the business. Liquidity ratios describe the firm's ability to meet short term obligations. Long-term risk ratios analyze the capital structure of a company and take a more macro-level approach to analyzing the company. Finally, stock market ratios deal specifically with publicly-traded companies and describe the company's position in the stock market. Regardless of the type of ratio used, a single ratio by itself does not accurately describe the firm; rather, a number of ratios should be used to help provide a broader perspective on the company. This point is exacerbated by the fact that there are multiple ratios that can be used to analyze the same part of the company. Therefore, there are no set criteria by which ratios should be used to analyze a company; however, the more ratios that are used in the analysis, the better the picture that is painted of the company.

This chapter explains the various ratios that might be used in performing ratio analysis by using these ratios to analyze the financial statements of Southwest Airlines. While all the ratios can be used to adequately describe the financial position of a company, the uniqueness of the airline industry requires additional calculations to understand the finances of an airline. Finally, based on the common and airline-specific financial calculations, an exercise in the benchmarking of various U.S. airlines is presented to show the merits of ratio analysis and to provide a better financial understanding of the airline industry.

## Profitability Ratios

As mentioned previously, profitability ratios help describe the success of the business by comparing the profits (or losses) generated against a variety of baselines. This helps standardize the profits of companies, making it easier to compare the profitability of one company against the profitability of another company. While this comparison helps standardize large and small companies alike, it is not necessarily the most useful tool in comparing companies across multiple industries, since the industry dynamics can vastly distort how companies generate a profit. The six profitability ratios that will be explained, using Southwest Airlines (Southwest is only a convenient example and the ratios themselves are applicable to any airline (or firm) as so desired) in 2008 as a concrete example, are:

- Operating profit margin ratio
- Profit margin ratio
- Return on assets
- Return on equity
- Asset turnover ratio
- DuPont Analysis.

*Operating profit margin ratio*   The operating profit margin (OPM) ratio compares the operating profit of a company with the total revenue generated. It enables a manager to determine how much operating profit is generated for every dollar of revenue. The operating profit margin can be particularly useful when analyzing a company as it excludes items such as interest expense and taxes, which are largely based on the macro-structure of the company. Excluding these items generally enables a greater in-depth analysis of the company's operations. Also, because we are excluding special items on the income statement in the calculation, this means that the operating profit margin ratio tends to remain more stable over time. The formula for calculating the operating profit margin ratio is:

$$\text{Operating Profit Margin} = \frac{\text{Operating Profit}}{\text{Total Revenue}}$$

Both items for calculating the gross profit margin ratio are found on the income statement. Operating profit is also commonly referred to as EBIT, or Earnings before Interest and Taxes. Referring back to the previous chapter, the gross profit margin for Southwest Airlines in 2008 was actually calculated in the common-size income statement, since the third column contained the line item as a percentage of total revenue. As a refresher, Southwest Airlines 2008 operating profit margin was:

$$\text{Operating Profit Margin} = \frac{\$449 \text{ million}}{\$11,023 \text{ million}} \times 100\%$$

$$\text{OPM} = 4.07\%$$

Based on the gross profit margin calculated above, every dollar of revenue generated by Southwest Airlines created roughly 4 cents of operating profit for the company. As a comparison, the gross profit margin for Southwest Airlines was 8.02% in 2007, 10.3% in 2006, and 9.5% in 2005. Obviously, Southwest Airlines was able to increase its gross profit margin during the period from 2005 to 2006, and this by itself is a positive signal; however, profit margins declined in 2007 and 2008. We can see from this ratio that revenue was increasing at a greater rate than unit costs from 2005–2006. However, while these values appear to display a strong company, they need to be compared with figures for the rest of the industry to understand Southwest Airlines position in the market.

*Profit Margin Ratio*   The profit margin ratio is similar in methodology to the gross profit margin ratio as it represents the net income of the company as a percentage of total revenue. The profit margin takes into consideration all facets of a company's financial structure and standardizes the financial bottom-line of the firm. The profit margin enables million dollar companies to be compared with billion dollar companies as it shows how much net income is generated for every dollar of revenue. The profit margin formula and Southwest Airlines 2008 profit margin are:

$$\text{Profit Margin} = \frac{\text{Net Income}}{\text{Total Revenue}} = \frac{NI}{TR}$$

$$\text{Profit Margin} = \frac{\$178 \text{ million}}{\$11{,}023 \text{ million}} \times 100\% = 1.61\%$$

Based on the audited financial statements of Southwest Airlines, every dollar generates 1.61 cents of profit for the company. This figure might seem miniscule, but the U.S. airline industry average for 2008 is at –15.23%.[2] Comparatively, 2007's figure was 6.5%, a one point increase over 2006's profit margin of 5.5%, and a significant increase over 2004's 3.3% profit margin ratio. Interestingly, this displays a slightly different perspective on the company than the gross profit margin ratio as this financial ratio displays profit generation increasing for every year during the period. This paradox is the result of a significant loss charge posted by Southwest Airlines in 2007 and 2005. This shows the importance of both calculations when performing ratio analysis, since the airline's gross profit margin declined from 2006 to 2007, while total profit margin increased. If only one of the ratios was calculated, the results could be potentially misleading when analyzing the company.

*Return on assets (ROA)*   Another profitability ratio that can be used to help standardize large and small companies is the return on assets ratio. This ratio measures the net income of the company after taxes against the fixed assets of the company. This shows the investment return that assets have provided. A company invests in fixed assets in an effort to generate increased profits, and therefore the return on assets ratio analyzes a company at one of the very fundamental elements of business. The formula for the return on assets and Southwest Airlines ROA is:

$$\text{Return on Assets (ROA)} = \frac{\text{Net Income}}{\text{Total Assets}} = \frac{NI}{TA}$$

---

2    The Airline Monitor, June 9th, 2009.

with Southwest Airlines 2007 return on assets being:

$$ROA_{2007} = \frac{\$178 \text{ million}}{\$14,308 \text{ million}} \times 100\%$$

$$ROA_{2007} = 1.24\%$$

Southwest Airlines 2008 return on assets ratio indicates that every $100 spent on assets yielded 1.24 cents of profit for the company. The return on assets ratio varies considerably by industries, since some industries are more highly capital intensive than others. The airline industry is highly capital-intensive, therefore the average industry return on assets is likely to be lower than in other industries. Because of this, the best way to compare the return on assets ratio is between companies competing within the same industry, providing a valuable benchmark by which to judge the firm.

*Return on equity (ROE)*   Similar in goal and methodology to the return on assets ratio, return on equity measures the company's performance against the total stockholders' equity in the company. If your airline has $500 million in net worth, and makes $100 million in annual profit, then the airline is making 5% ROE. This is helpful because the ratio you end up with is an indication of how well the airline turns its assets into income. The general formula for the return on equity formula and Southwest Airline's 2008 return on equity is once again found by referring back to both the income statement and balance sheet:

$$\text{Return on Equity (ROE)} = \frac{\text{Net Income}}{\text{Total Stockholders' Equity}}$$

$$ROE = \frac{\$178 \text{ million}}{\$4,953 \text{ million}} \times 100\% = 3.59\%$$

Unlike the return on assets ratio which may vary considerably from industry to industry, the return on equity ratio should not vary as much between industries. However, it may contain a larger variance between the companies competing within the industry. While this particular ratio is beneficial to investors, distortions may exist due to the financial structure of a company. For example, a company that is more heavily debt financed may have an artificially higher return on equity ratio than a company that is more equity financed. Therefore, there are multiple issues to consider when analyzing companies' return on equity ratios.

The 2008 ROE has been reduced from the previous ratios owing to the decrease in net income, while the equity structure remained relatively the same. Southwest Airlines 2007 return on equity ratio of 9.29% was slightly higher than 2006's return on equity of 7.74% and 2005's return on equity of 7.25%. Ideally, greater investment in the company should yield higher returns on equity since the company is able to take the equity gained and use it in areas where profits can be made. However, in a mature industry such as the airline industry, increased investment is not always possible as there may be very few areas that could generate new profits.

*Asset turnover ratio*    The asset turnover ratio measures total revenue against the total assets of the company. Similar in concept to the return on assets metric, the asset turnover ratio shows how much revenue assets generate for the company. Asset turnover is calculated using the formula and the results for Southwest for 2008 are calculated below:

$$\text{Asset Turnover} = \frac{\text{Total Revenue}}{\text{Total Assets}}$$

$$ATO = \frac{TR}{TA}$$

$$ATO = \frac{\$11{,}023 \text{ million}}{\$14{,}308 \text{ million}}$$

$$ATO = 0.7704$$

An asset turnover ratio of 0.7704 indicates that every $100 worth of assets generates $77.04 of revenue. An interesting relationship between three of the profitability ratios is the following:

$$\text{Return on Assets} = \text{Profit Margin} \times \text{Asset Turnover}$$

$$\text{ROA} = \text{PM} \times \text{ATO}$$

Therefore, only two of the three ratios above need be calculated to determine the remaining ratio. It also indicates how each ratio is looking at a similar component of the company, but goes about analyzing the company in a unique way. Understanding how a company's profits are generated from assets is a critical component to understanding the financial ratios and the concept of financial leverage.

*Du Pont analysis*    Although ratio analysis provides a detailed examination of the financial condition of a company, it does not provide the big picture or the links between the ratios to understand the raw financial data. The DuPont equation allows financial managers to summarize the data and the financial position of an organization. The DuPont equation shows that return on equity can be broken down into different segments. The breakdown of the ROE to produce the DuPont equity multiplier for Southwest Airlines (2008) is given below:

$$\text{ROE} = \frac{\text{Net Income}}{\text{Equity}} \times \frac{\text{Sales}}{\text{Sales}} \times \frac{\text{Total Assets}}{\text{Total Assets}}$$

$$\text{ROE} = \frac{\text{Net Income}}{\text{Sales}} \times \frac{\text{Sales}}{\text{Total Assets}} \times \frac{\text{Total Assets}}{\text{Equity}}$$

$$\text{ROE} = \text{ROA} \times \text{Equity Multiplier}$$

$$\text{ROE} = \frac{\$178 \text{ million}}{\$11{,}023 \text{ million}} \times \frac{\$11{,}023 \text{ million}}{\$14{,}308 \text{ million}} \times \frac{\$14{,}308 \text{ million}}{\$4{,}953 \text{ million}}$$

$$\text{ROE} = 0.0161 \times 0.7704 \times 2.888$$

$$\text{ROE} = 0.0358 = 3.58\%$$

## Liquidity Ratios

The second set of financial ratios used to analyze a business is liquidity ratios. These ratios analyze a company from a short-term perspective and focus on the company's ability to meet its current obligations. As mentioned in the previous chapter, liquidity refers to the ease and quickness by which assets can be converted into cash; therefore, the ultimate goal of liquidity ratios is the determination of how quickly the company can convert its assets into tangible cash. The seven liquidity ratios are:

- Working capital
- Current ratio
- Acid-test ratio (Quick ratio)
- Accounts receivable turnover ratio
- Days of accounts receivables
- Accounts payable turnover ratio/Days of accounts payables
- Inventory turnover ratio/Days of inventory

*Working capital*   Prior to calculating ratios, it is important to understand the concept of working capital, which is essentially the difference between current assets and current liabilities.

$$Net\ Working\ Capital = Current\ Assets - Current\ Liabilities$$

$$NWC = CA - CL$$

Referring back to previous definitions, current assets are assets which can be easily converted into cash, while current liabilities are short-term financial obligations. Therefore, working capital is the excess of short-term assets that are available for use and are not tied up by current liabilities. A company always wants working capital so that its short-term obligations are being met, since if short-term obligations are not met the company faces a solvency problem.

For Southwest Airlines in 2008, its amount of working capital was $87 million.[3] This indicates the company has sufficient assets to meet its short-term obligations. If working capital is negative, it means that current assets cannot satisfy current liabilities and either additional cash generation must be obtained or the time liabilities are due is pushed back.

*Current ratio*   One of the classic financial ratios, the current ratio measures the relationship between current assets and current liabilities. The current ratio analyzes the working capital of the company and helps determine if the company can meet its short-term obligations. However, unlike the amount of working capital which will vary considerably based on the company's size, the current ratio provides standardization of working capital, enabling industry comparison. The current ratio provides a proportion of how

---

3    Working Capital (2008) = Current Assets – Current Liabilities = $2,893 million – $2,806 million = $87 million.

much of the company's current liabilities are being met by the company's current assets (Ross, Westerfield and Jordan, 2008). The formula for the current ratio is:

$$\text{Current Ratio} = \frac{\text{Current Assets}}{\text{Current Liabilities}}$$

$$CR = \frac{CA}{CL}$$

Since it was previously determined that the amount of Southwest Airlines 2008 working capital was positive, the current ratio will be more than one, since all the current liabilities are being met by current assets. In fact, the 2008 current ratio for Southwest Airlines is 1.031.

$$\text{Current Ratio (2008)} = \frac{\$2,893 \text{ million}}{\$2,806 \text{ million}} = 1.031$$

A current ratio of 1.031 indicates that 103% of Southwest Airlines' current liabilities will be satisfied with current assets; therefore, the company will either attempt to defer their liabilities, or acquire short-term financing through a variety of options, such as a business line of credit. As a comparison, Southwest's 2007 current ratio was 0.92,[4] indicating that Southwest faced a short-term liquidity issue the previous year; however, it was able to overcome the issue.

*Acid-test ratio (quick ratio)*   A similar metric to the current ratio is the quick ratio, except that the quick ratio is a stricter measurement of the company's ability to meet its short-term obligations. The reason for this is the fact that not all current assets are used in the calculation. Current assets have a considerable range in their liquidity since some short-term investments can be converted into cash far more quickly than others, so these assets may be better indicators of the company's ability to meet its obligations. Therefore, in order to provide a more realistic view of assets that can be converted into cash to meet short-term obligations the acid-test ratio uses quick assets. While the classification of quick assets is ultimately at the discretion of the analyst, common current assets classified as quick assets are cash and cash equivalents, marketable securities, and current accounts receivable. Regardless of the classification of quick assets, inventory is almost always removed from the acid-test ratio, as inventories are more likely to be slow moving, indicating that the inventory is less liquid. Using a methodology where quick assets are simply cash, short-term investments, and accounts receivable, Southwest Airlines 2008 quick ratio was:

$$\text{Quick Ratio} = \frac{\text{Quick Assets}}{\text{Current Liabilities}} = \frac{CA - Inventory}{CL}$$

$$QR = \frac{QA}{CL}$$

$$QR_{(2008)} = \frac{(\$1,368 + \$435 + \$209) \text{ million}}{\$2,806 \text{ million}}$$

$$QR_{(2008)} = 0.717$$

---

4    Current Ratio (2007) = $4,443 million / $4,838 million = 0.92.

A quick ratio of 0.717 indicates that only 71% of Southwest's current liabilities can be quickly satisfied. Since the acid-test ratio is stricter than the current ratio, the quick ratio is always going to be less than the current ratio. Ultimately, the quick ratio provides a stronger analysis of a company's working capital since it removes some uncertainty over the composition of a company's current assets. How much liquidity an airline needs depends on its operating cycle. An airline's operating cycle is the time between when the cash is spent for goods and services to the time that investment generates cash.

*Accounts receivables turnover ratio*    Companies offer goods and services on credit to attract and maintain customers and we already know that a dollar today is worth more than a dollar tomorrow. Since most companies offer credit terms, it is important to monitor accounts receivables to make sure that payment is collected in a timely matter. It may be better for a company to offer long credit terms; however, if it takes the company a long time to collect accounts receivables, the company has been unable to use that money over the time period. Therefore, the accounts receivable turnover ratio is a measure of how many times accounts receivable are collected during a specified time period. When calculating the accounts receivable turnover ratio, net credit sales are usually used, since only the portion of revenue that is collected on credit should be analyzed. However, since few companies report revenue between cash and credit sales on their publicly available financial reports[5], total revenue usually has to be used as a proxy. This can lead to distortions in calculating the accounts receivable turnover ratio. Additionally, distortions can arise when using the accounts receivable balance at a point in time, since the balance could have varied significantly during the time period. However, since the average accounts receivable balance is only known internally, external analysis has to use the stated value on the balance sheet, and note the possible potential of distortions. Because the accounts receivable turnover ratio determines how quickly accounts receivables are turning over higher values indicate that accounts receivables are moving more quickly than lower values. Southwest Airline's 2008 accounts receivable turnover ratio is:[6,7]

$$\text{Accounts Receivable Turnover Ratio} = \frac{\text{Net Credit Sales}}{\text{Average Accounts Receivables}}$$

$$\text{Accounts Receivable Turnover Ratio (2008)} = \frac{\$11,023 \text{ million}}{\$234 \text{ million}} = 47.00$$

*Days of accounts receivables*    One of the problems with the accounts receivable turnover ratio is that the metric can be difficult to interpret. Therefore, an associated ratio is the days of accounts receivable, which converts the accounts receivable turnover ratio into the average time for accounts receivables during the period. In 2008, the days of accounts receivables for Southwest Airlines were:

$$\text{Days of Accounts Receivables} = \frac{\text{Number of Days in Period}}{\text{Accounts Receivable Turnover Ratio}}$$

$$\text{Days of Accounts Receivables (2008)} = \frac{365}{47} = 7.76 \text{ days}$$

---

5    The notes to the financial statements sometimes contain detail on the amount of revenue generated on credit.
6    Since net credit sales were unknown for Southwest Airlines, total operating revenue from the income statement is used instead.
7    The average accounts receivable balance for Southwest Airlines was the average of accounts receivable balance on December 31, 2007 and 2008.

A value for days of accounts receivables of 7.76 indicates that, on average, revenue generated by Southwest Airlines is collected in approximately seven to eight days. For many companies this is an extremely quick collection period; however, since the majority of airlines collect revenue on a fairly immediate basis,[8] the industry is expected to have short days of accounts receivables. For 2008, Southwest's days of accounts receivables was 7.776 days, and 9.62 for 2007, which means that days of accounts receivables did change from 2007 to 2008.

*Accounts payable turnover ratio/days of accounts payable*    Nearly identical in methodology to the accounts receivable turnover ratio is the accounts payable turnover ratio, which measures the number of times the accounts payable account turns over. While analyzing accounts payable is not as important, since the goal is to pay as late as possible, it is useful to compare the days of accounts payable with the days of accounts receivable, to help estimate the days of working capital. The formula for the accounts payable turnover ratio and days of accounts payable are:

$$\text{Accounts Payable Turnover} = \frac{\text{Period Purchases}}{\text{Average Accounts Payable}}$$

$$\text{Days of Accounts Payable} = \frac{\text{Number of Days in Period}}{\text{Accounts Payable Turnover Ratio}}$$

When referring to Southwest Airlines income statement, it is difficult to determine the purchases made by the company during the period; therefore, total operating expenses, less depreciation, which is a non-cash item, is used as a proxy for annual purchases. Using this methodology, the accounts payable turnover ratio and days of accounts payable for Southwest Airlines in 2008 was:

$$\text{Accounts Payable Turnover Ratio} = \frac{(\$10{,}574 - \$599)\text{ million}}{(\frac{\$668 + \$759 + \$643}{3})\text{ million}}$$

$$\text{Accounts Payable Turnover Ratio} = 14.45$$

$$\text{Days of Accounts Payable}_{(2008)} = \frac{365}{14.45} = 25.25 \text{ days}$$

Based on Southwest Airlines 2008 days of accounts payable, it appears the airline operates on a policy of paying their accounts in less than thirty days. Of note is the 17.5 day difference between the days of accounts receivable and accounts payable, indicating that the airline, on average, is able to use the revenue generated for nearly an additional 18 days prior to paying for the cost of flying the passenger. The days of working capital are increased by the fact that the majority of passengers book their travel significantly ahead of the departure date, further strengthening the airline's cash flow and providing the

---

8    For example, the majority of passenger travel is booked through the Internet, which collects credit card payment seemingly immediately. However, a lag does occur between when the credit card company dispatches the revenue collected for the flight to the airline, providing for short days of accounts receivable for credit-card generated revenue.

airline the opportunity to use the cash during that time period. Ideally, a company wants to maximize the difference between the days of accounts payable and accounts receivable to provide the company with short-term investment opportunities.

*Inventory turnover ratio/days of inventory*   The final area of liquidity to analyze is inventory. This is extremely important for manufacturing firms, but is less important in the airline industry, since a passenger seat is not inventoried. However, airline maintenance does contain inventoried parts to support the operation. Since there is a cost associated with warehousing inventory, it is important to make sure inventory is turning over quickly and not sitting idle in warehouses. On the other hand, the airlines want to make sure flights are not cancelled or delayed as a result of a lack of inventory, creating conflicting goals. The generic inventory turnover ratio and days of inventory calculations are:

$$\text{Inventory Turnover Ratio} = \frac{\text{Cost of Goods Sold}}{\text{Average Inventory}}$$

$$\text{Days of Inventory} = \frac{\text{Number of Days in Period}}{\text{Inventory Turnover Ratio}}$$

Since Southwest Airlines, or any airline, has no true cost of goods sold, the inventory turnover ratio uses the expense categories for which the inventory is required. Making the assumption that all inventory held by the airline are maintenance materials, the maintenance materials and repairs category can be used as a proxy for the cost of goods sold when calculating the inventory turnover ratio for airlines. Using this methodology, the inventory turnover ratio and days of inventory for Southwest Airlines in 2008 were:

$$\text{Inventory Turnover Ratio (2008)} = \frac{\$721 \text{ million}}{\$203 \text{ million}} = 3.55$$

$$\text{Days of Inventory} = \frac{365}{3.55} = 102.77 \text{ days}$$

For many industries, 103 days of inventory sitting idle would be unacceptable; however, in the airline industry this length of time is fairly common. This is largely a result of numerous parts that are required to support the operation and the fact that the usage of the parts is not very high. Additionally, since airlines operate globally, parts must be stocked in multiple cities to insure an on-time operation. This problem is compounded for Southwest Airlines which does not operate hubs and has sizeable operations at multiple airports. This type of operation probably requires increased inventory because of the numerous airports where maintenance problems might occur. Like most of the ratios, the days of inventory needs to be compared solely within the industry to determine how efficient the airline is operating.

## Long-term Risk Ratios

While liquidity ratios help analyze a company's financial position in the short-term, long-term risk ratios, or solvency ratios, analyze a company's ability to remain in business over the long-term. Of all the categories of ratios, long-term risk ratios tend to provide the greatest macro-perspective of a company. Because of this, the ratios focus on the underlying capital structure of the company, which ultimately helps determine the company's financial strength for the future. The three major long-term risk ratios are:

- Debt-to-equity ratio
- Debt-Asset ratio
- Times interest earned ratio.

*Debt-to-equity ratio*   The classic long-term risk ratio, the debt-to-equity ratio, determines the proportion of the company's capital structure that is composed of equity. It helps determine where the funding for the company exists, and how heavily weighted the company is to either debt financing or equity financing. The debt-to-equity structure of a company can also indicate the variability of future earnings, as more heavily debt financed companies will incur larger swings in profitability as a result of increased interest expenses. Additionally, the resultant financial structure of a company helps determine the cost of capital, an important metric used in financial decision-making. While numerous derivations of the debt-to-equity ratio exist, the generic formula is:

$$\text{Debt-to-Equity Ratio (D/E)} = \frac{\text{Total Liabilities}}{\text{Total Stockholders' Equity}}$$

Using the generic debt-to-equity ratio and the data from Southwest Airlines balance sheet, its 2008 debt-to equity ratio was 1.88.[9] This means that for every $1 of stockholders' equity, Southwest Airlines has been able to leverage $1.88 of debt finance. This ratio also indicates that Southwest Airlines is more debt financed than equity funded, as evidenced by a debt-to-equity ratio greater than one. Like so many other ratios, every industry and company are unique, therefore there is no universally optimal debt-to-equity ratio. Comparisons with similar companies competing in the same or similar industries help determine the potential for variability of future earnings.

*Debt ratio*   A common derivation of the debt-to-equity ratio is the debt ratio, which simply measures the proportion of debt that is financing the assets of the company. Since either liabilities/debt or stockholders' equity is used to finance assets, the debt ratio ultimately provides the percentage of debt in the capital structure. The debt ratio's formula and Southwest Airlines 2007 debt ratio is:

$$\text{Debt Ratio} = \frac{\text{Total Liabilities}}{\text{Total Assets}}$$

$$\text{Debt Ratio}_{(2008)} = \frac{\$9,355 \text{ million}}{\$14,308 \text{ million}}$$

$$\text{Debt Ratio}_{(2008)} = 0.6538 \text{ or } 65.38\%$$

Since both sides of the balance sheet must be equal, the debt ratio is merely comparing the proportion of liabilities held by the company against stockholders' equity—essentially the

---

9    Debt-to-Equity Ratio (2008) = $9,355 million / $4,953 million = 1.88.

debt-to-equity ratio. Southwest Airlines debt ratio of 65.38% indicates that a little over half of the company's assets were funded by debt. As a comparison, Southwest Airlines 2006 and 2007 debt ratios were 58.62% and 52.08%;[10] increasing steadily during the period. The comparison of debt ratios over time is an effective tool in helping understand the company's past and how it is positioning itself for the future. Based on a stable debt ratio, the airline appears satisfied with its mix of debt and equity in its capital portfolio, indicating a rather stable financial environment for the company. If a company were to make radical changes in its capital structure, such as dramatically increasing its proportion of equity, some financial implications could be drawn. These might include the fact that the cost of debt for the company may be prohibitively high (likely the result of poor bond ratings), or the company may be wishing to raise capital without having any set payment schedules. Therefore, changes in capital structure help to determine the company's ability to stay in business for the long-term.

*Times interest earned ratio*   The times interest earned ratio measures the company's ability to meet its interest payments. To debt holders, the times interest earned ratio is critical in determining the amount of risk the company presents to them. While calculated multiple ways, a simple method in calculating the times interest earned ratio is:

$$\text{Times Interest Earned Ratio} = \frac{\text{Earnings Before Interest and Taxes (EBIT)}}{\text{Interest Expense}}$$

Using information from the income statement, the times interest earned ratio for Southwest Airlines was 3.45 in 2008.[11] This value indicates that in 2008, Southwest Airlines operating income was nearly four times its annual interest expense, showing that they were in a fairly good position to be able to meet its interest payments. Therefore, the higher the times interest earned ratio, the better able the company is to meet their interest requirements. Having a higher times interest earned ratio ultimately helps lower the cost of debt as the company appears more stable to creditors. For comparison purposes, the times interest earned ratio in 2007 and 2006 was 6.64 and 7.30 respectively for Southwest Airlines.[12] Based on these values, Southwest Airlines position to meet its interest payments since 2006 has declined, displaying the results of decreased profitability.

## Stock Market Ratios

The final group of ratios that can be used to analyze a company are stock market ratios; these ratios are used to analyze a company in relationship to its equity position. Because stock market ratios analyze a company's position in the stock market, the ratios can only be used for public companies. The ratios provide good information when an individual is considering investing in a company, and are used extensively by the investment banking community in determining a company's value. Since ultimately a company's stock price is the result of analysis and projections by investors, stock market ratios are important in determining the fiscal health of a company. Since the goal of investing is to purchase low and have the company perform well in the future, stock market ratios help analyze the

---

10   Debt Ratio (2006) = Total Liabilities / Total Assets = $7,011 million / $13,460 million = 52.08%.
11   Times interest earned ratio (2008) = $449 million / $130 million = 3.45.
12   Times interest earned ratio (2007) = $791 million / $119 million = 6.64.
Times interest earned ratio (2006) = $934 million / $128 million = 7.30.

current value of a company. Listed below are four stock market ratios that are commonly used when assessing a company's position in the stock market:

- Earnings per share
- Price-earnings ratio
- Dividend payout ratio
- Dividend yield ratio.

*Earnings per share*   Since earnings per share was covered in the previous chapter, extensive explanation of the ratio is not required. As a refresher, earnings per share essentially state the net income of the company on a per share basis, reflecting the amount of income earned for every outstanding share of the company in the market. For example, assume DirectJet and EZjET both earn $150 million but company DirectJet has 100 million shares outstanding, while company EZjET has 50 million shares outstanding. We can calculate earnings per share for both airlines by taking the net earnings and dividing by the outstanding shares. DirectJet jet has an EPS of $1.50, while EZjET earnings per share are $3 per share. It makes more sense to look at earnings per share (EPS) for use as a comparison tool. You calculate earnings per share by taking the net earnings and divide by the outstanding shares. The simple formula for earnings per share is:

$$\text{Earnings per Share (EPS)} = \frac{\text{Net Income}}{\text{Average Number of Shares Outstanding}}$$

Earnings per share helps standardize a company's earnings based on its amount of equity. In financial circles, net income is always stated on an earnings per share basis, as it ultimately reflects the net income earned for every individual shareholder. Most publicly available income statements provide earnings per share and Southwest Airlines EPS for the period ending December 31, 2008 was $0.24.[13]

*Price-earnings ratio*   The price-earnings ratio is the ultimate assessment of a company's stock market value as it compares the relationship between the performance of the company according to the income statement and the stock market. Based upon the comparison of earnings and the stock price, the price-earnings ratio helps enable one to determine if the stock price of a company is either undervalued or overvalued. The P/E ratio is a measure every investor should be aware of to help find good stock market values. The price-earnings ratio is calculated using the following formula:

$$\text{Price-Earnings Ratio} = \frac{\text{Current Market Price}}{\text{Earnings per Share}} = \frac{P_s}{EPS}$$

Since the price-earnings ratio is calculated using the current stock market price of the company, the price-earnings ratio will be in constant flux based on the daily stock price. Based on Southwest Airlines earnings per share of $0.24, and its stock price of $8.61 on December 31, 2008, the price-earnings ratio of Southwest on December 31, 2008 was:

$$\text{Price-Earnings Ratio (2008)} = \frac{\$8.61}{\$0.24} = 35.87$$

---

13    Southwest Airlines, February, 2009.

A price-earnings ratio of 35.87 indicates that the stock price is 35.87 times greater than the earnings of the company. Like many other financial ratios, there is no target value for what the price-earnings ratio should be. The optimum price-earnings ratio is based on not only the industry the firm competes in, but also the overall stock market. A high price-earnings ratio may indicate that the stock price of the company is overvalued while the stock is probably undervalued for low price-earnings ratios. However, determining if a price-earnings ratio is high or low is ultimately a decision that the individual investor has to make, with the metric merely providing the investor with a methodology of helping assess the value of a company's stock.

The price-earnings ratio computed for Southwest Airlines on December 31, 2008 was backward looking since it used the historical financial performance of the company. The price-earnings ratio can also be forward looking by using projected earnings per share based upon a projection of future earnings. Forward looking P/E ratios help signal if the current stock price is either under- or overvalued for the company's future prospects. Obviously, this methodology is only as good as the accuracy of the forecast for earnings per share for a company in a future period, and these estimates can be influenced by a variety of factors.

*Dividend payout ratio*    An investor can earn a return on investment through two means: capital gains associated with selling a stock at a higher price than the price at which it was purchased and through the receipt of dividends issued by the company. The specific dividend policy of a company is usually complex, incorporating a host of factors; however, at a more general level, companies issue dividends (either cash payments or additional stock issues) in an effort to attract equity. Ultimately, the amount of dividends issued is reflected in the share price, with the assumption being that all information is disseminated.

The dividend payout ratio measures the percentage of earnings paid out as dividends reflecting the level of dividends that the company is distributing. A company with a high dividend payout ratio is attempting to signal that it is well off financially or that the company does not have the need to re-invest the earnings for other activities. Conversely, a low dividend payout ratio signals that a company is strapped for cash or wishes to re-invest the earnings in an attempt to realize even greater earnings in future periods. The dividend payout ratio is calculated with the formula:

$$\text{Dividend Payout Ratio} = \frac{\text{Dividends Distributed per Share}}{\text{Earnings per Share}}$$

Using Southwest Airlines $0.24 earnings per share in 2008 and cash dividends of $0.018 per share issued during the year, the dividend payout ratio for Southwest Airlines would be:

$$\text{Dividend Payout Ratio}_{(2008)} = \frac{\$0.018}{\$0.24}$$

$$\text{Dividend Payout Ratio}_{(2008)} = 7.5\%$$

A dividend payout ratio of 7.5% shows that Southwest Airlines decided to distribute 7.5% of its earnings during the period back to its shareholders. Once again, there is no optimum dividend payout ratio, and equally successful companies can have wildly divergent dividend payout ratios; however, the ratio does enable an investor to understand the dividend policy of the company, and this helps an investor determine an expected value for the stock.

*Dividend yield ratio*    The dividend yield ratio measures the relationship between dividends distributed and the market price of the company. The dividend yield ratio provides a similar level of analysis as the dividend payout ratio and is important to investors, particularly shareholders' dependent on dividends as a return on their investment. The dividend yield ratio is calculated using the following formula:

$$\text{Dividend Yield Ratio} = \frac{\text{Dividends Distributed per Share}}{\text{Current Market Price}}$$

Using the cash dividend of $0.018 per share being distributed during 2008 and a market price for Southwest Airlines stock of $8.61, the dividend yield ratio is 0.21%.[14] This indicates that less than 1% of the pricing of Southwest Airlines stock is a result of dividends being distributed, indicating a low dividend yield. Since there are other ways a stock can yield a return on investment (for example, capital gains), this ratio alone should not distract investors; however, investors seeking dividends should probably focus their attention elsewhere. By and large, the airline industry has very low dividend yield and payout ratios. This is due in part to the volatility of the industry and the need to invest in extensive capital projects. However, a few sectors, such as utility companies, are renowned for strong dividend yields, representing a relatively safe investment opportunity for risk-adverse investors who wish to earn returns from dividends. Further discussion of dividend policy is contained later in the text.

## FINANCIAL RATIOS: AIRLINE-SPECIFIC RATIOS

Since every industry is unique, certain industry specific ratios are developed that help provide a greater depth of analysis and understanding of the industry. The airline industry ratios are centered on two major measures of an airline's output: available seat miles (ASM) and revenue passenger miles (RPM). These two measures, combined with various items on the income statement and balance sheet, provide a substantial amount of airline-specific financial ratios.

Available seat miles is a measure of an airline's output, since it represents the number of miles that the airline has flown with its available seats, regardless of whether the seat is filled by a passenger. To illustrate, a 200-seat aircraft flying a 1,000 mile flight would represent 20,000 ASMs.[15] Available seat miles provides some standardization to an airline's output; however, ASMs do not provide a complete standardization since airlines can have the same amount of ASMs, but operate completely differently. For example, a short-haul airline with multiple frequent flights could end up with a similar amount of ASMs as a long-haul international airline with less frequent flights, yet the two airlines have completely different operating structures. By altering aircraft frequency,

---

14    Dividend Yield Ratio (2008) = $0.018 / $8.61 = 0.21%.
15    ASMs = Number of Seats per Aircraft × Flight Distance = 200 seats × 1,000 miles = 20,000 ASM.

aircraft density, and flight distance, airlines can adjust their output either upward or downward.

Revenue passenger miles represent the number of miles that revenue passengers fly on the airline. Whereas ASMs do not differentiate between whether the seat is occupied or not, RPMs are only calculated for seats occupied by revenue passengers. To further illustrate, the revenue passenger miles for the 200-seat aircraft flying the 1,000 mile flight with 140 revenue passengers would by 14,000 RPMs.[16] As a result, RPMs provides standardization for revenue while also allowing for easy calculation of an airline's load factor. Load factor is simply the proportion of an airline's seats that are filled by revenue passengers, and can be calculated by dividing RPM by ASM.

$$\text{Load Factor} = \frac{\text{RPM}}{\text{ASM}}$$

As an example, consider Southwest Airlines 2008 operating statistics:

**Table 7.1      Southwest Airlines 2008 operating statistics**

| | |
|---|---|
| Available seat miles (millions) | 103,271 |
| Revenue passenger miles (millions) | 73,491 |
| Average load factor | 71.20% |

*Source*: Compiled by the authors from Southwest Airlines 2008 annual report.

In the above example, Southwest Airlines 2008 load factor was 71.2%. While load factor provides an understanding of the airline's operation, it is not useful in determining the profitability of an airline since it omits the two critical factors in determining profitability: revenue and cost. Load factor merely highlights if seats are full, but high load-factors alone do not indicate profitability. For example, an airline could achieve a 100% load factor if it sold every seat for one dollar; however, the flight would not be profitable as the costs would far exceed the revenue. Two important airline-specific metrics that standardize revenue and costs are respectively Revenue per Available Seat Mile (RASM) and Cost per Available Seat Mile (CASM).

RASM standardizes revenue by calculating the amount of revenue that an airline receives for one available seat mile. It is calculated by taking the total passenger revenue generated and dividing by total ASMs. For Southwest Airlines, its RASM is calculated below and was 10.21 cents for 2008.

$$\text{RASM} = \frac{\text{Total Passenger Revenue}}{\text{Total ASM}}$$

$$\text{RASM}_{(2008)} = \frac{\$10,549 \text{ million}}{103,271 \text{ million}}$$

$$\text{RASM}_{(2008)} = 10.21 \text{ cents}$$

---

16    RPMs = Number of Revenue Passengers × Flight Distance = 140 pax × 1,000 miles = 14,000 RPM.

This implies that for every seat mile that Southwest Airlines flies, it generates 10.21 cents of revenue for that seat. Therefore, this ratio provides standardization for all airlines since their revenue generation is based on their level of output.

A similar metric is Cost per Available Seat Mile (CASM), which standardizes the costs of operating the airline, by providing the cost for one available seat mile. CASM is frequently calculated using both total expenses and just operating expenses. Additionally, CASM for individual line items can be calculated. For example, the maintenance, materials, and repairs CASM can be calculated, enabling a comparison of an airline's maintenance operations with other airlines. Regardless of which cost item is being compared, CASM simply provides the cost on a seat mile basis.

$$CASM = \frac{Total\ Costs}{Total\ ASM}$$

$$CASM\text{-}Total_{(2008)} = \frac{\$10,796\ million}{103,271\ million} = 10.45\ cents$$

$$CASM\text{-}Operating_{(2008)} = \frac{\$10,574\ million}{103,271\ million} = 10.24\ cents$$

For Southwest Airlines in 2008, its total CASM was 10.45 cents. This included all its operating expenses, other expenses (such as interest and gains/losses), and income taxes. Since items such as interest expenses and income taxes do not directly relate to the operation of the airline, and ultimately the company's output, a more accurate measure of an airline's cost structure is its operating CASM, which includes just operating expenses. As a result, all future references to CASM relate to operating CASM, as does any CASM numbers released by airlines. For 2008, Southwest Airlines operating CASM was 10.24 cents.

As described earlier, profit/net income is simply the resultant of total revenue less total costs. Since both revenue and expenses are standardized by the same metric (ASM), profit can also be stated in terms of available seat miles. Southwest Airlines total profit in 2008, stated in terms of available seat miles was:

Total Profit per ASM = RASM – CASM

Operating Profit (loss) per ASM (2008) = 10.21 cents – 10.24 cents = -0.03 cents[17]

Southwest Airlines lost 0.03 cents for every seat mile that was flown in 2008. Therefore, a 137-seat aircraft flying a 500-mile route in 2008 earned Southwest Airlines, on average, a loss of $4.11. Obviously, if Southwest Airlines RASM was greater than their CASM, the calculation would be the airline's profit per ASM.

A common misconception made about RASM is that it equals the average fare paid by a passenger for one mile. However, since RASM can be adjusted by either obtaining more revenue from the same number of passengers or by increasing the total number of passengers, it does not accurately reflect the revenue generated for just the paid seats. Thus, RASM reflects the revenue generated for both paid and unpaid seats. Therefore, in

---

17    Note that Southwest Airlines earned a profit in 2008 even though RASM – CASM was negative. This was a result of freight and ancillary revenue, which was not included in the RASM calculation.

order to determine the average amount of revenue received for a paid seat, Revenue per Revenue Passenger Mile (RRPM) or yield is calculated.

$$\text{R/RPM}_{\text{(Yield)}} = \frac{\text{Total Passenger Revenue}}{\text{Total RPM}}$$

$$\text{R/RPM}_{(2008)} = \frac{\$10,549 \text{ million}}{73,492 \text{ million}}$$

$$\text{R/RPM}_{(2008)} = 14.35 \text{ cents}$$

In 2008, Southwest Airlines on average was able to generate 14.35 cents of revenue from a paid passenger for one seat mile. Therefore, the average revenue received for a 500-mile flight on Southwest Airlines in 2008 was just $71.75. It is important to note that the average fare paid by the consumer was probably much higher as a result of taxes and fees. Yield is an important airline metric since it ultimately measures the airline's ability to maximize revenue. This is accomplished through effective yield management and by providing a product that consumers want and are willing to pay for.

As mentioned earlier, when calculating airline passenger load factor, the value is generally irrelevant unless compared to the breakeven load factor. Breakeven load factor is defined as the average percentage of an airline's capacity that must be covered for the airline to make zero profit. As a result, breakeven load factor takes into consideration the costs required to provide the product (Vasigh, Fleming and Tacker, 2008). Based on breakeven load factor, any actual load factor greater than the break even would provide a positive contribution, while any load factor less than breakeven would represent a loss. The basic formula for breakeven load factor is:

$$\text{B/E}_{\text{Load Factor}} = \frac{\text{CASM}}{\text{RRPM}}$$

$$\text{B/E}_{\text{Load Factor (2008)}} = \frac{10.24 \text{ cents}}{14.35 \text{ cents}}$$

$$\text{B/E}_{\text{Load Factor (2008)}} = 71.36\%$$

where:
RRPM = Revenue per revenue passenger mile (yield)[18]

Based on calculations of Southwest Airlines' actual load factor (71.2%) and breakeven load factor (71.36%), the airline should report an operating loss; however, owing to cargo and other revenue, which is not included in RRPM, Southwest was actually able to earn an operating profit. While an airline may report an operating profit, it may not necessarily represent a net profit since fixed overhead costs and interest income/ expenses would still need to be met. Therefore breakeven load factor is usually one of the more important factors employed by an airline when assessing routes and flights on an individual basis.

---

18    Yield or revenue per revenue passenger mile is the standard measure of average air ticket price.

## Airline Industry Benchmarking

As mentioned earlier, calculating various financial ratios is merely an academic exercise unless they are compared to other firms competing in the same industry. Therefore, the remainder of this chapter is devoted to using the financial ratios discussed above to benchmark (compare) twelve U.S. airlines to highlight their comparative effectiveness with respect to the financial ratios. The twelve U.S. airlines represent a mixture of low-cost and legacy carriers, providing an interesting contrast between the business models for the respective categories. Since it is mandatory that all U.S. airlines provide financial and operating statistics to the Department of Transportation (DOT), all the data are readily available from the Bureau of Transportation Statistics (BTS), simplifying the process for performing industry benchmarking.[19]

*Profitability analysis* Figure 7.1 provides the profit margin for twelve United States airlines for 2007. Profit margin helps determine the carrier's ability to turn revenue into profit. Based on the data for 2007, all U.S. airlines were profitable except for Frontier Airlines (F9). Of all the carriers, it appears that Northwest Airlines (NW) was the most successful, posting a profit margin that was nearly double the next best carrier, Delta (DL). However, since the data represent only one year, they could be distorted due to special charges or one-time gains. Based on historical experience, profit margins in excess of 10% are rare for the airline industry; therefore, it is likely that Northwest's statistics are distorted by some other factors.

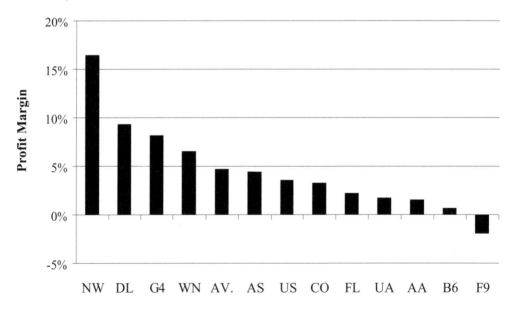

*Source*: Compiled by the authors from Bureau of Transportation Statistics (BTS) data.

**Figure 7.1　　U.S. airlines' profit margin: 2007**

19　It should be noted that the data obtained through the DOT and BTS are not perfect, as errors can exist in the data and carriers do not always group into similar categories.

Figure 7.2 shows that while most major U.S. carriers were profitable in 2007, almost all of the carriers posted losses in 2008. Only Allegiant Air (G4) and Southwest Airlines (WN) were profitable in 2008, with the average profit margin being approximately –13%. The reasons for the large negative profit margins include spiking fuel prices during the middle of 2008, reduced demand at the end of 2008 and in the case of Northwest and Delta, one-time costs associated with the merger.

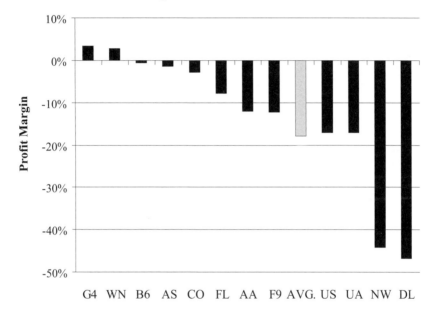

*Source*: Compiled by the authors using Back Aviation Form 41 data.

**Figure 7.2    U.S. airlines' profit margin: 2008**

As mentioned previously, a more accurate assessment of an airline's operations during the period is the operating profit margin ratio, which helps remove distortions in the data. Using the operating profit margin ratio, Figure 7.3 shows that Northwest Airlines (NW) dominance in 2007 over the industry was much less than if one had only examined the total profit margin. Northwest's gross profit margin was on par with Allegiant Air (G4) and Southwest Airlines (WN), with all three carriers around 8%. These three airlines present three divergent airline business models, with Northwest Airlines as a legacy international carrier, Allegiant as a leisure, quasi-charter airline, and Southwest Airlines as a national low-cost carrier. All three airlines found a way to turn roughly 8% of their revenue into an operating profit, highlighting their ability to maintaining a spread between unit revenues and unit costs in 2007.

Figure 7.4 highlights the change in operating profits by displaying the operating profit margins for the U.S. carriers in 2008. As with the total profit margin, the 2008 operating profit margins were much lower than they were in 2007 since only four major U.S. airlines were able to make an operating profit in 2008—Southwest, Allegiant, JetBlue and Delta. The average operating profit margin for all carriers in the figure was about -4%, a significant drop from the roughly positive 5% experienced in 2007.

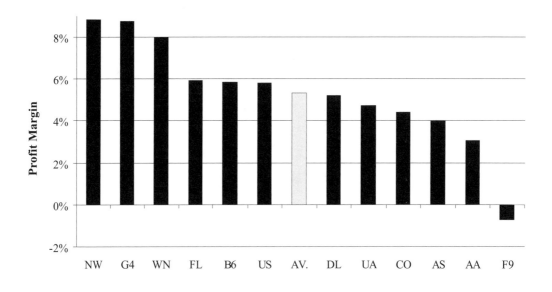

*Source*: Compiled by the authors from Bureau of Transportation Statistics (BTS) data.

**Figure 7.3      U.S. airlines' operating profit margin: 2007**

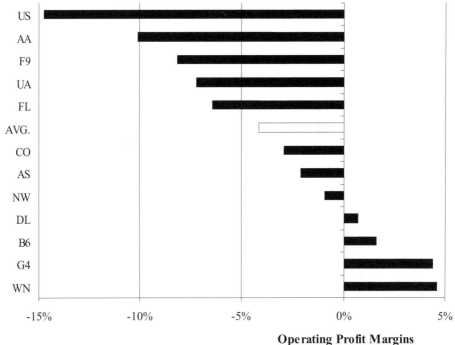

*Source*: Data Compiled by the Authors.

**Figure 7.4      U.S. airlines' operating profit margin: 2008**

Other methods for analyzing profitability are return on assets and return on equity. These metrics can be particularly important when deciding to invest in an airline, either through the purchase of equity or through capital leases. Figure 7.5 provides the 2007 return on assets for the twelve U.S. airlines that are being compared. Here both Allegiant Airlines (G4) and Northwest Airlines (NW) had very good returns on asset ratios. Their success could largely be attributed to the airlines having outright ownership of aircraft that are aging and are close to being fully depreciated. Since aircraft represent the largest asset pool for airlines, an airline that is able to generate decent returns with cheaper aircraft will generally have good ROA ratios. At the other end of the spectrum, both JetBlue (B6) and Frontier (F9) have new aircraft fleets, but were unsuccessful in 2007 parlaying these new aircraft into increased profitability.

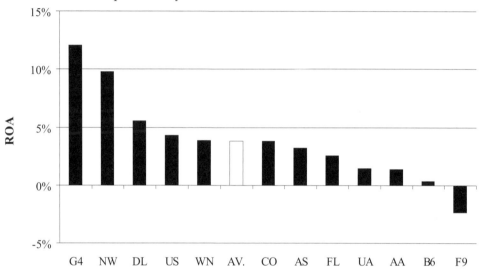

*Source*: Compiled by the authors from Bureau of Transportation Statistics (BTS) data.

**Figure 7.5      U.S. airlines' return on assets (ROA): 2007**

From a shareholders' perspective, an airline's ability to convert equity into profitability is one of the clear signals for the success of the company. Figure 7.6 shows that Allegiant Airlines (G4) had a tremendously high return on equity in 2007, while the rest of the industry also had solid ROE values. Clearly, equity investments in Allegiant Airlines translated into strong financial success in 2007. It is also worth noting that the grouping of carriers based on return on equity is similar to the return on asset ratios presented in Figure 7.5, with Allegiant and Northwest Airlines (NW) at the top and JetBlue (B6) and Frontier Airlines (F9) near the bottom.

Based on the four profitability metrics, a more in depth picture of the financial success of U.S. airlines is possible. This is particularly true when applied to Allegiant Airlines (G4), a small airline whose total profits only totaled $27 million, but whose financial performance was outstanding. This is a major benefit of benchmarking since it allows both small and large airlines, all with different operating philosophies, to be compared. Northwest Airlines (NW) displayed some strong financial results; this could be the culmination of financial restructuring and/or improved operational performance.

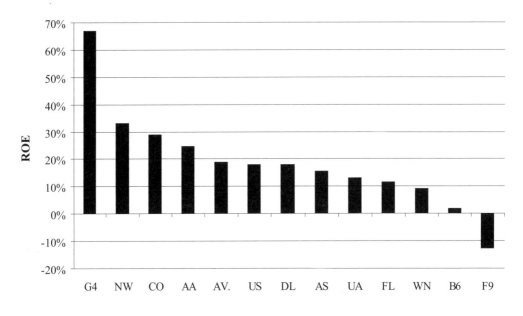

*Source*: Compiled by the authors from Bureau of Transportation Statistics (BTS) data.

**Figure 7.6      U.S. airlines' return on equity (ROE): 2007**

Southwest Airlines (WN) maintained steady financial results, proving yet again why it is continually regarded as one of the best managed U.S. airlines. As a whole, the U.S. airlines displayed solid financial results in 2007, particularly when compared to the disastrous financial performance of many previous years. However, 2008 saw a return to unprofitability for most carriers as a combination of high fuel prices and reduced demand reduced profit margins. While analyzing profitability helps one understand the historical performance of the airlines, more analysis is required to help predict future performance.

*Liquidity analysis*    As mentioned previously, the goal of liquidity ratios is to analyze the short-term solvency of an airline, in an effort to help determine if the airline can meet its short-term financial commitments. In an industry with such tremendous volatility, efficient cash management is critical to short-term success.

A key measurement of liquidity is the current ratio which compares the current assets of the company to its current liabilities. Ideally, an airline wants a current ratio greater than 1, indicating that its short-term liabilities can be covered by its current assets. For the twelve airlines sampled in Figure 7.7, only Northwest Airlines (NW) and Alaska Airlines (AS) had current ratios in excess of 1 in 2007. This indicates that for the other ten airlines, if all their current liabilities were to come due at once, they would not be covered. As it is, these airlines will have to take measures in the short-term to help satisfy their current liabilities. While the majority of the airlines have a current ratio in the 0.75 to 0.95 range, Allegiant Airlines (G4) has a current ratio of 0.39, which is very low. However, Allegiant's profitability ratios were above average for the industry, indicating that the airline may hope that future profits will generate cash, which in turn should help cover current liabilities. Regardless, Allegiant Airlines may need to do some restructuring of their current liabilities and assets to satisfy short-term requirements.

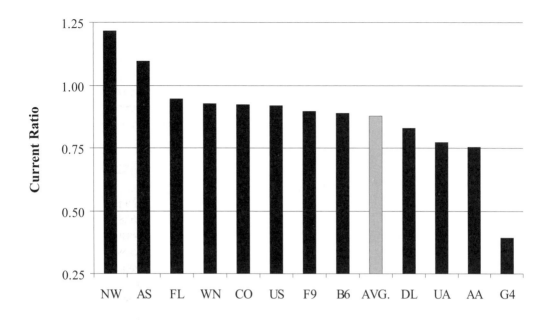

*Source*: Compiled by the authors from Bureau of Transportation Statistics (BTS) data.

**Figure 7.7    U.S. airlines' 200 current ratio: 2007**

While the current ratio and the quick ratio help analyze the overall immediate solvency of a company, three separate liquidity ratios analyze the financial structure of the airlines from an operational standpoint; these asses how effective the airlines are at cash management. Days of accounts receivables, days of accounts payable, and days of inventory are all metrics that analyze a different portion of an airline's cash management. When combined, they display the airline's overall cash management efficiency.

Figure 7.8 provides a comparison of the airlines' days of accounts receivables and days of accounts payable. These metrics should be analyzed together since an airline wants to receive its revenue as quickly as possible and pay its expenses as late as possible. Efficient cash management occurs when the airline's days of accounts receivables are low and when the airline's days of accounts payables are high. Based on Figure 7.8, American Airlines (AA), Continental Airlines (CO), and Allegiant Airlines (G4) all seem to have efficient cash management since their spans between days of accounts receivable and accounts payable are all in excess of 30 days. Through the introduction of electronic ticketing and the Internet, airlines have been able to reduce their days of accounts receivables considerably, as evidenced by the fact that the majority of the airlines have days of accounts receivable less than 20. The one exception is Alaska Airlines (AS), whose 58 days of accounts receivables is quite high. One possible reason behind Alaska Airlines high days of accounts receivables would be that a substantial portion of their operating revenue is derived from cargo, which has on average substantially longer days of accounts receivable than passenger revenue. At times, analyzing accounts payable can be misleading since suppliers may provide cost concessions if the airline pays earlier. Therefore, during negotiations with suppliers, purchasing departments must balance lower unit costs with shorter days of accounts payable. Figure 7.8 shows that most airlines have relatively short days of accounts payable. This is probably due to supplier negotiations for lower unit

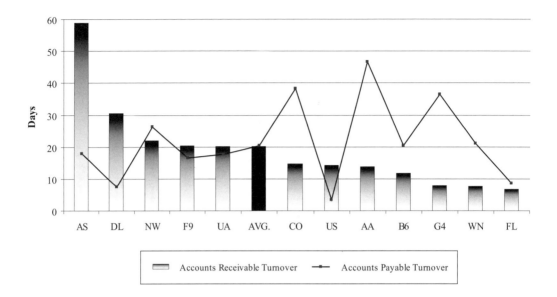

**Figure 7.8      U.S. airlines' days of accounts receivables and days of accounts payable: 2008**

costs (mentioned above) or other demands placed by suppliers on airlines because of the financial uncertainty of the airline industry. At the extreme of this is U.S. Airways (U.S.) where the days of accounts payable are 3 days. This makes it almost appear that the airline operates on a cash basis. Therefore, the airline receives very little benefit from credit and from the ability to hold onto cash.

The final metric used to analyze an airline's liquidity is the days of inventory, which determines how long, on average, inventory sits before being used. Inventory that is rarely used not only ties up cash that could be used elsewhere, but also incurs carrying costs for storing the inventory. However, too little inventory can cause operational problems resulting in either increased delays and cancellations or increased costs resulting from purchasing aircraft parts from other airlines. Figure 7.9 displays the days of inventory for the twelve U.S. airlines, with the assumption that all inventories are related to aircraft maintenance and repair expenses.[20] From Figure 7.9, Northwest Airlines (NW) holds inventory the longest while Alaska Airlines (AS) holds inventory the shortest. A possible explanation for Northwest Airlines long days of inventory is that its aging aircraft require more maintenance, and this in turn means that a greater stock of inventory is required. Another important factor that impacts the amount of inventory an airline holds is the number of different aircraft types in the fleet. Obviously, the greater the number of different aircraft types, the greater the inventory required. This means that inventory is one department where airlines can receive the benefits of economies of scale through operating streamlined aircraft fleets (i.e. operating less different types of aircraft). This reasoning could potentially explain the fact that four of the five highest airlines, in terms

---

20    While this assumption is not completely accurate, the majority of inventory held by airlines, in terms of dollars, is for aircraft maintenance. Other categories where inventory will be held include catering (if applicable) and general supplies.

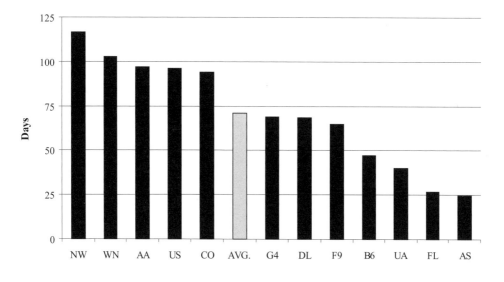

*Source*: Compiled by the authors from Bureau of Transportation Statistics (BTS) data.

**Figure 7.9      U.S. airlines' days of inventory: 2007**

of days of inventory, operate diverse fleets. The exception is Southwest Airlines and the possible reasons for this were discussed earlier in the chapter and  they relate to its extensive point-to-point route network.

*Long-Term risk analysis*    While solvency analysis deals with assessing an airline's ability to meet its short-term commitments, long-term risk analysis attempts to help predict the strength of the company in the future. Long-term risk analysis in the airline industry is usually analyzed using the debt to equity ratio, the debt ratio, and the times interest earned ratio. These will be covered in turn.

The heavy debt structure of the airline industry can be seen by comparing the debt-to-equity ratios of the twelve airlines. This heavy debt structure in the airline industry is ultimately the result of the immense amount of capital involved in operating an airline, with very large capital expenditures that are incurred for aircraft and facilities. Figure 7.10 shows the debt to equity ratio for twelve U.S. airlines. Note that all carriers have debt to equity ratios greater than 1, indicating that all of the carriers' capital structures are more heavily debt than equity weighted. The airline with the most balanced capital structure is Southwest Airlines (WN) as its debt to equity ratio is almost equal to 1. At the other end of the spectrum is American Airlines (AA), whose debt to equity ratio of 14 indicates that for every $1 in equity, American Airlines has $14 in debt. The cost of debt financing is reflected in interest expense. An airline that is highly leveraged in debt financing will incur a greater amount of interest expense, thus increasing the volatility of the company's earnings. On the other hand, the airline hopes that the use of debt financing will increase profits sufficiently to offset the increased interest expense.

Another debt based long-term risk metric is the debt ratio, which shows the total portion of assets financed by debt. A high debt ratio generally indicates a firm with greater risk since there are fewer assets that can be used to cover the debt. Also, this lack of assets may raise the cost of debt in the future since there may be more uncertainty and risk to the

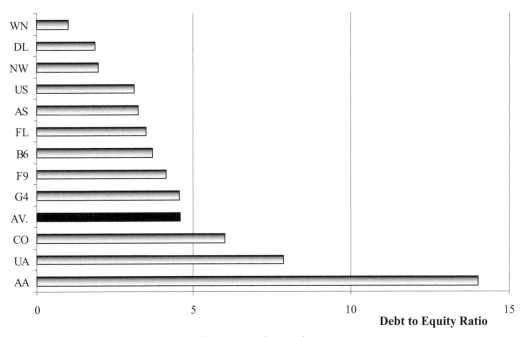

**Figure 7.10    U.S. airlines' debt-to-equity ratio: 2007**

lender. Therefore, from a long-term risk perspective, an airline with a lower debt ratio is generally less risky than a higher debt ratio airline. Based on the information contained in Figure 7.11, and using the rational explained above, the riskiest airline is United Airlines (UA) with a debt ratio greater than 0.80, and the least risky of the U.S. airlines is Southwest Airlines (WN) with a debt ratio of about 0.40. It is interesting to note that both Delta Air Lines (DL) and Northwest Airlines (NW) have relatively low debt ratios. This is likely the result of bankruptcy reorganization where the airlines could modify their debt structure. Note that Allegiant Airlines (G4), whose profitability ratios were some of the best in the industry, has the second highest debt ratio. Clearly Allegiant has used debt financing to generate increased profitability, but this has come with the increased risk of taking on too much debt. In the long-term, Allegiant must continue maintaining outstanding operational results, or the level of debt could be a problem in the future. This example highlights the fact that all of the ratios need to be analyzed when evaluating the financial strength or weakness of an airline.

Airlines with high debt ratios can expect increased interest expenses resulting from a larger debt load. The times interest earned ratio, displayed in Figure 7.12 for twelve U.S. airlines helps measure the airline's ability to meet its debt payments. A times interest earned ratio of less than one indicates that the airline does not generate enough earnings to cover its interest expense. A negative times interest earned (TIE) ratio indicates that the airline could fail to meet its interest payments and this could result in bankruptcy. Frontier Airlines' (F9) negative times interest earned ratio in 2007 was ultimately a signal of the airline declaring bankruptcy in 2008.

In 2008 the majority of the airlines shown in Figure 7.13 had negative times interest earned ratios. This indicates that these airlines have negative earnings, which severely impacts their ability to pay their debt. The only airlines which could comfortably pay their debt (had TIEs over 1) were Southwest Airlines and Allegiant.

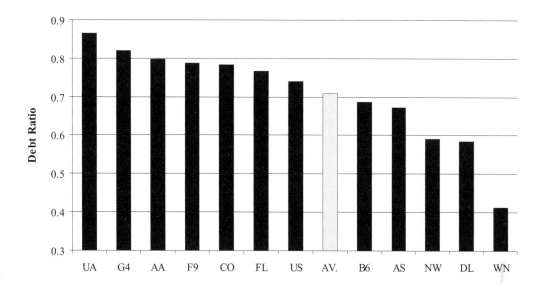

*Source*: Compiled by the authors from Bureau of Transportation Statistics (BTS) data

**Figure 7.11     U.S. airlines' debt ratio: 2007**

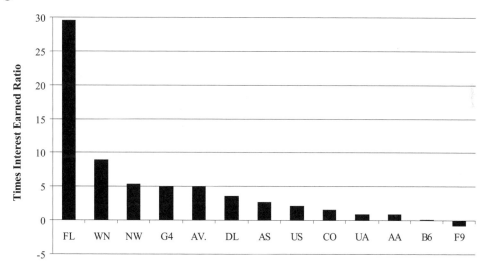

*Source*: Compiled by the authors from Bureau of Transportation Statistics (BTS) data.

**Figure 7.12     U.S. airlines' times interest earned ratio: 2007**

*Stock market analysis*   Another methodology used to analyze the airline industry is the external view of the airline. The price of the stock of a company, or an airline, varies according to the external perception of the company. The stock market is also the means by which airlines gain equity investment and it also helps signal the long term financial prospects of the airline. Since stock market prices change daily, ratios that contain these

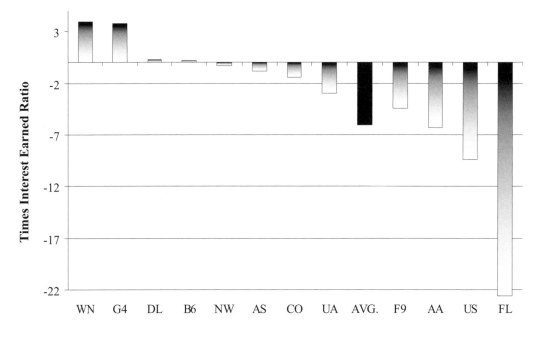

*Source*: Compiled by the authors using Back Aviation Form 41 Data.

**Figure 7.13     U.S. airlines' times interest earned ratio: 2008**

prices must be fixed at a certain point of time. Therefore, for comparison purposes, the data contained in Table 7.2 are based on market statistics generated at market closing on June 17, 2009. Owing to negative profits in 2008, all of the earnings per share (EPS) ratios are going to be negative except for the three carriers who made a profit in 2008, Allegiant, Republic and Southwest.

Based on the data compiled in Table 7.2, the price-earnings ratio can be calculated, which helps standardize the expectations of future earnings. Unlike many metrics which are backward looking, the price-earnings ratio provides some forward-looking information. This is because the price of the airline's stock is usually based on anticipated future cash flows. Table 7.3 displays the price-earnings ratio for eleven U.S. carriers. Investors want a higher price-earnings (PE) ratio, all other things equal, when investing in a company because it demonstrates that the company is using the money invested to generate earnings. Southwest Airlines had the highest PE ratio as of June 20, 2009 with a PE ratio of 100.29, with most of the carriers showing negative PE ratios.

Usually most stock market analysis of an industry would include calculating dividend yield and dividend payout ratios; however, of the airlines listed above, only Southwest Airlines issues dividends on a regular basis. Since dividends are usually issued by more financially stable companies, this is a good indication of the state of the industry; that is, of the carriers competing in the U.S. market. In this regard only Southwest Airlines felt it was financially stable enough to distribute dividends. This is probably not surprising considering the extreme volatility of the airline industry.

## Table 7.2      U.S. airlines' stock market data as of July 20, 2009

| Airline Name | Company Ticker Symbol | Market Price (@ 07/20/09) | EPS (@ 07/20/09) |
|---|---|---|---|
| AirTran | AAI | $6.18 | -1.80 |
| Alaska Airlines | ALK | $21.14 | -3.26 |
| Allegiant Airlines | ALGT | $45.77 | 2.64 |
| American Airlines | AMR | $4.33 | -3.78 |
| Continental Airlines | CAL | $9.75 | -5.69 |
| Delta Air Lines | DAL | $6.08 | -5.78 |
| Republic | RJET | $4.98 | 1.94 |
| JetBlue | JBLU | $4.61 | -0.23 |
| Southwest Airlines | LUV | $7.02 | 0.07 |
| United Airlines | UAUA | $3.39 | -39.05 |
| U.S. Airways | LCC | $2.04 | -19.65 |

Source: Compiled by the Authors.

## Table 7.3      U.S. airlines' price-earnings ratio as of July 20, 2009

| Airline Name | Market Price (@ 07/20/09) | EPS (@ 07/20/09) | PE Ratio |
|---|---|---|---|
| AirTran | $6.18 | ($1.80) | -3.43 |
| Alaska Airlines | $21.14 | ($3.26) | -6.48 |
| Allegiant Airlines | $45.77 | $2.64 | 17.34 |
| American Airlines | $4.33 | ($3.78) | -1.15 |
| Continental Airlines | $9.75 | ($5.69) | -1.71 |
| Delta Air Lines | $6.08 | ($5.78) | -1.05 |
| Republic | $4.98 | $1.94 | 2.57 |
| JetBlue | $4.61 | ($0.02) | -200.43 |
| Southwest Airlines | $7.02 | $0.07 | 100.29 |
| United Airlines | $3.39 | ($39.05) | -0.09 |
| U.S. Airways | $2.04 | ($19.65) | -0.10 |
| *Average* | | | *-8.57* |

Source: Derived from Data Compiled by the Authors.

*Operational analysis*    The final level of analysis of any company is operational efficiency. In the airline industry, analysis of operations can be quite involved; however, there are a few simple operational metrics that include the analysis of operating costs versus operating revenue.

Figure 7.14 displays the direct operating costs per available seat mile (CASM) for twelve U.S. carriers in 2007. Operating CASM standardizes the direct operating expenses associated with operating flights, providing a more accurate analysis of the airlines' operations. Not surprisingly, four of the five carriers with the lowest operating CASMs in 2007 are all classified as low-cost carriers. Of the major network carriers, Alaska Airlines (AS) and U.S. Airways (U.S.) had the highest cost structure in 2007, with the next five network carriers all having similar CASMs.

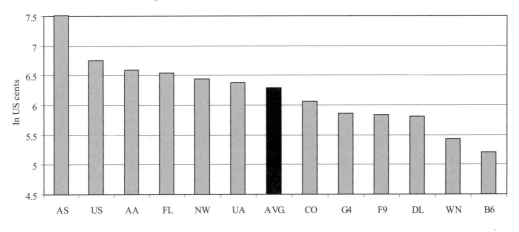

*Source*: Compiled by the authors from Back Aviation Form 41 Data.

**Figure 7.14    U.S. airlines' operating CASM: 2007**

Figure 7.15 shows the operating CASM for the same twelve airlines in 2008. As one can see by comparing Figure 7.15 with 7.14, operating CASM for 2008 went up from 2007. This is in large part due to the increase in fuel prices during 2008. One method to compare operating costs without the impact of fuel is CASM excluding fuel, which excludes the fuel line from the calculation. This metric ultimately then provides an analysis of an airline's core unit costs.

On the revenue side, the network carriers had the greatest revenue per available seat miles (RASM) in 2007, with Alaska Airlines and U.S. Airways leading the industry. U.S. Airways strong RASM should help offset their high operating costs. Part of the explanation for the revenue differentiation is the result of airlines catering to different market segments. Network carriers fly internationally where revenue yields are typically higher, and the network carriers can differentiate their product in this market segment by offering first class and business class service. The airline with the lowest RASM, Allegiant Airlines (G4), is able to compensate for their low revenue per available seat mile by having low operating costs. Therefore, both RASM and CASM need to be compared, since they both help explain the operational performance of the airlines.

Figure 7.17 shows revenue per available seat mile in 2008. The average RASM for the industry did not change much between 2007 and 2008. Northwest Airlines (NW) and American Airlines (AA) had the highest revenue per available mile during the year.

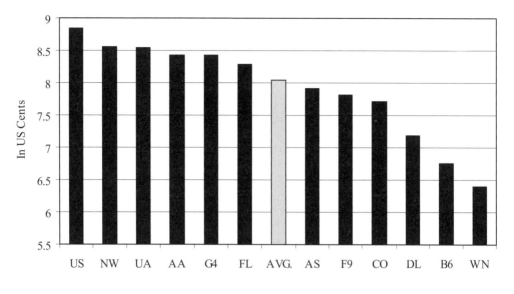

*Source*: Compiled by the authors from Back Aviation Form 41 Data.

**Figure 7.15    U.S. airlines' operating CASM: 2008**

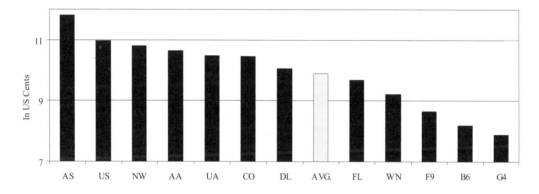

*Source*: Compiled by the authors from Back Aviation Form 41 Data.

**Figure 7.16    U.S. airlines' RASM: 2007**

Another revenue metric is revenue per revenue passenger mile (RRPM), which represents the average amount of revenue generated by a revenue passenger over one mile, also referred to as an airline's yield. Since RASM results can be impacted by load factor, RRPM measures how much revenue the airline can generate from a typical passenger without considering the problem of load factor. Figure 7.18 show that U.S. Airways (U.S.) had the greatest RRPM in the industry. Typically, airlines with short stage lengths are able to receive higher passenger yields, and this could help explain U.S. Airways lead in RRPMs, since U.S. Airways has several short-haul routes along the eastern United States seaboard. Airlines with relatively longer average stage lengths, like Frontier Airlines (F9) and JetBlue (B6) have lower yields when compared to the industry. Overall, most of the

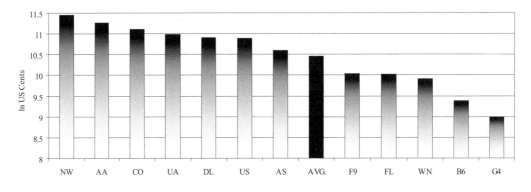

*Source*: Compiled by the authors from Back Aviation Form 41 Data.

**Figure 7.17     U.S. airlines' RASM: 2008**

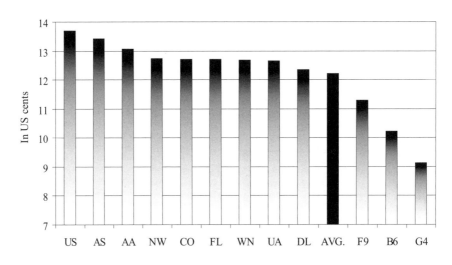

*Source*: Compiled by the authors using Back Aviation Form 41 Data.

**Figure 7.18     U.S. airlines' RRPM: 2007**

carriers are fairly close in terms of RRPMs, indicating fierce revenue competition that has resulted from fare matching. Because of this, it is very difficult for airlines to differentiate themselves in terms of revenue generation. For this reason, the industry has placed greater importance on controlling operating costs.

Figure 7.19 shows RRPM for 2008. In comparison to 2007, airline yields dropped from about 12 cents per revenue passenger mile to about 11 cents per revenue passenger mile in 2008. This indicates increased price competition across the industry, in part due to reductions in overall demand.

Finally, one of the most common, yet simplistic, measurements of an airline's operation is load factor. Load factor simply provides the percentage of an airline's inventory that is filled by revenue passengers. However, load factor does not take into consideration any of the revenue or operating costs of the airline; therefore, the metric alone is not terribly

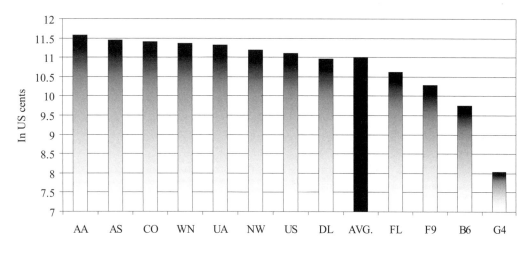

Source: Compiled by the authors using Back Aviation Form 41 Data.

**Figure 7.19     U.S. airlines' RRPM: 2008**

useful, as the passenger load factor can easily distort an airline's financial image. In order to be useful, load factor needs to be compared with the breakeven load factor (percentage of the plane which must be filled in order for the airline to breakeven at its current cost structure), with the difference between the two indicating the level of profitability. From Figure 7.20 we can see that most airlines were able to operate at a load factor greater than their breakeven load factor in 2007. At 64%, the airline with the lowest breakeven load factor was Southwest Airlines (WN) and interestingly, Southwest also had the lowest actual load factor in 2007. Southwest's industry-leading breakeven load factor is the result of its low operating costs and relatively high passenger yields.

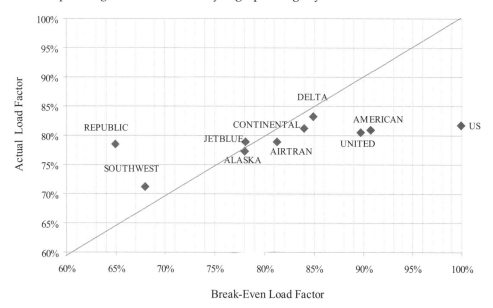

**Figure 7.20     U.S. airlines' load factors: 2008**

Figure 7.21 shows that the difference between actual load factor and breakeven load factor reveals a much different picture in 2008 than it did in 2007. U.S. airways has a breakeven point of 99.9%. This means that at their 2008 cost and yield structure U.S. airways will not be profitable even if they fill all of their seats on every flight. Therefore, U.S. will need to reduce costs and/or increase yield in order to maintain its level of operations. Several other airlines also had breakeven load factors greater than their actual load factor in 2007 and while not in as bad of a position as the U.S. Airways, these airlines will also need to lower costs or improve yields in order to return to profitability.

By benchmarking the U.S. airline industry through the use of profitability, liquidity, long-term risk, stock market related, and operational ratios, some general conclusions can be drawn about the industry and individual airlines. Overall, the industry was profitable in 2007; however, several of the operational, liquidity, and long-term risk ratios show an industry that has great difficulties and challenges, especially when compared to other industries. Of the low-cost carriers, both Southwest Airlines (WN) and Allegiant Airlines (G4) appear to have strong results, especially in terms of profitability; however, Allegiant does appear to have some liquidity issues that need to be addressed. Of the network carriers, Alaska Airlines (AS) had solid results throughout 2007, while U.S. Airways (U.S.) has some interesting operational results. The data for 2007 show that if U.S. Airways can reduce its costs, while maintaining its passenger yields, the airline could potentially have strong financial success. However, the reduction in operating expenses is very difficult, especially when the airline is struggling through a merger. Of all the airlines, Southwest Airlines appears the most stable and financially solid. This is not surprising considering its long history of financial success. However, Southwest Airlines is not immune from the multitude of challenges facing the airline industry—it may just be the best positioned airline to survive the challenges.

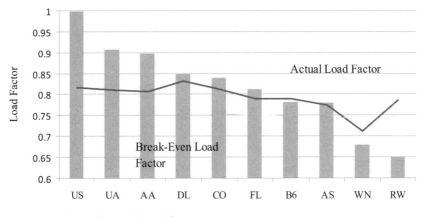

**Figure 7.21    U.S. airlines' load factors**

## PREDICTING INSOLVENCY

Airlines are known for their vulnerability to insolvency (Gritta, Adrangi, and Sergio, 2004). Many airlines have been under Chapter 11 bankruptcy protection and some airlines went bankrupt even when the market conditions were favorable. More than eleven airlines have already filed for bankruptcy or ceased operations since December 2007, with many airlines blaming the significant increase in fuel costs as a major contributing factor. Airlines such as Air Midwest, Aloha Airlines, ATA Airlines, Big Sky Air, Delta Air Lines, Northwest Airlines, Champion Air, EOS Airlines, Frontier Airlines, MAXjet Airways, and Skybus Airlines have filed for bankruptcy or have ceased operations (GAO, 2008).

In 2005 more than half of the U.S. airline capacity was with airlines that were acting under Chapter 11 bankruptcy protection (Isidore, 2005, and Gudmundsson, 2002). Chapter 11 allows U.S. airlines to break contracts and restructure under bankruptcy protection before emerging as a much leaner and better carrier. This fact has caused much concern, especially among the solvent airlines, as the following quote aptly demonstrates: "There is much concern that companies are taking advantage of the liberal U.S. bankruptcy laws, to the extent that incompetent executives keep their jobs, poorly managed companies survive, better managed companies are faced with unfair competition, and bankruptcy lawyers profit from unreasonably high fees… But the real problem may be that the stigma which once accompanied bankruptcy filing is gone" (Yang, Galen, 1993). With bankruptcy so prevalent in the airline industry, are there any indices or measures that might predict insolvency? Many ratios are useful in predicting the financial health of an airline.

## Altman's Z-score Model

For example, traditional ratio analysis is a frequently used tool for financial analysis. Presently, there are three theories that predict the likelihood of insolvency and these can be used to help investment decisions. They are: the Altman Z-score model, the Springate Z-score model, and the, Fulmer H-score model. Altman argued that the financial status of a firm is actually multidimensional, and no single ratio is able to reveal those dimensions; thus, a multivariate approach would be needed to capture the dimension crucial to capture the dimensions (Gudmundsson, 2002). Altman was the first person to successfully use step-wise multiple discriminate analysis to develop a prediction model with a high degree of accuracy and his model takes the following form (Altman, 1984):

Altman's Z-score Model for Private Industrial Companies:[21]

$$Z = 6.56A + 3.26B + 6.72C + 1.05D$$

with:

$$A = \frac{\text{Working Capital}}{\text{Total Assets}}$$

$$B = \frac{\text{Retained Earnings}}{\text{Total Assets}}$$

$$C = \frac{\text{EBIT}}{\text{Total Assets}}$$

$$D = \frac{\text{Market Value of Equity}}{\text{Book Value of Total Debt}}$$

The status of the company according to Altman's z-score model for private industrial companies is as follows:

- Healthy private company: z > 2.6
- Grey zone: 1.1 < z < 2.59
- Unhealthy company: Z < 1.1

---

21    Altman's original model takes the following form: Z = 1.2A + 1.4B + 3.3C + 0.6D + .999E.

## Springate's Z-score Model

Following procedures developed by Altman, Springate used step-wise multiple discriminate analysis to select four out of 19 popular financial ratios that best distinguished between sound businesses and those that actually failed (Springate, 1978).

$$Z = 1.03A + 3.07B + 0.66C + 0.4$$

with:

$$A = \frac{\text{Working Capital}}{\text{Total Assets}}$$

$$B = \frac{\text{Net Profit Before Taxes}}{\text{Total Assets}}$$

$$C = \frac{\text{EBIT}}{\text{Total Assets}}$$

$$D = \frac{\text{Sales}}{\text{Total Assets}}$$

A company may be classified as "failed" when the calculated Z value is less than .862.

## Fulmer's H-value Model

Fulmer also used step-wise multiple discriminate analysis to evaluate 40 financial ratios applied to a sample of 60 companies (Fulmer, et al., 1984). Fulmer chose a total of 60 companies and divided them equally among successful and failed businesses.

with:

$$V_1 = \frac{\text{Retained Earnings}}{\text{Total Assets}}$$

$$V_2 = \frac{\text{Sales}}{\text{Total Assets}}$$

$$V_3 = \frac{\text{EBIT}}{\text{Total Equity}}$$

$$V_4 = \frac{\text{Cash Flow}}{\text{Total Debt}}$$

$$V_5 = \frac{\text{Debt}}{\text{Equity}}$$

$$V_6 = \frac{\text{Current Liabilities}}{\text{Total Assets}}$$

$$V_7 = \log (\text{tangible total assets})$$

$$V_8 = \frac{\text{Working Capital}}{\text{Total Debt}}$$

$$V_9 = \frac{\log (\text{EBIT})}{\text{Interest Expenses}}$$

$$H = -6.075 + 5.528V_1 + 0.212V_2 + 0.073V_3 + 1.27V_4 - 0.12V_5 + 2.335V_6 + 0.575V_7 + 1.083V_8 + 0.894V_9$$

Companies with a negative H value may be a strong candidate for insolvency.

Table 7.4 shows Altman's Z-Score Model for Public Industrial Companies, Private Industrial Companies, Springate's Z-Score Model, and Fulmer's H-Score Model applied to U.S. Airlines for 2007 data.

**Table 7.4    Insolvency indexes for selected U.S. airlines**

|  | Altman public industrial | Altman private industrial | Springate | Fulmer |
|---|---|---|---|---|
| American Airlines | 0.9 | -0.4 | 0.3 | -2.6 |
| Alaska Airlines | 1.2 | 1.1 | 0.5 | -0.9 |
| JetBlue Airways | 0.7 | 0.3 | 0.2 | -2.6 |
| Continental Airlines | 1.4 | 0.4 | 0.6 | -1.3 |
| Delta Air Lines | 1.1 | 0.8 | 0.4 | -1.1 |
| AirTran Airways | 1.4 | 0.5 | 0.6 | -0.8 |
| Allegiant Air | 1.9 | -0.6 | 0.7 | -0.5 |
| Northwest Airlines | 1.2 | 1.5 | 0.6 | -1 |
| United Airlines | 0.9 | -0.2 | 0.3 | -2 |
| U.S. Airways | 1.5 | 0.5 | 0.6 | -1.3 |
| Southwest Airlines | 1.8 | 2.3 | 0.4 | 1 |

As Table 7.4 amply demonstrates, the airline industry is not in particularly good financial condition at least as far as these particular models are concerned. Once again, the most successful airline overall is Southwest Airlines, although even Southwest has some low scores. United and American Airlines appear to have the lowest scores from these models and this was also confirmed through some of the ratio analysis earlier in the chapter. This problem is consistent with the financial difficulty that the airline industry has experienced in this period.

All of the above models are suggestive indicators that show looming financial distress in the airline industry. However, these models alone cannot be totally relied upon as major predictors of airline bankruptcy (Adrangi, 2004). Airline management can perhaps take the necessary actions to improve the financial trends in the industry.

## SUMMARY

This chapter covered financial ratio analysis using measures of profitability, liquidity, stock market, and operational metrics. Comparisons of ratios with different industries would be meaningless. For example, comparing leverage ratios of stable companies such as Airbus with seasonal and cyclical airlines such as Alitalia would be useless. While financial ratios can provide us with important information about the financial performance of an airline, we should be aware that there are limitations to the use of financial ratios as an analytical tool in financial evaluations. The various ratios were defined and discussed individually and Southwest Airline's data for 2008 were used to give quantitative examples of how the ratios might actually be calculated. The results were then analyzed and discussed. Following this, the ratios were used to benchmark (compare) many of the largest airlines in the U.S. airline industry. Finally, three measures were introduced that might indicate a tendency toward an insolvency. These were then used to calculate the actual values for selected airlines that had previously been compared in the benchmarking process.

## DISCUSSION QUESTIONS

1. If an airline's ROE is low and management wants to improve it, explain why debt financing might be preferred to equity financing.
2. Explain why sometimes it is misleading to compare an airline's financial ratios with another airline which operates in the same route.
3. What are the most important determinants of an airline's return on stock holders' equity?
4. What is the major limitation of the current ratio as a measurement of an airline's liquidity?
5. What does a
   a.   debt ratio of 1.3 tell?
   b.   current ratio 1.5 tell?
   c.   quick ratio of 2.3 tell?
6. Discuss whether a high level of financial leverage is desirable.
7. Which financial leverage measure would be more desirable to evaluate Southwest airline's ability to pay its debt?
8. Discuss the limitations of ratio analysis and the cautions which must be taken when reviewing a cross sectional and time series analysis.
9. Describe the Z score suggested by Altman and calculate the Z score for EZjET airline with the following financial ratios:
10. Evaluate the limitations of ratio analysis and the steps which must be taken when reviewing financial and operational performance of airlines in different markets.
11. EZjET Airlines has the following financial data. Construct the DuPont system and determine which areas of the airline require additional analysis.

- $\dfrac{Sales}{Total\ assets} = 0.90$

- $\dfrac{Market\ equity}{Debt} = 0.10$

- $\dfrac{EBIT}{Total\ assets} = 0.10$

- $\dfrac{Retained\ earnings}{Total\ assets} = 0.2$

- $\dfrac{Working\ capital}{Total\ assets} = 0.08$

EZjET Airlines:

| | |
|---|---|
| Sales | $50,000,000 |
| Net profits after taxes | 40,000 |
| Total assets | 10,000,000 |
| Total liabilities | 6,000,000 |

Industry Averages:

| | |
|---|---|
| Total asset turnover | 0.50 |
| Debt ratio | 73.00% |
| Financial leverage multiplier | 2.50 |
| Return on total assets | 5.75% |
| Return on equity | 4.00% |
| Net profit margin | 3.50% |

12. Obtain the latest SEC 10-K filing for Continental Airlines and calculate the following metrics for the most current period:
   Operating margin
   Profit margin
   Return on assets
   Return on equity
   Asset turnover ratio
   Working capital
   Current ratio
   Debt-to-equity ratio
   Net debt-to-equity ratio
   Times interest earned ratio
   Basic earnings per share (If full year profit is a loss, calculate diluted earnings per share)
   Load factor
   Breakeven load factor
   Passenger revenue per available seat mile (PRASM)
   Total revenue per available seat mile (TRASM)
   Cost per available seat mile excluding fuel (CASM-ex fuel)
   Altman Z-Score

13. How can high risk, low ROA industries such as airline attract capital?

14. Assume DirectJet has an equity multiplier of 1.78, total asset turnover of 1.12, and a profit margin of 9 percent, what is its ROE?

15. EZjET has a long-term debt ratio of 0.85 and a current ratio of 1.30. Profit margin is 11%, ROE is 24.4%, current liabilities are $900 million, and sales are $5,600 million. What is the amount of the firm's net fixed assets?

# APPENDIX 1: FINANCIAL RATIOS

## *Financial ratios*

Profitability Ratios :

$$\text{Operating Profit Margin} = \frac{\text{Operating Profit}}{\text{Total Revenue}} = \frac{EBIT}{Sales}$$

$$\text{Profit Margin} = \frac{\text{Income } after\ taxes}{\text{Total Revenue}} = \frac{EAT}{Sales}$$

$$\text{Return on Equity (ROE)} = \frac{\text{Net Income}}{\text{Total Stockholders' Equity}} = \frac{EAT}{Equity}$$

$$\text{Return on Asset(ROA)} = \frac{EAT}{\text{Total Assets}} = \frac{EAST}{TA}$$

$$\text{Return on Assets} = \text{Profit Margin} \times Asset\ turnover$$

$$\text{ROE} = \frac{\text{Net Income}}{\text{Sales}} \times \frac{\text{Sales}}{\text{Total Assets}} \times \frac{\text{Total Assets}}{\text{Equity}}$$

$$\text{ROE} = \text{ROA} \times \text{Equity Multiplier}$$

Liquidity Ratios :

$$\text{- Current Ratio (CR)} \quad = \frac{\text{Current Assets}}{\text{Current Liabilities}} = \frac{CA}{CL}$$

$$\text{- Quick Ratio (QR)} \quad = \frac{\text{Quick Assets}}{\text{Current Liabilities}} = \frac{QA}{CL}$$

$$\text{- Net Working Capital} = \text{CA-CL}$$

Activity Ratios :

$$\text{- Accounts Receivable Turnover Ratio} = \frac{\text{Net Credit Sales}}{\text{Accounts Receivables (AR)}}$$

$$\text{- Days of Accounts Receivables} = \frac{\text{Number of Days in Period}}{\text{Accounts Receivable Turnover Ratio}}$$

$$\text{- } Average\ Collection\ Period = \frac{AR}{\dfrac{Total\ sales}{365}}$$

$$\text{- Accounts Payable Turnover Ratio} = \frac{\text{Period Purchases}}{\text{Average Accounts Payable}}$$

$$\text{- Days of Accounts Payable} = \frac{\text{Number of Days in Period}}{\text{Accounts Payable Turnover Ratio}}$$

$$\text{- Inventory Turnover Ratio} = \frac{\text{Cost of Goods Sold}}{\text{Average Inventory}}$$

$$\text{- Days of Inventory} = \frac{\text{Number of Days in Period}}{\text{Inventory Turnover Ratio}}$$

Leverage Ratios :

$$\text{Debt-to-Equity (D/E)} = \frac{\text{Total Debt}}{\text{Total Stockholders' Equity}}$$

$$Debet\ Assets\ Ratio = \frac{Total\ Debt}{Total\ Assets}$$

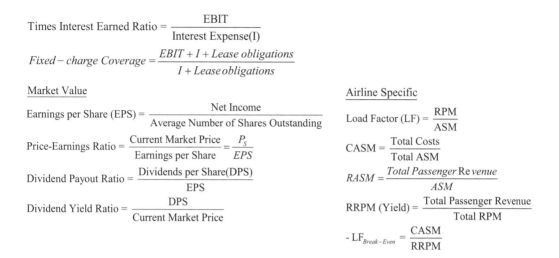

$$\text{Times Interest Earned Ratio} = \frac{\text{EBIT}}{\text{Interest Expense(I)}}$$

$$Fixed - charge\ Coverage = \frac{EBIT + I + Lease\ obligations}{I + Lease\ obligations}$$

Market Value

$$\text{Earnings per Share (EPS)} = \frac{\text{Net Income}}{\text{Average Number of Shares Outstanding}}$$

$$\text{Price-Earnings Ratio} = \frac{\text{Current Market Price}}{\text{Earnings per Share}} = \frac{P_S}{EPS}$$

$$\text{Dividend Payout Ratio} = \frac{\text{Dividends per Share(DPS)}}{\text{EPS}}$$

$$\text{Dividend Yield Ratio} = \frac{\text{DPS}}{\text{Current Market Price}}$$

Airline Specific

$$\text{Load Factor (LF)} = \frac{\text{RPM}}{\text{ASM}}$$

$$CASM = \frac{\text{Total Costs}}{\text{Total ASM}}$$

$$RASM = \frac{Total\ Passenger\ Re venue}{ASM}$$

$$\text{RRPM (Yield)} = \frac{\text{Total Passenger Revenue}}{\text{Total RPM}}$$

$$- LF_{Break-Even} = \frac{\text{CASM}}{\text{RRPM}}$$

# APPENDIX 2: DUPONT MODEL

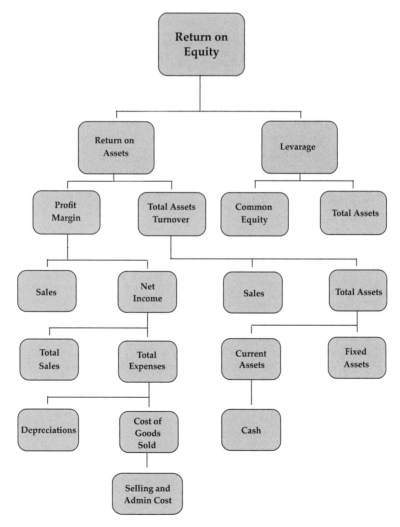

## REFERENCES

Adrangi, B. (2004). "Assessing the Financial Condition of the Major U.S. Passenger Airlines Over the 1993–2003 Period Using the P-Score and Z Score Discriminant Models", *Credit and Financial Management Review*.

Altman, E. (1984). "A Further Empirical Investigation of the Bankruptcy Cost Question." *Journal of Finance* 39:1067–1089

Fulmer, J., J. Moon, T. Gavin, M. Erwin "A Bankruptcy Classification Model For Small Firms." *Journal of Commercial Bank Lending*, 25–37.

Galen, M., and C. Yang (1993, January 25). "Legal affairs: a new page for Chapter 11?" *Business Week*, 3302, p. 36.

GAO, (2008). United States Government Accountability Office, Airline Industry, Potential mergers and acquisitions driven by financial and competitive pressures. GAO-08–845 Washington, D.C.: July, 2008.

Gritta, R., B. Adrangi, and D. Sergio (2004). "Assessing the Financial Condition of the Major U.S. Passenger Airlines Over the 1993–2003 Period Using the P-Score and Z-Score Discriminant Models", *Credit and Financial Management Review*.

Gudmundsson, S. (2002). "Airline Distress Prediction Using Non-Financial Indicators", *Journal of Air Transportation*, 7(2).

Isidore, C. (2005, September 15). Delta, Northwest file for bankruptcy: Spike in jet fuel sparks filings, putting almost half of U.S. airline capacity in Chapter 11. Retrieved July 29, 2008, from http://money.cnn.com/2005/09/14/news/fortune500/bankruptcy_airlines/

Ross, A., W. Westerfield, and D. Jordan (2008). *Fundamentals of Corporate Finance*, 8th ed. McGraw-Hill, Irwin Publishing Company.

Southwest Airlines (2008, February 1). Southwest Airlines 2007 Annual Report. Retrieved March 4, 2009 from http://www.southwest.com/investor_relations/annual_reports.html

Springate, G. (1978) "Predicting the Possibility of Failure in a Canadian Firm." Unpublished M.B.A. Research Project, Simon Fraser University.

# PART III

# Airline Capital Budgeting

# 8

# Airline Capital Budgeting

"Few businesses have as many variables and challenges as airlines. They are capital-intensive. Competition is fierce."

Joseph Weisenthal[1]

Airlines, maybe more so than other industries, require long-term capital expenditures for profitable, sustainable and efficient business operation. Commercial airlines are faced with many potential capital investment projects but limited financial resources, so many decisions must be made concerning projects with a long lifespan. The process of allocating capital and determining the profitability of long-term projects is called capital budgeting. Hence, capital budgeting is about deciding which projects are more profitable and add greater value to the airline. Therefore, airline managers must be competent in deciding whether an investment is worth undertaking and be able to choose intelligently between several different alternatives. In this chapter we look at different capital budgeting techniques and criteria such as payback period, net present value, internal rate of return, and break-even analysis. Applying these financial tools, the overall capital budgeting for an airline can be understood by first looking at capital decision-making on a more micro-level. The following topics are presented and discussed in the chapter:

- Airline Capital Budgeting and Cash Flows
- Project Classifications
  - Replacement vs. Expansion
  - Independent vs. Mutually Exclusive
- Payback Period
- Discounted Payback Period
- Net Present Value Method (NPV)
- Internal Rate of Return (IRR)
- Modified Internal Rate of Return (MIRR)
- Profitability Index (PI)
- Break-Even Analysis
  - Accounting Break Even
  - Economic Break Even
- Summary
- Discussion Questions.

---

1    Freelance economics and business journalist.

## AIRLINE CAPITAL BUDGETING AND CASH FLOWS

"Choosing the right investments to maximize the airline's position in the ever-changing marketplace is not a trivial task. Planning for capital expenditures is a vital element in ensuring future prosperity."

CA Advisors (Consulting Firm)

Capital budgeting is the backbone of financial management and making appropriate capital budgeting decisions is vital to achieving the goal of maximizing shareholders wealth. Capital budgeting is also important in cash flow analysis, as the timing of payments and financing ultimately impact a company's cash balance; however, the time value of money can impact a projects' perceived profitability. Applying these financial tools, the overall capital budgeting for an airline can be understood by first looking at capital decision-making on a more micro-level.

Capital budgeting is the process of identifying, evaluating and using capital to invest in long-term assets or projects. Airlines must decide how to use capital in order to provide value for the company and its shareholders.[2] For example, when Southwest Airlines replaces old aircraft with new and more fuel-efficient ones, the airline often reduces the operating costs associated with flying its new aircraft. In other words, capital budgeting is the process of identifying the best investment projects and the optimal allocation of resources. While in an ideal world any perceived profitable capital project should be undertaken, airlines are faced with financial constraints, so that the role of capital budgeting must include the rationing of capital.

The aviation industry is filled with numerous examples of projects requiring capital budgeting. For instance, when an aircraft manufacturer decides to introduce a new aircraft, it goes through a capital budgeting process to determine whether or not the project will be profitable. Consider Airbus's decision to build the new A380 airliner.[3] To determine whether to undertake the project, Airbus had to forecast expected future cash flows (inflows and outflows) and the prospects of obtaining the necessary financing. Airbus committed substantial resources to build A380 and if the capital budgeting has a flaw, it is difficult to reverse the decision owing to the massive initial cost and the initial contracts with subcontractors and the launch airline customers.

The cash flows for a typical long-term project, like the A380, involve cash outflows (payments) at the beginning of the project followed by cash inflows (revenues) in the latter half of the project. For the A380, design and development costs, followed by production costs would be major cash outflows. Cash inflows for the A380 would be initial aircraft purchase deposits from customers, full aircraft payment, and any additional support or spare parts revenue. In order to determine if the project was profitable or not, Airbus had to estimate the present and future cash flows of the project for the life of the aircraft, while keeping in mind the concept of time value of money. Research and development costs of the A380 were estimated to be around $13 billion U.S.D. (Sparaco, 2004). To offset development costs, Airbus may receive cash inflows for the next 40 years; however, because Airbus does not know the exact number of A380s they are going to sell in the

---

2    Capital budgeting preference decisions typically relate to choosing between several different alternatives, such as which type of aircraft to purchase.
3    The aircraft is listed at $300 million. The launch customers generally do not pay full list price, especially if they order large numbers of aircraft, so the average price could be anything between $200 and $250 million.

future, sales estimates are used based on a host of demand and economic factors. At full production Airbus is expected to produce about 50 A380s per year with the average sales price estimated at $225 million and a profit margin of 20% (Airbus A3XX, 2001). Based on these assumptions, at full production the cash flows would amount to $2.25 billion annually.[4] Assuming that Airbus does not produce at full capacity during the first two years, a cash flow diagram can be constructed (Figure 8.1) where the upfront development costs are borne in year zero, with positive cash flows depicted in future years.

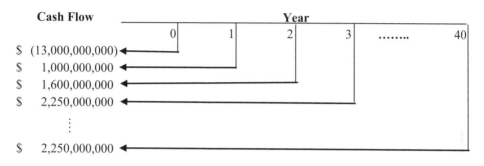

*Source*:  Harvard Business School, Case 9-201-028. Revised August 24, 2001.

**Figure 8.1     Potential cash flow: A-380**

While the above example displays equal cash flows from year three onwards, in many cases unequal cash flows will exist.[5] Unequal cash flows can be important as they impact the different methods that managers use to decide whether a project is accepted or rejected. Additionally, just because the capital budgeting process shows a project being profitable, that does not mean that it actually will be profitable, since many times reality differs from forecast. Cost overruns, incorrect demand assumptions, and unrealized costs are just many of the problems with forecasting capital budgeting projects; therefore, the goal is to make the analysis as accurate as possible, detailing all potential cash inflows and outflows. Before explaining the various capital budgeting methodologies, an understanding of project classifications is important, as it impacts the decision-making process.

## PROJECT CLASSIFICATIONS

There are many types of projects that a company can undertake. It is important for managers to distinguish between the types of projects in order to make the best decisions. Projects can be categorized into two different classifications:

- Replacement vs. expansion decisions
- Independent projects vs. mutually exclusive projects

---

4      Aircraft List Price × Annual Production × Contribution  Margin = Annual Cash Flow
                          $225MM × 50 a/c × 20% = $2.25B.
5      Numbers derived from "Airbus A380: Developing the World's Largest Commercial Jet (A)"; Case 9-201-028. Revised August 24, 2001; Harvard Business School.

## Replacement vs. Expansion Decisions

Capital assets can either be used to replace existing assets or to expand the business through the use of additional assets. A finance manager must know for which purpose the long-term assets will be used, since this impacts the capital budgeting analysis. In light of rising fuel prices, airline managers are facing numerous replacement decisions with respect to older, less fuel-efficient aircraft. For instance, Continental Airlines has decided to retire many of its older generation 737CL aircraft (–300, –500)[6] in favor of new 737NG aircraft (–700, –800, –900, –900ER) (Continental Airlines, 2008). Continental's replacement strategy is a result of believing the higher ownership costs of 737NG's are outweighed by the operating savings versus the 737CL aircraft. Additionally, Continental may also factor in residual cash inflows from the sale of 737CL aircraft. Continental's 737CL replacement plan is detailed in Table 8.1. On the other hand, Northwest's analysis differs from Continental's since it has chosen to retain 40-year old DC9 aircraft in lieu of new airplanes. This is probably the result of Northwest's aircraft being fully depreciated, minimizing the ownership cash outflows of the aircraft.

**Table 8.1    Continental Airlines Boeing 737 fleet plan as of June 5, 2008**

| Aircraft Model | Total at 6/30/08E | Net Changes 2H08E | Total at 12/31/08E | Net Changes 2009E |
|----------------|-------------------|-------------------|--------------------|-------------------|
| 737-900ER* | 10 | 10 | 20 | 18 |
| 737-900 | 12 | - | 12 | - |
| 737-800* | 111 | 6 | 117 | - |
| 737-700 | 36 | - | 36 | - |
| 737-300** | 47 | -24 | 23 | -23 |
| 737-500** | 55 | -13 | 42 | -7 |
| Total 737 Fleet | 271 | -21 | 250 | -12 |

* Final mix of new 737-800/-900ERs are subject to change
** Final mix and quantity of 737-300/-500 exits subject to change

Capital assets can also be used to expand operations by deriving increased profits from the asset. When the airline sees opportunities for additional growth, it may want to invest in expansion to obtain additional profits. Despite recent hardships in the airline industry, Southwest Airlines remains profitable, recording a profit of $179 million in 2008 (Southwest Airlines, 2008). In light of industry announcements of capacity reductions, Southwest Airlines has looked to expand its market share by adding service to new cities such as Denver, San Francisco, Boston, Minneapolis, Milwaukee, and New York LaGuardia where legacy carriers have scaled back their capacity. In order to expand, Southwest can either increase aircraft utilization or add additional aircraft. The capital budgeting process assesses the acquisition of new aircraft by comparing future profitability versus the

---

6       The Boeing 737 Classic is the name given to the B737-300, B737-400, and B737-500 series after the introduction of theB737-600 through B737-900 series.

acquisition costs of the aircraft. Southwest Airlines long-term aircraft orders are depicted in Table 8.2, displaying its fleet growth.

**Table 8.2     Southwest Airlines revises Boeing 737-700 delivery schedule as of January 22, 2009**

| Year | Firm | Options | Purchase Rights | Total |
|---|---|---|---|---|
| 2009 | 13 | - | - | 13 |
| 2010 | 10 | - | - | 10 |
| 2011 | 10 | 10 | - | 20 |
| 2012 | 13 | 10 | - | 23 |
| 2013 | 19 | 4 | - | 23 |
| 2014 | 13 | 7 | - | 20 |
| 2015 | 14 | 3 | - | 17 |
| 2016 | 12 | 11 | - | 23 |
| 2017 | - | 17 | - | 17 |
| Through 2018 | - | - | 54 | 54 |
| Total | 104 | 62 | 54 | 220 |

*Source*: Southwest SEC filings, January 2009.

## Independent Projects vs. Mutually Exclusive Projects

Capital projects can also be classified as either independent or mutually-exclusive, depending on the project's impact on other projects. A project is considered independent if the decision to accept or reject the project does not impact the decision of other projects. For instance, an airline could be assessing the installation of personal video entertainments systems at every seat. Such an analysis would consider the cost of the system, the maintenance of the system, any additional fuel burn resulting from incremental weight and the intangible customer satisfaction from the new entertainment system. This decision is probably mutually-exclusive as the decision is to install the entertainment system or not, with no other projects directly linked to the outcome. While most decisions will have ramifications on other projects, the key to independent projects is that no other projects await a decision as a result of the independent project.

Mutually exclusive projects are a set of projects where only one project will be accepted. When evaluating mutually exclusive projects, more than one project may prove to be profitable, satisfying the capital budgeting criteria; however, only the best project can be accepted. Mutually exclusive projects are created out of constraints, such as limited manpower or a lack of financial resources. In such cases, managers will compare all of the projects being proposed and determine which project they believe will deliver the most value for the company and its shareholders. An example of a mutually exclusive project was Boeing's decision to develop the 7E7 commercial airliner (now known as the

787 Dreamliner). At the time, Boeing was also considering a supersonic airliner and a stretch version of the 747 but determined that a medium-sized, wide-body, twin-engine jet airliner with greater fuel-efficiency would be the most profitable project. Such a decision was deemed mutually exclusive as such massive projects would utilize the majority of Boeing's engineering capabilities, while also consuming the majority of Boeing's capital resources. In other words, Boeing did not have the capabilities to pursue all three projects concurrently, even if the analysis showed that all projects would be profitable.

## PAYBACK PERIOD

There are several different methods that can be used by finance managers in determining whether or not an independent project should be undertaken or to choose between multiple projects. While each method has various strengths and weaknesses, the simplest methodology is payback period. A very simple example is the following: if you invest $15,000 and make $3,000 per month on that investment, the payback period will be 5 months. Hence, payback period is defined as the amount of time taken to recover the original investment. Using the payback period method, a manager sets the threshold in the time the project must return its original investment. Projects with a payback period shorter than the threshold are accepted. For instance, if the company requires all projects to recoup their initial investment within three years, a project with a payback period of four years would be rejected. In the case of mutually exclusive projects, the project with the shortest payback period will be chosen.

In order to understand the mechanics of calculating a potential project's payback period, consider two different proposals facing the maintenance department of a major airline. The first proposal would expand the airline's maintenance hangar allowing the airline to contract out maintenance services for other airlines. The second proposal requires the airline to redesign and improve its maintenance processes so that an aircraft's span days[7] are reduced and more aircraft can be accommodated. While the hangar expansion project will ultimately provide greater long-term benefit, the expansion project costs over twice as much and requires several years of ramp-up, creating uneven cash flows. Assuming the process revision can be implemented quickly, constant positive cash inflows are created. Table 8.3 provides the fully burdened cash flows for the two projects by year, as well as the cumulative cash flow.

The payback period is the point where the cumulative net cash flow equals zero. Depending on the nature of the cash flows, payback period can be computed simply. For projects with even cash inflows, payback period can be calculated using the following formula:

$$Payback\ Period = \frac{Initial\ Investment}{Annual\ Cash\ Inflow}$$

For the process revision project, the payback period is calculated to be 1.75 years, or one year and nine months.

$$Payback\ Period = \frac{\$7\,million}{\$4\,million} = 1.75\,years$$

---

7   Span days are the length of time that it takes to perform an aircraft's maintenance check.

**Table 8.3      Cash flows for maintenance project proposals**

| | Hangar expansion | | Process revision | |
|---|---|---|---|---|
| | Annual cash flow | Net cash flow | Annual cash flow | Net cash flow |
| Year 0 | ($15,000,000) | ($15,000,000) | ($7,000,000) | ($7,000,000) |
| Year 1 | $2,000,000 | ($13,000,000) | $4,000,000 | ($3,000,000) |
| Year 2 | $5,000,000 | ($8,000,000) | $4,000,000 | $1,000,000 |
| Year 3 | $10,000,000 | $2,000,000 | $4,000,000 | $5,000,000 |
| Year 4 | $25,000,000 | $27,000,000 | $4,000,000 | $9,000,000 |

For projects with uneven cash inflows, the cumulative cash flow needs to be compiled. If the cumulative cash flow in any period is equal to zero, then that period equals the payback period. However, if the zero cumulative cash flow value transcends two periods, then the value needs to be interpolated. Based on the net cash flow for the hangar expansion project, it is known that the payback period occurs between years two and three. Interpolating the cash flows provides the hangar expansion project with a payback period of 2.20 years.

$$PaybackPeriod = Year2 + \frac{(0 - Net\ Cash\ Flow_2)(Year\ 3 - Year\ 2)}{(Net\ Cash\ Flow_3 - Net\ Cash\ Flow_2)}$$

$$PaybackPeriod = 2 + \frac{(0 + \$8million)(3 - 2)}{(\$2million + \$8million)} = 2.80\ years$$

Based on the payback period method and assuming the projects are mutually exclusive owing to capital constraints, the manager will choose the process revision option. This is because the process revision projects will pay back its initial investments of $7 million in 1.75 years while the hangar expansion project has a longer payback period of 2.80 years. However, this example depicts one of the fundamental flaws in the payback period method, since it ignores all cash flows occurring after the payback point. In the maintenance example, the manager would be completing ignoring the $25,000,000 cash flow from the hangar expansion project in year 4 and all future years. Thus, one of the major flaws of the payback period method is that not all cash flows are taken into consideration, creating a short-term viewpoint of potential projects.

Why then do many managers like to use the payback method? For one it is very simple to understand and present to others without a financial background. A manager will be easily able to explain to another person that one investment returns the money within 1.75 years while the other takes 2.80 years. The sole belief that the shorter payback period is better revolves around the fact that the project appears less risky and that near-term cash flow forecasts are usually more accurate than long-term forecasts. Based on this, projects with completely different characteristics can have equal payback periods. Consider three unique projects with their respective cash flows contained in Table 8.4.

**Table 8.4     Projects with equal payback periods**

| Time | Project A | Project B | Project C |
|------|-----------|-----------|-----------|
| 0 | ($10,000) | ($10,000) | ($10,000) |
| 1 | $1,000 | $4,000 | $2,500 |
| 2 | $2,000 | $3,000 | $2,500 |
| 3 | $3,000 | $2,000 | $2,500 |
| 4 | $4,000 | $1,000 | $2,500 |
| 5 | $0 | $0 | $25,000 |

All three projects listed above have payback periods of four years. However the table illustrates that the cash flows for the projects are not all the same. If one were to claim that all three projects are equal because they have the equal payback periods, then he or she would be ignoring one critical finance concept, the time value of money. Project B has greater cash flows at the beginning of the project, while project A's larger cash flows are weighted toward the end of the project. Based on the time value of money, project B would be preferable to project A. If one were to claim that project A or project B were equal to project C, they would be ignoring project C's cash flows after the payback period. Project C would be preferable to the other two projects because of a very large cash flow in year 5.

To summarize, while the payback period methodology is easy to use and interpret, it does contain two critical flaws—ignoring cash flows after the payback period and ignoring the time value of money. Additionally, payback period really only applies to projects with sizeable initial cash outflows followed by periods of cash inflows. Fortunately, other methodologies alleviate these issues; therefore, simple payback analysis is typically used in conjunction with another capital budgeting methodology.

## DISCOUNTED PAYBACK PERIOD

The discounted payback method attempts to overcome one of the fundamental shortcomings of the simple payback period methodology by taking into account the time value of money. Using the simple present value formula, the discounted cash flows for each period are all discounted back to year zero

$$CF_0 = \sum_{t=0}^{n} \frac{CF_t}{(1+k)^t}$$

where:
$CF_0$ = the cash flow at year zero
$CF_t$ = the expected net cash flow at Period t
$n$     = the number of years
$k$     = the project's discount rate

The discounted payback method discounts all future cash flows to time period 0 so that cash flows over different time periods can be accurately compared based on the time value of money. To understand how the discounted payback method is used and differs from the simple payback method, reconsider the two options used above for the maintenance division of a major airline. A key consideration in the discounted payback period method is the appropriate discount rate to use. Typically, the company's weighted average cost of capital is used; however, if the appropriate interest rate for the financing method for the project is known, then that cost can be used. Table 8.5 displays the discounted cash flows using an assumed 8% discount rate.

**Table 8.5**    **Discounted cash flows of maintenance project proposals**

| | Hangar expansion | | |
|---|---|---|---|
| | Annual cash flow | DCF | NCF |
| **Year 0** | ($15,000,000) | ($15,000,000) | ($15,000,000) |
| Year 1 | $2,000,000 | $1,851,852 | ($13,148,148) |
| **Year 2** | $5,000,000 | $4,286,694 | ($8,861,454) |
| Year 3 | $10,000,000 | $7,938,322 | ($923,132) |
| **Year 4** | $25,000,000 | $18,373,746 | $17,450,614 |
| | Process Revision | | |
| | Annual cash flow | DCF | NCF |
| **Year 0** | ($7,000,000) | ($7,000,000) | ($7,000,000) |
| Year 1 | $4,000,000 | $3,703,704 | ($3,296,296) |
| **Year 2** | $4,000,000 | $3,429,355 | $133,059 |
| Year 3 | $4,000,000 | $3,175,329 | $3,308,388 |
| **Year 4** | $4,000,000 | $2,940,119 | $6,248,207 |

By discounting future cash flows the manager can examine which of the projects returns the initial investment more quickly in terms of today's dollars. Performing the same calculations as in the simple payback period method, the hangar expansion's discounted payback period is interpolated to be 3.05 years while the process revision is 1.96 years.

$$PaybackPeriod_{HE} = Year3 + \frac{(0 - NetCashFlow_3)(Year4 - Year3)}{(NetCashFlow_4 - NetCashFlow_3)}$$

$$PaybackPeriod_{HE} = 3 + \frac{(0 + \$923,132)(4 - 3)}{(\$17,450,614 + \$923,132)} = 3.05\, years$$

$$PaybackPeriod_{PR} = Year1 + \frac{(0 - NetCashFlow_1)(Year2 - Year1)}{(NetCashFlow_2 - NetCashFlow_1)}$$

$$PaybackPeriod_{PR} = 1 + \frac{(0 + \$3,296,296)(2 - 1)}{(\$133,059 + \$3,296296)} = 1.96\, years$$

Based on the discounted payback method we see that the maintenance process revision project still pays back the initial investment more quickly. While the discounted payback method has eliminated the time value of money issue, the problem of cash flows after the payback period still remains. The large cash flows in years 3 and 4 of the hangar expansion project are still not being taken into account in determining which project to select. The next method, net present value, eliminates this problem by taking into account all future cash flows.

## NET PRESENT VALUE (NPV)

The net present value (NPV) method is another financial tool that managers can use to evaluate the value that a project will return to the company and its shareholders. Like the discounted payback method, the NPV method uses discounted cash flows to compare projects; however, net present value utilizes all the relevant cash flows associated with the project, up until the end of the project's life. Hence, net present value is probably the most powerful capital budgeting tool available to financial managers. The net present value of a project is merely the present value of all expected cash inflows less the present value of all expected cash outflows. The steps in determining the net present value of a project are:

- Estimate the cash flows of the project
- Calculate the present value of cash inflows
- Calculate the present value of cash outflows
- Subtract present value of cash outflows from present value of cash inflows.

The generic formula for net present value is:

$$NPV = \frac{CF_1}{(1+k)^1} + \frac{CF_2}{(1+k)^2} + \quad + \frac{CF_t}{(1+k)^t}$$

$$NPV = CF[\frac{1}{(1+k)^0} + \frac{1}{(1+k)^1} + \quad + \frac{1}{(1+k)^t}]$$

$$NPV = \sum_{t=0}^{n} \frac{CF_t}{(1+k)^t}$$

Net present value calculations can be used for many different types of decisions in the airline industry. One type of decision where the net present value method is particularly useful is the decision on whether or not to expand. In order for an airline to grow, it needs to purchase or lease additional aircraft and hire extra crew members. Consider a regional airline that is looking to expand by leasing a larger aircraft, a Boeing 737, over a three-year period for $4 million annually. In addition to lease costs, there will be a one-time cost of $10 million to expand the maintenance hangar to accommodate a 737. The new route is expected to generate $40 million, $48 million, and $45 million in revenue respectively over a three year period. Direct operating expenses (fuel, salaries, and maintenance) are expected to be approximately $32 million, $38 million, and $36 million respectively. All future cash flows are discounted at the airline's weighted average cost of capital of 9%. Utilizing this information, the net cash inflows and outflows of the equipment lease are calculated in Table 8.6.

**Table 8.6    Cash flows for three-year 737 lease**

|                       | Year 0          | Year 1          | Year 2          | Year 3          |
|-----------------------|-----------------|-----------------|-----------------|-----------------|
| Capital Spending      | ($10,000,000)   |                 |                 |                 |
| Revenues              |                 | $40,000,000     | $48,000,000     | $45,000,000     |
| Expenses              |                 |                 |                 |                 |
| Fuel                  |                 | ($15,000,000)   | ($20,000,000)   | ($19,000,000)   |
| Salaries              |                 | ($15,000,000)   | ($15,000,000)   | ($15,000,000)   |
| Maintenance           |                 | ($2,000,000)    | ($3,000,000)    | ($2,333,333)    |
| Leasing Cost          |                 | ($4,000,000)    | ($4,000,000)    | ($4,000,000)    |
| Net cash flow         | ($10,000,000)   | $4,000,000      | $6,000,000      | $4,666,667      |
| Discounted cash flow  | ($10,000,000)   | $3,669,725      | $5,050,080      | $3,603,523      |

The net present value of the B-737 lease is the summation of every period's discounted cash flow.

NPV = Discounted Cash Inflows- Discounted Cash Outflows
NPV = $3,669,725 + $5,050,080 + $3,603,523 – $10,000,000
NPV = $2,323,328

While clearly a simplistic example, the net present value of the 737 lease is $2,323,328, meaning that in today's dollar value the project will net the airline $2,323,328. Since route expansion represents an independent project for the airline, the NPV merely needs to be equal to or greater than zero for the project to be accepted. Table 8.7 shows the decision that managers should make based on different net present values for independent projects. For mutually exclusive projects, the project with the greatest net present value should be selected.

**Table 8.7    Net present value decision-making table for independent projects**

| Net present value | Accept or reject? |
|-------------------|-------------------|
| Positive          | **Accept**: The project produces a return greater than the required rate of return |
| Zero              | **Accept**: The project produces a return equal to the required rate of return |
| Negative          | **Reject**: The project produces a return lower than the required rate of return |

Returning to the example of the two options facing the maintenance division (hangar expansion or process improvement), the net present value methodology eliminates the shortcomings of the payback period by taking into consideration the time value of money and all future cash flows. Table 8.8 provides the net present value calculation for the two options.

From Table 8.8, the four year net present value of the hangar expansion is $17,450,614 versus $6,248,507 for the maintenance process revision. If these two projects were independent projects they would both be accepted owing to their positive net present values; however, because they are mutually exclusive projects, only one project can be chosen, which in this case would be the hangar expansion. This conclusion is different from the conclusion the manager would have made using the discounted payback method as a result of the sizeable positive cash flows in years three and four of the hangar expansion project. The net present value method overcomes the shortcomings of the discounted payback method by factoring in all future cash flows and not just the cash flows until the payback period.

**Table 8.8     Net present value of mutually exclusive projects**

|  | Hangar expansion | | Process revision | |
|---|---|---|---|---|
|  | Cash flow | DCF | Cash flow | DCF |
| Year 0 | ($15,000,000) | ($15,000,000) | ($7,000,000) | ($7,000,000) |
| Year 1 | $2,000,000 | $1,851,852 | $4,000,000 | $3,703,704 |
| Year 2 | $5,000,000 | $4,286,694 | $4,000,000 | $3,429,355 |
| Year 3 | $10,000,000 | $7,938,322 | $4,000,000 | $3,175,329 |
| Year 4 | $25,000,000 | $18,373,746 | $4,000,000 | $2,940,119 |
| Net present value | | $17,450,614 | | $6,248,507 |

Additionally, assuming year four's cash flows extend into perpetuity, varying lengths of net present values can be calculated using the present value of a perpetuity formula. For instance, the ten-year net present value of the hangar expansion would be approximately $102 million and $20 million for the process revision. Ultimately, the length of the NPV is up to the financial manager; however, it should be of sufficient length to accurately depict the project.

A final important point to consider regarding the time value of money is that the net present value of the project is affected by the discount rate used to discount future cash flows. The net present value of future cash inflows will decrease as the discount rates increase. If a manager is unsure that the discount rate is the true rate at which capital can be raised, the manager should test a range of discount rates to determine the net present value of the project(s) at each discount rate.

## INTERNAL RATE OF RETURN (IRR)

The internal rate of return (IRR) is the rate of return the company receives from the project over its useful life. Internal rate of return is linked to net present value in that IRR is the discount rate where the net present value of the project is zero. This is the point where the initial investment has been returned, with the discount rate representing the return on investment. This link between IRR and NPV is represented mathematically in the following formula.

$$NPV = \sum_{t=0}^{n} \frac{CF_t}{(1+IRR)^t} = 0$$

While the internal rate of a project can be found using financial calculators or the IRR function in Microsoft Excel, internal rate of return can also be calculated mathematically by using the above formula where the NPV of the project is set to zero. In order to illustrate the IRR calculation, consider the simple cash flows contained in Table 8.9.

**Table 8.9      Simple cash flow**

| Time | Cash Flow |
|------|-----------|
| 0 | ($10,000) |
| 1 | $4,000 |
| 2 | $4,000 |
| 3 | $4,000 |

Since the internal rate of return is the point where net present value is equal to zero, to illustrate, the NPV is calculated using different discount rates in Table 8.10.

**Table 8.10     Simple cash flow NPV sensitivity**

| Discount rate | Net present value |
|---------------|-------------------|
| 0.00% | $2,000.00 |
| 9.00% | $125.20 |
| 9.50% | $35.62 |
| 10.00% | ($52.60) |

Interpolating the data contained in table 8.10, the internal rate of return for the simple project is found to be 9.70%. At this point the net present value is zero, showing that this project will yield a 9.70% return, based on the stated cash flows.

$$NPV = C_0 + \frac{C_1}{(1+IRR)} + \frac{C_2}{(1+IRR)^2} + \frac{C_3}{(1+IRR)^3} = 0$$

$$NPV = (10,000) + \frac{4,000}{(1+IRR)} + \frac{4,000}{(1+IRR)^2} + \frac{4,000}{(1+IRR)^3} = 0$$

As with all capital budgeting techniques, the internal rate of return is often used by firms to determine whether to accept or reject a project. There are two ways in which a firm can use IRR to analyze a project. The first way would be for a firm to set an arbitrary required rate of return for all internal projects. If the project's IRR exceeds the threshold requirement then the project would be accepted; if not, the project would be rejected. Conversely, the IRR could also be compared to the firm's weighted average cost of capital or the market rate on similar investments. Such a benchmark would ensure that the project at least returns the cost of capital required to fund the project.

In order to understand IRR's influence on decision making, consider another example involving a Car Rental Company that wishes to lease terminal space at a new airport. Assume that the Car Rental Company will incur $1,000 of one-time start-up costs with a one year lease and that the airport receives 25% of Car Rental Company's revenue, which is estimated to be $15,000 for the year. After the airport's share of revenue, the operating margin for Car Rental Company is 12.5% while taxes on operating income are 34%. Car Rental Company wants to determine if the project returns a greater rate of return than what it could receive from the market for investing the $1,000 at 12%.

**Table 8.11     Car rental company cash flows**

|                      | Year 0        | Year 1        |
| -------------------- | ------------- | ------------- |
| Capital expenditure  | ($1,000.00)   |               |
| Revenue              |               | $15,000.00    |
| Operating income     |               | $1,875.00     |
| Taxes                |               | $637.50       |
| Net income           |               | $1,237.50     |

In order to find the IRR of the project, we must set net present value equal to zero. Based on a net income of $1,237.50, as calculated in Table 8.11, the internal rate of return of the project for Car Rental Company is 23.75%.

$$NPV = C_0 + \frac{C_1}{(1+IRR)} = 0$$

$$NPV = -1000 + \frac{1237.50}{(1+IRR)} = 0$$

$$1000 = \frac{1237.50}{(1+IRR)}$$

$$IRR = 23.75\%$$

Since the internal rate of return for the one-year lease of the new location is 23.75%, Car Rental Company should accept the project since the internal rate of return exceeds the required rate of return of 12%, or the return the company could achieve elsewhere. For all projects in which a company is making an investment (initial cash outflows), the company should accept the project if the IRR is greater than the required rate of return. If the company is financing (receives an initial cash inflow), the company should accept the financing if the IRR is higher than the cost of borrowing money (interest rate).

There are problems, however, with using the IRR method to determine whether to accept or reject a project. If a project's net period cash flows change from cash outflows to cash inflows, and vice versa, more than once during the life of the project, there may not be one unique IRR for the project, but multiple IRRs (Ross, Westerfield, Jaffe, 2008). To provide an example of this problem, consider an airport that wants to install new flight information screens displaying flights' arrivals and departures. The project will require upfront construction costs as well as costs to replace the screens in two years when it is anticipated the screens will need replacing. Cash inflows are generated from airlines for the right to display their flights on the screens throughout the terminal. The cash flows for the project are depicted in Table 8.12.

**Table 8.12    Airport flight information screen cash flows**

|  | Year 0 | Year 1 | Year 2 |
| --- | --- | --- | --- |
| Capital expenditures | ($10,150) |  | ($20,000) |
| Fee collection |  | $23,000 | $7,000 |
| Net cash flow | ($10,150) | $23,000 | ($13,000) |
| Internal rate of return |  |  | 7.90% |

As the Table 8.12 shows, the airport has net cash outflows of $10,150 in year 0 and $13,000 in year 2 and a net cash inflow of $23,000 in year 1. Using Microsoft Excel, the IRR is calculated to be 7.90%; however, based on the switching cash flows, there is another solution whereby the NPV of the project equals zero at approximately 18.70%. Mathematically, both 7.90% and 18.70% satisfy the formula for internal rate of return.

$$NPV = C_0 + \frac{CF_1}{(1+IRR)} + \frac{CF_2}{(1+IRR)^2} = 0$$

$$For \ IRR_1 = 7.9\%$$

$$NPV = -10,150 + \frac{23,000}{(1+0.079)} + \frac{-13,000}{(1+0.079)^2} = 0$$

$$10,150 = 10,150$$

$$For \ IRR_2 = 18.70\%$$

$$NPV = -10,150 + \frac{23,000}{(1+0.187)} + \frac{-13,000}{(1+0.187)^2}$$

$$10,150 = 10,150$$

Instead of using Microsoft Excel, multiple IRRs can be solved for mathematically.

$$NPV = -10,150 + \frac{23,000}{(1+IRR)} + \frac{-13,000}{(1+IRR)^2} = 0$$

$$set \ \frac{1}{(1+IRR)} = X,$$

$$13,000 - 23,000X + 10,150X^2 = 0$$

Using the quadratic formula, the value of X is solved for:

$$X = \frac{-b \pm \sqrt{b^2 - 4ac}}{2a}$$

$$X = \frac{23,000 \pm \sqrt{(23,000)^2 - 4 \times 10,100 \times 13,000}}{2 \times 10,150}$$

$$X_1 = 1.1870$$
$$X_2 = 1.0790$$

*Hence,*

$$IRR_1 = 18.70\%$$
$$IRR_2 = 7.90\%$$

The two solutions for this problem can also be displayed using the NPV profile, which is a graphical representation of the NPV with varying discount rates. From the net present value profile, one can easily see how a project's NPV varies inversely with the discount rate, and sensitivity of the project to the discount rate. Figure 8.2 displays the NPV profile for the flight information screen project.

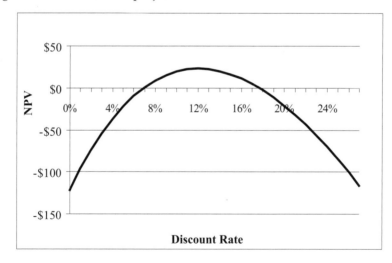

**Figure 8.2    NPV profile, airport flight information screen**

The NPV profile shows that for discount rates between the two IRRs (7.9% and 18.7%) the NPV of the project is positive and should be accepted; however, if the discount rate is less than 7.9% or greater than 18.7%, the project has a negative NPV and should be rejected. Clearly confusion arises in such a situation; therefore, in such circumstances the IRR provides no clear solution and should not be used in determining the fate of a project. Cash flows can be modified to return just one IRR value, a technique called modified internal rate of return, and this is discussed later on in the chapter.

Another problem arises with the internal rate of return when comparing mutually exclusive projects in that a conflict may arise between NPV and IRR. Depending on the method being used, NPV and IRR may recommend different mutually exclusive projects, creating uncertainty over which method to use. This problem can occur for two reasons:

- the projects have different scales
- the projects have different timing of cash flows.

When projects have different initial investments, the projects have different scales. To demonstrate the conflict of mutually exclusive projects with different scales, compare two projects to help alleviate aircraft congestion. The airline must choose whether to purchase a new tug to accommodate the push back of additional regional jet aircraft or build a new commuter concourse where the planes will be parked in such a way that they can power out of their parking spot on their own. Assume the discount rate for both projects is 10% with the cash flows, NPV and IRR of each project shown in Table 8.13.

**Table 8.13    Aircraft congestion projects NPV**

|  | Year 0 | Year 1 | Year 2 | Year 3 | Net present value |
|---|---|---|---|---|---|
| **New Tug** | ($30,000) | $15,000 | $15,000 | $15,000 | **$7,302.78** |
| **Regional concourse** | ($3,000,000) | $500,000 | $1,500,000 | $2,000,000 | **$196,844.48** |

The IRR calculation would shows that purchasing the new tug would be a better financial decision than building a new regional concourse; however, building the new concourse has a much greater NPV at a discount rate of 10%. The regional concourse obviously has a much larger scale with the initial investment 100 times larger than the investment for the new tug. This is a result of IRR normalizing results, whereas NPV is stated in absolute terms where larger projects will appear much better. When a conflict exists between IRR and NPV methods, the safe rule would be to choose the project with the larger NPV since this project adds greater value to shareholders than the project with a lower NPV. Assuming the airline has enough capital to build the regional concourse, this option should be chosen.

However, conflict may still occur between NPV and IRR methods when the initial investment for each project is the same. This problem will occur when cash flows occur at different points in time and is a result of the discount rate. To examine the importance of the discount rate when comparing mutually exclusive projects with the same scale, consider an airport examining two different ways to use excess space in one of its concourses. The airport can either use the space to add two additional gates or to build a new food court. The gates would earn revenue for the airport through a lease that a new airline would sign, while the food court would earn revenue through contracts with concessionaires, with the airport receiving a percentage of revenue. It is expected that construction of the new gates will not be finished until year two, while the food court will be ready in year one. Revenue for the food court is expected to be high in year one as airport passengers try the new food options, and is expected to fall off as some of the novelty has worn off.

The expected life of each project is five years. Table 8.14 provides the cash flows, IRR, and NPV with various discount rates for both the gate expansion and food court projects.

**Table 8.14    Concourse expansion project cash flows, NPV, and IRR**

| | | | Cash flows | | | |
| --- | --- | --- | --- | --- | --- | --- |
| | Year 0 | Year 1 | Year 2 | Year 3 | Year 4 | Year 5 |
| Gate expansion | ($2,000,000) | $0 | $500,000 | $800,000 | $1,000,000 | $1,000,000 |
| Food court | ($2,000,000) | $1,000,000 | $500,000 | $500,000 | $500,000 | $500,000 |

| | Net present value | | | | IRR |
| --- | --- | --- | --- | --- | --- |
| Discount rate | 5% | 10% | 15% | | |
| Gate expansion | $750,813 | $318,210 | ($26,985) | | 14.57% |
| Food court | $640,929 | $349,939 | $110,860 | | 17.68% |

Using IRR as a decision-making tool, the food court project would be accepted. The food court also has a greater NPV with discount rates of 10% and 15%; however, the gate expansion project has a greater NPV at a discount rate of 5%. Therefore, at a 5% discount rate, a conflict exists between the NPV method and the IRR method. What this tells us is that for lower discount rates the project to build new gates has a higher NPV, while at higher discount rates the food court project has a higher NPV. This conflict shows the importance of choosing the correct discount rate based on the riskiness of the cash flows and the comparable rate of return in the market. This relation between NPV values and the appropriate discount rate can be displayed with a NPV profile.

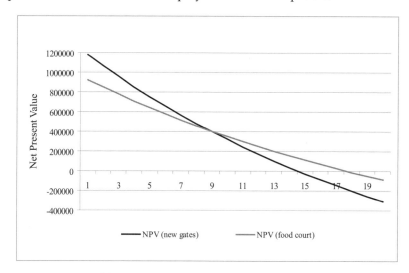

**Figure 8.3    NPV profile, concourse expansion project**

Figure 8.3 profiles the NPV of each project and also shows that there is a point at which the two lines intersect (at a discount rate of roughly 9%). For discount rates lower than the indifference point, the gate expansion project has a greater NPV while for discount rates greater than the indifference point, the food court project has a higher NPV. The indifference point is the point where both projects are equal, meaning that one is indifferent in choosing one project over the other. The indifference point can be calculated using the incremental IRR approach (Ross, Westerfield and Jaffe, 2008). The incremental IRR merely calculates the IRR for the differences in cash flows in each year of the projects. To calculate the incremental IRR for the gate and food court projects, subtract the cash flow of the food court project from the cash flow of the gate expansion project for each year, and then calculate the IRR for this new cash flow.

**Table 8.15    Concourse expansion projects' incremental IRR**

| | | Incremental cash flows | | | | |
|---|---|---|---|---|---|---|
| | Year 0 | Year 1 | Year 2 | Year 3 | Year 4 | Year 5 |
| Cash flow (new gates— food court) | $0 | ($1,000,000) | $0 | $300,000 | $500,000 | $500,00 |
| Incremental IRR | 8.75% | | | | | |

Based on Table 8.15, the incremental IRR for the two mutually exclusive projects is 8.75%. The incremental IRR tells us that the airport managers should choose the project to build the new gates if its discount rate is less than 8.75% and the food court if the discount rate is greater.

## MODIFIED INTERNAL RATE OF RETURN (MIRR)

As mentioned earlier, one of the problems with the internal rate of return method is that there can be multiple IRRs for one set of cash flows. Modified internal rate of return (MIRR) assumes that project cash inflows are reinvested or discounted at the opportunity cost of capital. In this method, future cash flows are combined so that only one change of sign exists. In order to combine future cash flows, future cash flows must first be discounted to the last year of the project.

$$\frac{\text{Terminal Value}}{(1+MIRR)^n} = PV(Costs)$$

$$\frac{\sum_{t=1}^{n} CF_t (1+k)^{n-t}}{CF_0} = (1+MIRR)^n$$

*Decision Rule for Modified Internal Rate of Return*

- Accept the project if MIRR > Cost of capital
- Reject the project if MIRR < Cost of capital

To illustrate how to use the modified internal rate of return, reconsider the project to install new flight information screens. Recall that in the flight information screen example, the sign of cash flows changed from negative to positive and then back to negative. In order to eliminate multiple IRR values, discount the cash flow in year two back to year one and then add the cash flow from year one. This assures that only one change of sign occurs within the project and only one IRR value is obtained. Table 8.16 details the steps of this calculation by using a discount rate of 10% for both stages of the modified internal rate of return methodology.

**Table 8.16     Airport flight information screen, modified IRR**

|  | | Cash flows | |
| --- | --- | --- | --- |
|  | Year 0 | Year 1 | Year 2 |
| Capital expenditure | ($10,150) |  | ($20,000) |
| Fee collection |  | $23,000 | $7,000 |
| Net cash flow | ($10,150) | $23,000 | ($13,000) |
| Year 2 cash flow dscounted to Year 1 |  |  | ($11,818.18) |
| Year 0 cash flow |  | ($10,150.00) |  |
| Year 1 Cash Flow |  | $11,181.82 |  |
| MIRR |  | 10.17% |  |

The modified internal rate of return of the flight information screen project is 10.17%. The fact that we had to specify a discount rate beforehand is the key difference from the simple IRR method. Therefore, the discount rate used affects the internal rate of return since different discount rates provide different MIRR values. A different discount rate may lead a manager to reject the project rather than accept it; therefore, just as in the NPV calculation, the discount rate is critical to the accuracy of the modified internal rate of return. However, since both methods require a discount rate, the NPV should probably be used for decision making and the MIRR calculation used for presentation purposes.

## PROFITABILITY INDEX (PI)

The profitability index (PI) is another technique used to measure the value that a project creates. The profitability index measures how much the investment returns compared to the original investment. It is defined as a ratio of the present value of the payback from all future cash inflows, divided by the initial cash outflows. The PI is frequently referred to as the benefit-cost ratio, since it is the ratio of the benefit from an investment to its cost.

$$PI = \frac{\sum_{t=0}^{n} \dfrac{CIF_t}{(1+i)^t}}{\sum_{t=0}^{n} \dfrac{COF_t}{(1+i)^t}}$$

where:
$PI$     = the profitability index
$CIF_t$  = the present value of cash inflows for time $t$
$COF_t$ = the present value of cash outflows for time $t$

For independent projects, a profitability index greater than 1 indicates that the project should be accepted since the present value of future cash flows will return more than the initial investment. Projects with a PI less than 1 should be rejected since the present value of future cash flows does not payback the initial investment. Put more simply, if the project does not pay for itself, then the project should not be accepted.

Typically, when comparing two mutually exclusive projects, the manager should choose the project with the greatest profitability index; however, the problem of scale reemerges. Projects with a higher initial investment may have a greater NPV, but have lower profitability indexes than projects with a lower initial investment. To demonstrate this problem and how to calculate profitability index, consider two projects that an airport can undertake that alleviate car parking congestion. One project would open an entirely new economy parking lot further away from the terminal and the other would expand the existing parking lot. Both projects are expected to be able to handle all demand for parking for the next five years. The discount rate for the projects is assumed to be 11%.

**Table 8.17     Airport parking lot profitability index ($ thousands)**

|  | Cash flows | | | | | | | |
| --- | --- | --- | --- | --- | --- | --- | --- | --- |
|  | Year 0 | Year 1 | Year 2 | Year 3 | Year 4 | Year 5 | P.I. | NPV |
| **New lot** | ($50,000) | $15,000 | $22,500 | $30,000 | $40,000 | $42,000 | | |
| **Discounted C.F.** | ($50,000) | $13,514 | $18,262 | $21,936 | $26,349 | $24,925 | 2.1 | $54,985 |
| **Expand lot** | ($25,000) | $20,000 | $20,000 | $22,000 | $22,500 | $22,500 | | |
| **Discounted C.F.** | ($25,000) | $18,018 | $16,232 | $16,086 | $14,821 | $13,353 | 3.14 | $53,511 |

Based on the cash flows in Table 8.17, the profitability index for each project is calculated as follows:

$$\text{PI (New parking lot)} = \frac{\left( \frac{15000}{1.11} + \frac{22500}{1.11^2} + \frac{30000}{1.11^3} + \frac{40000}{1.11^4} + \frac{42000}{1.11^5} \right)}{50000}$$

$$PI = 2.10$$

$$\text{PI (Expand existing lot)} = \frac{\left( \frac{20000}{1.11} + \frac{20000}{1.11^2} + \frac{22000}{1.11^3} + \frac{22500}{1.11^4} + \frac{22500}{1.11^5} \right)}{25000}$$

$$PI = 3.14$$

The calculations above show that the expanded lot has a greater profitability index than the new parking lot; however, as seen in Table 8.17, the NPV of the new parking lot is greater than the NPV of the parking lot expansion. In order to resolve this conflict one can simply accept the project with the higher NPV or compute the incremental profitable index (Ross, Westerfield and Jaffe, 2008). The incremental PI is similar to the incremental IRR calculated to account for scale differences earlier in the chapter. The incremental profitability index is calculated by subtracting the cash flows of the expanded lot from the cash flows of the new parking lot. Just like the original profitability index, all of the incremental cash flows are discounted, with all future incremental cash flows divided by the difference in initial investment (the larger amount that was invested in the new lot) to solve for the incremental PI. The incremental PI for the two projects is 1.06 as shown in Table 8.18.

**Table 8.18    Airport parking lot incremental profitability index**

|  | Cash flows | | | | | |
|---|---|---|---|---|---|---|
|  | Year 0 | Year 1 | Year 2 | Year 3 | Year 4 | Year 5 |
| New lot | ($50,000) | $15,000 | $22,500 | $30,000 | $40,000 | $42,000 |
| Discounted C.F. | ($50,000) | $13,514 | $18,262 | $21,936 | $26,349 | $24,925 |
| Expand lot | ($25,000) | $20,000 | $20,000 | $22,000 | $22,500 | $22,500 |
| Discounted C.F. | ($25,000) | $18,018 | $16,232 | $16,086 | $14,821 | $13,353 |
| Incremental D.C.F. | ($25,000) | ($4,505) | $2,029 | $5,850 | $11,528 | $11,572 |
| Incremental P.I. | 1.06 | | | | | |
| Incremental NPV | $1,474 | | | | | |

When examining an incremental profitability index, treat the incremental cash flows as an independent project. Therefore, an incremental PI of >1 indicates that the larger-scale project should be accepted over the smaller scale project. In the case of the parking lot example, the incremental PI of choosing the new parking lot over an expansion is 1.06; therefore, we should accept the new parking lot project. This decision is reinforced by the positive incremental NPV of $1,474.

## BREAK-EVEN ANALYSIS

Break-even analysis is an accounting concept that is typically used for manufacturing projects. It determines the minimum production level required to meet the costs of the project. Therefore, by definition, the break-even point is the point at which a company sells enough units of its product to make neither a loss nor a profit. The key to understanding break-even analysis is being aware of the difference between fixed and variable costs. Variable costs directly relate to varying levels of production while fixed costs exist for all levels of production. However, there are two different break-even points; the accounting break-even point and the economic (present value) break-even point (Ross, Westerfield and Jaffe, 2008). Most individuals are familiar with the first one but not very familiar with the second break-even point. Both break-even points are analyzed below so that we can be familiar with the strengths and weaknesses of each approach.

*Accounting Break-even Point*

The accounting break-even point of a project is the number of sales a company must make to cover the annual fixed costs and depreciation associated with a project. For example, Airbus has significant fixed costs and depreciation associated with research and development and the infrastructure to build a commercial aircraft like the A380. If Airbus wanted to calculate the number of A380s they need to sell to reach the accounting break-even point, the company should use the accounting break-even equation.[8]

$$Breakeven:$$
$$TR = TC$$
$$P \times Q = FC + Depreciation + VC \times Q$$
$$(P - VC) \times Q_{B-E} = FC + Depreciation$$
$$Q_{B-E} = \frac{FC + Depreciation}{Price - VC}$$

where:
FC  = annual fixed costs
VC  = variable costs per unit
P    = Price per unit

Assume that Airbus has fixed costs of $2 Billion and $100 million in equipment depreciation directly attributed to the A380. The average list sales price of the A380, as of June 2008, was $327.4 million (Airbus S.A.S., 2008). Variable costs are assumed to be $270 million per aircraft.

$$\text{Accounting Break-Even} = \frac{2,000,000,000 + 100,000,000}{327,400,000 - 270,000,000}$$

Accounting Break-Even = 36.59 planes per year

The accounting break-even point for Airbus is approximately 36.6 A380s produced per year, meaning that Airbus must produce and sell 37 or more A380s to make an accounting profit.

## Economic (Present Value) Break-even Point

Many managers only concern themselves with accounting profits and accounting break-even; however, managers who only concern themselves with accounting profit are not taking into account the opportunity costs of their initial investment. On the other hand, the concept of economic profit takes into account opportunity costs as well as accounting costs. The equation for economic profit is:

Economic Profit = Revenues – Costs (Fixed and Variable) – Opportunity Cost

In the case of a long-term project, the opportunity costs are the opportunity to have invested the initial cash outflows in another project. To calculate the economic break-even point, the initial investment must be discounted over the life of the project to determine the

---

8     As of February 9, 2010, Airbus has delivered 25 × A380 and received 202 firm orders.

yearly profit the project must make to compensate for the opportunity cost of foregoing other investments. This yearly profit is called the equivalent annual cost (EAC) and is calculated by taking the initial investment and dividing it by an annuity factor, since the annual cost is treated as an annuity (Ross, Westerfield and Jaffe, 2008). The formula for EAC is as follows:

$$\text{Equivalent Annual Cost (EAC)} = \frac{\text{Initial Investment}}{\text{Annuity Factor}}$$

The annuity factor is a function of the length of the project and the discount rate used. For the Airbus A380 example, assume the A380 is a 30-year project with a discount rate of 14%. The formula for the annuity factor is as follows:

$$\text{Annuity Factor} = \left[ \frac{1 - \dfrac{1}{(1+k)^t}}{k} \right]$$

where:
$k$   = the discount rate
$t$   = the length of the project, in years

For Airbus, the annuity factor of the A380 project is:

$$\text{Annuity Factor} = \left[ \frac{1 - \dfrac{1}{(1+.14)^{30}}}{.14} \right]$$

Annuity Factor = 7.00

Now that the annuity factor for the A380 project is known the EAC can be calculated assuming an initial investment of $13 billion.

$$\text{EAC} = \frac{\$13,000,000,000}{7.00}$$

EAC = $1,857,142,857

The equivalent annual cost, the yearly profit Airbus must make to compensate for opportunity cost, is approximately $1.86 Billion.

Now that the equivalent annual cost has been determined, the economic (present value) break-even point is found using the following formula:

$$\text{Economic Break-Even Point} = \frac{\text{EAC} + \text{FC} \times (1\text{-T}) - \text{Depreciation} \times \text{T}}{(\text{Price-VC}) \times (1-T)}$$

where:

$T$ = the corporate tax rate

Another key difference between economic and accounting break-even points is the fact that taxes are taken into consideration because any accounting profit is taxed at the tax rate. In the accounting break-even equation, the company makes zero accounting profit; however, in the economic break-even equation, a company makes an accounting profit and this is used to cover the project's opportunity costs.

Assuming a tax rate of 30% and based on the previously calculated value, the economic break-even point for the A380 project is:

$$\text{Economic Break-even} = \frac{\$1,857,142,857 + \$2,000,000,000 \times (1-0.3) - \$100,000,000 \times 0}{(\$327,400,000 - \$270,000,000) \times (1-0.3)}$$

$$\text{Economic Break-even} = 39.355$$

The economic break-even number shows that Airbus must average 39.355 A380s per year to break-even in terms of accounting and opportunity costs for the 30-year life of the project. In order to compensate for the opportunity cost of the project's investment, Airbus must sell approximately three more planes per year than previously calculated under accounting profit. The tax rate plays a significant role in this equation since depreciation is not taxed. The higher the tax rate, the larger the tax break Airbus will receive from depreciation expense, reducing the number of planes necessary to reach an economic profit.

Managers should consider the economic break-even point when making decisions about the feasibility of the project. The reason that the economic break-even point is also called the present value break-even point is because if the company has sales at the economic break-even level, the net present value of the project will be $0. Therefore, managers should only accept the project if the company will be able to meet or exceed the economic break-even sales level.


## SUMMARY

The chapter explained the various financial methods that can be used to accomplish airline capital budgeting. The simplest of these is the payback period where the manager picks a given amount of time for a capital budgeting project to return the initial investment. A slightly more sophisticated version of this method is the discounted payback period where the time value of money is taken into account for the payback period. Other more sophisticated methods were then introduced and explained. These included the net present value method and the internal rate of return method. Both of these methods take into account the time value of money over the entire assumed life of the project. In general, the net present value method is preferred over the internal rate of return when there is a choice between them. The chapter then covered the profitability index and variations of the internal rate of return and profitability index that eliminated the problem of multiple answers that could reprise with these methods. These were respectively called the modified internal rate of return and the modified profitability index. Each of the methods was explained with the use of quantitative examples.

## DISCUSSION QUESTIONS

1. What are the advantages and disadvantages of the payback method?
2. What is the net present value profile?
3. The DirectJet has installed 30 electronic kiosks at its Pittsburg hub. The kiosks expedite passengers to check-in, view seat assignments, make seat changes, review itineraries and print boarding passes. The net cost of each kiosk is $50,000 and the airline expects the following cash flows:

| Year | Cash Flow |
|------|-----------|
| 0 | –$50,000 |
| 1 | 6,000 |
| 2 | 9,000 |
| 3 | 12,000 |
| 4 | 15,000 |
| 5 | 20,000 |

   a. If the cost of capital is 8 percent, what is the net present value of each kiosk?
   b. What is the payback period?
   c. What is the discounted payback period?
   d. What is the internal rate of return (IRR)?
   e. Do you suggest that DirectJet purchase new electronic kiosks?
4. A survey has been commissioned by the Wi-Fi Alliance Association, a trade group representing companies in the industry indicating the need by frequent business travelers to use in-flight Wi-Fi. As a result of positive feedback, many airlines such as EZjET have signed a contract to install its satellite-based system in all of the fleet of A-320s. Calculate the NPV and PI for this project if the installation costs $100,000 per aircraft and the airline management expects the move will pay off through a user fee of $10.00 per connection, or $10,000 per aircraft annually for 30 years. The discount rate is 8%.
5. Ryanair, the third-largest European airline in terms of passenger numbers, has significantly enjoyed growth since its establishment in 1985. Ryanair has currently 199 Boeing B-377 with 113 back orders. Assume a new B-737NG costs $65 million, and it generates after-tax cash inflows of $8.50 million for the next ten years.
   a. Find the NPV if the airline uses a 12% opportunity cost of capital.
   b. What is the IRR?
   c. What is the payback period?
6. What is the difference between replacement and expansion projects?
7. What is the difference between independent and mutually exclusive projects?
8. DirectJet Airlines is planning to purchase a used B-757 for $10 million. Consider the following revenues and costs schedule, if the airline's cost of capital is 7% and the airline evaluates all projects on a cash flow basis.

| ($MM) | Year one | Year two | Year three | Year four | Year five |
|-------|----------|----------|------------|-----------|-----------|
| Total revenue | $12 | $21 | $35 | $41 | $38 |
| Aircraft fuel | $7 | $9 | $12 | $11 | $15 |
| Salaries | $5 | $5 | $9 | $9 | $9 |
| Aircraft maintenance | $2 | $3 | $4 | $5 | $6 |
| Depreciation expense | $3 | $3 | $3 | $3 | $3 |

    a. Calculate the payback period for the aircraft. If the airline requires all projects to be paid back in three years, would the project be accepted?

    b. Calculate the discounted payback period for the aircraft. If the airline requires all projects to be paid back in three years, would the project be accepted?

    c. Calculate the net present value of the aircraft. If all NPV positive projects are accepted, would the aircraft be purchased?

    d. Calculate the internal rate of return for the aircraft. If the airline requires all projects to meet or exceed its cost of capital, is the project accepted?

    e. Calculate the profitability index for the aircraft.

9. Consider an airline that is evaluating providing live television service on its aircraft for a nominal fee of $8 per flight. Assume the cost of installing the system is $2.5 million per aircraft with a variable cost of $2 associated with licensing use of the system.

    a. What is the accounting breakeven for the airline to install the system on a single aircraft?

    b. What is the economic breakeven assuming the airline could install an in-flight Internet service, in lieu of live television service, that is expected to generate a positive cash flow of $500,000 annually?

10. What is the difference between economic and accounting break-even?

11. EZjET is serving direct flight between Cairo and Amman, Jordan. The airline is planning to add, an additional Airbus A-320 to this route. The following table provides a summary of the after-tax cash flows associated with the acquiring of this aircraft:

**Net Cash flows**

| Year | Net Cash flow |
|------|---------------|
| 0 | ($80,000,000.00) |
| 1 | $18,000,000.00 |
| 2 | $24,000,000.00 |
| 3 | $20,000,000.00 |
| 4 | $12,000,000.00 |
| 5 | $8,000,000.00 |
| 6 | $2,000,000.00 |
| 7 | $1,500,000.00 |

    a. Calculate the project's Payback period.

    b. What is the project's NPV, assuming EZjET has a discount rate of 8%?

    c. What is the IRR?

    d. How do you interpret this number?

    e. Calculate the MIRR.

# REFERENCES

Airbus S.A.S. (2008). Press Centre. Retrieved June 18, 2008 from http://www.airbus.com/en/presscentre/

Continental Airlines (2008). Continental Airlines to reduce capacity, fleet, and staffing. Retrieved June 10, 2008 from http://www.continental.com/web/en-U.S./apps/vendors/default.aspx?i=PRNEWS

Esty, B. (2001, August 24). Airbus A3XX: Developing the World's Largest Commercial Jet (A). Harvard Business School, 9–201–028

Ross, S. A., R. W. Westerfield, and J. F. Jaffe (2008). *Corporate Finance* (8). New York: McGraw-Hill/Irwan.

Ryanair (2008). Ryanair announces biggest expansion ever. Retrieved June 10, 2008 from http://www.ryanair.com/site/EN/news.php?yr=08&month=jun&story=rte-en-050608

Southwest Airlines (2008). Southwest Airlines reports first quarter earnings. Retrieved June 10, 2008 from http://www.southwest.com/investor_relations/fs_quarterly_earnings.html

Vasigh, B., K. Fleming, and T. Tacker (2008). *Introduction to Air Transport Economics*. Burlington, VT: Ashgate.

# 9

# Airline Capital Structure and Cost of Capital

"Succession planning has been a major priority at Southwest for quite some time. We think we have come up with a winning combination of talent for our company reorganization."

Herb Kelleher, Founder of Southwest Airlines

Since the airline industry is highly capital-intensive and cyclical, an examination of an airlines' capital structure is critical to understanding the macro financial position of an individual airline. The industry is vastly susceptible to economic, political and/or environmental crisis. The recent outbreak of H1N1 virus will cost the industry around a billion dollars of revenue in 2009.[1] The industry needs for large amounts of capital has a profound impact on profitability and the survival of individual airlines. In the past, the industry has been able to generate only about half of its capital needs from internal cash flow and, the rest through issuing bonds and stocks. In this chapter we will explore the cost of raising capital and how to estimate these costs. Through an understanding of the cost of different types of capital, we can understand why an airline might use different capital sources. Using the weighted average cost of capital, the different capital costs (that is, common stock, preferred stock, debt, and retained earnings) are analyzed in detail. The following topics are covered in the chapter:

- Equity Financing
  - Common Stock
  - Preferred Stock
- Cost of Equity
  - Stock Valuation Models
  - Cost of Preferred Stock
  - Cost of Retained Earnings
- Bonds
  - Bond Valuation
- Airline Debt
- Cost of Debt
- Weighted Average Cost of Capital (WACC)
- Airline Debt and Equity

---

1    Robert Mann, president of R.W. Mann & Company, aviation consultants in Port Washington, N.Y.

- CAPM to estimate Cost of Equity $k_e$
- Business Risk vs. Financial Risk
  - Business Risk
  - Financial Risk
- Cost of Capital and Capital Budgeting
- Summary
- Discussion Questions.

## EQUITY FINANCING

As the old adage goes, if someone wants to be a millionaire, he or she needs to start out as a billionaire and then invest in an airline. The adage is largely a result of the extreme capital intensive nature of the air transport industry, with sizeable sums of capital needed from a variety of sources. While capital requirements are not unique to the air transport industry, the size and scope of the capital requirements for the aviation industry are what make the understanding of the cost of capital and capital structure so important. For instance, when aircraft manufacturer Airbus wanted to build a new commercial airliner, the A380 to compete with Boeing's B747, Airbus needed to raise over $10B in capital for the project for research/development and the construction of new production facilities (Wallace, 2007). Clearly, without effective capital structure policies, the behemoth A380 would never get off the ground.

Airports also commonly invest in large capital projects, some of which are partnered with airlines. For instance, Miami International Airport (MIA) underwent a $2.66B new North Terminal project to house American Airlines and its partner airlines with American Airlines contributing approximately 70% of the costs for the new terminal (Magcale, 2007). Similarly, Delta Air Lines plans to finance much of the $3B cost of a terminal construction project at its New York JFK hub, where terminals 2 and 3 would be combined and remodeled (Potkewitz, 2008, May 22). Further, airlines are required to finance aircraft purchases, aircraft modifications, and ground projects to operate an efficient and profitable business. While every business requires effective capital structure management, arguably the air transport industry faces one of the greatest burden from capital requirements.

Capital projects are usually funded through three different means: issuance of equity, issuance of debt, or cash obtained through the reinvestment of profits (retained earnings). As with anything, raising capital is not free, since there are different costs associated with each method of raising capital. The capital structure of a company is ultimately the mix between cash, debt, and equity that fund the company. The role of finance is the ability to fund all short-term and long-term capital needs at the lowest cost.

### Common Stock

Equity can be classified into two distinct categories, common stock and preferred stock,[2] based upon the shareholders' rights. Common stock represents a unit of ownership in

---

2    These stocks can be further subdivided by type such as blue chip stocks, cyclical stocks, penny stocks, over the counter (OTC) stocks, income stocks, interest-sensitive stocks and defensive stocks. Defensive stocks are stocks of companies whose earnings tend to remain fairly stable or perhaps even rise when the economy is slow.

the company and is commonly traded on public exchanges, such as the New York Stock Exchange (NYSE), the National Association of Securities Dealers Automated Quotations (NASDAQ), the Tokyo Stock Exchange (TSE), Paris stock exchange (known as Euronext Paris) and the London Stock Exchange (LSE). By being a proportional owner in the company, a common stockholder is afforded certain rights:

- Pre-Emptive Rights (First opportunity to buy new issues of shares)
- Vote on major issues and elect the Board of Directors
- Proportional ownership of assets if the company liquidates
- Proportional rights to dividends.

Shareholders are allowed first opportunity to buy new shares when a company decides to release additional shares of common stock. Shareholders may purchase a percentage of the new shares up to the proportion of existing shares that they own (i.e. if a person currently owns 1% of total shares outstanding, he or she will be allowed to purchase up to 1% of new shares). While an individual shareholder may have minimal influence over a company's operation, shareholders are afforded the right to vote on key issues at annual meetings and elect the board of directors, who act as the representative of the shareholders. Shareholders also have a right to the assets of the company; however, this is after debt creditors and preferred stockholders.

Companies raise equity capital by selling an ownership stake in the company. This is done either through an initial public offering (IPO), which is the first time an ownership stake in the company is publicly offered, or through subsequent share issuances. Any issuance in ownership is usually aided by an underwriter, who acts as a middle person between the company and publicly traded stock exchanges. Depending on the agreement, the underwriter will sometimes bear risk by providing the issuing company with a guaranteed issuance price.

In the airline industry, since most companies are publicly traded, there are numerous examples of airlines raising capital through equity issuances. For instance, in 2002 JetBlue's initial public offering raised $116 million by offering 5.5 million shares to the general public (Tsao, 2002). Airlines also routinely bolster their equity through subsequent share offerings, such as American Airlines 2008 offering of 27.1 million shares which provided $294 million of proceeds to the airline (American Airlines, 2008).

Many airlines issue common stocks to finance their growth during the expansion period. For example, Continental Airlines issued 18 million shares of its common stock on Oct 24, 2005 at $11.35 per share to the public.[3]

One important consideration to remember concerning stock issuance is that for every additional common stock offered, a stock's value decreases since an individual common share now represents a smaller portion of ownership. For example, consider a company whose equity consists of just two stocks. Under this scenario each stock represents approximately 50% ownership. However, if an additional stock was offered, each stock would now represent a 33% stake in the company, a significant reduction in value. Such stock dilution is ultimately reflected in lower stock prices. From a financing perspective, every subsequent common stock offering would therefore yield less capital received per share.

---

3    http://www.prnewswire.com

*Par value, stated value and market value*    When a company offers shares of stock there are two different values of the share of stock: the par value and the market value. Par value is an arbitrary value printed on the stock certificate that states the minimum value of the stock. As a result, the par value is usually very low, such as $0.01 or $1.00 per share. The par value of a stock is usually detailed on the balance sheet under shareholders' equity. Increasingly, companies are issuing stock without a par value.

The market value, what an individual actually pays for the stock, is almost always higher than the par value, reflecting the true intrinsic value of the stock. A company records any additional capital received from the issuance of stock above par value as additional paid-in capital on their balance sheet (Foerster, 2003). Table 9.1 shows the common stock section of the balance sheet for Continental Airlines. The balance sheet lists the par value of each share, shares the company is authorized to sell, the total number of shares outstanding and the additional paid-in capital from the sale of stock at a price greater than par. The average capital received from the issuance of common stock can be calculated by taking the additional paid-in capital divided by the number of shares issued. For Continental Airlines in 2007, the average capital received was $16.35.[4] This represents the capital received by CAL in excess of par from issuing common stock. While this price represents the market value at the time of issuance, the current market price is reflected by the stock market.

**Table 9.1      Shareholders' equity for Continental Airlines (U.S. $ Millions)**

|                                                                                              | 2008  | 2007  |
| -------------------------------------------------------------------------------------------- | ----- | ----- |
| Class B common stock - $.01 par; 400,000,000 share authorized; 123,264,534 and 98,208,888 shares issued and outstanding | 1.23  | 0.98  |
| Additional paid-in capital                                                                   | 1,997 | 1,606 |

*Source*: Compiled by the Authors from Continental Airlines Annual Report (2008).

In a situation where a company cannot fully reinvest retained earnings, companies will occasionally repurchase common stock in lieu of a dividend payment (Brigham and Gapenski, 1994). Stock that is internally held is called treasury stock and is usually located as a separate line item under the shareholders' equity section of the balance sheet. Stock repurchases are typically only done by companies with significant cash on hand since the company must purchase the stock at market value. Repurchasing ultimately reduces the number of shares outstanding, which is the total number of shares held by external investors. With fewer shares outstanding the intrinsic value of one share increases, and this ultimately increases a stock's value. However, a repurchase of shares decreases both assets and stockholders' equity on the balance sheet since cash is used in the stock repurchase. Table 9.2 shows the stockholders' equity section of Southwest Airlines balance sheet. From the table we can see that treasury stock reduces stockholders' equity based on the negative treasury stock values.

---

4      Average Capital Received = Additional Paid-In Capital / Total Number of Shares Outstanding
= $1,606 million / 98,208,888 = $16.35.

**Table 9.2       Stockholders' equity for Southwest Airlines (U.S. $ Millions)**

|  | 2008 | 2007 |
|---|---|---|
| Common stock - $1.00 par value; 2,000,000,000 shares authorized; 807,611,634 shares issued and authorized in 2008 and 2007 | 808 | 808 |
| Capital in excess of par value | 1,215 | 1,207 |
| Retained earnings | 4,919 | 4,788 |
| Accumulated other comprehensive income | -984 | 1,241 |
| Treasury stock, at cost – 72,814,104 and 24,302,215 shares in 2007 and 2006, respectively | -1,005 | -1,103 |
| **Total stockholders' equity** | **4,953** | **6,491** |

*Source*: Compiled by the Authors from Southwest Airlines Annual Report (2008).

Another key difference to note concerning equity is the difference between the book value of a company and its market value. The book value of a company is based on the actual amount of capital invested into the company, known as stockholders' equity (Brigham and Gapenski, 1994). Stockholders' equity is comprised of the book value of common and preferred stock, any capital in excess of par, and retained earnings less treasury stock.

Stockholders' Equity = Common Stock + Preferred Stock + Capital in Excess of Par + Retained Earnings – Treasury Stock

Retained earnings are profits obtained from prior periods and are reinvested in the company to earn more money for the company and its shareholders. The statement of stockholders' equity helps detail the retained earnings of company. The book value of a company is easily found by the total stockholders' equity line on the balance sheet. As an example, based on the information contained in Table 9.2, Southwest Airlines' book value at the end of 2008 stood at $4.9 billion.

The market value of equity, also commonly referred to as market capitalization, is based on the market value of common stock on an individual day. Based on the stock price, market capitalization is found from the total number of shares outstanding.

Market Capitalization = Stock Price × Number of Shares Outstanding

As a result of daily fluctuations in the stock price, market capitalization varies, resulting in companies getting "bigger" or "smaller" overnight. The current market price of a stock can be found by going to any number of financial websites such as Yahoo Finance[5] or MSN

---

5    http://finance.yahoo.com/

Money.[6] An example of the information provided by Yahoo! Finance is displayed in Table 9.3, showing the daily quote for Southwest Airlines stock market value.

**Table 9.3     Southwest Airlines daily quote**

| Southwest Airlines | | (NYSE: LUV) | |
|---|---|---|---|
| Last trade: | 7 | Day's range: | 6.77 - 7.00 |
| Trade time: | 23-Jul | 52wk range: | 4.95 - 16.77 |
| Change: | 0.08 (1.16%) | Volume: | 5,695,154 |
| Prev close: | 6.92 | Avg vol (3m): | 8,709,750 |
| Open: | 6.91 | Market cap: | 5.19B |
| Bid: | N/A | P/E (ttm): | 97.22 |
| Ask: | N/A | EPS (ttm): | 0.07 |
| First year target est: | 9.19 | Div & yield: | 0.02 (0.30%) |

*Source*: Complied by the Authors.

Using information gathered from Yahoo Finance, the market value of equity for Southwest Airlines can be calculated based on the stock price on July 23, 2009. While Table 9.4 displays the market capitalization calculation, as shown in Table 9.3, many financial tools already perform the simple market value calculation.

**Table 9.4     Southwest Airlines market capitalization**

| | |
|---|---|
| Stock price (as of 07/23/2009) | 7.00 |
| Number of shares outstanding | 774.2 Million |
| Market capitalization | $5.19 Billion. |

*Source*: Compiled by the Authors; 03/23/2009.

From Table 9.4 we see that Southwest Airlines' market value of equity is much higher than its book value ($5.19B compared to $4.95B); however these values are for different dates as the book value is based upon December 31, 2008 while the market value is on July 23, 2009. Regardless, appreciation in value indicates that the price of Southwest Airlines stock has increased since investors originally purchased the stock. Investors will require that a company has a higher market value than book value because it shows that investors are receiving a return on their investment.

Table 9.5 shows the book value and market value of equity of some major airlines. With the stock price based on future projections of financial return, the market capitalization of a company is one of the soundest tools to measure financial size, and, since return on investment is the major objective of investors, market capitalization is

---

a much more meaningful metric in terms of corporate valuation. Southwest Airlines has the largest market capitalization in the airline industry, even if they are not the largest carrier in terms of an airline's measure of output, available seat miles (ASMs). This market capitalization is the result of continual profitability. Ultimately, market capitalization reflects the financial health of a company, as perceived from the investment community.

**Table 9.5    Book value and market value of equity of major airlines***

| Airline | Book value ($ Millions) | Market value (capitalization) 22 July, 2009 |
|---|---|---|
| Southwest Airlines | $4,953.00 | $5,090.00 |
| Continental Airlines | $105.00 | $1,140.00 |
| United Airlines | -$2,465.00 | $489.00 |
| Alaska Air | $661.90 | $763.00 |
| American Airlines | -$2,935.00 | $1,200.00 |
| U.S. Airways | -$505.00 | $234.00 |
| Delta Air Lines | $874.00 | $4,550.00 |
| GOL | $457.00 | $1,540.00 |
| TAM | $605.00 | $1,920.00 |
| COPA | $632.00 | $1,740.00 |
| Allegiant Air | $233.92 | $771.27 |

*Source*: Compiled by the Authors.
* Millions of dollars.

## Preferred Stock

Preferred stock is a special form of equity ownership that has a fixed periodic dividend that must be paid before dividends are distributed to common stockholders. Preferred stock is often referred to as a hybrid security since it has many characteristics of both common stock and bonds. As with common stock, preferred stock has a stated par value, but trades at freely moving market values. Each preferred stock also has a stated preferred dividend which is the amount that will be distributed to stockholders' for one preferred share. Stated preferred dividends are usually expressed as a percentage of par value and are distributed in pre-determined periods (i.e. quarterly, yearly). Since preferred dividends are legally the first to be distributed to stockholders' (after debt payments), common stock is deemed more risky since common stock dividend payments are voluntary and paid after bondholders and preferred stockholders.

Other unique characteristics of preferred stock, acting as a hybrid between debt and equity are:

- Preferred stocks have no voting rights
- Preferred stocks receive dividends before common stock

- In case of liquidation, preferred shareholders are paid after bondholders, but before common stock holders
- Non-payment of dividend does not bring bankruptcy.

Owing to stated preferred dividends, preferred stock usually trades at a premium over common stock. While preferred stock issuance is common in a variety of industries, it remains rare in the airline industry. Since airlines tend to be never very financially stable, largely owing to the high degree of cyclicality in the industry, they are usually not in a position to distribute dividend payments, thereby reducing the airline's cash balance. Therefore, the issuance of preferred stock is not the most desirable method of raising equity in the airline industry.

Equity can also be raised through sources other than the issuance of stock. For smaller companies, the original founders/owners may decide to put additional equity into the business, thereby reducing the ownership percentage of the shareholders. Companies may also raise equity directly from another firm, bypassing the public issuance of common stock. Sometimes these private equity arrangements result in special conditions, transcending the line between common and preferred shares. For example, in October 2008, Warren Buffett invested $3 billion in General Electric (GE), providing his company with special preferred shares that gave a 10% annual dividend, voting rights, and callable rights (AP, 2008).

## COST OF EQUITY

An investor makes an investment in a company with the aim of achieving a healthy return on investment. The return on investment that shareholders require from a company represents the company's cost of equity. The cost of common stock ($k_E$) varies for each company based on risk factors such as variability in earnings, capital structure, and the macro-economic environment. The airline industry is probably deemed a "risky" investment owing to a high degree of volatility and cyclicality in earnings brought on from high fixed costs and significant exposure to the economy. As a result, one would expect higher costs of equity for an airline when compared to other companies that have more stable cash flows and earnings.

As mentioned previously in the text, investors receive a return on their investment through two means: dividends received and capital gains (increase in a stock's value). The total cost of common stock is found by combining the dividend yield and capital gains return. Dividend yield is the proportion of a stock's value that is attributed to dividends while capital gains return is the change in stock price over the period. As an example, consider a stock that is bought for $50 a share and pays an annual dividend of $2.50. After one year the stock increases in value to $55. Based on this information, the total return to the investor for the year was 15%, representing the historical cost of equity to the company. This total return of 15% can be broken down to 5% from dividend yield and 10% from capital gains. It should be noted that the future cost of equity is based upon perceived future dividends and capital gains. Therefore, the true cost of equity is based on investors' future perceptions of the company rather than for historical results.

$$k_e = \frac{D_1}{P_0} + \frac{P_1 - P_0}{P_0}$$

where:
D1  = Dividend at the end of year one
P1  = Stock price at the end of year one
P0  = Original stock price

$$k_e = \frac{\$2.50}{\$50.00} + \frac{\$55.00 - \$50.00}{\$50.00}$$
$$k_e = 0.05 + 0.10$$
$$k_e = 0.15$$

The goal of any company is to increase shareholder wealth. With investors investing to increase wealth, goal congruency should exist.[7] That is, the company achieves enough profitability to distribute dividends and increase share value. Based on these prospects, investors are willing to forego the time value of money to invest in the company and receive an appropriate rate of return. Since investors require compensation for their investment (time value of money) and for the risk involved, companies must achieve enough profit (return on equity) to pay dividends and/or increase the value of the company. Obviously, if profitability does not occur, the company will struggle in attracting additional investors and this in turn will make raising capital more difficult. A lack of such financial well-being will detract potential investors, thereby requiring higher rates of return to compensate for more risk. Ultimately, as Chapter 8 pointed out, the less risky the investment, the lower the cost of equity.

## Stock Valuation Models

As a general rule, the value of an asset, either financial or physical, is based on the perceived future net cash flows, or value. The cost of equity is ultimately based on investors' perceived future rate of return, which of itself is based on the risk and return paradigm. While the previous methodology calculated the historical cost of equity, the true corporate cost of equity needs to be computed based on perceived future earnings. To calculate investors' perceived rate of return, the dividend discount model can be used. The model can be derived depending on three different states of the stock's expected growth:

- Zero growth
- Constant growth
- Non-constant growth.

*Zero growth (constant dividend)*   A zero growth stock is a stock in which the dividends distributed are the same for every year with stockholders anticipating receiving the same amount of revenue per year forever. As a result, a zero growth stock is essentially a perpetuity with one constant payment (dividend) that extends into the foreseeable future

---

7     However, this is not always the case owing to a variety of agency issues.

(Brigham and Gapenski, 1994). As a result of no dividend growth, the equation can be simplified as:

$$P_0 = \frac{D_0}{(1+k_e)^1} + \frac{D_0}{(1+k_e)^2} + \ldots + \frac{D_0}{(1+k_e)^n}$$

$$P_0 = \sum_{n=1}^{\infty} \frac{D_0}{(1+k_e)^n}$$

$$n \to \infty$$

$$then: P_0 = \frac{D_0}{k_e}$$

where:
$P_0$ = the stock price today
$D_0$ = the dividend distributed today
$k_e$ = the cost of equity

Since the role of corporate finance is to satisfy all future financial requirements at the lowest cost, the cost of equity is probably the most important metric in the dividend discount model. Rearranging the formula provides:

$$k_e = \frac{D_0}{P_0}$$

While the zero dividend growth assumption is simple to understand, it is not very practical as dividend payments are likely to vary directly with financial performance over time. This assumption may be applicable to more or less stable companies (for example, utilities) and certainly does not apply to the air transport industry. Since the dividends remain constant, the dividend payout ratio (% of earnings paid out as dividends) is also assumed to be constant. Additionally, with capital gains not factored in, earnings per share are also assumed constant.

As an example of the dividend discount model with zero growth, consider DirectJet Airlines whose stock is currently trading at $25 per share and announced an annual dividend of $2.25 per share. Assuming that dividends are not expected to grow, the company's cost of equity equals is equal to 9%.

$$k_e = \frac{D_0}{P_0} = \frac{\$2.25}{\$25} = 0.09$$

*Constant dividend growth*   A constant dividend growth stock is one where the company is expected to grow over time. As a result, the corresponding dividend payments are expected to grow at a constant rate. The dividend growth rate can be found by comparing the current dividend payment versus the prior dividend payment and assuming that such growth will continue into perpetuity.

$$P_0 = \frac{D_1}{(1+k)^1} + \frac{D_2}{(1+k)^2} + \ldots + \frac{D_n}{(1+k)^n}$$

$$n \to \infty$$

$$then: P_0 = \frac{D_0(1+g)}{(k-g)} = \frac{D_1}{(k-g)}$$

$$k_e = \frac{D_1}{P_0} + g$$

Referring back to DirectJet Airlines, assume that the company's previous dividend was $2.18 per share. Based on the newly announced dividend of $2.25, this represents an approximate 3.2% growth rate.[8] Based on the company's expansion plans, one assumes this dividend growth will continue into the future. Using the current stock price of $25, DirectJet's cost of equity is found to be 12.48%.

$$k_e = \frac{D_0(1+g)}{P_0} + g = \frac{\$2.25(1+0.032)}{\$25} + 0.032 = \frac{\$2.322}{\$25} + 0.032 = 0.1248$$

*Non-constant growth*    While zero growth and constant dividend growth models are simple models, they are generally not the most realistic as companies invariably adjust their dividend payments over time. Stocks with non-constant dividend growth have growth rates that differ over time. Typically, this is representative of a start-up company with initial growth that is followed by a different growth rate as the company matures. To determine the cost of equity for non-constant dividend growth, future dividends need to be discounted back to the present time period (and the original dividend growth rate). The generic non-constant dividend growth model is:

$$P_0 = \frac{D_1}{(1+k)} + \frac{D_2}{(1+k)^2} + \frac{D_3}{(1+k)^3} + \ldots + \frac{P_n}{(1+k)^n}$$

where the last term represents the portion of constant dividend growth in the future and can be found using the constant dividend growth rate formula:

$$P_n = \frac{D_n}{(k-g)}$$

As an example of the non-constant dividend growth model in action, consider DirectJet once again. With DirectJet's stock currently trading at $40 per share and the previous annual dividend at $1.00 per share, the company expects the annual dividend to increase at a 3% rate for the next three years as the airline expands. For the fourth year, and onwards, the expectation is that dividends will increase at a more mature 7% rate. The first step in calculating the cost of equity for non-constant dividend growth is determining the dividend for each period.

---

8    Growth Rate = ($2.25 - $2.18) / $2.18 = 0.032 or 3.2%.

$$D_1 = D_0(1+g) = \$1.00(1+.03) = \$1.03$$
$$D_2 = D_1(1+g) = \$1.03(1+.03) = \$1.06$$
$$D_3 = D_2(1+g) = \$1.06(1+.03) = \$1.09$$
$$D_4 = D_3(1+g) = \$1.09(1+.07) = \$1.17$$

To determine the cost of equity, the value of the stock in the fourth year needs to be determined.

$$P_4 = \frac{D_4}{(k-g)} = \frac{\$1.17}{(k-0.07)}$$

Substituting the price of the stock in the fourth year into the non-constant growth model and solving for the cost of equity yields the following equation:

$$\$40 = \frac{\$1.03}{(1+k)} + \frac{\$1.06}{(1+k)^2} + \frac{\$1.09}{(1+k)^3} + \frac{\dfrac{\$1.17}{(k-0.07)}}{(1+k)^4}$$

Unfortunately, the cost of equity for non-constant growth cannot be solved without an iterative process. Fortunately, the goal seek function in Microsoft Excel can be used, where it is determined that the cost of equity for DirectJet was 9.20%.

As one may have noticed, the dividend discount model can also be used to calculate the fair market value of stock based upon an assumed cost of equity. This assumed cost of equity can be based upon the general market return, or what an investor would expect to receive from investing in the general market. In essence, this would represent the average cost of equity for all companies listed in a stock exchange. As an example, assuming a market return of 12%, a past dividend of $2.05 per share and an expected constant dividend growth rate of 9%, the theoretical fair market value of the stock would be approximately $75.

$$P_0 = \frac{D_1(1+g)}{(k-g)} = \frac{\$2.05(1+.09)}{(.12-.09)} = \frac{\$2.23}{0.03} = \$74.48$$

Any difference in the actual stock price versus the perceived market price could represent a buy or sell opportunity for an investor. However, there are multiple reasons why the fair market value of a stock may differ materially from the actual stock price:

- **Risk aversion (industry risk)**—Investors may perceive certain industries or the macro-economy as being more or less risky. As a result of risk, the perceived cost of equity will vary, affecting the market value of a stock. For example, when fuel prices rise, airline stocks tend to go down, even if the change in oil price is only expected to be temporary. This is a result of the perceived increased financial risk from the higher fuel prices.
- **Company risk**—Investors may require a higher rate of return because they fear that investing in that particular company is more risky. For example, U.S. Airways pilots continue to fight over their pay scale and seniority integration with former America West pilots (Kahn, 2008, March 3). Difficult labor negotiations and the possible threat of a strike tend to increase the risk for purchasing stock in U.S. Airways.

- **Inflation expectations**—Expectations for the amount of inflation in the economy may affect the required rate of return for investors. If inflation is expected to increase, investors will demand a greater rate of return to compensate for the time value of money.
- **Different stock valuation models**—Investors may use stock valuation models other than the dividend discount models. Other popular stock valuation models include the Discounted Cash Flow (DCF) and Earnings Growth (EG) models (Anuar, 2007, December 9), or other proprietary models.
- **Demand and supply/random events**—Individuals may like or dislike a stock on a certain day based on random events. News that may have no effect on financial issues, such as an emergency landing caught on video, like JetBlue in September of 2005, may cause the price to go up or down (MSNBC, 2005, September 22).

## Cost of Preferred Stock

The cost of preferred stock is similar to the cost of common stock with constant dividends as preferred stockholders receive a fixed dividend from the company into perpetuity. The cost of preferred stock is simply the stated dividend divided by the stock price, resembling the cost of common stock with zero dividend growth formula.

$$k_{ps} = \frac{D_{ps}}{P_{ps}}$$

As an example, DirectJet issued preferred stock paying a stated annual dividend of $5 per share. Based on the preferred stock trading at $40 per share, the cost of preferred equity for DirectJet would be 12.50%.

$$k_{ps} = \frac{\$5.00}{\$40.00}$$

$$k_{ps} = 12.5\%$$

## Cost of Retained Earnings

As mentioned previously, equity can be raised through two means: issuance of common/ preferred stock and through retained earnings. Whenever a company earns a profit, a decision needs to be made on the proportion of profits that are to be paid back to shareholders' through dividends or held by the company to reinvest in future expansion or other projects. Such a decision is usually the result of determining how much profitability the retained earnings can provide. A company that distributes no dividends believes that the earnings can be reinvested profitably within the company. As with anything, retained earnings bear a cost as investors must be compensated for the opportunity cost of foregoing a dividend. Recall that the rate of return for an investor is equal to the dividend yield plus the capital gains yield. Therefore, if a company is not paying dividends, then the capital gains yield must equal the investors' required rate of return. Thus, the formula for the cost of retained earnings is based on the value for the cost of equity calculated by using the dividend discount model discussed earlier.

$$k_{RE} = k = \frac{D_1}{P_0} + g$$

One difficulty in determining the cost of retained earnings is the growth rate of retained earnings. While in the cost of equity section we assumed a value for dividend growth, retained earnings can also be estimated based on the company's retention ratio and the cost of equity. The retention ratio is the historical proportion of net income that the company turns into retained earnings. The inverse of the retention ratio is the payout ratio, which is the proportion of profits that are distributed to shareholders' as dividends. The growth rate of retained earnings can be found using:

$$g = (Retention\ Ratio) \times (k)$$
$$g = (1 - Payout\ Ratio) \times k$$

As an example, DirectJet is a small airline looking at expanding and making inroads in the U.S. aviation industry. As a result, DirectJet has decided that its payout ratio will be only 10% of net income, resulting in an annual dividend of just $0.50 per share. Based on the constant dividend growth model, DirectJet's cost of equity is found to be 12.50%. Therefore if the current stock price is $20 per share, DirectJet's cost of retained earnings will be 13.75% as calculated below:

$$g = (1 - PayoutRatio) \times (k)$$
$$g = (1 - 10\%) \times (12.50\%) = 11.25\%$$
$$k_{RE} = \frac{D_1}{P_0} + g = \frac{\$0.50}{\$20} + 0.1125 = 13.75\%$$

## BONDS

"Airline industry seeks investors willing to finance billions of dollars of aircraft deliveries and other capital improvements. Will offer choice of junk bonds, stocks consistently underperforming the S&P 500, and uncertain aircraft residual values to those who apply."

Gerald J. Arpey, American AIrlines

The other major component used to raise capital is debt. While bonds are the most common corporate debt instrument, other financial debt instruments include corporate paper, lines of credit, and convertible bonds. A bond is a formal contract to repay borrowed money with interest at fixed, predetermined intervals. On July 17, 2009 British Airways announced it plans to issue a £300 million convertible debt to make sure it has sufficient cash to meet the current difficult economic environment.[9] A company will issue a bond, while the entity that buys a bond from a company is the bond- or debt-holder. An indenture is a written agreement between the company and its bondholders which discloses all of the rights

---

9      Bloomberg, July 17, 2009.

and privileges of bondholders as well as the terms of the bond. Common stipulations for bondholders' include the following:

- No voting rights
- Interest is paid to bondholders before dividends are paid to stockholders
- In case of liquidation, bondholders receive interest and face value of bond before preferred or common stockholders have access to assets.

In exchange for capital, the company agrees to pay the bondholder periodic interest payments, called coupon payments, until the bond has matured. The payments are called coupon payments because historically, when bonds were first issued, the bondholders would have to turn in the coupon with the bond to collect their interest payment. Nowadays companies have more modern systems of distributing interest payments; however, the name coupon payment remains the standard terminology. A bond is a legally binding agreement between a borrower and lender, with the borrower receiving first access to funds in the event of bankruptcy. Most corporations issue bonds in denominations of $1,000, the face value of the bond, with maturity between 10 to 30 years (Gitman, 2008). The cost of debt (coupon rate) depends on the market interest rate, the risk associated with the bond (possibility of bankruptcy) and the corporate tax rate. For example, on November 29, 2001, Standard and Poor's, the credit rating agency, downgraded British Airways' bonds to junk status, in a move that jacked up the airline's interest costs. The amount of the coupon payment is based on two items: the face value of the bond and the coupon rate.

The face value of a bond is similar to the par value of a stock, in that it is the basis of a bond's value and is printed on the bond certificate. The face value of the bond determines the amount that will be repaid at maturity, with maturity being the length of time remaining on the bond to payout the face value. Typically, bonds come with 1, 5, 10 or 30 year maturity periods; however, any maturity length can be created. Additionally, bonds can typically be bought or sold between the original investor and a third party at any time while the bond is still outstanding. In essence, just like stocks, bonds are publicly traded with various market values.

To understand the general dynamics of a bond, and the relationship between face value and coupon payment, consider a simple bond with a coupon rate of 8% and a par value of $1,000. The coupon rate, or the annual interest rate ($i$), is the rate determining the amount of interest paid annually. If the bond pays annual interest, the coupon payment (C) would be $80; however, if the bond pays interest biannually, the coupon payments would be $40.[10]

The type of bond mentioned above would be considered a fixed rate bond since the coupon rate remains at the same 8% throughout maturity. However, bonds will also have floating rates where a fixed value will be tied to some market indices. This is done to minimize swings in the bond's market value and have it more directly tied to the market. One of the most common market indices used in assessing a bond's coupon rate is LIBOR, or the London InterBank Offer Rate. The LIBOR is a daily reference rate at which banks borrow funds amongst themselves. As an example, consider a floating rate debt instrument with a $1,000 face value and a coupon rate of the 1-month LIBOR plus 4.50%. At the date

---

10    Annual Coupon Payment = Face Value * Coupon Rate = $1,000 * 8% = $80. Bi-Annual Coupon Payment = Face Value *(Coupon Rate / 2) = $1,000 * (8%/2) = $40.

of coupon payment, if the 1-month LIBOR was 0.50%, then the coupon payment would be $50.[11] However, if next year the 1-month LIBOR increased to 2.00%, then the coupon rate would increase to 6.50%, and the resulting coupon payment would be $65.[12] As a result, floating rate debt instruments will have different coupon payments over time.

In much the same way that stocks are not always traded at par value, bonds do not have to be sold at face value. There are three different types of bonds based upon their market value: par value bonds, premium bonds and discount bonds. Par value bonds are bonds that trade at face value, whereas premium bonds are bonds which trade at a market value greater than the face value and discount bonds are bonds which trade at a market value less than the face value.

The actual price that a bond sells at is based on current market interest rates (k) for bonds of companies with similar risk. Bonds sell at a premium if the coupon rate (i) is higher than the market interest rate (k). As the bond approaches maturity the market value approaches face value; the market value of the premium bond decreases. Discount bonds on the other hand sell for below face value because the coupon interest rates are lower than the market interest rate. As discount bonds approach maturity their market value also approaches face value; the amount of the discount below face value shrinks. Figure 9.1 shows how bond values approach par value as the bond nears maturity.

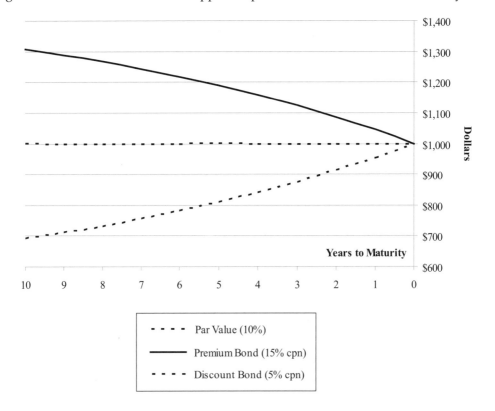

**Figure 9.1      Bond values with market interest rate = 10%**

---

11    Annual Coupon Payment = Face Value * Coupon Rate = Face Value * (1-month LIBOR + 4.50%) = $1,000 * (0.50% + 4.50%) = $50.
12    Annual Coupon Payment = Face Value * (1-month LIBOR + 4.50%) = $1,000 * (2.00% + 4.50%) = $65.

The theoretical value of a bond can be determined by using the annuity formula discussed in Chapter 7 and adding the face value discounted by the market interest rate.

$$\text{Market Value of Bond} = \sum_{t=1}^{n} \frac{C}{(1+k)^t} + \frac{FV}{(1+k)^n}$$

where:
C   = annual coupon payment
k   = market interest rate
t   = each payment period starting at t = 1
FV  = Face value of bond
n   = years to maturity

We should note that bond prices vary inversely with market interest rates. For fixed rate debt instruments, the higher the interest rates the lower the present value of the expected coupon payments, and thus the lower price of the bond (Clifford, 1979). Conversely, when the interest rate goes down, the price of the bonds goes up.

For example, consider a bond selling in 2009 for $1,000 with an annual coupon payment of $100 and ten years maturity. Now, suppose immediately after the bond was issued the interest rate drops to 8% and as a result the bond would appreciate to:

$$V_{Bond} = C \times [\frac{1}{k} - \frac{1}{k(1+k)^t}] + \frac{1000}{(1+k)^t}$$

$$V_{Bond} = 100 \times [\frac{1}{0.08} - \frac{1}{0.08(1+0.08)^{10}}] + \frac{1000}{(1+0.08)^{10}}$$

$$V_{Bond} = 100 \times 6.710 + 1000 \times 0.463$$

$$V_{Bond} = 671.00 + 463.00$$

$$V_{Bond} = 1,134$$

Thus, the bond has appreciated in value to $1,134, becoming a premium bond. This is a result of the coupon rate being greater than the interest rate, meaning an investor holding the bond would be earning a rate of return greater than the market.

## Bond Valuation

The purpose of theoretical bond valuation is to find out what price should be paid for a bond given the coupon payments, current discount rate, and the remaining time to maturity. Hence, the value of bonds depends on the amount and timing of the coupon payments, the creditors required rate of return, and the riskiness of these coupon payments.

To see the effects that the market value has on bond value, consider another example of a $1,000 par value bond with an annual coupon payment of $75 and five years to maturity.

Using the formula below and an 8% market rate, the bond's market value is $980, so that it is trading at a discount to the par value of $1,000.

$$\text{Market Value of Bond} = \sum_{t=1}^{n} \frac{C}{(1+k)^t} + \frac{FV}{(1+k)^n}$$

$$V_{bond} = \frac{\$75}{(1+.08)^1} + \frac{\$75}{(1+.08)^2} + \frac{\$75}{(1+.08)^3} + \frac{\$75}{(1+.08)^4} + \frac{\$75}{(1+.08)^5} + \frac{\$1000}{(1+.08)^5}$$

$$V_{bond} = \$980.04$$

The bond will continue selling at a discount as long as the market interest rate remains above the coupon interest rate. However, how much of a discount the bond sells for is dependent on the time to maturity and current yield on similar bonds. Table 9.6 shows the relationship between market rates and the price of bonds. In the above example, the assumed coupon rate is 7.50%, with the market interest rate varying. When the market interest rate is more than the coupon rate, bonds sell for less than face value. When the market interest rate is less than the coupon rate, bonds sell for more than face value (Brealey, Myers and Marcus 2007).

**Table 9.6     Bond market values as a result of market interest rates for 7.5% coupon bond**

| Market interest rate | Market value | Bond sells at: |
|:---:|:---:|:---:|
| 7.00% | $1,200 | Premium |
| 7.50% | $1,000 | Par value |
| 8.00% | $980 | Discount |

As market interest rates change, bond prices change, thus when the interest rate is the same as the coupon rate (7.50% in the example for a bond selling at par), the bond sells for its face value. However, if the market interest rate falls to 7%, the bonds' value increases the bond's interest rate is now greater than the market interest.

All the previous market value calculations have been predicated on knowing the market interest rate; however, in reality the underlying market interest rate can be found by knowing the current trading price for a bond. Known as yield to maturity, this is the interest rate that a bondholder will receive from purchasing a bond. As an example, consider a $1,000 face value bond, now trading at $1,049.95 that pays an annual coupon payment at the rate of 9% and matures in three years. Knowing that the bond is trading at a premium, the yield to maturity is expected to be less than the coupon rate of 9%. By reworking the market value of a bond formula, the yield to maturity is found to be 7.09%.[13]

---

13     As a result of the complexity of the calculation, the yield to maturity calculation is rarely performed by hand. Typically, either financial calculators or Microsoft Excel can help perform the yield to maturity calculation.

$$\text{Market Value of Bond} = \sum_{t=1}^{n} \frac{C}{(1+k)^t} + \frac{FV}{(1+k)^n}$$

$$\$1049.95 = \sum_{t=1}^{3} \frac{\$90}{(1+k)^t} + \frac{\$1000}{(1+k)^3}$$

$$k = 7.09\%$$

There are other reasons besides market interest rates that cause a bond to sell at a premium or a discount. Since bondholders have first access to a bankrupt party's assets, default risk is not as great a concern as it is to equity holders; however, it can play a role in bond market values. Bonds with increased risk will trade at a discount to the market. Additionally, special types of bonds will have different market values than their face values. For example, callable bonds with a call provision that gives the bondholder the option to collect the face value of the bond before the maturity date. These bonds sell at a premium because of the option to call in the face value early.

*Zero coupon bonds*    Other special types of bonds are zero coupon bonds, which do not pay interest payments during the life of the bond. Instead, zero coupon bonds are heavily discounted when bought so that the return occurs from receiving the face value at the bond's maturity date. The value of a zero coupon bond can be calculated (with the formula below) by finding the present value of the face value of the bond at maturity.

$$MV_{bond} = \frac{FV}{(1+k)^n}$$

As an example, consider a zero coupon bond whose face value is $1000 and that has 10 years until maturity. The calculation is shown below. Based on a market interest rate of 10%, the market value of the zero coupon bond would be $386.

$$MV_{bond} = \frac{\$1000}{(1+.10)^{10}}$$

$$MV_{bond} = \$385.54$$

Just as with discount bonds, zero coupon bonds' market value approaches face value as they get near to maturity. The value of zero coupon bonds as they approach maturity with different market interest rates is shown in Figure 9.2 overleaf. It shows that, as market interest rates increase, the market value of a zero-coupon bond decreases. Thus, the higher the market interest rate, the greater the built in capital gain of the bond as it approaches maturity.

## AIRLINE DEBT

Debt can be classified into two categories: unsecured and secured. For the airline industry, with highly capitalized assets, the distinction is critical to understanding financing. Secured debt is debt issued that is tied directly to some tangible asset, such as aircraft, engines, or spare parts. In the event of default and the inability to pay the debt's interest, the debt issuers have first right to seizing the assets. The cost of secured debt is ultimately based on the credit market and the secured assets' ability to cover the outstanding debt

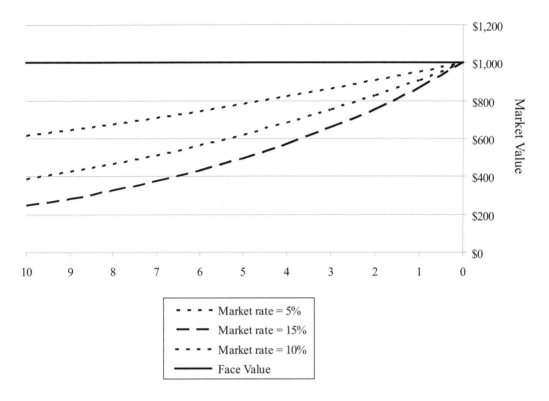

**Figure 9.2    Market value of zero-coupon bonds**

in the event of default. Unsecured debt is not directly tied to any assets, and as a result is usually more expensive than secured debt. Unsecured debt issuers have first right to any of the company's assets under default, but only after secured debt holders.

While there are many ways an airline can raise capital and debt, one increasingly common approach to aircraft financing is called enhanced equipment trust certificates (EETCs). EETCs have now become one of the more popular methods for financing aircraft, particularly in the United States (AF&AM, 2001). Basically, EETCs are securities that rely on the credit of a single corporate issuer. The credit is secured by aircraft as collateral and utilizes a liquidity facility to provide up to 18 months of missed interest payments (Scheinberg, 2008). EETCs are typically done in groups to finance a number of aircraft at one time, with multiple tranches issued (usually A, B, C, D) (Scheinberg, 2008). Each tranche will then possess a different cost of debt, with the A tranches typically being the lowest and D tranches the highest. Finally, each pass through certificate has the added protection of a liquidity facility, and these are revolving credit facilities made available from highly rated financial institutions (Scheinberg, 2008). These credit facilities help make timely interest payments in the event an airline fails to make an interest payment. Basically, they act as a sort of line of credit for the airline to use in the event of cash flow issues. These credit facilities help lower the cost of debt since they act as a safety net for certificate holders in the event of default. This is one of the principal reasons why EETCs are attractive to investors and so, ultimately, to airlines.

While EETCs are an increasingly common approach to aircraft financing, bank debt has long been the favorite of airlines. Bank debt is debt issued directly from a bank (instead of floated on the market) and it has many of the same features as bonds, but can be more customizable to a customers' needs. Other approaches to aircraft financing include simply paying cash for an aircraft (i.e. retained earnings), backstop financing from the manufacturer, or capital leases. Another popular method of having an aircraft is through an operating lease, which is a decision analyzed later on in the book.

## COST OF DEBT

As previously mentioned, the coupon rate of a bond is the rate of return to the investor. However, the cost of carrying debt is actually lower than the interest rate on the bonds since the interest a company pays is tax-deductible. Any interest a company pays reduces the company's taxable income, thus the cost of debt is the interest rate minus the tax shield savings.

To clarify the tax shield benefits of debt, consider the abbreviated income statements in Table 9.7 for two identical companies. However, assume company B has $200 more in interest expense as a result of increased debt. Interest expense acts as a tax shield since both company A and company B have identical operating incomes, but as a result of interest, company A has a greater pre-tax income and thus pays more taxes. While company's B interest expense is $200 greater, its net income is only $120 less than company A. This is a result of a tax shield of roughly $80.

**Table 9.7    Illustration of interest tax shield**

|  | Company A | Company B |
|---|---|---|
| Revenues | $2,050 | $2,050 |
| Expenses | ($1,000) | ($1,000) |
| Operating income | $1,050 | $1,050 |
| Interest expense | ($50) | ($250) |
| Pre-tax income | $1,000 | $800 |
| Income tax (@40%) | ($400) | ($320) |
| Net income | $600 | $480 |

In addition to interest payments depreciation allowances are also tax deductible expenses. The benefits of debt financing vs. equity financing favor a higher debt ratio since the tax benefits of debt typically mean that debt has a lower cost than equity. However, higher levels of debt may also carry higher costs. The first cost of higher debt derives from possible conflicts of interest between a firm's shareholders and creditors. The second cost is the higher probability of financial distress (Pinteris, 2003).

The cost of debt is simply the coupon rate of the bond less the interest effect of the tax shield. The generic formula for the cost of debt, taking into account taxes is:

$$k_d = c \times (1 - t)$$

where:
$k_d$ = cost of debt
$c$ = coupon rate of bond
$t$ = tax rate

As an example, take a company who issues bonds with a coupon rate of 8% and that has a marginal tax rate of 35%. The actual cost of debt for this company is 5.20%.

$$k_d = 0.08(1 - 0.35)$$
$$k_d = 0.0520$$

The tax benefit of debt makes acquiring capital through debt-financing more attractive to companies. In addition, bondholders have rights to be paid before shareholders and this normally makes bonds less risky than stocks. Because of the lower risk of a bond, the required rate of return is typically lower for a bondholder than for a shareholder.

## WEIGHTED AVERAGE COST OF CAPITAL (WACC)

Generally speaking, companies use a mix of the four sources of capital to fund operations: debt, preferred stock, common stock, and retained earnings. With various sources of capital having different costs, financial managers must use a combination of methods to provide the company with the lowest cost of capital. As a result, the total cost of capital of a company is the combination of the costs of the various sources of capital. The weighted average cost of capital takes into account the different costs of capital based on the company's capital structure. Each individual cost of capital is then weighted based on its proportion of the company's total capital structure. In essence, the WACC is the average of the cost of capital for all components contained in the capital structure.

The modus operandi for the WACC is a weighted combination of all the different cost of capital calculations. As seen from the formula below, the cost of common stock and retained earnings are combined into one component since they have similar properties. Additionally, not all companies have all components of the capital structure; therefore, in such situations, that component is merely zeroed out. The formula for WACC is shown below:

Weighted Average Cost of Capital

$$WACC = k_d(1 - T)(\frac{D}{V}) + k_{ps}(\frac{PS}{V}) + k_E(\frac{E}{V})$$

where:
$k_d$ = cost of debt (interest rate on bonds)
T = tax rate
D = market value of debt
V = total market value of the company
$k_{ps}$ = cost of preferred stock
PS = value of preferred stock
$k_E$ = cost of common equity (common stock, retained earnings)
E = market value of equity outstanding

To correctly calculate the weighted average cost of capital for a company, there are four necessary steps:

1. Calculate the value of each security as a proportion of the total value of the company.

2.  Determine the required rate of return of each security.
3.  Calculate the value weighting for each security.
4.  Calculate the weighted average of the rate of returns.

To understand the four steps required to calculate the weighted average cost of capital, consider a company that has a $20 million of 7.25% bonds outstanding, has issued 500,000 preferred stocks that pay an annual dividend of $2.25/share, and has one million common stocks outstanding that has historically paid a dividend of $1.25/share, but is expected to increase at a constant growth of 7%. Assuming a corporate tax rate of 40% and no retained earnings, the WACC can be calculated.

*Step One*   The value of each security is required to determine the appropriate weighting of the security in the capital structure. Since the bonds have $20 million outstanding, the debt value is simply $20 million. The stock's market values can be determined based on the number of shares outstanding and the current trading price. Assuming a preferred share price of $20/share and $50/share for common stock, the value of preferred shares is $10 million and value of common stock is $50 million.[14]

*Step Two*   The total capital structure for the company is $80M

$$V = D + PS + E$$
$$V = \$20 \text{ million} + \$10 \text{ million} + \$50 \text{ million} = \$80MM$$

Based on this, debt comprises 25% of the capital structure, preferred stock 12.50%, and common equity 62.50%.

$$D/V = \$20M / \$80M = 25\%$$
$$PS/V = \$10M / \$80M = 12.50\%$$
$$E/V = \$50M / \$80M = 62.50\%$$

*Step Three*   Using the various formulas to calculate the cost of the financial instruments, the cost of debt is found to be 4.35% after tax, the cost of preferred stock is 11.25% and the cost of common stock is 9.68%.

$$k_d = k \times (1-T) = 0.0725 \times (1-0.40) = 4.35\%$$

$$k_{ps} = \frac{D}{P} = \frac{\$2.25}{\$20} = 11.25\%$$

$$k_e = \frac{D_1}{P} + g = \frac{D_0(1+g)}{P} + g = \frac{\$1.25(1.07)}{\$50} + 7\% = 9.68\%$$

*Step Four*   Knowing the cost for each component of the capital structure and its value weighting, and using the formula below, the weighted average cost of capital is 8.55%.

$$WACC = k_d(D/V) + k_{ps}(PS/V) + k_e(E/V)$$
$$WACC = 4.35\%(25\%) + 11.25\%(12.50\%) + 9.68\%(62.50\%) = 8.55\%$$

---

14    Vps = Shares Outstanding × Stock Price = 0.50M × $20 = $10M.
Ve = Shares Outstanding × Stock Price = 1M ×$50 = $50M.

Debt clearly has the lowest cost of capital while preferred equity has the highest cost. Intuition might tell you that owing to the lower cost of debt, the company should have a larger percentage of its capital raised through debt financing; however, there are numerous reasons why the company may have considerably more capital financed through common equity instead of debt. The equity financing might consist largely of retained earnings. Retained earnings are good sources of finance since the capital already exists within the company and there is no need to search for investors. Another potential reason for this company's capital structure is the fact that the cost of debt will rise if the company finances too much capital through debt. The cost of debt is the cost associated with raising more capital by issuing debt. Bondholders may ask for higher interest rates if they see that lending capital is becoming riskier because the company is holding a large amount of debt. A higher cost of debt will also lead to the weighted average cost of capital rising as well. At certain debt ratios (called fences) the WACC "steps" up to a higher rate. Figure 9.3 shows the jumps in WACC that can occur when the debt-to-value ratio of a company increases.

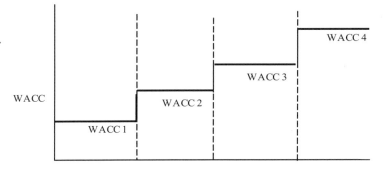

Debet-Asset Ratio

**Figure 9.3      IRR and WACC**

Figure 9.4 shows that the beta values for the majority of the airlines is positive, yet under one. This indicates less volatility when compared with the market as a whole; however, this could be influenced by the heavy volatility in the overall market in late 2008.[15] One carrier, Alaska Airlines, even has a beta of –0.03, which means that as the market declines, Alaska Airlines actually performs better than if the market increases. A few carriers such as YV and HA have a high degree of volatility, indicating increased market risk.

Engine manufacturers and aerospace defense companies tend to have lower betas than commercial aircraft manufacturers (with the exception being Rolls Royce which has a high beta). The reason for this is that demand for aircraft engines and defense spending is still high even in rough economic times and, while commercial aircraft manufacturers tend to fare better than the airlines in economic downturns, the tenuous nature of the airline industry still has a strong effect on commercial aircraft manufacturers (see Figure 9.5).

---

15    Beta has no upper or lower bound and betas larger than 3 will happen with voletile companies.

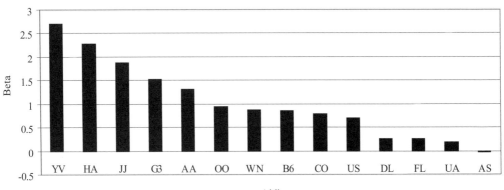

Figure 9.4    Airline stock betas

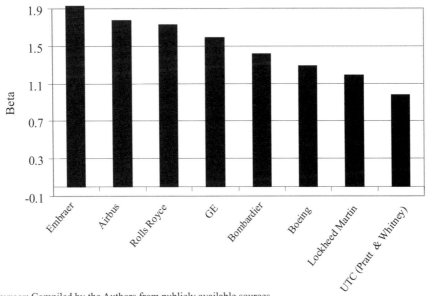

*Sources*: Compiled by the Authors from publicly available sources.

Figure 9.5    Aviation related companies

## AIRLINE DEBT AND EQUITY

Table 9.8 below shows the amount of debt and equity in different airlines. For airlines whose cost of debt is known, that information is also provided.

The information in Table 9.8 demonstrates that debt and equity structures vary from airline to airline. It is interesting to note that the larger carriers (American, Delta, and United Airlines) have very high amounts of debt compared to their amount of equity. Other airlines (Alaska, Southwest, TAM, and GOL) by comparison have much smaller debt-to-equity ratios.

Table 9.8      Airline debt and equity

| Airline | Total long-term assets ($ billions) | Long-term debt ($ billions) | Equity ($ billions) | $K_D$ |
|---|---|---|---|---|
| Alaska Airlines | 3.326 | 1.596 | 0.669 | 6.90% |
| American Airlines | 19.24 | 9.001 | 2.935 | |
| Continental Airlines | 8.339 | 5.371 | 0.105 | 7.10% |
| Delta Air Lines | 36.11 | 15.411 | 0.874 | |
| GOL Linhas Aereas | 2.39 | 1.041 | 0.457 | |
| Southwest Airlines | 11.419 | 3.495 | 4.953 | 6.73% |
| TAM Linhas Aereas | 4.642 | 3.11 | 0.605 | |
| United Airlines | 14.6 | 8.286 | -2.465 | 5.47% |
| U.S. Airways | 4.798 | 3.643 | -0.505 | 7.55% |

*Source*: Annual reports.

## CAPM TO ESTIMATE $K_E$

The Capital Asset Pricing Model (CAPM) was discussed in Chapter 8. The Capital Asset Pricing Model demonstrates that the expected rate of return on an investment is based on the risk-free rate, the average return in the market and the firm's beta. Beta is a measure of the market risk of a company as compared with the rest of the market. For example, a company whose beta is 1.2 signifies that as the market increases in value by 1%, the market value of the company's stock increases by 1.2%. The reverse is true if the overall value of the market where to go down by 1%. Figures 9.4 and 9.5 compare betas of airlines and aviation related companies.

In addition to beta, the WACC model requires the cost of equity to determine the overall cost of capital for a company. Suppose that we do not know or can't make a good assumption about what the cost of equity for a company is? When this is the case, we can use the Capital Asset Pricing Model to determine the cost of equity. In order to use the CAPM we must know the risk-free rate of interest, the rate of return for the market and the beta of the company. The use of CAPM to determine the cost of equity is demonstrated in the example below.

Capital Asset Pricing Model

The expected rate of return on the market is 12%

30-year Treasury Bonds have a yield of 6% (risk-free rate)

DirectJet has a beta of 1.2

Determine DirectJet's cost of equity

$$k_e = k_{rf} + (k_m - k_{rf})\beta$$
$$k_e = 0.06 + (0.12 - 0.06)(1.2)$$
$$k_e = 0.1320 = 13.20\%$$

In the example shown above, the return of the market, the beta of DirectJet and the yield of a 30-year Treasury bond are given to provide the three parameters needed for the Capital Asset Pricing Model. From this example we see that these three parameters can be used to estimate DirectJet's cost of equity and, performing the calculation, the model gives us a cost of equity of 13.20%. After using the CAPM equation to determine cost of equity, the WACC can be calculated as done in the previous section (Modigliani and Miller, 1958). Using the cost of equity calculated above the weighted average cost of capital can be calculated for DirectJet with a pre-tax cost of debt of 5.75%, a tax rate of 35%, no outstanding preferred stock and a capital structure with one half debt financing and one half equity financing.

$$WACC = I(1-T)(\frac{D}{V}) + k_E(\frac{E}{V})$$

$$WACC = .0575(1-.35)(\frac{1}{2}) + .1320(\frac{1}{2})$$

$$WACC = 8.47\%$$

From the WACC calculation, DirectJet is found to have a weighted average cost of capital of 8.47%. The weighted average cost of capital is obtained because airlines will often use their weighted average cost of capital to determine capital budgeting for capital-intensive projects that may be undertaken.

## BUSINESS RISK VS. FINANCIAL RISK

As previously mentioned in the more generic chapter on risk and return, investors require different rates of return for different companies based on the perceived amount of risk involved with investing in that company. More specifically, the risk of investing in a company can be broken down into two types of risk: business risk and financial risk. Business risk deals with the everyday operations of the company and the risk that its business plan will not be effective. Financial risk is the risk to shareholders (owners of the company) of raising capital through debt rather than common stock or retained earnings (Brigham and Gapenski, 1994).

### Business Risk

The business risk of an airline consists of the risk that the airline will not be able to generate a great enough return to stay in business. Business risk is applicable to all firms, including those without debt (Brigham and Gapenski, 1994). There are five areas that affect business risk:

1. Demand volatility—With other factors held stable, if a business has steady demand for its products and/or services the company will have less business risk.
2. Input cost volatility—If the price of supplies and other inputs to develop a product or service are constant, the company will have less business risk.
3. Sales price volatility—If a company is unsure of the price they will be able to charge for products and/or services, or if the price experiences a lot of variability, the business risk for the company increases.

4.  Ability to match price to input costs—If the company can quickly change its sales price to reflect changes in input costs the company can lower its business risk.
5.  Timely new product development- If companies are able to develop new products and/or services before their existing products become obsolete they will be able to reduce their business risk.

Unfortunately for the airline industry, all of these factors put the airline industry at a high level of business risk. Airlines face high demand volatility within the course of a year (summer and holidays busier than other times of the year) and even within the course of a week (Sunday, Monday and Friday are typically high demand days, while Tuesday and Wednesday are low demand days). The large amount of demand volatility means that airlines have a more difficult time projecting demand than companies in other industries. This high demand volatility increases business risk.

Sales price and input costs are also highly volatile in the airline industry. The price of fuel rises and falls on a daily basis and is quickly becoming the largest expense for airlines (over labor). The amount that airlines can charge is also extremely volatile. Because of the oligopoly structure of the air travel market, in order for airlines to increase fare levels, the competition must also increase its price so that the new prices will be sustained. These factors combined show that it is very difficult for airlines to adjust their prices in response to changes in the price of supply inputs. For example, airlines had a difficult time raising fares and fees in response to the fuel price crisis in early 2008.

Lastly, airlines are slow to receive new technology. While air travel as a whole remains attractive, many different aspects of air travel can become obsolete. Airlines have to constantly redesign and improve their first class and other premium cabins to attract the high-end business traveler. While the upgrades are expensive, airlines that do not improve their premium product will lose the high-yield customers and these are the customers that often help keep airlines afloat financially. In addition, airlines are not able to react to rising fuel prices with new technology as quickly as they would like. As fuel prices began to rise, airlines announced plans to retire old aircraft; however, replacing older aircraft with new aircraft from Boeing, Airbus, and so on takes many years to complete. The length of time it will take for an airline like American Airlines to replace its close to 300-airplane fleet of less fuel-efficient MD-80s may reach well into next decade (Mason, 2008, May 9). The inability to replace aging, less-efficient aircraft quickly puts airlines at a high level of business risk. Finally, owing to the high amount of regulation in the airline industry, any change requires an immense amount of bureaucratic wrangling.

*Operating leverage*   Operating leverage is a powerful tool that highlights the ratio between operating profit growth and sales growth. More directly, the degree of operating leverage is the sensitivity of the overall company's financial health with respect to sales growth. Operating leverage can also provide an indication of the company's cost structure, especially with respect to fixed costs. The general formula for the degree of operating leverage is:

$$DOL = \frac{\%\Delta \ in \ EBIT}{\%\Delta \ in \ Sales}$$

The explicit formulas are as follows:

$$DOL = \frac{Q(P-V)}{Q(P-V)-FC}$$

$$DOL = \frac{S-VC}{S-VC-FC}$$

where:
S      = initial sales in dollars
EBIT  = earnings before interest and taxes

The degree of operating leverage can vary considerably among companies in the same industry (Moyer et al. 2005). Companies with a high degree of operating leverage are much more sensitive to sales. This is partly a result of the company having sizeable fixed costs, which can either be leveraged effectively during times of increasing sales (because of decreasing average costs), or become a burden to the company during decreasing sales. As a concrete numerical example, suppose the degree of operating leverage is 2; this means that a 1% increase in ticket sales will result in a 2% increase in the airline's operating profit. In this case, there would be increasing returns to scale. Unfortunately, the reverse is also true during downswings in the economy, with the company experiencing a greater operating loss. Therefore, airlines with a high degree of operating leverage[16] will experience greater volatility of operating profit than airlines with smaller degrees of operating leverage.

Operating leverage can also be negative which indicates that when revenues increase, operating losses will decrease (and vice versa). Negative DOL indicates that the total costs exceed operating revenues. For example, a company with a degree of operating leverage of –1 will experience 100% increase in operating profit growth when the sales decline by 100%.

This scenario indicates decreasing returns to scale and it is probably due to the fact that the company has grown too quickly and is not effectively leveraging its fixed costs. Therefore, in order to improve its degree of operating leverage, the company should reduce its fixed costs while keeping the same level of output, or increase its output with the same fixed cost infrastructure. Additionally, changes to the company's contribution margin will also dramatically affect the company's degree of operating leverage. An airline may choose between a high or low level of fixed assets. For example, an airline may substitute's self-service check-in machines at different airports for check-in agents. If labor is not replaced with check-in machines, fixed costs are held lower, and variable costs are higher. With a lower level of operating leverage, the airline shows less growth in profits as sales rise, but faces less risk of loss as sales decline.

This overall understanding of an airline's cost structure is critical in the strategic planning phase of a company. It provides a comparison for the company between sales and operating profit, and depending on the value, can help guide strategic direction. It should be noted that operating leverage should not be confused with financial leverage, which deals with the amount of borrowed money that a company is using to finance its activities.

---

16    That is, companies that have higher fixed cost burden in relation to their overall profit.

## Financial Risk

> "The airline business is fast-paced, high risk, and highly leveraged. It puts a premium on things I like to do. I think I communicate well. And I am very good at detail. I love detail."

Robert L. Crandall

Shareholders bear financial risk when a company has a capital structure that includes debt. Including debt in a capital structure is known as leveraging the firm (Brigham and Gapenski, 1994). The risk that shareholders have from a firm becoming leveraged is that return on the equity will be reduced owing to the payment of interest to bondholders. In order for a company to place this risk on shareholders, there must be some potential benefit, otherwise the shareholders would never agree to allow the firm to finance through debt. While there is a risk that shareholders may receive a lower return on equity owing to interest payments, debt financing may also allow shareholders to receive a higher return on equity than could be achieved through equity financing alone.

To demonstrate the potential effects of leveraging, examine the figures in Tables 9.9 and 9.10. The company needs $500,000 in capital to operate, and expects earnings (EBIT) of $100,000 in the coming year. The company is trying to determine whether to finance their capital needs through a 50/50 ratio of debt and equity financing or rely solely on equity. The company pays 8% interest on debt financing and is taxed at a rate of 37%.

## Table 9.9     Leveraged firm vs. Un-leveraged firm (high EBIT)

|  | Leveraged firm | Un-leveraged firm |
|---|---|---|
| Expected EBIT | $100,000 | $100,000 |
| Interest (8% on $250,000 debt) | 40,000 | 0 |
| Earnings before taxes | $60,000 | $100,000 |
| Taxes (37%) | 22,200 | 37,000 |
| Net income | $37,800 | $63,000 |
| Expected ROE | $37,800/$250,000 = **15.12%** | $63,000/$500,000 = **12.6%** |

Investors receive a higher rate of return on equity when the company's earnings are high and debt financing is also used. The reason for the higher rate of return is that shareholders do not have to spread earnings over as large an equity base. In the example in Table 9.9, the amount of equity contributed in the leveraged firm is only $250,000 compared to $500,000 in the un-leveraged firm. While there are fewer earnings to distribute in a leveraged firm (owing to interest payments), the actual return on equity is higher, that is , 15.12% in our example compared to 12.6% for the un-leveraged firm.

What happens when a company has a bad year however? In Table 9.10 the same capital structures are used as in Table 9.9, but earnings do not meet expectations.

In Table 9.10 we see that the use of debt in the capital structure magnifies the negative effect on ROE when earnings are lower than expected. If the company was un-leveraged, the lower earnings would only reduce return on equity from 12.16% to 5.04%. However, with leveraged firms, the reduction in earnings means that interest payments make up

**Table 9.10      Leveraged firm vs. Un-leveraged firm (lower EBIT)**

|  | Leveraged firm | Un-leveraged firm |
|---|---|---|
| Expected EBIT | $100,000 | $100,000 |
| Actual EBIT | $40,000 | $40,000 |
| Interest (8% on $250,000 debt) | 40,000 | 0 |
| Earnings before taxes | $0 | $40,000 |
| Taxes (37%) | 0 | 14,800 |
| Net Income | $0 | $25,200 |
| Actual ROE | $0/$250,000 = **0%** | $25,200/$500,000 = **5.04%** |
| Expected ROE | $37,800/$250,000 = **15.12%** | $63,000/$500,000 = **12.6%** |

a larger portion of earnings. When leveraged firms have a lower EBIT than expected, their return on equity is often lower than if they were an un-leveraged. The relationship between return on equity, leveraged and un-leveraged firms, and EBIT can be demonstrated graphically as well. At lower earnings amounts, ROE is lower for leveraged firms, while at higher earnings ROE is higher for leveraged firms. This is shown in Figure 9.6.

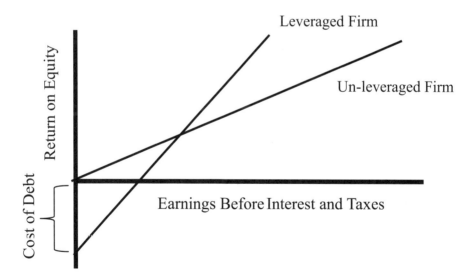

**Figure 9.6      Earnings and ROE for leveraged and un-leveraged firms**

Also as shown in the Figure 9.6, firms that are leveraged have lower (and even negative) returns on equity when EBIT is low. Shareholders of leveraged firms run the risk that the return on their investment will be lower than their required rate of return, or it might even turn into a negative return. Therefore, this risk of a poorer return on equity is the financial risk that shareholders assume when investing in a company with portions of both debt and equity financing.

*Financial leverage*   Financial leverage refers to the use of debt financing to enhance the chances for increasing the return on investment. Airlines must decide how leveraged they want to be, since increased leverage increases potential profitability but also the risk for financial distress.

Airlines that are highly leveraged may be at risk of bankruptcy if they are unable to make payments on their debt and they may also be unable to find new lenders in the future. However, financial leverage is not always bad as it can increase the shareholders' return on their investment and often there are tax advantages associated with borrowing. The degree of financial leverage (DFL) is defined as the percentage change in earnings per share that results from a given percentage change in EBIT:[17]

$$DFL = \frac{\%\Delta \, in \, EPS}{\%\Delta \, EBIT}$$

$$DFL = \frac{EBIT}{EBIT - Interest}$$

$$DFL = \frac{S - VC}{S - VC - FC - Interest}$$

As an example of calculating the degree of financial leverage, consider DirectJet Airlines generated an operating profit before interest and taxes of $500MM for the year. Based on its interest expense of $300MM annually, the degree of financial leverage is found to be 2.50. This means that for a 1% change in operating income, earnings per share increases 2.5%.

$$DFL = \frac{\$500}{\$500 - \$300} = \frac{\$500}{\$200} = 2.50$$

When operating profit exceeds interest, the airline is showing a net profit and DFL is positive. Conversely, once interest exceeds operating profit, the DFL becomes a negative number.

Table 9.11 opposite shows the estimated DOL and DFL for selected U.S. airlines for the years, 2007–2008. Several airlines have very high degree of operating leverages as measured by DOL.

## COST OF CAPITAL AND CAPITAL BUDGETING

The large amount of capital that is needed in the airline industry puts significant strains on the capital structure that an airline can operate under. With this capital situation, debt is often necessary for the airline to operate. Unless it can earn an internal rate of return

---

17   Technically, financial leverage is defined as the percentage change in EAT divided by the percentage change in EBIT.

**Table 9.11** **U.S airline leverages**

| Airline | Leverage | 2008 | 2007 |
|---------|----------|------|------|
| AA | DOL | 58.26 | 7.32 |
|    | DFL | 0.65 | 2.77 |
| AS | DOL | 69.20 | 1.25 |
|    | DFL | 0.63 | 1.30 |
| CO | DOL | 25.19 | -2.69 |
|    | DFL | 0.51 | -1.94 |
| UA | DOL | 505 | -419 |
|    | DFL | 0.90 | 1.92 |
| DL | DOL | 8.31 | 33.50 |
|    | DFL | 0.92 | 1.36 |
| U.S. | DOL | 39.46 | 3.92 |
|    | DFL | 0.89 | 1.63 |
| WN | DOL | -18.43 | 13.48 |
|    | DFL | 1.38 | 1.07 |
| B6 | DOL | -6.61 | 1.81 |
|    | DFL | -1.42 | 5.44 |
| FL | DOL | 17.84 | 3.29 |
|    | DFL | 0.75 | 1.76 |

Source: Compiled by the Authors from SEC 10K Filings.

(IRR) in excess of its cost of capital (WACC), the airline will not create economic value for its shareholders.

Therefore, as an operating rule of thumb, if the return from a project ($IRR_A$) exceeds the marginal cost of capital (MCC), then the project should be undertaken. The MCC is defined as the cost of the last dollar of new capital that the airline raises. Because of leverage and risk of debt financing MCC increases as more and more capital is raised by the airline (this concept was demonstrated in Figure 9.3). The concept behind the Investment Opportunity Schedule (IOS) is very similar to that of the MCC. The IOS represents the projects that are available for investment by an airline. It ranks them from the most attractive project to the least attractive project. In order to construct the IOS, the airline needs to first estimate the IRR of each of the project it is considering. Once they are identified, the financial manager can plot the IOS, and this is a chart of the IRRs of the airline's projects arranged from the highest IRR to the lowest IRR. Therefore, the IOS represents the projects that are available to the airline, ranking from the most profitable to the least. What is the optimal capital structure to operate at? MCC and IOS plotted together show which projects should be undertaken. Ideally, a firm should operate at the capital structure which causes their internal rate of return (IRR) and weighted average cost of capital to be equal to each other.

Airlines apply the marginal cost of capital in deciding whether or not to undertake a project or to expand.

For example, assume DirectJet is interested in four independent projects, the IRR and WACC for those projects is presented in the following investment opportunity schedule (IOS).

**Table 9.12    DirectJet investment opportunity schedule**

| Project | Internal rate of return | Capital investment | WACC |
|---------|-------------------------|--------------------|------|
| A | 20% | $500,000 | 9% |
| B | 17% | $700,000 | 12% |
| C | 15% | $1,000,000 | 15% |
| D | 10% | $1,500,000 | 18% |

The Marginal Cost of Capital (MCC) represents the cost of capital faced by the firm (ranking from the least to the most expensive). DirectJet will continue to accept projects as long as the marginal return generated by the project is higher than the marginal cost to DirectJet to pay to finance its needs. The airline will stop accepting projects once the marginal return generated by the project is exactly offset by the marginal cost faced by the airline. In Table 9.8 this point is reached at project C.

Aircraft manufacturers also examine the internal rate of return and marginal cost of capital. Frank Shrontz, the chief executive officer of Boeing in 1990, had to make the final decision on whether to launch the 777 project. Boeing had estimated the IRR of the 777 project to be 19% and had to determine the marginal cost of capital for the new commercial jet project (Bruner, 1992). One of the chief concerns for a company like Boeing is how to estimate the WACC. Boeing operates in two different sectors of the aviation industry, the defense industry and the commercial aircraft industry. Boeing had to decide whether to use the overall WACC for the company as a whole or whether to calculate a cost of capital specifically for its commercial aircraft division. Ultimately Boeing decided that the project would be profitable and the 777 turned into one of the most popular wide-bodied aircraft in the world.

When WACC equals IRR the company is not leaving behind any profitable projects and is also not engaging in any projects that are not profitable. Further discussion of the capital budgeting and long-term financing decisions is presented in the capital budgeting chapter. The internal rate of return of a company starts high since debt is low and then declines in a stepwise fashion as debt increases as a portion of the total value of the company. Therefore, IRR acts in an opposite fashion to WACC. Comparing the internal rate of return on projects to the weighted average cost of capital tells an airline if they should continue to add capital through debt. The optimal capital structure of a firm, based on IRR and WACC is shown in Figure 9.7.

## SUMMARY

Capital is extremely important in the airline industry. Airlines must have sufficient capital in order to maintain cash on hand and investment in infrastructure and equipment.

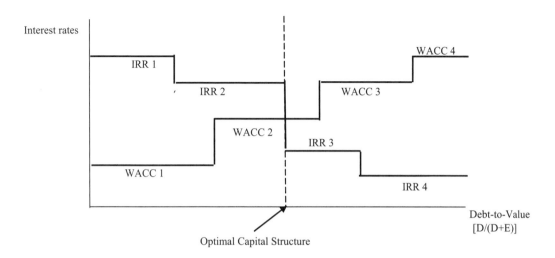

**Figure 9.7    Internal rate of return and weighted average cost of capital**

Capital can be raised either through debt or equity. Both debt and equity capital have costs associated with using investor's or creditor's money. While debt typically has lower initial costs than equity (due to tax benefits), as the proportion of debt financing increases, the average cost of capital (WACC) will also increase. However, the enormous cost of capital in the airline industry makes debt a necessary part of the financing of any airline.

## DISCUSSION QUESTIONS

1.  Could rumors of financial distress lead to a higher cost of capital? Do you think an airline must actually declare bankruptcy to have the higher costs associated with bankruptcy? DirectJet has recently issued $10 million zero coupon bonds. Knowing the fact that zero coupon bonds pay no interest, how does an investor expect to earn positive return on DirectJet's bonds?
2.  United Airlines, one of the oldest airlines in the world, was founded in 1926. United filed for Chapter 11 bankruptcy protection in December 2002, but managed to exit bankruptcy in February, 2006. UAL's financial performance was worse than expected, and losses widened in the fourth quarter of 2008 even though prices for jet fuel pulled back from record highs. Go to finance.yahoo.com. In the "Get Quotes" section, enter UAUA for United Airlines and record the following:
    a.  Recent price
    b.  52-week high
    c.  52-week low
    d.  52-week price change
    e.  What is the general direction of the United Airlines the stock price movement?
3.  What is the difference between common stock and preferred stock?
4.  What is the difference between par value and market value of a stock?
    a.  Using both recent SEC filings and online financial websites such as Google Finance, what is the par value and market value of JBLU's stock?
    b.  What is JBLU's market capitalization?

5.  Why could it be argued that market capitalization is the best measure of an airline's size instead of ASMs flown or aircraft operated?

6.  What generalizations can be made about the U.S. airline industry by analyzing the market capitalization of the major airlines in the industry?

7.  What is the cost of equity for an airline with a stock price of $16 per share and an annual dividend of $1.25 per share that is:
    a.  Not expected to grow?
    b.  Expected to grow at a constant rate based on its previous annual dividend which was $1.10 per share?
    c.  Expected to grow at the above rate for the first three years then 5% thereafter?

8.  What is the cost of retained earnings assuming the airline retains 95% of its earnings, its cost of equity is 14.25%, and it has a current stock price of $5.00 per share?

9.  Discuss the topic of debt securitization. Generally, why is secured debt cheaper than unsecured debt? Why is convertible debt generally cheaper the unsecured debt?

10. Discuss the rights of a bondholder in comparison to a stockholder.

11. What is the market value of a $1,000 face value bond which pays an annual interest rate of 6.5% with seven years to maturity assuming the current market rate is 2.75%? Is this bond trading at par, premium, or discount? What is its cost of debt to the company, assuming a 35% tax rate?

12. Calculate the weighted average cost of capital for EZjET assuming the following information:
    a.  The airline has debt outstanding at $1.1B, with an average cost of LIBOR + 2.75%
    b.  The airline has 20 million shares of preferred stock currently outstanding that is trading at $10 per share and pays an annual dividend of $0.80 per share.
    c.  The airline has 300 million shares of common stock outstanding that is currently trading at $2.00 per share paying an annual dividend of $0.10 per share, which is expected to grow at a rate of 12% for the foreseeable future.
    d.  The current LIBOR rate is 3%.
    e.  The airline does not expect to earn a profit for the year; therefore the airline will have no retained earnings. The airline's marginal tax rate, when profitable, is 40%.

13. Discuss the five areas that affect business risk and identify these factors for the airline industry.

14. What does it mean for a firm to be leveraged operationally or financially?

15. Obtain the latest SEC 10-K filing for Continental Airlines and using the two year income statement (exclude special items if necessary), calculate the:
    a.  Degree of operating leverage.
    b.  Degree of financial leverage.

## REFERENCES

Anuar, Z. (2007). Stock valuation model- 3 simple techniques to value stock. Retrieved August 27, 2008 from http://ezinearticles.com/?Stock-Valuation-Model---3-Simple-Techniques-to-Value-Stockandid=872014

Baker, K. and G. Powell (2005). *Understanding Financial Management: A Practical Guide*. Blackwell Publishing.

Bruner, R. (1992). *The Boeing 777-Teaching note*. (Report No. UVA-F-1017TN). Charlottesville, VA: University of Virginia Darden School Foundation.

Brealey, R., S. Myers, and A. Marcus (2007). *Fundamentals of Corporate Finance*, McGraw-Hill/Irwin.

Brigham, E. and C.Gapenski (1994). *Financial management: Theory and practice* (7). Fort Worth, Texas: The Dryden Press.

Clifford, S. and J. Warner. (1979). "On Financial Contracting: An Analysis of Bond Covenants." *Journal of Financial Economics*, 7, 3.

Dickinson, J. (2002, April 19). *JetBlue IPO aloft*. The Business Journal-Central New York. Retrieved September 4, 2008 from http://www.allbusiness.com/business-finance/equity-funding-sales-equity-to-public-ipo/1100458–1.html

Foerster, S. (2003). *Financial Management: A Primer*. W. W. Norton & Company.

Gitman, L. (2008). *Principles of Managerial Finance*. Pearson Publishing Company.

Kahn, C. (2008, March 3). Pilot seniority takes a long time to work out, says U.S. Air CEO.USA Today. Tempe, Arizona. Retrieved August 27, 2008 from http://www.usatoday.com/travel/flights/2008–03–03-usair-long-time_N.htm

Magcale, J. (2007, March 23). Miami's $1 billion construction increase request approved. Daily World EU News. Retrieved September 4, 2008 from http://www.turks.us/article.php?story=MIA

Mason, T. (2008, May 9). American Airlines in dilemma on when to replace aging fleet. The Dallas Morning News. Dallas, Texas. Retrieved August 21, 2008 from http://www.dallasnews.com/sharedcontent/dws/bus/stories/030908dnbusaaplanes.38acd8.html

Microsoft (2008). Southwest Airlines Co. (LUV). MSN Money. Retrieved August 27, 2008 from http://moneycentral.msn.com/detail/stock_quote?Symbol=LUV

Modigliani, F. and M. Miller (1958), "The Cost of Capital, Corporation Finance, and the Theory of Investment", *American Economic Review*, 48, 261–297.

Moyer, C., J. McGuigan, and W. Kretlow (2005). *Contemporary Financial Management*. West Publishing Company.

MSNBC (2005, September 22). Emergency landing televised on JetBlue flight: Passengers watched their terrifying drama live via satellite. MSNBC.com-Life Section. Retrieved August 27, 2008 from http://www.msnbc.msn.com/id/9430871/

Pinteris, G. (2003). Notes on Capital Structure, University of Illinois at Urbana-Champaign.

Potkewitz, H. (2008, May 22). Port Authority OKs study for JFK renovation. Crain's New York Business.com. Retrieved September 4, 2008 from http://www.crainsnewyork.com/apps/pbcs.dll/article?AID=/20080522/FREE/224234438/1066/keywords

Ross, S., R. Westerfield, and J. Jaffe (2009). *Corporate Finance*. McGraw Hill.

Shear, R. (2007, November). The airports: A rundown of the traffic in South Florida's friendly skies. South Florida CEO. Retrieved September 4, 2008 from http://findarticles.com/p/articles/mi_m0OQD/is_10_11/ai_n21168903

Smith, A. (2008, June 27). Fewer flights, higher fares. Cable News Network. Retrieved September 3, 2008 from http://money.cnn.com/2008/06/27/news/companies/airlines_capacity/index.htm?postversion=2008062714

Wallace, J. (2007, June 29). How the 'dream' was born. Seattle Post-Intelligencer. Seattle, Washington. Retrieved September 4, 2008 from http://seattlepi.nwsource.com/boeing/787/787primer.asp

# 10

# Working Capital and Current Asset Management

"The airline industry confronts some of the most challenging economic and operating conditions it has ever known. More than ever, airlines must reduce costs, maximize asset utilization, and enhance the customer experience so that they can retain and grow their customer base in an intensely competitive environment."

Oracle Corporation

In order to operate effectively, airlines must be aware of the short-term financial decision-making process. Concepts such as managing cash and working capital, short-term financing, current assets and liabilities management, and managing inventory are all important to the everyday operation of an airline. In order for an airline or any business to operate, the business must have sufficient current assets, such as cash, to be able to pay their liabilities as they come due; however, how much cash is enough? Can there be such a problem as having too much cash? We answer these questions and discuss other issues surrounding current assets and liabilities in this chapter. The following topics are covered in this chapter:

- Working Capital Policy
- Cash Management
  - Cash Shortages
  - Cash Surpluses
  - Liquidity (Cash) Management Models
- Baumol-Tobin Cash Inventory Model
- Miller-Orr Model : Fluctuations in Cash Flow
  - Fluctuations in Cash Flow
  - Foreign Exchange
  - Operating Cycle
- Accounts Receivable
- Current Liabilities Management
  - Terms of Credit
- Inventory Control Models
  - Inventory Carrying (Holding) Costs
  - Economic Ordering Quantity (EOQ)
  - Just-In-Time (JIT)
  - ABC Inventory Control
- Summary
- Discussion Questions.

# WORKING CAPITAL POLICY

"We believe that we currently have adequate cash on hand to meet our operating needs."

Chief Executive Sean Menke, Frontier Airlines, the day Frontier filed for bankruptcy

Before discussing the management of current assets, the concept of working capital must be explained. Working capital (WC) is defined as the difference between current assets and current liabilities. Therefore, working capital is the amount of current assets left over after subtracting current liabilities. It is also the amount of current assets that is being financed by long-term liabilities or equity. Without positive working capital an airline is likely to have problems paying its short-term liabilities which may include fuel bills, wages, or current rent for facilities. Additionally, a company that is unable to pay its bills in a timely manner is likely to not be able to receive credit from other companies. There have even been occasions in history where airlines have been refused refueling owing to issues with credit (Serling, 2008) or when pilots and/or passengers had to pay for the fuel with their own cash and credit cards as a result of airlines' working capital deficiency (*The Ottawa Citizen*, 1988, September 12). Maintaining working capital is so crucial for a company that many companies develop a working capital policy.

Developing a working capital policy is crucial to maintaining adequate reserves of current assets in order to pay current liabilities. Current Assets include:

- Cash
- Marketable Securities
- Accounts Receivable
- Inventory.

The airline industry provides a great example of an industry that experiences seasonal and fluctuating demand. By the nature of the travel industry, demand is strong during holiday periods with certain seasons, such as the summer, that have healthier traffic than the others. In Figures 10.1 and 10.2 we see the seasonality that occurs in the airline industry by examining the revenue passenger miles (RPM) data over a three-year period for two major U.S. carriers. Note that such seasonality exists for the U.S. airline industry and generally applies for northern hemisphere airlines. However, different airline industries may experience different patterns of seasonality trends that could potentially experience different peak periods.

From Figures 10.1 and 10.2, passenger demand typically falls off during the fall and winter months (Quarter 4 and Quarter 1) compared with the previous spring and summer (Quarter 2 and Quarter 3). While this trend holds true for these two carriers, other carriers may experience a different seasonality trend. Typically for U.S. carriers, those with a high exposure to the domestic market will see the second quarter being slightly greater than the third quarter, whereas for carriers with a greater proportion of international traffic, such as American and United, the third quarter will typically outperform.

The seasonality in passenger travel means that there will also be seasonality in the movement of cash. Since industry revenue is typically collected in advance, significant revenue is generated in the first two quarters of the year for travel during the second and third quarters. As a result, the first two quarters of the year typically generate positive working capital, while the latter two quarters experience increased costs and reduced revenue generation, resulting in cash burns during the last two quarters of the year. Such cyclicality makes it critical to effectively manage working capital.

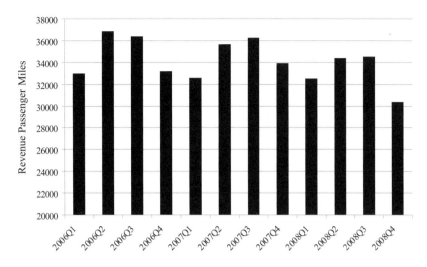

**Figure 10.1    American Airlines RPM (millions)**

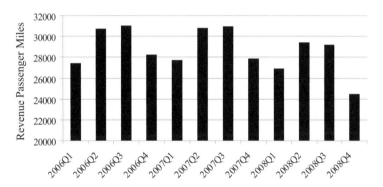

**Figure 10.2    United Airlines RPM (millions)**

Airlines must implement effective working capital policies to ensure solvency. The first of these is a working capital policy that is based on the current ratio of assets to liabilities. For example, a company may have a policy that the current ratio should be greater than or equal to 1.5. A working capital policy that states that the current ratio must be greater than or equal to 1.5 means that for every $1 in current liabilities there must be $1.50 in current assets.

Current Ratio ≥ 1.5
Current Liabilities = $1,000,000
Current Assets ≥ $1,500,000

The other method of developing a working capital policy is to develop a flat amount that must be maintained as a margin. For instance, a working capital policy may state that working capital must always be at least $1,000,000. Ultimately, some metric or goal must be stated to monitor working capital; however, such thresholds are ultimately at the discretion of management.

In the airline industry, a common judge of the amount of cash on hand is the ending cash balance to last twelve months of revenue metric (cash/LTM revenue). In essence, the metric standardizes the ending cash balance to revenue. Commonly, airlines' cash balance will exceed 10% of LTM revenue; however, if an airline's cash balance dips below this requirement, liquidity represents a major concern, as the airline has little flexibility in dealing with fluctuations in cash flow. In certain seasons, such as summer and winter holidays, demand for air travel is very high while in other seasons, such as after the winter's holidays and in the fall, demand is lower. Compounding the seasonal problem for airlines is the fact that the slow demand periods are also the times when airlines want to perform maintenance on aircraft so that they can keep the aircraft in service during the high demand periods. This means that maintenance costs rise when cash flow has decreased. The result is that the airline is left with higher costs and less cash coming in to pay for these costs.

## CASH MANAGEMENT

Cash is the most liquid of any current asset and must be available to pay liabilities as they come due. Since it is such an important asset, cash must be managed properly to ensure that there is neither too little, nor too much cash on hand at any given time. Airlines' treasurers face challenges in effectively managing their corporate cash flows. A strong cash position allows airlines such as Southwest Airlines and Singapore Airlines to internally finance purchases of new aircraft and reduce interest costs. Contrarily, cash shortage forced ATA Airlines into Chapter 11 bankruptcy protection. There are three reasons for holding cash: the *transaction motive*, the *speculative motive* and the *precautionary motive*. For airlines, the transaction motive concerns the use of cash to pay for everyday operating expenses such as payroll, aircraft fuel, and maintenance.

An airline also holds cash for precautionary reasons in order to weather seasonal trends, downturn economies, or emergencies. Referring back to the cash flow statement, an airlines' ending cash balance is the result of a combination of factors, such as net income, cash flow from operations, cash flow from investing, and cash flow from financing. While the latter two categories do not experience any significant seasonal patterns, both net income and cash flow of operations will. Depending on the carrier, usually either the second or third quarter will generate the greatest profit, a source of cash. Also, as previously mentioned, owing to the seasonality of demand, the first two quarters will typically generate positive cash flow from operations while the latter two quarters will experience cash burns from operations. As a result, assuming constant financing and investing constant, carriers must build up sufficient cash reserves in the first half of the year to weather the cash outflows in the latter half of the year. A slowing economy and high fuel prices have forced many airlines such as Aloha Airlines, ATA, and Champion Air out of business (International Herald Tribune, 2008, April 8). Therefore, airlines hold precautionary cash balances as a financial reserve in the event of unanticipated changes in cash outflows or cash inflows. A healthy precautionary cash balance may keep an airline from bankruptcy in more difficult financial times.

Finally, airlines hold cash to be in the right position to take advantage of attractive investment opportunities that may arise. For example, if some carriers go out of business, then the remaining airlines may be able to take advantage of market opportunities if they have cash available for expansion. After the failure of Aloha and ATA, Southwest Airlines took out additional cash reserves both as a precautionary measure and for the speculative motive that other carriers might fail. If this occurred then the strong cash reserves could leave Southwest with an opportunity to expand quickly (SmartBrief, 2008).

There are four basic problems that companies can experience with cash management:

- Shortage of cash
- Surplus of cash
- Fluctuations in cash flow
- Foreign exchange.

## Cash Shortages

Generally, cash deposits do not produce any great returns, but many airlines view the cash as a buffer against potential future insolvency. An airline with little cash may face potential insolvency if current liabilities outweigh the airline's ability to pay with an airline's cash shortage being a potential signal of bankruptcy. According to the WSJ several airlines including U.S. Airways and Air Tran most likely face some type of liquidity crisis before the end of 2009.[1] The aim of cash management is to allow airlines to have enough cash to pay the interest on their debt, as well as other current liabilities, and at the same time make investments in short term interest bearing assets (Besley and Brigham, 2009).

Treasurers have many different tools they can use so that a company does not become short on cash. In the short-term, managers can use tools such as:

- Cash forecasting
- Developing relationships with lenders
- Free financing
- Credit control.

Companies must forecast cash inflows and outflows each month based on historical projections of sales, collections of accounts receivable, payments made to suppliers/creditors, supplies needed, demand forecasts, and so on. Managing cash forecast, also called the cash budget, is one of a manager's most important tools in properly managing cash (Wensveen, 2007). Table 10.1 shows what sample cash forecast may look like for DirectJet Airlines in the first quarter of 2009.[2]

In Table 10.1, we see that DirectJet Airlines will run into a cash shortage at the end of February. Once managers identify, through forecasting, that cash problems may occur, they can first attempt to use one of the other three techniques to deal with projected shortages. If none of these techniques will alleviate the cash shortage, the company will have to raise additional capital through a variety of financing means, such as secured/unsecured debt offerings, equity offerings, or aircraft sale/leasebacks.

One technique that managers can use to deal with potential shortages of cash is to develop relationships with lenders. By developing relationships with lenders, a company can borrow money in the short-term during periods when additional cash is going to be necessary. A standing line of credit, for example, can be used to borrow cash in the short-term. Developing relationships with lenders also helps for longer-term cash needs, such as financing for capital projects.

---

1       Which Airlines Could Face a Cash Pinch in 2009? *The Wall Street Journal*, July 22, 2008.
2       The data in the table assumes:
         80% of Accounts Receivable (A/R) is retrieved in the month it is generated and 20% the next month.
         85% of Accounts Payable (A/P) is paid in the month it is incurred, 15% the following month.
         All sales are credit sales and all supply purchases are on credit.
         At the beginning of the quarter cash on hand is $1,000,000, A/R is $2,000,000 and A/P is $1,500,000.

**Table 10.1    Cash forecast 1st quarter 2009 DirectJet Airlines**

|                                  | Jan.         | Feb.         | Mar.         | Quarter      |
|----------------------------------|--------------|--------------|--------------|--------------|
| Beginning Cash on hand           | $1,000,000   | 2,000,000    | -3,375,000   | **$1,000,000** |
| Beginning Accounts Receivable    | 2,000,000    | 5,000,000    | 2,000,000    | **2,000,000** |
| Sales                            | 25,000,000   | 10,000,000   | 30,000,000   | **65,000,000** |
| Cash collections from receivables| 22,000,000   | 13,000,000   | 26,000,000   | **61,000,000** |
| Ending Accounts Receivable       | 5,000,000    | 2,000,000    | 6,000,000    | **6,000,000** |
|                                  |              |              |              |              |
| Beginning Accounts Payable       | 1,500,000    | 1,500,000    | 1,125,000    | **1,500,000** |
| Supplies/Inventory purchased     | 10,000,000   | 7,500,000    | 10,000,000   | **27,500,000** |
| Cash/Supplies Paid               | 10,000,000   | 7,875,000    | 9,625,000    | **9,625,000** |
| Ending Accounts Payable          | 1,500,000    | 1,125,000    | 1,500,000    | **1,500,000** |
| Wages paid                       | 5,000,000    | 4,500,000    | 5,000,000    | **14,500,000** |
| Rent/leases paid                 | 6,000,000    | 6,000,000    | 6,000,000    | **18,000,000** |
|                                  |              |              |              |              |
| Ending Cash on hand              | 2,000,000    | -3,375,000   | 2,000,000    | **$625,000** |

Airlines and other companies also take advantage of free financing from suppliers when available. Most suppliers offer financing terms that allow the net balance to be paid in 30 days. By taking advantage of these terms, a company can increase the amount of time from when the company pays its suppliers to the time that it receives cash from its customers. Additionally, the lines between lenders and suppliers have become blurred as airlines have successfully been able to raise capital from major suppliers. For instance, U.S. Airways has received financing from its primary aircraft supplier Airbus, its primary credit card supplier Barclays, and its regional carrier Republic Airways.

To reduce the time that it takes for a company to receive cash from customers, companies control the credit they extend to customers. Retail stores such as Best Buy, Old Navy and Sears practice credit control by looking at the credit ratings of customers who apply for a store credit card. Companies control credit for those who have lower credit ratings by charging a higher interest rate to compensate for the higher risk of extending credit to these customers (Best Buy, 2008). Airline ticket distribution is largely over the internet through an online travel agent (i.e. Orbitz) or on the airline's own website, so the one area that airlines have some control over is the speed at which they get paid by the credit companies. The speed at which airlines are paid is determined through contracts called covenants with banks and other financial institutions and typically, all of an airline's credit card transactions are processed by a limited number of banks or other financial institutions. The financial company may hold back a percentage of the revenue as collateral in case the individual credit companies do not pay the full amounts that their customers have charged. If airlines can demonstrate that a very high percentage of accounts receivable from their customers are collected, the company in charge of processing these transactions and collecting payment will generally hold back a lower percentage of the airline's revenue. For example, United Airlines announced that it was able to reach such an agreement with one of its credit card processors, Paymentech, and it is estimated that the agreement frees up $350 million in cash that was previously restricted (United Airlines, 2008, July 22). Therefore, airlines can potentially increase the amount of unrestricted cash on hand by negotiating with the credit card processing companies.

## Cash Surplus

While not having enough cash can be a major problem for businesses and airlines, having too much cash is also a problem. When a company has more cash than is needed, it means that cash is sitting idle when it could be invested, creating a profitable return for the company. If a company has more cash on hand than is necessary to pay current liabilities, that cash should be invested. While cash can be used to invest in longer term projects and activities, for short-term investing, marketable securities are frequently used. Marketable securities are short-term investments that can easily be sold and converted into cash and they are typically lower-yielding than bonds or stocks that are held for the long-term (Brigham and Gapenski, 1994). The idea behind investing in marketable securities is not to generate a huge rate of return, but rather to gain some return in lieu of cash sitting idle. The marketable security can then be sold in a period where the company needs cash to pay current liabilities, providing a high degree of liquidity. Some examples of marketable securities are U.S. Treasury Bills or CDs (Certificates of Deposit). Table 10.2 shows the daily yield of short-term Treasury Bills in March 2009.

## Table 10.2    Daily treasury bill yields—March 2009

| Date | 4 Weeks | | 13 Weeks | | 26 Weeks | | 52 Weeks | |
| | Bank Discount | Coupon Equivalent | Bank Discount | Coupon Equivalent | Bank Discount | Coupon Equivalent | Bank Discount | Coupon Equivalent |
| --- | --- | --- | --- | --- | --- | --- | --- | --- |
| 02/03/2009 | | 0.15 | 0.28 | 0.28 | 0.44 | 0.45 | 0.64 | 0.65 |
| 03/03/2009 | 0.14 | 0.14 | 0.27 | 0.27 | 0.43 | 0.44 | 0.65 | 0.66 |
| 04/03/2009 | 0.14 | 0.14 | 0.26 | 0.26 | 0.43 | 0.44 | 0.67 | 0.68 |
| 05/03/2009 | 0.1 | 0.1 | 0.2 | 0.2 | 0.39 | 0.4 | 0.63 | 0.64 |
| 06/03/2009 | 0.08 | 0.08 | 0.2 | 0.2 | 0.38 | 0.39 | 0.63 | 0.64 |
| 09/03/2009 | 0.11 | 0.11 | 0.23 | 0.23 | 0.46 | 0.47 | 0.66 | 0.67 |
| 10/03/2009 | 0.14 | 0.14 | 0.24 | 0.24 | 0.46 | 0.47 | 0.7 | 0.71 |
| 11/03/2009 | 0.14 | 0.14 | 0.23 | 0.23 | 0.45 | 0.46 | 0.7 | 0.71 |
| 12/03/2009 | 0.1 | 0.1 | 0.21 | 0.21 | 0.44 | 0.45 | 0.69 | 0.7 |
| 13/03/2009 | 0.08 | 0.08 | 0.19 | 0.19 | 0.41 | 0.42 | 0.66 | 0.67 |
| 16/03/2009 | 0.09 | 0.09 | 0.24 | 0.24 | 0.45 | 0.46 | 0.67 | 0.68 |
| 17/03/2009 | 0.14 | 0.14 | 0.24 | 0.24 | 0.44 | 0.45 | 0.67 | 0.68 |
| 18/03/2009 | 0.15 | 0.15 | 0.21 | 0.21 | 0.39 | 0.4 | 0.58 | 0.59 |
| 19/03/2009 | 0.09 | 0.09 | 0.2 | 0.2 | 0.39 | 0.4 | 0.58 | 0.59 |
| 20/03/2009 | 0.08 | 0.08 | 0.21 | 0.21 | 0.4 | 0.41 | 0.58 | 0.59 |
| 23/03/2009 | 0.08 | 0.08 | 0.22 | 0.22 | 0.4 | 0.41 | 0.58 | 0.59 |
| 24/03/2009 | 0.05 | 0.05 | 0.21 | 0.21 | 0.41 | 0.42 | 0.6 | 0.61 |
| 25/03/2009 | 0.02 | 0.02 | 0.19 | 0.19 | 0.4 | 0.41 | 0.58 | 0.59 |
| 26/03/2009 | 0.01 | 0.01 | 0.15 | 0.15 | 0.38 | 0.39 | 0.55 | 0.56 |

*Source*: U.S. Department of Treasury.

[1] Bank Discount refers to the quoted price on the secondary market based on a 360-day year; Coupon Equivalent refers to the purchase price and is based on a 365-day year.

Typically, investments in marketable securities are considered short-term investments (i.e. maturity under one year). As a comparison, Table 10.3 provides the average rate for certificates of deposit (CDs) with maturities of 3 months or longer. While the longer term maturities provide higher interest rates, they also provide less flexibility. Additionally, note that rates on CDs are market driven, and as such there is not necessarily a linear relationship between term and rate.

**Table 10.3     U.S. certificate of deposit (CD) averages as of 27 March, 2009**

| Term | Rate |
| --- | --- |
| 3 months | 3.15% |
| 5 months | 3.12% |
| 6 months | 3.23% |
| 9 months | 3.05% |
| 12 months | 2.94% |
| 18 months | 3.02% |
| 24 months | 3.02% |
| 30 months | 3.13% |
| 36 months | 3.08% |
| 48 months | 3.42% |
| 60 months | 3.33% |

*Source*: http://www.best-certificate-rates.com/site/national_averages

## Liquidity (Cash) Management Models

Since a company should not have too little cash or too much cash, what is the right amount of cash to have on hand? In practice, a wide variety of cash management models are used by firms in different industries to determine the appropriate level of cash to have on hand. In this section two different cash management methodologies are presented. The first of these models is called the Economic Order Quantity (EOQ).

*Baumol-Tobin cash inventory model*    We apply the Baumol-Tobin cash inventory model to the airline industry and allow for the possibility of investing cash for short term to earn interest. The EOQ model is a generalized version of the Baumol model and is also appropriate for different types of inventory as well as cash.[3] The model assumes that the company uses cash at a constant rate and the demand for cash is distributed evenly throughout the year. The Baumol model determines a quantity of cash that should be "ordered" or converted from marketable securities as the cash balance approaches zero. This quantity of cash is called the Economic Order Quantity (EOQ). In his paper Baumol derived the square root formula:

$$EOQ = \sqrt{\frac{2 \times C_o \times A}{C_h}}$$

---

3    William Baumol, "The Transactions Demand for Cash," *QJE*, Nov. 52, 545–556.

where:
$C_o$ = cost of converting marketable securities to cash
$C_h$ = opportunity cost of holding cash
$A$ = annual demand for cash

To understand the Baumol/EOQ model, consider that DirectJet has annual cash demand of $100,000,000 and assume that it can receive a return of 5% on marketable securities (opportunity cost of lost interest on marketable securities as a result of holding cash). Each transaction of converting marketable securities into cash costs DirectJet $200. We assume cash has an ordering cost (transaction) of shifting in and out of marketable securities.

$$EOQ = \sqrt{\frac{2 \times 200 \times (100,000,000)}{0.05}}$$

$$EOQ = 894,427$$

The EOQ model says that DirectJet should start the year with $894,427 and convert this amount from marketable securities to cash every time the cash balance reaches the conversion point. We can express the total costs, denoted TC, associated with cash balances for DirectJet as the sum of the carrying costs and the holding:

$$TC = \left(\frac{A}{Q}\right)C_O + \left(\frac{Q}{2}\right)C_h$$

Using the DirectJet data the total cost is:

$$TC = \left(\frac{100,000,000}{894,427}\right) \times 200 + \left(\frac{894,427}{2}\right) \times 0.05$$

$$TC = \$22,361 + \$22,361 = \$44,722$$

The amount of cash on hand for DirectJet will look like the diagram in Figure 10.3 throughout the year:

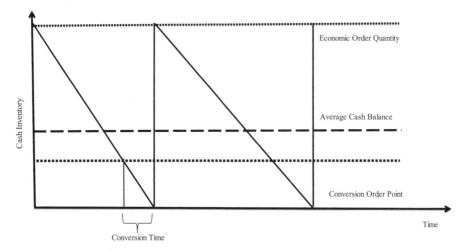

**Figure 10.3    EOQ order cycles over time**

The length of time that it takes to convert marketable securities to cash is called the conversion time. The conversion time determines the point at which an order is placed to convert marketable securities to cash. The *conversion order point* is the demand for cash during the conversion time. When the conversion order point is reached, a transaction to convert marketable securities to cash must be placed to avoid running out of cash. In Figure 10.3, the company begins the time period with a cash balance of (EOQ = Q). Naturally, the firm spends this money in equal amounts each period until the balance reaches zero. Then, the firm cannot operate unless it obtains additional liquidity. To acquire cash, the airline sells marketable securities and the receipts of the transaction are used to reach the optimal cash balances. Using the EOQ model, we can determine how many times throughout the year DirectJet would need to convert marketable securities into cash:

$$\text{No. of Cash Conversions} = \frac{\text{Annual Cash Demand}}{EOQ}$$

$$\text{No. of Cash Conversions} = \frac{\$100,000,000}{\$894,427}$$

$$\text{No. of Cash Conversions} = 111 \text{ times per year}$$

With 111 cash conversions from marketable securities throughout the year this equates to cash replenishment approximately every 3.2 days (360/111). Note that the frequency of cash conversions is a result of the relatively low transaction costs of converting marketable securities into cash. If the transaction cost were much higher, the economic order quantity would be significantly higher, resulting in fewer cash conversions throughout the year.

*Miller-Orr model*    The Baumol model is a simplistic method. Most importantly, it assumes predictable cash inflows and outflows, and it does not take into account variation in demand for cash. Many businesses experience fluctuations in cash flow since the demand and supply of cash is not always constant. There may be periods where more cash is needed or received than in other periods. Owing to seasonality and cyclicality, certain months are either cash generating or cash burning. This is a critical flaw of the EOQ model described above since it assumes a uniform burn of cash throughout the year. To account for fluctuations in cash flow and change in the demand environment, airlines will always want to maintain a minimum level of cash on hand. This can be incorporated into the EOQ model by simply adding the economic order quantity to a minimum threshold.

Businesses have various ways of trying to reduce the fluctuations in cash flow that they experience. Demand smoothing is one way to lower the fluctuation in cash flow. To reduce the fluctuation in demand airlines can set their fare structures so that lower fares are less available during peak demand seasons and more available during seasons that typically experience lower demand. In addition, airlines can structure maintenance contracts so that maintenance expenses for a year are divided into twelve equal payments per month, rather than having the cost for each month. While demand smoothing and other techniques to reduce fluctuations in cash flow may have some effect, the reality is that cash flows are not constant. To determine the amount of cash to keep on hand when cash flows are not constant we can use the Miller-Orr model.[4] Instead of prescribing a set amount of cash to convert from marketable securities each time like the Baumol model,

---

4      Merton Miller and Daniel Orr, "A Model of the Demand for Money by Firms," *Quarterly Journal of Economics*, Aug 1966, 413–435.

the Miller-Orr model sets upper and lower limits for the amount of cash a company should carry. Figure 10.4 gives a representation of the Miller-Orr model.

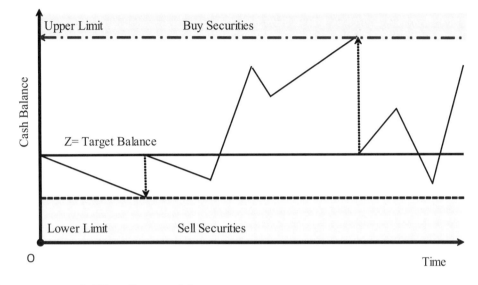

**Figure 10.4    Miller-Orr model**

*Fluctuations in Cash Flow*

In the Miller-Orr model a target balance for cash on hand is set for the month, year, and so on, and upper and lower limits are also set. As you can see from Figure 10.6, when the cash balance reaches the lower limit, marketable securities are sold to return cash on hand to the target balance. Conversely, when the cash balance reaches the upper limit, marketable securities are bought and the cash balance is returned to its target.

The target balance of a firm using the Miller-Orr model is established by comparing conversion cost and opportunity cost using an equation similar to the EOQ equation in the Baumol model.[5] In addition to conversion cost and opportunity cost, the variance of cash flows must also be known in order to calculate the target balance. Also, a lower limit (L) for the cash balance must be set; however, the lower limit may already be set for the company through a minimum cash covenant. As long as cash is between lower limit and the upper limit, no transaction is made. The equation for the target cash balance (Z) of a firm is shown in the equation below:

$$Z = \sqrt[3]{\frac{3 \times \text{conversion cost} \times \sigma}{4 \times \text{daily opportunity cost}}} + L$$

After a target balance and lower limit of cash have been determined, the firm can use the following equation to establish the upper limit (H) of their cash balance:

$$H = 3Z - 2L$$

---

5      For a review of test of the Miller-Orr model, see D. Mullins and R. Homonoff, "Applications of Inventory Cash Management Models," in S.C. Myers, ed., *Modern Developments in Financial Management*, New York: Frederick A. Praeger, Inc., 1976.

To demonstrate calculating the target balance and upper limit using the Miller-Orr model, consider a different example for DirectJet Airlines.[6] While the marketable securities conversion cost of $200 and an annual return of 5% are similar, DirectJet's bank requires a minimum balance of $1,000. The variance of daily cash flows has been calculated to be $50,000 based on historical data.

$$Z = \sqrt[3]{\frac{3 \times \text{conversion cost} \times \sigma}{4 \times \text{daily opportunity cost}}} + L$$

$$Z = \sqrt[3]{\frac{3 \times 200 \times 50000}{4 \times \dfrac{0.05}{360}}} + 1000$$

$$Z = 3780 + 1000 = 4780$$

$$H = 3Z - 2L$$

$$H = 3 \times 4780 - (2 \times 1000)$$

$$H = 12,340$$

Therefore, according to the Miller-Orr model with a lower limit of $1,000, DirectJet Airlines should have a target cash balance of $4,780 and an upper limit of $12,340.

## Foreign Exchange

In Chapter 5 we explained that airlines experience foreign currency risk. Since most currencies are freely traded, the exchange rate between currencies may not be the same at the time that airlines actually exchange currency as it was when the airline sold the ticket. If the exchange rate goes down, airlines receive less cash than they would have if the exchange rate had stayed the same or gone up. For example, suppose that Delta Air Lines sold a ticket from Paris-Atlanta to a person in France. If Delta Air Lines converted their fare of $750 from U.S. dollars to euros at an exchange rate of $1.50/euro, the ticket would cost 500 euros at the time of purchase. If the value of the euro declines as compared with the dollar between the time of purchase and the time Delta receives cash, then Delta will have lost money on the foreign currency exchange. For example, if a euro is now only worth $1.30 instead of $1.50 then Delta only receives $650 (500*1.50) for the ticket compared with the $750 they would have received from a passenger in the United States.

To combat fluctuations in exchange rates, airlines and other global companies can hedge exchange rates; that is, in much the same way as airlines hedge fuel, airlines may also hedge exchange rates.[7] When exchange rates are hedged, the airline could potentially receive a fixed dollar amount for every unit of foreign currency (FX Trademaker, 2008). An example comparing foreign exchange rates with or without a hedging strategy is shown in Figure 10.5.

As with other financial derivatives, exchange rate hedges have a premium; this is the amount that must be paid in exchange for the reduction in foreign exchange risk. Financial derivatives are explained further in Chapter 11.

---

6    D. Mullins and R. Homonoff, "Applications of Inventory Cash Management Models," in S.C. Myers, ed., *Modern Developments in Financial Management*, New York: Frederick A. Praeger, Inc., 1976.
7    Fuel and currency hedging are explained further in Chapter 11.

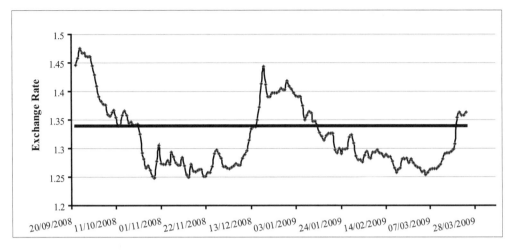

**Figure 10.5    Exchange rate \$/euro**

## *Operating Cycle*

A company's operating cycle is the time between ordering materials/inventory and collecting cash from customers after that inventory is sold. The operating cycle consists of purchasing inventory, producing the product, and selling the finished products (Moyer, McGuigan, and Kretlow, 2008). The time from when a company pays its suppliers to when the company receives payment from customers is called the *cash conversion cycle*. The cash conversion cycle is merely one part of the operating cycle of a business. Figure 10.6 shows both the operating cycle and the cash conversion cycle:

As we can see in the diagram, there are four parts to the operating cycle: the inventory period, the accounts receivable period, the accounts payable period and the cash conversion cycle (Ross, Westerfield and Jordan, 2008). The cash conversion cycle (CCC) can be expressed in terms of the other three parts of the operating cycle.

**CCC** = Inventory Period + Accounts Receivable Period – Accounts Payable Period

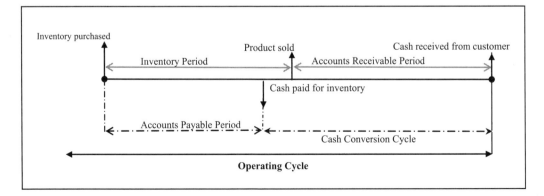

**Figure 10.6    Operating cycle**

Reducing the length of the cash conversion cycle is crucial to any business. Inventory must be sold and cash collected quickly from customers so that a business can buy additional inventory to sell to customers. From the equation for the cash conversion cycle shown above, we see that there are three methods that managers can use to reduce the cash conversion cycle:

1. Reduce inventory period
2. Reduce accounts receivable period
3. Increase accounts payable period.

In the next three sections we discuss the management of these three areas: accounts receivable, accounts payable and inventory.

The question arises as to whether airlines even have an operating cycle problem since the inventories that they sell (airline seats) are predominantly fixed. For all businesses effective accounts receivable and payable management are required, and while airlines' predominant inventory good is fixed, airlines still have other inventory such as food and beverages that are sold. And, it is especially important that food and beverages are turned into revenue quickly as spoilage is also a factor with food products. In addition, airlines carry inventory in their maintenance departments. Maintenance must have spare parts on hand to replace airplane parts that become inoperable. Without the necessary replacement parts, maintenance problems will not get fixed and airplanes will be stuck on the ground and airplanes on the ground result in tremendous amounts of lost revenue.

## ACCOUNTS RECEIVABLE

Accounts receivable are an important part of current assets; that is, managers must monitor the company's accounts receivable balance to determine if the company is efficiently converting sales into cash. One way of measuring the efficiency of accounts receivable is to determine the average amount of time it takes to convert sales into cash; this time is called the receivables collection (accounts receivable) period. Therefore, the formal definition of the receivables collection period (or days of sales outstanding) is the length of time required to convert a company's accounts receivable into cash.

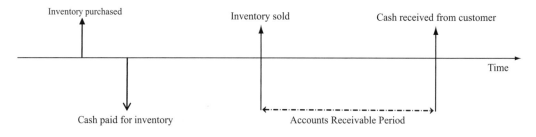

**Figure 10.7    Receivables collections period**

To determine the length of the receivables collection period, managers must know the percentage of sales that are made on credit. For retail and department stores the percentage of sales on credit may vary since some customers will pay cash while others will pay with a personal or store credit card. For the airline industry, nearly all sales are on credit. Passengers pay over the phone or on the internet with a credit card and very rarely does a passenger walk up to the ticket counter and pay cash for a ticket. Once managers know the percentage of sales made on credit, they can determine the annual credit sales by multiplying the percentage by total annual sales. Annual credit sales are then used to calculate the average receivables collection period using the following equation:

$$\text{Receivables Collection Period} = \frac{\text{Accounts Receivable}}{\left(\frac{\text{Annual Credit Sales}}{360}\right)} = \frac{\text{Accounts Receivable}}{\text{Average Daily Credit Sales}}$$

Assuming that an airline's sales are all on credit, we can determine the receivables collection period for different airlines by examining their income statements and balance sheets. The accounts receivable, annual sales and receivables collection period for six U.S. airlines and two Brazilian airlines (GOL and TAM) are shown in Table 10.4:

**Table 10.4     Airline accounts receivable, sales and receivables collection period**

| Airline | Accounts receivable ($ millions) | Annual sales ($ millions) | Receivables collection period (days) |
|---|---|---|---|
| American | 811 | 23,766 | 12.28 |
| Continental | 453 | 15,241 | 10.70 |
| Delta | 1,443 | 22,697 | 22.89 |
| GOL Lineas Aereas | 568 | 2,788 | 73.34 |
| Southwest | 209 | 11,023 | 6.83 |
| TAM S.A. | 1,086 | 4,597 | 85.05 |
| United | 1,086 | 20,194 | 19.36 |
| U.S. Airways | 291 | 12,244 | 8.56 |

*Source*: 2008 10-K SEC Filings except GOL and TAM, GOL and TAM data is for 2007.

By comparing the receivables collection period of the carriers above we see that Southwest Airlines does the best job of converting accounts receivable to cash. On average, Southwest Airlines is able to convert sales into cash in just under seven days. A possible explanation for this is Southwest's lack of reliance on a global distribution system, such as Sabre, and its degree of bookings made through its website. Delta on the other hand takes nearly 23 days to convert sales to cash, which could possibly be explained by its large international presence and the smaller proportion of bookings that are made on the Internet from international destinations. Receivables collection periods for the two Brazilian airlines were much higher than their American counterparts, 73 and 85 days. Companies like Southwest, which are able to convert their accounts receivable into cash quickly will have a higher degree of liquidity and a greater working capital margin than companies that have a longer receivables collection period.

The receivables collection period tells us how long, on average, it takes to receive payment from customers. An *aging schedule* breaks down the accounts receivable balance further and is necessary to develop an accurate cash forecast. The accounts receivable aging schedule tells a company, based on historical data, what percentage of accounts receivable is collected in the same month as sales, what percentage is collected in the following months, in two months, and so on.

Table 10.5 is an example of an aging schedule for DirectJet Airlines, assuming all sales are credit sales. Sales last January were $10,000,000 and the cash collected in each month for January's accounts receivable are shown in the table:

**Table 10.5    Accounts receive collections—DirectJet Airlines**

|                                   | January       | February    | March       | April     |
|-----------------------------------|---------------|-------------|-------------|-----------|
| Sales                             | $ 10,000,000  |             |             |           |
| Cash collections (January's sales)| $1,500,000    | $5,000,000  | $3,000,000  | $500,000  |

Table 10.5 shows that DirectJet collected 15% (1,500,000/10,000,000) of January sales in January, 50% in February, 30% in March and 5% in April. If this collection pattern holds true for other months, then DirectJet's aging schedule would be:

- 15% of accounts receivable is received in the month of sales
- 50% of accounts receivable is collected in the month following sales
- 30% is collected two months after sales
- 5% is collected three months after sales.

The above aging schedule shows that all credit sales were collected; however, it is not uncommon for a percentage of accounts receivables to not be collected. Frequently an accounting adjustment will be made (allowance for doubtful accounts) to account for accounts receivables that are not collected. Commonly, an aging schedule will also reflect a proportion of sales that are never collected.

Managing accounts receivable is important for any business because there is an opportunity cost associated with carrying accounts receivable. In order to extend credit to customers, businesses may need to borrow cash from financial institutions to maintain enough cash on hand to pay its own creditors. The cost of carrying accounts receivable (A/R) is shown in the following equation:

$$\text{Cost of carrying receivables} = \text{Cost of debt} \times (\% \text{ of A/R financed} \times \text{A/R})$$

If we look at the balances for accounts receivable in Table 10.6, we can compare each airline's cost of carrying receivables (if we assume they have the same cost of debt[8]). Continental and Delta Air Lines have similar annual sales figures; however, Delta has a much higher cost of carrying receivables because it has a much higher accounts receivable balance. If we assume that both airlines have a 5% cost of debt and that 75% of accounts

---

8    This is not necessarily an accurate assumption since different carriers have varying cost of debt; however, the range is rather close.

receivable are financed, then the cost of carrying receivables for Continental and Delta are:

$$\text{Cost of carrying receivables}_{CO} = 0.05 \times (0.75 \times \$453,000,000)$$
$$\text{Cost of carrying receivables}_{CO} = \$16,987,500$$
$$\text{Cost of carrying receivables}_{DL} = 0.05 \times (0.75 \times \$1,443,000,000)$$
$$\text{Cost of carrying receivables}_{DL} = \$54,112,500$$

Delta's higher accounts receivable gives Delta a higher cost of carrying receivables. This is because Delta must pay interest on the additional financing necessary to have the cash on hand to pay its current liabilities. This is a cost they would not incur if some or all of the accounts receivable were cash. This demonstrates the importance of collecting accounts receivable quickly, since a lengthy receivables collection period not only lengthens the cash conversion cycle, it also adds additional costs to doing business.

## CURRENT LIABILITIES MANAGEMENT

Just as important as managing current assets is the management of current liabilities since another way to increase working capital is to reduce the amount of current liabilities. In Table 10.6 we show the working capital for eight airlines:

**Table 10.6    Working capital and total liabilities (U.S. $ millions)**

| Airline | Current assets | Current liabilities | Total liabilities | Working capital |
|---|---|---|---|---|
| American | 5935 | 9374 | 28110 | -3439 |
| Continental | 4347 | 4474 | 12581 | -127 |
| Delta | 8904 | 11022 | 44140 | -2118 |
| GOL Lineas Aereas | 1767 | 1291 | 2612 | 476 |
| Southwest | 2893 | 2806 | 9355 | 87 |
| TAM S.A | 2840 | 1730 | 4528 | 1110 |
| United | 4861 | 7281 | 14727 | -2420 |
| U.S. Airways | 2359 | 3966 | 7175 | -1607 |

*Source*: 2008 10-k SEC Filings, except GOL and TAM are 2007 data.

From Table 10.6 we see that only Southwest, GOL and TAM have positive working capital, indicating that, of the airlines shown, only these three have sufficient current assets to cover current liabilities. The negative working capital margins of American, Continental, Delta, United and U.S. Airways show the financial trouble that U.S. legacy carriers are facing in the current industry and economic climate.

Because working capital is the amount of current assets financed by long-term liabilities or equity, using long-term debt or raising equity to purchase current assets reduces the need to use short-term debt to purchase supplies on credit. While it is true that long-term debt and equity also have costs associated them, it still may be less costly to manage current liabilities through understanding and taking advantage of longer term debt or equity. Working capital can also be better managed through taking advantage of the terms of credit associated with current liabilities.

## Terms of Credit

The competitive nature of business and the global economy means that businesses that do not offer terms of credit to their customers will probably lose out on business. Airlines and other businesses allow customers to purchase goods and services on credit. In business to business transactions, suppliers will not always require payment immediately upon delivery of inventory. Suppliers give an invoice and then the terms and time period under which the inventory must be paid. Common examples of credit terms provided include:

- Net 10: Entire balance must be paid within 10 days
- Net 30: Entire balance must be paid within 30 days
- 2/10, Net 30: Customer receives a 2% discount if invoice is paid within 10 days, otherwise the balance is due in 30 days.

There are two ways in which businesses can use terms of credit from suppliers to help manage current liabilities. The first method is to use the full term to pay the liability. If the terms of the invoice are Net 30, there is no reason to pay the supplier in 5 days. The reason that a business would want to use the full term to pay the invoice is to reduce the cash conversion cycle (CCC). By waiting to pay the supplier, the business increases the accounts payable period of the operating cycle thereby reducing the cash conversion cycle (CCC = Inventory period + Accounts Receivable period – Accounts Payable period). The other reason that businesses might not pay invoices before they are due is that they are foregoing the opportunity cost of using the cash that was used to pay the inventory. The cash could be earning a return as a marketable security until the time that the invoice is due.

Suppose DirectJet Airlines has an invoice for $10,000 from one of its parts suppliers that is due in 20 days. What would be the opportunity cost if the airline's investments in marketable securities have an annual return of 5%?

$$\text{Opportunity Cost} = (\text{Amount of invoice} \times \frac{\text{annual yield}}{360} \times \text{days paid early})$$

$$\text{Opportunity Cost} = (\$10,000 \times \frac{0.05}{360} \times 20)$$

$$\text{Opportunity Cost} = \$27.78$$

While losing $27.78 of investment return does not seem like a lot of money for a business, these amounts add up over time as businesses may receive hundreds or thousands of invoices a year. Taking advantage of credit terms is an easy way for a business to increase returns on investments and thereby create a better financial position for the company.

The second method by which airlines and other companies can take advantage of terms of credit is by utilizing cash or early payment discounts offered by suppliers. Assume that the terms of credit were modified for DirectJet Airlines' parts invoice, so that DirectJet received a 2% cash discount for paying twenty days early. The question becomes would the cash discount provide enough savings to compensate for the opportunity cost of investing the cash.

$$Savings = \text{Cash discount} - \text{Opportunity cost}$$
$$= (0.02 \times \$10,000) - \$27.78$$
$$= \$200 - \$27.78$$
$$= \$172.22$$

DirectJet should take advantage of the cash discount for early payment since it will net DirectJet $172.22 in savings. Taking advantage of the cash discount not only eliminates current liabilities from the balance sheet, it also increases net working capital by the amount of the savings (cash discount – opportunity cost).

In this section we have discussed two seemingly opposite strategies; one in which companies should take the full payment period to pay off invoices, and the other which states that companies should pay early when a cash discount is involved. How does a company know which strategy to use? If a cash discount is not offered for early payment, do not pay early. Paying early adds the opportunity cost of cash not being able to be invested over that time period. If a cash discount for early payment is offered, calculate the net savings of the cash discount (discount – opportunity cost). If net savings is positive, take advantage of the cash discount and pay early.

## INVENTORY CONTROL MODELS

To many businesses, inventory represents a necessary evil. Businesses do not want to have a considerable amount of inventory piled up in stores, warehouses or factories; however, businesses also know that if they do not have inventory available when customers want to purchase they will lose the sale. Inventory has costs associated with it and they are: the cost of purchasing the products from suppliers; the costs to place an order for inventory; the costs of holding the inventory and the costs of having a stock out (not having inventory available when a customer wants it). Therefore, inventory management is the practice of controlling inventory costs. Businesses want to be able to have enough inventories on hand to satisfy customer demand, but at the same time keep inventory levels down to reduce costs.

### Inventory Carrying (Holding) Costs

Sometimes it is assumed that once the inventory has been purchased that the cost of the purchase is the only cost associated with inventory. However, in reality there are many other costs associated with holding inventory. Some of these include:

- **Cost of capital**—The cash used to pay for inventory that could be invested in other projects or marketable securities.
- **Taxes and insurance**—Inventory is an asset, therefore any inventory that is on the balance sheet could represent a taxable asset. Insurance may be taken out on inventory to protect against damage or theft.

- **Spoilage, theft, obsolescence**—While waiting to be sold, inventory may spoil (become unusable) or fall victim to theft or obsolescence. Obsolescence occurs when new and better versions of the product or similar products become available to customers. For example, when Boeing introduced the 737NG, the 737 Classic became somewhat obsolete since the 737NGs had better fuel efficiency.
- **Cost of storage**—Inventory must be stored somewhere and a company may need to pay rent for a storage facility. In addition, there must be employees to man the storage facility and move inventory. Also, security guards may have to be hired to protect the company from theft of inventory. Increased wages for the manpower associated with holding inventory can be a major cost for a company.

In addition to holding costs, businesses also incur ordering costs each time they order inventory. The cost of ordering inventory arises from the fact that it takes the time of management, the purchasing department, or some other employee of the company to fill out the order forms, inspect the inventory for damage when it arrives, and to pay the bill for the inventory when it comes due. In addition, suppliers may charge an order processing fee with each order.

While airlines do not have a physical product to sell, since air travel is a service, an airline seat is still inventoried – just a very perishable product. However, in a sense airline seats are inventory, but a very perishable inventory. Once a flight leaves with empty seats, those seats can no longer be filled. While the number of seats on an airplane is relatively fixed, airlines can carry too many seats in their inventory, and this is called overcapacity. That is, there may be too many planes with unfilled seats, representing greater costs than necessary. In addition, many of the support activities of an airline must carry inventory. The maintenance department must carry spare parts to have them available if an aircraft needs a new part. Therefore, the maintenance department of an airline must make critical decisions about inventory levels of spare parts. Also, airlines must make inventory decisions on how much food and beverage to carry for in-flight service. In Table 10.7 and Figure 10.10 we show the percentage of current assets that inventory consists of for the eight airlines examined in the previous tables. As the tables depict, inventory represents a rather small portion of current assets for airlines.

## Table 10.7    Airline inventory as a percentage of current assets and sales

| Airline | Inventory ($ millions) | Current assets ($ millions) | Inventory/CA | Inv./sales |
|---------|------------------------|------------------------------|--------------|------------|
| American | 525 | 5935 | 8.85% | 2.21% |
| Southwest | 203 | 2893 | 7.02% | 1.84% |
| U.S. Airways | 163 | 2359 | 6.91% | 1.33% |
| GOL Lineas Aereas | 119 | 1767 | 6.73% | 4.27% |
| Continental | 235 | 4347 | 5.41% | 1.54% |
| United | 237 | 4861 | 4.88% | 1.17% |
| Delta | 388 | 8904 | 4.36% | 1.71% |
| TAM S.A. | 92 | 2840 | 3.24% | 2.00% |
| **Average:** | **245** | **4238** | **5.92%** | **2.01%** |

*Source*: 2008 10-K SEC Filings.

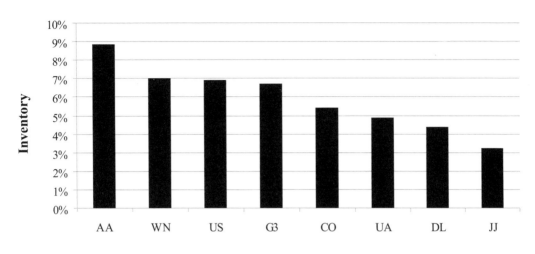

**Figure 10.8     Inventory as a percentage of current assets**

In the remainder of the chapter we present three inventory control models:

1.   Economic Order Quantity (EOQ)
2.   Just-In-Time (JIT)
3.   ABC Inventory Control.

## Economic Order Quantity (EOQ)

Several inventory methodologies determine when to reorder, and most of them rely on mathematical models to handle the optimal inventory level. Businesses must make a tradeoff between the costs of ordering inventory and the costs of holding inventory. This tradeoff process is captured in the economic order quantity model. The economic order quantity (EOQ) model uses the same formula as the Baumol cash management model that was discussed earlier in the chapter:

$$EOQ = \sqrt{\frac{2(\text{Annual Demand})(\text{Order or Setup Cost})}{\text{Annual Holding Cost}}}$$

EOQ Model

$$EOQ = \sqrt{\frac{2 \times C_o \times A}{C_h}}$$

where:
$C_o$ = cost of converting marketable securities to cash
$C_h$ = opportunity cost of holding cash
$A$ = annual demand for cash

There are several assumptions that must be fulfilled to use of the EOQ model with the graphical representation of the EOQ inventory model contained in Figure 10.9.

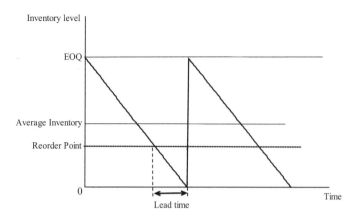

**Figure 10.9    Economic order quantity (EOQ) inventory model**

Assumptions of the EOQ model:

- All values are known with certainty and are constant over time.
- Inventory usage is uniform over time.
- Carrying costs change proportionally with changes in inventory levels.
- All ordering costs are fixed on a per order basis.

In order to demonstrate the economic order quantity model we again look at DirectJet Airlines. Assume that airline seats have movable parts (recline mechanisms) and are often in need of replacement owing to malfunction or wear and tear. DirectJet anticipates that 2000 seats will need to be replaced during a typical year. The cost of an airline seat is $1000 and the holding cost is 20% of the cost per seat. Each order for seats from the manufacturer costs DirectJet $500. Using the EOQ equation, the optimal size of every order placed with the manufacturer is 100 seats as follows:

$$EOQ = \sqrt{\frac{2 \times C_o \times A}{C_h}}$$

$$EOQ = \sqrt{\frac{2 \times 500 \times 2000}{0.2 \times 1000}} = 100 \text{ seats}$$

If the economic order quantity is known, other important information regarding a company's inventory position and ordering pattern can be determined. The average inventory, number of orders the company places for the product per year, and the total inventory cost of the product are:

$$\text{Average Inventory} = \frac{Q}{2}$$

$$\text{Number of orders per year} = \frac{A}{Q}$$

$$\text{Total Holding Cost (THC)} = C_h \times \frac{Q}{2}$$

$$\text{Total Ordering Cost (TOC)} = C_o \times \frac{A}{Q}$$

$$\text{Total Inventory Cost (TIC)} = THC + TOC$$

$$TIC = C_h \times \frac{Q}{2} + C_o \times \frac{A}{Q}$$

When the economic order quantity is used as the quantity ordered (Q), total holding cost (THC) and total ordering cost (TOC) are equal to each other (Ross, Westerfield and Jordan, 2008).

$$THC = TOC$$

$$When\ Q = EOQ$$

At the point where THC and TOC are equal the total inventory cost is minimized as shown in Figure 10.10:

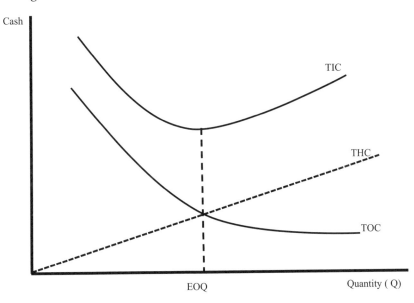

**Figure 10.10   Total inventory cost**

*Determining EOQ with Quantity Discounts*   Returning to our previous example of DirectJet Airlines ordering spare airline seats, what should DirectJet do if the seat manufacturer offers a $100 discount per seat on orders of at least 150 seats? Should DirectJet increase their order quantity to 150 or keep the EOQ of 100 seats? In order to determine the economically optimal decision, simply compare the total inventory cost (TIC) under each scenario and choose the order quantity which minimizes cost. Based on the comparison, DirectJet should continue ordering at the EOQ of 100 seats since the total inventory costs is less than ordering 150 seats with a price discount.

$$Total\ Inventory\ Cost\ (TIC) = C_h \times \frac{Q}{2} + C_o \times \frac{A}{Q}$$

$$Total\ Inventory\ Cost\ (TIC)_{100\ seats} = (0.2 \times \$1000) \times (\frac{100}{2}) + \$500 \times (\frac{2000}{100}) = \$20,000$$

$$Total\ Inventory\ Cost\ (TIC)_{150\ seats} = (0.2 \times \$900) \times (\frac{150}{2}) + \$500 \times (\frac{2000}{150}) = \$20,166.67$$

Once an appropriate order quantity has been determined, the next step in inventory management is to determine the reorder point. The reorder point is based on demand and the length of time it takes from the time an order is placed to the time the order is received (lead time). Therefore, the reorder point is the inventory level at which an order is placed to replenish inventory that has been used to fill customer demand. Reorder point is calculated based on demand and lead time.

$$\text{Reorder point} = \text{Demand} \times \text{lead time}$$

Returning to DirectJet's seats example, if the lead time for spare airline seats is two weeks, and it is based on constant demand, DirectJet should place an order of 100 seats (EOQ) when its inventory level reaches 77 seats remaining.

$$\text{Reorder point} = \text{Weekly Demand} \times \text{lead time}$$

$$\text{Reorder point} = \frac{A}{52 \text{ weeks/year}} \times 2 \text{ weeks}$$

$$\text{Reorder point} = \frac{2000}{52} \times 2 \approx 77 \text{ seats}$$

In order to protect against stock outs, some businesses implement an inventory policy that incorporates the element of safety stock. Safety stock is additional inventory that is carried to insure that when there is customer demand, the product will not be out of stock. Safety stock is common in businesses because demand is not always constant. Airline maintenance is a great example of the fluctuations in demand. A part for an engine may need to be replaced on five different engines in one week, but not needed on any engines the next week. Airlines may incorporate safety stock into parts inventory to ensure that the part will always be available. Additionally, the potential lost profits of having a stock out, or maintenance event, can impact the level of safety stock held. Because additional inventory is being held, the use of safety stock increases inventory holding costs and subsequently, the total inventory cost. In addition, the reorder point is also increased by the amount of safety stock. As a result, the reorder point and total inventory cost, when including safety stock is increased. Figure 10.11 opposite shows the EOQ model with the addition of safety stock:

### Total Holding Cost with Safety Stock (SS):

$$\text{Total Holding Cost (THC)} = C_h \times (\frac{EOQ}{2} + SS)$$

### Reorder Point with Safety Stock (SS):

$$\text{Reorder point} = (\text{Demand} \times \text{lead time}) + SS$$

## Just In Time (JIT)

In any inventory control model, the basic principle is that inventory has to be replenished.

Other inventory management methods besides the EOQ model can be used, including a Just-In-Time (JIT) system and an ABC inventory analysis. JIT is based on material planning and control and elimination of waste. The basic elements of JIT were developed by Toyota in the 1950s, becoming known as the Toyota Production System (TPS).[9] In a JIT system, a business works closely with suppliers to ensure that inventory arrives only when it is needed to satisfy customer demand. The goal of a JIT inventory system is to

---

9    Chase, Jacobs, and Aquilano, *Operations Management*, 11th edition, Irwin/McGraw-Hill.

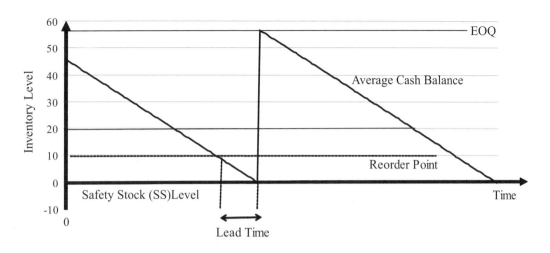

**Figure 10.11   EOQ model with safety stock**

operate without holding inventory or by holding as minimal inventory as possible. In
a JIT environment, each unit is organized so that parts arrive for the next job just when
others are completed, and therefore, the manufacturing process proceeds quickly. One
prominent example of a JIT system is Dell Computers. Dell works closely with suppliers
to reduce lead time and only orders computer components based on actual customer
orders for computers (Woodgrange Technologies, 2007). There are three components that
are necessary to implement a JIT system:

- Close coordination with suppliers
- Consistent quality production (no waste)
- Near zero lead time.

JIT can help commercial airlines compete in global markets when it saves inventory
warehousing costs. Just as JIT has many strong points, there are also weaknesses as
well. In this model everything is interdependent and each process relies on all the others
(Greenberg, 2002). This means that, if one process fails, then all others fail as well. However,
if a high degree of reliability in the individual processes can be achieved, then just-in-time
is a source of great strategic advantage and can provide large savings. Therefore, there
are a great number of companies and industries that have implemented JIT inventory
systems or derivatives of the system, including Boeing. The implementation of the JIT in
maintenance helps to provide an efficient, service oriented aircraft overhaul system for
most airlines.

## ABC Inventory Control Model

An ABC inventory system classifies different items in a company's inventory into three
different categories that are based on the cost, importance and frequency of use of each
inventory item. In an ABC inventory system, inventory that is worth a greater dollar
amount and is of great importance to the company is placed in the A category (the

category with the highest level of oversight and control). Less important inventory items are then categorized together and inventory levels are monitored less closely (Block and Hirt, 2005). "A" items are roughly the top 15%, and B items are next 35%. Finally, Class C items represent a small percentage of the total dollar value, up to approximately 25%, but a high percentage of the total number of items, 50 to 100%. This method analyzes the items according to their value and not according to their importance in the production process. It may, therefore, sometimes generate difficulty. The ABC model is an inventory management model where the inventory is divided into three categories:

- **A category**—Inventory that has the highest value, usage or importance to the company. Inventory levels of "A" items are kept higher and are monitored more closely.
- **B category**—Inventory items that have less importance, value or demand than the A items. There is less control and monitoring of inventory levels than the A category.
- **C category**—Inventory items that have the lowest value or importance. For these items there is minimal control and monitoring of inventory levels.

Many airline maintenance departments find that the ABC inventory approach works best for them. Critical aircraft parts are placed in the A category and inventories of these parts are kept high and monitored daily or weekly. More common, less-expensive items like nuts and bolts may be put in the C classification and placed in a bin for easy access and/or retrieval. An order to replace C inventory items may not be made until the bin is near empty.

## SUMMARY

This chapter has discussed the basics of working capital and current asset management. The major topics discussed included: cash management, operating cycle, and current asset/liability management. Cash is the most important current asset to manage as it is used to pay current liabilities, but at the same time does not yield a return to the company unless invested. Other current assets, such as accounts receivable and inventory, must also be managed effectively since insufficient management of accounts receivable and inventory can result in additional costs that airlines and other businesses should avoid.

## DISCUSSION QUESTIONS

1. Describe the typical cash conversion cycle for an airline in relation to the calendar year.
2. What are the three reasons for any airlines to hold cash? Provide an example of why an airline may wish to hold cash for each reason.
3. What are the four basic problems an airline may experience with cash management?
4. What is the economic order quantity (EOQ) assuming the annual demand for cash is $1 million, the cost of converting marketable securities to cash is $1,000 per transaction, and the market bearing interest rate is 4.5%? What is the number of cash conversion per year?

5.  Describe the difference between the operating cycle and the cash conversion cycle.
6.  An aircraft seat manufacturer generates $500,000 in monthly sales with 95% of sales done on credit. Assuming the cost of debt is 6%, what is the manufacturer's monthly cost of carrying accounts receivable?
7.  An airline is being offered credit terms of 3/15, net 45 for a $225,000 invoice. Assuming an opportunity cost of 3%, should the airline accept the credit terms?
8.  An airline MRO (Maintenance, Repair, Overhaul) facility currently holds $80,000 worth of inventory of 200 aircraft parts. Assuming an annual demand of 150 units for the part, an order cost of $2,000, and a holding cost equal to 35% of the parts value, what is the optimal ordering quantity for the part?
    a.  How many orders are made in a year?
    b.  What is the average inventory (in dollars) on hand in units?
    c.  What is the total holding cost of inventory?
    d.  What is the total ordering cost of inventory in a year?
    e.  What is the total inventory cost in a year?
    f.  Assuming a lead time of one month, what is the reorder point?
    g.  Assuming the MRO wishes to maintain a safety stock of ten units, what is the new reorder point and total inventory holding cost?
9.  Describe the three levels of the ABC inventory system, and provide examples of inventory that would be classified in each category.
10. What is the transaction cost for cash as an asset?
11. EZjET utilizes the Baumol to model to estimate its cash balance. The airline requires $5,000,000 in cash each time it converts marketable securities into cash. What is the average cash balance if the holding cost is $500,000, and the transaction costs are $60,000?

# REFERENCES

Baumol, W. (1952). "The Transactions Demand for Cash," *QJE*, Nov., 545–556.

Besley, S. and E. Brigham (2009). *Principles of Finance*, 4th, South-Western.

Best Buy (2008). Financing offers. Retrieved September 16, 2008 from http://www.bestbuy.com/site/olspage.jsp?id=cat12125andtype=pageandfCode=10#.

Block, S. and G. Hirt. (2005). *Foundations of Financial Management*, 11th ed.

Brigham, E. and L. Gapenski (1994). *Financial Management: Theory and practice* (7). Orlando: Dryden Press.

Chase, R., R. Jacobs, and J. Aquilano (2005). *Operations Management for Competitive Advantage*, 11th ed. McGraw-Hill/Irwin.

FX Trademaker (2008). Hedging Forex. Retrieved September 18, 2008 from http://www.fxtrademaker.com/hedging_forex.htm#

Greenberg, D. (2002). "Just-In-Time Inventory System Proves Vulnerable to Labor Strife." *Los Angeles Business Journal*, October 7, 2002.

International Herald Tribune (2008, April 8). String of airline bankruptcies prompts questions of which carrier could be next. Retrieved September 30, 2008 from http://www.iht.com/articles/ap/2008/04/08/business/NA-FIN-U.S.-Airline-Bankruptcies.php?page=1

Merton, M. and D. Orr (1966). "A Model of the Demand for Money by Firms," *QJE*, Aug, 413–435.

Moyer, C. J. McGuigan, and W. Kretlow (2008). *Contemporary Financial Management*, (10). Cengage Learning.

Ross, A., W. Westerfield, and D. Jordan (2008). *Fundamentals of Corporate Finance* (8). New York: McGraw-Hill/Irwin.

Serling, J. (2008). *Character and Characters: The spirit of Alaska Airlines*. Seattle:Documentary Media.

SmartBrief (2008). Southwest bolsters cash position with $600 million in loans. SmartBrief, Inc. Retrieved September 30, 2008 from http://www.smartbrief.com/news/ASTA/companyData.jsp?companyId=679andc=summary2005

The Ottawa Citizen (1988, September 12). Pilot credit card refused, passengers chip in for fuel, p. D17. Retrieved September 12, 2008, from ProQuest Newsstand database.

United Airlines (2008, July 22). *United Airlines reaches agreement in principle to enhance liquidity by approximately $1.2 Billion*. Chicago: UAL Corporation.

Weensven, J. (2007). *Air Transport: A management perspective* (6). Ashgate Publishing.

Woodgrange Technologies (2007). Business2000 case study: Dell- A different way of doing business. Woodgrange Technologies, Ltd. Retrieved October 1, 2008 from http://www.business2000.ie/cases/cases/case409.htm

# PART IV

# Practical Applications of Airline Finance

# 11

# Fuel Hedging and Risk Management

"The reason we did it wasn't to make money. We're not that smart. We're a long-lead-time business. We have to know how many airplanes to order, and we have to put out our schedules months in advance. You don't want to go into a situation where prices are out of your control. We wanted to be able to build a business plan where we would pretty well know what our costs would be. We thought of it as insurance."

Laura Wright[1]

As in life, the airline industry is filled with risks. One of the greatest risks to the airline industry is the price of jet fuel, as jet fuel is the largest cost component and its spot price is largely out of an airline's control. Hedging is a technique used to minimize risk by offsetting one's exposure to fluctuations in prices. For instance, an airline can lock in costs by buying crude oil futures at a pre determined price. By not hedging, airlines are taking on the risk of rising fuel prices into their operations. In order to hedge against fuel and currencies, one needs to utilize various financial derivatives. Thus this chapter will provide detail on financial derivatives, such as options and future contracts, while detailing the benefits of hedging for airlines. On the other hand, hedging it is not always a "win-win" solution, as losses can be borne from hedging. Cathay Pacific Airways posted a record $1-billion loss on fuel hedging last year and this was the biggest loss in the airline's history. United Airlines also lost $544 million on fuel hedges in the last quarter of 2008. The losses included $472 million in unrealized losses and $72 million in realized losses. The gains and losses from hedging are also analyzed through a brief examination of hedge accounting, while the appendix provides insight into the powerful Black-Scholes options pricing model. The chapter covers the following topics:

- Financial Derivatives and Options
  - Hedging
  - How to Hedge
- Airline Industry and Fuel Hedging
  - Swaps (Plain vanilla and differential)
  - Call options
  - Collars (Zero-cost and premium)

---

1    CFO, Southwest Airlines, regarding fuel hedging.

One of the most recent shifts in the airline industry has been the increasing proportion of jet fuel costs to an airline's cost structure. Uncertainty about the future liabilities or future cash flows exposes airlines to risk. Previously, wages, salaries, and benefits represented the greatest expense to airlines; however, as the price of crude oil has continued rising airlines have been subjected to a cost that has increased nearly sevenfold in just five years (IATA, 2008). One way to manage this risk is through the use of financial derivatives. Airlines enter into different forms of derivative instrument transactions in order to manage potential financial risks, including fuel price risk, interest rate risk, and exchange rate risk. For example, Southwest Airlines fuel expense in 2008 was $3.71 billion, more than double their fuel costs in 2005 (Southwest Airlines, 2008). Southwest's fuel hedges during this time allowed the airline to compensate for fuel price increases, contributing to cash savings of almost $1.3 billion during 2008. JetBlue's CEO David Barger in his report to shareholders in relation to the company's $76 million loss in 2008 said, "While we're never happy to report a loss, given that our 2008 fuel expense increased $400 million compared with 2007, I truly believe our team did an excellent job."[2] Figure 11.1 depicts the cost of fuel from January 2003 to March 2009. The year 2008 began with mounting oil prices, where crude oil price reached a peak of $147 a barrel in July, but then fuel prices spiraled downward to about $40 a barrel.

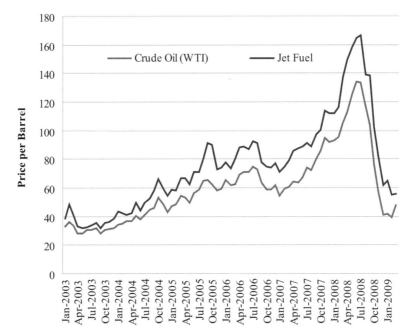

**Figure 11.1    Jet fuel and crude oil prices**

---

The major problem concerning fuel for airlines is that, unlike some other costs, jet fuel prices are largely out of an airline's control. The reason for this is the simple fact that the price of jet fuel is ultimately the result of a market clearing price. An airline's inability to have control over its largest cost is the source of an immense amount of risk. In fact, jet fuel in the airline industry is probably one of the largest costs that any firm has no direct control over. However, airlines do have ways of controlling the amount they pay for jet fuel since they can hedge against the soaring costs of oil. Hedging is a strategy that involves taking an opposite position in a security (sell vs. buy) in order to minimize risk. Ultimately, hedging is performed to minimize the volatility and risk of a major input or cost to a firm. While jet fuel represents the largest hedging opportunity to airlines, currency hedging is also routinely performed to minimize the volatility in world currency prices. For airlines operating to a multitude of countries, currency hedging can help separate a good business decision from a disastrous one. Fuel and currency hedging are types of financial options and, in order to understand them, we must first understand options.

## FINANCIAL DERIVATIVES AND OPTIONS

Options, futures and forwards are all financial derivatives. They are called derivatives because their value is derived from an underlying security. The most basic and probably most understood derivative is an option. An option is a contract which gives the holder the right, but not the obligation, to buy or sell an asset at a given price during a given period of time. There are two different options: a call option and a put option.

- **Call options** are the right, but not the requirement, to buy a particular asset at a predetermined fixed price (strike price) at a time up until the maturity (expiration) date of the option.

Buyers of call options pay a premium for the right to buy the commodity at the specified price (Hull, 2008). Call options act as caps on the price of a commodity (such as jet fuel). If the market price of the commodity is less than the strike price, the holder of the call option will not exercise his/her option and will simply buy the commodity at market price. However, if the market price of the underlying security is above the strike price, the holder of the call option will utilize his/her call option in order to buy the commodity at the lower strike price, ultimately resulting in a gain.

- **Put options** are the right, but not the requirement, to sell a particular asset at a predetermined fixed price (strike price) at a time up until the maturity date of the option.

Put options are the opposite of call options. Put options protect the seller of a commodity by placing a floor on the price they will be able to sell the commodity for; therefore, a put option will only be exercised if the market price falls below the strike price.

There are always two parties involved in the purchase of an option. There is the writer (seller) and the buyer. The buyer pays the writer a premium for the contract to compensate the writer for the risk that the option may be exercised. The amount of this premium depends on the value of the underlying commodity, the volatility of its price, and the time to maturity of the option. Table 11.1 shows the potential obligation for the buyer and the seller of call and put options.

**Table 11.1    Seller and buyer obligations**

|  | Writer | Buyer |
|---|---|---|
| Sell | Obligation to Sell | Option to Buy |
| Buy | Obligation to Buy | Option to Sell |

In order to better understand the value of options, let us examine the following example which involves options in a non-hedging scenario. Suppose you were to buy ten April call contracts for DirectJet stock, which currently trades at $40/share, with a strike price of $40 and a $6.50 premium for this call option.[3] Each call option contract is for the purchase of 100 shares of DirectJet stock. The option is quoted at a premium of $6.50 per share, so the contracts cost $650 each. You would spend a total of 10 × $650 = $6,500. You wait until the expiration date (EXP) in April; Table 11.2 tells you the option value and profit per share for exercising the call option on an individual basis.

**Table 11.2    Call option values/share**

| Stock price | Option value | Premium | Profit |
|---|---|---|---|
| $0 | $0.00 | -$6.50 | -$6.50 |
| $10 | $0.00 | -$6.50 | -$6.50 |
| $20 | $0.00 | -$6.50 | -$6.50 |
| $30 | $0.00 | -$6.50 | -$6.50 |
| $40 | $0.00 | -$6.50 | -$6.50 |
| $50 | $10.00 | -$6.50 | $3.50 |
| $60 | $20.00 | -$6.50 | $13.50 |
| $70 | $30.00 | -$6.50 | $23.50 |
| $80 | $40.00 | -$6.50 | $33.50 |
| $90 | $50.00 | -$6.50 | $43.50 |
| $100 | $60.00 | -$6.50 | $53.50 |
| $110 | $70.00 | -$6.50 | $63.50 |

This scenario can also be shown graphically, as in Figure 11.2. As can be seen, the payoffs are directly proportional, one to one, after the asset rises above the exercise price. When the stock price is less than the exercise price ($40), the call option is referred to as out of the money and the option would expire as worthless. In this case your loss is limited to the premium paid to purchase the contract and nothing more.

As mentioned earlier a put option does the exact opposite of a call. A put option gives the holder the right to sell a stock at a predetermined value on or before the expiration .The contract holder does not necessarily hold any stock at the time of the contract. Consider an

---

3    Options expire on a specific date and the time to expiration is known as its maturity.

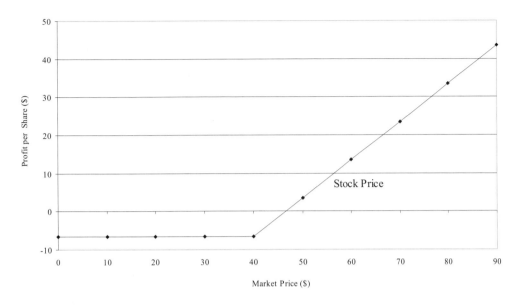

**Figure 11.2    Call option profit**

investor who purchases ten put options, with a stock price of $40 per share, and a premium of $6.50 per stock. Assume the strike price was determined to be $40 per share and each contract is for 100 shares. Therefore, each contract will cost $650, with the ten contracts amounting to $6,500. At the expiration of the put, assume the stock price is $30 and the Seller will exercise his/her right to sell the stock at $40 dollars, which after the premium is deducted will give a profit of $3.50. Now assume the stock prices rise to $50 at the expiration. In this case the seller will not exercise his/her options and his/her loss is only the premium. Table 11.3 depicts the option values and profit at different stock price for this put option.

**Table 11.3    Put option values per share**

| Stock price | Option value | Premium | Profit |
|---|---|---|---|
| 0.00 | 40.00 | -6.50 | 33.50 |
| 10.00 | 30.00 | -6.50 | 23.50 |
| 20.00 | 20.00 | -6.50 | 13.50 |
| 30.00 | 10.00 | -6.50 | 3.50 |
| 40.00 | 0.00 | -6.50 | -6.50 |
| 50.00 | 0.00 | -6.50 | -6.50 |
| 60.00 | 0.00 | -6.50 | -6.50 |
| 70.00 | 0.00 | -6.50 | -6.50 |
| 80.00 | 0.00 | 6.50 | -6.50 |
| 90.00 | 0.00 | -6.50 | -6.50 |
| 100.00 | 0.00 | -6.50 | -6.50 |
| 110.00 | 0.00 | -6.50 | -6.50 |
| 120.00 | 0.00 | -6.50 | -6.50 |

Table 11.3 reveals that as the stock prices decrease it will be beneficial to the buyer and vice versa if the stock price increases above the exercise price, at which time the buyer will lose only the premium of $6.50 per share. Therefore the put option allows an investor to reduce the risk and occurs when one has a bearish outlook on the stock. Figure 11.3 details the gain/loss of the put option of DirectJet.

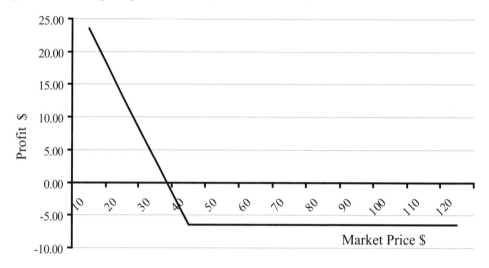

**Figure 11.3    Put option profits**

To understand the various scenarios for the option again, remember the purchased DirectJet April $40 call option. At expiration, assume DirectJet's stock price is $50 per share, which means the buyer can exercise the call option at $40 per share, resulting in a gain of $10 per share, or $1,000 total per call contract. Since your initial call premium was $650, the net profit is $350 per contract. Obviously, if the share price goes up further, your return on investment can be much greater. Conversely, one could also simply sell the option back in the market, at any time before expiration, and take the profit on the option sale itself. Figure 11.4 plots the profit of a call option at expiration against the stock price; hence, a call option has value to its owner only if the price of the underlying asset is above the strike price. If the value of the asset is below the strike price, the owner of the option simply lets it expire unexercised.[4] The primary advantage of buying options is that the investor cannot lose more than the premium of $6.50 per share. If you buy the shares outright and the price goes below $40, you are of course exposed to the full amount of the loss.

## Hedging

Now that we understand how financial options work, we can look at how the hedging of fuel prices and foreign currencies works. In effect, hedging is a transfer of risk similar to buying insurance policies. Hedging diminishes the volatility of a portfolio returns and

---

4    The option value would be negative.

**Call Option**
Strike Price = $40

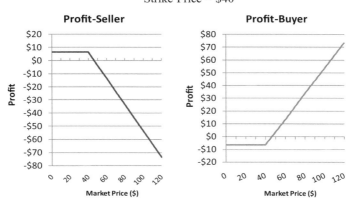

**Put Option**
Strike Price = $40

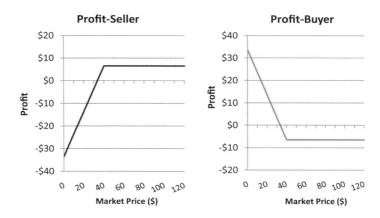

**Figure 11.4    Profitability of call and put options**

reduces the risk of loss. Hedging is also comparable to buying and selling options since the objective is to reduce risk.

In order to understand hedging, three critical questions must be answered:

- Should the firm hedge?
- How to hedge?
- How much to hedge?

*Should the firm hedge?*

> "Jet fuel is a very significant part of the cost structure of an airline. Jet fuel prices are traditionally very volatile. They have gone from $2 a gallon in 2007 to $4 in July 2008. In February 2004, it was still $1 a gallon."

Christian Terwiesch

"Its operation in a world beset by fuel and energy crises makes no sense at all."

Senator Cranston of California, About the Concorde, 1974

Senator Cranston's comments regarding the Concorde were not only true, since the Concorde ultimately became uneconomical at high fuel costs, but could apply to some of the fuel inefficient aircraft of today. American still operates a very large MD-80 fleet and the newly combined Delta/Northwest still operate large MD-80 and DC-9 fleets.[5] It may not be feasible, operationally or financially, to replace a large number of airplanes at once; therefore, airlines with older, less fuel-efficient planes are going to be more heavily impacted by rising fuel prices. In order to protect against rising fuel prices, even airlines with newer fleets, may enter into fuel hedging contracts.

As CFO Wright of Southwest Airlines said, fuel hedging is an insurance policy, and the sole purpose of hedging is to minimize risk (Wharton School of Business, 2008 November 12). Therefore, any cost that might fluctuate widely, and over which an airline has no control, represents a cost for which hedging should be analyzed. Ultimately, hedging is a mechanism used to reduce or eliminate the fluctuations in costs, providing an airline with a more assured cost structure, thereby reducing an airline's risk exposure. Fuel costs represent the greatest opportunity for hedging in the airline industry, since the price of jet fuel is largely out of an airline's control and it also fluctuates widely. Since exchange rates can fluctuate significantly, airlines routinely hedge foreign currency.

Once financial risks have been identified, a decision needs to be made as to whether or not the airline should hedge. There is no universally correct answer as to whether an airline should hedge jet fuel and/or currencies. Historically, airlines have both prospered (i.e. Southwest Airlines) and been hurt through hedging strategies.[6] Ultimately, the success of hedging actions is determined by the outcome of events far in the future. Since the future price of jet fuel or a currency exchange rate is unknown, the outcome of the hedging strategy is unknown; however, hedging can significantly help reduce the range of prices, thereby reducing an airline's exposure to risk.

In order to be successful at hedging, one requires a hypothesis about the price of jet fuel or the currency exchange rate in the future. To form a reasonable hypothesis, an understanding of the factors affecting the risk item is essential. As basic economic theory states, the price of any good is the equilibrium point between the supply and demand for the good. Related to crude oil, the price of oil should be the equilibrium between the supply of crude oil and the demand for crude oil. However, in financial markets, speculation might comprise a substantial portion of a commodity's price.

- **Speculation** is the buying (selling) of a good today with the expectation that the future price of the good will go up (down). Therefore, speculation will affect the price of the good today. Buying drives up the price (increase in demand) and selling drives the price down (decrease in demand).

Since commodities are traded on exchanges, if the current belief is that the price of oil will be high in the future, then speculators will be taking stances on oil today that

---

5       Sources: www.delta.com and  www.aa.com
6       Southwest entered into hedging in 1999 when oil was at $11 a barrel (Los Angeles Times, May 30, 2008). The airline chose to hedge only 10% of its long-term fuel requirements after losses on fuel hedging in the fourth quarter of 2008.

ultimately drives up the price of crude oil today. Therefore, speculation is the component of a commodity's price that is the result of future expectations about the commodity's price. Unlike supply and demand, which contain fundamental underlying market principles, speculation not only creates significant swings in the price of a commodity, but is also difficult to assess and determine.

Given that jet fuel represents the greatest risk exposure for an airline, an understanding of the factors impacting the supply and demand for jet fuel is crucial in helping determine a hedging strategy for jet fuel. Since jet fuel is a derivative of crude oil, the variables that impact the price of crude oil ultimately affect the price of jet fuel.

## How to Hedge

If it has been deemed beneficial to hedge a commodity, the next question involves how to actually hedge. Hedging involves using financial derivatives which, as discussed previously, are instruments whose payoffs and values are derived from an external source. While hedging involves multiple financial derivatives, it is all based upon forward and future contracts.

- **Forward contract:** an agreement between two parties to buy or sell a specified amount of a commodity at a specific price at a specific time in the future.

For illustration purposes, suppose an airline agrees to buy 10,000 gallons of jet fuel in three months at a price of $3.00 per gallon. At the time of maturity, the airline would physically receive 10,000 gallons of jet fuel and pay the supplier $30,000 for the commodity. The "profitability" for either party would be determined by calculating the difference between the spot price, the price of the commodity at the contract's maturity, versus the forward price, the price of the commodity stated in the forward contract. Assuming that the price of jet fuel at maturity was $2.80 per gallon, the airline would incur a loss of $2,000[7] as a result of entering the forward contract, while the supplier would have recorded a gain of $2,000.[8]

Regardless of the gain/loss position of either party at maturity, both sides are expected to perform their end of the agreement.[9] However, while an agreement can be enforceable in a court of law, both sides are taking on some level of credit risk as either party has the potential to default on the forward contract. While credit risk may not be as extensive for some parties, the ultimate goal of hedging is to reduce risk, and therefore forward contracts are not always the best mechanism to use in a hedging strategy.

The other major problem with forward contracts as a hedging mechanism in the airline industry is that in order for the contract to be honored, the supplier must deliver the commodity. In the example, the supplier would have to provide the airline with 10,000 gallons of jet fuel on a single day. Aside from the logistical problems of delivering 10,000 gallons of jet fuel to the airline, other issues such as the variability of supply and demand create inefficiencies in the hedging strategy.

---

7    Loss = (Spot Price − Forward Price) × Quantity = ($2.80 − $3.00) × 10,000 = ($0.20) × 10,000 = ($2,000)
8    Gain = (Forward Price − Spot Price) × Quantity = ($3.00 − $2.80) × 10,000 = $0.20 × 10,000 = $2,000
9    The airline is expected to pay the supplier $30,000 and the supplier is expected to provide the airline with 10,000 gallons of jet fuel.

As a result of these shortcomings, future contacts are one of the more desirable financial derivatives used in hedging since they are similar to forward contracts, but feature more formalized and standardized characteristics.

- **Future contracts**: Standardized contracts with set criteria of the amount, price, and future delivery date of a currency, security, or commodity that are bought and sold at futures exchanges.

The differences between forward contracts and future contracts are shown:

| Futures Contract | Forward Contract |
|---|---|
| • Terms and conditions are standardized<br>• Traded on organized exchanges<br>• Lower default risk<br>• Buyer and seller do not contract directly with each other | • Not standardized (parties set terms)<br>• Traded in the "over the counter" market<br>• Higher default risk<br>• The buyer and seller are dependent upon each other |

Just like a stock market, futures markets have real-time listings on the future prices for various durations of future contracts. In the United States, the Chicago Mercantile Exchange (CME) is the largest exchange with future contracts available on a wide range of commodities and currencies, ranging from corn to weather (CME, 2008). However, for the airline industry, the New York Mercantile Exchange (NYMEX) is probably the most important since that is where crude oil futures are exchanged. Outside of the United States, other major futures markets include the Tokyo International Financial Futures Exchange and the London International Financial Futures Exchange.

As was mentioned, future contracts are standardized contracts with many specifications. The contracts for light sweet crude oil that are traded on the NYMEX are for 1,000 U.S. barrels (42,000 gallons) of light sweet crude oil; however, the future prices are listed in U.S. dollars on a per barrel basis (NYMEX, 2008). All settlements for contracts occur on the $25^{th}$ of the month, or the next appropriate business day. Additionally, the light sweet crude oil futures specify in detail delivery options for the contracts and the appropriate acceptable grade for the crude oil.

Table 11.4 displays six different futures contracts, ranging from one to six months in duration. Regular market trading on the NYMEX occurs from 9 a.m. to 2 p.m.; however, electronic trading occurs almost 24 hours, 7 days a week and this creates differences between the last trade (electronically) and the last settlement (regular trading) (NYMEX, 2008). Generally, the future prices for light sweet crude oil increase over duration, reflecting possible market positions about crude oil and the fact that, with an increase in duration, suppliers bear an increased amount of risk.

Looking at the 4-month futures contract for light sweet crude oil (December 2009), to purchase the contract on July, 2009 would cost approximately $68,100 based on the settlement price.[10] Based on this fact, futures markets are clearly not for the individual, but are markets more aimed at institutional investors and corporations looking at hedging. While institutional investors and corporations could theoretically take receipt of their futures contract, this is almost never done since buyers and sellers regularly offset

---

10    Order Cost = Futures Price (Aug 09) * 1,000 barrels = $68.10* 1,000 = $68,100 (Trading unit = 1000 U.S. Barrels, 42,000 Gallons).

**Table 11.4    Futures for light sweet crude oil, July 29, 2009**

|          | High  | Low   | Recent settle | Volume  |
|----------|-------|-------|---------------|---------|
| Sep-09   | 67.01 | 63.04 | 63.35         | 315,414 |
| Oct-09   | 68.53 | 64.98 | 65.23         | 89,949  |
| Nov-09   | 70.06 | 66.61 | 66.9          | 34,811  |
| Dec-09   | 71.1  | 67.8  | 68.1          | 51,929  |
| Jan-09   | 71.77 | 68.83 | 69.06         | 11,260  |
| Feb-09   | 71.19 | 69.73 | 69.92         | 3,967   |

*Source*: Compiled by the authors using New York Mercantile Exchange (NYMEX) data on July 29, 2009.

their position prior to maturity. Future contracts are settled daily through the market clearinghouse ("mark-to-market"). This is substantially different from forward contracts which are only settled at maturity. This settlement process involves buyers and sellers taking positions on the commodity (Bessembinder, 1991). A position is a financial stance on a stock or financial derivative.

- **Long position (Long):** An agreement to purchase
- **Short position (Short)**: An agreement to sell.

For the airline industry, a major issue for hedging is that their largest and most unpredictable cost, jet fuel, is not a widely traded commodity and is not traded on the New York Mercantile Exchange. While over the counter forward contracts can be created for jet fuel, futures contracts are a much more effective medium (for the reasons described previously), to hedge with. Because no futures market exists for jet fuel, another widely traded commodity must be used instead. In choosing the commodity with which to hedge, the goal is to find a traded commodity whose prices fluctuate in the same way as jet fuel. Because jet fuel is a byproduct in the refining process of crude oil, other refining byproducts (such as heating oil) are likely to have similar pricing characteristics. Therefore, this makes them suitable hedging commodities for jet fuel.

A methodology for determining a suitable hedging commodity for jet fuel is to take the historical prices for various commodities and calculate the correlation coefficient. The correlation coefficient is a scale free measure of the association between two variables. In practical terms, the correlation coefficient describes how closely the prices of two variables move. A positive correlation indicates that the variables move in the same direction, while a negative correlation implies that they move in the opposite direction. Based on weekly historical spot price data, Table 11.5 provides the correlation coefficient to U.S. Gulf Coast Jet Fuel for three NYMEX –traded commodities over one, five, and ten year time periods.

From the correlation coefficients contained in Table 11.5, New York Heating Oil would appear to be the best liquid commodity as its correlation coefficients are greater for all periods of time than Light Sweet Crude Oil and Mont Belvieu Propane. Based on heating oil's one-year correlation coefficient of 0.9978, approximately 99.78% of price fluctuations in Gulf Coast Jet Fuel are also experienced in New York Heating Oil. Since there is no minimum requirement for the correlation coefficient, any of the three liquid commodities could be used in a jet fuel hedging scheme; however, by choosing Mont Belvieu, TX Propane, one would be assuming an increase in basis risk since the correlation coefficient

**Table 11.5    U.S. Gulf Coast spot price correlation**

|                      | 1-Year | 5-Year | 10-Year |
|----------------------|--------|--------|---------|
| New York heating oil | 0.9978 | 0.9925 | 0.9954  |
| Light sweet crude oil | 0.9906 | 0.9855 | 0.9928  |
| Mont Belvieu, TX     | 0.9026 | 0.9698 | 0.9763  |

*Source*: Compiled by the Authors; August 29, 2008.

for propane is much lower than New York Heating Oil. Basis risk describes the risk that the value of the commodity being hedged may not change in tandem with the value of the derivative contract. In essence, basis risk is the proportion of fluctuations in jet fuel prices that are not related to changes in the spot price of the liquid commodities. Using the correlation coefficient the amount of basis risk can be determined by simply subtracting the correlation coefficient from 1. Using the one-year time period, the basis risk for New York Heating Oil is 0.0022 or 0.22% while the basis risk for Mont Belvieu Propane is 0.0974 or 9.74%. Since the goal with any hedging program is to reduce the amount of risk being borne, choosing to hedge jet fuel with the commodity that provides the lowest basis risk is usually the best solution. By reducing basis risk the chance that a fluctuation in the price of jet fuel that does not correspond to a fluctuation in the price of the derivative is minimized. Such fluctuations could potentially cause significant loss on the hedge. However, it should be noted that in order to hedge jet fuel in the futures market, some degree of risk must be borne since jet fuel is not a highly liquid commodity. Based on the correlation coefficients contained in Table 11.3, the majority of U.S. carriers that do hedge jet fuel should utilize a combination of both New York Heating Oil and Light Sweet Crude Oil.

While the basis risk described above simply refers to the proportion of risk that is borne owing to the diversion of price fluctuations between jet fuel and the derivative commodity, basis risk can also broken into three primary components: product basis risk, time basis risk, and location basis risk. Product basis risk occurs when there is a mismatch in the quality, consistency, or weight of the underlying product. In terms of the airline industry, while crude oil and jet fuel are similar, they are two separate commodities with different product and market characteristics and this could potentially cause distortions in pricing. Time basis risk occurs when there is a mismatch in the timing of the hedge. Since futures contracts have set time periods, time basis risk can occur when the desired time frame of the hedger differs from the stated contract dates. Finally, location basis risk is the result of a mismatch in the price of the product from one location to another. This is particularly common in the aviation industry, where the spot price of jet fuel can vary significantly not only from one location to the next in the United States, but also from country to country.

## AIRLINE INDUSTRY AND FUEL HEDGING

"We view our program as insurance; our goal is to minimize the volatility of fuel expenses. To do that, you've got to be in the market actively without an opinion as to what energy prices will do."

Paul Jacobson, Delta Air Lines Inc

While the majority of this chapter's focus has been on jet fuel hedging, currency hedging is also extensively practiced in the aviation industry. Whereas jet fuel is not a highly liquid commodity, currencies are. This significantly reduces the basis risk in currency hedging and enables one to participate in the futures market directly. Regardless of whether one is hedging international currencies or jet fuel, four major derivative instruments are commonly used to help reduce one's risk:

- Swaps (Plain vanilla and differential)
- Call options
- Collars (Zero-cost and premium)
- Futures contracts.

It should be noted that derivative strategies are not limited to the four instruments listed above. In fact, there are endless variations of strategies that can be effectively used in a hedging strategy. However, the four major strategies listed above form the basis for the majority of variant derivative instruments.

## Swaps (Plain Vanilla and Differential)

The basis behind any swap is to exchange a floating price for a fixed price over a period of time. A swap is entered into by two parties, with one party assuming the variable price while the other assumes the fixed price. In the case of the airline industry, an airline wishes to reduce its variability in the price of jet fuel; therefore, the airline will assume the fixed price portion of the swap. Since a swap contract does not involve either party taking physical control over the commodity, a swap is deemed an off-balance-sheet financial arrangement where both parties settle their contractual obligations through a transfer of cash. As a result, a swap contract ultimately results in one party "winning" and another party "losing"; therefore, when a swap contract is entered, both parties must have divergent viewpoints on the price fluctuations of the commodity since both parties will enter a swap contract with the sole goal of being the "winner".[11]

Swap contracts can be conducted either through the over-the-counter market or through organized exchanges. In either case, a swap bank is commonly utilized, where a financial institution acts as a facilitator between the two parties. In the over-the-counter market, a custom contract is created between two parties whereby the quantity, settlement, and time period of the contract are all customizable. These swaps, called plain vanilla swaps, are the most basic and do not cost any money if a swap bank is not used. While it is difficult for airlines to find potential partners, swap contracts can be created directly for jet fuel, and in this case direct swap contracts for jet fuel reduce the basis risk involved in the hedging strategy. Swap contracts are also routinely formed through organized exchanges for highly liquid commodities. Here, the New York Mercantile Exchange (NYMEX) acts as the swap bank, with the swap contracts containing fixed quantities and settlement dates. While the futures market does not contain jet fuel, the NYMEX does list a Gulf Coast Jet Fuel Calendar Swap, in addition to the commonly traded Gulf Coast Heating Oil Calendar

---

11    This, of course, is exactly the same thing that happens in the stock market when the buyers and sellers of stocks conclude a sale.  The buyer believes that the stock will go up while the seller believes that the stock will go down.

Swap (NYMEX, 2008). A swap contract where another commodity is being used, such as using heating oil instead of jet fuel, is commonly referred to as a differential swap.

In order to better understand the hedging principles of a swap contract, consider an airline that negotiates a one year swap contract with another party for 100,000 barrels of jet fuel monthly for a fixed price of $130/barrel with settlement performed monthly. The floating price of jet fuel for the swap is based on the monthly average of the spot price of jet fuel according to the Platt's New York Harbor Jet Fuel Price Index (Carter, Rogers, and Simkins, 2003). For the first month after the swap contract was entered, the monthly average spot price for jet fuel was $132/barrel. During the month, the airline would continue to pay the spot price for jet fuel; however, at the settlement date, the airline would make financial arrangements with the other party to provide the airline with a fixed price for the month. For the airline, the monthly settlement amount can be determined by using the formula:

Settlement Credit (Cost) = (Monthly Average Spot Price − Fixed Price) × Quantity

For the first month, the airline would receive a payment from the other party for $200,000 as a result of the spot price for jet fuel increasing over the amount of the fixed price of $130/barrel.

Settlement Credit (Cost)$_1$ = ($132/barrel − $130/barrel) × 100,000 barrel = $200,000

For the second month of the contract, assume the average spot price of jet fuel drops significantly to $125/barrel. In this scenario, the airline will be forced to pay the other party $500,000 as a result of the significant decrease in the spot price of jet fuel.

Settlement Credit (Cost)$_2$ = ($125/barrel − $130/barrel) × 100,000 barrels = ($500,000)

While the airline may experience substantial variation in settlement payments from month to month, since the airline would continue purchasing jet fuel at the spot price, the settlement payments act as a mechanism to ensure that the airline continues paying a single fixed price for the duration of the contract.

Because of the swap contract, an airline's variability in jet fuel prices is reduced, since the airline is guaranteed to pay an average of $130/barrel for 1.2MM gallons of jet fuel over the one year period of the contract. As a result of this fixed price, determining the "winner" and "loser" in a swap contract is simple. If the average annual spot price for jet fuel exceeds $130/barrel, the airline would receive a gain from hedging activities, while if the average annual spot price was below $130/barrel, the airline would record a loss on hedging activities. Because a swap contract is a zero-sum game (there's only one winner and one loser), the exact opposite win/loss scenario applies to the other party. Figure 11.5 graphically displays the win/loss scenario for the airline utilizing a $130/barrel jet fuel swap contract.

## Call Options

As stated earlier, because of the small size and lack of liquidity in jet fuel demand,[12] there is not an organized market where jet fuel options are traded. Therefore, airlines use options

---

12    This is in contrast to other financial derivatives.

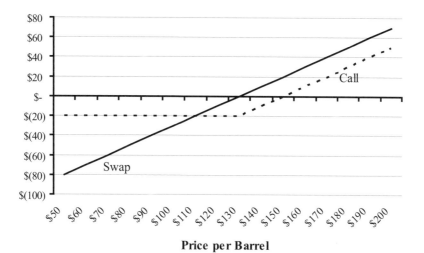

**Figure 11.5    Airline hedging profit (loss)/barrel for $130/barrel jet fuel swap**

on heating oil or diesel fuel whose prices are highly correlated with jet fuel prices and are therefore effective hedges for jet fuel. Many airlines such as Southwest and JetBlue have traditionally hedged their jet fuel costs using heating oil and crude options, swaps, and futures.

If it is believed that the price of jet fuel is going to increase in the future, a call option can limit an airline's exposure to soaring jet fuel prices. However, the major benefit of call options is that if the spot price of jet fuel does not exceed the strike price, the airline does not record a hedging loss, except the cost of the options' premiums (Baker, 2007). Therefore, unlike a swap, where an airline records a hedging loss if the price of jet fuel dips below the fixed price, options still provide the airline with the benefit of lower than expected spot prices.

For the airline industry, options are traded on the NYMEX for futures contracts; therefore, options cannot be purchased for jet fuel and must instead be purchased for either heating oil or crude oil. The majority of commodity options are typically available for just the next three months; however, a few long-run oil options can potentially be purchased. Table 11.6 displays a few of the options available on the NYMEX for light sweet crude oil, the most liquid oil option that is traded on the NYMEX, for April 16, 2009. The typical size of an options contract on the NYMEX is for 1,000 barrels of oil, which is 42,000 gallons of oil, the standard size of a futures contract on the NYMEX.

Based on the data from Table 11.6, there are a complete range of options available for hedging. The maturity month for an option represents the period in which the holder of the option has the right to purchase the commodity at the strike price. The actual expiration date of the option varies from month to month (depending on holidays and weekends), but usually falls around the middle of the month of the preceding month (NYMEX, 2008). For instance, the maturity date for the June 2009 light sweet crude oil option is actually May 14, 2009 (NYMEX, 2008).

The strike price for an options contract represents the price at which an asset can be purchased. From a hedging standpoint, the strike price represents the ceiling for crude oil and is the maximum that one would pay for crude oil. If the price of crude oil is above the strike price, a hedging gain is recorded (less the premium) while, if the price of crude

**Table 11.6     NYMEX light sweet crude oil call options, July 30 2009**

| Maturity month | Strike price / barrel | Premium / barrel | Volume |
|---|---|---|---|
| 9-Jun | $40 | $12.80 | 0 |
| 9-Jun | $50 | $4.80 | 207 |
| 9-Jun | $55 | $2.10 | 4 |
| 9-Jun | $60 | $1.03 | 318 |
| 9-Jun | $65 | $0.35 | 10 |
| 9-Jul | $67 | $1.30 | 50 |
| 9-Jul | $70 | $0.97 | 23 |
| 9-Jul | $75 | $0.50 | 16 |
| 9-Dec | $65 | $6.55 | 4 |
| 9-Dec | $73 | $4.30 | 1 |
| 9-Dec | $90 | $1.40 | 2 |

[1] Strike prices are actually listed in cents; therefore the strike price of $120 is actually listed as 12000 on the NYMEX. The strike price has been converted in figure 13.7 for the reader's convenience.

*Source*: Compiled by the authors using NYMEX data.

oil is below the strike price, the option is not exercised and the only financial loss to the airline is the premium paid. This win-loss scenario is depicted in Figure 11.6 for the June 2009 option with a strike price of $60 per barrel and with a premium of $1.03 per barrel.

An important factor to consider when hedging using call options is that while a hedging loss may not be recorded, cash needs to be spent upfront to purchase call options at the premium price. The issue of spending cash upfront is a major deterrent to many companies,

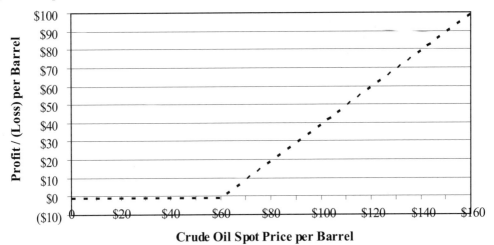

**Figure 11.6     Airline hedging profit (loss) per barrel for a $60 strike price call option with a $1.03 Premium**

especially airlines, since the company may not have sufficient funds for the investment. This was particularly important after September 11, 2001 when only Southwest Airlines had sufficient funds to invest in jet fuel hedges (Associated Press, 2008, June 30). As the price of oil rose dramatically, only Southwest Airlines benefited from hedges, and this was largely a result of its strong financial position in the past. The amount of money spent on hedge premiums in the airline industry is significant, as Southwest Airlines alone spent $52 million on hedging premiums in 2007 (Associated Press, 2008, June 30).

In order to better understand the impact of option premiums on the win/loss scenario, as depicted in Figure 11.6, consider an airline that purchases a 1 June 2009 call option with the strike price of $60 per barrel and a premium of $1.03 per barrel. On the date of purchase, the airline would spend $1,030 to purchase the call option.[13] Assume that on May 6, 2009 (8 days prior to the maturity date of the June 2009 option contract) the spot price for a barrel of oil is $58. Assuming this price for crude oil remains constant until maturity, the airline would not redeem the call option and simply lose the premium of $1,030.

$$\text{Hedging Gain (Loss)}_1 = (\text{Spot Price} - \text{Strike Price, or 0 if Spot Price below Strike Price}) \times \text{Quantity} - (\text{Premium} \times \text{Quantity})$$

$$\text{Hedging Gain (Loss)}_1 = (\$0) \times 1,000 - (\$1.03 \times 1,000) = \$0 - \$1,030 = (\$1,030)$$

In a second scenario, assume that at maturity the price of light sweet crude increases to $61.03 per barrel. Since the spot price for crude oil exceeds the strike price, the option would be exercised and the airline would "receive" 1,000 barrels of crude oil at $60 per barrel. The hedging gain for this call option would be $1,030; however, when the option premiums are taken into consideration the total gain is zero and the airline is no better off from their hedging activities.

$$\text{Hedging Gain (Loss)}_2 = (\text{Spot Price} - \text{Strike Price}) \times \text{Quantity} - (\text{Premium} \times \text{Quantity})$$

$$\text{Hedging Gain (Loss)}_2 = (\$61.03 - \$60) \times 1,000 - (\$1.03 \times 1,000) = \$1,030 - \$1,030 = \$0$$

Finally, consider a third scenario where the price of crude oil spikes unexpectedly to $70 per barrel. In this situation, the airline's hedging strategy will have worked as it will record a gain from hedging activities in the amount of $8,970.

$$\text{Hedging Gain (Loss)}_3 = (\text{Spot Price} - \text{Strike Price}) \times \text{Quantity} - (\text{Premium} \times \text{Quantity})$$

$$\text{Hedging Gain (Loss)}_3 = (\$70 - \$60) \times 1,000 - (\$1.03 \times 1,000) = \$10,000 - \$1,030 = \$8,970$$

## Collars (Zero-cost and Premium)

A collar involves purchasing a call option and at the same time selling a put option, providing both upside and downside protection. Collars require the sale of a put option to compensate for the premium associated with purchasing a call option. Usually, the call

---

13    Purchase Cost = Call Premium per barrel × 1,000 barrels (call option contract) = $1.03 × 1000 = $1,030.

and the put are both out-of-the-money when this strategy is implemented, and have the same expiration date. While the purchase of call options provides a significant ceiling for a commodity's price, the expense of option premiums either pushes a firm to not using call options, or pushes the strike price to such a high level that it merely guards against a catastrophic increase in the price of the commodity. While the notion of not recording a significant hedging loss is comforting, going long with (purchasing) call options provides a relative amount of volatility, especially if the strike price is substantially above the current spot price. One potential solution to minimize price volatility are collars; these involve going long on a call option, while subsequently going short (selling) on a put option. When combined, both a price ceiling and a price floor are created providing the airline with increased cost certainty. Depending on the specific call and put options that are bought and sold, a collar hedging strategy can be cost free.

**Zero-cost collar**: A collar in which the premium received from selling the put option exactly offsets the cost of purchasing a call option.

**Premium collar:** Occurs when the premium of the purchased call option exceeds the cash flow gained from selling the put option; this is typically more common than a zero-cost collar.

Table 11.7 provides a listing of various put options available for light sweet crude oil on April 16, 2009.

**Table 11.7    NYMEX light sweet crude oil put options as of April 16, 2009**

| Maturity month | Strike price / barrel | Premium / barrel | Volume |
|:---:|:---:|:---:|:---:|
| 9-Jun | $40 | $0.40 | 13 |
| 9-Jun | $45 | $1.07 | 23 |
| 9-Jun | $50 | $2.73 | 12 |
| 9-Jun | $52.50 | $3.86 | 24 |
| 9-Jul | $38 | $0.50 | 1 |
| 9-Jul | $40 | $0.80 | 1 |
| 9-Jul | $41 | $1.00 | 2 |

*Source*: Compiled by the Authors using NYMEX data.

In order to construct a zero-cost collar, the premiums for both the call and put options must match. Based on data contained in Tables 11.6 and 11.7, one zero-cost collar opportunity exists with a July 2009 maturity. In order to construct the zero-cost collar, an airline would need to sell the July 2009 $38 strike price put option receiving the premium of $0.50 per barrel. Using these proceeds, the airline would then purchase the July 2009 $75 strike price call option. As a result of these transactions, the airline has created a price ceiling of $75 for zero-cost, which is a significant improvement over merely purchasing a call option. The only tradeoff in doing so is that a price floor is established at $38, where if the spot price for crude oil falls below $38, a hedging loss will be recorded. In this particular example, an increased level of oil price certainty is provided to the airline for zero-cost; and they will not pay more than $75 per barrel for crude oil and not less than $38 per barrel. This win/loss scenario is depicted in Figure 11.7.

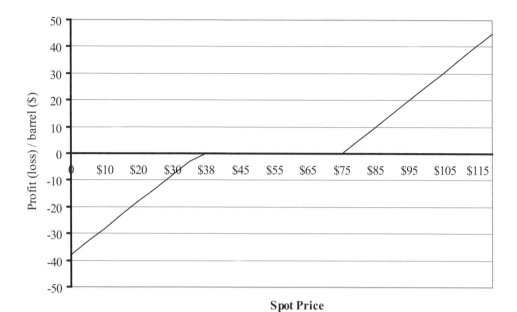

**Figure 11.7    Airline hedging profit (loss) per barrel for a zero-cost collar
with a call option strike price of $75/barrel and a put option
strike price of $38/barrel**

While zero-cost collars are an ideal situation, the majority of the time the spread in the strike prices is rather wide. If a much narrower collar is desired, or a collar more heavily weighted to where the price ceiling is closer to the market spot price, then the premium for the purchase of the call option is probably going to exceed the premium received from the sale of the put option.

Consider a scenario where the airline wishes to have a price ceiling much closer to the spot price on May 8, 2009 in our previous scenario of $58, but wants to reduce their hedging premium cost. By selling one June 2009 $50 per barrel strike price put option, the airline receives a premium of $2,730.[14] Using this revenue, the airline then proceeds to purchase one June 2009 $50 per barrel strike price call option for $4,800.[15] Since the strike price of the put and the strike price of the call are the same, the airline has effectively locked in oil prices at $50/barrel for less than the price to purchase a standalone call option. In order to understand the gain/loss implications of a premium collar, consider three scenarios where the spot price of light sweet crude oil at maturity:

- Increases to $62 per barrel
- Falls to $52.07 per barrel
- Falls to $50 per barrel.

*Scenario One*    When the price of crude oil jumps to $62 per barrel, exceeding the strike price of the call option, the collar strategy provides a hedging gain as the collar premium

---

14    Based on April 16, 2009 data: $2.73 Premium × 1000 = $2,730.
15    $4.80 Premium × 1000 = $4,800.

is offset by the gains incurred from the call option. The hedging gain under this scenario is $9,930.

$$\text{Hedging Gain (Loss)}_1 = (\text{Put Option Premium} - \text{Call Option Premium}) + G/(L) \text{ Call Option} + G/(L) \text{ Put Option})$$

$$\text{Hedging Gain (Loss)}_1 = [(\$2.73 \times 1000) - (\$4.80 \times 1000)] + [(\$62 - \$50)\ 1000 + 0]$$

$$\text{Hedging Gain (Loss)}_1 = [\$2,730 - \$4,800] + [\$12,000] = \$9,930$$

*Scenario Two*   While the price of crude oil falls to $52.07 in scenario two, exceeding the strike price of the call option, the gain from hedging merely offsets the collar premium, making the airline no better off by hedging. Such a scenario does not exist for zero-cost collars, as there are no premiums to offset. The hedging gain under this scenario is $0.

$$\text{Hedging Gain (Loss)}_2 = (\text{Put Option Premium} - \text{Call Option Premium}) + G/(L) \text{ Call Option} + G/(L) \text{ Put Option})$$

$$\text{Hedging Gain (Loss)}_2 = [(\$2.73 \times 1000) - (\$4.80 \times 1000)] + [((\$52.07 - \$50)\ 1000) + 0]$$

$$\text{Hedging Gain (Loss)}_2 = [\$2,730 - \$4,800] + [\$2,070] = \$0$$

*Scenario Three*   The price of crude oil falls to the strike price of $50, with neither the put option nor the call option being exercised. As a result, the airline would only lose the premium in creating the collar, which is $2,070.

$$\text{Hedging Gain (Loss)}_3 = (\text{Put Option Premium} - \text{Call Option Premium}) + G/(L) \text{ Call Option} + G/(L) \text{ Put Option})$$

$$\text{Hedging Gain (Loss)}_3 = [(\$2.73 \times 1000) - (\$4.80 \times 1000)] + [0 + 0]$$

$$\text{Hedging Gain (Loss)}_3 = [\$2,730 - \$4,800] + 0 = (\$2,070)$$

Figure 11.8 displays the hedging gain/loss for a particular premium collar on a per barrel basis.

While a collar is the typical method of hedging, combinations of going long or short with both put and call options can create a host of options available that can help protect against different risk factors. Each combination of put and call options provides different gain/loss scenarios that may provide a hedging gain or loss depending on the spot price of the commodity. Since the ultimate goal of hedging is to reduce one's risk to volatility in the price of a commodity (and hopefully minimize the cost in doing so), each unique combination of put and call options might ultimately serve the purpose.

## Futures Contracts

As has been discussed previously, a fourth potential hedging strategy would be to enter into a futures contract providing the airline with a known, hedged price for crude or

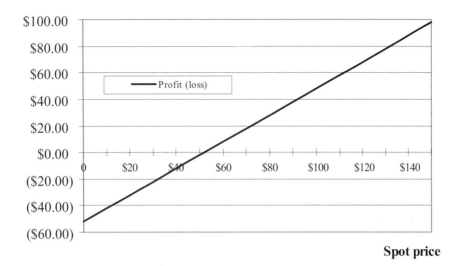

**Figure 11.8    Airline hedging profit (loss)/barrel for a swap strategy**

heating oil at a predetermined point in the future. One of the major benefits of futures contracts is that they are widely traded for as far out as eight years, making them an attractive solution for a long-term hedging strategy (NYMEX, 2008). Since no premiums exist for purchasing and selling futures contracts, futures contracts represent an absolute gain/loss scenario, where if the spot price of the commodity exceeds the futures price at maturity, a hedging gain is recorded and a hedging loss is recorded when the spot price falls below the future price. In essence, a futures contract acts in a similar way to a swap, but does not involve settlements as the contract is for only a month.

As with any decision regarding hedging, the correct amount to hedge is ultimately determined by the spot price of the commodity at the hedges maturity. Ultimately, if the hedge was "in-the-money" an airline would have wanted to hedge the maximum amount as the hedge provided them with a gain; however, if the hedge was "out-of-the-money" then the airline would not have wanted to hedge at all. In fact many airlines, including United and Northwest Airlines, are losing money on their current fuel hedges as they bet that fuel prices would continue to rise after going up to a high of about $140/barrel (Freed, 2008, September 17). Since the hedging has great volatility, the optimum level of hedging rests where the benefits/costs of hedging are offset by any considerable increase/decrease in the commodity's spot price.

Another factor involved in the decision-making concerning the amount to hedge is cash flow. Fuel hedging costs money, and for some strategies, requires premiums to be paid up-front. For airlines, cash flow is always a critical issue and the magnitude of jet fuel purchases requires a significant cash outlay for the airlines to hedge. For instance, in 2007 Southwest Airlines spent $52 million on hedging premiums (Associated Press, 2008, June 30). Since hedges are also commonly purchased on credit, cash and good credit are the major requirements for engaging in hedging activities, and, if an airline has neither of them, it may not be able to hedge to its optimal amount. This is the primary reason why Southwest Airlines was the only U.S. airline that benefited greatly from fuel hedging in the early 2000s after the industry downturn following the terrorist attacks of 2001. As a result of the industry downturn, "…*most carriers had terrible creditworthiness and couldn't hedge. Counter-parties feared that carriers would renege on their trade*" (Associated Press, 2008, June 30). Today, Southwest

Airlines has changed its fuel hedging strategy after large drops in the price of jet fuel at the end of 2008. Southwest has eliminated its unprofitable fuel hedging contracts; and has re-hedged at lower prices with only 10% of its expected fuel requirement for 2009–2013 (Southwest Airlines, 2009, February 2).

Based on the two factors of risk minimization and cash flow, airlines might pursue different levels of jet fuel hedging. Figure 11.9 displays the percentage of jet fuel requirements that are hedged for nine U.S. airlines, including Southwest, based on filings reported to the Securities Exchange Commission (SEC) at the end of 2008. From the filings, Delta Air Lines has the greatest proportion of their jet fuel expenses hedged while most of the other airlines have a roughly equal proportion of their jet fuel requirements that are hedged and not hedged. This balance enables them to reap any potential benefits of drops in jet fuel spot prices while also receiving the benefit of hedges if the spot prices increase dramatically. Alaska Airlines (AS) is hedged perfectly at 50% for 2009, indicating they may have a set strategy where they hedge exactly half their fuel requirements prior to the beginning of the year. Such set strategies, as opposed to speculation, are typically more successful in the long-run and provide the greatest decrease in the volatility of fuel prices. A potential explanation for the large proportion of hedging at Delta could be their average fleet age. Delta inherited many of Northwest's older fleet after the merger, causing relatively poor fuel efficiency. Poor fuel efficiency could cause Delta to be the most susceptible to changes in jet fuel prices. As a result, their increased jet fuel price volatility would cause them to have a higher optimum level of hedging to minimize price variability.

Another interesting hedging dynamic is how far in the future airlines should hedge. Based on publicly released financial information, the majority of carriers tend to have

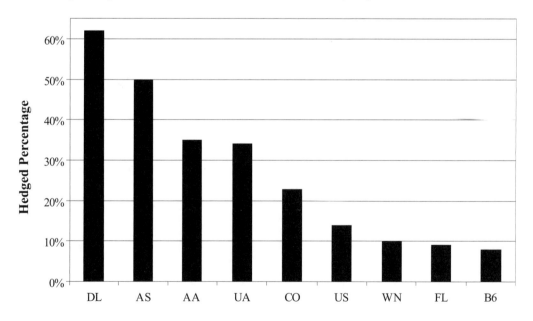

*Source*: Compiled by the authors using 10-K SEC filings.

**Figure 11.9    Percentage of airline fuel requirements hedged: 2009**

short hedging time frames where jet fuel requirements are only hedged approximately six months forward. While this shorter time frame typically reduces the probability of large hedging gains, it also reduces the amount of speculation, and risk, that the airline is bearing by hedging far into the future. While long-term hedges can provide lower strike prices, the amount of risk that is being borne is not substantially reduced. Of the nine airlines contained in Figure 11.9, only two other carriers besides Southwest reported hedges beyond 2009; these were Alaska Airlines with 14% of 2010's jet fuel requirements hedged, while Delta Air Lines had just 5% of 2010's requirements hedged. Such long-term hedges are potentially risky if jet fuel prices take sharp declines; however, the structure and minimal size of these particular hedges could help to reduce the risk. Such long-term hedges have paid off extremely well before (for Southwest Airlines) and could do so again for both of these carriers. However, in 2008 and the first quarter of 2009 Southwest Airlines posted three consecutive quarterly losses due in part to losses on its fuel-hedging contracts (Koenig, 2009, April 16). Another aspect observed is the reduction in the fuel hedging by many of the LCC s, owing to the sharp drop in the oil price from $147 in July, 2008 to $32 within a few months. During this period, Southwest, JetBlue and Airtran hedged only about 10% of the fuel requirements for 2009. The appendix to this chapter discusses the Black-Scholes asset pricing model and presents a quantitative example of how this model might be used to value a financial option.

## FUEL HEDGE ACCOUNTING

In the United States, there are two methods in how the values of an airline's fuel hedges are represented in the financial statements: with hedge accounting or without hedge accounting. According to FASB[16] 133 "Accounting of Derivative Instruments and Hedging Activities", all airlines, regardless of if they use fuel hedge accounting or not, are required to recognize the fair value of all their financial derivatives as either an asset or liability on the balance sheet (FASB, 2008). Whereabouts on the balance sheet is up to the discretion of the airlines, but is always stated in the notes to the financial statements. While Southwest Airlines has a special line item on their balance sheet under current assets for their fuel derivative contracts, other airlines, such as Continental Airlines represent their hedges on the balance sheet under other current assets when in an asset position, and accrued current liabilities when in a liability position (Continental Airlines, 2008).

The key difference in accounting practices concerning hedge accounting is the recognition of gains and losses on the fuel derivative contracts. Fuel hedge accounting allows an airline to only report the realized hedge gain or loss in the accounting period, even if the fair value of the derivative contracts changes significantly from one period to the next. The hedging gain or loss is recorded on the income statement, usually as either a special item, or a part of the fuel expense line, which is detailed in the notes to the income statement.

Accounting for hedging gains and losses without hedge accounting is a bit more difficult since the realized portion of the airline's fuel hedge portfolio needs to be accounted for, but also the unrealized hedging gain/loss of hedging contracts that have not yet been settled. In essence, the gain or loss of all future hedging contracts needs to also be shown on the income statement. The unrealized hedge gain or loss represents the mark-to-

---

16    Financial Accounting Standards Board.

market change in the fair value of the hedging portfolio. As a result of changes in the price of the underlying commodity (i.e. crude oil), the unrealized hedge gain/loss can experience significant swings in value, which are ultimately going to be reflected on the income statement.

In order to understand the difference in accounting methodologies and their impact on earnings consider the following scenario for an airline. On December 31, 2007 the spot price for crude oil was $80/bbl, resulting in a $100 million hedging gain for the fourth quarter of 2008.[17] Based on the forward crude oil curve, the airline expects to have hedging gains of $80 million in First Quarter, 2008, $40 million in Second Quarter, 2008, $20 million in Third Quarter, 2008, and a hedging loss of $10 million in Fourth Quarter, 2008. From this information, the unrealized hedge gain on December 31, 2007 was $130 million, with the realized hedge gain being $100 million. While fair valuation techniques are much more complex, assume that the fair value of fuel hedging derivatives is equal to the realized and unrealized hedge gains, resulting in a fair value of $230 million at December 31, 2008.

In the next quarter, the spot price of crude oil declines to $60/bbl, significantly reducing the value of the hedge portfolio. As a result, the realized hedge gain in First Quarter, 2008 is only $40 million, with the forward crude oil curve projecting zero hedge gain/losses in Second Quarter, 2008 and hedging losses of $20 million in Third Quarter, 2008, $40 million in Fourth Quarter, 2008, and $10 million in First Quarter, 2009. As of March 31, 2008 the fair value of the airline's hedging portfolio now stands as a liability of $30 million. As a result of the decline in the price of crude, many airlines, especially in Asia Pacific, could lose about $10 billion owing to fuel hedging contracts.

From this information, the accounting entries made as of March 31, 2008 will vary depending on the hedge accounting methodology. Using hedge accounting, the current liabilities account on the balance sheet will contain a value of $30 million (the fair value of the derivative portfolio), while the fuel expense line on the income statement will contain a $40 million gain on hedging activities (realized hedging gain as at March 31, 2008). Without hedge accounting, the current liabilities account on the balance sheet will also contain a value of $30 million; however, the fuel expense line will contain an entry of a $260 million loss on hedging activities (mark-to-market change in the fair value of the fuel hedge portfolio).

Clearly from this example, a lack of hedge accounting will result in greater volatility of earnings as a result of changes in the underlying price of the hedge commodity. As companies wish to minimize volatility in earnings, there is a benefit to airlines in adopting hedge accounting. Airlines are free to adopt hedge accounting; however, complex work must be undertaken to prove that the underlying commodity acts as a direct hedge. For airlines, it must be proved both historically and forward-looking that the hedged commodity (i.e. crude oil) is acting as a direct hedge against jet fuel. This process is time-consuming and is the reason why roughly half of U.S. airlines have implemented hedge accounting. A byproduct of hedge accounting is hedging ineffectiveness which results when certain derivative instruments are no longer "effective", or when the relationship between the underlying commodity and the cash flow do not match. As a result, airlines may post hedge ineffectiveness charges on the income statement when portions of the hedge portfolio no longer qualify for hedge accounting. However, usually most hedges are effective and therefore hedge ineffectiveness charges are usually minimal for airlines.

---

17    Assume that the airline is using crude oil as a substitute for hedging jet fuel.

## SUMMARY

In this chapter we have discussed financial derivatives. We have looked at call and put options as well as forward and future contracts. Airlines may use financial options to reduce uncertainty and/or risk. One area in particular that airlines engage in is hedging. Hedging is ultimately about reducing one's exposure to variability in the price of a commodity. For the airline industry, jet fuel now represents one of the largest costs, and with the spot price of jet fuel out of the airlines' control, hedging can be a necessary practice for airlines. The reason for this is the desire to reduce risk and to have more constant financial earnings. While many airlines have touted their hedging success stories, jet fuel hedging is not a "win-win" solution with significant hedging losses possible.[18] Singapore Airlines lost $225 million owing to fuel hedging contracts in 2008 and other airlines such as Cathay Pacific, Shanghai Airlines, Thai Airways, China Eastern, and Air China have all posted losses because of extreme fuel price volatility. Additionally, hedging is not free with airlines either having to pay premiums or heightened strike prices to participate. In general, the benefit of increased levels of price certainty that hedging provides sometimes outweigh the potential of hedging losses for most airlines. While the principles of hedging presented here have focused on jet fuel for airlines, the hedging strategies are universal, applying to multiple industries with any commodity with price variability. In such cases, hedging is an effective tool to minimize risk and provide the company with increased cost/revenue certainty. The appendix to the chapter presents the Black-Scholes Option Pricing Model. This quantitative model can be used to estimate how much an airline might have to pay in premiums for a given hedging strategy. The model does this by calculating the market value of the options that the airline might purchase in pursuing their hedging strategy.

## DISCUSSION QUESTIONS

1.  What are the basic differences between futures contract and forward contract and do you think speculation has impacted the price of oil?
2.  What is the basic difference in strategy between buying and selling an option?
3.  What is the basic difference between speculators and hedgers?
4.  How can airlines enter fuel hedging markets?
5.  Describe the difference between a call and a put option.
6.  What is a collar?
7.  Many major airlines have posted millions of dollars in one-time losses as falling oil prices have reduced the value of their hedge contracts in 2008. The Hong Kong based airline, Cathay Pacific, lost $1 billion on fuel hedging contracts due to significant decreases in the oil prices.
    a.  Discuss the advantages and disadvantages of hedging.
    b.  Why do airlines not always engage in hedging practices?
    c.  Why should an airline not hedge 100% of a hedge asset?
8.  Using the data contained in Table 11.6, what is the total call option premium paid to hedge 168,000 gallons of light sweet crude oil at $70 / barrel with July 2009 delivery?
    a.  Assuming the price of oil was $75 / barrel in July, what was the total gain/(loss) of the hedge?

---

18 · A Merrill Lynch report predicts nine Asian carriers will report $3.8 billion in estimated losses from contracts tied to fuel hedging in 2008.

b.   Assuming the price of oil was $60 / barrel in July, what was the total gain/(loss) of the hedge?

9.  Using recent data obtainable from the NYMEX, construct a costless collar using light sweet crude oil.

10. Using recent data obtainable from the NYMEX, construct a collar that deviates $10 from the current spot price. What is the total premium paid / (earned) to hedge 252,000 gallons using this collar?

11. What conclusions or comments can be made about the airline industry based on the analysis of the current hedge portfolios of major carriers?

12. Assume that three months ago you bought a put option on EZjET stock for $5 with an exercise price of $85. If the stock price at expiration of this option is $75, calculate the rate of return on this investment.

13. Explain what risk an investor is exposed to, if he/she owns the stock and has purchased a put option on the stock.

14. Explain how an airline gains a benefit by buying heating oil options.

## APPENDIX 1: THE BLACK-SCHOLES OPTION PRICING MODEL

As previously mentioned the cost (premium) of a financial option depends on the value of the security, the volatility of the security, the strike price and the time until the option expires (time to maturity). In this section we present a model to value financial options called the Black-Scholes Option Pricing Model. If an airline wants to adopt a fuel hedging strategy by purchasing options on commodities such as heating or crude oil it must determine how much the options are going to cost in order to determine the correct strategy. The Black-Scholes Model is one of the tools used to determine the market value of an option. The model takes into account the current price of the asset, the strike price of the option, the risk-free interest rate, the volatility of the price of the asset and the time to maturity to calculate the market value of an option (Marshall, 1989). The Black-Scholes Model may be confusing because of all the different terms involved in the equations. Therefore, to better understand the model, we present the equations involved, a quantitative example of the model and a graph showing how variations in some of the variables change the value of a financial option.

*Black-Scholes Option Pricing Model*

$$P_{option} = S_{price} \times N(d_1) - S_{strikeprice} \times e^{-r_{RF} \times t)} \times N(d_2)$$

$$d_1 = \frac{ln(\frac{S_{price}}{S_{strikeprice}}) + (r_{RF} + \frac{\sigma^2}{2}) \times t}{\sigma \times \sqrt{t}}$$

$$d_2 = d_1 - \sigma \times \sqrt{t}$$

where:
$S_{price}$    = current market price of security
$N(d_1)$    = normal probability distribution of d1
$S_{strikeprice}$ = strike price of financial option

$r_{RF}$        = risk-free interest rate
$t$          = time to maturity(expiration) of the option (in years)
$N(d_2)$     = normal probability of distribution of d2
$\sigma$          = instantaneous standard deviation (volatility) of the security

Suppose that DirectJet wants to purchase an option for heating oil as part of a fuel hedging strategy. Using the following information, determine the market price of the option according to the Black-Scholes Option Pricing Model.

$$S_{strikeprice} = \$100$$

$$S_{price} = \$100$$

$$t = 1$$

$$r_{RF} = 12\%$$

$$\sigma = .1$$

**Step 1** We should calculate $d_1$

$$d_1 = \frac{Ln(\frac{S_{price}}{S_{strikeprice}}) + (r_{RF} + \sigma^2/2) \times t}{\sigma \times \sqrt{t}}$$

$$d_1 = \frac{Ln(\frac{100}{100}) + (.12 + .1/2)^2 \times 1}{0.1 \times \sqrt{1}}$$

$$d_1 = 1.25$$

**Step 2** Calculate $d_2$

$$d_2 = d_1 - \sigma \times \sqrt{t}$$
$$d_2 = 1.25 - .1 \times \sqrt{1}$$
$$d_2 = 1.15$$

**Step 3** Determine $N(d_1)$ and $N(d_2)$ by using a standard normal probability distribution table. Looking at a standard normal distribution table we can determine that $N(d_1)$ and $N(d_2)$ equal 0.8944 and 0.8749 respectively:

- $N(d_1) = 0.8944$
- $N(d_2) = 0.8749$

**Step 4** Calculate the fair market price of the option:

$$P_{option} = S_{price} \times N(d_1) - S_{strikeprice} \times e^{-r_{RF} \times t)} \times N(d_2)$$

$$P_{option} = 100 \times 0.8944 - 100 \times e^{-.12 \times 1)} \times 0.8749$$

$$P_{option} = \$11.84$$

In Figures 11.10, 11.11 and 11.12, we show the effects of time to maturity and volatility on the value of an option. If the volatility of the security or the time to maturity of the option changes, there are large effects on the value of the option; as time to maturity or volatility increases, the price of the option also increases.

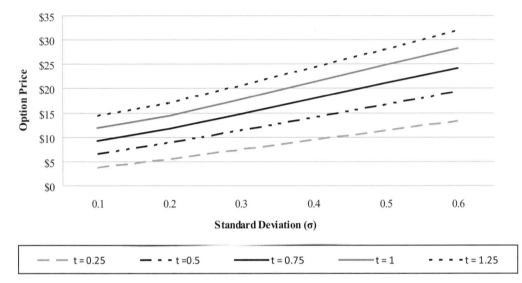

**Figure 11.10   Effect of time to maturity on option price**

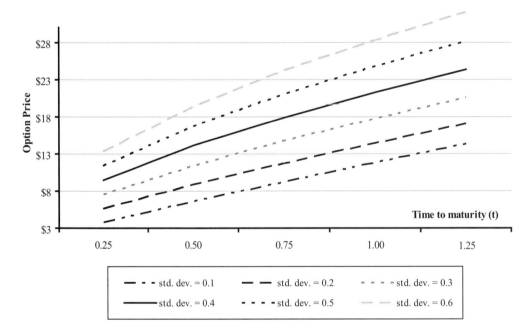

**Figure 11.11   Effect of volatility (σ) on option price**

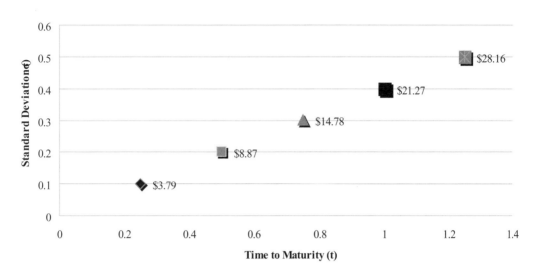

Figure 11.12    Cumulative effect of time to maturity and volatility

## REFERENCES

Associated Press (2008, June 30). *Airlines hedge against soaring fuel costs*. Dallas: The Associated Press.

Baker, A. (2007). *The Options Book*, 8th ed. National Center for Employees Ownership.

Bessembinder, H. (1991). "Forward contracts and firm value: Investment incentive and contracting effects". *Journal of Financial and Quantitative Analysis*, 26:519–532.

Carter, A., D. Rogers, and J. Simkins (2003). "Does fuel hedging make economic sense? The case of the U.S. airline industry", *Journal of Finance*, 1–48.

Chance, M. (2003*)*. *An Introduction to Derivatives and Risk Management*, 6th ed. New York: Thomson Learning.

CME (2008). Trade CME products. Chicago Mercantile Exchange. Retrieved October 10, 2008 from http://www.cme.com/trading/

Freed, J. (2008, September 17). United may not be alone with fuel hedge loss. The Associated Press. Retrieved October 10, 2008 from http://www.forbes.com/feeds/ap/2008/09/17/ap5438768.html

Hull, J. (2008). *Options, Futures, and Other Derivatives*, 7th ed. Prentice Hall.

IATA (2008). Jet fuel price development. International Air Transport Association. Retrieved October 7, 2008 from http://www.iata.org/whatwedo/economics/fuel_monitor/price_development.htm

Koenig, D. (2009, April 16). Southwest Airlines posts 1Q loss, plans buyouts. Associated Press. Retrieved April 16, 2009 from http://finance.yahoo.com/news/Southwest-Airlines-posts-1Q-apf-14944901.html?sec=topStoriesandpos=8andasset=andccode=

Marshall, F. (1989). *Futures and Option Contracting*. Cincinnati, Ohio: South-Western Publishing Co.

NYMEX (2008). NYMEX ClearPort product slate. New York Mercantile Exchange. Retrieved October 10, 2008 from http://www.nymex.com/cp_produc.aspx?

Southwest Airlines (2009, February 2). Southwest Airlines Co 10-K 2008. Dallas: Southwest Airlines Co.

Wharton School of Business (2008, November 12). For Airlines and Others, Even the Best Fuel-price Bets Can Lead to Turbulence. Retrieved December 11, 2008 from http://knowledge.wharton.upenn.edu/article.cfm?articleid=2087

# 12

# Buy versus Lease Decision-Making

"The current challenging financial and market environment have made it much more capital efficient for airlines to lease aircraft."

Robert Martin, Chief Executive BOC Aviation, an aircraft leasing company

The largest and most expensive assets for an airline are the aircraft, and many airlines depend on external resources to finance aircraft purchase. How to finance those assets is a major decision for any company or airline. While multiple options exist, fixed assets such as aircraft can commonly either be purchased or leased. Much of this decision will hinge on the cost of capital and the availability of cash for the airline. If the airline has a high cost of capital, or is short of liquidity, it may be cheaper and more advantageous for the airline to lease rather than buy. Additionally, the decision will impact where the aircraft appear on the financial statements. There are also other advantages and disadvantages to leasing that may impact the buy versus lease decision, and these are covered in this chapter. This chapter also covers the buy versus lease decision in quantitative detail, along with the different types of leases and major aircraft leasing companies. The following topics are covered in the chapter:

- Types of Leases
  - Wet Lease
  - Sale and Leaseback/ Leveraged Leases
  - Operating Lease
  - Financial (Capital) Lease
  - Cross-Border Leases
- Buy vs. Lease Analysis
- Major Commercial Aircraft Leasing Companies
- Summary
- Discussion Questions
- Appendix 1: Key Provisions of an Operating Lease
- Appendix 2: Key Provisions of Operating a Wet Lease (ACMI).

## TYPES OF LEASES

A lease is an agreement whereby the lessor transfers to the lessee, in return for a payment or series of payments, the right to use an asset for a given period of time. The lease transfers ownership of the property to the lessee to the end of the lease term. Before the 1980s, many airlines chose purchase. By 1990, leasing had become far more popular, with approximately one half of the entire aircraft fleet under some form of lease. Leasing aircraft is also the most common way for start-up airlines to acquire aircraft. Before discussing specific types of leases, the basic terminologies surrounding an aircraft lease are:

- Lease: A lease takes place when the owner of an aircraft agrees to rent out the use of the aircraft to another party for a series of payments over a period of time.
- Lessor: The owner of the aircraft who leases the asset out to another party.
- Lessee: The party that rents the aircraft from the lessor for his/her own use.

In the airline industry, an airline is typically the lessee while a financial institution or third party corporation will be the lessor. However, this may not always be the case as airlines sometimes lease aircraft to another airline; therefore, understanding the correct terminology is important when understanding such a transaction.

A general classification for a lease depends on whether the asset is represented on the balance sheet or off the balance sheet. If the asset is an on-balance sheet item, it means the company carries the item on its balance sheet as an asset and must depreciate the asset over time. If the asset is an off-balance sheet item, the company does not record the asset on their balance sheet and does not have to record depreciation expense. However, rental payments will still appear on the income statement. There are both advantages and disadvantages to having an asset on the balance sheet. Having an asset on its balance sheet increases the value of assets and ultimately the value of the firm. Depreciation on the asset acts as a tax shield as the depreciation expense is deducted from operating income, reducing the taxable amount of income. However, as the asset side of the balance sheet increases so does the liability side. In order to carry the asset on the balance sheet, long-term liabilities, in the form of loans and notes, are needed to finance the asset and are held on the balance sheet. Therefore, an important factor in deciding whether to lease an aircraft, or the type of lease an airline wants to enter into, is whether or not the airline wants the aircraft to be on the balance sheet or off the balance sheet asset. There are empirical examples that show owning an aircraft is less costly than leasing; however, many airlines choose to lease aircraft for the following reasons:

- conservation of airline's working capital and credit capacity
- provisions of finance, that may include no deposits or pre-payments
- shifting risk to lessor (short term leases)
- no aircraft trading experience needed
- possibility to exclude lease finance from balance sheet
- volume discounts for aircraft purchase can be passed on to airlines.

### Wet Lease

A wet lease provides an airline with an aircraft and everything that is needed to operate the aircraft, including crew, maintenance and insurance for the aircraft. Typically called an ACMI lease (Aircraft, Crew, Maintenance, Insurance), the lessors are typically either specialized airlines or airlines with too much capacity. Wet leases typically are for a short period of time in order to provide the lessee with immediate capacity without fleet induction and training costs. In some circumstances, wet leases can extend for a period beyond a year owing to either political or labor restrictions. ACMI leases are just one type of wet lease, which can be customizable. For instance, the lessor may provide the flight crew for the aircraft; however, the cabin crew may be supplied by the lessee. Such a lease, where the cabin crews are not provided by the lessor, has on occasion been called a damp lease.

Airlines may require a wet lease for a host of reasons, such as:

- The aircraft is needed for a temporary (seasonal) capacity increase.
- The cost of acquiring a new aircraft is too great.
- The aircraft is needed in service before additional crew can be hired and trained.
- The airline is circumnavigating certain government regulations.
- One of the airline's aircraft is out of service for a period of time.
- The wet lease is cheaper than operating the aircraft themselves.

Seasonal increases in capacity are a common cause for wet leasing. For instance, during the winter there is a peak in demand for charter flights from Canada to sunny destinations in Mexico and the Caribbean. Since it may not be financially wise for Canadian charter airlines to acquire the aircraft and associated personnel for the entire year, aircraft can be wet leased for the winter period when demand is great and then have the lease end when demand falls off. While wet leasing an aircraft is probably more expensive for airlines than operating it themselves, if the aircraft is not in demand for eight months of the year, then it does not make financial sense to have that aircraft.

Certain onetime events may also be a potential reason for wet leasing an aircraft. Sporting events such as the World Cup, Super Bowl, or the Olympics could all potentially require an airline to wet lease additional aircraft to cope with the demand. Another common source of demand for wet leased aircraft is the Islamic Hajj, which is the annual pilgrimage to Mecca. Aircraft are wet leased from all over the world to support the annual influx of passengers into Saudi Arabia.

The cost of acquiring aircraft, and the necessary permits and certificates, can for some airlines be considerable; therefore some start-up airlines engage other airlines to operate flights on their behalf. One example of this could be Hooters Air, which used Pace Airlines to operate the flights under a wet lease agreement, even though the aircraft were painted in the Hooters Air color scheme.

Many times airlines are faced with the problem of lead time between when the airline wants the aircraft and when the airline can have the aircraft. Most of the time this is the result of delivery delays or order backlogs; however, crew training may also stall an airline from being able to operate a new aircraft type. In such scenarios, short-term wet leases can provide the immediate capacity while the airline gets up to speed to be able to operate the aircraft themselves. An example of this would be Turkish Airlines who wet leased B777-300ER aircraft from Jet Airways until they had sufficient crew to be able to operate the flights themselves.

Sometimes airlines receive government sanctions or restrictions on flying, such as the European Union's Airline Blacklist. If an airline is placed on the EU's blacklist, they are not permitted to operate flights to Europe, even if they operate flights within their own country/region. If the airline desires flights to Europe, they may wet lease aircraft from another airline to operate flights just to Europe where they cannot operate.

Sometimes airlines, particularly small carriers, will not have great fleet flexibility; therefore, when an aircraft goes out of service or is required to undergo heavy maintenance, the airline must wet lease an aircraft to keep the schedule intact.

Finally, airlines may wet lease aircraft as a result of the lease being cheaper. While this does not pertain to all agreements, sometimes regional airlines, while operating under capacity purchase agreements, operate aircraft on behalf of major airlines. As a result of contractual labor restrictions, such as pilot scope clauses, regional airlines can occasionally operate aircraft more cheaply than major carriers, and do so under the guise of a wet lease.

Airlines that wet lease aircraft fall into two categories: regular airlines with too much capacity or specialized ACMI airlines, such as Air Atlanta Icelandic. Air Atlanta Icelandic is a charter airline based in Iceland that specializes in wet leasing aircraft to other airlines (Aerospace Technology, 2008). Air Atlanta Icelandic leases different types of narrow- and wide-body aircraft to charter and scheduled airlines around the world. When an airline needs extra passenger or cargo capacity, they work out a lease agreement with Air Atlanta Icelandic or another airline to do some of their flying for them. Among Air Atlanta Icelandic's many contracts, the airline has extended wet lease agreement with Saudi Arabian Airlines for two B747-300 passenger until the end of 2009. Another example of an airline wet leasing aircraft owing to overcapacity is United Airlines which wet leases a Boeing 747-400 aircraft to Air Pacific to ensure that its schedule is maintained while one of the carrier's own aircraft undergoes refurbishment as part of a planned maintenance program.

## Sale and Leaseback/Leveraged Leases

From time to time airlines may decide to change their aircraft ownership structure, usually as a result of requiring immediate liquidity. Therefore, airlines will engage in a sale and leaseback transaction where the airline will sell an aircraft that they own to another party (lessor) and then lease the aircraft back from the lessor. As a result, an airline's ownership structure will shift to more leases. Because of the transaction, the airline will receive a cash inflow which will then be used to pay down the debt associated with the aircraft. If the sale value is greater than the amount of debt against the aircraft, the airline will receive a positive cash flow. For example, European tour operator and charter airline TUI Travel announced a $526 million deal with AerCap Holdings in 2008 to sell and leaseback 19 of its aircraft to pay down its debt (MoneyWeek, 2008).

A leveraged lease is a special type of leaseback transaction. A leveraged lease allows the leasing company to spread the cost of acquiring the aircraft over a seven year period (*The Economist*, 2005 May). This allows the leasing company to receive tax benefits from the reduction in net income from buying the aircraft for the first seven years of the lease rather than only in the first year. Combined with the tax benefits of interest on loans paid to finance the aircraft, a leveraged lease becomes a very attractive option to leasing companies.

For an airline, the sale and leaseback of the aircraft provides an infusion of cash which can be particular helpful in economic downturns. But why would a leasing company or other party agree to such an agreement? For leasing companies, they are provided with an asset and an established customer without having to buy a brand new aircraft, but still generate lease income from the airline. The leasing company believes it can make a profit through the interest received from lease payments and from the residual value of the aircraft at the end of the lease. The time value of money concept particularly applies here. The airline is willing to pay a premium, through the form of interest payments to the lessor, in order to have the cash from the sale of the aircraft today rather than some time in the future.

## Operating Lease

Aircraft can be leased for the long-term under two different types of leases; operating leases and capital leases. While aircraft leasing can be broadly placed into these two categories, aircraft leasing is a complicated process and there are numerous occasions that can make the leasing process more complicated since there are different types of leasing options and different tax laws under cross-border lease agreements. Under an operating lease, the airline (lessee) rents the use of an aircraft from the leasing company (lessor) for a period of time. Sometimes it is also called a service or maintenance lease since maintenance and insurance are usually included in the contract. The length of the contract between the leasing company and the airline is usually less than the useful life of the airplane. At the end of the contract the airline returns the aircraft to the lessor. The lessor can then either lease the aircraft to somebody else or sell the aircraft. Even while the aircraft is in the lessee's possession, the leasing company retains ownership of the aircraft. In summary, an operating lease is frequently used to acquire aircraft for a term of 2–7 years.

Because the lessor retains ownership of the aircraft, the airplane remains on the lessor's balance sheet. For the airline, the aircraft is an off-balance sheet asset as they do not own the aircraft. The only part of an operating lease that effects the financial statements of the airline is the rental expense that is recorded on the income statement for the payments the airline makes to the lessor. The airline does not receive the tax benefit associated with depreciation because the asset is not on their balance sheet and therefore does not have a depreciation expense.

The advantage of an operating lease for the airline is that there is less risk involved as the airline does not take full control of an asset. Under an operating lease, the lessor is usually responsible for insurance on the aircraft as the asset is bearing risk by being rented out and used by another company. The airline also has less economic risk because the operating lease is usually for a shorter term than the useful life of the aircraft. During economic downturns the aircraft can be returned to the leasing company either at the end of the lease or the airline could potentially terminate the lease for a penalty. Additionally, under bankruptcy protection, airlines typically renegotiate lower lease rates or are able to break lease contracts without penalty. Owing to the cost of fuel in 2008, many airlines cut capacity by returning leased aircraft. U.S. Airways for example returned six 737s and four A320s, as well as canceling future leases for two wide-body A330s (Michaels, June 12, 2008). Another advantage of operating leases is that the airline does not run the risk of recording a loss on the aircraft's salvage value at the end of its useful life. If the estimated salvage value of the aircraft is $1 million but is only able to be salvaged for $700,000, a leasing company bears that loss and not the airline.

In return for the risk borne, the leasing company receives rent payments from the airline that are probably greater than the cost of interest payments associated with financing the aircraft. The leasing company also receives a tax benefit from any interest they are paying in order to finance the purchase of the aircraft from the manufacturer. In addition, the leasing company receives the tax shield from the expense of the aircraft's depreciation.

To summarize, the advantage of an operating lease is that the airline does not make long-term commitments. The disadvantage is that the lease price is not fixed in the long-term since the length of the lease is less than the life of the aircraft and could substantially increase in price in the future. When United Airlines filed for Chapter 11 bankruptcy protection, it showed $22.8 billion of assets and $21.2 billion of liabilities[1], and what was not included was $24.5 billion in non-cancellable operating-lease commitments, mostly for aircraft.

**Table 12.1     Operating lease characteristics**

| Item | Accounting action |
| --- | --- |
| Lessor's accounting treatment | On-balance sheet |
| Lessee's accounting treatment | Off-balance sheet |
| Interest in residual value | To lessor on-balance sheet |
| Cross-border | Frequently |
| Leveraged | Via lessor's balance sheet |
| Cancelable | Usually not, some lessor permit (in return for a fee) after a non-cancelable period |

## Financial (Capital) Lease

A financial, or capital, lease differs slightly from an operating lease in that the asset is carried on the balance sheet of the lessee, causing different tax implications. A financial lease acts as an alternative to debt financing an aircraft with a financial lease being non-cancelable and with the lessee usually responsible for maintenance, insurance, and property taxes. In essence, the lessee owns the aircraft, but still makes payments to the lessor as it acts as the financer of a loan. A financial lease is differentiated from an operating lease if the lease agreement has one of the following four conditions:

- The lessee takes ownership of the leased property by the time the lease terminates.
- The lease contains a bargain purchase option.
- The lease term is equal to 75% or more of the estimated economic life of the leased property.
- The present value of the minimum lease payments is equal to or more than 90% of the fair market value of the property.

If the lessee receives ownership of the asset or can purchase the asset at a heavily discounted cost at the end of the lease then the lease must be considered a financial lease (Hawkins, 1999). Similarly if the value of the lease is more than 90% of the fair market

---

1     Source: The Associated Press (2002, December 9)

value or the term of the lease is three-quarters of the useful life of the asset or longer, the lease is a capital lease. If any of these four conditions are met, the asset is "owned" by the lessee and the asset must be held on the company's balance sheet and depreciated over the asset's useful life. Unique difference of capital leases, when compared with operating leases are:

- The airline is considered owner of aircraft.
- The aircraft is shown as an asset on airline balance sheet.
- The payments are shown as a liability on the airline balance sheet.
- The airline is generally responsible for insurance, maintenance and other costs of ownership.
- The interest and depreciation tax benefits accrue to the airline.
- The lease term is usually near the useful life of the aircraft.
- The lease is usually not cancelable.
- The specifications of the aircraft are usually set by airline.
- The payout is usually near the cost of buying.

Why are airlines attracted to financial leases when they bear the risks of ownership that the lessor would have to bear under an operating lease? As mentioned, the aircraft is listed on the airline's balance sheet and as such, the airline receives the tax benefits of interest and depreciation expenses. In addition, the airline gets to specify the features and specifications of the aircraft, such as galley layout and engine choice which are customizable for the airline. Under operating leases, this level of customization usually does not occur; however, an airline could potentially "cherry pick" aircraft that are suited to them.

The following illustration depicts the effect on the balance sheet as the result of different aircraft acquisition methods (for ten Boeing 737-600, priced at $60,000,000 per aircraft).

**Balance Sheet**

**Aircraft purchased with debt (Airline owns the Aircraft)**

| Assets | | Liabilities | |
|---|---|---|---|
| Aircraft | $450,000,000 | Debt | $450,000,000 |
| Other Assets | $150,000,000 | Equity | $150,000,000 |
| Total Assets | $600,000,000 | Total | $600,000,000 |

**Capital Lease**

| | | | |
|---|---|---|---|
| Aircraft | $450,000,000 | Capital Lease | $450,000,000 |
| Other Assets | $150,000,000 | Equity | $150,000,000 |
| Total Assets | $600,000,000 | Total | $600,000,000 |

**Operating Lease**

| | | | |
|---|---|---|---|
| Aircraft | $0 | Debt | $0 |
| Other Assets | $150,000,000 | Equity | $150,000,000 |
| Total Assets | $600,000,000 | Total | $150,000,000 |

However, there are also disadvantages to a financial lease. The cost of the lease is likely to approach the cost of buying the aircraft as the length of the lease approaches the useful life of the aircraft. On the other hand, some aspects of a lease make the present value of the lease likely to be cheaper than a loan. Leasing companies may receive better terms from aircraft manufacturers than an airline can, owing to better credit ratings or discounts from manufacturers for buying in bulk. These savings may be passed on from the leasing company to the airline, thus making leasing a more attractive option for the airline than buying the aircraft outright. However, some of these savings may be tempered by the fact that the leasing company will look to pass on some of its risk, including the salvage value risk. The airline also has to take into account the fact that the long-term nature of a financial lease means that, unlike an operational lease, the aircraft cannot be returned if financial conditions worsen.

**Table 12.2     Financial lease characteristics**

| Item | Accounting action |
| --- | --- |
| Lessor's accounting treatment | Depending on the juristication concerned |
| Lessee's accounting treatment | On-balance sheet |
| Interest in residual value | Generally to lessor, sometimes shared |
| Cross-border | Commonly in order to tap in to tax incentives, or non-resident investors |
| Leveraged | Frequently, but tax laws make leveraged leasing uneconomic in many jurisdictions |
| Cancelable | Usually not, some lessor permit (in return for a fee) after a non-cancelable period |

## Cross-border Leases

A cross-border lease occurs when two parties from different countries agree to a lease agreement. The airline industry is an industry in which cross-border transactions occur quite frequently. This is mainly due to the global nature of the aviation industry and the prominence of many western leasing companies making cross-border leasing profitable for both leasing companies and foreign airlines. Cross-border leases are more complicated owing to differing tax laws between countries. However, sometimes these tax differences can be used to the advantage of the airline. For example, Aeroflot signed an agreement with Natexis Aircraft Finance in Europe to lease seven A321s in 2006 (Trade Finance, 2006 December). The agreement was achieved in large part owing to the tariffs Aeroflot would face if they bought a new non-Russian aircraft. By leasing the A321s, Aeroflot avoided paying the 42% tariff and was able to operate a western-built aircraft which they might feel is more fuel-efficient than Russian-built aircraft.

Cross-border leasing will continue to be popular both for airlines and leasing companies. Many tax-friendly jurisdictions such as Ireland, Singapore, and the Middle-Eastern region have attracted and retained aircraft leasing companies owing to their friendly leasing laws and extremely low corporate tax rates. As an example, Ireland has a corporate tax rate of 12.5%, as compared with that of 35% for the United States and the Irish tax rate allows for an eight year write off of assets (Airline Fleet). The U.S. MACRS systems currently allows for 7-year depreciation of assets and a 12-year straight line method for financial statements. In addition to these attractive tax rates, the passage of bilateral tax treaties has increased the ability of companies to utilize the benefits of cross-border leasing. In addition, Ireland has a wealth of knowledge and experience with regard to cross-border aircraft leasing. For instance, KPMG (an organization which specializes in international tax matters) has a large presence in Ireland that is specifically dedicated to the aircraft leasing industry (Airline Fleet). KPMG has also been involved in cross-border leasing since the early days of aircraft leasing and is considered to be the expert on the subject.

The following table illustrates the aircraft fleet ownership structure for different airlines from the U.S. and other countries. The table shows that different airlines have different strategies when it comes to leasing or owning aircraft. Brazilian airlines GOL and TAM, for example, lease all of their aircraft. In the U.S., U.S. Airways also has nearly all of its aircraft on lease. This high percentage could be due to a lack of capital available to finance the purchase of new aircraft and could be an overall indication of an airline's health. Other airlines, like Southwest and Ryanair, own a very high percentage of the aircraft they operate. About 35% of all jetliners are under a leasing contract and this percentage is likely to grow "as airlines and other customers look to expand without the commitment of buying aircraft" (*Wall Street Journal*, 2007). Later in this chapter we discuss the advantages and disadvantages of leasing and owning.

**Table 12.3    Airline fleet ownership structure**

| Airline | Aircraft Type | Owned | Lease | | |
|---------|---------------|-------|-----------|-----------|---------|
| | | | Operating | Financial | Unknown |
| Air Canada | A32X | 26 | 51 | 17 | 20 |
| | 767 | 11 | 18 | 6 | 6 |
| | 777 | 7 | 1 | - | - |
| | Embraer 175/190 | 57 | - | - | - |
| Alaska | 737 Classic | 9 | - | - | 28 |
| | 737NG | 66 | - | - | 7 |
| American | A300 | 10 | 24 | - | - |
| | 737NG | 67 | 10 | - | - |
| | 757 | 87 | 31 | 6 | - |
| | 767 | 50 | 12 | 11 | - |
| | 777 | 47 | - | - | - |
| | MD-80 | 126 | 107 | 67 | - |
| Continental | 737 Classic | 14 | - | - | 51 |
| | 737NG | 80 | - | - | 101 |
| | 757 | 24 | - | - | 34 |
| | 767 | 23 | - | - | 3 |
| | 777 | 8 | - | - | 12 |

**Table 12.3     *Continued***

| Airline | Aircraft Type | Owned | Lease | | |
|---|---|---|---|---|---|
| | | | Operating | Financial | Unknown |
| Delta/ Northwest | A32X | 96 | 30 | - | - |
| | A330 | 32 | - | - | - |
| | 737NG | 76 | - | - | - |
| | 747-400/-200F | 11 | 15 | - | - |
| | 757 | 108 | 49 | 35 | - |
| | 767 | 75 | 26 | - | - |
| | 777 | 10 | - | - | - |
| | DC-9 | 71 | - | - | - |
| | MD-88/MD-90 | 79 | 21 | 33 | - |
| GOL | Total Aircraft (737 Classic, 737NG, 767) | - | 84 | 28 | - |
| Ryanair | 737NG | 128 | - | - | 35 |
| Southwest | 737 Classic | 128 | 82 | - | - |
| | 737NG | 318 | - | 9 | - |
| TAM | A32X | - | 60 | 32 | - |
| | A330/A340 | - | 2 | 12 | - |
| | 767 | - | - | 2 | - |
| | Fokker 100 | - | 2 | - | - |
| | MD-11 | - | 3 | - | - |
| United | A32X | 79 | - | - | 73 |
| | 737 Classic | 18 | - | - | 28 |
| | 747-400 | 18 | - | - | 9 |
| | 757 | 32 | - | - | 65 |
| | 767 | 17 | - | - | 18 |
| | 777 | 45 | - | - | 7 |
| U.S. Airways | A32X | 31 | - | - | 180 |
| | A330 | 4 | - | - | 5 |
| | 737 Classic | - | - | - | 70 |
| | 757 | 3 | - | - | 36 |
| | 767 | - | - | - | 10 |
| | Embraer 190 | 25 | - | - | - |

*Sources*: 2007 Annual Report, 2008 10K or U.S. GAAP filing ex. Ryanair; Ryanair from FY2008 Annual Report.

## BUY VS. LEASE ANALYSIS

At the heart of any discussion on leasing is the question of whether an airline should lease or buy. As Table 12.3 above displays, airlines have divergent policies on aircraft leasing. Additionally, leasing policies vary by aircraft type within an airline's fleet. The buy versus lease decision is also common in everyday life as one must decide whether to lease or buy when shopping for a car. Airlines must make this decision on a much larger scale since the prices of new aircraft are in the millions of dollars. In order to understand the buy versus lease decision it is important to examine the benefits leasing holds for airlines.

Why airlines lease:

- Cheaper financing (through tax shield)
- Reduce the risks of asset ownership
- Implicit interest rates
- Maintenance may be included (operational lease)
- Convenience and flexibility
- Capital budgeting restrictions
- Financial statement effects.

In essence, all of these reasons above can be categorized into both cost and risk. In the area of cost, the lessee considers the cost of credit or the expense of income taxes (Eades, 1991). If cost is the primary factor in the buy versus lease decision and the interest rate is less or the tax benefit is greater for the lease, the airline will choose to lease. On the other end of the decision making process, if the airline is primarily worried about economic risk, it may decide to lease in order to have the flexibility to return the aircraft before the end of its useful life and to avoid salvage value risk.

In order to analyze the financial component of the buy versus lease decision, an approach comparing the net present value (NPV) of buying and leasing can be used. The NPV of buying and leasing can be examined by looking at all cash flows for each method of financing or by looking at the incremental cash flows (the difference between buying and leasing). If the net present value of the incremental cash flows is positive, buying the aircraft is the better financial option. If the NPV of incremental cash flows is a negative, the financial advantages of leasing outweigh aircraft ownership. Therefore, when comparing the overall NPV numbers of leasing and purchasing, the method with the higher NPV cost should be chosen.

To examine the decision of buying or leasing, consider an airline attempting to buy (through equity financing) or lease, a Boeing 737-800 that costs $65 million. Depreciation and maintenance expenses subtract from the airline's taxable income. The airline (lessee) receives the tax benefit of lease payments in an operating lease, but only receives the depreciation and maintenance tax savings if they purchase the aircraft. Assume the tax rate is 35%. In this example, assume maintenance costs are $2,000,000 per year. The aircraft is depreciated using the straight line method with an expected salvage value of 50% of the purchase price at the end of seven years. A depreciation schedule, using straight line depreciation, for ownership is shown in Table 12.4. The net present value of the cost of each method is examined from the airline's point of view using a discount rate of 12%, which is assumed to be the airline's cost of equity. The operating lease is for a seven-year period with payments for each year due at the end of the previous year.

**Table 12.4    Depreciation schedule for 737-800 under ownership**

| Year | Depreciation rate | Depreciation | Book value | Tax savings |
|------|-------------------|--------------|------------|-------------|
| 0 | | | $65,000,000 | |
| 1 | 7.14% | $4,642,857 | $60,357,143 | $1,625,000 |
| 2 | 7.14% | $4,642,857 | $55,714,286 | $1,625,000 |
| 3 | 7.14% | $4,642,857 | $51,071,429 | $1,625,000 |
| 4 | 7.14% | $4,642,857 | $46,428,571 | $1,625,000 |
| 5 | 7.14% | $4,642,857 | $41,785,714 | $1,625,000 |
| 6 | 7.14% | $4,642,857 | $37,142,857 | $1,625,000 |
| 7 | 7.14% | $4,642,857 | $32,500,000 | $1,625,000 |

From the two scenarios contained in Table 12.5, the operating lease option appears to be the most favorable and this is largely because aircraft ownership is hindered with additional costs, even with the tax shield benefit. Additionally, the original purchase price does not justify the cash flow savings over the lease option.

In both examples (lease or buy), any cost item that reduces profitability receives the tax shield benefit of 35% of the cost item. As a result of increased expenses, profitability is reduced; however, the exposure to taxes is also reduced (but only by 35%). Note that in the purchase option, the cash flow calculation excludes non-cash items such as depreciation expense; however, it does include the depreciation tax shield savings (Brigham and Ehrhardt, 2008).

In the above example, the aircraft was purchased through equity; however, most airlines have a higher portion of their capital structure as debt rather than equity and typically use debt to finance aircraft. Assuming the aircraft was purchased using debt would change the comparison since the interest on debt is tax deductible. Table 12.6 readdresses the buy versus lease decision, except that the aircraft is debt financed and an interest rate of 10% is assumed. The discount rate used in the calculation will be the after-tax cost of debt (10%) × (1-T).

From Table 12.6, and because of debt financing, the difference between buy versus lease is much closer; however, the net advantage of leasing is still $3,291,000. The major difference under the equity financing versus debt financing is in the discount rate used to lessen the cash flows. In the previous example, the discount rate was 12%, which was assumed to be the company's cost of equity. In the above example, the discount rate was the after-tax cost of debt, which was 6.5%. As a result of the smaller discount rate, the impact of the positive cash flow from the tax shield savings has a greater impact and can offset the net purchase price. However, debt financing is still higher than the leasing option for this example.

**Table 12.5    Lease versus equity financing NPV analysis (thousands of dollars)**

|  | Year 0 | Year 1 | Year 2 | Year 3 | Year 4 | Year 5 | Year 6 | Year 7 |
|---|---|---|---|---|---|---|---|---|
| **Cost of Owning (equity financing)** | | | | | | | | |
| Net purchase price | ($65,000) | | | | | | | |
| Maintenance cost | | ($2,000) | ($2,000) | ($2,000) | ($2,000) | ($2,000) | ($2,000) | ($2,000) |
| Maintenance tax savings | | $700 | $700 | $700 | $700 | $700 | $700 | $700 |
| Depreciation | | ($4,643) | ($4,643) | ($4,643) | ($4,643) | ($4,643) | ($4,643) | ($4,643) |
| Depreciation tax savings | | $1,625 | $1,625 | $1,625 | $1,625 | $1,625 | $1,625 | $1,625 |
| Residual value | | | | | | | | $32,500 |
| Residual value tax | | | | | | | | ($875) |
| Net cash flow | ($65,000) | $325 | $325 | $325 | $325 | $325 | $325 | $34,450 |
| Discounted cash flows | ($65,000) | $290 | $259 | $231 | $207 | $184 | $165 | $15,583 |
| NPV cost of owning | | | | | | | | ($48,080) |
| **Cost of Leasing (operating lease)** | | | | | | | | |
| Lease payment | ($10,000) | ($10,000) | ($10,000) | ($10,000) | ($10,000) | ($10,000) | ($10,000) | |
| Payment tax savings | $3,500 | $3,500 | $3,500 | $3,500 | $3,500 | $3,500 | $3,500 | |
| Net cash flow | ($6,500) | ($6,500) | ($6,500) | ($6,500) | ($6,500) | ($6,500) | ($6,500) | $0 |
| Discounted cash flows | ($6,500) | ($5,804) | ($5,182) | ($4,627) | ($4,131) | ($3,688) | ($3,293) | |
| NPV cost of leasing | | | | | | | | ($33,224) |
| **NAL** | | | | | | | | $14,856 |

Based on the above analysis the airline decides to the lease the Boeing 737-800 aircraft. However, what is the financial impact of the lease to the lessor and does the buying of an asset and then leasing that asset out to another party bring value to the lessor and its shareholders?

To examine the impact of leasing the aircraft to the lessor, a similar analysis is undertaken with the lease payments the airline paid in Tables 12.3 and 12.4 as the income for the lessor. The depreciation, maintenance costs and salvage value will be the same as the airline would incur if it was the owner of the aircraft. The leasing company can finance

**Table 12.6    Lease versus debt financing NPV analysis (thousands of dollars)**

|  | Year 0 | Year 1 | Year 2 | Year 3 | Year 4 | Year 5 | Year 6 | Year 7 |
|---|---|---|---|---|---|---|---|---|
| **Cost of Owning (debt financing)** | | | | | | | | |
| Net purchase price | ($65,000) | | | | | | | |
| Maintenance cost | | ($2,000) | ($2,000) | ($2,000) | ($2,000) | ($2,000) | ($2,000) | ($2,000) |
| Maintenance tax savings | | $700 | $700 | $700 | $700 | $700 | $700 | $700 |
| Depreciation | | ($4,643) | ($4,643) | ($4,643) | ($4,643) | ($4,643) | ($4,643) | ($4,643) |
| Depreciation tax savings | | $1,625 | $1,625 | $1,625 | $1,625 | $1,625 | $1,625 | $1,625 |
| Residual value | | | | | | | | $35,000 |
| Residual value tax | | | | | | | | ($875) |
| Net cash flow | ($65,000) | $325 | $325 | $325 | $325 | $325 | $325 | $34,450 |
| Discounted cash flows | ($65,000) | $305 | $287 | $269 | $253 | $237 | $223 | $22,169 |
| NPV cost of owning | | | | | | | | ($41,258) |
| **Cost of Leasing (operating lease)** | | | | | | | | |
| Lease payment | ($10,000) | ($10,000) | ($10,000) | ($10,000) | ($10,000) | ($10,000) | ($10,000) | |
| Payment tax savings | $3,500 | $3,500 | $3,500 | $3,500 | $3,500 | $3,500 | $3,500 | |
| Net cash flow | ($6,500) | ($6,500) | ($6,500) | ($6,500) | ($6,500) | ($6,500) | ($6,500) | $0 |
| Discounted cash flows | ($6,500) | ($6,103) | ($5,731) | ($5,381) | ($5,053) | ($4,744) | ($4,455) | |
| NPV cost of leasing | | | | | | | | ($37,967) |
| **NAL** | | | | | | | | $3,291 |

the purchase of the aircraft through bonds with an interest rate of 7%. The company's tax rate is 35%, making the after-tax cost of debt 4.55% [7% × (1-T)].

Using the after-tax cost of debt as the discount rate, the operational lease has a net present value of $686,000 for the leasing company because of the lessor's lower financing costs. Leasing companies generally have a better credit rating than airlines since they largely act as banks; therefore, leasing companies can finance the purchase of an aircraft at a lower cost and pass some of this savings on to the airlines. The cost of debt savings that the leasing company does not pass on to the airline is the profit margin for the leasing company.

Because of the risk involved in owning assets and differences in credit ratings between airlines and leasing companies, there is a great potential for profit in the aircraft leasing industry. The increasing popularity for leased aircraft among airlines means that the leasing and financing of aircraft is a large and growing industry. However, leasing

**Table 12.7    Financial analysis from lessor's viewpoint**

| | Year 0 | Year 1 | Year 2 | Year 3 | Year 4 | Year 5 | Year 6 | Year 7 |
|---|---|---|---|---|---|---|---|---|
| **Value of Lease (thousands)** | | | | | | | | |
| Net purchase price | ($65,000) | | | | | | | |
| Maintenance cost | | ($2,000) | ($2,000) | ($2,000) | ($2,000) | ($2,000) | ($2,000) | ($2,000) |
| Maintenance tax savings | | $700 | $700 | $700 | $700 | $700 | $700 | $700 |
| Depreciation | | ($4,643) | ($4,643) | ($4,643) | ($4,643) | ($4,643) | ($4,643) | ($4,643) |
| Depreciation tax savings | | $1,625 | $1,625 | $1,625 | $1,625 | $1,625 | $1,625 | $1,625 |
| Lease payment | $10,000 | $10,000 | $10,000 | $10,000 | $10,000 | $10,000 | $10,000 | |
| Tax on lease payment | ($3,500) | ($3,500) | ($3,500) | ($3,500) | ($3,500) | ($3,500) | ($3,500) | |
| Residual value | | | | | | | | $35,000 |
| Residual value tax | | | | | | | | ($875) |
| Net cash flow | ($58,500) | $6,825 | $6,825 | $6,825 | $6,825 | $6,825 | $6,825 | $34,450 |
| Discounted cash flows | ($58,500) | $6,528 | $6,244 | $5,972 | $5,712 | $5,464 | $5,226 | $25,230 |
| NPV of lease | | | | | | | | $1,876 |

companies need to place aircraft with customers at profitable levels to generate income. Aircraft without customers are not earning revenue, while paying interest and tying up capital. Therefore, just like airlines, lessors will experience cyclicality in their business. Additionally, if the cost of capital rises for the lessors, they could find themselves in a less competitive position.

## MAJOR COMMERCIAL AIRCRAFT LEASING COMPANIES

There are several companies who lease aircraft to different clients all over the world. Aircraft leasing is an industry that deals with sizeable amounts of capital; therefore, many of the world's largest financial institutions are involved in aircraft leasing. Since leasing companies' main source of profitability growth is the expansion of their fleet, raising capital is extremely important to their success. Because of the large volume of capital needed, leasing companies must have exceptional relationships with financial institutions and an exemplary credit rating. The largest aircraft leasing companies include General Electric Commercial Aviation Services (GECAS), International Lease Finance Company and CIT Aerospace. In addition, in order to facilitate sales of their aircraft, Boeing and Airbus also have their own leasing divisions: Boeing Capital Corporation and Airbus Asset Management.

GECAS is a division of the General Electric Company and provides operating and financing leases to over 225 different airlines worldwide (General Electric Commercial Aviation Services, 2008). The commercial aviation services division offers A320s, A330s,

Boeing 737s, Boeing 767s, Boeing 777s, CRJ-700s and Embraer 170s. Since GE is also an engine manufacturer, the majority of the GECAS fleet is GE powered. Additionally, this provides GECAS with opportunities to bundle services together and can allow favorable lease terms to generate additional engine sales. In addition to passenger aircraft, GECAS also offers freighter aircraft for lease. An April 2008 deal with China Cargo Airlines gave the airline six Boeing 777 freighters and a sale leaseback agreement for six of the airline's MD-11 freighters (General Electric Commercial Aviation Services, 2008). Since it provides both passenger and cargo aircraft for lease, GECAS can quickly respond to growth in either sector. In addition to having cargo aircraft available for lease, GECAS also performs conversions on 737s and 767s to convert the aircraft from a passenger configuration to a cargo configuration or a mixed configuration. Much of GECAS success is tied to GE, which based on the parent company's current financial difficulty, makes obtaining capital at reasonable rates that much harder for GECAS.

International Lease Finance Company (ILFC) is another very large aircraft leasing company with a wide range of aircraft.[2] ILFC offers all of the commercial models from Boeing and Airbus in its fleet of nearly 1000 aircraft (ILFC, 2010). The company was founded in 1973 by Leslie and Louis Gonda along with Steven Hazy.[3] In 1990, American Insurance Group (AIG) purchased ILFC. The company believes that the large variety of aircraft available means that an airline can find exactly the right type of aircraft to fit their fleet needs by leasing through ILFC. The ILFC fleet is also one of the youngest in the world (International Lease Finance Company, 2008). This factor is more attractive to the airlines since it reduces the fuel costs through newer and more efficient aircraft. In addition to offering aircraft leasing and finance services, ILFC also offers risk management and insurance solutions. As with all leasing companies, ILFC's success is tied to being able to acquire attractive financing through AIG. However, with AIG's financial troubles, ILFC has been put up for sale.

CIT Aerospace is an up and coming company in the aircraft leasing industry. CIT offers regional jets from Bombardier and Embraer in addition to the standard fleet of Boeing and Airbus commercial aircraft. CIT leases its fleet of over 300 aircraft to over 100 different airlines around the world (CIT Aerospace 2010). CIT offers more than just leasing of aircraft, since it also offers many different types of loan and finance options to airlines. In addition to leasing and finance of aircraft, CIT also offers advisory services to airlines on financial issues and asset management (CIT Aerospace, 2010). Just as with the previous two companies, CIT Group has also faced financial difficulties, creating issues for CIT Aerospace.

Boeing and Airbus' leasing divisions take opposite approaches from each other. Boeing Capital Corporation works in much of the same way as a traditional aircraft leasing company like GECAS or ILFC. Boeing Capital Corporation offers operating and capital leases to airlines as well as working with third-party lenders, such as commercial banks and other financial institutions, to secure financing for aircraft purchases (Boeing Capital Corporation, 2009). By offering financial solutions to airlines for new aircraft, Boeing Capital works with the commercial aircraft division to ensure that Boeing continues to sell new airplanes. On the other hand, Airbus Asset Management works to maintain a high residual value of used Airbus aircraft and sells and leases these aircraft (Airbus S.A.S., 2009). By concentrating on the used aircraft market, Airbus Asset Management

---

2       www.ilfc.com
3       On February 3, 2010, Mr. Hazy informed the Chairman of the Board of the Company that he will retire as a director, effective from February 5, 2010.

attempts to increase Airbus' sales by entering the used aircraft market, a segment generally dominated by the traditional aircraft leasing companies. In addition to used aircraft sales and leasing, Airbus Asset Management works with airlines to develop financial and risk-management solutions.

DAE Capital is a new entrant in the aircraft leasing market. DAE Capital, part of state-controlled Dubai Aerospace Enterprise, placed orders for 228 Boeing and Airbus aircraft in 2007 (*Wall Street Journal*, 2007). This instantly brought DAE to the top ten of aircraft lessors with regard to value and fleet size. DAE was founded in Dubai in May 2007 and currently has a fleet of 36 single aisle and wide-body aircraft.[4]

Figure 12.1 displays the top 10 leasing companies by their fleet value. Note the considerable variation in fleet values between the top two companies and the rest of the survey. These results were derived from Airline Business' annual aircraft leasing survey and account for total aircraft in the fleet. These rankings will surely change as some of the larger aircraft orders placed by such companies as DAE are received into their fleet. Regardless of DAE's entry into the leasing market, it is clear that aircraft leasing is dominated by two companies: GECAS and ILFC. Such power in the leasing market enables both companies to have significant influence not only on airlines, but also aircraft manufacturers. One of the original design goals of the B787 was to be able to interchange engine types on the airframe. Such requirements were ultimately at the request of the aircraft lessors as this flexibility ultimately helps increase residual aircraft value.

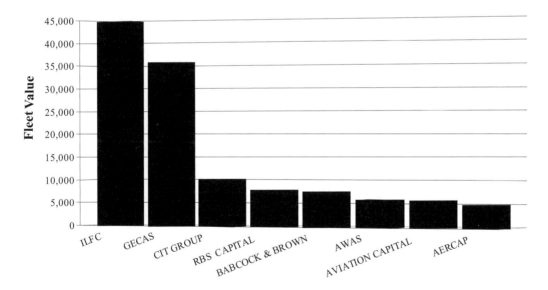

**Figure 12.1    Top ten aircraft leasing companies by fleet value (millions)**

Figure 12.2 displays the current size of each of the aircraft leasing companies that were displayed in Figure 12.1. It is interesting to note that, although the ILFC current fleet value is considerable higher than that of GECAS, the company currently has a significantly

---

4    United Arab Emirates, August 02, 2009.

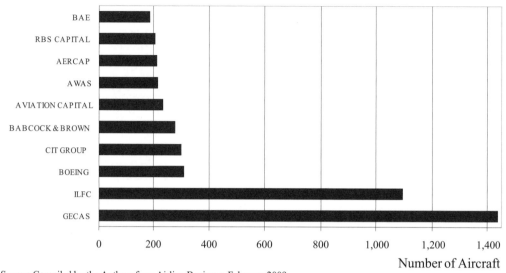

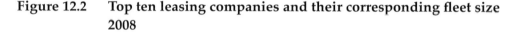

*Source*: Compiled by the Authors from Airline Business, February 2009.

**Figure 12.2    Top ten leasing companies and their corresponding fleet size 2008**

larger fleet size. It is expected that, with the development of emerging regions in the aircraft leasing market, the mix of companies in the top ten will change in the coming years. Established companies will probably be challenged by new entrants that are backed by financial entities with large amounts of capital.

Table 12.8 shows the top five narrowbody lessors by fleet value in 2009 which include narrowbody aircraft offered by Boeing and Airbus as well as regional jets. ILFC and GECAS are by far the leading leasing companies for narrowbodies in terms of value and fleet size, which is not surprising considering their overall size. Here again ILFC and GECAS "flip-flop" as one is larger based on aircraft value while the other is larger based on aircraft count. Based on this divergence, it could be stated the GECAS has a greater proportion of older aircraft in their portfolio.

Table 12.9 shows the top five widebody lessors by fleet value in 2008, which includes the Airbus A330, A340 and A380; Boeing B747, B767, B777 and B787; and the MD-11. ILFC and GECAS are the two leaders again, but for the widebody aircraft ILFC is by far the leading company with over $20 billion U.S.D. in leased aircraft value.

About 35% of all jetliners are under a leasing contract and this percentage is likely to grow (*Wall Street Journal*, 2007). This means that leasing companies are poised to grow in the future to meet the increasing demand from airlines for leased aircraft. It is also expected that more aircraft leasing companies will appear in China because of new banking regulations that now allow commercial banks to have financial leasing companies. In fact, the Bank of China has acquired a Singapore based leasing company and renamed it BOC Aviation. It will remain based in Singapore owing to the beneficial tax structure there. It remains to be seen how an economic powerhouse such as China will affect this truly global industry.

The value of the leased aircraft fleet, the number of units and the average value per aircraft unit are shown in Table 12.10 for the major aircraft manufacturers. Boeing and Airbus are by far the leading brands in leased aircraft for the medium and long haul. Boeing

**Table 12.8      Top narrow body lessors by fleet value (2009)**

| Rank | Company | Value (millions US$) | Number in fleet |
|------|---------|----------------------|-----------------|
| 1 | ILFC | 23,653 | 792 |
| 2 | GECAS | 21,800 | 956 |
| 3 | RBS Aviation Capital | 7,363 | 187 |
| 4 | CIT Group | 6,426 | 218 |
| 5 | Babock & Brown | 6,178 | 258 |

*Source*: *Airline Business*, July 2009.

**Table 12.9      Top wide body lessors by fleet value (2009)**

| Rank | Company | Value (millions US$) | Number in fleet |
|------|---------|----------------------|-----------------|
| 1 | ILFC | 21,034 | 300 |
| 2 | GECAS | 9,070 | 165 |
| 3 | CIT Group | 3,418 | 59 |
| 4 | AWAS | 2,605 | 54 |
| 5 | Aircastle | 2,208 | 39 |

*Source*: *Airline Business*, July 2009.

**Table 12.10      Leased mainline aircraft fleet by manufacturer (2008)**

| Manufacturer | Value (millions US$) | Fleet units | Average value (millions US$) |
|--------------|----------------------|-------------|------------------------------|
| Airbus | 62,576 | 1,821 | 34.4 |
| Boeing | 75,139 | 3,443 | 21.8 |
| Bombardier | 2,458 | 216 | 11 |
| Embraer | 2,959 | 146 | 20 |

*Source*: *Airline Business*, February 2008.

is leading in units while Airbus is leading in average value. The leading manufacturers for leased regional jets are Bombardier and Embraer.

The 2008 and 2009 economic crisis has profoundly affected the aircraft leasing industry. Many leasing companies are bracing for the imminent airline bankruptcies and consequently a glut of aircraft in the market. Crisis in the airline industry compounded with the lower government interest rates has significantly reduced the leasing rates and with it the returns to the leasing companies. As a solution, many of the lessees are restructuring their financing with the manufacturers and the banking sector. Aircraft manufacturers are willing to renegotiate the delivery and pre-delivery payments, since leasing clients conduct the majority of the aircraft purchases.

# SUMMARY

In this chapter we have examined the aircraft leasing market. Different types of aircraft leases, including operational and financial leases, were discussed. For any new aircraft acquisition, airlines are faced with the choice either to purchase the aircraft or lease the aircraft. When determining whether to lease or buy, an airline will examine the present value of cash flows of each method taking into account cost of debt and tax considerations. Leasing may have a lower cost than purchasing owing to the ability of leasing companies to raise capital at a lower cost than the airline can. Finally, we examined some of the major aircraft leasing companies and the different products and services they offer. This is an industry which is expected to continue to grow and expand worldwide, especially as more countries change their legislation regarding finance-leasing companies.

# DISCUSSION QUESTIONS

1. What is the difference between a wet lease, an operating lease and a financial lease?
2. Assume that both EZjET and DirectJet are practically identical airlines. The only difference between the two airlines is that EZjET leases most of its aircraft whereas DirectJet owns its aircraft and finances it by debt. Compare and contrast their balance sheets.
3. Why might an airline be interested in lease aircraft?
4. Explain why an airline may be interested in an aircraft sales and leaseback provision.
5. Provide at least three reasons for the attractiveness of leasing in the airline industry.
6. Explain the responsibilities and function of the lessee and lessor in an aircraft lease agreement.
7. Jet bridges are being manufactured and have been installed at many airports around the world. DirectJet is considering whether to borrow money and purchase the jet bridge or to lease it from the manufacturer under an operating lease agreement. If the airline purchases the jet bridge, the cost will be $500,000. DirectJet can borrow funds for four years at 10% interest. The airline uses the three year MACRS depreciation and has a 38% tax rate. The alternative is to sign an operating lease agreement for annual payments of $100,000 for the first two years and $200,000 for the last two years. Compute the:
   a. after-tax cost of the operating lease agreement.
   b. present value of the alternatives after tax.
   c. annual payments for the loan.
   d. amortization schedule for the loan.
8. DirectJet is evaluating a lease agreement for an aircraft push truck that costs $150,000 and falls into the MACRS 5-year class and is in 35% tax bracket. DirectJet can borrow the money at 8% and amortize the loan over the 6-year period if it decides to borrow money and buy rather than lease the truck. The loan payments would be made at the end of the year. The truck has a 6-year economic life, and its estimated residual value is $70,000. If DJ buys the push truck, it would purchase a maintenance contract that costs $3,500 per year, payable at the end of each year. The lease terms, which include maintenance, call for a $35,000 lease payment at the beginning of each year. Should DirectJet buy or lease?
9. Discuss how different tax rates between lessor and lessees might promote leasing.

# APPENDIX 1: KEY PROVISIONS OF OPERATING LEASE

*Key Provisions of Operating Lease*[5]

1. Offer to Lease Aircraft
2. Names of Lessor and Lessee
3. Aircraft Type, Model, Engines, Configuration
4. Monthly Rent
5. Term of Lease
6. Delivery Date
7. Deposits
    a. Booking and Lock Out Agreement
    b. Refundable, Interest, Escrow or Comingled with Operating Funds
    c. Term
8. Security Deposit
9. Representations
10. Delivery Conditions
    a. Fresh from C-Check (Zero Hours)
    b. Delays?
    c. Positioning Costs
    d. Inspection of Records, aircraft and test flight
11. Registration Requirements
12. Insurance Minimums
13. Indemnities and Warranties
14. Maintenance Issues
    a. Hour/Cycle Ratio
    b. Maintenance Program to be used—MPD compliant
        i. Line Maintenance, Base Maintenance
        ii. In-House or Outsourced
        iii. FAA/CAA Type Certification
        iv. Outsource Maintenance Provider Delegated Duty in Contract
    c. AD/SB compliance
        i. Lessor Responsibilities/Lessee Responsibilities
        ii. Costs and Payment
    d. Records and Logs—Back to Birth Traceability
    e. Maintenance Reserves
        i. Airframe, Engines, Landing Gear, APU, LLP
        ii. Lessee Pay? Escrow?
15. Lessor Inspections During Term of Lease
16. Changes During Lease Term
17. Redelivery
    a. Condition
    b. Location
    c. AD/SB Compliance
    d. No defects
    e. Return of Records

---

5    Jamie Baldwin, J.D., 2009.

18.   Governing Law
19.   Dispute Arbitration—IATA Procedures
20.   Events of Default and Remedies
21.   Lessor/Lessee Contact Details
22.   Expiration of Offer and Mode of Acceptance
23.   "Subject to Contract"
24.   Signature Blocks.

## APPENDIX 2: KEY PROVISIONS OF OPERATING A WET LEASE (ACMI)

*Key Provisions of Operating a Wet Lease (ACMI)*[6]

1. Offer to Lease Aircraft
2. Names of Lessor and Lessee
3. Aircraft Type, Model, Engines, Configuration
4. Block Hour Rate
    a. Summer Rate/Winter Rate
    b. Payment Terms
5. Minimum Guaranteed Block Hours and Hourly Cost Per Hour Above Minimum
6. Hour/Cycle Ratio
    a. Additional Cost if fall below ratio
7. Term of Lease
8. Delivery Date and Location
    a. Positioning Costs
9. Deposits
    a. Booking and Lock Out Agreement
    b. Refundable, Interest, Escrow or Comingled with Operating Funds
    c. Term
10. Security Deposit
11. Representations
12. Lessor To Provide
    a. Aircraft
    b. Cockpit Crew (number of sets)
    c. Cabin Crew (number of sets)
    d. Engineers/Maintenance Personnel
    e. Aircraft Maintenance
    f. Insurance for hull, aircraft, third party
    g. Company Representative at Lessee Base
    h. Galley Equipment
13. Lessee To Provide
    a. Landing, Parking and Airport Fees
    b. Navigation and Overflight Charges
    c. Flight Plans, Charts
    d. Fuel, Oil, Lubricants
    e. Ground Handling in accordance with IATA Ground Handling Agreement
    f. Aircraft Interior and Exterior Cleaning
    g. Additional Cabin Crew required by Lessee
    h. Crew Hotel Accommodation at night stops in accordance with Lessor Standards
    i. Crew Accommodation at Lessee Base in accordance with Lessor Standards
    j. Crew Transportation
    k. Crew Per Diem
    l. Crew Home Travel Leave
    m. Crew Positioning

---

6    Jamie Baldwin, J.D., 2009.

    n.    Passenger, Cargo, War Risk Insurance
    o.    Airfreight of Spare Parts
    p.    Customs Clearance
    q.    Government Taxes
    r.    Security Passes, Visas, Work Permits, Airport Passes
    s.    Office Space for Lessor with Communications Facilities at Lessee Base
    t.    Storage Space for Spare Parts
    u.    Hanger to Carry Out Maintenance
    v.    Costs for Lessor Crew Training of Lessee Crew
14. Livery Provisions (delivery/redelivery)
15. Registration Requirements
16. Insurance Minimums
17. Indemnities and Warranties
18. Redelivery Date and Location
    a.    Costs
19. Governing Law
20. Dispute Arbitration—IATA Procedures
21. Events of Default and Remedies
22. Lessor/Lessee Contact Details
23. Expiration of Offer and Mode of Acceptance
24. "Subject to Contract"
25. Signature Blocks.

# REFERENCES

Aerospace Technology (2008). Air Atlanta Icelandic-Aircraft wet lease B737, B747, B757, B767, A300 and A310. SPG Media Limited. Retrieved June 26, 2008 from http://www.aerospace-technology.com/contractors/leasing/air_atlanta/

Airbus S.A.S. (2008). Managing the Airbus portfolio. Retrieved July 2, 2008 from http://www.airbus.com/en/services/asset/

Bianchi, S. and D. Michaels (2007, November 20). "Dubai Jump-Starts Aerospace Ambitions; State-Controlled Firm Buys 228 Jets to Lease, Move Could Prove Costly". *Wall Street Journal*, p. A12.

Boeing Capital Corporation (2008). Aircraft financial services. Retrieved July 2, 2008 from http://www.boeing.com/bcc/sitemap/af.html

Brigham, E. and M.Ehrhardt (2008). *Financial Management: Theory and practice* (12th). Thomson Learning.

Center for Asia Pacific Aviation (2007). Air Malta wet-leases A320s to Etihad Airways. Retrieved June 26, 2008 from http://middleeastaviation.aero/news/index.php?option=com_content&task=view&id=4714&Itemid=59

CIT Aerospace (2007). Products and Services for the Aerospace Industry. Retrieved July 2, 2008 from http://www.citaerospace.com/CF/Products.aspx

Dubai Aerospace Enterprise (2008). http://www.dubaiaerospace.com/portal/HOME/tabid/100/Default.aspx.

Eades, K. (1991). *Burlington Northern Railroad Company: Equipment leasing*. (Report No. UVA-F-0969). Charlottesville, VA: University of Virginia Darden School Foundation.

General Electric Commercial Aviation Services (2008). Commercial aircraft leasing and financing. Retrieved July 2, 2008 from http://www.gecas.com/commercial.asp

Hawkins, D. (1999). *Lease accounting and analysis*. (Report No. 9-100-003). Boston, MA: Harvard Business School Publishing.

International Air Transport Association (2007). *Airline Finance & Accounting Management*. International Air Transport Association, Montreal.

International Lease Finance Company (2008). http://www.ilfc.com/introduction.htm.

Joyce I, and J. Wilding, (2008, February). "Top 50 Leasing Survey". *Airline Business*. p. 44.

Michaels, J. (2008, June 12). More Capacity Cuts at U.S. Airways. Aviation Week. Retrieved June 23, 2008 from http://www.aviationweek.com/aw/generic/story_channel.jsp?channel=comm&id=news/USCUT06128.xml

MoneyWeek (2008). TUI in sale and leaseback deal. Retrieved June 26, 2008 from http://www.moneyweek.com/file/49186/tui-in-sale-and-leaseback-deal.html

*The Economist* (2005, May). Business: Flying on empty; Aviation in America. 375 (8427), 73. Retrieved September 10, 2008, from ABI/INFORM Global database.

*Trade Finance* (2006, December). Time to release the brakes. Trade Finance, 38–40. Retrieved September 10, 2008, from ABI/INFORM Global database.

# 13

# Aviation Industry Valuation

"Using the "per-enplaned passenger basis," an industry rule of thumb that ties the value of an airport to the number of passengers it serves each year, the potential worth of the top 71 U.S. airports falls somewhere between $90 billion and $100 billion."

Ronald D. Utt, Ph.D., Heritage Foundation

The growth of air transportation around the world is remarkable considering the various random shocks which the industry has been subjected to. Air transportation plays an important role in economic prosperity and progress. According to Airports Council International (ACI), the number of passengers is expected to grow by an average of more than 4% per year over the next 20 years. By putting all of the previous topics together, the valuation of the various parts of the aviation industry (i.e. airlines, airports, and aircraft) can be accomplished. Since aircraft and airports are high-value assets, the valuation of each can have significant financial impacts on the aviation industry. This chapter presents the various factors that affect valuation in the aviation industry, and provides a method for forecasting the future value of differing aviation entities. The following topics are covered in the chapter:

- Commercial Airport Systems
  - U.S. Commercial Airport System
  - Canadian Commercial Airport System
  - European Commercial Airport System
  - Airport and Airline Financial Agreements
- Aviation Infrastructure Privatization and Methods to Accomplish It
  - Full or Partial Divesture
  - Contracting Out
  - Contract Management and Long-Term Lease
- Airport Valuation
- Aircraft Valuation
  - Aircraft Valuation Model
- Summary
- Discussion Questions.

This chapter covers the valuation of physical assets. This is an especially critical topic in aviation finance because of the pervasiveness of government control of the major aspects of the air transport industry, including, but not limited to, airports, air traffic control, some specific airlines, and most significantly, international airline routes. While there is a reasonably robust market for aircraft, the purchase of aircraft is still an extremely expensive capital expenditure decision; hence, the valuation of aircraft is critical in determining fair asset value and projected salvage value. This fact, together with the government ownership of airports in most major countries and the resultant nonexistence of any formal market for these resources, means that there are generally no good market benchmarks for these specialized assets. Added to this we have the present tendency of governments in many countries to privatize either these assets or the aviation infrastructure or both , and the question of the value of the resources becomes even more critical. Therefore, it would be helpful to develop a theoretical model or technique to approximate the value of the resources as, at the very least, a starting point for any market transfer of the resources. The chapter covers some of the more important models and techniques for valuation of resources in the aviation industry.

## COMMERCIAL AIRPORT SYSTEMS

Airports are crucial for the well-being of the global economy since air transportation is an important indicator of the economic situation of, not only various countries or regions, but the entire global economy. Figure 13.1 depicts the global distribution of passengers by region worldwide. This information is based upon the Airports Council International (ACI) report for the first four months of 2009. As is evident from Figure 13.1, North America currently has the highest percentage of passengers for the four months of 2009; however, it is not the highest growth region. Instead, the Middle East has had by far the highest growth rate over 2008 at 5.8%, followed by Africa at 4.8% and Asia Pacific at 1.2%. Just like the overall economy, these growth rates illustrate that areas like North America have already experienced their high growth rates and are mature industries, while Asia and the Middle East are experiencing higher growth rates that are expected to continue for the foreseeable future as the industry and economy grow in these regions.

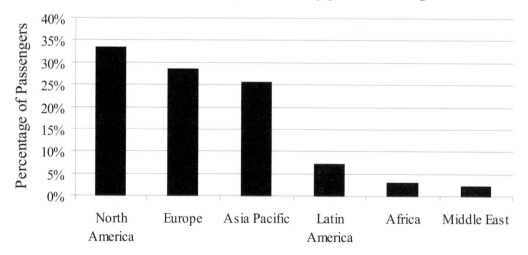

Source: ACI, 2009.

**Figure 13.1    Percentage of passenger volume by region, April 2009**

Figure 13.2 compares the world's distribution of aircraft movements by region. And, although North America once again has the highest percentage of aircraft movements, its growth rate for 2009 was negative. For this category, the Middle East had the highest growth rate, followed by the Asia Pacific region. These data also demonstrate the importance of air-transportation on a global scale, especially in developing regions of the world.

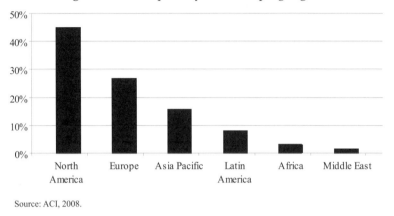

Source: ACI, 2008.

**Figure 13.2    Percentage of world aircraft movements, year to date April 2009**

The rapid growth in these regions of the world can also be seen by comparing the ten fastest growing airports in the world and, as reported by ACI, the vast majority of these airports are located in Asia. To illustrate, Figure 13.3 provides the top ten 2008 airport growth rates. Since growth at smaller airports can be misleading when comparing percentage improvements, these are the top ten fastest growing airports for 2008 that handle more than five million annual passengers. Airports that post large percentages of year over year growth normally mirror the economic performance of an area. This means that, in most cases, the surrounding geographic areas are also experiencing a significant increase in their economic performance. However, the soaring fuel prices in 2008 and the resulting decrease in capacity, could provide some distortion of the airport growth rates.

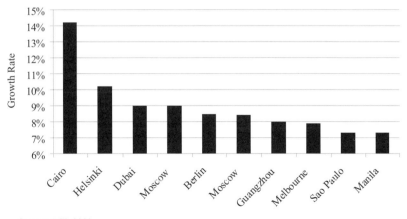

Source: ACI, 2008.

**Figure 13.3    Top ten fastest growing airports 2008**

Table 13.1 provides the top 15 airports by passenger movement for 2008. Among the 15 top airports, seven are found in the United States, which reaffirms the data in Figure 13.1 displaying North America as the largest aviation market in the world. The typical driver of passenger traffic is the economy; however, with the development of the hub and spoke system, airport traffic can be above what the local economy would generate. For instance, ATL, ORD, and DFW, are all hub airports with that being the primary reason for their inclusion in the top 15 worldwide airports.

**Table 13.1    Top 15 airports worldwide by passenger volume, 2008**

| Rank | City | Airport Code | Number of passengers |
|---|---|---|---|
| 1 | Atlanta | ATL | 90,039,000 |
| 2 | Chicago | ORD | 69,354,000 |
| 3 | London | LHR | 67,056,000 |
| 4 | Tokyo | HND | 66,736,000 |
| 5 | Paris | CDG | 60,852,000 |
| 6 | Los Angeles | LAX | 59,542,000 |
| 7 | Dallas/Fort Worth | DFW | 57,069,000 |
| 8 | Beijing | PEK | 55,662,000 |
| 9 | Frankfurt | FRA | 53,467,000 |
| 10 | Denver | DEN | 51,436,000 |
| 11 | Madrid | MAD | 50,823,000 |
| 12 | Hong Kong | HKG | 47,898,000 |
| 13 | New York | JFK | 47,790,000 |
| 14 | Amsterdam | AMS | 47,430,000 |
| 15 | Las Vegas | LAS | 44,075,000 |

*Source*: Compiled by the Authors using data from Airline Business June 2009.

## U.S. Commercial Airport Systems

The Federal Aviation Administration (FAA) classifies commercial airport systems in the U.S. using a number of different metrics. As part of the FAA classification system, the National Plan of Integrated Airport Systems (NPIAS) was developed to classify airports. The purpose of this report is to identify the airports which are of value to the aviation system in the U.S. and may therefore receive federal funding.[1] This classification is based on specific metrics that categorize airports for various purposes, some of which include the availability of funding from the federal government.[2] The NPIAS for 2009–2013

---

1    The funding is mainly based on the Airport Improvement Program (AIP).
2    NPIAS is compiled by the Department of Transportation and Federal Aviation Administration on a yearly basis. This report is a five-year forecast of the aviation system specifically from an airport perspective.

includes 3,411 airports out of the 5,190 airports that are currently open to the public in the U.S. (NPIAS 2009-2013). The NPIAS further classifies airports into subsets based upon their passenger enplanements with the two major categories being primary commercial service and non-primary commercial service airports. These categories contain 383 and 139 airports respectively. The 522 commercial service airports account for 100% of the annual enplanements, within the U.S. (NPIAS, 2009-2013). Based upon their number of annual emplaned passengers, the 383 primary commercial service airports are further broken down into the categories of large, medium, small, and non-hub airports. The FAA's definitions of large, medium and small hubs are as follows:

- Large hubs: Airports that account for 1% or more of the total enplanements within the U.S.
- Medium hubs: Airports that account for between 0.25% but less than 1% of the total U.S. enplanements.
- Small hubs: Airports that account for between 0.05% but less than 0.25% of total U.S. enplanements.
- Non-hubs: Airports that have at least 10,000 annual enplanements but less than 0.05% of the total U.S. enplanements.
- Non-Primary Commercial Service Airports: Airports that have 2,500 annual enplanements but less than 10,000.

Figure 13.4 lists the 30 large-hub airports for the year 2008. The results are based upon the FAA reports for the year 2008. As Figure 13.4 shows, even within the category of large-hub airports, there is still a large amount of variance between the largest Atlanta (ATL), with almost 6% of U.S. enplanements, and the smallest, Chicago Midway (MDW), with just slightly over 1% of U.S. enplanements for the observation period.

The distribution of the FAA airport classification is put into further perspective in Table 13.2. It displays the number of airports in each category based upon results filed by the FAA in the NPIAS. The data were compiled using 2008's operating results (FAA, 2009).

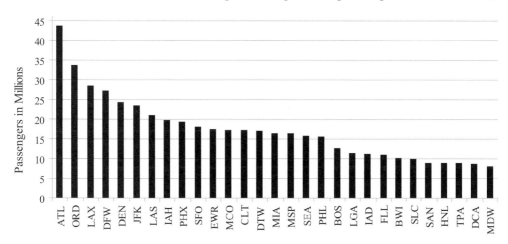

*Source*: Compiled by the Authors.

**Figure 13.4    U.S. enplanements: Large hub airports, 2008**

**Table 13.2    Number of U. S. airports within each classification**

| Airport type | Number of airports |
|---|---|
| Large hub | 30 |
| Medium hub | 37 |
| Small hub | 72 |
| Non-hub primary | 244 |
| Non-primary commercial service | 139 |
| Total | 522 |

*Source*: Compiled by the Authors using data from NPIAS 2009-2013.

## Canadian Commercial Airport Systems

Similar to that of the United States, airports in Canada are broken into categories based upon their operating status and geographic locations. Listed in descending order, the categories are as follows: National Airports Systems (NAS), Regional / Local Airports, Small Airports, and Arctic Airports.

The airport ownership structure in Canada is unique and innovative when compared with that of other large western countries. In Canada the government retains ownership of the 26 largest airports and these 26 airports (known as the National Airport System or NAS) handle roughly 96% of all passenger and cargo. Although the government retains the ownership of these airports, their financial and operational management have been transferred to Canadian Airport Authorities (CAA's) on a long term basis. The CAA's are not-for-profit organizations with a board of directors and other requirements as set by the Canadian government (Transport Canada).[3] The idea behind this transfer is that it will shift responsibility for the airports away from taxpayers to the actual users of the airport (Transport Canada). This structure can be compared with long-term leases because the government still retains ownership of these airports. However, the operation of the airport is given to the actual users of the system who provide the funding through various revenue sources (i.e. user fees).

## European Commercial Airport Systems

Europe is now a "test bed" of airport management techniques for the rest of the world. Several textbooks and papers have been published on the British Airport Authority (BAA); therefore, this textbook will only briefly discuss the BAA and instead focus on other systems around Europe. The discussion on European Commercial Airports is broken into two sub-categories:

- United Kingdom
- Continental Europe.

---

3    *The Journal of America Enterprise Institute*, December 5, 2008.

*United Kingdom* The vast majority of all major commercial service airports in the United Kingdom are under some form of privatization. The major example of this is the privatization of BAA airports which occurred in the 1980s and was followed by other airport groups. The BAA privatization serves as an example for the rest of the world and is discussed in later parts of this chapter.

To further highlight Britain's approach to aviation matters, the Civil Aviation Authority (CAA) was made into a government corporation in the 1970s and is completely funded by the aviation system (CAA). This means that the British taxpayers do not directly fund the air transport system in Britain. Instead, the actual users of the system fund it. The CAA is responsible for all economic oversight, airspace policy, safety regulation, and consumer protection of the air-transport system in Britain (CAA). This model has been applied by other countries, most notably by the Canada, where the users of the system also pay (instead of the public funding).

*Continental Europe* The Netherlands serves as another example of European airport privatization innovation. The unique approach to privatization taken in this country is that the various government organizations, both on the national and local levels, are the major shareholders here. This is further illustrated with the case of the Amsterdam Schiphol Airport that is covered later in the chapter. Table 13.3 shows the major European Airports by annual passengers for 2008.

In the following section a further description of the BAA and Amsterdam airport privatizations is given, as well as the reasons for privatization.

**Table 13.3     Top ten European airports by passenger volume, 2008**

| Rank | City | Airport Code | Number of Passengers |
|------|------|--------------|----------------------|
| 1 | London/Heathrow | LHR | 67,056,000 |
| 2 | Paris | CDG | 60,852,000 |
| 3 | Frankfurt | FRA | 53,467,000 |
| 4 | Madrid | MAD | 50,823,000 |
| 5 | Amsterdam | AMS | 47,430,000 |
| 6 | Rome | FCO | 35,133,000 |
| 7 | London/Gatwick | LGW | 34,214,000 |
| 8 | Barcelona | BCN | 30,196,000 |
| 9 | Paris | ORY | 26,208,000 |
| 10 | Dublin | DUB | 23,467,000 |

*Source*: Compiled by the Authors using data from Airline Business June 2009.

## Airport-airline Financial Agreements

As a result of the changing airline industry structure and diversification of operations, airport operators in the U.S. have begun to shift from residual cost to compensatory fee pricing structures. Under a residual cost approach, airport fees incurred by airlines are adjusted so as to allow the airport to fully recover its operating costs after subtracting landside revenues. Under such a structure the airlines bear the financial or equity risk of the airport. In contrast to the residual approach, a compensatory fee approach occurs when the airport fees incurred by the airlines are contractually established between the airport and airline. The compensatory approach tends to shift financial risk to the airport and not the airline. As such, improvements in operating efficiency or landside revenue benefit the airport. Residual agreements were typical during the era of airline regulation, with the first such agreement occurring between O'Hare International Airport (ORD) and United Airlines (Wells and Young, 2004). After deregulation, compensatory approaches have become common place in the United States.

This shift by airports from residual to compensatory agreements allows airport operators to profit from landside operations, while being adequately compensated for airside operations, thus enabling airports to be privatized. Furthermore, many examples of airport privatization provide support for the argument that divestiture can enhance the efficiency of airport operations (Truitt and Michael, 1996). Hamzaee and Vasigh (1998) show the benefits of privatization of airports in Western Europe, Latin America, and Asia. This may inspire officials in search of new economic opportunities to consider transforming airports from publicly run into private businesses. At the time of this publication, Chicago Midway Airport (MDW) was in the process of becoming the first large-hub airport in the U.S. to enter into a type of privatization under a form of a long-term lease agreement (Gilroy, 2008). Implementation of this process was expected to take some time; however, because of current federal regulations and global financial credit crunch, Midway's privatization plan collapsed.[4] The $2.5 billion, 99-year lease agreement for Midway Airport fell apart since private investors could not raise the necessary money and the Midway deal was never approved by the FAA.[5]

## AIRPORT INFRASTRUCTURE PRIVATIZATION

The increasing capital needed to build and maintain commercial airports has created pressure on the public sector to relinquish control and ownership of these airports to the private sector. Governments are increasingly turning to the private sectors for its efficiency in managing the operation, financing, and development, as well as providing security for airports.

Privatization is now much more common around the world, with the initial wave of airport privatization having started in England.

In 1987 the British government privatized its seven major airports when it offered British Airport Authority (BAA) to the public for $2.5 billion. Attracted by the positive results from the UK model, the trend of airport privatization migrated to other countries. Austria's Vienna Airport was listed on the Vienna Stock Exchange in 1992.

Since then, many airports have been privatized. In Europe, airports such as Belfast, Brussels, Budapest, Copenhagen, Dusseldorf, Frankfurt, Hamburg, and Rome, have been privatized. In Latin America many countries, such as Argentina, Chile, Colombia, and

---

4       Associated Press, April 21, 2009.
5       The Huffington Post, April 9, 2009.

Mexico, have privatized their airports. Asia-Pacific has also been engaged in privatization with airports such as Auckland, Brisbane, Melbourne, and Sydney.[6]

In 1994 two Danish Airports were privatized as Copenhagen Airports Ltd. and listed on the Copenhagen Stock exchange. In both of these examples, the respective government sold slightly less than 50% of the shares to the private sector (Poole, 1999). In Italy the Leonardo Consortium won the bidding process to become the major shareholder of Aeroporti di Roma. This airport had previously been privatized and was being publicly traded (Airports International, 2000). Since this time, Macquarie Airports have bought and sold 45% of the airport, with the major shareholder now being the firm Gemina SpA (Gilroy, 2008).

The Schiphol Group controls and operates the Amsterdam Schiphol Airport, Rotterdam, Eindhoven, and Lelystand Airports. The Schiphol Group's major shareholders are comprised of the following entities: the State of Netherlands, the City of Amsterdam, and the city of Rotterdam, with respectively 75.8%, 21.8%, and 2.4% of ownership shares (Schiphol). The Schiphol Group's alliance partner, the Frankfurt Airport Company (FAC), currently named Fraport Worldwide, was fully privatized in June 2001 through the initial public offering of its shares. According to the latest Reason Foundation report, Fraport has annual revenue in excess of $2.8 billion. To put this amount in perspective, Grupo Ferrovial (the current owners of the BAA) has annual revenues in excess of $5.3 billion (Gilroy, 2008).

Australia has privatized the three major airports of Brisbane, Perth, and Melbourne. The plan was initiated in July 1997 as the Federal Airport Cooperation offered the sale of long-term leases (Forsyth, 1997). These leases are for a term of 99 years. These three airports are some of Australia's busiest and were leased for a combined AU $3.337 billion (Cook, 1997). Flughafen Frankfurt/Main AG and its alliance partner, Schiphol Group, acquired the long-term lease for the Brisbane airport, the first instance of these two firms working together (Financial Times, 2000). The privatization of the Sydney Kingsford Smith International Airport was also completed through the sale of a 99-year lease for $3.1 billion (Rimmer, 2002). Melbourne airport was leased for AU $1.3 billion to a consortium headed by the then British Airport Authority (BAA) (Daily Deal, 2002). In addition to the privatization of the original Australian airports, the privatization of the Sydney Kingsford Smith International Airport was also completed through the sale of a 99-year lease for $3.1 billion (Rimmer, 2002). Like its neighbor Australia, New Zealand has also privatized its major airports. The methods through which New Zealand has privatized its airports are different, however, from those of Australia. For instance, New Zealand, instead of using long-term leases, has sold large stakes of its airports (Gilroy, 2008).

Malaysia has begun the process of airport privatization and it is the first Asian country to do so. Other privatization efforts are also under way in other various Asian countries. The Omani government is evaluating the privatization of two major airports (Air Finances Journal, 1999). China is also involved with airport privatization and has even allowed outside firms to participate in such ventures. Xi'an Airport is a Chinese airport which is already fully privatized (Gilroy, 2008). According to the 2008 Annual Privatization report by the Reason Foundation, Fraport has a 24.5% stake in Xi'an Airport and is responsible for airport operations and commercial development at that airport.

---

6    Reason Foundation, January, 2001.

In Mexico, Grupo Aeroportuario del Sureste,[7] has operated nine Mexican airports since early 1998, and is a publically traded company on the New York Stock Exchange under the symbol ASR. ASR's portfolio includes the following airports: Cancun, Cozumel, Huatulco, Merida, Minatitlan, Oaxaca, Tapachula, Veracruz, and Villahermosa Airports. The three other major Mexican Airport Companies are OMA GAP, and ASUR. These airports are concentrated by geographic region, with OMA airports in the central and northern regions, while GAP is in the pacific region, and ASUR are in the southeastern region (Gilroy, 2008).

In early 1999 the Santiago International Arturio Benitez Airport in Chile was privatized with a 15-year management concession to SCL Aeropuerto de Santiago and this company has a number of large shareholders. Argentina also awarded a 30-year operating license to a consortium led by U.S. based Ogden Aviation Group (Ogden Corporation, 1999) for 33 of Argentine's airports although these airports are still currently under the control of Aeropuertos Argentina 2000. Elsewhere in Latin America, Peru's Lima's Jorge Chavez International Airport was under the ownership of Fraport which increased its ownership share from 42.7% to 100% (Gilroy, 2008).

However, airport privatization is not always successful. Stewart International Airport in Newburgh, N.Y., was operated by the UK-based National Express Group. Because the airport did not generate acceptable revenue, the lease was sold to the Port Authority of New York and New Jersey. British Airports Authority's lease was not extended with the Indianapolis International Airport because the airport argued that it paid the British firm $21 million to bring brand-name stores and restaurants to a terminal and this was not done.[8]

## PRIVATIZATION TECHNIQUES

There are several different approaches to airport privatization. These approaches differ in the degree to which control and ownership is relinquished. Generally, one can differentiate among the following forms:

- full divestiture and sale of shares
- contracting out
- contract management and long-term lease.

### Full or Partial Divestiture and Sale of Shares

With this method, government transfers the ownership of the airport along with management and investment responsibilities to private owners. This can be achieved through full or partial divestiture. Full divestiture allows the government to generate funds while transferring operational responsibilities to the private sector. However, the sale of the airport may limit the possibility of future state or government intervention (The World Bank, 1996).[9] Partial divestiture allows for the possibility of government intervention in the future if necessary. The best known example of full divestiture is the privatization of

---

7    S.A.B. de C.V. (ASUR).
8    C. O'Malley, Indianapolis Business Journal, Monday, July 23 2007.
9    The World Bank, Note No. 82, June 1996.

the British Airport Authority through the creation of BAA PLC and the sale of its shares to the private sector. In 2006, BAA was acquired by the Spanish firm Grupo Ferrovial and renamed BAA Limited (BAA), for over $15.57 billion (10 billion pounds). BAA owns and operates seven UK airports, including London Heathrow, Gatwick, Stansted, Southampton, Aberdeen, Edinburgh, and Glasgow. Now, Britain's Competition Commission is forcing BAA to sell three of its U.K. airports, including Gatwick and Stansted, and Scotland's Edinburgh airports, by arguing that BAA's monopoly power is hurting airlines and their passengers.[10] Britain's Manchester Airport Group, Germany's Fraport, as well as Virgin Atlantic, have all said they will consider a bid for Gatwick.[11] The privatization of Vienna International Airport and Copenhagen are also examples of full or partial divestiture.

## Contracting Out

This is a traditional tool to privatize state-owned enterprises and to relinquish public control. It involves contracting out for the provision of selected services such as restaurants, parking, security services, cargo, baggage handling, fueling services, and so on. In addition, governments establish business policies and negotiate contracts with private firms to provide selected services. This privatization technique has been applied at the airports managed by the U.S. division of BAA (now Grupo Ferrovial). In addition, BAA's U.S. division (BAA U.S.A.) has developed the AIRMALL concept and uses this to manage retail development at airports including Pittsburgh International, Boston Logan, and Baltimore-Washington (BAA U.S.A., 2008).

## Contract Management and Long-term Lease

The third tool for airport privatization is involvement of the private sector in management contracts, where the state retains the ownership and investment responsibilities. Several United States airports currently are operated under management contracts. These include Westchester County Airport and Albany County Airport in New York and Sanford-Orlando International Airport. In the case of Orlando-Sandford, TBI Management Co. handles the operations within the terminal building. The management contract model is attractive because it reduces government's involvement in the day-to-day functioning of the airport, yet allows it to retain ultimate control over the airport's operation. In this case, the state retains ownership and investment responsibility, and the private sector is responsible only for operations and implementation of managerial strategies.

Under long-term leases, the government can turn over operations and management as well as investment responsibilities. Examples of this privatization model are the three Australian airports of Brisbane, Melbourne, and Perth, and various airports in Argentina. Stewart International Airport in New York operated under this model as well until the NY/NJ Port Authority bought out the remaining years of its 99-year lease in 2007 (The Port Authority of NY/NJ, 2007, November). Under a long-term lease agreement the airport operator may be responsible for financing the construction of the airport but must relinquish control at the end of the lease term. The main objective for a government is to

---

10    Ferrovial's BAA must sell 3 airports, Reuters, August 20, 2008.
11    Reuters, December 17, 2009.

increase funding while at the same time transferring operational responsibilities. Build-Operate-Transfer (B.O.T) is a commonly used technique for designing and constructing a complete project such as an airport, power plant, and seaport. A variation of this is Build-Own-Operate and Transfer (B.O.O.T). In addition, there is also Build-Own-Operate (B.O.O), where the private sector is not only responsible for current investments but is also is in charge of financing the construction of the airport. Amman is planning to privatize the Kingdom's airports. The contract is expected to be based on a BOT or BOOT.

Also, the lack of private ownership may impose difficulties in raising and investing large amounts of capital from the private sector. Instead, partnerships between local government and private enterprise may be developed. Several examples of this type of public-private partnership already exist in the United States, including airports in Atlantic City and Morristown, New Jersey (Atlantic City International Airport, 2008).

## AIRPORT VALUATION

Two general methodologies are commonly used for estimating the enterprise value of a firm. The first is a "direct valuation" approach, which provides an estimate of firm value based upon the cash flows the firm is expected to generate. The second is a "relative valuation" approach in which value estimates of the company are obtained by examining the price of comparable firms. This approach involves applying a market-based multiple to an accounting measure of profit to secure a value estimate.[12]

Financial theory recognizes the superiority of the "direct valuation" approach, commonly referred to as the discounted cash flow (DCF) model. Common variations of DCF include the dividend discount model (DDM) and the residual income model (RIM). These models involve a present value computation of forecasted future cash flows (e.g. dividends, earnings, etc.). Accordingly, these models derive estimated enterprise value from the economic value to be generated and received by the purchaser of the firm. On the other hand, "relative valuation" methodologies tend to be based upon historical accounting measures, and ignore differences in accounting methodologies and future prospects between the firms.

DCF valuation begins with a forecast of future cash flows to be generated by the firm or asset under consideration. For purposes of valuing an operating entity such as an airport, the appropriate cash flows to consider include operating revenue, operating expenses, and incremental investments or divestitures. While operating income may be used as a proxy for cash flow, non-cash items such as depreciation and amortization should be excluded from the calculation, and adjustments for taxes must be made. Forecast operating income is a function of growth from period to period and operating profit margins. Management decisions and policies affect incremental investment or divestiture of fixed and working capital. While the estimations can be complex and require certain assumptions and estimations, periodic cash flow may be simply defined as:

$$CF_t = R_{i,t-1}(1 + g_t)(1 - T_t) - \Delta R(f_t + w_t)$$

where:
$CF$  = cash flow applicable to period t.
$R$    = revenue

---

12    For example, price-to-earnings, price-to-book, or price-to-sales ratios from the comparable firms.

$g$      = annual growth rate in revenue
$T$      = income tax rate
$f$      = incremental fixed capital investment required per dollar of revenue increase
        [investment net of replacement of existing capacity estimated by depreciation]
$w$     = incremental working capital investment required per dollar of revenue increase
        i = 1 or 2, 1 = landside revenue, 2 = airside revenue.

Each of the future periodic cash flows represents value to be received by the buyer. However, the longer it takes to receive this cash flow, the less valuable it becomes to the buyer today. As such, these future periodic cash flows must be discounted to determine the value of that cash flow to the buyer today. The sum of these discounted future cash flows defines the maximum amount the buyer should be willing to pay for the asset, and thus the value of the asset. In this case the value of an airport can be defined as:

$$V_{Airport} = \sum_{t=0}^{n} \frac{[R_{t-1}(1+g_t)(1-T_t)-\Delta R(f_t+w_t)_t](1+g_t)}{(1+k_t)^t}$$

where:
$V_{Airport}$    = the current or present value of the airport.
$k_t$         = discount rate applicable to period $t$.
$n$         = the number of periods over which cash flows are expected to be generated.
$g_t$        = expected growth component in period $t$.

We assume that the overall market rate of return ($k_t$) will be greater than the expected growth component ($g_t$).

Clearly, estimating the future periodic cash flows for an airport over an extended period of time can be a cumbersome process. In fact, given the nature of the operation, an airport essentially has an unlimited time horizon. As such, if growth rates are assumed to be constant, along with operating margins and rates of investment, the cash flows represent constant growth perpetuity, and the value of the airport may be estimated using a variation of the *Gordon Growth Model*.[13]

The discount rate, or required rate of return, reflects prevailing market rates of return adjusted for the risk associated with the investment. Typically, financial managers estimate the required rate of return on investment projects as a function of the firm's *weighted average cost of capital (WACC)*. Based on the prevailing market returns for the firm's financial securities, the WACC reflects both the prevailing market rates of return, as well as the risk specific to the company. The general formula for the *weighted average cost of capital* is:

$$WACC = w_d \times k_d \times (1-T) + w_e \times k$$

where:
$w_d$    = proportion (weight) of debt funding
$k_d$    = cost of debt
$T$     = corporate tax rate

---

13     More complete discussion and derivation of the Gordon Growth Model is available in most managerial finance textbooks such as Intermediate Financial Management by E.F. Brigham and P.R. Daves, 7th edition, published by Thompson Learning in 2002.

$w_e$ = proportion (weight) of equity funding
$k$   = cost of equity

The relevant cost of debt is the interest rate required by investors to earn their desired return given the risk associated with the investment. Computed in this way, the cost of debt ($kd$) is expressed by the following formula:

$$\text{Debt Premium} = \beta_d\,(MRP) + EDL + LP$$

where:
$\beta_d$   = Beta of Debt
$MRP$ (Market Risk Premium) = $k_m - k_{rf}$
EDL  = Estimated Default Losses
LP    = Liquidity Premium

The debt premium determines the premium over and above the risk-free rate that is required by investors for holding the debt. It reflects marketability and exposure to the possibility of default. It also represents the incremental cost of raising debt. Practically speaking, the cost of debt ($k_d$) can be determined by calculating the yield to maturity on the firm's outstanding debt issues.

A number of methods are available to estimate the cost of equity. However, the Capital Asset Pricing Model (CAPM) is the most popular, owing to its intuitive appeal and relative ease of application. The CAPM develops a relationship between the non-diversifiable risk of an asset (measured by its beta) and the opportunity cost of investing in that asset. The CAPM links the risk-free rate, the asset's non-diversifiable risk and the expected return on the market portfolio. The standard CAPM model for return on equity ($ke$) is expressed by the following formula:

$$k_e = k_f + \beta_e(MRP)$$

where:
$k_f$   = risk-free rate[14]
$\beta_e$   = equity beta
Market Risk Premium $(MRP) = k_m - k_{rf}$[15]

Risk relates to the possibility that expected returns may not actually materialize. The total risk of an asset or business is made up of both diversifiable risk and un-diversifiable risk. Diversifiable (or unsystematic) risk is unique to the asset or firm and can be mitigated by diversification of investments.

Using the WACC is an effective means for determining the appropriate required rate of return at which to discount the expected cash flows from an investment, provided that the risk of the investment is similar to the average risk of the firm's existing investments.

---

14    The risk-free rate is the interest rate that an investor would earn on a risk-less investment. However, in reality there is no such thing as the risk-free rate. Governments are typically the only entities in the market for funds considered to have such a low level of risk. Therefore, rates for Government bonds are usually used to approximate the risk-free rate.
15    Market Risk Premium (MRP) represents the additional premium that investors require to hold the market portfolio—a diversified basket of 'risky' assets—over and above the return that can be obtained from investing in risk-free assets. It is not affected by firm specific factors.

To the extent that the risk of the investment is greater (or lesser) than the firm's average investment, the required rate of return must be adjusted up (or down) from the WACC. Although a discussion of the methodologies for making this adjustment is outside the scope of this chapter, these include risk adjustment of the expected cash flow, adding to (or subtracting from) the required rate of return on an educated estimation basis, or estimating the beta specific to the investment by looking to "pure play" firms in the market.

## AIRPORT VALUATION APPLICATION

Table 13.4 below lists examples of airport valuations based upon the theoretical valuation methods listed in this chapter. The airports chosen for the theoretical valuation are: John F. Kennedy, Atlanta, and the BAA Group consisting of Heathrow, Gatwick, Stansted, Southampton, Glasgow, Edinburgh, and Aberdeen airports. Table 13.4 is based on actual data for 2008 and, for this example, the monetary units used for airports JFK ATL and BAA are in millions of U.S.D.[16]

**Table 13.4    Operating revenues, expenses, and profit ($ millions)**

| Metric | JFK | ATL | BAA* |
|---|---|---|---|
| Operating revenues | 950.6 | 386.2 | 3444.2 |
| Operating expenses | 657.5 | 175.7 | 2048 |
| Operating profit | 293.1 | 210.5 | 1395 |
| Net profit | 174.5 | 323.3 | 940 |

*Source*: Complied by the Authors using data from FAA Report 127 and Statistical Series: The UK Airports Industry.

Based upon historical data, it is assumed that the net income growth rates for these airports will not exceed (on average) over 4% per year for the next 30 years. Therefore, the following calculations have been completed based upon growth rates of 0%, 2%, and 4%. Based upon the performance of these airports, calculations were undertaken using discount rates of 5%, 8%, and 10%. Tables 13.5 and 13.6 reflect the estimated values of these airports based upon the information and assumptions listed above. Notice the negative impacts that the increasing discount rates have on the estimated values of the airports. This reinforces the concept that was illustrated in previous chapters of this text, which is, the higher the discount rate, the lower the present value of future cash flows. It should also be noted that if these values were computed using operating profit and not net income, then Atlanta would have a considerably lower value and the other airport's values would increase dramatically. This shows the impact that non-operating revenues and expenses can have on an airport.

To further illustrate this concept Figure 13.6 depicts the anticipated yearly net income for the three entities assuming a 2% yearly growth combined with a 5% discount rate.

---

16    BAA is a UK-based company that owns and operates seven major airports including London Heathrow (LHR) and Gatwick (LGW).

**Table 13.5    Airport values at different financial conditions**

| Airport | 5% | 8% | 10% | Growth rate |
|---|---|---|---|---|
| JFK | $2,680.86 | $1,963.29 | $1,643.99 | 0% |
| ATL | $4,970.05 | $3,639.74 | $3,047.80 | |
| BAA Group | $14,494.29 | $10,614.68 | $8,888.40 | |
| JFK | $3,376.79 | $2,383.35 | $1,953.63 | 2% |
| ATL | $6,260.25 | $4,418.51 | $3,621.84 | |
| BAA Group | $18,111.31 | $12,783.04 | $10,478.22 | |
| JFK | $4,352.01 | $2,954.58 | $2,366.30 | 4% |
| ATL | $8,068.20 | $5,477.50 | $4,386.90 | |
| BAA Group | $23,486.82 | $15,945.18 | $12,770.42 | |

**Table 13.6    Estimated value in thirty years at various discount rates assuming 2% growth rate based on operating profit**

| Airport | 5% | 8% | 10% |
|---|---|---|---|
| JFK | $5,675.57 | $4,005.84 | $3,283.58 |
| ATL | $4,066.23 | $2,869.96 | $2,352.50 |
| BAA Group | $27,036.72 | $19,082.63 | $15,641.98 |

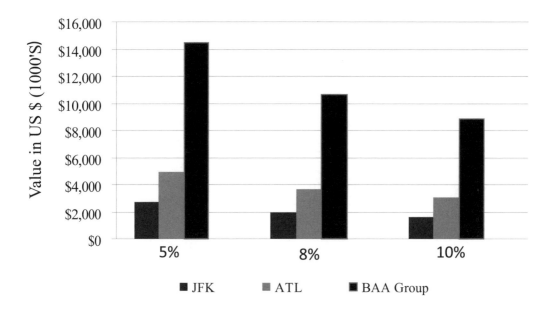

**Figure 13.5    Estimated value of the airports assuming 0% growth**

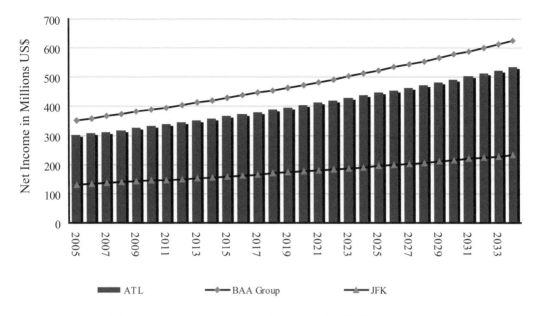

**Figure 13.6    Net income at 2% growth rate and 5% discount rate**

Figure 13.7 displays the predicted growth in operating profit for the three groups assuming the same rates as the example above.

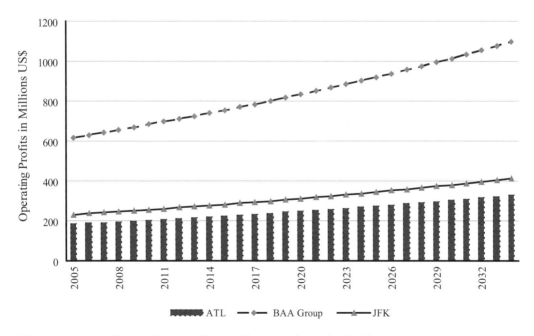

**Figure 13.7    Operating profit at 2% growth and 5% discount rate**

This further illustrates the effects that non-operating items and accounting methods can have on the net-income of an airport. If we were to base the value of the airports solely upon the operating profit, rather than net profit, the BAA group would have a considerable advantage.

## AIRCRAFT VALUATION

Aircraft valuation is another application of valuation in the airline industry and the Discounted Present Value (DPV) model can be applied to estimate the theoretical value/hedonic price of commercial aircraft.[17] We know that an airline executive would never purchase an aircraft that is calculated to return only $10 million over its useful life if the purchase price is more than $10 million. How then do airlines evaluate the price they should pay for an aircraft? The best way to understand the valuation process is to build the DPV concept from its simplest form and then apply it to more complex applications. It is a straightforward matter to extend this definition to the somewhat more complex process of valuation. That is, rather than the single time period valuation, the DPV valuation takes place over the number of time periods that cover the life of the asset (annuity). In the valuation process, the future values make up of the difference between the revenues and costs of operating the aircraft for the time period in question. Each time period has its own calculation, but all of them use the same discount rate. Furthermore, each time period also has both revenues and expenses associated with it, producing a rather complicated looking equation when written out, but the basic concept is still fairly simple. That is, the idea is to balance the discounted stream of profits (revenue minus cost) over the assumed life of the asset and then compare this with the cost of the asset. Since the cost is incurred in the present time, the returns from the stream of profits must exceed the required rate of return in order to make the investment worthwhile.

### Aircraft Valuation Model

The following example is based primarily on a paper by Vasigh that discusses a methodology for aircraft valuation. The example is a practical application of the valuation technique discussed above. The model allows the user to disaggregate revenues and costs for various types of aircraft and then estimate the value of the aircraft over an expected asset life span (about 30 years). First, the formulas are presented and then the results are compared with a list price for the aircraft type. To estimate total revenues per year the following formula is used:

$$TR = \text{Revenue from Passengers} + \text{Revenue from Cargo}$$

$$TR = \beta \times \left[ \left( \frac{RPM}{\beta} \times RRPM \right) + \left( \frac{RTM}{\beta} \times RRTM \right) \right]$$

where:
TR      = total revenues
β       = block hours[18]

---

17    The basic principle of the hedonic pricing technique is that the price of an aircraft is related to its characteristics such as; fuel efficiency, comfort, speed, maintenance expenses, etc.
18    Typically includes taxi time plus airborne time.

RPM    = Revenue passenger mile[19]
RTM    = Revenue tone mile[20]
RRPM   = revenue per revenue passenger mile (passenger yield)[21]
RRTM   = revenue per revenue ton mile (cargo yield)[22]

To improve their revenue streams, many airlines in the United States and around the world have turned to the ancillary revenue by charging passengers for different services. Moreover, in the past few years such revenue has become an important component of airlines' income. Airlines such as Ryanair, easyJet and Allegiant are targeting a higher percentage of their income to come from non-ticket sources. Ryanair's ancillary revenue grew 40 percent to $562.6 million in the nine months to the end of December 2009.[23] The airline aims to raise that to 20 percent over the next three years. And, although not in the above model, this revenue can easily be incorporated by adding the appropriate terms. To estimate costs the following formula was used:

$$TC = ASM \times \left\{ \left[ \frac{\theta \times \frac{\gamma}{\beta}}{\frac{ASM}{\beta}} \right] + \left[ \frac{\frac{\lambda}{\beta}}{\frac{ASM}{\beta}} \right] + \left[ \frac{\frac{\mu}{\beta}}{\frac{ASM}{\beta}} \right] + \left[ \frac{\iota}{ASM} \right] + \left[ \frac{\varpi}{\frac{ASM}{\beta}} \times \beta \right] \right\} + Admin$$

where:
TC      = total costs
Admin   = administration costs, such as servicing, sales, and general cots
ASM     = available seat miles[24]
$\theta$       = fuel cost per gallon
$\gamma$       = gallons of fuel consumed
$\lambda$       = flight personnel cost
$\mu$       = maintenance labor and materials cost
$\iota$       = indirect costs
$\omega$       = total capital cost of aircraft
k       = cost of capital (required rate of return / risk of the estimated cash flow)
t       = year
n       = expected aircraft life

Finally, the revenues and costs are combined over the assumed useful life of the asset (profits = revenues minus costs) and discounted using the weighted average cost of capital discussed above. Recall from the earlier discussion that this rate includes the market discount factor adjusted for the risk factor of the individual firm or firms. The final formula for valuation is the following:

$$V_{aircraft} = \sum_{t=0}^{n} \frac{\left( \left\{ \beta \times \left[ \left( \frac{RPM}{\beta} \times RRPM \right) + \left( \frac{RTM}{\beta} \times RRTM \right) \right] \right\} - \left[ ASM \times \left\{ \left[ \frac{\theta \times \frac{\gamma}{\beta}}{\frac{ASM}{\beta}} \right] + \left[ \frac{\frac{\lambda}{\beta}}{\frac{ASM}{\beta}} \right] + \left[ \frac{\frac{\mu}{\beta}}{\frac{ASM}{\beta}} \right] + \left[ \frac{\iota}{ASM} \right] + \left[ \frac{\varpi}{\frac{ASM}{\beta}} \times \beta \right] \right\} + Admin \right] \right)_t}{(1+k)^t}$$

---

19    One fare-paying passenger carried one mile.
20    One ton carried one mile.
21    A measure of unit revenue, calculated as the gross revenue generated per RPM.
22    RRTM is a measurement of revenue earned on the movement of a ton of freight over one mile.
23    Reuters, February 01, 2010.
24    One seat transported one mile.

While this formula appears to be extremely complex, it is nothing more than a concrete application of the discounted valuation process described in the earlier part of the chapter. That is, the first part of the numerator is made up of the individual revenue components that can be expected over the lifetime of aircraft, while the second part of the numerator is made up of the individual cost components that are expected to occur over the lifetime of the aircraft. These components are then subtracted and summed over the predicted useful life of the aircraft. Finally, the entire stream is discounted by the weighted average cost of capital.

Table 13.7 below, contains the valuation calculated from the above equation and shows the sensitivity of the valuation to changes in various factors in the above equation.

## Table 13.7    Theoretical new aircraft value ($)

| Factor | Applied growth rate | Airbus A320-200 | Boeing 737-700LR |
|---|---|---|---|
| Discount rate | 12% | 77,781,964 | 55,335,194 |
| | 9% | 99,205,432 | 70,575,004 |
| | 10% | 91,028,574 | 64,758,315 |
| | 11% | 83,948,914 | 59,722,124 |
| | 13% | 72,378,665 | 51,491,491 |
| Fuel cost (price per gallon) | 2% | 70,232,335 | 50,037,702 |
| | 1% | 74,251,463 | 52,857,880 |
| | 1.50% | 72,308,001 | 51,494,174 |
| | 3% | 65,638,426 | 46,814,206 |
| | 5% | 54,293,483 | 38,853,583 |
| Maintenance expenses | 3.75%; 7.10% | 73,008,644 | 50,192,222 |
| A320-200; | 1%; 1% | 76,730,505 | 54,876,052 |
| B737-700LR; | 2,5%; 4% | 74,872,627 | 53,070,329 |
| | 5%; 6% | 70,786,590 | 51,367,213 |
| | 8%, 11% | 63,441,202 | 43,954,374 |
| Passenger yield | 1.25% | 97,221,004 | 70,506,204 |
| | 1% | 93,079,311 | 67,273,860 |
| | 1.50% | 101,500,158 | 73,845,828 |
| | 2% | 110,493,837 | 80,864,857 |
| | 3% | 130,398,835 | 96,399,519 |
| Block hours | 0.10% | 79,723,589 | 56,894,052 |
| | 0% | 77,781,964 | 55,335,194 |
| | 0.05% | 78,749,726 | 56,112,174 |
| | 0.50% | 87,740,075 | 63,330,174 |
| | 0.75% | 92,961,749 | 67,522,442 |

Although the results in Table 13.7 are, of course, subject to the assumptions contained in the example, they are nonetheless interesting in their own right. In all cases the discounted net present value approach produced values that were less than the average listed sale price. This is not surprising since we would expect the aircraft manufacturer to attempt to obtain the highest sale price for an individual aircraft. What is interesting is the fact that the DPV approach produced valuations that were very close to the average list price in many instances and not exceptionally far away in others. In the end of course, the actual sale price will be a compromise between the buyer and the seller but the valuation process produces a useful benchmark for both.

Table 13.8 lists the effects that variations in different variables have on the price of both wide- and narrow-body aircraft. These values are based upon one% variations in the costs of the variables. For example, a 1% increase in the discount rate will cause the value of the Airbus A-320 to decrease by over $5,403,298 where as an increase in the block hours (utilization) of this aircraft by 1% will cause an increase of over $1,940,246.

**Table 13.8   Net aircraft value-trend changes**

| | Discount rate +/- 1% | Fuel cost +/- 1% | Maintenance +/- 1% | Pax yield +/- 1% | Block hour +/- 0.1% |
|---|---|---|---|---|---|
| **Narrow body** | | | | | |
| + | (5,403,298) | (4,593,908) | (1,771,205) | 17,973,530 | 1,940,246 |
| A320-200 | | | | | |
| - | 6,166,951 | 4,019,128 | 1,490,406 | (15,821,149) | (1,941,626) |
| + | (3,843,702) | (3,223,495) | (1,253,484) | 14,047,544 | 1,578,608 |
| B737-700 | | | | | |
| - | 4,386,930 | 2,820,178 | 1,076,017 | (12,327,185) | (1,558,858) |
| **Wide body** | | | | | |
| + | (12,994,586) | (13,254,621) | (2,850,478) | 48,316,101 | 4,643,621 |
| A330 | | | | | |
| - | 14,831,102 | 11,596,230 | 2,410,339 | (42,398,980) | (4,585,520) |
| + | (12,753,537) | (12,140,706) | (3,496,076) | 44,273,757 | 4,554,906 |
| B767-400 ER | | | | | |
| - | 14,555,985 | 10,621,686 | 2,954,928 | (38,851,689) | (4,497,915) |

Table 13.9 lists the various arc elasticities for the aircraft compared in Table 13.8. Keep in mind that the arc elasticity is a measure of elasticity between two points.

From 13.9 we see that for every 1% increase in block hours per day, the aircraft increases in value by 24% or more. In order to fully illustrate the effect that aircraft utilization has on an airline consider the following concepts. An aircraft is a huge financial expense for an airline and this asset must be used, therefore an aircraft on the ground is a "waste of

**Table 13.9    Arc price elasticity for various aircraft**

|                | Discount rate | Fuel cost | Maintenance | Pax yield | Block hour |
|----------------|---------------|-----------|-------------|-----------|------------|
| **Narrow body** |               |           |             |           |            |
| A320-200       | -7.4          | -6.16     | -2.24       | 17.19     | 24.35      |
| B737-700       | -7.4          | -6.06     | -2.32       | 18.48     | 27.57      |
| **Wide body**  |               |           |             |           |            |
| A330           | -7.4          | -7.56     | -1.52       | 18.73     | 24.07      |
| B767-400ER     | -7.4          | -6.99     | -1.95       | 17.75     | 24.06      |

money" for the airline; this is due to the fact that when an aircraft is on the ground it is not generating revenue. Figure 13.8 depicts the aircraft utilization (in block hours per day) of four airlines: American, Continental, Northwest and Southwest.

Since Southwest is the only U.S. airline that has posted a profit every year of its existence, Figure 13.8 shows that this may be due to their relatively high utilization rate. If we now compare this figure with the data provided in Table 13.8 for the 737-700 (which comprises the majority of Southwest's fleet), then it is apparent that for every 0.1% change in utilization the airline will experience an increase of close to 1.6 million U.S.D. In the above figure, Southwest is the only point-to-point airline of the four shown and for the vast majority of the observation periods, Southwest has had a higher rate of aircraft utilization over its hub and spoke counterparts. One can therefore conclude that, owing

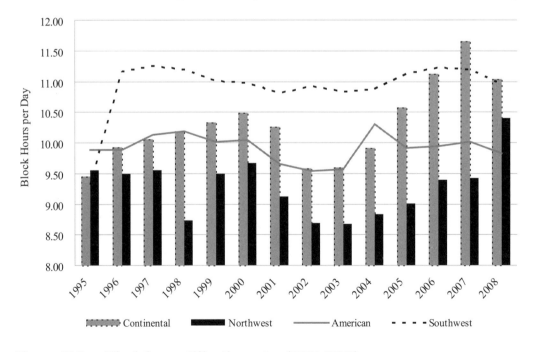

**Figure 13.8    Block hour utilization rates (1995–2008)**

to a high rate of aircraft utilization, Southwest places a higher value on aircraft use than its competitors.

## SUMMARY

This chapter extends the earlier discussion of NPV and IRR to encompass the concept of valuation of high value assets such as airports and aircraft. Valuation is important in the airline industry since many resources are government owned or controlled and do not have consistent market-based valuations. Therefore, it is important to have models or methods that can provide benchmark valuations for these resources. NPV is the preferred method for estimating the theoretical value of resources. Finally, the chapter introduces methods for using discounted cash flows to value aircraft based on measures of revenue and cost such as block hours, RRPM and ASM.

## DISCUSSION QUESTIONS

1.  Detail the FAA's classification of airports. Where does your hometown airport fall within the FAA's classification?
2.  What are some of the benefits of airport privatization?
3.  Is there any unique techniques we should use to measure the value a commercial airport?
4.  Explain, in relative valuation, terms, how to estimate the value of an airport by looking at how the market prices similar airports.
5.  Comment on the following statement and do you agree or disagree with it:

    "Valuation modeling may not be an objective practice, since any presumptions and partiality that an analyst brings to the process may find their way into the value."

6.  If you, as a government agency, are planning to privatize your local airport, how would you be able to protect the airport users, mainly passengers and the airlines, from monopolistic practices?

## REFERENCES

Air Finances Journal. (1999) Omani Government Appoints CSFB for Airport Privatization. September.

Airport and Port Program. Retrieved September 23, 2008, from Transport Canada Web site: http://www.tc.gc.ca/programs/airports/status/menu.htm

*Airport World*, News, June-July 2000, 5(3), 7

Atlantic City International Airport (2008). Atlantic City International Airport since 1942. South Jersey Transit Airport Retrieved September 19, 2008 from http://www2.sjta.com/acairport/

BAA. Retrieved September 19, 2008, Web site:
http://www.baa.com

BAA U.S.A. (2008). Retrieved September 19, 2008, Web site: http://www.baausa.com/Content/Locations.aspx

Cook, B. (1997, September/October) "Australia: On top of Privatization Down Under." *Airport Magazine*. (on-line). Available: http://www.airportnet.org/depts/publications/airmags/Am91097/Australia.htm

*Daily Deal*. (2002, March 11). Sydney Airport Deal Restarted. New York.

Federal Aviation Administration (FAA). Airports and Air traffic, Retrieved September 16, 2008, from FAA Web site: http://www.faa.gov/airports_airtraffic/

Federal Aviation Administration (FAA). Data and Statistics, Retrieved September 16, 2008, from Federal Aviation Administration Web site: http://www.faa.gov/data_statistics/

Federal Aviation Administration (FAA). (2006). National Plan of Integrated Airport System (NPIAS) 2007–2011.Accessed September 16, 2008 from http://www.faa.gov/airports_airtraffic/airports/planning_capacity/npias/reports/media/2007/npias_2007_narrative.pdf

*Financial Times*. (2000, September 25) 'Going down under: Frankfurt Airport Company acquires Strategic Stake in Brisbane International Airport.'

Forsyth, P. (1997). Price Regulation of Airports, June 27.

Gilroy, L. (2008). Annual privatization report. Reason Public Policy Institute, Retrieved October 15, 2008 from http://www.reason.org

Grupo Aeroportuario del Sureste, S.A.B. de C.V. (ASUR). Retrieved September 22, 2008, from Grupo Aeroportuario del Sureste, S.A.B. de C.V. (ASUR) Web site: http://www.asur.com.mx/asur/index.asp

Hamzaee, R. and B. Vasigh (1998). "A Comparative Analysis of Economic Performance of U.S. Commercial Airports." *Journal of Air Transport Management*, 4, 209–210.

Hamzaee, R. and B. Vasigh, (2006). "A Collective Airport—Airline Efficiency Strategic Model," *International Journal of Applied Management Technology*, 4,1, 67-78.

Morristown Municipal Airport. Retrieved September 19, 2008, Web site: http://www.mmuair.com/management.html

Ogden Corporation, News, (on-line) Available: http://www.Invertir.com/news/nr3821.html

O'Malley, C., *Indianapolis Business Journal*, July 23 2007.

Poole, Jr., R. (1999, June 30). "Comments on Airport Privatization Pilot Program presented to the House Aviation Subcommittee." Reason Public Policy Institute Retrieved from http://www.rppi.org/speeches/airports.htm.

Schipol Group. Retrieved September 22, 2008, from Schipol Group Web site: http://www.schipholgroup.com/Homepage/Homepage.htm

The Port Authority of NY/NJ (2007, November). Stewart International Airport (SWF) facts. Retrieved October 18, 2008 from http://www.stewartintlairport.com/CommutingTravel/airports/html/swf_info.html.

Top Airports (2008). Retrieved October 7, 2008, from Air Transport News Web site: http://www.airtransportnews.aero/analysis.pl?id=541

Transport Canada. Retrieved September 23, 2008, from Transport Canada Web site: http://www.tc.gc.ca/air/menu.htm

Truitt, L. and E. Michael (1996). "Airport privatization: Full divestiture and its alternatives." *Policy Studies Journal*, Urbana, 24, 100-124.

United States General Accounting Office (GAO, 2003). Airport Financing, Testimony before the Subcommittee on Aviation, Senate Committee on Commerce, Science, and Transportation.

Wells, A. and S. Young (2004). *Airport Planning and Management* (5ed). McGrawHill.

# Appendix A:
# Airline Data Sources

This section outlines some of the data sources commonly used in the aviation industry. The information also indicates whether the data is freely accessible or can be obtained only through subscription fees and, where appropriate, the web addresses are provided.[1] While the majority of data sources described are from the United States, data sources for international aviation are also provided. The major data sources discussed are:

- U.S. Department of Transportation (DOT) / Bureau of Transportation Statistics (BTS)
- Federal Aviation Administration (FAA)
- International Air Transport Association (IATA)
- International Civil Aviation Organization (ICAO)
- Official Airline Guide (OAG)
- Airports Council International (ACI)
- Air Transport Association (ATA)
- Air Transport Intelligence (ATI)
- Airline Monitor
- UK Civil Aviation Authority (CAA)
- Transport Canada (TC)
- Eurocontrol
- The Aircraft Owners and Pilots Association (AOPA)
- Bureau of Economic Analysis (BEA)
- Bureau of Labor Statistics (BLS)
- Organization for Economic Cooperation and Development (OECD).

## U.S. DEPARTMENT OF TRANSPORTATION (DOT)/ BUREAU OF TRANSPORTATION STATISTICS (BTS)

One of the best sources for aviation-specific data for U.S. aviation activity is the United States Department of Transportation (DOT), through the Bureau of Transportation Statistics (BTS). There are multiple DOT databases that provide a wealth of statistics and financial information for the airline industry.

One database that is used throughout this book is Form 41, which provides a wealth of information concerning U.S. airlines ranging from general airline financial data, specific airline cost data, general traffic data, and airport activity statistics. All U.S. registered airlines are required to provide the data to the DOT and it can be useful for evaluating airlines.

---

1    Website addresses were current as of 2009.

Another useful database is O&D, which stands for Origin and Destination. Using a ten percent sample of actual tickets, various statistics are provided for individual U.S. domestic city pairs. The O&D database shows on what airline passengers traveled, the average ticket price, and a large amount of other data. As might be expected, the O&D data is very useful for demand estimation.

The T100 database is similar to O&D, but for international city pairs. However, the data is presented in a slightly differently format and is not as extensive. This data enables demand estimation for international routes.

In addition to these three major databases, the DOT also provides additional databases such as Schedules, Fleet, and Commuter.[2] While DOT statistics are technically public information and can be obtained free, unless the user has advanced Excel and Access skills, the data is very difficult to access. Therefore, in order to use most of the DOT data, airline database packages such as Back Aviation are required. Unfortunately, these products require a paid subscription.

## FEDERAL AVIATION ADMINISTRATION (FAA)

The Federal Aviation Administration is another good source for U.S. data. In particular, the FAA is a good source for information and data concerning aviation accidents and safety. The FAA also provides data concerning aviation forecasts and other issues such as terminal space usage, passenger facility charges, and airline service indexes. All this data can be obtained without charge through the Federal Aviation Administration's website, http://www.icao.int.

## INTERNATIONAL AIR TRANSPORT ASSOCIATION (IATA)

The International Air Transport Association highlights issues and provides information concerning issues affecting airlines globally. The free economic analysis section provides information concerning the industry outlook, cost comparisons, traffic analysis, and fuel prices. In addition to the free data, IATA provides a wealth of additional subscription information that compares international carriers and provides airline rankings in terms of a variety of statistics. Through IATA's website, http://www.iata.gov, a wealth of information, (particularly concerning global aviation issues) can be collected.

## INTERNATIONAL CIVIL AVIATION ORGANIZATION (ICAO)

The International Civil Aviation Organization, an arm of the United Nations, is the source for pertinent legal issues, particularly international air service agreements. However, probably the most valuable source from ICAO is ICAO data, a subscription database; this database provides international data, including origin and destination passenger statistics, airline financial data, and airport activity statistics. ICAO data is a useful backup source to fill-in any data not covered by DOT O&D and T100 databases in the United States and

---

2     It should be noted that additional aviation data is provided through the Department of Transportation (http://www.dot.gov) and the Bureau of Transportation Statistics (http://www.bts.gov) websites.

a primary source for other international demand analysis. Information concerning ICAO and ICAO data can be obtained through the website, www.icao.int.

## OFFICIAL AIRLINE GUIDE (OAG)

The Official Airline Guide is a compilation of over 1,000 airline schedules, creating the definitive source on airline schedules. Users can access date-specific schedule information through www.oag.com without charge. However, for airlines, a complete historical OAG database is more useful. Through this database, ASMs can be easily determined for a large number of city pairs.

## AIRPORTS COUNCIL INTERNATIONAL (ACI)

Airports Council International is a community of international airports that collectively lobbies on various issues concerning airports. Through ACI's website, www.airports. org, data and rankings can be obtained concerning the number of passengers handled by various airports, the cargo movements through the airports, and the number of international passengers, to name just a few; therefore, ACI helps collate information concerning airports worldwide.

## AIR TRANSPORT ASSOCIATION (ATA)

The Air Transport Association (ATA) is an airline trade association representing the United States' leading airlines. Through the association's website www.airlines.org, a broad overview of information concerning the U.S. aviation industry is provided, notably fleet information, economic impact studies, and labor statistics. However, probably the most useful report from ATA is the monthly traffic report which traffic statistics and industry RASM/yield. As a result, the monthly ATA report is a highly anticipated report by financial analysts; however, unfortunately it is only provided on a fee basis.

## AIR TRANSPORT INTELLIGENCE (ATI)

Air Transport Intelligence (ATI) is a database encompassing a wealth of information on the aviation industry. ATI provides a database of aviation-specific journal articles from such publications as *Airline Business* and *Flight International*, which can be quite helpful in any qualitative analysis. ATI also provides searchable databases on information concerning airlines, airports, aircraft, suppliers, and schedules. While ATI does not provide quantitative data, it is a valuable resource when initially researching specific areas. ATI is only available to subscribers, and more information can be gathered at www.rati.com.

## AIRLINE MONITOR

Another subscription database is Airline Monitor, which reviews trends in the airline and commercial jet aircraft industries. Airline Monitor provides a variety of reports, in a variety of formats, over issues such as block hour operating costs, airline financial results, and commercial aircraft production. Airline Monitor also provides historical data, which is especially helpful in constructing time series data with numerous observations. More information concerning the products offered by Airline Monitor can be found at www. airlinemonitor.com.

## UK CIVIL AVIATION AUTHORITY (CAA)

The UK Civil Aviation Authority provides a function similar to the FAA, except in the United Kingdom. Using www.caa.co.uk, information covering the entire UK aviation industry can be obtained. Through the economic regulation and statistics portion of the CAA's website, a wealth of statistical data can also be accessed.

## TRANSPORT CANADA (TC)

Transport Canada is the governing body for all transportation related activities in Canada. Statistics, data, and regulations concerning the commercial aviation industry can all be obtained through Transport Canada and StatsCan. More information concerning Transport Canada can be found at www.tc.gc.ca.

## EUROCONTROL

Eurocontrol, standing for the European Organization for the Safety of Air Navigation, is the primary provider of air traffic control services throughout Europe. While specific data can be difficult to obtain from Eurocontrol, their website does provide a variety of information concerning the aviation industry in Europe.[3] More specifically, Eurocontrol can provide detailed information pertaining to airport traffic, delays, and capacity management initiatives.

## THE AIRCRAFT OWNERS AND PILOTS ASSOCIATION (AOPA)

The Aircraft Owners and Pilots Association is a membership community that promotes and advocates for the general aviation industry. Recently, AOPA has been involved in the fight over fuel surcharges and restrictions concerning the use of general aviation aircraft in congested airspace. The AOPA website, www.aopa.org, is split into two sections: public and members. While the general public can receive basic information from AOPA, members can obtain a more thorough investigation of issues facing the general aviation community. Additionally, members receive information pertaining to weather and flight planning.

---

3    Eurocontrol—www.eurocontrol.int

## BUREAU OF ECONOMIC ANALYSIS (BEA)

The U.S. Bureau of Economic Analysis is an essential source when forecasting demand for air transportation services. The BEA provides detailed statistics of the state of not only the U.S. economy, but regional economies. Since GDP is a suitable proxy for consumer income, data from BEA can help in any regression analysis. The Bureau of Economic Analysis provides additional macroeconomic indicators such as balance of payments, unemployment, and industry-specific economic accounts. Data can be freely obtained at www.bea.gov.

## BUREAU OF LABOR STATISTICS (BLS)

The U.S. Department of Labor's Bureau of Labor Statistics is the definitive source concerning the labor force in the United States. BLS provides data on such factors as unemployment, consumer price indices, wages, and labor demographics. The level of data can be quite detailed, with the various statistics broken down into industries and regions. For any analysis involving labor, www.bls.gov should be consulted.

## ORGANIZATION FOR ECONOMIC COOPERATION AND DEVELOPMENT (OECD)

The Organization for Economic Cooperation and Development is comprised of thirty member countries which have active relationships with over seventy countries and multiple non-governmental organizations (NGOs). OECD is primarily concerned with social and macroeconomic issues; therefore the selection of data from www.oecd.org encompasses these categories. Statistics are sorted into various industries and enable comparisons between countries. Unfortunately OECD does not publish any reports concerning the aviation industry; therefore, much of the useful data from the OECD will be general macroeconomic data, usually displayed on a monthly or quarterly basis.

# Appendix B:
# Top 100 Commercial Airports

| Rank | City | Country | Iata Code | Passenger (Millions) |
|---|---|---|---|---|
| 1 | Atlanta | USA | ATL | 90.039 |
| 2 | Chicago | USA | ORD | 69.35 |
| 3 | London | UK | LHR | 67.05 |
| 4 | Tokyo | Japan | HND | 66.754 |
| 5 | Paris, Charles de. | France | CDG | 60.87 |
| 6 | Los Angeles | USA | LAX | 59.5 |
| 7 | Dallas/Ft.Worth | USA | DFW | 57.09 |
| 8 | Beijing | China | PEK | 55.93 |
| 9 | Frankfurt | Germany | FRA | 53.46 |
| 10 | Denver | USA | DEN | 51.54 |
| 11 | Madrid | Spain | MAD | 50.84 |
| 12 | Hong Kong | China | HKG | 47.84 |
| 13 | New York | USA | JFK | 47.8 |
| 14 | Amsterdam | Netherlands | AMS | 47.43 |
| 15 | Las Vegas | USA | LAS | 43.21 |
| 16 | Houston | USA | IAH | 41.71 |
| 17 | Phoenix | USA | PHX | 39.9 |
| 18 | Bangkok | Thailand | BKK | 38.6 |
| 19 | Singapore | Singapore | SIN | 37.7 |
| 20 | Dubai | UAE | DXB | 37.4 |
| 21 | San Francisco | USA | SFO | 37.23 |
| 22 | Orlando | USA | MCO | 35.66 |
| 23 | Newark | USA | EWR | 35.36 |
| 24 | Detroit | USA | DTW | 35.13 |
| 25 | Rome | Italy | FCO | 35.13 |
| 26 | Charlotte | USA | CLT | 34.74 |
| 27 | Munich | Germany | MUC | 34.53 |
| 28 | London | UK | LGW | 34.21 |
| 29 | Miami | USA | MIA | 34.06 |
| 30 | Minneapolis/St Pa | USA | MSP | 34.06 |
| 31 | Tokyo | Japan | NRT | 33.46 |
| 32 | Guangzhou | China | CAN | 33.45 |
| 33 | Sydney | Australia | SYD | 33.31 |
| 34 | Toronto | Canada | YYZ | 32.33 |
| 35 | Jakarta | Indonesia | CGK | 32.23 |
| 36 | Seattle/Tacoma | USA | SEA | 32.19 |
| 37 | Philadelphia | USA | PHL | 31.83 |
| 38 | Barcelona | Spain | BCN | 30.19 |
| 39 | Seoul | So. Korea | ICN | 30.16 |
| 40 | Istanbul | Turkey | IST | 28.62 |

| Rank | City | Country | Iata Code | Passenger (Millions) |
|------|------|---------|-----------|----------------------|
| 41 | Shanghai | China | PVG | 28.23 |
| 42 | Kuala Lumpur | Malaysia | KUL | 27.53 |
| 43 | Mexico City | Mexico | MEX | 26.21 |
| 44 | Paris,Orly | France | ORY | 26.2 |
| 45 | Boston | USA | BOS | 26.1 |
| 46 | Melbourne | USA | MEL | 24.89 |
| 47 | Mumbai | India | BOM | 24.33 |
| 48 | Washington | USA | IAD | 23.7 |
| 49 | Dublin | Ireland | DUB | 23.46 |
| 50 | Delhi | India | DEL | 23.24 |
| 51 | New York | USA | LGA | 23.07 |
| 52 | Shangahi | China | SHA | 22.87 |
| 53 | Palma | Spain | PMI | 22.82 |
| 54 | Fort Lauderdale | USA | FLL | 22.62 |
| 55 | London | UK | STN | 22.35 |
| 56 | Zurich | Switzerland | ZRH | 22.04 |
| 57 | Manila | Philippines | MNL | 22.03 |
| 58 | Taipei | Taiwan | TPE | 21.93 |
| 59 | Copenhagen | Denmark | CPH | 21.47 |
| 60 | Manchester | UK | MAN | 21.41 |
| 61 | Shenzhen | China | SZX | 21.4 |
| 62 | Sao Paulo | Brazil | GRU | 20.99 |
| 63 | Baltimore Washin | USA | BWI | 20.88 |
| 64 | Salt Lake City | USA | SLC | 20.79 |
| 65 | Moscow | Russia | DME | 20.45 |
| 66 | Vienna | Austria | VIE | 19.74 |
| 67 | Oslo | Norway | OSL | 19.34 |
| 68 | Milan | Italy | MXP | 19.22 |
| 69 | Brisbane | Australia | BNE | 19.03 |
| 70 | Antalya | Turkey | AYT | 18.84 |
| 71 | Honolulu | USA | HNL | 18.81 |
| 72 | Johannesburg | South Africa | JNB | 18.63 |
| 73 | Brussels | Belgium | BRU | 18.48 |
| 74 | Tampa | USA | TPA | 18.26 |
| 75 | Stockholm | Sweden | ARN | 18.17 |
| 76 | Dusseldorf | Germany | DUS | 18.15 |
| 77 | San Diego | USA | SAN | 18.12 |
| 78 | Vancouver | Canada | YVR | 18.04 |
| 79 | Washington | USA | DCA | 18.02 |
| 80 | Sapporo | Japan | CTS | 17.66 |

| Rank | City | Country | Iata Code | Passenger (Millions) |
|------|------|---------|-----------|---------------------|
| 81 | Chicago | USA | MDW | 17.34 |
| 82 | Fukuoko | Japan | FUK | 17.3 |
| 83 | Chengdu | China | CTU | 17.25 |
| 84 | Athens | Greece | ATH | 16.49 |
| 85 | Osaka,Kansai | Japan | KIX | 16.01 |
| 86 | Kunming | China | KMG | 15.82 |
| 87 | Osaka,Itami | Japan | ITM | 15.63 |
| 88 | Jeddah | Saudi Arabia | JED | 15.343 |
| 89 | Moscow | Russia | SVO | 15.21 |
| 90 | Okinawa | Japan | OKA | 15.11 |
| 91 | Berlin | Germany | TXL | 14.86 |
| 92 | St Louis | USA | STL | 14.43 |
| 93 | Cairo | Egypt | CAI | 14.36 |
| 94 | Portland | USA | PDX | 14.29 |
| 95 | Seoul | So. Korea | GMP | 14.26 |
| 96 | Sao Paulo | Brazil | CGH | 13.66 |
| 97 | Cincinnati | USA | CVG | 13.63 |
| 98 | Lisbon | Portugal | LIS | 13.6 |
| 99 | Bogota | Colombia | BOG | 13.45 |
| 100 | Helsinki | Finland | HEL | 13.44 |
| Source: Airport Council International , 2009 | | | | |
| Ranked accordingly to Passenger embarkation and disembarkations annually. | | | | |

# Appendix C:
# Airlines Vital Statistics

| Rank | Airline | Fleet Size | US Cents/RPM | Load Factor | IATA Code | Country |
|------|---------|-----------|--------------|-------------|-----------|---------|
| 1 | American Airlines | 610 | 5.3406 | 80.60% | AA | USA |
| 2 | Air France-KLM | 374 | 10.03536 | 79.70% | AF/KL | FRANCE |
| 3 | Delta Airlines | 444 | 6.14169 | 81.50% | DL | USA |
| 4 | United Airlines | 378 | 6.47703 | 81.00% | UA | USA |
| 5 | Continental Airlines | 350 | 5.71941 | 80.20% | CO | USA |
| 6 | Northwest Airlines | 312 | NA | 83.80% | NW | USA |
| 7 | Lufthansa | 249 | NA | 78.60% | LH | Germany |
| 8 | Southwest Airlines | 544 | 5.53932 | 71.20% | WN | USA |
| 9 | British Airways | 233 | 7.11045 | 77.00% | BA | UK |
| 10 | Quantas | 136 | 6.93036 | 80.70% | QF | Australia |
| 11 | Emirates | 133 | 5.53311 | 75.80% | EK | UAE |
| 12 | US Airways | 351 | 7.04835 | 81.70% | US | USA |
| 13 | Cathay Pacific | 120 | 5.0922 | 78.80% | CX | China |
| 14 | Singapore Airlines | 106 | NA | 76.30% | SQ | Singapore |
| 15 | Japan Airlines | 197 | NA | 64.70% | JL | Japan |
| 16 | China Southern Airlines | 288 | 5.43375 | 73.80% | CZ | China |
| 17 | Air Canda | 197 | 6.94899 | 81.40% | AC | Canada |
| 18 | Air China | 212 | 5.88708 | 74.90% | CA | China |
| 19 | Ryanair | 197 | 3.30372 | 82.20% | FR | Ireland |
| 20 | Thai Airways | 87 | 5.25987 | 76.80% | TG | Thailand |
| 21 | All Nippon Airwys | 147 | NA | 65.40% | NH | Japan |
| 22 | Korean Air | 127 | 6.07338 | 71.40% | KE | South Korea |
| 23 | China Eastern Airlines | 231 | 5.70699 | 70.80% | MU | China |
| 24 | Iberia | 115 | 7.27812 | 80.00% | IB | Spain |
| 25 | Air Berlin | 88 | 6.39009 | NA | AB | Germany |
| 26 | easyjet | 163 | 5.78772 | 82.70% | U2 | UK |
| 27 | jetblue Airways | 150 | 4.52709 | 80.40% | B6 | USA |
| 28 | Virgin Atlantic Airways | 38 | NA | 76.90% | VS | UK |
| 29 | TAM  Linhas Aereas | 131 | 7.53894 | 71.10% | JJ | Brazil |
| 30 | Qatar Airways | 65 | 5.07978 | 72.60% | QR | Qatar |
| 31 | Malaysia Airlines | 92 | 4.44015 | 67.80% | MH | Malaysia |
| 32 | THY Turkish Airlines | 120 | 7.44579 | 73.90% | TK | Turkey |
| 33 | Thomson Airways | 62 | NA | 91.10% | BY | UK |
| 34 | China Airlines | 62 | 4.27869 | 76.80% | CI | TAIWAN |
| 35 | Saudi Arabian Airlines | 103 | NA | 63.40% | SV | Saudi Arabia |
| 36 | Airtran Airways | 136 | 4.91211 | 79.60% | FL | USA |
| 37 | Alaska Airlines | 115 | 6.07338 | 77.30% | AS | USA |
| 38 | Air New Zeland | 47 | 6.21 | 79.30% | NZ | New Zealand |
| 39 | Alitalia | 156 | NA | 68.50% | AZ | ITALY |
| 40 | SWISS | 61 | 9.01692 | 80.40% | LX | Switzerland |

| Rank | Airline | Fleet Size | US Cents/RPM | Load Factor | IATA Code | Country |
|------|---------|-----------|--------------|-------------|-----------|---------|
| 41 | Thomas Cook Airlines | 41 | NA | 90.00% | MT | UK |
| 42 | SkyWest Airlines | 280 | 7.8246 | 77.70% | OO | USA |
| 43 | Aeroflot | 101 | 6.93657 | 70.90% | SU | Russia |
| 44 | LAN Airlines | 56 | 5.95539 | 76.60% | LA | Chile |
| 45 | Asiana Ailines | 68 | NA | 73.70% | OZ | South Korea |
| 46 | GOL Transportes Aereos | 86 | 7.91154 | 62.40% | G3 | Brazil |
| 47 | Ethiad Airways | 42 | NA | 75.40% | EY | UAE |
| 48 | EVA Air | 45 | 4.30353 | 79.50% | BR | Taiwan |
| 49 | South African Airways | 50 | NA | 74.30% | SA | South Africa |
| 50 | Hainan Airlines | 61 | NA | 78.30% | HU | China |
| 51 | Westjet Airlines | 79 | 6.06096 | 80.10% | WS | Canada |
| 52 | TAP Portugal | 54 | 7.56378 | 67.00% | TP | Portugal |
| 53 | Finnair | 69 | 7.80597 | 75.20% | AY | Finland |
| 54 | Condor Flugdienet | 22 | NA | 88.90% | DE | Germany |
| 55 | Jet Airways | 75 | NA | 67.50% | 9W | India |
| 56 | Austrian | 32 | 10.69362 | 75.20% | OS | Austria |
| 57 | Virgin Blue Airlines | 69 | 6.42114 | 80.50% | DJ | Australia |
| 58 | TUIFly | 41 | NA | 0.86% | X3/HF | Germany |
| 59 | Mexicana | 63 | NA | 72.10% | MX | Mexico |
| 60 | Philippine Airlines | 39 | NA | 76.00% | PR | Philippine |
| 61 | Transaero Airlines | 45 | NA | 82.60% | UN | Russia |
| 62 | El AL Israel Airline | 35 | 6.28452 | 82.30% | LY | Israel |
| 63 | Air Europe | 39 | 6.58881 | 80.20% | UX | Spain |
| 64 | Shenzhen Airlines | 79 | NA | 77.60% | ZH | China |
| 65 | Garuda Indonesia | 65 | 5.32818 | 76.50% | GA | Indonesia |
| 66 | Egyptair | 48 | NA | 66.90% | MS | Egypt |
| 67 | AerLingus | 46 | 6.45219 | 83.60% | EI | Ireland |
| 68 | Monarch Airlines | 31 | NA | 83.60% | ZB | UK |
| 69 | Frontier Airlines | 51 | 4.80654 | 80.60% | F9 | USA |
| 70 | Air India | 124 | NA | 58.00% | AI | India |
| 71 | Jetstar Airways | 42 | NA | 76.10% | JQ | Australia |
| 72 | Aeromexico | 49 | 5.68215 | 71.90% | AM | Mexico |
| 73 | ExpressJet | 244 | 5.1543 | 75.90% | XE | USA |
| 74 | S7 Airlines | 34 | 0 | 79.00% | S7 | Russia |
| 75 | Vietnam Airlines | 51 | NA | 71.90% | VN | VietNam |
| 76 | Pakistan I'ntl Airlines | 39 | 5.06115 | 71.30% | PK | Pakistan |
| 77 | Gulf Air | 36 | NA | 74.90% | GF | Bahrain |
| 78 | Air Transat | 18 | NA | 88.80% | TS | Canada |
| 79 | AirAsia | 45 | NA | 72.00% | AK | Malaysia |
| 80 | Hawaiian Airline | 33 | 5.45238 | 82.60% | HA | USA |

| Rank | Airline | Fleet Size | US Cents/RPM | Load Factor | IATA Code | Country |
|---|---|---|---|---|---|---|
| 81 | Shanghai Airlines | 53 | NA | 69.50% | FM | China |
| 82 | American Eagle Airlines | 223 | 11.51955 | 71.10% | MQ | USA |
| 83 | Xiamen Airlines | 53 | 5.10462 | 77.20% | MF | China |
| 84 | CorsairFly | 7 | NA | NA | SS | FRANCE |
| 85 | Transavia Airlines | 31 | 5.4648 | 78.00% | HV | Netrherland |
| 86 | Sprit Airlines | 28 | 3.86883 | 80.30% | NK | USA |
| 87 | Royal Air Maroc | 39 | NA | 65.90% | AT | Morroco |
| 88 | SAS International | 155 | 6.03612 | 83.50% | BU | Sweden |
| 89 | Mesa Airlines | 132 | 6.7689 | 74.60% | YV | USA |
| 90 | Avianca | 45 | NA | 76.50% | AV | Colombia |
| 91 | Atlantic Southeast Airlines | 160 | 9.47646 | 79.80% | EV | USA |
| 92 | Copa Airlines | 43 | 7.9488 | 78.00% | CM | Panama |
| 93 | Iran Air | 50 | NA | 78.50% | IR | Iran |
| 94 | Aerolenas Argetinas | 38 | NA | 72.20% | AR | Argentina |
| 95 | Sichuan Airlines | 43 | NA | 76.00% | 3U | China |
| 96 | Spanair | 48 | 8.11026 | 68.50% | JK | Spain |
| 97 | Ethiopian Airlines | 34 | 5.37165 | 70.30% | ET | Ethiopia |
| 98 | Onur Air | 25 | NA | NA | 8Q | Turkey |
| 99 | Sri Lankan Airlines | 14 | 3.81294 | 72.70% | UL | Sri Lanka |
| 100 | Kenya Airways | 26 | 6.65712 | 70.80% | KQ | Kenya |

# Index